A
SAN FRANCISCO
RESTAURANTS 97/98

MW01277233

San Francisco

to Marin County
(including Sausalito,
Belvedere, and Tiburon)

Golden Gate Bridge
(southbound toll)

San Francisco
Bay

Pacific
Ocean

Golden Gate
Nat'l Rec. Area

Marin
Blvd

The Exploratorium
& Palace of
Fine Arts

Lincoln Blvd.

Washington Blvd.

Baker
Beach

South Bay

China
Beach

Presidio

West Pacific Ave.

Clay St.

Presidio
Heights

Golden Gate
Nat'l Rec. Area

Lake St.
California St.

Pt. Lobos Ave.

Sutro
Heights
Park

Geary Blvd.

The Richmond

Balboa St.

Fulton St.

M. H. de Young
Museum

J. F. Kennedy Dr.

Turk Blvd.
Golden Gate Av
Fulton St.

Golden Gate
Park Stadium
(Polo Field)

Golden Gate
Park

Stow
Lake

California Academy of
Sciences & Steinhart
Aquarium

The
Haight

Lincoln Way

Kezar Dr.

Frederick St.

Cole
Valley

Judah St.

Lawton St.

Lawton
St.

University of
California,
San Francisco

Uppe
Mark

The Sunset

Mount
Sutro

Noriega St.

Pacheco St.

Sunset
Reservoir

Twin
Peaks

Ocean
Beach

Rivera St.

Twin
Peaks

Taraval St.

Woodside
Ave.

Glen
Canyo
Park

Vicente St.
Wawona St.

West
Portal

Mount
Davidson
Park

Pine Lake
Park

Stern
Grove

San
Francisco
Zoo

Sloat Blvd.

Ocean Ave.

Bosworth
St.

Monterey Blvd.

Lake
Merced

Winston Dr.

San Francisco
State University

Judson Ave.

City College of
San Francisco
Ocean
Ave.

Harding Park
Municipal
Golf Course

Holloway Ave.

Fort
Funston

John Muir Dr.

Brotherhood Way

Montana St.

Randolph St.   Farallones St.

San Francisco
Golf Club

Hanover St.

N

km
mi
1/2
1
2

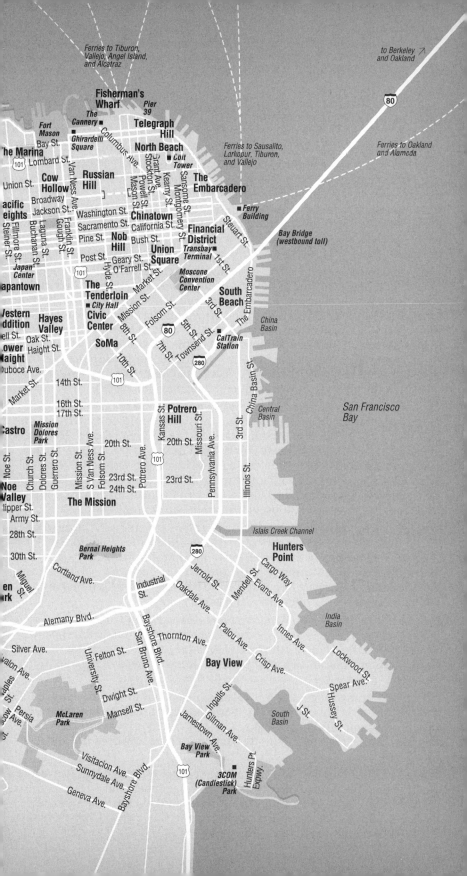

Orientation

From the aroma of roasting coffee that wafts through the air of **North Beach**, to the sights of fresh fish on ice in **Chinatown**, to the colorful pyramids of organic produce in the chic shops of **Pacific Heights**, to the host of great *taquerías* that dot the **Mission**, it's obvious that this city loves food. Residents here spend more money in restaurants than do their counterparts anywhere else in the country—easy to do in a city that boasts one restaurant for every 230 people, the highest proportion in the country.

Food has a long and colorful history in San Francisco. In 1849 the Gold Rush brought thousands of fortune seekers, mostly men, to the West Coast. There were enough saloons to intoxicate a city five times its size, and barkeepers soon figured out a way to attract customers and get them to rack up a bigger bar bill at the same time: the free lunch. It wasn't long before miners began to factor the quality of the food into their patronage, and the San Francisco restaurant trade was under way.

Restaurants also began to spring up in another male bastion: the bordello. In fact, Sally Stanford, one of the city's most renowned madams, became both a successful restaurateur and a mayor. Stanford, who ran her business out of an impressive Victorian house on **Pine Street**, retired from the world's oldest profession in 1950 and then opened **Valhalla**, a plush Victorian restaurant in **Sausalito**, a charming community just across the **Golden Gate Bridge.** In 1972 she won a seat on the Sausalito city council and was so popular that she became mayor in 1976. Later she was named honorary vice-mayor for ife, which she jokingly turned around to "the mayor of vice."

Though the madam's restaurant is long gone, there are restaurants all over the city that are still thriving after more than a century: **Tadich Grill** opened its doors in 1849, followed by **Sam's Grill** in 1867. **Maye's Oyster House** also opened in 1867, and **Ristorante Fior d'Italia** dates to 1886. The restaurants of each succeeding decade provide a cultural blueprint of the city's growth: **Schroeder's**, a German restaurant near the **Embarcadero**, was established in 1893; **Bardelli's**, an old-style Italian restaurant near **Union Square**, dates to 1909; and in the Mission, **Roosevelt Tamale Parlor** set up shop in 1922.

The city's rich culinary tapestry is enhanced by its location in the heart of one of the country's richest agricultural areas and its proximity to some of the best wine regions in the world, including **Sonoma** and **Napa** to the north and **Santa Cruz** and **Monterey** to the south. California wine, which many oenophiles now compare in quality to the best French labels, is making a strong showing on the international market.

And the fog, which San Francisco residents love to complain about, is another factor that fuels our passion: The cool temperatures stimulate the appetite. Where else in the country can you feel at home having a rich lamb stew, a hearty glass of wine, and a loaf of yeasty sourdough bread in the middle of August?

No longer mining for gold, today's visitors talk about the weather, the hills, and the European flavor of the city, but more than anything else they talk about the restaurants: from **Masa's**, **Rubicon**, and **Boulevard** to **Stars** and **Betelnut.** And no wonder. The city has come a long way from its Gold Rush roots.

When two dozen food writers around the country were asked for five words to describe San Francisco–style cooking, every one of them put "fresh" at the top of their list. In 1971 Alice Waters made that connection between land and plate and started a nationwide revolution when she opened **Chez Panisse** in

Berkeley, which may be the only restaurant in the country with a full-time forager on staff to search for the best fresh products.

Today diners also can keep tabs on the way their meals are prepared. With a proliferation of places with open kitchens—among them **Stars, VIVANDE, Porta Via, Boulevard, Hawthorne Lane, Postrio,** and **One Market Restaurant**—the city has turned eating out into something of a spectator sport; in many cases you'll feel as though you have front-row seats at a master cooking class.

In keeping with this personal touch, chefs often identify the produce and the grower's name on the menu: Laura Chenel goat cheese, Liberty duck, or Star Route farms lettuce, to name a few. Good, fresh bread is another essential. Many restaurants bake their own, and the Bay Area nurtures at least a dozen small artisan bakeries. Look for breads by **Bakers of Paris, Boudin, Acme, Metropolis, Bread Workshop, Semifreddi's, Il Fornaio, Grace Baking,** and **Tassajara Bread Bakery.** And then there's the coffee: Specialty roasters abound—**Peet's Coffee & Tea, Spinelli Coffee Company, Capricorn Coffees, Caffè Trieste, Graffeo Coffee,** and **Peerless,** just to name a few—and everyone can tell you why his or her favorite is the best.

San Francisco is one of the most ethnically diverse cities in the country, and its culinary repertoire reflects that fact. Chinese restaurants have become so sophisticated that some specialize in one of the regional styles: Chiu Chow, Shanghai, Canton, Hakka, Hunan, Mandarin, Szechuan, and Peking. Diners can sample the native dishes of Burma, Cambodia, Laos, Malaysia, and Singapore. The rustic cuisine of Istria is explored at **Albona Restaurant,** and **YaYa Cuisine** features the exotic flavors of Mesopotamia. The latest trend is Mediterranean, a style that freely blends the flavors of France, Greece, Italy, Spain, Egypt, and Morocco. **Lhasa Moon,** in the **Marina,** is the only Tibetan restaurant west of the Rockies. And **La Paz Restaurant and Pupuseria** in **SoMa** is one of the many places in the city that serve Salvadoran cuisine.

If the number of dining options listed within this guide overwhelms you, try sampling from among the restaurants we've chosen as our personal favorites in "ACCESS Top 10" on page 9.

So whether it's a dinner of grilled veal chop with parmesan-potato puree in the stylish surroundings at **Postrio,** or a midday cappuccino and biscotti break at **Caffè Trieste,** San Francisco is still going for the gold.

How To Read This Guide

SAN FRANCISCO RESTAURANTS 97/98 ACCESS®
is arranged so you can see at a glance where you
are and what is around you. The numbers next to
the entries in the following chapters correspond to
the numbers on the maps.

The star ratings system takes into account the
quality, service, atmosphere, and uniqueness of
the restaurant. An expensive restaurant doesn't
necessarily ensure an enjoyable evening; while a
small, relatively unknown spot could have good
food, professional service, and a lovely
atmosphere. Therefore, on a purely subjective
basis, stars are used to judge the overall dining
value (see star ratings below). Keep in mind that
chefs and owners often change, which sometimes
drastically affects the quality of a restaurant. The
ratings in this guidebook are based on
information available at press time.

The restaurant price ratings, as categorized
below, describe general price-range relationships
among other restaurants and are based on the
average cost of an entrée for one person,
excluding tax and tip.

Restaurants

★	Good
★★	Very Good
★★★	Excellent
★★★★	Extraordinary Experience
$	The Price Is Right (less than $10)
$$	Reasonable ($10-$15)
$$$	Expensive ($15-$25)
$$$$	Big Bucks ($25 and up)

Wheelchair Accessibility

Wheelchair accessibility is noted by a ♻ at the end
of the entry. An establishment is considered
wheelchair accessible when a person in a wheelchair can easily enter a building (i.e., no steps, a
ramp, a wide-enough door) without assistance *and*
if the rest rooms are on the same floor as the
dining area and their entrances and stalls are wide
enough to accommodate a wheelchair.

Symbols

Everything from soup to nuts, the following
symbols indicate where you can stop or shop:

baked goods   ice cream/candy shops

coffee/tea   markets/food shops

wine/liquor   tableware

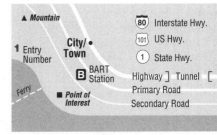

cooking supplies/cookbooks

Map Key

▲ *Mountain*	80 Interstate Hwy.
1 Entry Number	101 US Hwy.
City/ Town ●	1 State Hwy.
B BART Station	Highway] Tunnel [
Ferry	Primary Road
■ *Point of Interest*	Secondary Road

FYI

Area code 415 unless otherwise noted.

Drinking

The legal drinking age is 21. Bars stay open until
2AM. Wine and liquor are widely available and can be
purchased in most grocery stores and supermarkets.

Hours

It's a good idea to call ahead to find out if a particular
restaurant or shop will be open the day and time you
plan to visit. Generally shops are open Monday
through Saturday 9AM to 6PM, but keep in mind that

schedules may change with the seasons, the
economy, or even the whim of the owner. Opening and
closing times for shops, coffeehouses, and tearooms,
etc. are listed by day(s) only if normal hours apply
(opening between 8 and 11AM and closing between 4
and 7PM). In all other cases, specific hours are given
(e.g., 6AM-2PM, daily 24 hours, noon-5PM).

Reservations

Most restaurants within the city accept reservations.
Calling ahead is always a good idea, especially if the
restaurant is popular. It's easier to get a table Monday

through Wednesday nights than Thursday through Saturday, and earlier or later in the evening than the prime dinner hour of 7 to 8PM. Always call as far ahead as possible, but if you are shut out of the day and time you want, ask to leave your name on a waiting list. If you are staying in a large hotel, sometimes the concierge can secure a reservation for you at an always-busy restaurant. Many places have dining counters overlooking the kitchen to accommodate drop-in customers—they're also great for the single diner. But if you still can't get in to the hot spot of choice for dinner, go there for lunch—it will probably be less expensive and uncrowded enough for you to actually see the room and hold a conversation.

Smoking
In San Francisco, it is currently legal to smoke only in the bar area of restaurants and in freestanding bars and taverns. In addition, many eateries prefer to be entirely smoke-free; always ask before lighting up. On 1 January 1998, a state law will be implemented that prohibits smoking in all restaurants, bars, and taverns. A number of places, however, have tapped into the cigar-smoking fad that has swept the country by adding separate cigar rooms (see "The Return of the Smoke-Filled Room," on page 118, for details).

Tipping
A 15 percent gratuity to wait staff is standard in most dining spots, though 20 percent for good service is becoming more common. Generally, there is no need to tip the maître d' or the sommelier separately.

Food Tours
The best way to acquire an insider's view of two of the most food-intense neighborhoods—North Beach and Chinatown—is on a guided walking tour.

GraceAnn Walden (397.8530), a food columnist for the *San Francisco Chronicle* (and also the reviser of this book), leads a four-hour walking tour of North Beach each Saturday, including lunch at **Enrico's.** On the third Saturday of each month, she also offers a tour that goes behind the scenes of the fishing industry at **Fisherman's Wharf,** including a visit to a smokehouse (with samples of smoked salmon) and lunch at **Alioto's.**

Shirley Fong Torres (355.9657), known as the "Wok Wiz," offers a 3.5-hour tour of Chinatown daily, which includes a walk through an herb shop, an Asian supermarket, and a noodle factory, and concludes with a dim sum lunch. On Saturday, she expands the walk, calling it "I Can't Believe I Ate My Way Through Chinatown Tour."

For coffee lovers, **Elaine Sosa** (673.WALK) conducts "Javawalk," a two-hour tour of coffeehouses Tuesday through Saturday in spring and summer and Thursday through Saturday in fall and winter. The tour starts at Union Square and winds through Chinatown and North Beach. Sosa covers the history and rituals of coffeehouse culture, stopping at a couple of North Beach cafes for a quick java fix, as well as at a coffee purveyor's where participants can watch the beans being roasted.

Fabulous Food Festivals and Street Fairs

San Francisco's fascinating ethnic diversity is joyously reflected in its many food festivals and street fairs held throughout the year. A few events that are located outside the city are unique—for example, the celebration of wine in **Healdsburg,** and of mustard in the **Napa Valley**—and give people a wonderful reason to get into their cars and go to a party. All of the celebrations tend to be crowded, noisy, fragrant, and colorful, brimming with local pride. The following are some of the most prominent, regularly scheduled festivities:

February
The **Chinese New Year Festival and Parade** is a two-week celebration from the end of February into early March, climaxing in a colorful parade that snakes through **Chinatown.** It draws thousands of visitors and is aired live on local television stations. Traditional Chinese foods— sweet bean buns and dumplings, among others— are featured. ♦ Bounded by Kearny and Powell Sts, and Bush St and Broadway. 982.3000

Clam Chowder Cook-Off and Chowder Chase has, in addition to the cook-off, a number of booths along the boardwalk that sell clam chowder; fairgoers can do their own taste tests. ♦ Santa Cruz Beach Boardwalk, off Beach St (between the San Lorenzo River and Cliff St). 408/423.5590

The **Russian Festival** celebrates Russian culture and showcases food, music, and crafts. Celebrants feast on kasha, pierogi, blini, and caviar, and wash it down with a variety of vodkas. ♦ 2450 Sutter St (between Divisadero and Broderick Sts). 921.7631

The **Tet Festival** commemorates the Vietnamese New Year and features such traditional foods as shrimp and pork spring rolls, hot rice noodles, and fish soups. ♦ Larkin St (at O'Farrell St). 885.2743

Masters of Food & Wine, an annual event held just outside **Carmel-by-the-Sea,** brings together world class vintners, spotlights local and Northern California chefs, and welcomes culinary luminaries from all over the US and the world, such as Julia Child and Robert Mondavi. The six-day festival is a gourmand's dream, with wine tastings, celebrity chef cooking classes, and multicourse dinners accompanied by premium wines.

At the Highlands Inn (on Hwy 1, 4 miles south of Carmel-by-the-Sea), Carmel Highlands. 408/624.3801; fax 408/626.1574 &

March

The **Napa Valley Mustard Festival** takes place in communities throughout the valley

when the wild mustard blooms on the local hillsides. The festival features winery tours, wine tastings, and gourmet foods, most involving mustard in some guise. Vendors sell jars of mustard, and area restaurants offer intimate dinners of such dishes as quesadillas made with mustard, and salmon with mustard sauce. ♦ Napa, Yountville, St. Helena, and Oakville, among other towns. 707/938.1133

April

Cherry Blossom Festival is held in **Japantown** and celebrates Japanese art, film, and Kabuki theater; it features teriyaki and tempura, among other favorite foods. There's also a traditional Japanese tea ceremony. ♦ Bounded by Octavia and Fillmore Sts, and Geary Blvd and California St. 563.2313

May

Carnaval Parade and Festival emphasizes multiculturalism and outrageousness in its parade, costumes, and cuisine. Food ranges from Brazilian to Thai to Creole to Filipino. ♦ Harrison St (from 21st to 16th Sts). 826.1401

Cinco de Mayo Parade and Festival commemorates Mexico's defeat of the French in 1862. Traditional Mexican and other Latin music is played, and food vendors offer barbecue, burritos, *flautas* (fried, stuffed tortillas), Mexican ices, margaritas, and beer. ♦ Civic Center Plaza, in front of City Hall (bounded by Larkin and Polk Sts, and Grove and McAllister Sts). 826.1401

Norway Day Festival is staged to promote cultural and economic cooperation between Norway and the United States. It showcases arts and crafts, music, and such Norwegian foods as open-face sandwiches featuring shrimp, salmon, or meatballs. Cooks prepare waffles, served with jam, and *lefse* (a crepe served with sugar and butter). ♦ Herbst Pavilion at Fort Mason (bounded by Bay St and San Francisco Bay, and Van Ness Ave and Laguna St). 510/676.4708

Russian River Wine Festival stages wine tastings and intimate dinners at the wineries, featuring such entrées as salmon cakes and grilled Sonoma free-range chicken breast. Participants can also snack on more casual foods. ♦ Healdsburg Plaza (bounded by Matheson and Plaza Sts, and Center St and Healdsburg Ave), Healdsburg. 707/433.6935

June

North Beach Street Fair reflects the area's Italian-immigrant roots, as well as its past and present status as a mecca for artists and writers. The scene consists of music, paintings sold on the street, and plenty of eating and drinking (sausage and pepper sandwiches, garlic chicken sandwiches, shish kabobs, cannoli, pizza, and cappuccino). ♦ On Grant Ave (between Columbus Ave and Union St), 403.0666

Union Street Spring Festival is essentially a garden party held in historic **Cow Hollow.** The street is closed to traffic from Gough to Steiner Streets, and a fashion show, waiters' race, and tea dancing are among the festivities. From the plethora of street vendors, you can buy tasty bagels with cream cheese, lace onions, gourmet sausages, focaccia stuffed with prosciutto or vegetables, fajitas, and hamburgers.

July

Jazz & All That Art on Fillmore is an enormous free jazz concert held on Fillmore Street. While you're moving to the groove, feast on buffalo wings, barbecued pork sandwiches, jambalaya, gumbo, and cheesesteaks. ♦ Fillmore St (between Post and Jackson Sts). 346.4446

Sonoma Salute to the Arts also features wine-country gourmet foods, especially goat cheese and foie gras; one of the two producers of foie gras in the United States is located in **Sonoma.** ♦ Sonoma Plaza (bounded by First St E and First St W, and Napa and Spain Sts), Sonoma. 707/938.1133

September

Folsom Street Fair is not for the timid—the booths here are devoted to leather, body piercing, and the like. This is where you can sample a variety of traditional Indian specialties, as well as knishes, barbecued oysters, steak and chicken tacos, and pizza.

ACCESS Top 10

Within these pages you will find more than 1,200 restaurants and coffee and wine bars (plus food and housewares shops)—an overwhelming dining dilemma indeed. To ease your way, we at ACCESS have gone out on a limb and selected from among these legions of food emporia our choices of the top ten dining spots in the city. In making our selections we have not limited ourselves only to places carrying high price tabs or offering haute cuisine. Instead we have chosen those establishments that, each in its own special way, afford diners a particular level of excellence, be it the best ambience, best value for the dollar, or the best cuisine when money is no object. Rest assured that all the places listed within the pages of this book have earned the ACCESS seal of approval. Of the many, however, these few stand out. Bon appetit!

Bruno's Chef James Ormsby presents seared *ahi* tuna on perfumed lentils and salmon with a mushroom "roof" served in quinoa in a 1950s retro setting complete with huge red leather booths and a Marilyn Monroe lookalike, who hosts.

Enrico's Sidewalk Cafe This lively place on busy Broadway is perfect for people watching, pizza eating, and listening to jazz. The menu also features tapas, and main courses with Asian, Spanish, and Italian influences.

La Folie Chef/owner Roland Passot has hit his stride in this elegant, yet casual dining place with such luscious dishes as boneless quail stuffed with foie gras—as lovely to look at as they are to eat.

Fringale An authentic bistro with the finest in French fare—haute cuisine at low prices.

Great Eastern Simply the best Chinese restaurant in Chinatown, this is the place for prawns, fish, and abalone plucked fresh from the tanks—steamed or stir-fried, it's a treat.

The Heights Located in a sedate townhouse, this is the perfect venue for Charles Solomon's refined French/Californian cuisine. Save room for the apple napoleon with green apple sorbet.

Jasmine House Wonderful Vietnamese food from this family-owned and -operated restaurant includes grilled catfish, whole crab done with butter and black pepper, and fresh spring rolls. A helpful staff can guide you through the menu.

Oritalia Fusion cuisine at its finest, this is the place where Asian meets Italian in style.

Saji Real sushi lovers come to this place, where artistic flair and fresh fish fill the bill. Chicken teriyaki, tempura, and soft-shell crab are other standouts.

Zarzuela For the most delicious tapas in the Bay Area, this neighborhood haunt offers a cozy setting, friendly service, and a good wine list to boot.

Downtown/Union Square

The epicurean epicenter of San Francisco is the downtown area, encompassing Union Square and the **Financial District.** On any given weekday, about 225,000 people come here to work, play, shop, and eat. As

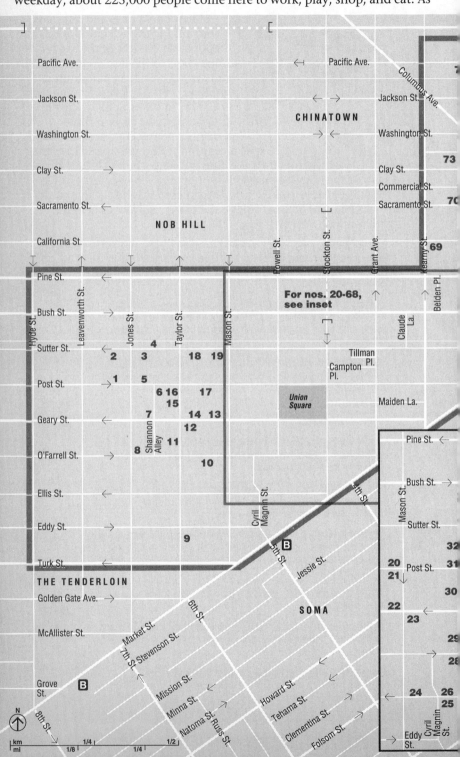

one of the country's top financial centers, and encompassing its third-largest shopping district (after New York and Chicago), downtown also claims the lion's share of the city's three- and four-star restaurants. They're splashy and special, and they lure San Franciscans and tourists to the area specifically to dine. Downtown is home to **Aqua**, probably the city's most beautiful restaurant, with its stunning architecture, lofty ceilings, and towering flower arrangements. The extraordinary **Redwood Room** in the **Clift Hotel** is a bar cloaked in aged redwood and featuring large reproductions of Gustav Klimt paintings on the rich-wood interior. Other destinations are the romantic, exotic **Fleur de Lys**, which cossets guests under its tent of flowered fabric; the elegant, red-walled **Masa's**; and the exuberant **Postrio**, with its glitz and glamour.

Yet the fast pace of the area has also bred hundreds of places that cater to the quick-lunch crowd. Some aren't worth the price, while others are expert at preparing hearty deli sandwiches and bountiful salads.

The Financial District's heyday began on 12 May 1848, when Sam Brannan, editor of the town's first newspaper, announced that gold had been discovered in the foothills of the Sierras. The Gold Rush turned the local shopkeepers into bankers, since they had scales that could weigh the gold and safes for storing it. Other businesses proliferated here as well, including eateries catering to lusty appetites. One San Francisco classic in particular, the no-nonsense "men's grill," harks back to this era, when lucky miners came to town for a thick steak, Champagne, and the company of a Barbary Coast damsel. These historic eateries exude a masculine ambience characterized by dark wood, tile floors, and bentwood chairs; most offer a simple French–Italian–inspired menu. Several of these old-timers are still popular (and today both women and men are welcome), including the **Tadich Grill**, serving classic preparations of seafood; and **Sam's Grill**, with its warren of private booths for discreet encounters.

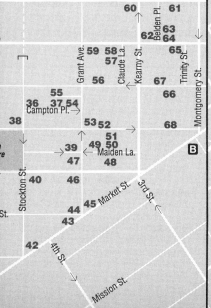

By the time of the Civil War, genteel Union Square had become a hub of retail commerce, exemplified by the **City of Paris** department store. It was known for its basement food hall, not unlike the one at Harrods in London and a precursor of **Macy's Cellar.** When the Dallas-based **Neiman Marcus** department store took over the space in the early 1980s, the **City of Paris** was demolished except for its impressive glass dome. Today people can sip a demitasse of bouillon and munch on hot popovers under the dome at **The Rotunda** and enjoy a civility that harks back to the top hat and white gloves era.

A host of fine merchants surrounds the square. But though branches of **Tiffany, Saks**, and **Macy's** can now be found in cities across the nation, the restaurants in Union Square retain their unique character. An innovative breed of dining establishment has arrived on the scene: **Rumpus,** tucked away in an alley off **Grant Avenue**, boasts a party atmosphere, and **Cafe Akimbo** on **Maiden Lane** offers unusual East/West combinations in bright, modern surroundings. In Union Square, you can pick up just the right cookie cutter or catch a cooking demonstration by a local chef in **Macy's Cellar**, buy exotic condiments from **The Epicurean Shop** at **Neiman Marcus**, or indulge in a luscious bonbon from **The Candy Jar.**

The **Embarcadero Center**, an eight-block complex of retail offices and residential space, contains some top-flight restaurants, including **Harbor Village**, one of the city's handsomest Chinese eateries, and **Splendido**, a Mediterranean oasis in the concrete jungle. An ever-increasing number of eateries near the complex draws diners from all over the Bay Area to the concrete caverns of the Financial District. There's **L'Olivier**, with its classic French country dishes; **Rubicon**, backed by celebrities Robert De Niro and Robin Williams; and **MacArthur Park**, which boasts an all-American bill of fare. **Sol y Luna** has great tapas, and several evenings a week it becomes a sizzling nightclub. Another popular watering hole (if a more sedate one) is the **London Wine Bar** on **Sansome Street**; established in the mid-1980s, it was the first of its kind in California.

Admittedly, this is an expensive area of town to eat in. However, there are several great lunch spots which cater to downtown workers, such as **Kelly's on Trinity, Nosheria**, and **360° Gourmet Burritos.** In addition, patrons of such reasonably priced alfresco cafes as the charming **Cafe Bastille** and **Plouf** can enjoy the illusion of dining on a Parisian boulevard.

1 Burma House Cuisine ★$ The exotic flavors of Myanmar are showcased in a utilitarian environment distinguished only by the artificial vines twisting around the ceiling beams. Salads are highlights, particularly the ginger salad, tossed tableside with tender young ginger, lentils, yellow peas, fried garlic, sesame seeds, and chilies, balanced by a squeeze of fresh lime. Or choose the refreshing tea salad, which has a peaty quality. Good options for the main course are the panfried string beans, with a wallop of chilies, and the Rangoon squid, which is scored and steamed, topped with peanuts, and served on a bed of spinach with a pungent sweet-and-sour sauce. The low prices and convenient location make this a good destination for theatergoers. ♦ Burmese ♦ M-F lunch and dinner; Sa-Su dinner. 720 Post St (between Jones and Leavenworth Sts). 775.1156 &

2 Cafe Titanic ★$ Entrepreneur Chip Conley has bought and refurbished small hotels all over San Francisco, adding restaurants to each. Now, he's replaced the ordinary coffee shop at the **Commodore International Hotel** with a delightful diner-cafe. The name, **Cafe Titanic,** fits in well with the nautical decor of the hotel in general, and the basic American fare is tasty. For breakfast (served until the restaurant closes), try eggs served with applewood-smoked bacon, home fries, and fresh-baked muffins or scones; or ricotta-stuffed French toast served with warm fruit and real maple syrup. Good lunch choices include the "life preserver" burger, the exotic vegetarian Vietnamese sandwich with five-spice tofu, and the chicken prosciutto sandwich with melted fontina accented with sun-dried tomatoes and basil. The homemade soups are terrific, too. ♦ American ♦ Daily breakfast and lunch until 2:30PM. 825 Sutter St (between Jones and Leavenworth Sts). 923.6800; fax 923.6804

3 Fleur de Lys ★★★★$$$$ Famed designer Michael Taylor, who defined the California look, decorated this elegant restaurant in 1969, yet it remains right up-to-date. Flowered fabric is fashioned into a room-size tent at the center of the room over an impressive arrangement of fresh flowers, making a perfect setting for the stunning French-Californian menu. Hubert Keller, who has worked with the great French chef Roger Verge, has removed much of the butter and fat from his cuisine. In addition to the impressive à la carte selections, he offers a four-course tasting menu beginning with a spectacular "Symphony of Fleur de Lys Appetizers" (which may include a crab cake, a sushi roll slice prepared with quinoa, and a slice of foie gras studded with pecans) and followed by an entrée such as venison tournedos on braised endive, potato-wrapped lamb chops on roasted shallots, or seared swordfish on chive mashed potatoes. There's also an inventive, four-course vegetarian tasting menu that might feature a light cauliflower mousseline; handmade pasta with wild mushrooms and thyme; and braised celery hearts. Save room for an elegant, delicious dessert, such as fresh raspberry sabayon soufflé with vanilla ice cream or pumpkin–cream cheese pie with nutmeg-cinnamon ice cream. The wine list is pricey. ♦ French/Californian ♦ M-Sa dinner. Reservations recommended; jacket required. 777 Sutter St (between Taylor and Jones Sts). 673.7779; fax 673.4619

4 Lehr Brothers Bistro & Grill ★$$ This dining room in the **Canterbury Hotel** has been a San Francisco institution since 1970, but it has undergone a complete makeover. Now the space encompasses a bistro, grill room, oyster bar, and even a cigar room (one of the city's latest restaurant fads). One of the bistro's unique features is an entire wall stacked with premium spirits and liqueurs. A new chef, Philipe LaMancusa, has re-energized the menu; good choices are the grilled Hawaiian Big Eye Tuna on warm Maui onion-tomato concasse; and aged Delmonico steak with

truffle sauce. In addition to the Delmonico, there are five other cuts of steak: the locally grown Niman-Schell, Omaha Certified, Harris Ranch, and Nebraska. But skip the dreadful desserts. ♦ Continental ♦ Grill: daily breakfast, lunch, and dinner. Bistro and oyster bar: daily lunch and dinner.740 Sutter St (between Taylor and Jones Sts). 474.6478 ᕐ

WISHART

5 Wishart In business for over 20 years, this delightful shop with an English feel is a find for the food lover who has everything. How about a silver-plated pizza cutter, ice-cream scoop, or Tabasco-sauce holder? There are also silver place-card holders, bottle stoppers, crystal brandy snifters and wineglasses, salt and pepper shakers, and other accessories. One of the top draws: a special silver-plated coffeepot, a favorite of connoisseurs. ♦ Tu-Sa. 664 Post St (between Taylor and Jones Sts). 474.7442 ᕐ

6 Ar Roi ★★$ With a Deco-inspired interior and extremely friendly service, this Thai eatery is a cut above most of the neighborhood competition. While many Thai chefs in this country tone down their spices, the one here embraces fiery flavors. The chicken salad is pungent and sinus-clearing, with the citrus overtones and the spiciness a refreshing contrast to the crisp, cold iceberg lettuce and the profusion of ground chicken. Shrimp with red curry in coconut milk hits the palate tasting sweet but leaves in a blaze of fire that can only be doused by rice. Other worthy dishes are the chicken with coconut milk soup (a classic starter) and chicken wings with chili sauce topped with crisp, fried basil leaves. ♦ Thai ♦ M-Sa lunch and dinner; Su dinner. 643 Post St (between Taylor St and Shannon Alley). 771.5146

7 City of Paris ★★$$ Named after the legendary department store (which is now **Neiman Marcus**), this Art Nouveau bistro turns out some excellent straightforward food. The open kitchen is dominated by a rotisserie. To start, the cabbage salad combines salty lardons of bacon and chunks of blue cheese, with a lemony dressing bringing everything together. One of the top main-course choices, and by far the best value, is the roast chicken, served with crunchy double-cooked fries. Wine prices are excellent, but the service can be a little disjointed. ♦ Californian/Bistro ♦ Daily breakfast, lunch, and dinner. 101 Shannon Alley (at Geary St). 441.4442; fax 928.6813 ᕐ

That's some dough: Thirty-five years ago, a plain slice of pizza cost 15¢; today it's $2.

Dottie's TRUE BLUE CAFE

8 Dottie's True Blue Cafe ★$ Pancakes and homemade breads are the lure of this breakfast and lunch spot. A recent change in ownership has brought an increase in vegetarian offerings, especially at lunch, like the roasted eggplant sandwich with goat cheese and tomatoes, a black bean chili, and vegetable-filled tarts. ♦ American ♦ M lunch; Tu breakfast; W-F breakfast and lunch; Sa-Su breakfast. 522 Jones St (between O'Farrell and Geary Sts). 885.2767 ♿

9 Original Joe's Italian Restaurant ★$ This Italian-American spot has a strong following despite its location in the Tenderloin, a slowly improving neighborhood that still carries a rather rough reputation. The excellent hamburger—a huge, loosely formed log of ground meat served on a chewy, hollowed-out French roll—may be one of the reasons for its appeal. (Ask for your burger to be flame-grilled rather than fried.) The red vinyl booths and moody lighting likewise speak of another era. The waiters in vintage tuxedos are as classic as the retro food, and the cooks working behind the counter in the open kitchen are as crusty as the bread. ♦ Italian ♦ Daily lunch, dinner, and late-night meals. 144 Taylor St (between Turk and Eddy Sts). 775.4877; fax 775.6563

10 Cityscape Restaurant ★★$$$ Located on the 46th floor of the **San Francisco Hilton and Towers,** this restaurant affords diners one of the best views of the city—a stunning 360° panorama. You can have a good dining experience here, too, if you stick to the classics like prime rib, surf and turf, Maine lobster, or New York steak. The desserts, however, are only adequate. ♦ Californian ♦ M-Sa dinner; Su brunch and dinner. Reservations recommended. 333 O'Farrell St (between Mason and Taylor Sts). 771.1400; fax 673.5163 ♿

11 Napa Valley Winery Exchange In keeping with its name, this shop stocks mostly Napa Valley wines among its 500 selections. The staff also helps customers plan trips to the Napa Valley and arranges personal appointments for winery tours and tastings and will ship purchases, too. A quarterly newsletter includes the staff's pick of those wines introduced in the last three months. ♦ M-Sa. 415 Taylor St (between O'Farrell and Geary Sts). 771.2887; fax 441.9463 ♿

12 French Room ★★$$$$ With a massive crystal chandelier and Louis XV decor, this beautiful restaurant in the **Clift Hotel** is popular with hotel guests and other visitors to the city, but is overlooked by locals. The menu choices span the globe, which probably reflect the hotel's many international guests. For breakfast (as well as Sunday brunch), there's Belgian waffles, *huevos rancheros* (fried eggs served over a corn tortilla with spicy tomato sauce), smoked-salmon eggs Benedict, egg-white frittatas for the low-cholesterol set, and even a full Japanese menu. The lunch and dinner menus concentrate on classic American dishes superbly prepared—the dry-aged New York steak, for example, is nearly perfect. The extensive, award-winning wine list features French, Italian, and American vintages. ♦ International ♦ M breakfast; Tu-Sa breakfast and dinner; Su brunch. 495 Geary St (at Taylor St). 775.4700; fax 441.4621 ♿

12 Redwood Room ★★$$$ One of the best examples of Art Deco design in America, this dining room in the **Clift Hotel** is entirely paneled in redwood from a 2,000-year-old tree. Soaring 22-foot fluted columns and an elegant 75-foot bar decorated with fine Italian marble highlights and Klimt reproductions complete the magnificent look. The "bistro" menu lists a nice selection of snacks and light lunch choices. Start with a traditional French onion soup or a hearts of romaine salad with creamy Caesar dressing. The terrific entrées include the Clift burger with crisp Canadian bacon and melted Swiss cheese, smoked turkey club sandwich with avocado, and chicken or shrimp stir-fry with Shanghai noodles. This is a great place to relax over Champagne and a light meal while listening to the nightly jazz piano music. ♦ Californian/French ♦ Bistro menu 11AM-11PM. 495 Geary St (at Taylor St). 775.4700; fax 441.4621 ♿

13 California Pizza Kitchen ★$ Put on dark glasses to enter this chrome yellow, black, and white world of strange pizzas. In the worst of California tradition, this chain's parlor offers thin, slightly sweet crusts topped with such idiocies as barbecued chicken, Thai chicken with peanuts, duck with hoisin sauce, and Canadian bacon with pineapple. Stick with the traditional and you'll have no regrets, especially since the prices for pizza and pasta are reasonable for the area. ♦ Gourmet Pizza

♦ Daily lunch and dinner. 438 Geary St (between Mason and Taylor Sts). 563.8911; fax 563.2143 ♿

14 David's Delicatessen ★★$ The true deli connoisseur may be disappointed by this place, the city's most famous Jewish deli. However, the sandwiches are generous, piled high with lots of pastrami or corned beef, and the Reuben and the blintzes are standouts. Full dinners include Hungarian goulash, stuffed cabbage, and beef brisket. For dessert, you can choose among any of more than a hundred homemade pastries, including dense cheesecake and "decadence," a gooey concoction made with five kinds of chocolate. Service is efficient and friendly. ♦ Deli ♦ Daily breakfast, lunch, and dinner. 474 Geary St (between Mason and Taylor Sts). 771.1600; fax 931.5442 ♿

14 La Scene Cafe and Bar ★★$$$ A pleasant spot before or after the theater, this richly appointed room is graced with sketches of performers who have appeared at the **Curran Theatre.** The food here has been unreliable in the past, but now Natalie Sellers (formerly of **Stars Cafe**) has taken over in the kitchen—a harbinger of very good things to come. The à la carte menu changes regularly, but has featured such appetizers as crispy calamari with romesco sauce, and hummus with mint pesto accompanied by lentil chips and onion confit tart. Entrées include sautéed yellowtail with creamy polenta, marinated pork chops, braised lamb shanks, and a truly outstanding New York strip steak. The pretheater three-course fixed-price menu is a great deal. ♦ Provençal/ Mediterranean ♦ Daily breakfast; Tu-Sa dinner; daily bar (with a limited menu M, Su). Reservations recommended. 490 Geary St (at Taylor St). 292.6430; fax 441.8788 ♿

Floréal®

15 Floréal This charming flower shop fashions unique, sophisticated centerpieces, with the unusual touch of fruits and vegetables; an arrangement might include pomegranates, kiwi, and a profusion of fragrant lavender. It's worth a visit for inspiration alone; check out the

whimsical art pieces featuring fruit and food motifs, freeze-dried produce that looks great in arrangements, and elegant garlands for all seasons. ♦ M-Sa. 533 Taylor St (between Geary and Post Sts). 885.4261; fax 885.0342 ♿

16 Gold Leaf The theme at this store is food and flowers, with thousands of miniature ceramic fruits, vegetables, and flowers that are so detailed they look like shrunken versions of the real thing. The collection also includes wonderful button covers, mini-teapots, earrings, bells, and magnets that follow the same food-obsessed theme. ♦ M-Sa. 611 Post St (between Taylor and Jones Sts). 885.4004; fax 673.6177 ♿

17 Postrio ★★★★$$$ Wolfgang Puck's Northern California outpost looks like a slice of LA. With customers who appear to be from central casting descending a dramatic staircase into the impressive dining room, it's a great place to people watch. However, although the ambience is influenced by Hollywood, the inventive food is rooted in San Francisco's strong Italian and Asian heritage. Chefs (and brothers) Steven and Mitchell Rosenthal have put their own spin on Puck's signature cuisine with such creations as leg of lamb with garlic potato puree and nicoise olive sauce; tuna sashimi with salmon tartare and uni vinaigrette (a vinaigrette made with sea urchin roe); and a yummy charcuterie plate. Other standouts include Puck's version of roasted Chinese duck, served with a changing array of sauces such as spicy mango and crispy lotus root. The service is smooth and professional. While everyone seems to come here for lunch or dinner, most people don't realize it's also a great downtown breakfast spot. Don't miss the oyster and pancetta omelette. ♦ Californian ♦ M-F breakfast, lunch, and dinner; Sa-Su brunch and dinner. 545 Post St (between Mason and Taylor Sts). 776.7825; fax 776.6702 ♿

18 Yakety Yak Coffee House Brightly painted in primary colors, this rambling, rustic cafe attracts an artistic crowd, especially the students at the **Academy of Art College** across the street. The counter is lined with all kinds of delicious pastries and munchies, and the coffee has a marvelously strong and bitter edge. ♦ Daily. 679 Sutter St (between Mason and Taylor Sts). 885.6908

19 White Horse Tavern ★★$ This tavern, in the **Hotel Beresford,** replicates an Edinburgh pub, and as might be expected, the cooks do a splendid job with grilled meats. Portions are large, preparations are straightforward, and prices are excellent. The large hamburger is a serious challenge to finish, and the corned beef and cabbage, which consists of a half-dozen thick slices of meat and half a head of cabbage cut into wedges and arranged on the plate with a boiled potato, makes for a pleasant dining experience. ♦ British ♦ M breakfast and lunch; Tu-Sa breakfast, lunch, and dinner. 635 Sutter St (between Mason and Taylor Sts). 673.9900; fax 474.0449

SAN FRANCISCO

20 Pacific ★★★$$$ This restaurant at the **Pan Pacific** hotel has undergone some major changes, including the erection of a new etched-glass partition that makes the space feel more intimate and closed-off from the lobby. Chef Yoshi Kojiima, an up-and-coming local star, has revamped the menu, adding appetizers such as lightly smoked sturgeon paired with a salad made with mache (field greens); tuna tartare with osetra caviar; and a perfectly grilled scallop with fava-bean-soup puree. The entrées continue in this modern vein, particularly the roast beef fillet with portobello mushrooms and grilled striped bass with curried apples. Tasty desserts are featured as well; if you have room, be sure to try the wild berry napoleon with silky mascarpone cheese, or the refreshing curried pineapple with mango sorbet. ♦ Californian ♦ M-F breakfast, lunch, and dinner, Sa-Su brunch and dinner. 500 Post St (between Mason and Taylor Sts). 929.2087; fax 921.4756 ♿

ZiNGARi
r i s t o r a n t e

21 Zingari ★★$$$ Formerly the **Ristorante Donatello** (which was one of the top Italian eateries in the city several years ago), this dining room in the **Donatello Hotel** continues to serve excellent Italian fare. Owner/chef Giovanni Scorzo has chosen to feature dishes from all over Italy, presented in an elegant, refined style with such menu offerings as broiled calamari topped with fresh tomatoes and basil, grilled and smoked mozzarella cheese served with portobello mushrooms and radicchio (which the menu calls "wild chicory"), and veal loin stuffed with truffles and fontina cheese, as well as risotti, pasta dishes, and salads. Named after the Italian word for "gypsies," the decor of the intimate dining room features Venetian marble accents. ♦ Italian ♦ Daily breakfast, lunch, and dinner. 501 Post St (at Mason St). 441.7100; fax 885.8842 ♿

22 Christophe ★$$$ Classic French food in a pink-washed Art Deco setting makes this restaurant a festive spot for dining before or after the theater. The best deal is the pretheater fixed-price menu, which might consist of ravioli with sun-dried tomatoes, mixed salad, thin medaillons of pork piccata, and a fresh-fruit pudding. ♦ French ♦ M, Su dinner; Tu-Sa lunch and dinner. Reservations recommended. 405 Mason St (between Geary and Post Sts), Second floor. 771.6393; fax 771.6496 ♿

22 Biscuits and Blues ★$$ Well-known restaurateur Regina Charboneau specializes in "hot biscuits and cool blues." The biscuits, shrimp and corn fritters, and vinegar-laced greens *are* exceptional, but otherwise the kitchen can be uneven. Among the main courses on the abbreviated menu are grilled or fried catfish and chicken, a daily special such as jambalaya, Caesar salad topped with crisply fried shrimp, and a vegetarian plate of pickled black-eyed peas, mashed potatoes, pureed sweet potatoes, and those wonderful greens. The walls of this basement-level speakeasy are covered with shrines to blues singers, and masses of candles flank the slightly raised stage. For added pleasure, there is live music every night. ♦ Southern ♦ Cover from 9PM to 1AM. Tu-Sa dinner. 401 Mason St (at Geary St). 292.2583; fax 834.2754 ♿

23 Sushi Bune ★★$ Popular and fun for a quick lunch, this spot's chefs place sushi and sashimi on little boats that float around the sushi bar's moat; diners at the counter grab as little—or as much— as they want as it sails by. At the end of the meal the server counts up what the diner has consumed, calculating the prices by the size or shape of the raft. Other choices include a full dinner menu, and the tempura is better than average. ♦ Japanese ♦ Daily lunch and dinner. 389 Geary St (at Mason St). 781.5111 ♿ Also at: 181 O'Farrell St (between Stockton and Powell Sts). 392.5111 ♿

24 New Delhi Restaurant ★★$$ Set in a former hotel ballroom, this eatery is graced by elaborate columns that lend it a vestige of grandeur. Among the offerings the tandoori chicken and the vegetable turnovers stand out. For a quick bite, sit at the ornate mahogany bar and order appetizers. ♦ Indian ♦ M-Sa lunch and dinner; bar daily until 2AM. 160 Ellis St (between Powell and Mason Sts). 397.8470; fax 397.1024

25 Puccini & Pinetti ★$ Operated by the Kimpton hotel group, which manages more than a dozen restaurants around town, this casual dining spot presents a menu that emphasizes straightforward pasta dishes, a few salads, and well-prepared panini, all at reasonable prices. Particularly good menu choices are angel hair pasta with roasted vegetables and basil oil, spicy spaghetti alla putanesca, and grilled chicken breast with rosemary potatoes. ♦ Californian/Italian ♦ Daily lunch and dinner. 129 Ellis St (at Cyril Magnin St). 392.5500; fax 392.2650 ⅋

26 Kantaro ★$ Light wood columns and white walls hung with lanterns give this Japanese restaurant style that belies its low prices. The best dish is teriyaki; the chicken version is moistened with a sauce that adds only a touch of sweetness. The tempura are crisp and excellent in flavor, although the coating is on the heavy side. Sushi or sashimi are fine for a quick lunch, and also popular is the Chirashi-sushi or scattered sushi, a bowl of vinegary rice topped with sliced raw fish, daikon, pickled ginger, cucumbers, and other fresh-tasting ingredients. ♦ Japanese ♦ Daily lunch and dinner. 124 Ellis St (between Powell and Cyril Magnin Sts). 986.2339; fax 986.4312 ⅋

27 John's Grill ★★$$ A classic San Francisco grill established in 1908, this eatery caters to the two-martini-lunch businessman. With a moody, dark wood and brass interior, it's no surprise that this was a favorite hangout of author Dashiell Hammett (as well as his fictional character Sam Spade). Like all grills of the period, its food has an Italian flavor. Specialties include steaks and pork chops with baked potatoes (one of Sam's favorites). The chicken Jerusalem (with artichokes and mushrooms) is a good rendition of a classic; and the seafood dishes are satisfying, especially the shrimp louie (tiny Bay shrimp on a bed of lettuce topped with a dressing of mayonnaise, red chili sauce, chopped green pepper, and green onion). To wash down your food, try the "Bloody Brigid," a sweet and sour vodka drink named for the dame that "done in" Sam Spade's partner, Miles Archer, in *The Maltese Falcon*. ♦ American ♦ M-Sa lunch and dinner; Su dinner. 63 Ellis St (between Stockton and Powell Sts). 986.0069; fax 982.2583

28 Dojima An ★★$$ Noodles are the specialty at this sleek, minimally decorated Japanese spot. The menu lists 23 different combinations made with either *udon* (thick, chewy white noodles) or *soba* (spaghetti-like buckwheat noodles), along with 11 *donburi* (rice topped with meat and vegetables). Best bets include the Japanese mountain vegetables and the cold noodles with grated daikon. The tempura, teriyaki, and other choices aren't nearly as special. ♦ Japanese ♦ Daily breakfast, lunch, and dinner. 219 O'Farrell St (between Powell and Cyril Magnin Sts). 956.0838

KULETO'S

29 Kuleto's Italian Restaurant ★$$ The large open kitchen gives this trattoria a boisterous feel. Sitting at the counter can be fun: Watch the always-harried chefs pull wonderful pizzas from the oven and exceptional roasted meats from the rotisserie. Pastas are good, too—especially the penne with lamb sausage and red chard in a marinara sauce—though on particularly busy nights the food can be lackluster. The adjoining **Caffè Kuleto** serves espresso drinks, focaccia, panini, and gelato at outdoor tables during the day. ♦ Italian ♦ Daily breakfast, lunch, and dinner. 221 Powell St (between O'Farrell and Geary Sts). 397.7720; fax 986.7050 ⅋

30 Compass Rose ★$$$ Formerly just an afternoon tea spot, this place in the lobby of the **Westin St. Francis Hotel** is now a full-service restaurant. Both the dining area and the adjacent bar feature dark wood paneling, high ceilings, and a quiet, subdued atmosphere; the bar also has hand-crafted, cut glass accents. The menu offers typical California cuisine presented with somewhat inconsistent quality. Featured as appetizers are shrimp tempura, grilled chicken winglets, and caviar; pizzas with inventive toppings such as smoked chicken are also available. A full tea is still served in the afternoon. ♦ Californian ♦ Daily lunch, afternoon tea, and dinner. 335 Powell St (between Geary and Post Sts). 774.0167; fax 403.6850 ⅋

30 Dewey's ★$ Also in the lobby of the **Westin St. Francis,** this sports bar is a fun place to grab a bite and catch your favorite team on one of the many TV sets. Decent cappuccino and excellent homemade pastries hit the spot at breakfast, and at lunch there's an all-you-can-eat buffet salad and sandwich bar. In the evening the menu features typical pub grub: burgers, sandwiches, and pizzas. Decorated in traditional pub style, with wood paneling, scattered tables, and bar stools, the bar features over 50 different beers. ♦ Sports Bar ♦ Daily breakfast, lunch, snacks, and dinner. 335 Powell St (between Geary and Post Sts). 774.0169; fax 403.6850 &

30 St. Francis Cafe ★★$$ This informal bistro was recently redecorated, and the atmosphere is now much lighter and airier. At breakfast, there's a traditional Japanese buffet as well as American dishes. The dinner menu begins with light appetizers such as greens with roasted garlic vinaigrette and a delightful Caesar salad with rosemary croutons; main courses include prime rib, grilled red snapper, and an interesting wild mushroom cioppino. Fans of classic comfort food shouldn't miss out on the traditional meatloaf, roast chicken, or braised lamb shank. To finish the meal on a sweet note, try cheesecake with strawberry sauce, apple jack Bavarian cake, or "liquored-up" bread pudding. ♦ American Bistro ♦ Daily breakfast and dinner. 335 Powell St (between Geary and Post Sts). 774.0264; fax 403.6850 &

30 My Sister's Garden Ceramic plates from Portugal and Italy, including the Nino Brucca collection, bring the southern European countryside to this shop in the lobby of the **Westin St. Francis** hotel. ♦ Daily. Main entrance 427 Post St (between Powell and Mason Sts). 397.0550 &

31 Morton's of Chicago ★$$$$ Although this upscale steak chain offers a great piece of beef, diners pay an exceedingly high price. And even at that price, the meat comes ungarnished; every side dish carries a separate price tag. Waiters are trained like seals to "tell" the menu, punctuating their recitation by displaying the raw ingredients—a potato, a bunch of broccoli, and a live lobster, for instance. For dessert, avoid the soufflés and stick with the Key lime pie. The basement setting, with dark woods and low lighting, has a retro mood. ♦ Steak house ♦ Daily dinner. 400 Post St (at Powell St). 986.5830; fax 986.5829 &

According to the National Restaurant Association, San Franciscans spend $978 per person annually for food consumed outside of the home.

World Famous
Sears FINE Food
BREAKFAST LUNCH

32 Sears Fine Foods ★★$$ Hordes line up at this no-nonsense breakfast and lunch spot. With its classic breakfasts, bare-bones environment, and motherly waitresses, the place is an institution. The most popular dish is the Swedish pancakes. ♦ American ♦ W-Su breakfast and lunch. 439 Powell St (between Post and Sutter Sts). 986.1160

33 Cafe SFA ★★$$ On the fifth floor of **Saks Fifth Avenue,** this department-store dining room is among the best of its kind. Booths curve around the room, affording a bird's-eye view of Union Square, and the convivial mix of well-dressed buyers, executives, and ladies-who-lunch provides ample opportunities for people watching. The imaginative menu includes a delicious crab sandwich, grilled Asian pork chops with a wild rice and spinach pancake, and smoked chicken and arugula salad with tarragon vinaigrette. ♦ Californian ♦ Daily lunch. 384 Post St (at Powell St). 986.4758; fax 986.0643 &

34 Scala's Bistro ★★★$$ In the **Sir Francis Drake** hotel, this dining room has quickly become one of Union Square's top restaurants and a magnet for the fashion crowd. The tin ceiling, Craftsman-looking lights, and striking open kitchen combine to spectacular effect. The bilevel dining area is broken up with booths and partitions that make just about every table seem intimate. The menu features both French country and Italian influences, including one of the best versions of fried calamari in town. Carpaccio is enhanced by shaved raw artichokes and nutty parmesan cheese, and linguine with fresh manila clams, toasted garlic, and oven-roasted tomatoes never fails to satisfy. Meat courses include marinated pork tenderloin with shoestring potatoes and wilted greens, and seared salmon fillet with buttermilk mashed potatoes. The lamb daube with spring vegetables is great on a chilly day. Among the memorable desserts is the Bostini cream pie—actually a bowl of rich custard topped with a tender cupcake of orange chiffon, all doused in chocolate sauce. ♦ Italian ♦ Daily breakfast, lunch, and dinner. 432 Powell St (between Post and Sutter Sts). 395.8555; fax 395.8549 &

34 Harry Denton's Starlight Room ★★$$ Harry Denton has a long history in San Francisco as a great host, bar-and-restaurant owner, and party animal, and now he has brought his boisterous personality to the rooftop nightclub at the **Sir Francis Drake** hotel. The room is decorated in sumptuous glamour reminiscent of classic 1930s movies, with voluminous silk drapery in ruby red and gold, crystal chandeliers, and high-backed velvet booths. But undoubtedly the major asset is the spectacular 360° view, which can be had from almost every table in the place. The menu features elegant appetizers and light entrées, including caviar, jumbo shrimp cocktail, oysters on the half shell, and chilled smoked beef tenderloin. Desserts here range from the light (angel food cake) to the deliciously decadent ("Death by Chocolate," a sinfully rich chocolate mousse cake), and a dizzying array of cocktails, specialty drinks, and wines is available. A full orchestra and vocalists perform dance music Monday through Saturday nights, and taped music is played on Sundays. ♦ American ♦ Cover. Daily dinner. 432 Powell St (between Post and Sutter Sts). 395.8595; fax 391.8719 ♿

34 Cafe Espresso ★★$ Few coffee bars are as pretty as this corner cafe in the **Sir Francis Drake.** At breakfast, grab a newspaper from the racks at the front window, order a bowl of granola or a pastry, and settle back for a gentle morning wake-up. The rich yellow walls, bistro-style chairs with marble tables, and the Old World marble-topped bar give the interior a sophisticated look. The straightforward fare includes sandwiches on fresh rolls or focaccia and such salads as Caesar, Chinese chicken, and Thai shrimp. End the meal with Snicker Doodle cookies and a cup of cappuccino or espresso. ♦ Cafe ♦ Daily breakfast, lunch, and dinner. 432 Powell St (between Post and Sutter Sts). 395.8585 ♿

35 Masa's ★★★★$$$$ Julian Serrano uses his Spanish heritage and French training to create some of the most innovative food in town. Instead of an à la carte menu, a four-course and a six-course tasting menu are offered. Serrano sautés chunks of rich foie gras to a crisp veneer and serves them with perfect vegetable morsels bathed in a truffle sauce with a hint of sweetness from Madeira. Lamb noisettes with green peppercorns in a velvety Zinfandel sauce is perfectly complemented by a rich Bordeaux. More than 20 vintages on the award winning wine list (including the exquisite Château d'Yquem) can be enjoyed by the glass, which facilitates matching the right wine to each course. The dining room has a sleek elegance, with modern art on the red walls and Hutschereuther china and Christofle silver table settings. Though the service is smooth and efficient, it can also be a bit cold and impersonal. ♦ French ♦ Tu-Sa dinner.

Reservations recommended; jacket required. 648 Bush St (between Stockton and Powell Sts). 989.7154; fax 989.3141 ♿

36 Campton Place Restaurant ★★★$$$$ Probably the best-known and most elegant hotel restaurant in the city, this establishment in the **Campton Place** hotel elevated its former chefs Bradley Ogden and Jan Dirnbaum to national stature. The present chef is Todd Humphries, who worked at Lespinasse in New York, and he has brought a French flair to dishes such as roast lobster with sweet corn risotto and summer truffles; and grilled Day Boat scallops with tomato confit and saffron gnocchi. Some of the dinner entrées also appear on the lunch menu at considerably lower prices. Another specialty is power breakfasts: The corn sticks are famous, but the prices are steep. ♦ American ♦ M-Sa breakfast, lunch, and dinner; Su brunch and dinner. Reservations recommended; jacket recommended. 340 Stockton St (at Campton Pl). 955.5555; fax 955.5596 ♿

37 Anjou ★★$$ A charming French ambience pervades this two-level dining room. The menu created by chef-owner Pierre Morin strikes a balance between tradition and innovation: There's moist duck confit on portobello mushrooms and herb polenta; asparagus with puff pastry in a morel-studded cream sauce; a casserole of prawns and artichokes; and lamb chops with fresh flageolets. On the classic side, consider such dishes as the thin-cut New York steak with extra-crisp fries, calves' brains sautéed with sage, or *tarte tatin* (upside-down apple tart) for dessert. ♦ French bistro ♦ Tu-Sa lunch and dinner. 44 Campton Pl (between Grant Ave and Stockton St). 392.5373

38 Napper's ★★$ Located on the ground floor of the **Grand Hyatt Hotel** on Union Square, this cafeteria has such whimsical touches as tables set on mannequin legs. On nice days, dine around a fountain on a brick terrace overlooking Union Square. Sandwiches are fairly priced and include shrimp salad, crab salad, and roast turkey; there are also hot dogs and chili dogs. Salads are another good luncheon value: The cobb has grilled chicken, bacon, blue cheese, and vegetables, and the creamy Caesar is available plain or with chicken. There's also a daily changing soup special and hearty chili con carne. ♦ American ♦ Daily breakfast, lunch, and early dinner. 345 Stockton St (between Post and Sutter Sts). 398.7687; fax 403.4888 ♿

Seeds of Change

On menus all over the Bay Area, you will see fruits and vegetables such as tomatoes, corn, apples, and beans described as "heirloom." The standard definition of the word is "something of special value passed along from generation to generation"; in agricultural terms, it takes on a different meaning: an heirloom tomato, for example, is one whose variety has been specially preserved because of its outstanding flavor.

Most people don't realize this, but up to 90 percent of the fruit and vegetable varieties that were grown in this country at the turn of the century have now disappeared. With the decline of the family farm in favor of agriculture run by large corporations, many of these varieties were discontinued in favor of hardier hybrids that were easier to grow and more suited to shipping over long distances and storing for long periods of time.

Most of these decisions were purely business-related; taste was almost never a factor and was sometimes deliberately disregarded for more practical considerations. The most egregious example was during the 1960s, when researchers at the **University of California at Davis** cultivated a square tomato that would fit better into shipping containers. That variety never made it into the marketplace, but other similarly pedestrian ones did.

And as the number of available varieties decreased, the spectrum of quality narrowed as well. In addition, there was the danger of extinction to consider: "Mono-crops," or crops based on only one or two varieties, have a higher chance of dying out if attacked by a pest or disease. For example, Ireland's Great Potato Famine in the 19th century occurred because there were only two types of potatoes grown there, and both were wiped out by blight.

Alarmed by this disturbing trend, a group of home gardeners called Seed Savers began to promote the preservation of plant varieties. The organization eventually swelled to 8,000 members, and it had a major impact on the policies of the produce industry. Thanks largely to the group's efforts, about 1,800 varieties have now been preserved and designated as "heirloom." And with America's increased awareness of food quality and freshness, there has been no shortage of consumers and restaurants willing to purchase these superior-tasting fruits and vegetables—even at their often-higher prices.

38 Plaza ★$$ Like **Napper's** (see page 19), this grand, full-service restaurant is in the **Grand Hyatt Hotel,** but the same cobb salad costs more than twice as much here. However, the mezzanine-level room is impressive: A stained-glass dome, latticework walls, a fountain, and a slate floor create a garden pavilion, complete with coconut palm trees, and the wall of windows overlooking **Union Square** provides picture-postcard views. Aside from sandwiches, there are such well-prepared hot dishes as roast chicken in a golden brown gravy or shrimp-chicken-vegetable stir-fry over rice. Evenings bring a fixed-price menu and free valet parking at the hotel entrance. And the Sunday Champagne brunch is popular. ◆ American ◆ Daily breakfast, lunch, and dinner; Su brunch. 345 Stockton St (between Post and Sutter Sts). 398.1234; fax 392.2536 ♿

39 Cafe Akimbo ★★$$ East and West meet comfortably at this 38-seat, third-floor cafe tucked away on Maiden Lane. Although the walls and support beams across the ceiling are painted in a rainbow of colors, the atmosphere is serene. Few chefs do as good a job with cross-cultural cooking as Daniel Yang, a former flight attendant who is the co-owner and (self-taught) chef. Starters include chilled soft tofu with a confetti of dried flowers and shrimp, all accented with a lemon-soy dressing, and grilled flank steak, drizzled with a honey-sesame vinaigrette. Among the entrées, pan-cooked chicken is paired with a sweet-potato and curry sauce, and a confit of duck leg is imaginatively served with an apricot sauce and ginger-glazed carrots. The ginger crème caramel makes a refreshing and comforting finish. ◆ Californian ◆ M-Sa lunch and dinner. 116 Maiden La (between Grant Ave and

Stockton St), Third floor. 433.2288; fax 433.2298 &

40 The Epicurean Shop The top floor of **Neiman Marcus** is the place to go for high-quality (and expensive) provisions, including smoked salmon, caviar, wine and spirits, cheeses, cookies, pies, cakes, and specialty products. Designer table accessories are also available. Made-to-order gift baskets are a specialty. ♦ Daily. 150 Stockton St (at Geary St), Fourth floor. 362.3900 ext 2177; fax 291.9616 &

THE
ROTUNDA ℠

40 The Rotunda ★★$$ The centerpiece of this elegant restaurant on the fourth floor of **Neiman Marcus** is the impressive stained-glass dome from the **City of Paris** department store, the site's former occupant. The dome lends a warm, romantic glow to the tiered dining room that wraps around the atrium. Other nice touches are the tiny cups of bouillon and delicious popovers with flavored butters that automatically appear on each table. Popular dishes include the lobster club sandwich, the oven-roasted chicken with mustard sauce, and the smoked-salmon salad. Desserts range from a tall root-beer float to an impressive lemon layer cake sprinkled with coconut. ♦ Californian ♦ Daily lunch and tea. Reservations recommended. 150 Stockton St (at Geary St), Fourth floor. 362.4777 &

THE
FRESHMARKET ℠

40 Fresh Market Cafe ★$ Relatively inexpensive, this third-floor cafe at **Neiman Marcus** is popular with the retail crowd, which comes for sandwiches (chicken curry in pita, tuna-pecan salad), salads (cobb, Caesar, or that 1950s classic, sweet lemon soufflé), and the soups (which change daily). Carrot cake and pound cake are both good ways to cap a meal or enjoy a midday respite from shopping. ♦ Cafe ♦ M, Th-F breakfast, lunch, and early dinner; Tu-W, Sa-Su breakfast and lunch. 150 Stockton St (at Geary St), Third floor. 362.3900 ext 2169 &

41 Macy's Cellar Just about everything any at-home cook needs can be found in this huge basement-level department of **Macy's.** It boasts walls of pottery dishes, appliances, cutlery, bar stools, gadgets, and a whole section of specialty food products, including oils, mustards, pastas, and condiments. Non-cooks will be happy, too, with the take-out deli

featuring Wolfgang Puck's pizza, **Boudin** breads and cakes, and Tom's cookies (they're fabulous). There's even a wine shop. Every Saturday a free cooking demonstration is given by a local or visiting chef (past partici-pants have included Jan Birnbaum of **Catahoula Saloon and Restaurant** and Roy Yamaguchi of the **Roy's** chain of restaurants). ♦ Daily. 170 O'Farrell St (between Stockton and Powell Sts). 397.3333 &

42 Ghirardelli Chocolates Chocoholics who don't want to fight the crowds at **Ghirardelli Square** can buy a wide range of chocolates in more peaceful surroundings here. Many of the choices are great for giving: A 10-ounce milk chocolate cable car may be the ultimate edible gift, and the 10-ounce can of unsweetened cocoa makes unbeatable hot chocolate. ♦ Daily. 44 Stockton St (between Market and O'Farrell Sts). 397.3615; fax 397.7626 &

42 Planet Hollywood ★$$$ Number 25 in the worldwide chain of eateries owned by Sylvester Stallone, Arnold Schwarzenegger, and Bruce Willis, this spot is more for the fanatical movie buff than the gourmet. Cluttered with movie photos, costumes, and artifacts (including the ark from *Raiders of the Lost Ark,* one of the half-human robots from the *Terminator* series, and a represent-ation of Stallone's *Demolition Man* character frozen in a block of ice), it's more of a theme park than a restaurant; gastronomically, your best bet is the simple hamburger, followed by a classic ice-cream soda. But kids (and kids at heart) will probably have a good time. (You might want to bring earplugs, though—the sound system continually blasts high-decibel rock music.) And don't forget to buy a T-shirt. ♦ American ♦ Daily lunch and dinner. 2 Stockton St (at Market St). 421.7827 &

43 Eppler's Bakery ★$ This 111-year-old enterprise, now with five branches, feels like a cozy hometown bakery. Its ovens turn out more than 300 products, including cakes, cookies, Danish, and doughnuts. Nothing is a standout, but the pastries are sweet and gooey. Coffee drinks, pastries, sandwiches, and other light lunch fare can be eaten in-house. ♦ Cafe ♦ M-Sa 6AM-7PM; Su 7AM-6PM. 750 Market St (at Grant Ave). 392.0101. Also at: Numerous locations throughout the city

44 Armani Cafe ★$$ For light eaters, a horseshoe-shape espresso bar right in the middle of **Emporio Armani** offers great coffee drinks, wine, aperitifs, focaccia sandwiches, designer pizzas, freshly made salads, and fresh-grilled seafood and meats. The tables are set up in a circle around the preparation/ serving area. ♦ Cafe ♦ Daily lunch. 1 Grant Ave (at O'Farrell St). 677.9010; fax 677.9212 &

45 Cafe Dolci Cramming a lot into a closet-size space, this black-and-white, high-tech espresso bar/candy shop offers three kinds of chewy caramels, truffles, bags of sweets, biscotti, and great cups of Spinelli coffee— all to go. Easy to miss, it's next door to the **Wells Fargo Bank.** ♦ M-Sa. No credit cards accepted. 740 Market St (at Grant Ave). 392.9222 &

46 Morrow's Nut House Innumerable nuts fill this tiny specialty shop, and all kinds of fancy nuts line the walls behind the glass-covered bins of fresh-roasted nuts. The legumes are always fresh, and unsalted varieties are offered for the benefit of people watching their sodium intake. There's also trail mix and fleshy dried apricots and papayas, among other fruits. ♦ M-Sa. 111 Geary St (between Grant Ave and Stockton St). 362.7969 &

47 Crate & Barrel This Chicago-based retail chain has an excellent selection of stylish merchandise for the kitchen, bath, and beyond, including dishes and wineglasses in just about every shape and size. On the lower level, there's also furniture, candles, and toys. Prices are generally lower than at department stores, too. ♦ Daily. 125 Grant Ave (between Geary St and Maiden La). 986.4000; fax 986.8280

NOSHERIA

48 Nosheria ★$ A good place for a quick bite, this cafeteria-style eatery offers gigantic sandwiches with six to eight ounces of roast meats, cold cuts, and tuna or chicken salad. (Smaller helpings are also available, for those watching their waistlines.) In nice weather, umbrella-topped tables are set outside. ♦ American ♦ M-Sa breakfast and lunch (until 4:30PM). 69 Maiden La (between Kearny St and Grant Ave). 398.3557 &

48 Sur La Table This Seattle-based emporium of cookware, cooking utensils, and dinner-ware has just opened its first outpost in San Francisco. The 12,000 products the store carries (including knives, small appliances, linens, and bakeware) are housed in an enormous building with 14,000 square feet of selling space. An 850-square-foot

demonstration kitchen hosts cooking classes by guest chefs. ♦ Daily. 77 Maiden La (between Kearny St and Grant Ave). 632.7900; fax 732.7797 &

49 Christofle Known for its beautiful sterling silver flatware, tea sets, trays, and wine buckets, this branch of the French chain also presents a fine collection of china, all in elegant surroundings. ♦ M-Sa. 140 Grant Ave (at Maiden La). 399.1931; fax 399.1779 &

50 Candelier A veritable inspiration for setting a beautiful table, this shop features more than a thousand candles (and various holders), displayed cunningly in seasonal exhibits. For one, an entire table was covered with what appeared to be a bountiful array of fruits and vegetables, interspersed with cookbooks; closer inspection revealed that the grapes, raspberries, asparagus, corn, pears, and tarts were actually candles. There's also a well-chosen assortment of dinnerware, place mats, napkins, soaps, and bath products (the scent of the vanilla soap is addictive). ♦ M-Sa. 60 Maiden La (between Kearny St and Grant Ave). 989.8600; fax 989.9263

51 Gump's This retailer, which has been selling luxury goods since 1861, is one of the premier stores on Union Square. Within its beautifully remodeled 1910 Beaux Arts building, a spectacular 32-foot-high atrium vaults over a museum-quality 18th-century Ching dynasty Buddha; the selling area lies around the perimeter. No other store in San Francisco has as impressive a selection of fine crystal, silverware, and china; the "Great Wall of China" on the second floor offers more than 200 patterns. The extensive tabletop collection includes such treasures as antique Georg Jensen gravy boats ($13,000), an artistic Sabbatini silver tea service ($2,100), and Steuben glass from the 1920s and 1930s (priced from $525 to $25,000). The Baccarat collection features such unique pieces as a crystal and cobalt-blue chandelier ($38,000). In addition to its exquisite displays of jade jewelry and pearls, the store is known for fine Chinese porcelains and modern European and American art glass. A bed, bath, and linen department offers a wealth of elegant place mats and napkins. Even if you can only afford to browse, it's a not-to-be-missed San Francisco classic. ♦ M-Sa. 135 Post St (between Kearny St and Grant Ave). 982.1616; fax 984.9379 &

52 Williams-Sonoma The well-known cookware chain got its start in 1956, when it was launched by Chuck Williams. (Williams originally owned a hardware store in Sonoma, hence the name.) The merchandise at this flagship store, beautifully displayed on two floors, offers the serious cook the best in equipment. Lately, however, the china and glass made in Europe specifically for the chain store is less unique in design than it used to be, and in many cases it can't go into the dishwasher or microwave. ♦ Daily. 150 Post St (between Kearny St and Grant Ave). 362.6904; fax 362.2852 ᵬ Also at: Numerous locations throughout the city

53 The Candy Jar This tiny shop has been an institution in Union Square since the late 1970s. The display cases hold truffles, bonbons, marzipan fruits, and other tempting sweets, some made without sugar. Individually wrapped candies and toffees line the shelves and bins, and everything can be beautifully gift-boxed. ♦ M-Sa. 210 Grant Ave (between Post and Sutter Sts). 391.5508 ᵬ Also at: 2065 Oakdale Ave (between Rankin and Selby Sts), Bay View. 550.8846; fax 550.8359 ᵬ

54 Teuscher Chocolates of Switzerland In business since the 1930s, this tiny, expensive chocolate shop has a glittery, party atmosphere. Of the hundred varieties of chocolates flown in from Zurich weekly, the most popular is the Champagne chocolate, containing a splash of Dom Pérignon in the center. All the chocolates can be elaborately boxed for impressive gifts. ♦ M-Sa. 255 Grant Ave (between Campton Pl and Sutter St). 398.2700; fax 398.2631 ᵬ

55 Rumpus ★★★$$ Noisy and bright, as its name implies, this stylish spot nevertheless has a civilized edge. And great food streams from chef Charles Price's glass-enclosed kitchen: onion tart with black olives and sun-dried tomatoes; butternut-squash ravioli with sage-vegetable sauce; juicy roast chicken enlivened with garlic, and New York steak with mashed potatoes and onion demi-glacé. The Caesar salad is one of the best in town, and the wine list, which concentrates on Rhône and Italian varietals from California wineries, is tops. For dessert, order the chocolate brioche bread pudding or the apple tart, which is composed of lightly browned slices of fruit draped over a mound of custard resting on a crisp circle of puff pastry; the latter takes 20 minutes, but is well worth the wait. ♦ American ♦ M-Sa lunch and dinner; Su dinner. 1 Tillman Pl (off Grant Ave, between Campton Pl and Sutter St). 421.2300; fax 421.2316 ᵬ

56 Sonoma Valley Bagel Co. ★★$ The latest addition to San Francisco's growing number of bagelries, this pleasant eatery boils its bagels in a kettle instead of oven-baking them, which makes them nice and chewy. There are 13 varieties, including jalapeño, cranberry, and sun-dried tomato with basil, and low- and no-fat spreads to go with them. The menu is rounded out with hot dogs served on bagel buns, bagel sandwiches, soups, and salads. There's both indoor and outdoor seating, or you can get your bagel to go. ♦ American ♦ Daily breakfast and lunch. 266 Sutter St (between Kearny St and Grant Ave) 951.0133; fax 951.8540 ᵬ

57 Café Claude ★$$ The zinc bar, where patrons can linger as long as they like, and the lively ambience make this a French haven, especially for lunch. Nighttime often brings live jazz. The menu revolves around typical bistro fare, with a few specials chalked on a blackboard. The onion soup is hearty and delicious, and the *croque monsieur*, a puffy delight of warm cheese and ham, is served with a small salad. Grazers will love the charcuterie platter, which includes pâté. If cassoulet is on the menu, don't pass it up, and wash it down with a Côtes du Rhône. And for dessert, what else but chocolate mousse? ♦ French ♦ M-F breakfast, lunch, and dinner; Sa dinner. 7 Claude La (off Bush St, between Kearny St and Grant Ave). 392.3505 ᵬ

58 Le Central ★$$ On a chilly night, come to this brasserie for soul-warming comfort food. The crab cakes are as good here as in Maryland, and the beet salad topped with sieved egg makes a light, tasty appetizer. At its best, the cassoulet with beans, confit, and juicy pieces of sausage is great; the quality is sometimes inconsistent, though. The best dessert is the crème caramel, which has a brûlée-like consistency. The narrow room lined with tables and rough brick walls has a European feel. One drawback is that the staff can be cold and impersonal. ♦ French ♦ M-Sa lunch and dinner. Reservations recommended. 453 Bush St (between Claude La and Grant Ave). 391.2233; fax 391.3615 ᵬ

58 Rendezvous du Monde ★★$$ Tiny and cute, this family-owned, 50-seat spot has a hideaway appeal. The changing menu lists some interesting salads and such simple noshes as roasted potatoes with aioli, caponata with grilled focaccia, or *brandade* (a puree of salt cod and potatoes) with toast

points. The fish selection might include halibut with an olive-and-lemon paste on a bed of corn and sugar snap peas. Don't miss the *pots de crème* (custard) for dessert. ◆ French/Italian ◆ M breakfast and lunch; Tu-F breakfast, lunch, and dinner; Sa brunch and dinner. 431 Bush St (between Claude La and Grant Ave). 392.3332

59 **Cafe de la Presse** ★★$ The atmosphere is oh-so-European at this newsstand/cafe, and it has become the cornerstone of an emerging "French Quarter." Linger over cereal, pastries, pancakes, or simple egg dishes in the morning and straightforward salads, sandwiches, and cold plates at lunch. Just so you'll know you're still in America, there are hamburgers, as well as quiches and pasta. ◆ American/French ◆ Daily breakfast, lunch, and dinner. 352 Grant Ave (at Bush St). 398.2680; fax 249.0916 &

60 **360° Gourmet Burritos** With nine locations in the Bay Area, this take-out place (formerly **The Hot Shop**) does for burritos what California chefs have done for pizza, stuffing them with all kinds of nontraditional ingredients. Here are such fillings as lamb Mediterranean, Chinese chicken, sweet-and-hot duck, and Bombay curry, to name a few. ◆ M-Sa. 359 Kearny St (at Pine St). 989.8077; fax 989.8078 & Also at: Numerous locations throughout the city

61 **Occidental Grill** ★★$$ Here's a new twist on the traditional San Francisco grill. Even though a restaurant has operated on this site since 1909 and its latest incarnation evokes those old days with a dark wood bar, green-glass lights, and semiprivate booths, the food has a 1990s pedigree dubbed "contemporary grill fare." Stick with the simpler offerings: grilled double chicken breast with summer tomato salad, smoked pork chop with horseradish mashed potatoes and cranberry ketchup, and skirt steak with three-cheese-stuffed chili. If you're sensitive to smoke, beware—the bar here is popular with cigar smokers, and the smoke tends to drift into the dining room. ◆ American ◆ M-F lunch and dinner. 453 Pine St (between Montgomery St and Belden Pl). 834.0484

Supper Club

61 **Fizz** ★★$$ Under the same ownership as **Cafe Tiramisù** (see page 25), this supper club brings a touch of class to the neighborhood. The place has got it all—interesting food, a retro Italian-style decor (featuring 1950s-era pewter metal tables and chairs, frosted metal table tops, etc.), jazz music, and outdoor seating. Try the silky gravlax, which comes house-cured with grappa; or wontons stuffed with shrimp and served with nectarines and jicama-plum dipping sauce. Main courses include roast chicken ravioli and braised rabbit with goat cheese polenta. ◆ Contemporary ◆ M-F lunch and dinner (F to 1AM); Sa dinner (to 2AM). 471 Pine St (between Montgomery St and Belden Pl). 421.3499 &

62 **Specialty's Cafe and Bakery** At lunchtime, Financial District workers line up to take out sandwiches, soups, and salads from this carryout shop, which has four locations around the city. It has made a name for itself by its practice of baking all its breads and pastries in-house, although sometimes the bread can be leaden and the sweets somewhat disappointing. ◆ M-F 6AM-6PM. No credit cards accepted. 312 Kearny St (between Bush and Pine Sts). Daily specials 896.BAKE; catering, delivery, and customer service, all locations 512.9550 & Also at: Numerous locations throughout the city

63 **Cafe Bastille** ★★$$ Perfectly capturing the atmosphere of a French bistro, this charming cafe on a pedestrian street attracts both a business clientele and a good share of young bohemians, who come in for the nightly live jazz as well as the food. Try the onion soup, steamed mussels, roast chicken breast, or pâté. Even though the cafe is in the shadow of the 52-story **Bank of America** monolith, you can sit at one of its outdoor tables and pretend you're in Paris. ◆ Bistro ◆ M-Sa lunch and dinner. 22 Belden Pl (between Bush and Pine Sts). 986.5673; fax 986.1013

63 Cafe Tiramisù ★★★$$ The captivating smells of sautéed garlic and onions alone would lure passersby into this chic cafe, whose walls look as if they're painted with ancient frescoes. Everyone receives a friendly welcome, and the Italian food is just as warming: risotto with earthy mushrooms, osso buco with soft polenta, and roasted whole fish with nuances of smoke. In all, this eatery is one of the best places in the area for a hearty Italian meal. Outdoor seating is available, too. ♦ Italian ♦ M-F lunch and dinner; Sa dinner. Reservations recommended. 28 Belden Pl (between Bush and Pine Sts). 421.7044; fax 421.3009

63 Plouf ★★★$$ Local restaurateurs Eric Klein and Olivier Azancot, along with French-born Jocelyn Bulow, operate this tiny dining spot dedicated to seafood in general and mussels and oysters in particular. (The name, appropriately, is the French word for "splash.") Featured here are mussels prepared in several different sauces and accompanied by crisp french fries, as well as an oyster bar and a number of seafood dishes, all at bargain prices. There are some tables outside in the pedestrian alleyway. ♦ Bistro ♦ M-F lunch and dinner; Sa dinner. 40 Belden Pl (between Bush and Pine Sts). 986.6491 ♿

64 Sam's Grill ★★$$ In business since 1867, this is the best of the old-time grills; it's so retro, it's come back in style. The masculine, clubby decor has dark wainscoting and enough coat hooks to accommodate an army. The back is lined with curtained booths, just right for a clandestine meeting. It's the perfect stage for the veteran waiters, who work hard to maintain a gruff demeanor (underneath they're really quite charming). Top choices include sweetbreads served on toast points with crisp slices of bacon and roasted potatoes, minute steak, celery Victor, French pancakes (thin crepes drizzled with lemon juice and powdered sugar), and comforting rice pudding (the fish dishes, however, are sometimes overcooked). Wines are fairly priced. ♦ American ♦ M-F lunch and dinner. 374 Bush St (between Montgomery St and Belden Pl). 421.0594; fax 421.2632

65 Kelly's on Trinity ★★$ Kelly Mills, who won acclaim as chef at the **Four Seasons Clift** hotel, gave up the fast track to open this cafeteria-style lunch spot several years ago. The pastel green and yellow color scheme, printed upholstery, and windows overlooking Trinity Street make it more pleasant than most quick-hit restaurants. Chili and three types of soup are offered each day, and the salads range from steak with mushrooms, green beans, and croutons to Asian chicken with celery, eggplant, and a Thai dressing. Sandwiches are prepared on freshly made rolls, and the cookies and desserts—particularly the apple bread pudding—are excellent. ♦ Cafeteria ♦ M-F breakfast and lunch. 333 Bush St (at Trinity St). 362.4454; fax 362.2813 ♿

66 FAZ ★★$$ The business-lunch crowd flocks to this sleek spot in the **Crocker Galleria.** Light wood partitions divide the long, narrow room, adding intimacy; the color scheme of ocher accented with plum and olive provides an earthy, rustic ambience. The menu blends the flavors of the Middle East and California: Homemade potato chips share top billing with a salad topped with pomegranate seeds, toasted walnuts, and a pomegranate vinaigrette. At lunch, portobellos on rosemary focaccia make a popular sandwich, and any of the pastas—such as *riso* (rice-shaped pasta) with baby artichokes in a light tomato sauce—are good choices. For dessert there's honey-soaked baklava with three kinds of nuts, and black-and-white chocolate torte with a buttery crust served in a pool of caramel sauce. ♦ Middle Eastern/Californian ♦ M-F lunch and dinner; Sa dinner. Reservations recommended. 161 Sutter St (between Montgomery and Kearny Sts). 362.0404; fax 362.5865 ♿

John Walker & Co.
WINE AND SPIRITS SINCE 1933

66 John Walker and Co. Liquors Thick burgundy carpets and richly paneled cases that display wine as elegantly and meticulously as art set this wine and spirits store apart. There's a special emphasis on Bordeaux and other French wines, although the Italian and California offerings are nothing to dismiss, either. More than 150 customers store wine with the shop; some have overbought, and their older vintage wines are listed on a sheet at the counter for resale. The selection of half bottles, large bottles, and miniatures is impressive. The staffers are particularly adept at locating hard-to-find wines; they also will gift wrap and ship purchases. ♦ M-Sa. 175 Sutter St (between Montgomery and Kearny Sts). 986.2707; fax 421.5820 &

66 **Perry's Downtown** ★★$$ Perry's, one of the city's most popular watering holes, has been a fixture on trendy Union Street since 1969. Not content to rest on his laurels, Perry Butler, the legendary restaurateur/barman behind that operation, has opened a downtown version that's every bit as good as the original establishment. It's got the same look (hardwood and tile floors, wood panels, and brass accents reminiscent of East Side New York) and the same menu of all-American classics (burgers, chili, Caesar salad, *ahi* tuna club sandwich, soups, and salads). For dessert, be sure to try the apple brown Betty. ♦ American ♦ Daily lunch and dinner. 185 Sutter St (between Montgomery and Kearny Sts). 989.6895; fax 433.4409 & Also at: 1944 Union St (between Laguna and Buchanan Sts), Cow Hollow. 922.9022

67 **Metropol** ★★★$ Albert Rainer, who built a loyal clientele at **Hyde Street Bistro** in Nob Hill, has expanded his empire with this stylish eatery. It offers more bang for the buck than just about any other. The dark wood molding, marbleized walls, black marble floors, polished cherry tables, and whimsical Italian lights make a dashing setting for the delicious fare. Highlights include roasted eggplant salad with goat cheese and greens, and seafood salad with fennel, carrots, and celery in a tarragon vinaigrette. Homemade bread is the foundation for such sandwiches as roast beef with pickled onions and horseradish. Another good choice is the calzone bursting with artichokes. For grazers, almost every savory course can be ordered in a half portion. The desserts are made in-house: Try the dark-and-white chocolate mousse torte. ♦ Californian ♦ M-Sa lunch and dinner. 168 Sutter St (between Trinity and Kearny Sts). 732.7777; fax 732.7778 &

Chicken Tetrazzini—that rich, delicious mélange of chicken, macaroni, cheese, and a mushroom velouté sauce—was created in honor of a famous San Francisco–based coloratura soprano, Luisa Tetrazzini.

68 **Gloria Jean's** The heady coffee aroma in this bean-and-brew store in the **Crocker Galleria** is infused with a chocolaty raspberry scent—a tip-off to the shop's focus on flavored coffees, including such unusual selections as hazelnut cinnamon, butter pecan, and banana cream. Flavored coffee is anathema to the local coffee connoisseur, so few of the retailers in the area carry as wide a selection (50 varieties) as this fast-growing chain. ♦ M-Sa. 50 Post St (between Montgomery and Kearny Sts). 391.7755; fax 391.8965 & Also at: Numerous locations throughout the city

69 **Carnelian Room** ★★$$$ Panoramic views of the Golden Gate and Bay Bridges dazzle diners at this eatery on top of the **Bank of America World Headquarters** building. At night the room is dark and romantic, the brass chandeliers and dark wood paneling giving it a solid, traditional feel. The food has taken some pretty hard knocks over the years, but a meal here can be a pleasant experience if you order simply. The best way to go is the three-course, prix-fixe menu; it's not only a good value but also offers the most straightforward dishes, with three choices in each category. The starting course may be sautéed Dungeness crab cakes or sautéed foie gras. Entrée selections may include veal loin pillows stuffed with mushrooms; grilled New York steak with a red wine and peppercorn sauce; or house-smoked and roasted sturgeon with a Champagne sauce. For dessert, the chocolate hazelnut semifreddo and the custardy crème caramel are both good choices. The award winning wine list is one of the most extensive in all of California. ♦ French ♦ M-Sa, cocktails and dinner; Su brunch and dinner. 555 California St (at Kearny St), 52nd floor. 433.7500; fax 291.0815 &

70 **Palio d'Asti** ★★★ $$ One of the city's best spots for pasta, it's a handsome place, with cement beams making a dramatic contrast to the polished wood trim and the gleaming white, glass-enclosed kitchen. Many of the pastas are homemade, and they're all dressed creatively with such flourishes as artichoke

hearts, parmesan cheese, mint, and Italian parsley. The pizzas and soups are also satisfying. Unfortunately, the restaurant is now open only for lunch (it can be rented in the evening for special functions). ♦ Italian ♦ M-F lunch. Reservations recommended. 640 Sacramento St (between Montgomery and Kearny Sts). 395.9800; fax 362.6002 ♿

71 **Paninoteca Palio d'Asti** ★★$ A lower-priced offshoot of **Palio d'Asti** (see above), this spot features stylish fare to carry out or eat in. The panini made on homemade breads are excellent. Choices run from the *san rocco* (roast of the day) to the *tanaro,* a rich combin-ation of mascarpone cheese, chives, and smoked salmon. Be sure to try the dense biscotti. ♦ Italian ♦ M-F breakfast and lunch. 505 Montgomery St (between Sacramento and Commercial Sts). 362.6900; fax 362.0700 ♿

72 **Vertigo Restaurant & Bar** ★★★$$$ Named for the famous movie Alfred Hitchcock filmed in the city, this restaurant was an instant hit when it opened a few years ago. Located on the ground floor of the **Transamerica Pyramid,** it is as spectacular as the much-photographed building. Copper mesh covers the peaked ceiling, and a dramatic light fixture snakes overhead. The rich woods, huge flower arrangements, circular banquettes, and open kitchen give the three-tiered dining room an expansive feel. The seasonal menu features local organic ingredients and highlights French, Italian, and Asian cuisines. The chef, Jeff Inahara, has cooked at Patina in Los Angeles and the **Coconut Grove** in San Francisco. Inahara puts his own spin on California cuisine, including such entrées as red curry bouillabaisse with scallops, mussels, clams, and monkfish; and herb-roasted chicken with lemon-scented mashed potatoes. The extensive wine list includes Californian and imported labels. ♦ Californian ♦ M-F lunch and dinner; Sa dinner. Reservations recommended. 600 Montgomery St (at Clay St). 433.7250; fax 732.7270 ♿

73 **Alfred's** ★★★$$$ The dimly lit room says "classic steak house," and indeed this is a classic; it's been in business since 1928. The specialty here is the delicious New York cut, grilled over mesquite and accompanied by ravioli, baked potato, or french fries. Or choose from such pastas as cannelloni and fettuccine Alfredo. Appetizers have an Italian

bent and include antipasto; the Caesar salad is made table-side. ♦ Steak house ♦ Daily dinner. 659 Merchant St (between Montgomery and Kearny Sts). 781.7058

74 **Tommy Toy's** ★$$$ The main dining room here is fashioned after the 19th-century Chinese empress dowager's reading room, an opulent setting of ornate carved archways and porcelain vases and lamps. The enthusiastic regulars insist this is one of the city's top restaurants. Those who go expecting authentic Chinese food, however, will be disappointed. The menu is a mishmash of Chinese and French specialties; two of the most popular dishes are seafood bisque in fresh coconut crowned with puff pastry and whole lobster sautéed with pine nuts and mushrooms in a peppercorn sauce. ♦ Chinese/French ♦ M-F lunch and dinner; Sa-Su dinner. Reservations recommended; jacket required. 655 Montgomery St (at Washington St). 397.4888; fax 397.0469 ♿

75 **Cypress Club** ★★★$$$ Pull back the massive door and step into a whimsical 1930s supper club, with sensuous, breastlike light fixtures, faux–stained glass murals, massive columns that look like ginger jars, and custom-designed chairs upholstered in plush velvet. The surroundings set an appropriate stage for chef Alan McLennan's imaginative food. Try the *matsutake* mushroom (which grows near pine trees that give it a particular scent) served with tomato *concasse* (peeled and diced) and marjoram *jus.* Other distinctive dishes include oven-roasted Maine lobster with a tarragon polenta napoleon, Chilean sea bass with a potato crust perfumed with cream truffle sauce, and venison loin with a ragout of sunchokes (Jerusalem artichokes). Round out the meal with a dessert such as silky Valrhona chocolate crème brûlée or mango tart accented with saffron sabayon. ♦ American ♦ Daily dinner. Reservations recommended. 500 Jackson St (at Montgomery St). 296.8555; fax 296.9250 ♿

76 **Thomas E. Cara, Ltd.** Long before San Francisco was captivated by coffee, Thomas Cara began importing espresso machines. He also stocked Italian polenta pots, ravioli makers, French duck presses, and fish poachers, none of which was locally available when he opened in 1946. Cara's sons now run the business out of a stylish shop that displays top-of-the-line coffee-makers (both home and commercial models)

on glass shelves against the white walls as if they were works of art. The staff's service and familiarity with the products are beyond compare. The store also maintains a supply of parts, and still services machines purchased 50 years ago. ♦ M-F; Sa noon-3PM. 517 Pacific Ave (between Montgomery and Kearny Sts). 781.0383; fax 781.7224 ﾋ

77 Bix ★★$$$ The location on quiet Gold Street, in the shadow of the **Transamerica Pyramid,** sets the mood at this posh 1930s-style supper club, where people sip martinis at the elegant bar, backed by a bigger-than-life mural, and a torch singer croons in the corner. Massive columns support a mezzanine from which diners look down on the action. In such a dramatic setting, the American-style food can be a bit of a letdown. The menu changes seasonally, but always includes such reliable standbys as Waldorf salad, updated with roquefort cheese, and chicken hash. Other homey dishes might include grilled pork chops served with mashed potatoes, grilled lamb chops with mustard and mint, duck confit, and sturgeon with roast vegetables. In these drop-dead surroundings, you might be inclined to splurge on the Russian *osetra* caviar with crème fraîche and toast points. The downside is that the well-selected wines can be rather expensive, though a few reasonably priced reds are available. ♦ American ♦ M-F lunch and dinner; Sa-Su dinner. Reservations required. 56 Gold St (between Sansome and Montgomery Sts). 433.6300; fax 433.4574 ﾋ

John C. Kirkpatrick, the manager of the palace hotel in San Francisco around the turn of the century, is said to have created oysters Kirkpatrick. Here is the recipe: Carefully open six oysters and place them on a bed of rock salt. Mix one teaspoon of minced green pepper with one teaspoon of celery, and add to six tablespoons of chili sauce. Cover the oysters with the sauce; top with slices of cooked bacon and a generous sprinkling of parmesan cheese. Bake at 375 degrees for 10 minutes and serve.

78 London Wine Bar $ This establishment, which opened in the mid-1980s, claims to be the oldest wine bar in California. It has a classic look, with dark wood, racks and boxes of wine lining the walls, and a clientele that likes to swirl wine and nibble on bread sticks in relaxed surroundings. More than three dozen wines are offered by the glass and are well complemented by light lunches and snacks. You can't beat the pâté and cheese plate or the salmon rillettes. ♦ Wine bar ♦ M-F 11:30AM-9PM. 415 Sansome St (between Sacramento and Commercial Sts). 788.4811

79 Rubicon ★★★$$$ With a glitzy list of investors that include Robert De Niro, Francis Coppola, and Robin Williams, this dramatic space has the look of a New York loft. The striking decor features earthquake-protection beams crisscrossing the oversize windows, white walls, and dark wood accents. The original chef was Traci Des Jardins, one of Joachim Splichal's most talented protegés, but at press time she was planning to leave to open a place of her own. Scott Newman, her sous-chef, is slated to take over the kitchen, and since he is well versed in Des Jardin's culinary style, not much change is anticipated. The French-inspired à la carte menu offers such excellent starters as duck confit with spicy greens and cracklings, and portobello mushroom salad; entrées may include pork tenderloin with sweet potatoes, grilled fish with a barley "risotto," or a seared *ahi* tuna sandwich. The business lunch—a two-course, prix-fixe special—is a great bargain, especially considering the quality of the food. Larry Stone, one of the country's master sommeliers, offers a marvelous wine list. ♦ Californian ♦ M-F lunch and dinner; Sa dinner. Reservations required; jacket required. 558 Sacramento St (between Sansome and Montgomery Sts). 434.4100; fax 421.7648 ﾋ

79 Snookies Cookies Cookies are tops here, and you can't miss with the chocolate peanut butter, butter pecan, oatmeal walnut, or chocolate chip. The chockablock shop also features whimsical ceramic cookie jars, including a replica of the *Mona Lisa,* a pig eating a watermelon, the Flintstones' home, a cactus, and a cowboy boot. ♦ M-F; Sat 10AM-3PM. 560 Sacramento St (between Sansome and Montgomery Sts). 788.1878; fax 788.1783 ﾋ

80 Silks ★★$$$ The excellent East-West fare here draws a good lunch crowd, but this restaurant at the luxurious **Mandarin Oriental San Francisco** hotel has had a hard time attracting diners to the Financial District at night. In its short life, the dining room has been remodeled several times; now it is casual, but still elegant and lively, with plush carpeting, dramatic lighting, and paintings and sculptures by local artists. Starters include seared Day Boat scallops and (in season, which is June through October) an heirloom tomato salad with Maui onions and Thai basil vinaigrette. Entrees include grilled lamb chops in an Indonesian marinade; roasted quinoa with grilled mushrooms; and sesame-seed-crusted sea bass. The extensive wine list has received awards from the *Wine Spectator*. ♦ Californian/Asian ♦ Daily breakfast, lunch, and dinner. Reservations recommended. 222 Sansome St (between Pine and California Sts). 986.2020; fax 433.0289 ♿

81 Sol y Luna ★★$$ Stick with the tapas and avoid the entrées—especially the gummy paella—at this relentlessly modern-looking Spanish spot. Among the "little plate" standouts are roasted, then grilled, red and purple Peruvian potatoes with chipotle aioli and meaty crab cakes. Or try the tiger prawns with a splash of vodka and a tomato sauce. Wednesday through Saturday, the restaurant becomes a supper club with live entertainment that has proved to be very popular with locals. ♦ Spanish ♦ M-F lunch and dinner; Sa dinner. Reservations recommended. 475 Sacramento St (between Battery and Sansome Sts). 296.8696 ♿

82 Park Grill ★★$$$ This dining room, on the third floor of the **Park Hyatt** hotel, has elegant, understated appointments that make it ideal for a quiet business meal. Entrées, which change regularly, might include horseradish-crusted halibut with mashed potatoes and a flurry of crispy leeks; mustard roasted chicken with whipped sweet potatoes; or grilled lamb chops accented with dates and a roasted-garlic flan. ♦ Californian ♦ Daily breakfast, lunch, and dinner. 333 Battery St (between Sacramento and Commercial Sts). 296.2933; fax 296.2919 ♿

83 Yank Sing Restaurant ★★★$ Though the food at this clean, well-appointed dim sum parlor is good, aficionados of genuine Chinese fare may find the menu and the surroundings too Americanized and lacking in ethnic flavor. It's ideal for novices at the dim sum experience, however, because the staff is willing to explain each dish. Dumplings are a specialty, but other treats include individual servings of Peking duck in warm, steamed buns and minced squab spooned into crisp lettuce cups. The restaurant is accessible to wheelchairs, but only through the freight elevator. ♦ Dim sum ♦ Daily lunch. 427 Battery St (between Clay and Washington Sts). 362.1640; fax 391.3003 ♿

84 MacArthur Park ★$$$ This stylish, loftlike place with exposed brick walls has been serving up American regional food since the early 1970s. The baby back ribs are inconsistent, but the crispy, thin onion "strings" are nothing short of addictive. Other choices include smoked duck with Vermont maple glaze, apricot chutney, and braised greens; and smoked pork chops with Santa Catalina sweet potatoes and glazed apples. The desserts are mostly too dense and heavy, but if you must have a sweet, choose the creamy tapioca pudding. ♦ American ♦ M-F lunch and dinner; Sa-Su dinner. Reservations recommended. 607 Front St (between Jackson St and Pacific Ave). 398.5700; fax 982.2424 ♿

84 Ciao ★$$ One of the first to bring modern Northern Italian fare to San Francisco, this trattoria is still a popular stop. The contemporary, hard-edged room has clean white walls and a brightly lit interior. Service can be hit-or-miss, and sometimes the staff can be a bit patronizing. Nevertheless, people come here for wonderful bread sticks and the homemade pasta. Don't miss the fresh fruit granita (Italian ice) if it's available: It's great. ♦ Californian/Italian ♦ M-Sa lunch and dinner; Su dinner. Reservations recommended. 230 Jackson St (between Front and Battery Sts). 982.9500; fax 982.2424 ♿

85 Freed Teller & Freed's Like the original store on Polk Street, this store with more modern decor enjoys the company's long-standing reputation as a fine purveyor of coffee and coffee-making accessories. ♦ M-F 6AM-6PM. 1 Embarcadero Center (Sacramento St, at Battery St). 986.8851; fax 986.8853 ♿ Also at: 1326 Polk St (between Bush and Pine Sts), Nob Hill. 673.0922; fax 673.3436 ♿

85 Pottery Barn People with lots of dash and a little cash have come to rely on this chain's constantly changing array of accessories for the home. This branch is a pilot store for the company's catalog sales, so it stocks items that can't be found at the other locations here and around the nation. ♦ Daily. 1 Embarcadero Center (Battery St, between Sacramento and Clay Sts). 788.6810; fax 788.4819 ♿ Also at: 2100 Chestnut St (at Steiner St), The Marina. 441.1787; fax 441.5311 ♿

86 Pasqua The first shop to be established by the San Francisco chain in 1983, this branch is strictly takeout. However, it offers such sandwiches as roast turkey with pesto sauce, sun-dried cranberries, and greens on a seeded baguette. In addition, this place offers dependably good croissants and muffins. The coffee, blended from six different beans, is generally milder than others around town and is a part of many locals' week day ritual. ♦ M-F. 303 Sacramento St (between Front and Battery Sts). 788.4441 ♿ Also at: Numerous locations throughout the city

A Q U A

87 Aqua ★★★★$$$$ Without a doubt the city's most creative seafood restaurant, it is also the prettiest, with clean architectural lines, dramatic lighting, and a half-dozen towering bouquets of fresh flowers. The service strikes the proper balance between relaxed friendliness and sharp professionalism. The food, orchestrated by executive chef Michael Mina, is a tour de force of juxtaposed flavors that rarely misses the mark. Examples include potato-wrapped Idaho trout with a foie gras and apple stuffing; the signature tuna and foie gras medallions with a pinot noir sauce; and steamed Maine lobster with smoked sturgeon ravioli. Most of the sauces forgo butter and cream, deriving their intense flavors from the extraction and reduction of vegetable or meat juices. Flavored oils also are used to add color and tang. The ever-changing desserts look as spectacular as they taste, and the wine list is expertly matched to the imaginative menu. ♦ Seafood ♦ M-F lunch and dinner; Sa dinner. Reservations recommended. 252 California St (between Front and Battery Sts). 956.9662; fax 956.5229 ♿

Tadich Grill

THE ORIGINAL COLD DAY RESTAURANT ®

87 Tadich Grill ★★$$ A San Francisco classic, this fish house began in 1849 as a coffee stand in a tentlike structure on what is now Commercial Street. It has been at its current location since 1967, with a wood bar (popular for quick lunches), booths, and tables that give it a no-nonsense feel. The brusque service is all part of the act that attracts tourists and locals alike. The clam chowder is a popular beginning, followed by the rex sole, petrale, or sand dabs that are boned on request. The fish is served with a now-legendary potato-based tartar sauce. Another classic is the Hangtown fry—a scramble of oysters, bacon, and eggs. For dessert, nothing's more soothing than the creamy rice pudding. ♦ Seafood ♦ M-Sa lunch and dinner. Reservations recommended. 240 California St (between Front and Battery Sts). 391.1849; fax 391.1373 ♿

88 Schroeder's ★$$ One of the oldest restaurants in the Financial District, it has been serving solid (read heavy) German food for more than a hundred years. Specials are featured daily (roast turkey and mashed potatoes on Wednesdays, oxtail on Thursdays, for example), and there's always the tried-and-true Wiener schnitzel, sauerbraten, and sausage platters with sauerkraut and boiled potatoes. Near the **Embarcadero Center,** it's a good spot for a quick lunch; hefty plates of food appear within minutes of ordering. ♦ German ♦ M-F lunch and dinner. 240 Front St (between California and Sacramento Sts). 421.4778 ♿

89 Chevys ★★$ This ever-expanding local chain serves up very familiar, if bland, Mexican food. But the tortillas are freshly made, and the fajitas are tops. Although the decor—empty beer cases serving as partitions, a splash of bright colors—seems a little too studied to be authentic, the spirit is fun. The kitchen uses no lard, and some dishes are low-fat, too. A cautionary note: Avoid the margaritas, which are pre-mixed and dispensed from a machine. ♦ Mexican ♦ Daily lunch and dinner. 2 Embarcadero Center (Front St, between Sacramento and Clay Sts), Promenade level. 391.2323; fax 391.4404 ♿ Also at: Numerous locations throughout the city

89 The Holding Company ★$$ A popular watering hole, it also serves food that goes beyond the burger genre. Daily specials might include herb roasted chicken with cauliflower gratin; sautéed sea scallops with fresh pasta; Louisiana gumbo; or rock shrimp ravioli with lobster sauce. The real draw is the free Happy-Hour buffet, featuring fruit, cheese, dips, and a hot tidbit or two. The liquor and beer selections are impressive. ♦ American ♦ M-F lunch and dinner. 2 Embarcadero Center (Front St, between Sacramento and Clay Sts). 986.0797; fax 986.7412

90 L'Olivier ★★$$$ Convivial and charming, with friendly service and the muffled comfort of thick draperies and cushioned chairs, this is ideal for a quiet, civilized classic French repast. The terrace room is a lovely spot for lunch. The kitchen is known for its bouillabaisse; beyond that, consider lobster bisque, calves' liver with meltingly sweet onions, roast duckling, and soufflés. The prix-fixe dinner menu is a bargain and might include crab cakes, a soup or salad, such entrées as grilled salmon with ginger sauce or a casserole of rabbit, and a dessert from the pastry tray. ♦ French ♦ M-F lunch and dinner; Sa dinner. 465 Davis Ct (at Jackson St). 981.7824; fax 981.2904

SCOTT'S
SEAFOOD
GRILL & BAR

91 Scott's Seafood ★$$$ The terrace here is a popular spot for lunch; the inside dining room is country French. Unfortunately, the food never soars. The selection of fresh fish changes daily; grilled sand dabs and local petrale sole, served with lemon-caper butter, are among the specialties. ♦ Seafood ♦ M-Sa lunch and dinner; Su dinner. 3 Embarcadero Center (Sacramento St, between Drumm and Davis Sts). 981.0622; fax 296.9501 ♿ Also at: 2400 Lombard St (at Scott St), The Marina. 563.8988; fax 563.1897 ♿

92 Confetti le Chocolatier Cases of truffles and shelves of imported chocolate bars, jelly beans, and marzipan (the pig faces are particularly fun) fill this candy shop; pastry and coffee are also served. A center display features seasonal and holiday-themed treats. ♦ Daily. 4 Embarcadero Center (Drumm St, between Sacramento and Clay Sts). 362.1706 ♿

92 Splendido ★★★$$$ Tucked away in a high-rise shopping center is this Mediterranean oasis, with a domed brick ceiling at the entry, a rough rock fireplace, whimsical lights, and an open kitchen. The kitchen recently was taken over by Giovanni Perticone (formerly of the **Armani Cafe,**

Scala's, and **Frantoio Ristorante**), and the food has never been better. Start with a tasty appetizer like oak-roasted mussels in a tomato saffron broth. Entrées like the grilled veal chop with caramelized pears and zante currants have a wonderful balance of flavors, while the grilled salmon with fresh corn polenta is set off with a spicy tomato-thyme butter sauce. ♦ Mediterranean ♦ M-F lunch and dinner; Sa-Su dinner. 4 Embarcadero Center (Drumm St, between Sacramento and Clay Sts). 986.3222; fax 434.3530 ♿

92 Harbor Village ★★$$ Elegantly appointed with rosewood and teak, and somewhat pricier than other Hong Kong–style restaurants, this place features excellent dim sum at lunch. At night the waiters resolutely try to steer non-Asian patrons to the most mundane dishes, so stand firm. Some popular choices include the minced squab and Peking duck, but ask about any seasonal or chef's specialties. The prearranged banquets also can be exceptional, and the half-dozen opulent private dining rooms are perfect for celebrations. The best way to get the full impact of this dining experience is in a group, where you can order lots of dim sum dishes or several entrées and share. There's a patio area for those who prefer the outdoor take-out dim-sum kiosk. ♦ Cantonese ♦ Daily lunch and dinner. 4 Embarcadero Center (Drumm St, between Sacramento and Clay Sts). 781.8833; fax 781.8810 ♿

92 SRO! ★$ Designed for the eat-quick and take-out crowd (hence the name), this spot offers varied and interesting lunches, including lasagna, chicken, salads, and cheeses; the same foods are available in the early evening (for takeout only). There's also a breakfast menu. The wine section features Californian and European selections and hosts regularly scheduled tastings. There are tables inside, but the choice dining spots are outside over-looking the impressive **Villancourt Fountain** in **Justin Herman Plaza.** ♦ Cafe/Takeout ♦ Daily breakfast, lunch, and early dinner. 4 Embarcadero Center (Drumm St, between Sacramento and Clay Sts). 986.5020; fax 399.1267 ♿

93 Levy's Bagels & Co. This recent arrival brings a New York twist to the deli business with its traditional boiled and baked bagels (plus such unconventional, unnecessary varieties as blueberry). The turkey is house-roasted, and the chopped liver, tongue, and knishes round out the hit parade. Owners Marie and Robert Levy urge busy customers to fax in their orders. ♦ M-W 6AM-6:30PM; Th, F 6AM-5PM; Sa 7:30AM-2PM; Su 7:30AM-1PM. 21 Drumm St (between California and Sacramento Sts). 362.5580; fax 362.5581 ♿

Chinatown

Stand on the corner of **Stockton Street** and **Broadway** on a Saturday or Sunday morning to see the real Chinatown. The sidewalks overflow with shoppers going about their everyday chores. Spending one afternoon here will teach you more about Asian food than a year of studying all the latest Chinese cookbooks. Stand beside a woman as she carefully chooses snow peas—one by one—for her family's dinner. Or strike up a conversation about where to get the best barbecued pork in town and watch the sparks fly (people can get pretty passionate about their favorite barbecue spot).

The second most densely populated area in the United States (behind New York City's Harlem), Chinatown is home to the largest concentration of Asian residents outside of Asia. Popular with both tourists and locals, it attracts about 10 million visitors annually. And it's the weekend destination for

Chinese-Americans from all over the Bay Area, whether they live in San Francisco itself or drive here from the suburbs. Bounded approximately by **Kearny** and **Powell Streets**, and **Bush Street** and Broadway, the area is like a small foreign country, especially once you get away from the trinket and T-shirt shops. Even the alleyways teem with activity; everywhere you walk there's something to pique the senses.

When it comes to food, follow your nose through these colorful streets and keep a lookout for eateries that attract a sea of Chinese faces. **Jackson Street**, with its wealth of excellent dining choices, is the Restaurant Row of this neighborhood. At the impressive **Great Eastern Restaurant**, the server will bring a live fish to the table for inspection before it is prepared for your meal. Here too is **J & J Restaurant**, one of the best dim sum parlors in the city. At **Feng Huang Pastry**, the rice noodles, rolled and stuffed with barbecued pork or dried shrimp, are unsurpassed—tender, but with a bit of elasticity. And at **Hunan Homes** restaurant, you might catch a glimpse of movie director Francis F. Coppola and his staff at the table next to yours, enjoying sizzling Hunanese smoked pork or velvety eggplant with garlic sauce.

In fact, food lovers can discover joyous eating experiences all over Chinatown—just don't judge a place by its looks; some of the finest gems are tucked into drab storefronts. Not to be missed are **Kam (H.K.) Po Kitchen**, where the ducks in the window have a perfect cherry wood glaze; **Hing Lung**, whose whole roast pigs have skin as crisp as glass; and **Mee On Company**, a candy store renowned for its candied ginger and other sweet treats. Some Chinatown bakeries or shops have become famous for a single specialty. For example, for moon cakes (dense, round pies with sweet or savory fillings), people turn to **New Ping Yuen;** and for sweet Chinese pork or duck sausage, connoisseurs head for **Kwong Jow Sausage Manufacturing Company.**

Food is so important to the Chinese people—after all, it was famine in the province of Canton in 1848 that spurred the first Chinese immigrants to America—that Zao Wang, the Kitchen God, is revered by both Buddhists and Taoists. Usually represented by a strip of paper with his name in Chinese characters, he is an important fixture in kitchens throughout Chinatown. His job is to watch over the family, and at Chinese New Year's, he is burned so that his spirit may rise to heaven and report on the family's behavior—both good and bad. So enjoy Chinatown with curiosity and a spirit of adventure, and say a prayer to the Kitchen God, because you can never have enough influential friends.

1 Lotus Garden ★$ Strictly vegetarian, this second-floor establishment is perched beneath the lovely stained-glass dome of a Buddhist temple. The decor is otherwise pretty generic, with chrome lights and Formica-topped tables, but carpeting and windows overlooking the street add an upscale feel. A lighted menu board at the hostess stand advertises the daily specials, which might include sizzling-rice soup with eight assorted vegetables, various rice plates, chow mein, and taro chips with sweet-and-sour sauce. The deserts are just as satisfying: Save room for the hot walnut pudding. ♦ Chinese/Vegetarian ♦ Tu-Su lunch and dinner. 532 Grant Ave (between Pine and California Sts). 397.0130

2 R & G Lounge ★★$$ Though it's still one of the best Cantonese restaurants in the city, this spot has slipped a little since its longtime chef left. Like most eateries of its type, it specializes in seafood. One reliable dish is the steamed prawns, which are served with a dipping sauce. Other temptations include curried prawns, ginger and green-onion squid, and homey clay-pot dishes of oxtail, oysters, or onion and chicken. The downstairs restaurant is strictly utilitarian, with a tile floor and plain tables; banquets—which this place does particularly well—are held upstairs in a more formal dining room, brightly lit with chandeliers. Top executives from the Chinese business community also use the upstairs dining room for power lunches. One specialty banquet item is a duck soup presented in a winter melon (which has a zucchini-like flavor); the server spoons out some melon with the soup to create a luscious, refreshing dish. ♦ Chinese ♦ Daily lunch and dinner. 631-B Kearny St (at Commercial St). 982.7877

3 The Wok Shop Woks are only a small part of the cooking equipment carried in this store, which is so crammed that pots, pans, kitchen gadgets, and other wares hang from the ceiling for lack of space on the shelves. There is also a good selection of Chinese cookbooks, many written in English. ♦ Daily. 718 Grant Ave (at Commercial St). 989.3797 ♦

4 Eastern Bakery Despite its name, this popular Chinese bakery/cafe, in business for more than 60 years, displays numerous Western-style confections (inspired, perhaps, by the fact that one of the owners used to work at the late, lamented Blum's bakery). There's crumb cake, chocolate cream cake, strawberry cheesecake, and a decent napoleon. The fat doughnuts are a little dense, but the flavor is quite good. The shop also stocks bags of candied kumquats, ginger, and melon. ♦ Daily. No credit cards accepted. 720 Grant Ave (at Commercial St). 982.5157 ♦

5 Oriental Pearl Restaurant ★★$ One of the city's prettiest dim sum parlors, this second-floor spot features a soothing gray-and-white color scheme with vertical window blinds, plush carpeting, comfortable black chairs set at tables with white cloths, and a fish tank in a brass wall. Unlike at most dim sum places, customers order from a menu. The dumplings aren't the best choices here; instead, go for the salt-baked prawns and the Chiu Chow–style marinated duck, braised in soy sauce and served with a pungent vinegar

dipping sauce. The dinner menu is even more enticing. The house special, chicken meatballs, are a mix of chicken, shrimp, water chestnuts, and Smithfield ham in a delicate, egg-white wrapper. Seafood in a crispy nest of taro is extraordinary in both taste and presentation, and a dish of mustard greens gets just the right amount of salt flavoring from the Virginia ham. And the service, by waiters in white shirts and bow ties, is as attentive as at the finest French restaurant. ♦ Chinese ♦ Daily lunch and dinner. 778 Clay St (between Kearny St and Grant Ave). 433.1817; fax 433.4541 ♦

6 Empress of China ★$$ Dining at this dramatic sixth-floor establishment is like being entertained in an imperial palace. A carved 13th-century panel stands at the elegant entrance, which widens into a "garden pavilion," with an impressive wooden pagoda and a black-and-white marble floor laid in a star-burst pattern. Three romantic and elegant dining rooms, all with beautiful views of the city, are arranged around the pagoda. The quality of the food ranges from serviceable to uninspired, and the dishes are somewhat Americanized. But you can get a cocktail here, which is a rarity in Chinatown restaurants. ♦ Chinese ♦ Daily lunch and dinner. 838 Grant Ave (between Clay and Washington Sts), Sixth floor. 434.1345; fax 986.1187 ♦

6 Chong Imports This basement store is easy to miss: It's in a mall, and the entrance is at the bottom of a curved stairway. But those who make their way down the stairs will find woks up to 30 inches wide, 11.5-quart saucepans, and huge steamer baskets, as well as items scaled to the home kitchen. There's a good selection of dishes, and a shelf of imported Chinese candies and other foods. ♦ Daily. 838 Grant Ave (between Clay and Washington Sts). 982.1432 ♦

6 Bow Hon ★$ Despite the unimpressive, faded surroundings and the cramped quarters, people in the know come here for clay-pot dishes (the best in the city) and the roast pork. Skip the rest—it's mediocre. ♦ Chinese ♦ Daily breakfast, lunch, and dinner. 850 Grant Ave (between Clay and Washington Sts). 362.0601

7 Sam Wo $ Readers of Armisted Maupin's *Tales of the City* may remember one scene set in a Chinatown restaurant, in which a crusty waiter browbeats the customers, ordering them to set tables, wash their hands, etc. This is that place, but the waiter has died, taking his act with him. Nevertheless, the restaurant, which opened in 1914, remains one of Chinatown's most venerable, and the reasonable prices and okay food keep it well patronized. Try the *congee* (rice porridge), noodle dishes, and wonton soup with duck.

♦ Chinese ♦ M-Sa lunch and dinner. No credit cards accepted. 813 Washington St (between Grant Ave and Waverly Pl). 982.0596

8 Kowloon Vegetarian Restaurant ★$
The window displays of figurines and pastries are deceptive; this is a vegetarian spot, one of the few that serve meatless dim sum. An array of vegetables, soy products, and wheat gluten stand in for the meat in traditional dishes. The egg rolls are delicious, with a mushroom-vegetable filling that's packed with flavor. Dumplings are equally good, filled with mushrooms, faux chicken, and vegetables; the *siu mai* (pork dumplings), made with taro root, mushrooms, and carrots, are terrific. You won't even miss the poultry in the *kung pao* "chicken," with tofu, green peppers, peas, corn, celery, carrots, mush-rooms, and a handful of crunchy toasted peanuts in a slightly spicy sauce. Other preparations include curried "pork," assorted "gluten-over-rice" concoctions, and fried, crispy walnuts. ♦ Chinese/Vegetarian ♦ Daily lunch and dinner. No credit cards accepted. 909 Grant Ave (at Washington St). 362.9888

8 Mee On Company Barely big enough to notice, this candy shop, which has been in business since the 1920s, is a storehouse of preserved and sugared treats: coconut, lotus nuts, water chestnuts, winter melon, kumquats, ginger (the best), and lotus roots, to name a few. They're stashed in bins and sold by the quarter pound. Also available are chewy dried papaya and preserved plums. ♦ Daily. No credit cards accepted. 812 Washington St (between Grant Ave and Ross Alley). 982.4456 &

9 Silver Restaurant ★$ The glittering silver marquee raises expectations of glamour, so the utilitarian interior here is something of a letdown. The main draw is the inexpensive food, especially during crab season (November through April), when a whole crab is usually priced at about $9; also attractive are the round-the-clock service and friendly, attentive staff. Overall, the food is okay, and the *congees* and the thin noodles with wontons and a choice of toppings (including excellent barbecued pork or duck) make a fine end to a long night of partying. The place is usually packed at 2AM, when the bar crowd stops by for "breakfast." ♦ Chinese ♦ Daily 24 hours. 737 Washington St (between Portsmouth Sq and Grant Ave). 433.8888 &

10 World Ginseng Center This supermarket-size ginseng emporium is a good place to buy the aromatic, gnarled roots of that medicinal herb. There's ginseng from America, China, and Korea in just about every form: extract for tea, tea bags, medicinals, and candies. Prices go as high as $1,000 a pound for the prized Wisconsin wild ginseng. ♦ Daily. 801 Kearny St (at Washington St). 362.0928 &

11 J & J Restaurant ★★★$ Crowds line up outside this top dim sum parlor. Inside, the decor is much like other Hong Kong–style restaurants, with paneled walls and crystal chandeliers. But the dumplings here have some of the best fillings around, boldly flavored by their main ingredients: The *ha gow* (shrimp dumplings) taste only of shrimp and ginger, for example. The pork balls are encased in a flour dumpling and served with a red vinegar sauce; the dumplings shaped like cocks' combs contain chopped shrimp, cilantro, and fresh water chestnuts, which add a sweet, crunchy burst of flavor; and the silken bean-curd skins have a tender interior. When the dim sum carts are stored for the evening and the full menu is offered, look to the seafood specialties, which are fresh as can be; their key ingredients are scooped up live from the fish tank. ♦ Chinese ♦ M dinner; Tu-Su lunch and dinner. 615 Jackson St (between Kearny and Wentworth Sts). 981.7308 &

12 DPD Restaurant ★★$$ Some of the best Shanghai noodles in the city are served at six well-worn Formica tables in a battered yellow-and-green building. The spicy, thick noodles, which turn mahogany-colored in the wok, are like manna when served with Chinese cabbage and strips of pork. The noodle soups are just as enticing, whether topped with pork chops, beef tendon, or smoked fish. On the seafood menu try the hot braised prawns and the scallops in garlic-and-ginger sauce. Daily specials often include vegetable wontons with pork and such non-noodle dishes as steamed fish. The blackboard specials can be excellent, but the noodle dishes are not to be missed. ♦ Chinese/Shanghai ♦ Daily lunch and dinner. No credit cards accepted. 901 Kearny St (at Jackson St). 982.0471

13 House of Nanking $ This tiny, grungy place has inexplicably developed a cult following, mostly of Caucasian college students. Customers line up outside for as long as an hour for the privilege of squeezing in at a small table and being rushed through a meal that will probably last half as long as the wait. The dishes, a mishmash of culinary styles, are prepared with the same hot, salty sauce and presented sloppily, with no finesse. ♦ Chinese ♦ M-Sa lunch and dinner; Su dinner. No credit cards accepted. 919 Kearny St (between Jackson St and Columbus Ave). 421.1429

14 Tandoori Mahal ★★★$$ At the very edge of Chinatown, near North Beach, this new Indian spot is a welcome addition to the area. The atmosphere is romantic, thanks to glittering, sequin-covered wall hangings, soft lighting, and pleasing Indian music playing in the background. The service is polite and attentive, too. Don't miss the tandoori dishes, which are the house specialty. The nan bread is good and fluffy, while the dals (soups) are filling and savory starters. There's also a small bar in the back of the long dining room. The all-you-can-eat buffet lunch is a particularly good value. ♦ Indian ♦ Daily lunch and dinner. 941 Kearny St (at Columbus Ave). 951.0505

15 Hunan Homes ★★$ Decorated in shades of pink, this dining spot boasts a fun, comfortable atmosphere and first-rate cuisine. Among the dishes are Hunan-style smoked ham, stir-fried with cabbage, leeks, and green pepper; and eggplant doused with garlic and mixed with bits of ground pork. Platters of prawns or beef with green pepper and onions are tossed with chili sauce and ground pork and served sizzling. It's a popular hangout for celebrated director Francis Coppola and his entourage. ♦ Chinese ♦ Daily lunch and dinner. 622 Jackson St (between Kearny and Beckett Sts). 982.2844

16 Jackson Pavilion ★$ One of only a handful of Chinese-owned restaurants specializing in American food (known as sai choy), this is where local Chinese-Americans go for omelettes and prime ribs. Try the omelette with strips of ham, turkey, onions, bell peppers, and mushrooms, served with commercial preshaped hash browns (crisp and greasy) and lavishly buttered toast. The menu runs to pork chops and the like, but there are a few ramen noodle combinations. ♦ American ♦ Daily breakfast, lunch, and dinner. 640 Jackson St (between Kearny and Beckett Sts). 982.2409

17 Great Eastern Restaurant ★★★$$ Fish is the thing to order at this typically noisy bilevel eatery with ornate crystal chandeliers: It couldn't be fresher. The tanks are filled with crabs, abalone, prawns, oysters, scallops, frogs, and various fin fish, which are priced by the pound. Order a whole steamed fish and the waiter will bring the flopping creature to

the table for your inspection. The kitchen literally makes the most of its ingredients, transforming the bones of a cod, for instance, into a rich soup with a spicy bite, then cutting the rest of the fish into chunks to stir-fry with sugar snap peas and other vegetables. The prawns, fresh from the aquarium, are incredible steamed in the shell (you peel them yourself) and prepared with a generous dose of minced garlic. Among the nonseafood dishes, both quail and squab are popular. ♦ Chinese ♦ Daily lunch and dinner until 1AM. 649 Jackson St (between Kearny and Wentworth Sts). 986.2500 ♿

18 Golden Flower Restaurant ★$ One of the few Vietnamese spots in Chinatown, it's popular for pho (Vietnamese noodle soup made from pork bones and oxtails). Choose among 12 beef preparations, each presented in a big bowl with side garnishes of bean sprouts, mint, cilantro, chilies, lemon wedges, and chili sauce. The classic finish is filtered coffee, which slowly drips into a cup containing spoonfuls of sweet condensed milk. ♦ Vietnamese ♦ Daily lunch and dinner. No credit cards accepted. 667 Jackson St (between Kearny St and Grant Ave). 433.6469 ♿

19 New Woey Loy Goey Restaurant ★$ This modest place has built a reputation for its rice and noodle dishes at rock-bottom prices. More than 60 rice plates and 35 noodle dishes are offered; try the cashew chicken rice plate and the garlic chicken with crispy noodles. ♦ Chinese ♦ Daily lunch and dinner. No credit cards accepted. 699 Jackson St (at Grant Ave). 399.0733

20 Ten Ren Tea Company of San Francisco, Ltd. Ellen and Mark Lill's pretty shop specializes in green tea, which has become the darling of the health-conscious. More than a dozen varieties are sold from large gold-metal cans lining the rich wood shelves. Two glass cases along one side hold an impressive display of teapots for sale. The other half of the store is devoted to ginseng, also reputed to have healing qualities. The shop is orderly and very clean, and a carved table sits in the center for free tea tastings; a raised area in back is reserved for the Chinese tea ceremony, which is performed every morning for city-tour groups (or for private groups—call to make arrangements). The staff are helpful and willingly answer questions. ♦ Daily 9AM-9PM. 949 Grant Ave (between Washington and Jackson Sts). 362.0656; fax 750.8242 ♿

Shopping in Chinatown—
A Flavorful Adventure

Whether you're a seasoned master of Chinese cookery or don't know soy sprouts from bean sprouts, a visit to San Francisco's **Chinatown** can be educational. It gives you a terrific opportunity to explore another community's history, culture, and cuisine. The need for food is common to all people; the only difference between societies is in the ways they satisfy that need.

In China, many foods are seen as curative, almost medicinal, as well as simply nutritious. The old adage "You are what you eat" could be translated in Chinese culture as "Eat to stay healthy." A nursing mother, for example, is encouraged to eat silver carp in order to stay healthy and strong. The use of herbal therapy to relieve pain and other symptoms of illness has begun to take root in the US.

The best way to shop in Chinatown is to start with a recipe that you would like to prepare. Draw up your shopping list of ingredients and set out. Need a canned or bottled sauce? **May Wah Trading Company** is sure to have it. Does your recipe call for a bit of Smithfield ham? Pick up a slice or two at **Metro Foods Company**. Want to roast fresh quail or squab? Go to **Ming Kee Poultry,** where you can either buy the live bird and do the killing, plucking, and processing yourself or else have it done for you in the shop.

This element of Chinatown's food markets—the custom of keeping animals alive until the moment they are bought as food, when they are slaughtered—has attracted a lot of attention recently. The practice provides the buyer with absolute proof that the meat is fresh, which is an important consideration in Asian culture. But animal-rights activists object to this, as well as to the sometimes cramped and unsanitary conditions in which the animals are kept. In response, some spokespeople from the Asian community have decried the protests as a racist attack on their culture, saying that much worse abuse takes place in butcher shops and large-scale meat-proces-sing plants. The San Francisco Com-mission of Animal Control and Welfare has held many meetings on the subject, and many newspaper articles have explored the issue at length. At press time, the controversy had not been resolved; however, it's unlikely that live animals will disappear from the markets here.

With its bustling streets and foreign atmosphere, Chinatown can be somewhat intimidating to venture into. Many of the people you are dealing with are recent immigrants, so they haven't had a chance to learn much English. But patience, friend-liness, and persistence pay off in the end.

You can communicate volumes by smiling, gesturing, and pointing. But if you really need some good advice or help, seek out young staffers, who are usually English-speaking. Relax and let yourself be swept up in all the activity, and you'll undoubtedly find shopping in Chinatown a unique, fascinating experience.

21 Yong Kee For more than 30 years this bakery has produced superior steamed pork buns, with moist, light dough and finely ground fillings. The noodle rolls, however, are thick and almost mushy, lacking that bit of rubber band resistance that marks the best. ♦ Tu-Su. No credit cards accepted. 732 Jackson St (between Grant Ave and Stockton St). 986.3759

22 Ginn Wall Company An all-purpose Chinese cookware store, it stocks a little bit of everything: bowls, some cookbooks, tart molds, moon-cake presses, steamers, woks, rice cookers, cast-iron grill pans, and a surprisingly wide variety of knives, cleavers, pastry tips, and cookie cutters. There's even a selection of seeds for Chinese vegetables. The owners are cheerful and friendly. ♦ M-W; F-Su. 1016 Grant Ave (between Jackson St and Pacific Ave). 982.6307 &

23 Golden Gate Bakery Yellow custard tarts are displayed at just about every bakery and on every dim sum cart in the city, but the best are at this tiny, crowded shop. The tart shells are made with butter for a crust as flaky as puff pastry, and the seductively good custard has just a hint of salt (typical of Chinese pastries). They're kept warm so they always taste freshly baked—and they're good enough to delight even the finest French pastry chef. ♦ Daily. No credit cards accepted. 1029 Grant Ave (between Jackson St and Pacific Ave). 781.2627

24 Mayerson Food Company Always crowded, this produce-and-meat market is known for its high-quality Chinese ingredients. Fat taro root, massive radishes, and sweet *dau meu* (pea sprouts) vie for space. Most of the hard-working employees do not speak English, so you're on your own if you have questions. ♦ Daily. No credit cards accepted. 1101 Grant Ave (at Pacific Ave). 398.4618 &

25 Four Sea Supermarket One of the most impressive fish markets in Chinatown (or in the city, for that matter), it displays 25 kinds of fish on ice and in tanks; meat is sold along one side. Here you can find eel curled like snakes ready to strike, live turtles up to 18 inches long, live frogs, blue crab, tiny catfish, geoduck (pronounced *gooey*-duck), and silver-skinned pike three feet long. Everything is butchered to order, which is no sight for the squeamish but certainly ensures freshness. ♦ Daily. No credit cards accepted. 1100 Grant Ave (at Pacific Ave). 788.2532 &

26 New On Sang Poultry Company The front window is stacked with wire cases holding guinea fowl and blue chickens (they have blue skin and white feathers); the latter, reputed to have curative powers, are a popular ingredient for soup. Inside, the poultry that has made this place famous is quickly cut up behind glass windows. Chicken and parts are displayed on one side, fish on the other. The same company owns **San Francisco Chicken/New On Sang Market,** a stylish rotisserie and deli on Clement Street in the Richmond district. ♦ Daily. No credit cards accepted. 1114 Grant Ave (between Pacific Ave and Broadway). 982.9228 & Also at: 617 Clement St (between Seventh and Eighth Aves), The Richmond. 752.4100; fax 750.8242 &

The fortune cookie was invented in San Francisco around the turn of the century by Makota Hagiwara, the chief gardener of the Japanese Tea Garden in Golden Gate Park.

A typical Chinese breakfast (and late-night snack) is *juk,* or thick rice porridge, rather than ham and eggs. At Hing Lung, the house special *juk* is chock-full of seafood; another version features pork innards (liver, spleen, etc.); yet another, a cut-up thousand-year-old egg (a duck egg that has been preserved for three months). For the uninitiated, the *juk* with prawns is a good introduction. Add a dab of hot chili paste and a splash of soy sauce to this rib-sticking dish.

27 Yuen's Garden ★★$ As at so many Chinatown shops, the windows at this restaurant/store are decked with hanging roasted birds, but these have a particularly good color, and the selection is above average. The tea-roasted quail has an exquisite five-spice taste, and even the chicken wings retain their succulence. The shop also offers walnut-hued squab cooked with the head on, soy-sauce chicken, poached chicken, roasted Rock Cornish game hens, tea-smoked duck, and pressed duck. Rice-flour crepes, chewy and delicious, are made to order in the window by a friendly old woman, then filled with sugar, chopped peanuts, and coconut, or savory pork, peanuts, and dried shrimp. The food can be taken out or eaten at one of the tables (the place seats 50). ♦ Chinese ♦ Daily lunch. No credit cards accepted. 1131 Grant Ave (between Pacific Ave and Broadway). 391.1131 &

28 New Hop Yick Meat Market Fresh meats line one side of this popular market, while the other side is reserved for sausage, pressed ducks, and Smithfield ham, which is very popular in Chinese cooking. Mountains of crisp pork skins fill the window. ♦ Daily. No credit cards accepted. 1155 Grant Ave (between Pacific Ave and Broadway). 989.0247 &

28 Kwong Jow Sausage Manufacturing Company Connoisseurs recommend this place for its Chinese-style sausage called *lop cheong.* Made from beef, pork, or duck liver, the chewy, slightly sweet sausages cover an entire wall of the shop; smoked bacon and other cured products are also sold. The rest of the space is occupied by the butcher shop, where the sausage meat is prepared. ♦ Daily. No credit cards accepted. 1157 Grant Ave (between Pacific Ave and Broadway). 397.2562 &

29 Taiwan Restaurant ★★★$ The Northern-style food is so good at this dining spot that people should be lining up at the door for it. Unfortunately, many pedestrians walk on by because the restaurant looks as though it's part of a bank. But the steamed dumplings are superb: With just the right amount of meat and cabbage, they gush slightly as you bite into the tender, slightly chewy shell. Crispy chicken and Shanghai noodles are also excellent, as are the turnip cakes, which are crunchy outside and creamy just below the surface. If you've never been a fan of tripe soup, try the version here: It's tender and mild, with long strips of greens and pickled vegetables in a delicate broth with just a hint of spice. The decor is straight-forward: A brass hood separates the kitchen from the entrance, and the small dining room in back is decorated in gray and plum with faux-granite Formica tables. This place also has an extremely popular and equally good sister restaurant in the Richmond district. ♦ Chinese ♦ M-F lunch and dinner; Sa-Su brunch and dinner. 289 Columbus Ave (at Broadway). 989.6789. Also at: 445 Clement St (at Sixth Ave), The Richmond. 387.1789 &

30 New Sun Hong Kong ★★$ Even if the food weren't good, it would almost be worth visiting this two-level corner restaurant for its views of Columbus and Broadway, where the worlds of Chinatown and the predominantly Italian North Beach collide. *Congee* is the most popular dish at every meal. Hot pots are another specialty, and they're always earthy and comforting. One of the best features smoky chicken with mushrooms and onions in a rich sauce that's spicy with flecks of coarsely ground black pepper. If the street view becomes dull, focus attention on the glass-enclosed kitchen, which gets a bit steamy during peak hours. All in all, it's a satisfying show. This place is great for night owls, too—it stays open until 3AM. ♦ Chinese ♦ Daily breakfast, lunch, and dinner until 3AM. 606 Broadway (at Grant Ave). 956.3338; fax 956.3345 &

31 Kim Do Company A hodgepodge of garish ceramic figurines, shaving cream, garden tools, kitchenware, and trinkets can be found here, much of it stacked in the middle of the floor. The discerning shopper can unearth some bargains, such as huge coffee mugs with lids, individual soy bowls, china spoons, white platters, and all kinds of kitchen gadgets. ♦ Daily. No credit cards accepted. 638 Broadway (between Grant Ave and Stockton St). No phone

31 Gold Mountain Restaurant ★★★$ The blush-colored dining room with red accents is so long and so crowded that the captains carry walkie-talkies. Crowded rooms, however, mean crowded carts, brimming with all kinds of fresh dumplings. The *ha gow* here is simple but delicious: the plump shrimp is lightly accented with ginger. The *siu mai,* traditional steamed dumplings, are dressed up with whole shrimp on top. One of the most unusual preparations is a ground shrimp mixture, dotted with carrots and a whole cilantro leaf, dipped in a tempuralike batter and deep-fried. Soup carts dish up *congee;* others have griddles so that the pot stickers

can be warmed and crisped before serving. Noodle dishes, served at dinner, are also excellent. Try the *chow fun,* wide white noodles that are nearly paper-thin. This is probably one of the two most popular dim sum palaces with the city's Chinese residents. ♦ Chinese ♦ Daily breakfast, lunch, and dinner. 611 Broadway (between Grant Ave and Stockton St). 296.7733; fax 296.7782 &

31 Hing Lung Chinese Cuisine ★★$ Fans converge here mainly for the *juk* (a thick rice porridge offered 17 ways). The house special stirs a delicate blend of shellfish and fish into the thick, steaming mixture. Other *juk* dishes include pork liver with sliced pork; fresh clams with abalone, which has a clean, fresh flavor; and pork-blood curd, with musty nuances. The kitchen is sequestered behind glass at the entrance; the dining room in back is outfitted with bamboo chairs and slick glass bricks in the ceiling. ♦ Chinese ♦ Daily breakfast, lunch, and dinner until 1AM. 674 Broadway (between Grant Ave and Stockton St). 398.8838; fax 398.8893 &

32 Metro Foods Company Bright, modern, and packed with merchandise, this must-stop shop for packaged goods contains endless rows of chili sauces and other bottled condiments, myriad dried mushrooms and fungi, and an incredible array of dried fruits and candies, Asian liquors, pickled products, Smithfield hams, and vacuum-packed sliced Chinese hams. ♦ Daily. No credit cards accepted. 641 Broadway (between Grant Ave and Stockton St). 982.1874 &

33 VIP Coffee and Cake Shop Many Chinatown bakeries make cream cakes and rolls with basic sponge cake, but none does them as well as this generic-looking shop with a green linoleum floor. The roll cakes come with a choice of fillings, including lemon, chocolate, and strawberry. There also is a layer cake with a whipped cream–egg white frosting, each piece crowned with a strawberry. The chicken buns are unrivaled: Glazed golden brown, they taste like old-fashioned yeast dinner rolls stuffed with creamed chicken and mushrooms. ♦ Daily. No credit cards accepted. 671 Broadway (between Columbus Ave and Stockton St). 989.7118

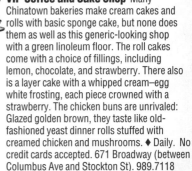

Restaurants and Institutions, a magazine that covers the restaurant industry, reports that 1.5 billion people worldwide eat with a knife, fork, and spoon; 1.2 billion use chopsticks; 350 million use a knife and their hands; and 250 million eat with only their hands. In San Francisco, which has the largest Chinese population in the US (127,140 at last count), the use of chopsticks is most likely higher than in most other cities.

Regional Chinese Cuisine

If your idea of good Chinese food is chop suey and egg foo yong, a visit to San Francisco can awaken your tastebuds to a whole new world of Asian cooking. (As a matter of fact, chop suey is more of an American dish—it was invented in 1856 by an immigrant Chinese cook in San Francisco.) **Chinatown** is the obvious place to go for authentic Chinese food, but it can also be found in other areas, such as **North Beach, SoMa,** the **Richmond,** and even **Japantown.** Here is a detailed guide to the most popular cuisines of China, including specific places in San Francisco to find them.

Cantonese

The first Chinese people who emigrated to the US in the mid-19th century came from the southern province of Canton, which at the time was suffering widespread famine. For quite a while afterwards, the majority of Chinese immigrants in America were Cantonese; as a result, Cantonese is the most widely known style of Chinese cooking. The preparations are usually quite colorful, using thin, clear sauces so as not to detract from the individual ingredients. Stir-frying is a popular method of cooking fish, poultry, pork, and vegetables; and dumplings are often steamed. Flavorings include oyster sauce, light soy, and black beans. The quintessential Cantonese dish is a stir-fry that concentrates on vegetables and either seafood or chicken. Other choices include fried rice; rice noodles; fish, crab, or oysters that have been steamed and served with either ginger and green onions or with black beans; dim sum; and delicate soups.

San Francisco eateries with great Cantonese food include **Harbor Village** (Drumm St, between Sacramento and Clay Sts, 781.8833; 781.8810 &) downtown; **Yuet Lee Seafood** (1300 Stockton St at Broadway, 982.6020) and **Hing Lung Chinese Cuisine** (674 Broadway between Columbus Ave and Stockton St, 398.8838; fax 398.8893 &) in Chinatown; and the **Mayflower Seafood Restaurant** (6225 Geary Blvd at 27th Ave, 387.8338; fax 387.1760) in the Richmond.

Chiu Chow

Chiu Chow is the name of a coastal region in the province of Guangdong. Its residents are nicknamed "the tidelands people" because many of them emigrated from here to parts of southeast Asia. Many Chiu Chow dishes feature seafood flavored with piquant sauces, such as steamed lobster with tangerine jam, fish served with broad-bean paste, and spicy goose with garlic and vinegar sauce. Vegetables are often carved into intricate shapes and designs, including dragons, birds, and flowers. Crab rolls, prawn rolls, oysters, fried pompano, and whole lobster and crab are other characteristic foods.

There aren't many places in San Francisco that specialize in this kind of cuisine, but try **Narai** (2229 Clement St between 23rd and 24th Aves, 751.6363 &) in the Richmond district.

Hakka

The Hakka people were a nomadic northern tribe that migrated to southern China (the word *hakka* means "guest people" in Chinese dialect). The most famous Hakka dish is salt-baked chicken. Other typical items include stuffed tofu, dishes flavored with fermented wine, and mustard greens cooked in a clay pot with unsmoked Chinese bacon.

In San Francisco, the **Ton Kiang** restaurants are the top places to go for this cuisine. There are two locations: one in **Presidio Heights** (3148 Geary Blvd at Spruce St, 752.4440) and one in the Richmond (5821 Geary Blvd at 22nd Ave, 386.8530 &).

Hunan

Like Szechuan cooking, Hunan cuisine is spicy, but it uses heavier sauces and its meats are frequently marinated or smoked. Look for garlic chicken and Hunan-smoked ham and bacon.

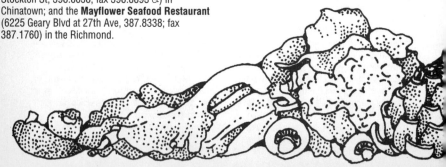

The **Hunan Restaurant** (924 Sansome St between Broadway and Vallejo St, 956.7727; fax 956.5772 ♿) in North Beach offers a wide variety of hot and spicy Hunan delicacies.

Mandarin/Northern Chinese

Northern China is where Peking, the court city of the emperor, was located, and Peking (now called Beijing) had a significant impact on the region's cooking. Its characteristic cuisine developed from the elaborate banquets held in the emperor's court, and naturally the most talented chefs were employed. Dishes are light and delicate, with the starch represented by noodles rather than rice. Many entrées are served with pancakes, such as Beijing duck and moo shu pork. Other typical items are minced squab in lettuce cups; hand-pulled noodles; Beggar's chicken, which is made by cooking a whole chicken in clay; boiled dumplings filled with either pork or shrimp; and pan-fried wheat noodle dishes.

To sample outstanding Mandarin fare, head for **The Mandarin** (900 North Point St across from Aquatic Park, 673.8812; fax 673.5480 ♿), on the fourth floor of the **Woolen Mill** in **Ghirardelli Square**; **No. 1 Dumpling House** (832 Clement St between Ninth and 10th Aves, 221.2699) in the Richmond, which specializes in boiled dumplings; or **San Wang Restaurant No. 1** (1682 Post St at Laguna St, 921.1453) in Japantown, which has great hand-pulled noodles.

Shanghai

This populous province lies at the mouth of the Yangtze River in Eastern China. Its cuisine is characterized by braised dishes and heavy sauces. Duck or chicken prepared using the "dark cooking" method—that is, braising in wine, dark soy, and star anise—is a typical favorite. Other common dishes are vegetarian goose, made from a soy product; chicken or fish marinated with Shaoxing wine; and juicy pork dumplings that are steamed and eaten with black vinegar and ginger.

To sample the tastes of Shanghai, visit the **Fountain Court** (354 Clement St at Fifth Ave, 668.1100; fax 668.1123), in the Richmond, and the **Wu Kong Restaurant** (101 Spear St at Mission St, 957.9300; fax 957.0696 ♿), in **SoMa**'s **Rincon Center.**

Szechuan

Located in the southwestern part of China, the Szechuan province has a very hot climate. Therefore, spicy dishes are favored here, in the belief that eating hot food will help cool the body. If a dish is described as "Szechuan style," it is likely to contain hot peppers, garlic, and/or tomatoes.

In San Francisco, it is difficult to find a restaurant that specializes in authentic Szechuan cuisine, although many places have a few dishes from that region on their menus. Your best bet is to go to the **Szechwan Village Restaurant** (3317 Steiner St between Lombard and Chestnut Sts, 567.9989) in the **Marina** district.

Taiwan

The political status of this island south of mainland China has been controversial since 1949, when Chiang Kai-shek and his Nationalist government took refuge here after the rise of Mao Tse-tung. To this day, it is considered part of China, but it stubbornly clings to its own identity. The food of this region seems to echo that dichotomy: Both original Taiwanese creations and traditional dishes from Northern China are featured in this cuisine. Look for items such as pickled greens with shredded pork tripe; omelettes made with taro flour, eggs, and oysters; and boiled dumplings.

For this distinctive fare, turn to the **Taiwan Restaurant,** which has two outlets: one in Chinatown (289 Columbus Ave at Broadway, 989.6789) and the other in the Richmond (445 Clement St at Sixth Ave, 387.1789 ♿).

34 Yuet Lee Seafood ★★★$ Standing like a beacon at the busy corner at Broadway and Stockton, this place with a lime-green-and-orange exterior and equally bright interior stands out. Open until 3AM, it's a refueling stop for club prowlers, and the staff is always welcoming. Among the best-sellers are the stir-fry combinations, but these don't really show off the kitchen's talents. The salt-and-pepper squid, quickly stirred in a dry wok, is a must-order dish, as are the steamed rock cod and Dungeness crab; however, the rice *congee* is better at nearby **Hing Lung** (see below). For a late-night snack, the shrimp with scrambled eggs will hit the spot. ♦ Chinese/Seafood ♦ M, W-Su lunch and dinner. No credit cards accepted. 1300 Stockton St (at Broadway). 982.6020

35 Hing Lung Under the same ownership as **Hing Lung Chinese Cuisine** (see page 39), this take-out shop does its own roasting and is best known for its roast pork. It is also a butcher shop. ♦ Daily. 1261 Stockton St (at Broadway). 397.5521

36 May Wah Trading Company Non-Chinese Asian products fill this market run by Vietnamese native Jimmy Wong and his family. They import foodstuffs from Cambodia, Laos, India, the Philippines, Vietnam, and Thailand, including Thai basil, fresh lemongrass and galangal (a pungent root), tamarind pods, and all the chili and fish sauces so important to Asian cuisines. This place is a great source for fresh fish, meat, produce, and a variety of packaged products. The mostly English-speaking staff is friendly and helpful. A red-carpeted stairway leads to a spacious selling floor stocked with cooking paraphernalia and wonderful porcelain dishes: Look for the celadon rice bowls decorated with pale leaves and lavender grapes. The prices are low, too. Large, lidded stockpots go for less than half of what they fetch in the Union Square area. For an interesting gift, check out the red jalapeño-shape chopstick rests. ♦ Daily. No credit cards accepted. 1230 Stockton St (between Pacific Ave and Broadway). 433.3095; fax 433.7876 ♿ Also at: Numerous locations throughout the city

37 Meriwa ★★$ In **Meriwa Center,** a commercial building with a tiny mall, this ballroom-size restaurant boasts crystal chandeliers and dark molding. Rows of pink-clothed tables are well spaced to allow the dim sum carts to make their way comfortably through. The diners here tend to be Asian, which may be evidence of the food's quality and authenticity. The staff is charming, and the dim sum carts hold some unusual preparations: One cart carries soup, and another holds a selection of noodle dishes and plates of roast duck. Here the *siu mai* has a dense pork texture and bold flavor; the bean-curd skins are dark brown and are rolled around matchstick-thin slices of ginger and bamboo shoots; and the delicate half-moon tapioca turnovers are stuffed with sweet shrimp, pale green Chinese chives, and crisp bits of fresh water chestnuts (which bear no relation to the flavorless canned version). ♦ Chinese ♦ Daily breakfast and lunch. 728 Pacific Ave (between Grant Ave and Stockton St). 989.8818; fax 989.3908 ♿

37 Pacific Court Cafe ★$ One of the rare Chinese-owned restaurants that serve *sai choy* (American food), this cafe in the **Meriwa Center** offers crisp, garlic-fried chicken, thick prime ribs, pork chops, and hamburgers. Meals are accompanied by soup and salad, which aren't that good, but the servers are so charming that you would like to love everything. Although the food is American, the room is generally filled with Chinese faces. The open kitchen, tiled walls, carpeting, and two-level dining area are reminiscent of a small-town Holiday Inn. It's not fancy, but it's pleasant. ♦ American ♦ Daily breakfast, lunch, and dinner. No credit cards accepted. 728 Pacific Ave (between Grant Ave and Stockton St). 781.8312 ♿

37 Hong Kong Deli This tiny kiosk just inside the **Meriwa Center** looks like a ticket booth, but its display case holds many flavors of jerky: chicken, five-spice beef chunks, beef with oyster sauce, beef with curry; and beef topped with duck liver or pork teriyaki. The Chinese version is cut so thin that it's almost translucent, moist, and just a bit chewy. ♦ Daily. No credit cards accepted. 728 Pacific Ave (between Grant Ave and Stockton St). 391.4968 ♿

38 Hop Sang Company Pork is the specialty at this popular full-service meat market. The staff waits on customers behind a sales counter and also butchers meat in a glass-enclosed work area. ◆ M-Sa. No credit cards accepted. 1199 Stockton St (at Pacific Ave). 781.1692 ♿

NEW PING YUEN

39 New Ping Yuen This bakery specializes in moon cakes, which look like dense, round pies with a design embossed on the crust. These pastries are traditionally exchanged at the Autumn Buddhist Moon Festival in September and at family celebrations from birthdays to anniversaries. Here they come in all sizes and with various fillings, including red bean paste, sweet sesame seeds, lotus seeds, salty pork, egg yolk, and chicken. The bakery also is known for its baked buns, which have either a juicy pork filling, or drier chicken or beef filling. ◆ Daily. 1125 Stockton St (between Jackson St and Pacific Ave). 433.5571 ♿

40 Sun Duck Market A case in back of this top-rated fish and poultry market holds a selection of chickens and ducks, including Petaluma-raised Peking duck. Dried and fresh fish fill the rest of the cramped quarters. The doorway is usually tended by an employee overseeing a plastic tub filled with flopping black bass; they're sold almost as fast as they can be caught. ◆ Daily. No credit cards accepted. 1107 Stockton St (between Jackson St and Pacific Ave). 956.8030 ♿

40 Golden Gate Meat Company Considered the best meat market in Chinatown, it specializes in pork; there's a small selection of beef and poultry, too. Like most other shops in the area, the interior isn't much to look at, but the meat here is and with good reason. Each display is lined up just so, and everything tastes just as good as it looks—which is to say, much better than the meat at other area markets. The staff is very helpful and willingly answers questions about the most economical cuts of meat and best ways to prepare them. ◆ Daily. No credit cards accepted. 1101 Stockton St (at Jackson St). 392.0940 ♿

41 JR New Orange Land One of the top shops for Chinese produce, its bins line both sides of the sidewalk, creating traffic jams that make bumper cars seem civilized. If it's a Chinese vegetable and it's in season, it'll probably be here, and at an excellent price. For years, this place has been known for its bargain-priced oranges and other citrus fruits. ◆ Daily. No credit cards accepted. 1055 Stockton St (at Jackson St). 982.8188 ♿

42 Feng Huang Pastry While most pastry shops in Chinatown are Cantonese, this 28-year-old bakery prefers the Mandarin style. Here are *the* best rice-noodle rolls in the city, which come stuffed with various meat combinations (this shop even supplies many Bay Area Chinese restaurants with the rice-noodle dough for *chow fun*). And don't overlook the turnovers filled with coconut and fried to a crisp crunch. The buns are wonderful, too, with a dry, firm texture and a slightly sweet pork filling. The place is nothing to look at, but the quality of the ingredients and the final products are beyond compare. ◆ Daily (but the shop closes some Thursdays; call to check). No credit cards accepted. 761 Jackson St (between Ross Alley and Stockton St). 421.7885 ♿

43 Golden Gate Fortune Cookie Company The aromas of almond and sugar waft down Ross Alley, where this cramped factory has been making fortune cookies for more than 30 years. The process is relatively straightforward. Batter is poured into a mold and baked on a circular conveyer belt. Grandmotherly workers pluck up each hot, flat disk, place a paper fortune in the center, and quickly fold it into the distinctively shaped cookie. In addition to the usual predictions of health and wealth, X-rated fortunes are available. Visitors can watch the cookies being made and, for a glimpse into the future, buy them here, too. ◆ Daily. No credit cards accepted. 56 Ross Alley (off Jackson St, between Grant Ave and Stockton St). 781.3956 ♿

Want to learn more about Chinese vegetables, calligraphy, or the Chinese zodiac? You can buy books and posters on these subjects at the Chinese Culture Center located on the third floor of the Holiday Inn at 750 Kearny Street. In addition to cards, books, and jewelry, there are rotating exhibits of art and crafts. The center is open Sunday from noon to 4PM and Tuesday through Saturday from 10AM to 4PM. Admission is free.

The Chinese have picturesque names for some dishes that have become popular menu mainstays. Moo shu pork means "wooden whiskers pork," which refers to the fact that its ingredients are all finely shredded. And a dish consisting of chopped meat with bean thread noodles is called "ants climbing tree"—the "ants" are the bits of ground meat, climbing a noodle "tree."

44 Gourmet Kitchen With so many shop windows hung with ducks, ribs, and other roast meats, it's hard to decide which is best; however, this place has won legions of fans for its roast pig and duck. A close look reveals that the skin is evenly colored and crisp. ♦ Daily. No credit cards accepted. 1051 Stockton St (between Washington and Jackson Sts). 781.7988 &

44 New Golden Daisy Company Roast suckling pig is the specialty of this take-out deli. The butcher slices pieces to order from an upside-down hanging pig. The skin is darker and crispier than most, making the meat seem all the more rich and succulent. Pans stacked in the front window proffer chicken feet in a rich brown sauce, as well as fried chicken wings, pork ribs, and delicious smoked bacon. The pressed duck, which looks like a cartoon character flattened by a steamroller, has an intense, salty flavor and is used to make soup. The deli also makes superb "Chinese tamales"—rice and other ingredients wrapped in lotus leaves and steamed. ♦ Daily. No credit cards accepted. 1041 Stockton St (between Washington and Jackson Sts). 392.0111 &

45 Lucky Creation ★★★$ Shared tables are the norm in this blue-tiled hole-in-the-wall, but the food is something to savor: This is, by far, the best vegetarian restaurant in town. One of the tastiest dishes is mixed vegetables in a golden nest—a crisp potato basket lined with perfectly cooked broccoli florets and filled with oyster, button, and straw mushrooms, wood ears, and white fungus, all bathed in an intense brown sauce. Another standout is an array of mushrooms, celery, green bell pepper, and carrots, all cut like stars and daisies. Taro is shaped like a goldfish, deep-fried until crisp, and served with a sweet-and-sour sauce. Another good choice is fresh-tasting pan-fried noodles topped with mushrooms, bean sprouts, and celery. ♦ Chinese/Vegetarian ♦ M-Tu, Th-Su lunch and dinner. 854 Washington St (between Ross Alley and Stockton St). 989.0818

SUPERIOR ®

46 Superior Trading Company Established in the 1950s, this business is one of the city's most respected purveyors of Chinese medicinal herbs and teas. The wood drawers that line the wall make the place look like a cross between an old-time bank and an apothecary. ♦ Daily. No credit cards accepted. 837 Washington St (between Waverly Pl and Stockton St). 982.8722 &

47 Wycen Foods Inc. Off the beaten path, but going strong since 1948, this meat-processing plant sells cured duck gizzards, chicken liver sausage, cured dried duck, Chinese-style bacon, and pork rinds. Smoked fish and beef jerky also are available. ♦ Daily. No credit cards accepted. 903 Washington St (at Stockton St). 788.3910 &

48 Little Paris Coffee Shop ★★$ This tiny, modest shop is a good place to try one of the most distinctive cross-cultural foods to be embraced by the Asian population here, *bahn mi.* Part Vietnamese and part French, these sandwiches are much cheaper than their American counterparts, and usually a lot more interesting. They're constructed on a French roll (crisp outside, chewy inside) that's slathered with mayonnaise and stuffed with such fillings as pâté, smoked chicken, barbecued pork, and pork sausage, then piled with shredded pickled daikon, carrots, cilantro, onions, and cucumbers and splashed with chili vinegar. There are also big bowls of *pho* with all kinds of fresh garnishes, including cilantro, bean sprouts, and lemon slices, and a dozen puddinglike desserts. Altogether, it makes a quick, filling, and inexpensive meal. ♦ Vietnamese/Cafe ♦ Daily lunch and dinner. No credit cards accepted. 939 Stockton St (between Clay and Washington Sts). 982.6111 &

49 L & H Seafood This seafood market is particularly notable for its large selection of live crabs. ♦ Daily. No credit cards accepted. 838 Jackson St (between Stockton and Powell Sts). No phone &

50 New Hong Kong Noodle Company The raw wood shelves and boxes in back make this look more like a warehouse than a noodle factory, but it turns out fresh, thick, and chewy Shanghai noodles to cook at home. Also on hand are all kinds of frozen dim sum, including sesame rice balls and pot stickers, and packages of dried noodles. ♦ Daily. No credit cards accepted. 874 Pacific Ave (at Powell St). 433.1886 &

51 Mee Heong Bakery With one case filled with soft drinks, another with pastries, and a single row of tables, what's the draw at this bakery-cafe? Steamed buns. They're made with airy, moist dough and have such fillings as pork and lotus paste. ♦ Daily. No credit cards accepted. 1343 Powell St (between Pacific Ave and Broadway). 781.3266

52 Kam (H.K.) Po Kitchen ★★$ People from all walks of life can be seen enjoying the wholesome, tasty fare at this exceptionally

clean corner cafe. Most of the *congee* dishes are very cheap; even more elaborate preparations are a bargain. Try soup, lo mein, or rice dish that features barbecue. The take-out section in front offers roast pig, poultry, and ribs. If you're planning a large buffet party, this is the place to get enormous pans of chow mein or roast meat at a pittance.
◆ Chinese/Takeout ◆ Daily lunch and dinner. No credit cards accepted. 801 Broadway (at Powell St). 982.3516

53 Imperial Tea Court A calming oasis in between Chinatown and North Beach, this modern tea shop with dark wood accents offers high-quality teas and tables where people can sip. For a fee, tea masters guide tastings that demonstrate how the brew changes character as it goes from the first steeping to the fourth and final one; connoisseurs consider the second and third prime. Many teas here cost more than $100 a pound: The Junshan Yinzhen is $545; Sword of the Emperor is $365; and the popular Imperial Dragon Well is $280 (small samples are also available at a reasonable price). The staff is so helpful that a visit here seems like a college course in the myriad qualities of tea. ◆ Daily 11AM-6:30PM. 1411 Powell St (between Broadway and Vallejo St). 788.6080; fax 788.6079

54 Des Alpes Restaurant ★★$ The dining room behind the cozy bar looks just as a Basque dining hall should: packed with tables, crowded with families having a good time, and imbued with a warm, comfortable ambience. The seven-course prix-fixe menu is keyed to the days of the week and features staggering quantities of such fare as sweetbreads, oxtail stew, lamb stew, and trout—all at an incredible price. This is one of the best deals in the city, and the waiters have a spirit as bountiful as the food. ◆ Basque ◆ Tu-Su dinner. Reservations recommended Friday through Sunday. 732 Broadway (between Stockton and Powell Sts).

In Chinese restaurants, the adventurous and budget-minded diner should bypass the Americanized "family dinners"—a multicourse fixed-price menu—and ask for the *wo choy* menu. It also offers a prix-fixe meal, but usually provides more authentic dishes. If the *wo choy* is not in English, ask a waiter to translate it for you.

Dim sum, the name for the array of Chinese delicacies served at many restaurants in Chinatown, is Cantonese for "heart's delight."

Bests

Boz Scaggs
Rock Singer/Owner of Slim's, a San Francisco nightclub

The **Bay Area** has so many great restaurants—inventive cooking, the best ingredients—but I seem to wind up at these places more than any others:

Hayes Street Grill—the best seafood the Bay Area has to offer—no mean feat—plus great salads and dessert. My European friends' favorite.

Zuni Cafe—Drop-dead direct hits from the wood ovens, exquisite martinis, and the best selection of oysters in town. Good people watching, including requisite art victims and some of the city's best chefs.

Hawthorne Lane—An elegant, cushy room, beautiful bar. Innovative menu, with many dishes having Asian twists—all beautifully presented. Even the wait staff is excited by the food.

Oliveto—Chef Paul Bertolli rules! Reading his inspired menus is half the fun. Fantastic wine list.

Tommaso's—Anytime. Great, hearty Italian food, Neapolitan style and pizzas cooked in a wood-burning oven. A family-run trattoria.

Don Ramon's Mexican Restaurant—authentic Guadalajara-style Mexican food. Terrific margaritas. Another inviting family-run place.

Linda Lee
All About Chinatown! Walking Tour Leader

Gold Mountain—This is the best place for dim sum in **Chinatown** and you can rub elbows with the local Chinese . . . grandmas with grandkids gathered around banquet tables.

Harbor Village—The best dim sum outside of Chinatown.

Lucky Creation—This is my favorite vegetarian recommendation. All the vegetable dishes come out tasting fresh and vibrant, and the meat substitute dishes are tasty and intriguing.

R & G Lounge—This is a reliable place for Cantonese food . . . fresh seafood, salt-and-pepper roasting, and clay pot dishes, all consistently prepared.

Mastering the Dim Sum Experience

No San Francisco culinary experience is complete without a sampling of dim sum. These delicious tidbits are a local institution; only Hong Kong has more dim sum parlors, and that's where the tradition originated.

Generally, dim sum are served for brunch; most dim-sum houses open around 10AM and close in the middle or late afternoon. Typically, waiters circle the dining room pushing carts stacked with covered bamboo or stainless- steel containers filled with steamed or fried dumplings, shrimp balls, spring rolls, steamed buns, and Chinese pastries. Just point to the items that look appealing as they roll by; the dim sum won't be listed on a menu, and the waiters often speak no English, so ordering is done by gesture.

Although dim sum may appear to be exotic, most fillings are pretty straightforward—pork, shrimp, cabbage, mushrooms, and ginger appear in many guises. Such unfamiliar delicacies as duck or chicken

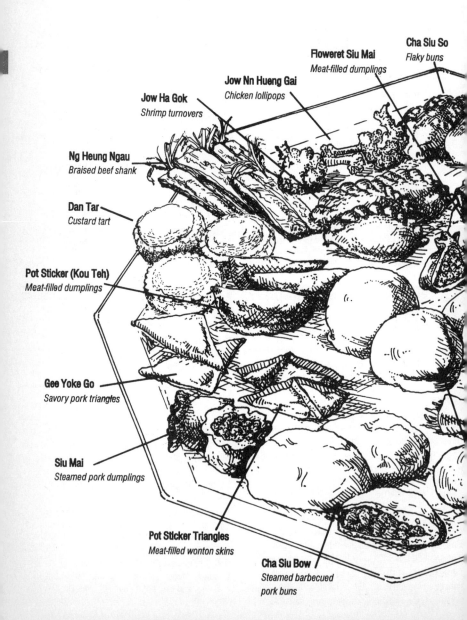

Cha Siu So
Flaky buns

Floweret Siu Mai
Meat-filled dumplings

Jow Nn Hueng Gai
Chicken lollipops

Jow Ha Gok
Shrimp turnovers

Ng Heung Ngau
Braised beef shank

Dan Tar
Custard tart

Pot Sticker (Kou Teh)
Meat-filled dumplings

Gee Yoke Go
Savory pork triangles

Siu Mai
Steamed pork dumplings

Pot Sticker Triangles
Meat-filled wonton skins

Cha Siu Bow
Steamed barbecued pork buns

feet are sometimes offered, but they are easy to detect and reject, if you so desire. Noodle dishes may also be available, but they will be listed on a menu with English translations, rather than offered from the cart.

Each table is set with a container of brick-red chili oil, bottles of soy sauce, and white vinegar. Chili sauce and vinegar are mixed to make a sauce for pot stickers, and soy sauce and chili oil are blended to accent just about everything else.

The carts circulate continuously, so you can order in stages, taking a few items each time they pass. In the old days, the bill was figured by the number of little plates left on the table, but today, a printed bill is updated by the servers as the meal progresses. It never adds up to much, though—you'll have to eat a lot of food to spend more than $10 a person.

Every dim sum restaurant does things a little differently, but here's a thumbnail guide to some of the most popular items.

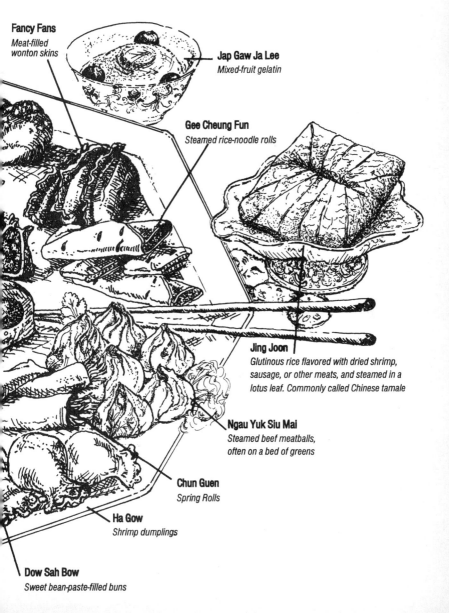

Fancy Fans
Meat-filled wonton skins

Jap Gaw Ja Lee
Mixed-fruit gelatin

Gee Cheung Fun
Steamed rice-noodle rolls

Jing Joon
Glutinous rice flavored with dried shrimp, sausage, or other meats, and steamed in a lotus leaf. Commonly called Chinese tamale

Ngau Yuk Siu Mai
Steamed beef meatballs, often on a bed of greens

Chun Guen
Spring Rolls

Ha Gow
Shrimp dumplings

Dow Sah Bow
Sweet bean-paste-filled buns

North Beach

North Beach is fueled by coffee. The dense concentration of quaint coffeehouses and the heady aroma of roasting beans scenting the air practically mesmerize strollers into passing first one hour, then two, over a leisurely cup.

According to local lore, the first cappuccino in the United States was served in North Beach in 1956 by John Giotta at **Caffè Trieste**. The cafe, now run by his son, still attracts a diverse group with its dark Italian espresso, made at the roasting facility next door. North Beach also boasts two other roasters: **Caffè Roma Coffee Roasting Company** and **Graffeo Coffee**, which has been selling coffee since 1935. Comparing coffees and absorbing the different atmosphere at each cafe is an excellent way to experience the area's essence.

Certainly coffee, as well as North Beach's European, laid-back atmosphere, helped seduce the Beat Generation into taking root here in the 1950s, particularly at **Enrico's** on **Broadway**. The bohemian spirit lingers today, with many writers and painters clinging to rent-controlled apartments around **Telegraph Hill.**

There's more than just java here, though, as the scent of bread baking and the perfume of sautéed garlic attest. North Beach is virtually synonymous with "Little Italy," and its Italian culinary history reaches back to the first immigrants from Genoa, who arrived in the 1840s, followed by the Ligurians, the Luccans, and finally, in the late 1880s, the Sicilians.

Despite their strong presence in North Beach today, Italians were not the first to settle the area. The original Gold Rush–era settlers were Chinese fishermen, who later gave way to Irish and German immigrants who clustered on Telegraph Hill. The first Italians called this section of San Francisco "Little City" and recreated Italy here, with legitimate theaters and concerts and three newspapers all in Italian. The Genovese established truck farms and got into the produce business, the Luccans were storekeepers, and the Sicilians established many of the eateries along **Fisherman's Wharf.** The Sicilian influence on the neighborhood is apparent every October, when a procession honoring the Madonna del Lume (Madonna of Light), a religious observance from that part of Italy, departs from **Saints Peter and Paul Catholic Church** and heads toward Fisherman's Wharf for the blessing of the fishing fleet.

Look no farther for evidence of North Beach's Italian soul (or, at least, stomach) than the focaccia at **Liguria Bakery;** biscotti from the **Italian/French Bakery;** air-dried sausage from **Molinari Delicatessen;** fat cotechino sausages and delicious mascarpone tortas from **Prudente Meat Market and Deli;** the irresistible *sacripantina* at **Stella Pastry;** and a rum-soaked *zuccotto* at **Victoria Pastry Co.** And after you've taken in the culinary sights, don't miss **Biordi**, where owner Gianfranco Savio has gathered a magnificent assortment of traditional and modern Italian pottery.

Capp's Corner and **LaFelce** provide the classic Italian family-dining experience, complete with red-and-white-checkered oilcloths, walls covered with photographs and mementos, and bargain-priced five-course meals. But even in North Beach, that kind of old-style eatery is beginning to give way to trendier, more tourist-oriented spots, including **The Stinking Rose**, which offers an all-garlic menu.

Other shifts are evident, such as the latest twist in North Beach's demographic profile. The neighborhood abuts **Chinatown**, and ever since Chinese immigration to San Francisco peaked in the 1980s, the Asian influence in the area has grown. The 1990 census revealed that only about 12 percent of North Beach residents were of Italian heritage. Chinatown, traditionally demarcated from North Beach by Broadway, has begun creeping across the divide. The two worlds collide at Broadway and **Grant Avenue**, in a dizzying kaleidoscope of language, sights, and smells. The growing Asian influence has resulted in a bit of cross-pollination at some North Beach restaurants. **Enrico's** serves steamed clams in a broth perfumed with lemongrass, while **the house** on Grant Avenue serves soba noodles and roasted garlic sauce for pasta.

Nevertheless, in spite of new influences such as that of the Asian community, and the addition of strip clubs and flashing neon which has made this area nearly as colorful as Las Vegas, plenty of classic European flavor remains. In fact, during the 1990s a new wave of Italian immigrants has been opening restaurants in the neighborhood, including **Steps of Rome, L'Osteria del Forno,** and **Ristorante Ideale.**

No tour of North Beach would be complete without a cappuccino finale. For the best cup, head for **Mario's Bohemian Cigar Store.** This 19th-century hangout makes a fitting spot for the inevitable realization that even the most leisurely day spent exploring the neighborhood has somehow rushed by. Well, relax and linger a little longer; you've just discovered the magic of North Beach.

湖 南 小 喫

Hunan Restaurant

1 Hunan Restaurant ★★$$ Owner Henry Chung introduced spicy Hunan food to San Francisco in a 20-seat hole-in-the-wall back in 1974. Since then, it's expanded several times, but the restaurant is still always filled to the rafters. Devotees keep coming back for "Diana's Special" (which is named after Henry's wife), a deep-fried pie filled with pork, cheese, and onions; the house-smoked duck; and ham with peppers and onions, which is hot enough to clear the sinuses. ♦ Chinese ♦ Daily lunch and dinner. Reservations recommended. 924 Sansome St (between Broadway and Vallejo St). 956.7727; fax 956.5772 ♿

ESSEX

SUPPER CLUB

2 Essex Supper Club ★★★$$$ Set in the previous location of the famous **Ernie's** restaurant, this new supper club appeals mainly to the younger set. On the lower level is a cigar room/bar, with premium stogies, fine liqueurs, and billiards tables. The first-floor dining room, whose sedate decor is brightened by some colorful contemporary artwork on the walls, presents an innovative menu of continental dishes by chef David Lawrence. Among the top picks are heirloom tomato salad with *haricots verts,* Maine lobster timbale with mango and chutney accents, oven-roasted Muscovy duck breast served with an unusual chocolate-raspberry vinegar gastrique, and seared salmon accompanied by a lobster-potato hash. Upstairs, there's another smoking room that also features performances of live music. ♦ Supper Club ♦ Tu-Sa dinner. 847 Montgomery St (between Jackson St and Pacific Ave). 397.5969; fax 397.3215 ♿

3 The Helmand Restaurant ★★★$$
Afghani food, little known in this part of the world, is worth exploring in this pretty, romantic place with flowers on each table and low-key service.

A specialty is lamb, served three ways: sautéed with yellow split peas, onions, and vinegar; speared into kabobs, marinated with onion and sun-dried baby grapes, and charbroiled; or marinated, sliced, and served on Afghan bread with sautéed eggplant. *Aushak* is a kind of Afghan ravioli, tender pillows of pasta stuffed with leeks and served with a yogurt sauce, carrots, yellow split peas, and a beef sauce. The combinations seem exotic, but the flavors are sublime, and a good wine list matches the refined food. ♦ Afghani ♦ Daily dinner. 430 Broadway (between Montgomery and Kearny Sts). 362.0641 ♿

BRANDY HO'S

4 Brandy Ho's ★★$ This glitzy Chinese eatery, located in a building featuring award-winning modern architecture by **John Goldman,** is wrapped with enough neon to rival the flashing lights that snake down Broadway. The facade has 23-foot red columns topped with a porcelain garland of red peppers (which figure prominently in the restaurant's cuisine). The Hunan menu features pungent house-smoked meats, including chicken, duck, and ham served with whole cloves of garlic. Most of the dishes have a fiery undercurrent, but some are listed as "Not Hot With Pepper." One of the most popular preparations is the *kung pao* chicken, which is sautéed with peanuts, bamboo shoots, water chestnuts, and onions. The staff is happy to help customers make selections. ♦ Hunan ♦ Daily lunch and dinner. Reservations recommended Friday and Saturday. 450 Broadway (between Montgomery and Kearny Sts). 362.6268. fax 362.3098 ♿ Also at: 217 Columbus Ave (between Pacific Ave and Broadway). 788.7527; fax 788.7528

F lunch and dinner; Sa dinner. 1020 Kearny St (between Pacific Ave and Broadway). 397.3066 &

5 Enrico's ★★★$$ From a safe perch on the heated outdoor patio, diners can observe the bawdy goings-on of the neon jungle around them while enjoying chef/owner Rick Hackett's Italian-inspired fare. (There's also indoor seating, with live entertainment nightly.) The pizzas, cooked to a turn in the wood-burning oven, have a yeasty, thin crust. They are available in classic versions, like the margherita (with roasted garlic and tomato sauce), or topped with such creative combinations as shrimp, corn, and ricotta. The mussels with olive oil, garlic, and Italian parsley are among the best in the city. Another excellent dish is the Tuscan-style T-bone steak served with white beans. Hackett also offers an outstanding tapas menu featuring such savories as smoked salmon with cucumber jam; Spanish tortillas; house-cured olives; grilled fruit with proscuitto; and velvety tripe. And diners with a sweet tooth will appreciate the tasty desserts, particularly the brûlées and any of the fruit and chocolate items. ♦ Italian/Mediterranean ♦ Daily lunch and dinner. Reservations recommended. 504 Broadway (at Kearny St). 982.6223; fax 397.7244 &

6 Tommaso's ★★$ *People* magazine proclaimed it one of the country's top three pizza places, but success hasn't spoiled this little spot, which is credited with producing San Francisco's first brick-oven pizza in the 1930s. All of the crisp, thin-crust pizzas, spread with exactly the right amount of topping, are superb. So is the pasta, served with freshly made, sensible, traditional sauces. When you do plain and simple as well as this, there's no need to do anything else. ♦ Italian ♦ Tu-Su dinner. 1042 Kearny St (between Pacific Ave and Broadway). 398.9696; fax 989.9415

6 Cho-Cho Restaurant ★$$ One of the oldest Japanese restaurants in the city, this place has developed a following among the Hollywood set. It was featured in the movie *Rising Sun,* and regular customers include Francis Coppola and George Lucas. It has the atmosphere of a well-worn Japanese country inn, with rough wood beams, baskets, and massive tables. The open kitchen is framed by shelves holding hand-thrown pottery. Top food choices include sukiyaki, tempura, and a spinach salad with roasted red peppers, tantalizing bacon, sesame seeds, and a special, ginger-laden sauce. ♦ Japanese ♦ M-

7 Caffè Macaroni ★★$$ The quality of the food at this cute but modest trattoria has deteriorated a bit in the past few years, but it has remained a popular neighborhood spot. Reliable entrées include a dish of crab, mussels, and octopus served over black pasta flavored with squid ink, puffy gnocchi with gorgonzola sauce, pork with fennel-seed sauce, and chicken breast sautéed with porcini mushrooms. ♦ Italian ♦ M-F lunch and dinner; Sa dinner. Reservations recommended. No credit cards accepted. 59 Columbus Ave (between Washington and Jackson Sts). 956.9737

8 San Francisco Brewing Company This brewpub offers 20 types of specialty beers, plus house brews, and caters to the Financial District crowd. The interior is virtually the same as it was at the turn of the century. Suspended above the impressive mahogany bar, with its gilded top and beveled-glass mirrors, is a long fan that looks like a Willy Wonka contraption and gently turns a series of palm fans. The tile moat around the bar is actually the original spittoon. There's history here, too: Boxer Jack Dempsey worked as a bouncer, and Babyface Nelson was captured in what is now the women's room. On most nights you can hear blues, jazz, and other live music. The experience is great, but the food is an afterthought, though you can't go wrong with a hamburger and all the fixings. ♦ Daily. 155 Columbus Ave (at Pacific Ave). 434.3344 &

9 Campo Santo ★$ Looking like a folk-art celebration of the Day of the Dead, with kitschy Madonnas and candles everywhere, this quirky spot is a find for those who have overdosed on Italian food and want to enjoy Mexican-inspired fare. Unfortunately, a change in ownership has caused a downturn at this once very popular alternative in the trattoria-dense North Beach. The food is less exciting now than it used to be, and the flavors are somewhat muddied. The menu currently includes several vegetarian entrées, as well as burritos, chicken mole, and a few creative variations of traditional Mexican dishes, such as salmon tacos with grilled onions and prawn quesadillas with tomatoes and cactus—all delicious as they sound.
♦ Mexican ♦ M lunch; Tu-F lunch and dinner; Sa-Su dinner. Reservations recommended for parties larger than four. 240 Columbus Ave (between Pacific Ave and Broadway). 433.9623

9 Tosca Cafe The special cappuccino in this popular hangout is actually made without coffee: It's a frothy cup of steamed milk with brandy and chocolate. The bar is also known for its "white nun," made with steamed milk, Kahlúa, and brandy. No food is served, but things are always hopping here. The gleaming copper espresso machine at the end of the bar, the dark, spacious interior, and the Italian opera on the jukebox give the place a unique character. (Best nights to hear the arias are Monday, Tuesday, and Wednesday; disco music blasting from a nearby nightclub the rest of the week greatly diminishes the experience.) You might see Nicolas Cage lounging by the bar when he is in town or exchange thoughts with an up-and-coming book author. ♦ Daily 5PM-2AM. No credit cards accepted. 242 Columbus Ave (between Pacific Ave and Broadway). 986.9651

10 Vesuvio ★$ One of the most popular gathering places for the 1950s Beat generation, this bar still has a bohemian, beatnik feel. ♦ Bar ♦ Daily. No credit cards accepted. 255 Columbus Ave (at Jack Kerouac St, near Broadway). 362.3370

11 Little Joe's ★$$ The menu proclaims "Rain or shine, there's always a line," which is a bit of hyperbole these days, with other Italian restaurants opening almost every week. The food here is hearty and straightforward in a 1950s way. Specialties include sautéed calamari steaks with white wine, garlic, and tomato sauce; fish stew in a garlicky tomato sauce (served with a bib, if you wish); and pasta with prawns, tomato, and cheese.
♦ Italian ♦ Daily lunch and dinner. 523 Broadway (between Kearny St and Columbus Ave). 982.7639; fax 433.7066 ♿

12 Yee Cheong General Contractors Although this crammed shop doesn't look like much, it's excellent for bargain-priced Asian cookware. You'll find a good selection of woks, tongs, and other kitchen tools and gadgets. ♦ Daily. No credit cards accepted. 1319 Stockton St (between Broadway and Vallejo St). 398.7395 ♿

13 the house ★★★$$ Modern in both look and food, this cross-cultural restaurant is the brainchild of Larry Tse, an accountant who put away his calculator to tie on an apron. Choose among such appetizers as shrimp in a heady Chinese barbecue sauce with hot sesame oil; Caesar salad strewn with golden bay scallops; wonderful taro spring rolls, no bigger than a pinkie; garlicky fried chicken wings; and tempura with a substantial batter. Outstanding main courses include sea bass with ginger soy sauce, served with gingery bok choy and roasted or mashed potatoes; veal chop with oyster sauce and shiitake mushrooms; warm noodles with strips of barbecued pork; and stir-fried calamari with bean-paste noodles. Desserts might be a dense chocolate-truffle torte or a thick apple crumb pie. The decor—granite floors, honey-colored tables, and modern Italian lights hanging from the ceiling—makes an appropriate setting for the cutting-edge food. ◆ Asian/Californian ◆ Tu-Sa lunch and dinner. 1230 Grant Ave (at Columbus Ave). 986.8612 ᕑ Also at: 1269 Ninth Ave (between Irving St and Lincoln Way), The Sunset. 682.3898; fax 682.3892 ᕑ

14 The Stinking Rose ★$$ The name refers to garlic, and the tag line on the menu—"We season our garlic with food"—isn't stretching the truth. The most popular dish is the *bagna calda* (a hot skillet of oven-roasted garlic in olive oil and butter with a hint of anchovy), which spreads on bread like butter. The nongarlic dishes on the menu are marked with a vampire, but lasagna is the only savory course safe for Dracula. For dessert, skip the garlic ice cream with caramel mole sauce and chill out on the lemon sorbet. The restaurant has an enormous following, primarily tourists. Those who haven't had their fill of garlic can buy products made from the pungent cloves. ◆ Italian/American ◆ Daily lunch and dinner. Reservations recommended. 325 Columbus Ave (between Grant Ave and Vallejo St). 781.ROSE; fax 781.2833 ᕑ

15 Steps of Rome ★$
A young, attractive Italian crowd gathers here to meet over cups of espresso. Good antipasto salads and pasta dishes are also available. ◆ Cafe ◆ Daily breakfast, lunch, and dinner. No credit cards accepted. 348 Columbus Ave (between Grant Ave and Vallejo St). 397.0435

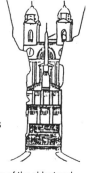

16 Columbus Cutlery One of the oldest and most respected cutlery stores in the city, this is where many professional chefs buy their knives and have them sharpened. The shop packs a complete selection of knives, scissors, and utensils into a space that feels no bigger than a phone booth. There's always a crowd waiting for service, and the couple who own the shop can be a bit cranky—

though they will answer your questions. ◆ M-Tu, Th-Sa. 358 Columbus Ave (between Grant Ave and Vallejo St). 362.1342

17 Molinari Delicatessen This Italian deli, which dates from 1896, is so crammed with fresh and packaged food that it can be claustrophobic. But squeeze yourself in to pick up some of the fresh tortellini and ravioli and the air-dried salami. The display case contains a mouthwatering assortment of meats and such cheeses as gorgonzola, *cambozola,* and Italian fontina. Fresh sausage selections include hot or mild Sicilian; French, which is made with white wine; and excellent *bresaola* (air-dried beef). You'll also find a wonderful selection of olive oils, vinegars, and pastas, and the imported wines are a real bargain. ◆ Daily. No credit cards accepted. 373 Columbus Ave (between Grant Ave and Vallejo St). 421.2337 ᕑ

18 Biordi Hand-painted Italian pottery fills this large ceramics shop that's been here since the 1940s. The display is an education in classic and modern majolica designs; trying to decide among the lovely items that pack the floor-to-ceiling shelves can lead to sensory overload. Shoppers will find dishes, bowls, platters, vinegar and oil cruets, pitchers, vases, and even tables. Look for the Renaissance-style plates from Deruta and the beautiful pastel fruit and flower pottery patterns of Castelli. ◆ Daily. 412 Columbus Ave (at Vallejo St). 392.8096; fax 392.2608 ᕑ

18 Figaro ★★$$ A popular addition to the neighborhood, this new, reasonably priced trattoria (on the site of the now-closed **Caffè Roma**) is usually packed with a young crowd, especially on Saturday nights. The walls have been painted gold, there's a dark wood bar, and much of the artwork that had decorated the former cafe has been restored. The pastas are very good, particularly the angel hair pasta with sun-dried tomato; and the lightly fried calamari with garlicky aioli is terrific, too. The osso buco in a tomato-based sauce is sometimes a bit undercooked, but it's seasoned with a nicely piquant gremolata (minced garlic, lemon peel, and Italian parsley). The service is efficient and attentive, though sometimes rushed at peak hours. ◆ Italian ◆ Daily lunch and dinner. 414 Columbus Ave (between Vallejo and Green Sts). 398.1300

19 Caffè Puccini The strains of Italian opera emanating from this popular cafe (nicknamed "The Pooch" by its loyal patrons) attract a diverse, music-loving, and artistic crowd. The bar that stretches along the back wall is surrounded by displays of pastries and sweets; the tortes and tarts are particularly good. ◆ Daily. 411 Columbus Ave (between Vallejo and Stockton Sts). 989.7033 ᕑ

Beyond Spaghetti and Meatballs: A Culinary Tour of Italy

In the mid-19th century, immigrants from several areas of Italy (including Genoa, Sicily, Liguria, and Umbria) started coming to San Francisco, settling in and around the **North Beach** area. Many of these new arrivals decided to open restaurants that would showcase their homeland's cuisine. In a very short time, North Beach became synonymous with "Little Italy" in the minds of San Francisco residents.

Regional dishes would frequently undergo changes en route to their American incarnations. In some cases, the chef would deliberately tone down a spicy recipe to satisfy the more conventional tastes of American diners; other times the chef couldn't acquire the traditional ingredients or wanted to include local meat, seafood, or produce. Although this sometimes led to unadventurous menus centered around spaghetti and pizza, sometimes an exciting new dish would be created. For instance, cioppino, which is said to have been invented in San Francisco, is based on a Ligurian fish stew reworked to incorporate Dungeness crab, squid, mussels, and clams.

These days, the focus is definitely on authenticity and innovation in menu planning and execution. The result is that San Francisco now boasts countless restaurants where Italian dishes are being re-created and re-invented for the benefit of their discerning diners. The kitchen may be run by a recent arrival from the province in question or by an American-born chef who has received first-hand training in Italian cooking, but the result is always *magnifico*.

One of the best places to sample the various tastes of Italy is **Il Fornaio,** a chain with outposts in San Francisco and throughout Northern California. During the first two weeks of every month, a different region is highlighted on the dinner menu—appetizers, entrées, desserts, and wines. The San Francisco branch is in the **Embarcadero** (1265 Battery St at Greenwich St, 986.0100; fax 986.2210 &); there is also a location in **Carmel-by-the-Sea** (Ocean Ave at Monte Verde Ave, 408/622.5100; fax 408/624.3030 &). A variety of Italian cuisines is also served at the elegant **Zingari** (501 Post St at Mason St, 441.7100; fax 885.8842 &), located in **Downtown** San Francisco.

The following North Beach eateries concentrate on the foods from particular regions of Italy: **Rose Pistola** (532 Columbus Ave between Stockton and Union Sts, 399.0499 &) features the cuisine of Liguria; **North Beach Restaurant** (1512 Stockton St between Green and Union Sts, 392.1587; fax 392.0230 &) offers Tuscan fare; **Ristorante Volare** (561 Columbus Ave between Green and Union Sts, 362.2774; fax 362.1353) presents Sicilian favorites; **Albona Restaurant** (545 Francisco St at Taylor St, 441.1040; fax 441.5107) is the only restaurant in the city that serves Istrian cuisine; and **Ristorante Ideale** (1309 Grant Ave at Vallejo St, 391.4129) has a menu of Roman dishes.

But what's the difference between the cooking of one region and the cooking of another? To help you sort out the various styles, descriptions of the regions and their specialties can be found below.

Emilia-Romagna

This region produces parmesan cheese, balsamic vinegar, and many of the best wines in Italy (including Sangiovese). Bologna, its capital, is said to be the culinary heart of the country; dishes from this area include sauce Bolognese, rich with beef and sometimes pork; tortellini; and *prosciutto di Parma*.

Istria

Situated just below Trieste, this peninsula belonged to Italy until its ownership was transferred to Yugoslavia after World War II. Because of its location on the spice-trade route, almonds, honey, dates, raisins, cumin, and paprika have become integral parts of the area's food, and the influences of central Europe added goulash, strudel, and sauerkraut to its culinary repertoire. One interesting dish is the *brodetto,* a ragout of fish, squid, and shellfish in a balsamic sauce.

Lazio

This region, which includes the capital city of Rome, is characterized by sophisticated, simple cooking.

One lovely dish is saltimbocca, which is veal stuffed with prosciutto and sage; its name means "jump in the mouth." Gnocchi, whether made with potato or spinach, and fried artichokes are quintessentially Roman fare.

Liguria

The majority of Italian immigrants to San Francisco in the early 19th century came from this region, located on a narrow strip of Italy's west coast. Stuffed calamari, stuffed pasta, and pastries made with chestnut flour are characteristic dishes, and Ligurians are famous for using lots of basil in their cooking, especially in pesto.

Piemonte

In Northwest Italy, Piemonte is a prime wine-growing region; among the most famous vintages that come from here are Barolo, Barbaresco, and Barbera. Look for dishes that use freshwater fish, as well as polenta, gnocchi, risotto, and the ever-popular white truffles.

Sicily

The largest island in the Mediterranean, Sicily lies south of the toe of Italy's "boot." During its long history, it has been overrun by invaders from many different countries (including Greece, Normandy, North Africa, and several Arab nations), and all of them have left their mark on the cuisine. Typical dishes may incorporate rice, semolina, raisins, pine nuts, anchovies, hot peppers, tuna, swordfish, citrus fruits, fennel, and tomatos. Other major ingredients include the spicy, peppered pecorino cheese, used to complement pasta, and creamy ricotta.

Tuscany

Located in Northwestern Italy, it is one of the largest regions of the country. Tuscany is known for its wines (particularly Chianti and Brunello), olives (and olive oil), and specialty beef dishes. The cuisine is simple, avoiding heavy sauces that would obscure the taste of the individual ingredients. Very often fresh herbs are used in dishes. *Pappa al pomodoro,* a tomato and bread soup, is one of the area's most famous dishes, and meringue is a popular dessert.

Umbria

Sandwiched between Tuscany and Marche, Umbria is known for its fine white wines, specifically from Orvieto. The cooking here is hearty and makes good use of the beautiful perfumed black truffle that is native to this region. Pancetta (unsmoked bacon) also makes frequent appearances, whether wrapped around game, stuffed into pastas, or used in sauces. Other ingredients used frequently are olives and fresh trout.

20 Calzone's ★$$ Black tile and bright neon accents give the facade a space-age look that seems jarring alongside the more traditional storefronts here. But past the doorway, this place is strictly Old World: green walls lined with foodstuffs, a bare tree wrapped in tiny white lights, and a bar positioned under a canopy of miniature liquor bottles. The food isn't a standout, although the pizza is better than average. One luxurious plus: Complimentary limo service is offered to and from the Financial District for parties of up to 15. ♦ Italian ♦ Daily lunch and dinner. 430 Columbus Ave (between Vallejo and Green Sts). 397.3600; fax 397.3446

20 Stella Pastry Everything has been made on the premises since this traditional Italian bakery opened in 1942. Be sure to try the specialty, *sacripantina,* layers of sponge cake brushed with maraschino liqueur and zabaglione. Other noteworthy selections include tiramisù, a creamy dessert with layers of ladyfingers, liqueur, mascarpone, and cocoa; biscotti; amaretti, macaroonlike cookies topped with pine nuts; cannoli; and panettone. ♦ M-F 7:30AM-7PM; Sa 7:30AM-midnight; Su 9AM-6PM. No credit cards accepted. 446 Columbus Ave (between Vallejo and Green Sts). 986.2914

21 U.S. Restaurant ★★$ The topsy-turvy arrangement of the rooms, the well-worn interior, and the long-cooked Italian/American food offer up a classic slice of North Beach. This is a popular spot for strapped college students, tourists looking for a bargain, and officers from the nearby police station. Hotcakes are a specialty at breakfast, and ham and two eggs make a filling, low-cost start to the morning. Each day brings four or five specials, all at rock-bottom prices. Regulars come on Wednesday for the stewed tripe or baked ham with ravioli, and on Friday for the stewed rabbit or crispy fried calamari. ◆ Italian/American ◆ Tu-Sa breakfast, lunch, and dinner. No credit cards accepted. 431 Columbus Ave (between Vallejo and Stockton Sts). 362.6251

22 Caffè Trieste ★$ An eclectic clientele—bohemians, musicians, white-collar types, and tourists—flocks here to relax, converse, and enjoy some of the best coffee in North Beach. They can also find pastries and, at lunch, a limited number of sandwiches, like turkey or ham and cheese on focaccia. The company imports, roasts, and distributes its own beans. The retail shop next door often is covered in a haze from the beans roasting out in the open for all to see. The favorite brew here is the Italian roast espresso, a rich, smooth blend that's just on the edge of bitterness. Every Saturday afternoon, the restaurant holds a singalong, with patrons and staff performing arias together. ◆ Cafe ◆ Daily. 601 Vallejo St (at Grant Ave). 392.6739

23 North Beach Pizza ★$ A full menu is available (heavy on pasta), but most diners concentrate on the pizza, which many claim is the best in the city (though we find it to be inconsistent). Ten combinations are offered, including one with pepperoni, mushrooms, and cheese, and another with clams, garlic, and cheese—all smoothed over the slightly doughy crust. You can call for pizza delivery 24 hours a day. ◆ Pizzeria ◆ Daily lunch and dinner. 1310 Grant Ave (between Vallejo and Green Sts). 433.2444; fax 433.7217. Also at: 1499 Grant Ave (at Union St). 433.2444; fax 433.7217

24 Ristorante Ideale ★★★$$ Maurizio Bruschi, who was a part-owner of **Bonta** in the Marina district and **Pazzia** on Third Street, spotlights the foods of Rome at his restaurant, which is decorated in warm pumpkin tones. The one-page menu is filled with not-to-be-missed selections. Start with a simple salad or fried Arborio rice dumplings stuffed with mozzarella. For pasta, try the *pappardelle* (broad noodles) with a tomato-based lamb sauce, or penne with a combination of fresh and smoked salmon in a creamy tomato sauce. Delicious entrées include the baby lamb chops, grilled pork loin with wild fennel, and Cornish hen roasted with herbs. ◆ Italian ◆ Tu-Su dinner. Reservations recommended. 1309 Grant Ave (between Vallejo and Green Sts). 391.4129

25 Mo's Gourmet Hamburgers ★★$ The top hamburger in the area, prepared over a revolving coal-fired grill, it has a slightly smoky flavor with a crusty exterior and juicy interior. The old-fashioned shakes, served in the metal containers, are winners, too. And nostalgia buffs go wild for the frothy root-beer float. ◆ Hamburgers ◆ Daily breakfast, lunch, and dinner. 1322 Grant Ave (between Vallejo and Green Sts). 788.3779 &

26 The Nature Stop This natural-foods grocery is a godsend for local residents. There's a deli featuring mostly vegetarian selections and sandwiches, a juice bar with wheat-grass shooters, and a small produce section with five kinds of mushrooms and other choice seasonal items. Bread comes from **Tassajara, Semifreddi's,** and **Metropolis.** A whole wall of bins has foods in bulk, including a dozen granolas, and shelves hold nonfat snacks, a half-dozen flavors of honey, and an herbal tea section that includes "Daily Detox . . . For today's toxic environment." ◆ M-F 9AM-10PM; Sa-Su 10AM-9PM. 1336 Grant Ave (between Vallejo and Green Sts). 398.3810; fax 398.1537 &

27 La Bodega ★$ Decorated in bright, bold colors, this Spanish restaurant features a lovely abstract brush painting of flamenco dancers. A complimentary bowl of olives sets the stage for the rest of the meal. Try the thinly sliced chorizo, and follow it with the paella or the chicken served over vegetable-studded rice. Every night after 8PM, there's live entertainment. ♦ Spanish ♦ Daily dinner. 1337 Grant Ave (between Vallejo and Green Sts). 433.0439 ₺

28 Figoni Hardware Co. Here is a classic: a vintage 1907 hardware store, complete with scarred wood floors, bare lightbulbs hanging from the 15-foot ceiling, and helpful salespeople who are almost courtly in their long, blue coats. The surprise is the wide array of great kitchenware, including cast-iron grill pans, gadgets, and basic Italian pottery. Among the Italian food-making equipment look for ravioli rolling pins, pasta machines, and parmesan cheese graters. ♦ M-Tu, Th-Sa. 1352 Grant Ave (between Vallejo and Green Sts). 392.4765

29 Maykedeh ★★$$ By most accounts this is the best Persian restaurant in the city, a rating based somewhat on the pleasant decor: White tablecloths and fresh flowers lend an airy atmosphere. To start, try the tender lamb tongue with lime, sour cream, and saffron, or the dolmas (stuffed grape leaves). Among the best dishes are such house specials as the marinated *poussin* (broiler chicken), slightly charred by flames, or the hefty skewers of perfumed ground lamb and beef, which have been marinated in lime and onions. ♦ Persian ♦ Daily lunch and dinner. Reservations recommended Friday and Saturday. 470 Green St (between Varennes St and Grant Ave). 362.8286 ₺

29 Bocce Caffè ★$$ This stylish restaurant has open-beam ceilings, swirling fans, terra-cotta floors, and an attractive patio surrounding a fig tree. The menu includes a good selection of inexpensive dishes, including lasagna, cannelloni, gnocchi, and pizza. But watch out for the house specials: They can cost twice as much, but don't taste twice as good. Stick with the basics and you'll be happy, especially in such nice surroundings. ♦ Northern Italian ♦ Daily lunch and dinner. 478 Green St (between Varennes St and Grant Ave). 981.2044 ₺

29 North End Caffè The atmosphere here is a real throwback to the time when Beat Generation artists and poets regularly held public performances of their work in coffeehouses like this one, which has worked its way into the fabric of local life. Readings are held regularly by all kinds of people—even former mayor Joe Alioto has been known to drop by once in a while to read a poem or two.

The young crowd seems content to play chess or backgammon and ponder existence over a strong cup of coffee. ♦ Daily. No credit cards accepted. 1402 Grant Ave (at Green St). 956.3350

30 Danilo Italian Bakery An all-purpose bakery specializing in Tuscan recipes, this shop makes a lot of things very well, among them breads, bread sticks, biscotti, focaccia, and panettone (including the very special anise-flavored *buccelatto*). One of the unique treats is a *torta di verdura,* a dense pie made with Swiss chard, liqueur, raisins, and pine nuts. ♦ Daily. No credit cards accepted. 516 Green St (between Grant Ave and Stockton St). 989.1806 ₺

31 New Pisa Restaurant ★$ A classic North Beach restaurant that serves family-style food, this place is a sister to the better-known **Capp's Corner** (see page 63). The fixed-price menus (including salad, soup, pasta, main course, and spumoni) are the same at both, but the atmosphere here is more refined, with booths that afford some privacy. Go on Friday for the crab cioppino. Throughout the week, the leg of lamb, herb chicken with mushrooms and rosemary, and homemade sausage score points. ♦ Italian ♦ Daily lunch and dinner. 550 Green St (between Grant Ave and Stockton St). 989.2289; fax 989.2025

32 Savoy Tivoli In business since 1907, this watering hole for the postcollegiate singles crowd has a "rec room" with three pool tables, a well-worn bar, and a very European feel. Bar food is available, but young people really come to drink, mingle, and hang out. ♦ Tu-Th 5PM-2AM; F-Su 3PM-2AM. No credit cards accepted. 1434 Grant Ave (between Green and Union Sts). 362.7023

33 Cafe Jacqueline ★★★$$ Soufflé's the thing at this cozy, romantic restaurant with candles and flowers on the tables—in fact, it's the only thing. Owner Jacqueline Margulis stations herself behind a big bowl of eggs, ready to whisk them by hand into airy, flavorful delights. Each soufflé is designed to serve two; they aren't cheap, but they're absolutely wonderful. Savory selections might include salmon and asparagus, shiitake mushrooms, or white corn with ginger and garlic. The dessert soufflés—raspberry, Grand Marnier, and chocolate—are too good to choose among. The only other dishes offered are salad and soup to enjoy before the soufflé extravaganza. ♦ French ♦ W-Su dinner. 1454 Grant Ave (between Green and Union Sts). 981.5565

34 Prudente Meat Market and Deli
An institution, this great market has been in the Rossi family since it opened in 1910 as **R. Iacopi and Co.** A couple of years ago, it was sold to a goddaughter of former owner Leo Rossi and the name was changed. Among the delicacies prepared on the premises are pancetta, Parma-style prosciutto, and house-cured dry jack cheese. The family also has a longstanding tradition of sausage making; the excellent varieties sold here include hot Calabrese, aromatic, garlicky Toscana, and slightly sweet Sicilian. Rossi's ex-wife, Darlene, originated the famous *tortas:* homemade mascarpone cheese layered with such fillings as basil and sun-dried tomatoes, smoked salmon, porcini mushrooms, black olives and pine nuts, and figs and almonds. Don't miss the nightly entrées (chicken cutlets, roasted vegetables and garlic, and rich gourmet sandwiches), which are available only for takeout. ♦ Daily. 1462 Grant Ave (between Green and Union Sts). 421.0757; fax 421.0759 &

35 Italian/French Bakery
The *bastone* (club loaf) here repeatedly earns top marks in tasting contests. This bakery also has a deserved reputation for its Dutch crunch sourdough, bread sticks, and crisp biscotti in such flavors as walnut, hazelnut, chocolate chip, anise, and almond. ♦ Daily 7AM-6PM. 1501 Grant Ave (at Union St). 421.3796 &

In *How to Cook a Wolf,* the writer M.F.K. Fisher tells a true story of a San Francisco college student who lived for two years during the Depression on about seven cents a day by eating ground wheat at every meal and drinking a gallon of milk each week. He supplemented his diet almost every day with a piece of fruit stolen from a nearby Chinese-owned pushcart. After he graduated from college, he sent the pushcart owner ten dollars; he received four dollars in change, and an invitation to a New Year's party in Chinatown. He went.

36 Lo Coco's Restaurant ★★$$
Few restaurants prepare lusty Sicilian food as well as this intimate spot. Many of the sauces are intensely flavored. The *pasta con sarde,* from a recipe that dates back more than a thousand years, is made of saffron pasta tossed with anchovies, fennel, pine nuts, currants, and bread crumbs. The flavor is haunting. Also satisfying are any of the pastas with a hearty Neapolitan tomato sauce. The pizzas here are wonderfully light and crisp; the crust is so good, in fact, that the simplest toppings are best. The pepperoni and green-onion pizza, for instance, comes out crisp around the edges and with a fresh-tasting tomato sauce. The homemade cannoli, stuffed with ricotta cheese and preserved cherries, also is excellent. All these delights are served up amid a comfortable, cafelike atmosphere, with brick walls, terra-cotta floors, and windows that open onto the street. ♦ Italian ♦ Tu-Sa dinner. Reservations recommended Friday and Saturday. 510 Union St (between Grant Ave and Stockton St). 296.9151 &

37 Gelato Classico ★$
Specializing in Italian ice cream, which has a dense and almost sticky texture, this popular chain offers some interesting flavors: spumoni, caffè mocha, coconut macadamia, and *stracciatella,* with Oreo-like cookies. Sorbets and coffee drinks also are featured. ♦ Ice-cream parlor ♦ M-Th, Su 11AM-11PM; F-Sa 11AM-midnight. No credit cards accepted. 576 Union St (between Grant Ave and Stockton St). 391.6667 &

38 Caffè Malvina ★★$
Compared to others in the area, this cafe has an expansive feel: A sea of well-spaced tables and bent-wood chairs is surrounded by a curving bar and windows that open to the bustle of passersby. The coffee, roasted and ground at the restaurant's facility south of Market Street, is rich and bracing. Another reason to come here is for the terrific salads: Sweet rock shrimp are combined with sliced button mushrooms, bacon, and baby spinach with a warm lemon dressing. Another winner is the *quattro stagione,* featuring marinated garbanzo and kidney beans, artichoke hearts, roasted peppers, mushrooms, and avocado on a bed of mixed greens. Sandwiches and *pizzetta* are better than average. ♦ Cafe ♦ Daily. 1600 Stockton St (at Union St). 391.1290 &

39 Moose's ★★★$$ Ed and Mary Etta Moose, former owners of the popular **Washington Square Bar and Grill,** have created an impressive eatery here. Popular with the city's prime movers and shakers for power lunches and dinners, it's modern and airy, with windows overlooking the street, an expansive open kitchen, arches separating the bar from the dining area, and a piano that supplies dinnertime jazz. Chef Fabrice Canelle, formerly with the Ritz-Carlton hotel restaurant in Orange County, offers an interesting menu, including Mediterranean fish soup with rouille; and small gnocchi with smoked salmon, *pistou* (basil, garlic, and olive oil) sauce, and crème fraîche and caviar. The private dining room upstairs is great for parties of up to 40. ♦ Californian/Italian ♦ M-Sa lunch and dinner; Su brunch and dinner. Reservations recommended. 1652 Stockton St (between Union and Filbert Sts). 989.7800; fax 989.7838 ﹩

40 Liguria Bakery This is the best place to buy focaccia, either plain, raisin, green onion, or tomato with green onions and raisins. In fact, the Ligurian pizza bread is the only product sold here. It's baked throughout the day in the brick oven, just as it has been since 1911. ♦ Daily; Su until noon. No credit cards accepted. 1700 Stockton St (at Filbert St). 421.3786 ﹩

41 Mama's Girl ★$ After 30 years in business as **Mama's,** Mama Sanchez's restaurant was taken over by her daughter Elena. It's one of the most popular breakfast stops in the area—the cooks are adept at omelettes. In 1990s fashion they also feature such low-cholesterol specials as an egg-white omelette with mushrooms and green onions. This is the kind of place every neighborhood should have. ♦ American ♦ Tu-Su breakfast and lunch. No credit cards accepted. 1701 Stockton St (at Filbert St). 362.6421

43 Ristorante Fior d'Italia $$$ Opened in 1886, this establishment claims to be America's oldest Italian restaurant, which may well be true. Casual diners can eat in the bar at tables with checkered cloths. The dining room, with red vinyl–tufted booths and gilded mirrors, is a perfect backdrop for risotto, a dozen homemade pastas, and many veal dishes. The price tends to be high for the rather average fare, but the place is popular with tour groups. ♦ Italian ♦ Daily lunch and dinner. Reservations recommended. 601 Union St (at Stockton St). 986.1886; fax 986.7031 ﹩

43 LaFelce ★★★$$ An ultratraditional place, complete with white cloths and red carnations on each table, plus a glass-globed chandelier that is firmly rooted in the early 1970s. The menu is just what you'd expect, too, with such well-executed specialties as veal saltimbocca,  fettuccine Alfredo, osso buco, and spinach gnocchi. ♦ Italian ♦ M, W-F lunch and dinner; Sa-Su dinner. 1570 Stockton St (between Green and Union Sts). 392.8321

44 North Beach Restaurant ★★★$$ A recent $1-million renovation brings a fresh, up-to-the-minute look to this North Beach eatery. The two main dining rooms feature handsome wood wainscotting and cabinetry, and skylights and a curved cathedral ceiling are dramatic additions. There's also a smaller basement space called "The Prosciutto Room," which seats up to 12 people at one table; it doubles as the curing room for the restaurant's hams. The menu, created by longtime chef/co-owner Bruno Orsi, presents some of the most delicious Northern Italian food in the city. Standouts include chicken cooked under a brick, homemade pasta, house-cured prosciutto, and any veal dish. A cigar room—the latest trend at San Francisco restaurants—has been added, and there are several private dining rooms. ♦ Northern Italian ♦ Daily lunch and dinner. 1512 Stockton St (between Green and Union Sts). 392.1587; fax 392.0230 ﹩

45 Caffè Sport ★★★$$$ Formerly infamous for its surly, aggressive waiters, this place has turned over a new leaf—now the service couldn't be nicer or more accommodating. And chef Antonio Latona's rustic Italian food is simply among the best the city has to offer. Popular dishes include cioppino and any of the pastas, which may be paired with lobster, pesto, calamari, shrimp, scallops, or four kinds of cheese. It's worth a visit just to see the wealth of colorful, Sicilian-inspired artwork covering the walls and ceiling and competing for attention with the Christmas lights that crisscross overhead. This alone will get you in a festive spirit. ♦ Italian ♦ Tu-Sa lunch and dinner. Reservations recommended. No credit cards accepted. 574 Green St (between Grant Ave and Stockton St). 981.1251

46 Dianda's Bakery $ Best known for its wedding cakes, Danish pastries, almond torte, and panettone, this is also a good place to relax with a cup of espresso and a pastry, soup, or quiche. Other excellent offerings are St. Honoré cake, eclairs, and "bunches," delectable custard-filled rum balls stuck together with honey, should satisfy any sweet tooth. ♦ Cafe ♦ Daily. No credit cards accepted. 565 Green St (between Grant Ave and Stockton St). 989.7745 &

49 Florence Ravioli In addition to the eponymous ravioli factory, groceries and a delicatessen are on-site, providing everything needed to put an authentic-tasting Italian meal on the table. The pasta is excellent, and so are the *prosciutto di Parma,* 35 kinds of cheese, imported olives, and wines. ♦ Daily; Su until 3PM. No credit cards accepted. 1412 Stockton St (between Vallejo St and Columbus Ave). 421.6170; fax 421.7633 &

50 Little City Market/Meats Locals drive across town to this full-line butcher shop for veal and a variety of homemade sausages. It's one of the few places in San Francisco where you can buy hard-to-find cuts like veal tongue and breast of veal. The helpful staff always provides tips and information, but if you still don't know just what to do with the meat you just bought, recipes are plastered all over the walls. To round out a meal, polenta in bulk and imported dried pasta also are available. ♦ M-Sa. 1400 Stockton St (at Vallejo St). 986.2601 &

49 Victoria Pastry Co. Many restaurants, including **Caffè Trieste** and **Caffè Puccini** (see page 56 and page 53), fill their pastry displays and bread baskets at this bakery, which turns out both Italian and French specialties. The panettone is baked year-round, and the *cornetti* (crescent-shaped, brioche-like pastries) are a popular morning treat. The St. Honoré cake, cream puffs, eclairs, and amaretti (soft, almond-flavored cookies) have also garnered legions of fans, and we think the cannolis are the best in the whole city. ♦ Daily. 1362 Stockton St (at Vallejo St). 781.2015; fax 781.CAKE &

50 Panelli Brothers' Delicatessen It's a treat to pick up a sandwich here for a leisurely lunch alfresco in nearby Washington Square. This deli also produces excellent party trays of cold cuts and is a good place to find fresh goat cheese. It's a popular "cop stop" for police officers at the nearby precinct. ♦ Daily; Su until 2:30PM. 1419 Stockton St (between Vallejo and Green Sts). 421.2541 &

51 Ristorante Firenze ★★$$ The interior design gets high marks here: The ceiling in the bar area is painted to look like the ruins of the top of a building, with a huge crack and blue sky and clouds showing through. You feel as if you're actually standing in the ruin. The dining room walls are marbleized, with wispy clouds overhead, and below, a shelf trailing ivy vines. Unfortunately, the food doesn't live up to the fanciful decor, though you can't go wrong with the vegetable soup or the thick noodles doused in a tomato-based rabbit sauce. ♦ Italian ♦ Daily dinner. 1429 Stockton St (between Vallejo and Green Sts). 392.8485; fax 421.5813 &

52 Mara's Italian Pastry Not all of the pastries are baked in-house, but this shop has developed a large following nevertheless. Every one of the sweets filling the window looks good, but do as locals do and choose the homemade cannoli, apricot twists, raspberry rings, and macaroons. ♦ Daily. No credit cards accepted. 503 Columbus Ave (between Green and Union Sts). 397.9435

53 Grazie ★★$$ Don't let them take you to the upstairs dining loft; sit at the counter in front of the open kitchen, where you can feel the warm glow of the flames dancing beneath each skillet, and watch the chefs perform their magic. Pastas are some of the best in North Beach; each sauce is made before your eyes.

And the meat dishes, including the thick, stuffed veal chop and the thin piccata, are not to be missed. ◆ Italian ◆ Daily dinner. 515 Columbus Ave (between Green and Union Sts). 982.7400; fax 982.7401

L'Osteria del forno

54 L'Osteria del Forno ★★★$ If we had to pick one "find" in North Beach, this little hole-in-the-wall would be it. Few places have such a wonderful feel, with tables wedged into the front windows and friendly, casual service. The kitchen turns out *the* best focaccia sandwiches, excellent pasta, and a roast of the day, usually beef or a delectable pork that has been marinated and braised in milk. All this for what amounts to small change. ◆ Italian ◆ M, W-Su lunch and dinner. Reservations recommended. No credit cards accepted. 519 Columbus Ave (between Green and Union Sts). 982.1124

55 Caffè Roma Coffee Roasting Company Java gets no fresher than at this popular coffeehouse, which is dominated by its roasting machine. The aromatic, bitter-tinged coffees go well with the pastry selection here. The cafe portion has been remodeled to create an idealized 1990s version of a 1920s cafe: a black-and-white tile floor, swirling fans, and dark wood shelves holding all kinds of coffee-related merchandise. In the retail area you can also purchase coffee by the pound. Note, however, that there are no public restrooms here. ◆ Daily. 526 Columbus Ave (between Stockton and Union Sts). 296.7662; fax 800/296.ROMA

56 Rose Pistola ★★★$$ Restaurateur/chef Reed Hearon has had no trouble keeping busy in San Francisco the past few years. First he opened the hot, hip **Lulu** in the SoMa district, then he and partner Louis Clement created **Cafe Marimba,** a new-wave presentation of Mexican food. Now Hearon has opened this Italian eatery in North Beach. The food is in the tradition of the early Ligurian and Genoese immigrants to North Beach—highlights include great cioppino, porcini risotto fritters with fontina cheese, braised calamari and artichokes with polenta, and pizzas baked in a wood-burning oven. The whole baked fish is overpriced, but good. The dining room is accented with Italian glass tile, chrome, and mahogany. Live jazz is offered after 9PM. ◆ Italian ◆ Daily lunch and dinner (to 1AM Friday and Saturday). 532 Columbus Ave (between Stockton and Union Sts). 399.0499 ♿

57 Ben & Jerry's It caused quite a controversy when this East Coast–based chain opened a branch here several years ago. Residents worried that the neighborhood would soon turn into Anytown USA. Well, North Beach has managed to hold on to all its individuality even as this shop dishes up its famous ice cream as well as baked goods and espresso drinks. The top seller here is the ice cream studded with chocolate-chip cookie dough. ◆ Daily. 543 Columbus Ave (between Green and Union Sts). 249.4684; fax 249.2655 ♿ Also at: Numerous locations throughout the city

57 Il Pollaio ★$ The grilled chicken can be very good at this pie-shaped cafe, but sometimes it comes overcooked. Other entrées—such as lamb chops, pork chops, and rabbit—are spiced and grilled in the traditional Argentine manner. Don't miss either of the side orders: crisp french fries or marinated eggplant. Soup, a couple of salads, and two desserts round out the short—but tasteful—menu. The large picture windows give diners a good look at the bustling traffic on Columbus Avenue. ◆ Argentine/Italian ◆ M-Sa lunch and dinner. 555 Columbus Ave (between Green and Union Sts). 362.7727

57 Ristorante Volare ★$ Since the mid-1980s, Giovanni Zocca has operated **El Menudo,** one of the best *taquerías* in the Outer Mission. Now, in keeping with his Italian heritage, he has opened this Sicilian eatery in North Beach. The waiter may try to "help" you by steering you to the more traditional, mundane dishes, but insist on ordering the Sicilian specialties, such as penne served with a sauce made from tomatoes and fresh ricotta, or Sicilian antipasti featuring *bottarga* (preserved tuna roe), crabmeat, and vegetables. And make sure that you leave room for the deliciously prepared tiramisù, which is so heavenly it's almost sinful. ◆ Italian ◆ Daily lunch and dinner. 561 Columbus Ave (between Green and Union Sts). 362.2774; fax 362.1353

58 Mario's Bohemian Cigar Store ★★★$ For many locals this 19th-century cafe encapsulates everything that's right about North Beach: The surroundings are comfortable but unpretentious, the staff is friendly, and the cappuccino is the best in the area. When the Crimani family took over the bar in 1971, they added windows that overlook Washington Square Park and transformed it from a hangout for elderly Italian men into an upbeat, bustling spot where diners can enjoy a light meal. The focaccia sandwiches are excellent, the ricotta cheesecake perfect for a midafternoon snack. The place stays open until midnight most evenings (except Sunday, when it closes at 11PM). ◆ Cafe/Italian ◆ Daily breakfast, lunch, and dinner. 566 Columbus Ave (at Union St). 362.0536. Also at: 2209 Polk St (between Vallejo and Green Sts), Russian Hill. 776.8226; fax 776.3388 ⑁

59 Michaelangelo Cafe ★$$ With all the people inside and lines often snaking outside, this cafe can be as busy as Grand Central Station at rush hour. While waiting for a seat, peek in through the large windows to see an impressive tableau: The tables are covered with prints of some of Michelangelo's ceiling work, the walls with elaborately framed oil paintings. Top menu choices include the calamari salad, served on lettuce with a lemony dressing, and the pastas, which are sometimes oversauced (fans nonetheless favor the thick bolognese sauce with meat and mushrooms). One of the best dishes is the potato gnocchi in a creamy tomato sauce. ◆ Italian ◆ Daily dinner. No credit cards accepted. 579 Columbus Ave (between Green and Union Sts). 986.4058

59 Coit Liquors A knowledgeable staff and a great selection of Italian wines set this wine-and-liquor store apart from the rest. The staff prides itself on tasting wines at least four nights a week, and the experience shows: When customers ask questions, they get the right answers. ◆ Daily until midnight. 585 Columbus Ave (at Union St). 986.4036; fax 296.7825 ⑁

59 Pasta Pomodoro ★★$ This pasta house offers incredible deals and generous portions. Plus, the gnocchi, coated in gorgonzola sauce and spiked with diced tomato, are better than preparations that cost twice as much. The dozen or so pastas include *penne putanesca* (with black and green olives and a slightly spicy tomato sauce); rigatoni with roast chicken, cream, mushrooms, and sun-dried tomatoes; and spaghetti with calamari, mussels, and scallops in a light tomato sauce. The Caesar salad is light on the garlic and anchovy, but big shavings of parmesan compensate. A few sandwiches round out the menu, and for dessert there's tiramisù, biscotti, or gelato. Clean and spare, with seating at a U-shaped counter or tables along the walls, the place is designed to ensure quick turnover. ◆ Italian ◆ Daily lunch and dinner. No credit cards accepted. 655 Union

St (at Columbus Ave). 399.0300; fax 399.0377 ⑁ Also at: Numerous locations throughout the city

Gira Polli

59 Gira Polli ★★$ The stippled walls and high-tech lighting make an interesting juxtaposition to the wood-fired rotisserie, where diners can watch the flames lick at the dozens of chickens lazily bronzing. Few places do chicken better; here it's served with Palermo-style potatoes, cooked in broth and baked with white wine and herbs until they're tender. There are a few salads, soups, and pastas, and they are fine, too—but not nearly as special as the chicken. For dessert, the light, lemon-flavored cheesecake will satisfy any sweet tooth. A popular take-out menu offers complete family-style dinners for four (with garden salad, pasta with pesto, two chickens, potato and vegetable, and biscotti) at an amazing price. ◆ Italian/Takeout ◆ Daily dinner. 659 Union St (between Columbus Ave and Powell St). 434.4472; fax 434.3762

60 Little City Antipasti Bar ★$$ One of the first restaurants in the city to cash in on the grazing trend, this place offers dozens of small Italian appetizers, in the tapas mode. They may include grilled tuna on white beans with a dollop of aioli; ground lamb patties accentuated with an Arabic salad of cucumbers, peppers, and croutonlike pita chips; or grilled baby artichokes with a tomato-tarragon aioli. But the best-seller is straight out of the 1980s: roasted garlic with baked brie. The decor is warmed by brick walls, a bar that takes up a good portion of the room, and fine paintings by local artists. An overflow dining room, often set up for private parties, opens at peak times; it's less interesting, but has a great collection of photos from North Beach and Italy. ◆ Italian ◆ Daily lunch and dinner. 673 Union St (at Powell St). 434.2900; fax 434.1501

61 Washington Square Bar and Grill ★★ $$ This place has been a political and celebrity hangout since it opened in 1973, thanks to its jovial former owner, Ed Moose, who sold it in 1990 and opened up **Moose's** (see page 59) just across the square. After a few tough years, the "Washbag," as locals fondly call this establishment, was given a new lease on life when Peter Osborne—who also owns the **Buchanan Grill** in the Marina—bought the restaurant and spruced up the interior. But he left all the memorabilia that gives it the feel of a casual men's club, and has kept up the tradition of live piano music at night. The crowds have returned, and the place captures the spirit of North Beach, particularly with its classic Italian/Californian menu. Standout dishes include smoked salmon with warm potato pancakes, fried calamari, petrale sole with capers and lemon, veal chop with mushrooms, and a warm apple tart with caramel sauce. ♦ Italian/Californian ♦ M-F lunch and dinner; Sa-Su brunch and dinner. 1707 Powell St (between Union St and Columbus Ave). 982.8123; fax 982.5718

62 Capp's Corner ★$$ At this quintessential neighborhood Italian joint, the rows of red-and-white–checkered tables are so close that you nearly eat with your neighbor. Completing the picture, a group of buddies at the long wooden bar seems perpetually engaged in animated conversation, half watching the TV suspended overhead. The waitresses may seem a bit brusque at first, but actually they're very friendly. The food has that old-style appeal, with a multicourse bargain that includes soup and salad, pasta, a main course, and spumoni. The leg of lamb is good, as are the braised veal shanks served with baked polenta. The braised pork loin with mushroom sauce can be a tad dry, but the flavor is outstanding. ♦ Italian ♦ M-F lunch and dinner; Sa-Su dinner. Reservations recommended. 1600 Powell St (at Green St). 989.2589

63 O'Reilly's Bar & Restaurant ★★$$ Owned by Irish-born restaurateur Miles O'Reilly, this eatery gives the mostly Italian neighborhood of North Beach a taste of the "aulde sod." O'Reilly has introduced some genuine Irish objects into the decor, including an 18th-century globe-shaped street lamp from Dublin and a handsome mahogany bar topped by stained-glass canopy from Cork. On the walls are pen-and-ink drawings of prominent Irish men and women; most striking is the whimsical mural depicting some of Ireland's greatest writers, including Yeats, Joyce, Wilde, and Brendan Behan. Chef Larry Doyle (who formerly worked at **Stars** and **Stars Cafe** under Jeremiah Tower) wants to put Irish food on the map—and he doesn't mean corned beef and cabbage (which is actually an American creation). His menu features traditional dishes, such as lamb stew, "boxty" (smoked salmon draped over a light potato cake), and a "fry-up" of fish, chips, cockles, and mussels. At the bar, you can get Guinness and other varieties of ale, served warm at 45 degrees the way they do in pubs back in Ireland. ♦ Irish ♦ M-Sa dinner; Su brunch and dinner. 622 Green St (between Columbus Ave and Powell St). 989.6222

Contadina

64 Trattoria Contadina ★★$$ Somewhat off the beaten path, this restaurant draws mostly locals with its well-prepared Italian food and warm and welcoming service. (Celebrities dine here too, or so the framed glossies of Kirstie Alley, Melanie Griffith, and Jack Scalia attest.) The menu has been changed to emphasize lighter foods and sauces. Few dishes in North Beach are as appealing as the veal medaillons covered with a cream sauce infused with the earthy, nutty flavors of porcini mushrooms. If you want something more substantial, begin with the paper-thin carpaccio or the marinated calamari. All meals come with a salad. ♦ Italian ♦ Daily dinner. Reservations recommended. 1800 Mason St (at Union St). 982.5728

The Goods on a Special Sauce

Rick Hackett, the chef-owner of **Enrico's** (504 Broadway at Kearny St, 982.6223; fax 397.7244 ♿) in **North Beach,** has created a red-pepper ketchup that nicely complements a hamburger or a grilled chicken sandwich. Here is the recipe:

8 sweet red bell peppers, seeded and sliced

2 yellow onions, peeled and sliced

2 whole jalapeños

3/4 cup granulated sugar

3/4 cup red wine vinegar

Place all ingredients in a covered pot and simmer for 30 minutes. Remove jalapeño and puree the rest. Refrigerate.

The Italian/French Bakery in North Beach bakes approximately 6,000 loaves of bread a day. Its most popular product is a half-sour, crusty bread called the "bastone." In Italian *bastone* means "the club," which is precisely what the long, thick loaf resembles.

All Aboard

In case breathtaking views and great food aren't enough, diners in Northern California can also enjoy a relaxing meal while sailing around **San Francisco Bay** or on a train cutting through the magnificent **Napa Valley** wine country. The following are a few options:

Hornblower Dining Yachts (788.8866) offers cruises around the bay at lunchtime on Friday, brunch break on Saturday and Sunday, and the dinner hour nightly. The service can't be beat, the vintage three-floor boat is wonderful—with a stately, cruise-liner feel—and the views set the mood for romance. The food on the limited American menu, however, is pretty mundane. Reservations are required. Boats leave from **Pier 33** (at Bay St and The Embarcadero).

Pacific Marine Yachts Charters and Dining Cruises (788.9100) boasts a bountiful Sunday brunch cruise. The two-hour excursion includes not only a buffet and sparkling wine, but a close-up view of sea lions and pelicans in the bay. Food is cooked on board, so the brunch selections—ranging from eggs and Belgian waffles to salads, a meat carvery, and fish dishes—taste fresh. Book early, especially if you want a table by the window. There are also dinner-dance cruises on Saturday nights, and many customized private yacht charters are available. The boat leaves from **Pier 39.**

The **Napa Valley Wine Train** (707/253.2111, 800/427.4124) offers reservations-only brunch, lunch, or dinner excursions aboard a 1915 vintage train with Pullman lounge and dining cars. Over the course of a three-hour trip, a French/California–inspired three- or four-course meal is served to the passengers. Half the diners enjoy wine or cocktails in the lounge while the others sit down to eat at elegant damask-covered tables. Midway through the trip, the second group begins the meal (ending with dessert and coffee), while the first has their dessert and coffee in the cocktail lounge. Board the train for lunch Monday through Friday, brunch on Saturday and Sunday, or dinner Tuesday through Sunday. Those passengers who want to be more spontaneous can order food à la carte or taste wines in the deli car, also by reservation. The train leaves from the **Napa** railroad station (1275 McKinstry St, between First St and Soscol Ave).

preparing rabbit. (His two specialties come together marvelously in the fettuccine with house-smoked rabbit.) Fans have a hard time choosing among rabbit entrées, whether it's roasted with grappa and oyster mushrooms; or grilled, seasoned with rosemary, and accompanied by roasted potatoes with balsamic vinegar; or sautéed with porcini mushrooms, sage, garlic, and wine. Those who think of rabbits as cute little bunnies rather than as a meal will be very happy with the scampi with oyster mushrooms or the lamb medaillons with black olives and capers. Also be sure to order white beans seasoned with olive oil, garlic, and fresh herbs. The tiramisù makes a perfect ending. ♦ Italian ♦ Tu-Sa dinner. Reservations required. 800 Greenwich St (at Mason St). 776.7766

65 Graffeo Coffee Mention great coffee and the name Graffeo always comes up; this retail store, which dates from 1935 and roasts its own beans, has a cultlike following. The rich house blend combines beans from Colombia, Costa Rica, and New Guinea, and connoisseurs consider the Swiss water–process decaffeinated Colombian to be the best of its kind. ♦ M-F 9AM-5PM; Sa 9AM-6PM. 735 Columbus Ave (between Filbert and Greenwich Sts). 986.2420, mail order 800.222.6250; fax 986.1577

66 Buca Giovanni ★★★$$$ A romantic, cavelike setting showcases terrific Italian dishes and grilled meats. All pastas are made on the premises, and the chef is a master at

67 Caffè Freddy's Eatery ★$ Just a few blocks from the North Beach hubbub, this brightly painted corner restaurant caters to a young clientele with what the staff refers to as "affordable gourmet" Italian fare. The menu comprises mostly salads, sandwiches, and pizzas, all served in large portions. Some of the more unusual offerings include an open-face sandwich of hot goat cheese and smoked salmon with a spinach vinaigrette, and a *pizzetta* with slices of new potatoes, mozzarella, parmesan, provolone, and a sprinkling of fresh rosemary. There's also a selection of low-calorie dishes made without oil or dairy products. One drawback: Service can sometimes be brusque. ♦ Italian/American ♦ Daily breakfast, lunch, and dinner. 901 Columbus Ave (at Lombard St). 922.0151 ♿

68 Zax ★★★$$ Husband-and-wife team Mark Drazek and Barbara Mulas share culinary duties at this quintessential city bistro. An out-of-the-way place, it has a soothing, modern decor: A wide celadon stripe painted around the room subtly contrasts with the gray walls, while the apricot ceiling adds a pleasant glow; the large flower arrangement and polished wood chairs complete the look. Starters on the changing menu might include a puffy goat cheese soufflé to complement a mixed green salad dressed with a cider vinaigrette. The entrée might be well-peppered salmon cooked to a bronze finish and served either propped on mashed potatoes infused with garlic or with a ragout of artichokes and new potatoes. For dessert, don't miss the wonderful *gallette,* an old-fashioned apple tart in which a delicious buttery crust curls over the top. ♦ French/Mediterranean ♦ Tu-Sa dinner. 2330 Taylor St (between Columbus Ave and Francisco St). 563.6266 ♿

RISTORANTE·ISTRIANO

69 Albona Restaurant ★★★$$ Owner Bruno Viscovi re-creates the intriguing food of his homeland at the only Istrian restaurant in Northern California. (Istria, a peninsula below Trieste, belonged to Italy for 2,000 years before becoming part of Yugoslavia after World War II.) Thanks to Istria's position on the spice-trade route, almonds, honey, dates, raisins, cumin, and paprika were integrated into its cuisine. Central European influences added goulash, sauerkraut, and strudel. Viscovi prepares uncommon fare, and he describes his dishes with such a poetic cadence that diners hang on his every word. The ravioli filled with cheese, pine nuts, and golden raisins are served in a browned sirloin-tip sauce with a hint of sweet spices and cumin. The panfried gnocchi, served in the same sirloin sauce, are puffy, slightly crispy mouthfuls that are so specific to Viscovi's hometown that they are unknown even 10 miles away. One of his top recommendations is the roasted free-range chicken cooked with a wine glaze; also worth trying is the *brodetto,* a ragout of fish, squid, and shellfish in a rich balsamic sauce. The moody lighting and comfortable chairs make a pleasant backdrop to the dramatic food. ♦ Istrian ♦ Tu-Sa dinner. Reservations recommended Friday and Saturday. 545 Francisco St (between Mason and Taylor Sts). 441.1040; fax 441.5107

70 Julius' Castle ★$$$$ With its richly paneled interior, soft lighting, and panoramic vista of the bay, this place perched on the hills near **Coit Tower** has probably kindled more romantic flames than any other dining spot in the city. Unfortunately, the food fails to live up to the surroundings. Pasta with broccoli rabe and garlic isn't nearly as special as it should be, and the kitchen insists on using mealy potatoes to showcase sautéed scallops in a refreshing cucumber sauce. Sea bass, served with garlic mashed potatoes and a mountain of fried leeks, is dry and overcooked, while the pheasant comes to the table blood-red in the middle. Despite its culinary drawbacks, the restaurant continues to be popular—especially with tourists. ♦ Continental ♦ Daily dinner. Reservations required; jacket required. 1541 Montgomery St (at Greenwich St). 392.2222; fax 986.8197

71 Dalla Torre ★$$$ Under the same ownership as **Julius' Castle** (see above), this place offers somewhat better food accompanied by the same great views of the bay and nearby gardens. Sitting at the foot of **Coit Tower** (the name is Italian for "at the tower"), the restaurant has peach-colored walls and some beautiful frescoes that distinguish the lower-level dining room from the bar on the mezzanine. As for the menu, stick with the simple dishes, such as roast chicken in herb-flecked sauce, grilled lamb noisettes with couscous pasta, and a satisfying minestrone. There's also a bar. The service is very efficient and warm, which is much appreciated by the mostly tourist clientele. ♦ Italian ♦ Daily dinner. Reservations recommended. 1149 Montgomery St (between Union and Filbert Sts). 296.1111; fax 982.2055

Fisherman's Wharf/ The Embarcadero

Ever-popular with tourists, Fisherman's Wharf is mostly avoided by locals, probably because of the amusement-park atmosphere it has acquired over the years. But they don't know what they're missing; this area has a long history of seafaring and fishing, and it also has a number of fine restaurants, many of which boast patios or wharfside windows that make the most of their spectacular views of the **Golden Gate Bridge**, the **Bay Bridge**, **Alcatraz**, and the shimmering water of **San Francisco Bay**.

The bay was once so rich with fish and shellfish that archaeologists have been able to identify Native American settlements (such as that of the Ohlone people, who lived here for centuries until they died out in the 19th century) by the mounds of oyster shells contained in the substrata of the banks. From around the time of the Gold Rush in the mid-19th century until the early 20th century, fisherfolk streamed here from Italy and used their own time-honored traditions to net, hook, or scoop a living from the sea. The main catches were salmon and crab. As recently as 1970, more than 300 vessels regularly fished the waters. Today, only about 120 boats are moored in the harbor, and most of those travel beyond the bay to nab their daily catch of

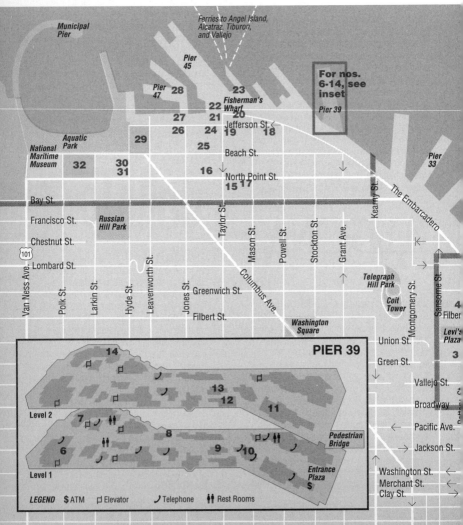

rock cod, salmon, and Dungeness crab. And there hasn't been much shipping or receiving on the docks here since the 1960s, when the advent of container ships caused most of this activity to shift across the bay to Oakland, a more convenient location. What remains is almost a honky-tonk caricature of a bustling port, with lots of touristy T-shirt and souvenir shops, a wax museum, and dance clubs.

Nevertheless, the area still evokes some of the romance of the time when San Francisco's economy was linked to the sea—particularly if you visit in the early morning. Just stroll over to **Pier 45** (which has recently evolved into the center of the wholesale fish industry), where each day's catch is cut and filleted for sale to the city's markets and restaurants. Or go to **Pier 47** and watch as the fishing boats—each fitted with enormous net-retrieving equipment and topped by towering outriggers—chug out of the harbor. Farther down the Embarcadero, pilot ships are sent out to guide cruise ships and large container freighters through the bay's tricky waters.

And the wharf can still sate any appetite for fresh seafood in every incarnation—from the simplest, purest oysters on the half shell at **A. Sabella's Restaurant** to juicy *ahi* tuna steak at **Scoma's** to "walkaway" crab cocktail or tasty fish-and-chips to go at **N. Alioto's** streetside stand. All three spots have been family-owned and -operated for generations.

In the past, the food proffered by the wharf's seafood houses was traditional almost to the point of stuffiness. Nowadays, though, a wide variety of cooking styles can be found here. Even stalwarts such as **A. Sabella's**, **The Waterfront Restaurant**, and **Alioto's No. 8** have updated their menus and added more contemporary creations. (So no one will look at you strangely if you ask for your fish to be cooked medium rare.) A bit apart from the wharf's hubbub, you can sample the inventive fare at the popular and stylish **Fog City Diner.**

The wharf area is also home to three distinct retail-entertainment-dining hubs: **Ghirardelli Square**, the **Cannery**, and **Pier 39.** The buildings that make up Ghirardelli Square were once manufacturing plants owned by Domingo Ghirardelli, the Italian-born confectioner who arrived in San Francisco in 1849 and is best known for the chocolate that still bears his name. In the 1960s, the Ghirardelli family sold the business, the new owner moved the chocolate production to San Leandro (in the East Bay), and the square underwent an impressive redevelopment. Today it bustles with free entertainment and an interesting assortment of shops and eateries. The only remnant of its chocolaty past is the **Ghirardelli Chocolate Manufactory**, a wondrous combination of seductive soda fountain, elegant chocolate shop, and miniature chocolate factory.

The brick building that houses the **Cannery** was built at the turn of the century as a fruit- and vegetable-packing plant; under the Del Monte company's ownership, it became the world's largest peach-canning facility. It was sold in 1964 and reopened in 1967 as a collection of shops, galleries, and restaurants.

Pier 39, which was developed in 1978, attracts more than 10 million visitors a year to its shops and food vendors and restaurants. It's the place to pick up such snacks and souvenirs as flavored coffees at **San Francisco Tea and Coffee Co.** and delicious peanut-butter fudge at **The Fudge House**.

Despite its excessive commercialization, Fisherman's Wharf remains an area worthy of notice by anyone who loves the sea and seafood. And plans are underway to make it more attractive and easier to visit for both visitors and residents. Future improvements (scheduled to be completed by the end of 1997) include the redesign of the Embarcadero and the addition of a trolley line to the wharf.

1 The Waterfront Restaurant ★★$$
Popular for lunch and brunch, this favorite (which is undergoing a lengthy remodeling) capitalizes on its grand view of the Bay Bridge and Treasure Island. The menu is dominated by fresh fish, naturally, and the preparations have been updated and Asian flavors incorporated into the formula. ♦ Seafood ♦ M-Sa lunch and dinner; Su brunch and dinner. Pier 7 (at The Embarcadero and Broadway). 391.2696; fax 391.7125 ♿

de Stijl (de stil') n. [1]An art movement that originated in the Netherlands in 1917.[2]Style as an attitude to life. A utopian faith in the new rather than the old. CAFE

2 deStijl Cafe ★★$ Whether you call it hip or cutting edge, this busy cafe is a magnet for television talent and local architects who work in the area. The room has a cool feel, with a color scheme of black, faded red, and orange, dramatic wood-back chairs, and light wood tables. Breakfast choices include granola, excellent waffles, and fresh fruit dishes. The lunch menu tends to be inspired by the Middle East: It might include red lentil *kibbeh*, a lentil patty stuffed with chickpeas and spinach and topped with a creamy yogurt sauce; a sandwich of grilled chicken topped with tahini-and-cumin sauce; and a clear vegetable broth with cracked wheat, spinach, and a touch of cumin and cinnamon. For dessert, try

the oatmeal cookies, and don't miss the incredible strawberry-rhubarb pie if it's available. ♦ Californian ♦ M-Sa breakfast and lunch; Su breakfast. Reservations required on Thursday. 1 Union St (at Front St). 291.0808

3 Pastis ★★★$$ This is the second San Francisco restaurant operated by chef/entrepreneur Gerald Hirigoyen (the wildly popular **Fringale** in SoMa was the first). Although the food here is not as exciting as **Fringale**'s, it's still very good. The decor is simple, with banquette seating and brick walls; one wall is painted with brightly colored geometric designs. Fail-safe appetizers include seared oxtail with gribiche (a mayonnaise-based sauce with chopped hard-boiled eggs and pickles) and sautéed foie gras with grapes and verjus. The steamed salmon is a good selection for health-conscious diners, but those who like heartier meat dishes will adore the pork tenderloin with mashed potatoes and curry or the crispy chicken with citrus-cumin jus and dates. Save room for the green apple tart. There's some outdoor seating in good weather. Another plus is that there is lots of street parking in this waterfront business district. ♦ Contemporary French ♦ M-F lunch and dinner; Sa dinner. 1015 Battery St (between Union and Green Sts). 391.2555; fax 391.1159 ♿

4 Happy Valley Chinese Seafood Restaurant ★★★$$ This stylish restaurant located near Levi's Plaza specializes in Mongolian hot pot, but unlike the less-expensive wannabes in the Richmond district, it uses nothing but high-quality ingredients. The hot-pot process is similar to preparing fondue: A pot of bubbling broth is brought to your table, as well as some just-caught seafood, a selection of ground dumpling pastes, noodles, and fresh vegetables. You pick up your food with chopsticks or small baskets and put it into the pot (it's done when it floats to the top). Drink the flavorful broth at the end. For those who want their meals already cooked, the menu also features typical Cantonese stir-fry and braised dishes. ♦ Chinese ♦ M-F lunch and dinner; Sa-Su dinner. 1255 Battery St (between Filbert and Greenwich Sts). 399.9393; fax 399.9399 ⅋ Also at: 2346 Lombard St (between Pierce and Scott Sts), The Marina. 922.9179 ⅋

4 Il Fornaio ★★$$ One of the prettiest Italian restaurants in the city, the dining room looks out on the well-manicured Levi's Plaza. There's outdoor seating for dining on sunny days, but there is also a heated patio that's pleasant in chilly weather, as well as an attractive, popular bar. The pizzas are appealing, as is any meat or pasta dish that emerges from the wood-burning oven. Try the eggplant pizza with black olives and smoked mozzarella, or the focaccia pizza with gorgonzola, pine nuts, and sweet onions. Other specialties include ravioli stuffed with lobster and ricotta and topped with a lemon-cream sauce, and spinach linguini with rock shrimp and tomatoes. It's also a great place for a weekend brunch. The homemade breads are wonderful; pick up a loaf to go at the adjoining bakery. ♦ Italian ♦ M-F breakfast, lunch, and dinner; Sa-Su brunch and dinner. Reservations recommended. 1265 Battery St (between Filbert and Greenwich Sts). 986.0100; fax 986.2210 ⅋ Also at: Numerous locations throughout the Bay Area

In the latter part of the 19th century, the top lunch spot in North Beach was La Gianduja. And the dish that drew the customers in was the 35-cent pot roast dinner. The top round or chuck was flavored with lemon, garlic, thyme, tarragon, oregano, and bay leaves, and the sauce consisted of red wine, tomatoes, bacon, and beef stock.

5 Fog City Diner ★★$$ One of the most visited restaurants in the city, it fueled the diner trend when it opened more than a decade ago. At night the chrome exterior and neon glow like a space station in orbit; the interior, swathed in rich wood and brass, looks more like a stylish 1930s men's club. Yes, there's such diner fare as burgers, fries, and "black cows," but with a decidedly upmarket flair; the ketchup is homemade and the menu is rounded out with numerous Californian specialties, including crab cakes, stuffed *pasilla* (fresh chili peppers), and all kinds of California-style fish and meat dishes. ♦ American ♦ Daily lunch and dinner. 1300 Battery St (at Greenwich St). 982.2000; fax 982.3711 ⅋

6 The Fudge House This locally owned shop makes fudge and candy-dipped fruits before your eyes. There are dozens of fudge flavors (the peanut butter is excellent), as well as caramel apples, chocolate-covered strawberries, white chocolate–covered red licorice, chocolate-dipped bananas, English toffee, peanut clusters, and pecan logs. ♦ Daily. Pier 39 (Building K, Level 1). 986.4240; fax 743.1485 ⅋

7 Alcatraz Café and Grill ★$ The prison cell at the entrance (go ahead, step inside and take a picture) and the sign that asks, "Have you done time in our retail shop?" let you know right away that this is a tourist haunt. Still, it has some of the most reasonably priced fare on Pier 39, if you can get by the pun-filled menu: The "Preliminary Hearings" include good onion rings and deep-fried calamari with a popcornlike crunch. The "Warden's Dinner Menu" includes clam chowder or tossed salad with such main courses as "killer shrimp" (spicy prawns served with rice). There are also burgers and pizzas, and other cutely named categories, but if we continue on with the theme any further we might have to cop a plea. ♦ American ♦ Daily lunch and dinner. Pier 39 (Building M, Level 1). 434.1818; fax 434.2266 ⅋

8 We Be Knives Pocketknives and hunting and kitchen knives fill the display cases and cover the walls of this specialty shop. All the best brands for cutting up in the kitchen are here, including Wüsthof and Gerber. ♦ Daily. Pier 39 (Building O, Level 1). 982.WEBE; fax 331.1479 ⅋

Here's the Punch Line

In the 1870s the most popular drink in San Francisco was the Pisco Punch, first served at the famous Bank Exchange Saloon. Although the precise recipe died with its creator, bar owner Duncan Nichol, here's an updated version.

    1 tablespoon Pernod
    1½ ounces brandy
        (Pisco Peruvian
        brandy, if
        available)
    1 ounce grape juice
    shaved ice
    6 ounces chilled pineapple juice

Coat the inside of a tall glass with the Pernod, pouring out the excess. Add the brandy, grape juice, and ice. Top with pineapple juice to the brim.

9 Chocolate Heaven The sign over the door proclaiming this "The Greatest Chocolate Store in the World" is only a bit exaggerated; the shop does boast an incredible selection of imported and domestic chocolates. Rarely will you find boxes of Hawaiian Host, Perugina, Lindt, Ghirardelli, Joseph Schmidt, Blum's, Cremaretto from Italy, Ferrero Rocher, and Nob Hill under one roof. The walls are lined with bins of chocolates sold by the piece. Novelties include jalapeño jam chocolates and cream-filled seashells from Belgium. ♦ Daily. Pier 39 (Building D, Level 1). 421.6551 ♿

10 Blue Chip Cookies Be warned: These big, gooey cookies can be addictive. The chocolate chip is a winner. ♦ Daily. Pier 39 (Building B, Level 1). 989.9411 ♿ Also at: Rincon Center, 101 Spear St (at Mission St), Financial District. 896.5267; fax 989.1746 ♿

11 Eagle Cafe ★$ Once a ticket office and baggage room for the **McCormick Steamship Line,** this rustic, turn-of-the-century building looks like a longshoreman's hangout. It became a cafe in 1928 and was lifted and moved to the present location in 1978. A century of scars shows on the walls, which are covered with white railroad car siding. The tiny kitchen, set behind a green Formica counter, turns out bountiful breakfasts and lunches. French toast, homemade corned-beef hash, and fluffy buttermilk pancakes are top morning choices. At lunch there's a list of sandwiches and hearty, reasonably priced blue plate specials, including meat loaf or roast beef with mashed potatoes, vegetables, and sourdough bread. ♦ American ♦ Daily breakfast and lunch; bar until 10PM. Pier 39 (Building A, Level 2). 433.3689 ♿

Old Swiss House

12 Old Swiss House ★★$$$ This place looks like a little slice of the Alps: Swiss-style stencils decorate the perimeter of the pitched room, which is dominated by a hexagonal fireplace, and lace curtains soften the oceanfront view. Although most menus on the wharf are almost carbon copies of one another, this one is distinguished by such hearty European specialties as medaillons of pork sautéed in butter and topped with cognac-infused morels; lamb, served with a cranberry glacé; and pan-fried veal stuffed with ham. ♦ Swiss/Continental ♦ Daily lunch and dinner. Pier 39 (Building C, Level 2). 434.0432 ♿

13 San Francisco Tea and Coffee Co. Geared to the tourist, this shop stocks more flavors of coffee and tea than just about any other in the city. Coffee flavors include peaches 'n' cream, macadamia nut, and Irish cream. Coffeepots, teapots, and other related equipment are for sale, including mugs with handles in the shape of toucans, dinosaurs, fish, and alligators. ♦ Daily. Pier 39 (Building D, Level 2). 421.5119 ♿

14 Yet Wah $ The only Chinese restaurant on Pier 39, its menu has a middle-of-the-road appeal, but the lunch buffet can get sorry-looking by 3PM. It is part of a chain known for generic, yet well-prepared, food; however, each branch is individually owned, so the quality varies from one to the other. ◆ Chinese ◆ Daily lunch and dinner. Pier 39 (Building M, Level 2). 434.4430 ♿

15 Cost Plus World Market A one-stop bargain-shopping paradise, this warehouse-size store stocks everything from country- or Shaker-style tables and chairs, to all kinds of glassware and pottery, to an enormous selection of specialty foods, including coffees, teas, and wines. With a large collection of baskets, napkins, and the like, it's easy to gather all the makings of a beautiful gift basket. ◆ Daily 9AM-9PM. 2552 Taylor St (between Bay and North Point Sts). 928.6200; fax 921.2657 ♿

16 Foggy's A good cup of coffee isn't easy to come by in this neighborhood, which makes this spot (which used to be called **Foggy Bay Coffee Company**) a real find for those who need to refuel. Tea is also available, and there is a nice selection of pastries to enjoy with a "cuppa" at one of the small tables. ◆ Daily. 540 North Point St (between Taylor and Jones Sts). 474.2070 ♿

17 Cafe Pescatore ★$$ One of the most attractive dining options in the wharf area, this place has a welcoming trattoria atmosphere, with an impressive exhibition kitchen. The wood-burning oven turns out crisp-crusted pizzas (accompanied by either soup or salad, they're a real bargain). Some dishes can be uneven; stick with the stews and roasts, including the roast chicken breast with mixed greens, pancetta, and a balsamic vinaigrette. The location, a block away from the crowds, adds a civilized note. ◆ Italian/Seafood ◆ Daily breakfast, lunch, and dinner. 2455 Mason St (between Bay and North Point Sts). 561.1111; fax 561.1199 ♿

BEN& JERRY'S

18 Ben & Jerry's Largely a walk-and-lick operation, this popular ice-cream shop does offer inside tables to those who want to relax with a sundae; the shop also shares the patio in back of the **TraveLodge at the Wharf** hotel with **Johnny Rockets** (see below). Wheelchair access is through the hotel. ◆ Daily. 79 Jefferson St (between Powell and Mason Sts). 249.2662 ♿ Also at: Numerous locations throughout the city

18 Johnny Rockets ★★$ At this 1950s-style diner/hamburger joint, you can enjoy a root-beer float and fries while seated around the poolside patio. On a sunny day, looking at the pool ringed by palm trees will make you think you're in Florida. ◆ American/Hamburgers ◆ Daily breakfast, lunch, and dinner. 81 Jefferson St (between Powell and Mason Sts). 693.9120; fax 693.9404 ♿ Also at: 1946 Fillmore St (at Pine St), Pacific Heights. 776.9878; fax 776.1189 ♿

19 N. Alioto ★★$ Here's a streetside stand with a difference: The fish-and-chips and other seafood offerings look fresh and taste it, too. If you can't visit the wharf without indulging in a crab cocktail, this is the place for it. The squid salad is also very good. ◆ Seafood ◆ Daily. 155 Jefferson St (between Mason and Taylor Sts). 776.7300 ♿

19 A. Sabella's Restaurant ★★★$$$ When the Sabella family emigrated here from Sicily in 1871, they made their living by fishing the bay. They opened this seafood restaurant in 1920, and they've been in business here ever since. Today, the third generation of Sabellas runs the place. The huge banquet-style room has floor-to-ceiling windows overlooking the wharf, and a bar in the back is warmed by a fireplace that would look right at home in an Aspen ski lodge. Chef Michael Sabella's menu boasts several dishes with an Asian influence, such as whole cracked crab with a light, fermented black-bean sauce. The fresh seafood offerings change daily, but outstanding entrées include crab cioppino with shrimp, clams, and mussels; a huge crab–and–bay shrimp louie that also includes lobster and avocado; bouillabaisse; and sautéed fresh Monterey calamari. The abalone Dore with a lemon-garlic beurre blanc and sautéed spinach is another succulent choice. The lounge next door features live entertainment on weekends and mystery-theater packages that include the whodunit, as well as a three-course meal, tax, and parking. ◆ Seafood ◆ Daily lunch and dinner. 2766 Taylor St (at Jefferson St), Third floor. 771.6775; fax 771.6777 ♿

20 Boudin Sourdough Bakery & Café ★$ Since opening on North Beach's Grant Avenue back in 1849, this bakery chain has expanded to 18 locations in San Francisco. This branch offers a glimpse, behind glass, of the sourdough bread–making process. It also houses two eateries, the original in front, with a few tables, and a cafe/bakery in the parking area behind (Taylor Street between Jefferson Street and Fisherman's Wharf). The menu is the same at both, and offers sandwiches on sourdough bread. A specialty at all **Boudin** cafes is clam chowder served in a hollowed-out sourdough loaf, allowing diners to eat the bowl, if that's their pleasure. ◆ Cafe ◆ Daily breakfast, lunch, and light dinner until 8PM. 156 Jefferson St (between Mason and Taylor Sts). 928.1849; fax 776.1778. Also at: Numerous locations throughout the city

21 Tarantino's ★$$$ A view of the boat basin is assured, thanks to the tiered seating at this restaurant, which has been here since 1946. But although the food can be fine, the preparations often seem slipshod. Pasta is made in-house and is used as a bed for some of the specialties, including scallops and prawns in a smoky tomato sauce, redolent of garlic. Best bets include steamed clams with butter and garlic; grilled sand dabs; rex sole, served boned; and abalone, dipped in an egg batter and served with a butter sauce. ♦ Seafood ♦ Daily lunch and dinner. 206 Jefferson St (between Taylor and Leavenworth Sts). 775.5600; fax 749.2097 ♿

22 Alioto's No. 8 ★★★$$$ Not to be confused with **N. Alioto,** this is the oldest restaurant on the wharf and one of the most popular as well. It is *the* place for cioppino (prepared here with generous amounts of crab and shellfish). The streetside stand offers cracked crab, while **The Oysteria,** an oyster bar on the first floor, is fine for a light repast. Menu offerings range from typical Californian/Italian fare (such as ziti with pine nuts, raisins, tomatoes, and flakes of fresh fish) to unusual Sicilian specialties like calamari with *muddica* (a topping of bread crumbs, garlic, and anchovies). The seafood risotto here is one of the best in town; another great entrée is abalone wrapped in a light egg coating. Nunzio Alioto is one of the top sommeliers in San Francisco, and his list of excellent wines includes many bargains, particularly among the Italian vintages. The upstairs dining room was being remodeled at press time, but whatever the new look will be,

it's likely that diners will still be able to enjoy the great views of the fishing-boat activity in the harbor. ♦ Seafood ♦ Daily lunch and dinner. 8 Fisherman's Wharf (at Taylor St). 673.0183; fax 673.3894 ♿

23 The Franciscan ★★★$$$ This venerable wharfside restaurant has recently received a complete renovation. The overall look is sleek and classy, with small shaded lamps on the tables, classic wood columns, and stunning views of the San Francisco Bay, ship activity in the harbor, and Alcatraz, which can be seen from every seat in the house. The food has been made over as well, with great success: appetizers include a delicious *ahi* tuna carpaccio dressed with wasabi crème fraîche; seafood spring rolls with a port-ginger dipping sauce; and sparkling fresh oysters on the half shell. Main courses include spaghetti Bolognese, fettucine Alfredo with crabmeat, angel hair pasta with rock shrimp and eggplant in a spicy tomato sauce, fish-and-chips, and sautéed scallops with sweet pepper risotto. And unlike most other restaurants on the wharf, this place makes its desserts in-house—don't miss the yummy chocolate mousse cake. ♦ Seafood ♦ Daily lunch and dinner. Pier 43½ at the Embarcadero (on the water). 362.7733; fax 362.0174 ♿

24 Tokyo Sukiyaki Restaurant and Sushi Bar ★★$$ After a day at the garish wharf, you'll welcome the serenity of this sleek spot decorated with celadon walls and movable bamboo screens. Sit Western-style, kneel on tatami mats at low tables, or perch at the elevated sushi bar. Two menus are offered, regardless of where the diners are seated: One lists such typical dishes as tempura and teriyaki, and a smaller menu, written in Japanese and English, presents traditional rice and noodle dishes and a variety of sake and spirits. Sushi is better elsewhere, but do try the beef sukiyaki with scallions, mush-rooms, tofu, and noodles; *shabu shabu* (slices of beef cooked in broth and served with sesame and vinegar sauces); and some of the cooked fish dishes, including the salt-broiled flounder. ♦ Japanese ♦ M-F dinner; Sa-Su lunch and dinner. 225 Jefferson St (between Taylor and Jones Sts). 775.9030; fax 775.3872

25 Everyday Cafe ★★$ A big hit with both locals and visitors, this coffee shop offers three kinds of java, as well as tea and Lappert's ice cream, an exotic brand that is imported from Hawaii (try the Kona coffee-fudge flavor). Owner Holly Smith offers bagel sandwiches, fresh pastries, and croissants at breakfast, and the rest of the day she serves a wide variety of sandwiches, homemade soups, and salads. ♦ American ♦ Daily breakfast, lunch, and dinner (to 7PM Oct-

May). 448 Beach St (between Taylor and Jones Sts). 346.6047 ♿

26 The Sweet Factory Big Plexiglas tubes, on the walls display an extravaganza of hard candies in such eye-catching colors as lime green, Pepto Bismol pink, and passionate purple. Snacking on these Day-Glo–hued morsels is a high-tech way to get low-tech cavities. Other sweets include chocolates, jelly beans, and gummies. ♦ Daily. 333 Jefferson St (between Jones and Leavenworth Sts, in the Anchorage Mall). 474.4731 ♿

26 The Candy Barrel Wine barrels brimming with all kinds of treats give this sweetshop a nostalgic feel. There are more than 25 flavors of locally produced saltwater taffy, including watermelon, coconut, passion fruit, caramel pecan, and licorice swirl, as well as individually wrapped hard candies. Another local specialty not to be missed is Judy's coconut almond brittle—simply marvelous. Just down the street, and under the same ownership, **Doc's International Candy Shoppe** (131 Jefferson St, between Mason and Taylor Sts, 771.8908) offers an equally vast selection. ♦ Daily. 333 Jefferson St (between Jones and Leavenworth Sts, in the Anchorage Mall). 771.5526 ♿

27 Pompei's Grotto ★$$ Compared to the banquet-size dining rooms that predominate in the area, this quaint room, decked out in checkered tablecloths, paneled walls, and gently whirling fans, has an intimate, almost romantic ambience (but it's popular with families, too). The restaurant dates from 1946, and the food has a similar pedigree—the menu includes all kinds of seafood mixed in with Italian specialties. ♦ Italian ♦ Daily

lunch and dinner. 340 Jefferson St (between Taylor and Leavenworth Sts). 776.9265; fax 776.9646 ♿

27 Lou's Pier 47 Club This noisy, boisterous nightclub offers live blues music performances and dancing, along with a full bar and a pub-style menu of burgers and snacks. With its funky, hip atmosphere, it has become very popular very quickly. There's also a restaurant that serves meals during the day, but it's nothing special. ♦ Restaurant: daily breakfast, lunch, and dinner. Club: daily 4PM-2AM. 300 Jefferson St (between Taylor and Leavenworth Sts). 771.0377

28 Scoma's ★$$ Believe it or not, this venerable but rundown seafood house is the highest-grossing restaurant in San Francisco, packing people in just about every day of the year. It's the kind of joint where indifferent waiters sling your food at you on the run and present the check before dessert even arrives. But it attracts locals (who frequently are seated without waiting) and tourists alike. Much of the charm of this place is its dockside location. As for the food, the fish is very fresh, and portions are generous, but the presentation is fatally flawed. Oysters on the half shell, for instance, are mishandled, buried in ice, and sloppily served. Best bets are the grilled fish steaks served with simple sauces. ♦ Seafood ♦ Daily lunch and dinner. Pier 47 (on the water). 771.4383; fax 775.2601 ♿

⊛THE CANNERY©

29 The Cannery Constructed in 1909 as the Del Monte Fruit Company's peach-canning plant, this building was remodeled in 1968 by **Joseph Esherick & Associates** following the successful redevelopment of Ghirardelli Square (see page 74). The three-story complex contains shops, restaurants, a comedy club, galleries, and a movie theater. Its sunken courtyard, which is filled with flowers and century-old olive trees, hosts musicians, mimes, and other talented street performers. ♦ 2801 Leavenworth St (at Beach St). 771.3112; fax 771.2424 ♿

Within The Cannery:

Cannery Wine Cellar and Gourmet Market This sprawling market, with an exposed network of pipes and wires overhead, seems an unlikely place for a serious wine-and-liquor store. But amid the clutter of tourist merchandise are stocked more than 300 kinds of beers, 160 single-malt scotches, and a good collection of California wines. Shelves of gourmet products, including mustards, jams, olive oils, and vinegars, round out the food selections.
♦ Daily. 673.0400; fax 673.0161 &

handmade ceramic studio One of the latest additions to **The Cannery,** this is the first San Francisco branch of a chain of paint-your-own-pottery shops based in the Mill Valley. You can create an individually designed souvenir of the city, for yourself or as a special gift. It's a great place to indulge your nascent artistic impulses. Kids will love it, too. ♦ Daily. 440.2898 &

30 **Buena Vista Cafe** ★$ You haven't had Irish coffee until you've had it here, because of the drink's quality as well as its history. That soul-satisfying brew, blended with Irish whiskey and topped with whipped cream, was first served in the United States at this place in 1952, after Stan Delaplane, a longtime *San Francisco Chronicle* columnist, tasted it at the airport in Shannon, Ireland, and brought the idea back. The cafe's not much to look at: Round wooden tables sit on an old tile floor, and the scarred walls look as if they've seen a hundred coats of glossy paint. The bar menu offers casual, tasty fare, such as hamburgers with cheddar or outstanding Reuben sandwiches, and blackboard specials include corned beef and cabbage, and macaroni and cheese. ♦ American ♦ Daily breakfast, lunch, and dinner; bar until 2AM. No credit cards accepted. 2765 Hyde St (at Beach St). 474.5044; fax 474.2207 &

30 **Little Rio Cafe and Pizzeria** ★$ This is one of many similar restaurants around the Bay Area that offer a menu of pizza and Brazilian cuisine. Colorful Latin flair wins out in the decor department with splashy tablecloths, but pizza is clearly the most popular item. There's even a Carmen Miranda dessert pizza, slathered with butter, cinnamon, sugar, bananas, and cheese (order at your own risk). Pasta and Brazilian dishes round out the menu, which includes marinated beef sautéed with onions and served with rice and beans, and, every weekend, *feijoada,* a black-bean and pork stew that is considered the national dish of Brazil. A good selection of bottled beers from Brazil, El Salvador, Peru, and other exotic places also is showcased. ♦ Brazilian/Pizzeria ♦ Daily lunch and dinner. 2721 Hyde St (between North Point and Beach Sts). 441.3344 &

31 **Chez Michel** ★★★$$$ A complete departure from the usual wharf-area restaurant, this upscale establishment has pale gray walls, matching plantation shutters at the windows, mirrors, and wood beams. Indirect lighting illuminates an eye-catching domed ceiling. However, the overall mood is cold and the color scheme unflattering, casting a gray wash onto diners' faces. A new chef, Alain Redelsperger, has taken over the kitchen, and he has changed the menu dramatically. The seafood pearl pasta (similar to couscous) is perfumed with curry and features tender, tiny mussels and clams; another good appetizer is crispy sweetbread salad. If you like rabbit, the rabbit loin wrapped in pancetta on braised fennel with olive sauce is a must; and the entrée of tournedos of lamb shank is a tasty dish. The wine list could be more interesting, but the prices are reasonable. ♦ French/Californian ♦ Tu-Su dinner. 804 North Point St (between Hyde and Larkin Sts). 775.7036; fax 775.1805 &

32 **Ghirardelli Square** During the Civil War this was the site of a woolen mill, but it was the famous chocolate factory built here in 1896 by Domenico Ghirardelli that gave the square its name. The factory was converted into the city's most attractive commercial complex by **Wurster, Bernardi & Emmons Inc.** and **Lawrence Halprin & Associates** from 1962 to 1967. The location is blessed with a view of the bay, and at night the buildings are festively outlined by strings of lights. The **Mermaid Fountain** in the central plaza, designed by local artist Ruth Asawa, is a good resting and meeting spot. Free entertainment is usually taking place somewhere within the square, and the information booth (located smack in the middle of the square) has a detailed guide to the shops and restaurants. ♦ 900 North Point St (at Larkin St, across from Aquatic Park). 775.5500; fax 775.0912 &

Within Ghirardelli Square:

Ghirardelli Chocolate Manufactory ★★$ You're unlikely to find better ice-cream concoctions than those at this magical combination of soda fountain, chocolate shop, and chocolate factory. The soda fountain dishes up huge, scrumptious sundaes and steaming mugs of delicious hot chocolate topped with mounds of whipped cream; on warm days try the strawberry or vanilla soda. Next door, the elegant chocolate shop's dark wood cases are filled with sweet temptations. The mini-factory is in back; there, three exposed belts gently rotate a paddle that stirs the vat of molten chocolate. ♦ Ice-cream parlor ♦ Daily. Clocktower Building, First floor. 771.4903; fax 775.0912 &

The Mandarin ★$$$ With its brick walls, windows overlooking the bay, country-style setting, and formal service, this has been one of the city's most beautiful and elegant Chinese restaurants for many years. It's gone through a number of changes in ownership since its glory days in the 1970s, and the menu has evolved into an odd mix of good (if unadventurous) Chinese fare and "fusion" dishes that miss the mark. Our advice: Stick to the classics and enjoy the gorgeous view. ♦ Chinese ♦ Daily lunch and dinner. Woolen Mill, Fourth floor. 673.8812; fax 673.5480 &

McCormick & Kuleto's ★$$$ Far and away the most impressive-looking restaurant in the area, this seafood house has a view of the lighted **Aquatic Park** and a striking design by **Pat Kuleto,** who has worked his magic on many of the city's best restaurants. The tiered interior features rich wood-and-brass appointments and tortoiseshell-glass lights shaped like boats. The food can be excellent, but with 400 seats plus private receptions and banquets, consistency is a problem. Dozens of fresh fish are featured each day. Order what looks simplest and you may well have a very good meal. ♦ Seafood ♦ Daily lunch and dinner. Webster Building, Courtyard level. 929.1730; fax 567.2919 &

Adjoining McCormick & Kuleto's:

Crab Cake Lounge ★★$ It looks like a typical wharfside bar, its brick walls covered with pictures, but this place serves up plenty of good, affordable eats. More than a half-dozen varieties of oysters are offered on the half shell, as well as salads, crab, mussels, grilled trout, hamburger, and a dozen or so pizzas cooked in the brick oven. The bar features at least 10 single-malt scotches and as many Cognacs, Armagnacs, and bottled beers, including a special seasonal draft. ♦ Seafood ♦ Daily lunch and dinner. 929.1730; fax 567.2919 &

Gaylord India Restaurant ★$$$ No Indian restaurant in the city matches the elegance of this one, awash in pink and red and mahogany, with a wall of glass overlooking the bay. The food has become a bit sloppy and tired, although the tandoori

selections are still outstanding. ♦ Indian ♦ Daily lunch and dinner. Chocolate Building, Third floor. 771.8822; fax 771.4980 &

Operetta Italian dining and kitchen accessories are the backbone of this store, along with a few well-chosen food items and antiques. Be sure to look for the tapestry table runners and tablecloths that incorporate a vegetable-and-fruit motif into the design. ♦ Daily. Woolen Mill, Third floor. 928.4676 &

Scan Trends This shop carries tabletop accessories by such important Scandinavian names as Royal Copenhagen and George Jensen. You'll find more than 30 dinnerware patterns, flatware, candlesticks, serving trays, and other items to set a beautiful table. ♦ Daily. Woolen Mill, Third floor. 775.2217; fax 707.996.7790 &

Timo's Norte ★★★$$ Under the same ownership as **Timo's Tapas Bar** in the Mission, this excellent tapas eatery is a welcome addition to Ghirardelli Square. (Its presence is part of a concerted effort by local businesses to increase resident patronage of the Wharf by attracting branches of well-regarded restaurants from other neighborhoods.) Owner/chef Carlos Corredor has created a reasonably priced menu of tapas ranging from tender veal kidneys in a sherry sauce to Catalan-style spinach with pine nuts and raisins. There are also Spanish entrées such as *ajiaco,* a filling and hearty chicken-and-potato soup which is the national dish of Colombia; a refreshing avocado and *ahi* tuna ceviche; and prawns sautéed with garlic. On the weekends, Corredor also prepares whole roast pigs. Tasty sangrias, a good wine list, and classic desserts such as flan round out the offerings. Although the menu is Spanish, the restaurant still has the Caribbean-flavored look of **Cha Cha Cha,** which it replaced: bright colors, fake palm trees, tin accents. ♦ Spanish ♦ Daily lunch and dinner. Mustard Building, Second floor. 440.1200; fax 440.3192 &

Nob Hill/Russian Hill

Nob Hill and Russian Hill, two of San Francisco's most famous areas, have completely different personalities. Russian Hill, which is closer to the water, has always enjoyed a bohemian spirit that attracts artists. It has nurtured such famous writers as George Sterling, Ambrose Bierce, and Robert Louis Stevenson. It's also home to the **San Francisco Art Institute**, which was founded in 1871, and squiggly **Lombard Street**, known as the "crookedest street in the world." But Russian Hill's artsy unconventionality is not reflected in the food found here. The restaurants tend to be small and cater to a neighborhood clientele that ranges from well-heeled executives to blue-collar families.

Polk Street, the main shopping strip that serves both neighborhoods, has undergone something of a revival, especially the northern end stretching toward the bay. It houses a four-star French restaurant, **La Folie**, and a popular singles' bar and restaurant, **Johnny Love's.** Several ethnic restaurants and elegant carryouts have added a gourmet patina to the street: **Leonard's** offers up great cheeses; **Pure T** churns up tea-flavored ice cream (which may sound weird but is delicious); **The Real Food Company** features just-picked organic produce; and **The Jug Shop** stocks a wide selection of wines at competitive prices.

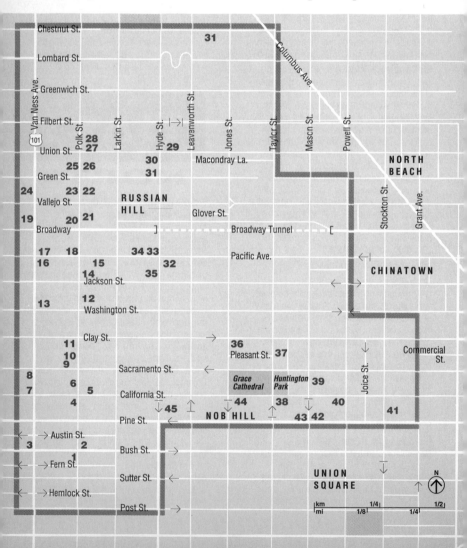

Higher up, near Nob Hill, the scene is somewhat tattered. Known as "Polk Gulch," it was the center of gay culture before the Castro emerged in the 1970s. It still has a smattering of bars, but the merchants are struggling to find an equilibrium.

Farther up still, the best doughnuts in the city can be found at **Bob's Donut and Pastry Shop.** And don't miss the wonderful take-out seafood at the venerable **Swan Oyster Depot,** which has a marble counter where you can enjoy a bowl of clam chowder, fresh cracked crab, or oysters.

A more exclusive ambience pervades Nob Hill. Rising steeply from Polk Street, Nob Hill is distinguished on the skyline by its landmark **Grace Cathedral.** Built on the spoils of commerce, the area began to attract visitors after the advent of the cable car, which made scaling the hills easier. This is where the "Big Four" staked their claims: Here Charles Crocker, Leland Stanford, Mark Hopkins, and Collis Huntington all raised hilltop mansions, which were destroyed in the 1906 earthquake and fire. Today the area is home to some of the city's most distinctive hotel restaurants: **The Big Four** at the **Huntington;** the campy **Tonga Restaurant and Hurricane Bar** (whose South Seas theme extends to hourly rainstorms) at the **Fairmont;** the tony **Nob Hill Restaurant** and the panoramic **Top of the Mark** at the **Mark Hopkins Inter-Continental San Francisco;** and **The Dining Room** and **The Terrace** at the **Ritz-Carlton San Francisco.** Then there's the stunning **Charles Nob Hill,** whose fabulous food and attentive service made it a hit from the moment it opened a few years ago.

Tucked away in the residential sections of both Russian Hill and Nob Hill are some of the cutest restaurants in town, such as the popular **Zarzuela.** Other interesting eateries are situated along the **Hyde Street** cable car line and are frequented mostly by locals: They head to the **Hyde Street Seafood House and Raw Bar** for its good food and welcoming atmosphere; **Café Chaise** for a good light meal; and **Sushi Grove** for Japanese fare.

---

1 Maye's Oyster House $$ Dating back to 1867 and at this location since 1904, this Italian-style seafood restaurant blazes no new culinary trail, but if you stick to the simplest dishes you'll do just fine. ♦ Italian/Seafood ♦ M-F lunch and dinner; Sa-Su dinner. 1233 Polk St (at Fern St). 474.7674

2 Freed Teller & Freed's One of the oldest specialty coffee merchants, this establishment is still the Rolls-Royce of purveyors. The knowledgeable staff can explain all the different beans and roasts in great detail. Another bonus: rows of jars holding bulk spices, including a terrific selection of whole peppercorns from exotic-sounding places. Ask and they will help you create your own blend of tea or coffee. ♦ M-Sa. 1326 Polk St (between Bush and Austin Sts). 673.0922; fax 673.3436 & Also at: 1 Embarcadero Center (Sacramento St, at Battery St), Financial District. 986.8851; fax 986.8853 &

3 Coconut Grove ★★$$ Entering this elegant supper club is like walking into a 1930s movie. A massive dome painted with screen legends of the 1930s and 1940s, stylized metal palms scattered about the two-story dining room, a center stage, white leatherlike booths, and exquisite crystal and silver on every cloth-draped table foster a pleasantly decadent atmosphere. The place was recently acquired by partners who lowered the food prices, eliminated the cover charge, and created an interesting menu of New Orleans– and Caribbean-style dishes. Among the better appetizers are red curry coconut bouillabaisse with shellfish, and entrées include blackened catfish with an apple-jicama slaw and grilled chicken breast spiced up with a mango-ginger barbecue sauce. The desserts, such as coconut–passion fruit Bavarian tart in a macadamia-nut crust with prickly pear coulis, are quite good as well. There's live entertainment nightly. ♦ American ♦ Tu-Su dinner (F-Sa until 2AM). 1415 Van Ness Ave (between

Bush and Austin Sts). 776.1616; fax 776.7416 &

4 Crustacean ★★$$$ Roast crab is the dish to order at this upscale Vietnamese restaurant. On the third floor of a glass-fronted building, diners enjoy a neon-lit, vaguely Deco-looking space and have a bird's-eye view of the bustling shopping activity on Polk Street. Try the roast Dungeness crab, flavored with butter; royal tiger prawns; garlic noodles; and ravioli. ◆ Seafood ◆ Daily dinner. 1475 Polk St (at California St), Third floor. 776.2722; fax 776.1069 &

5 Cordon Bleu ★$ Bare bones all the way, this Vietnamese restaurant compensates with extremely low prices and excellent five-spice chicken. While not a place to linger (smoke from the kitchen sometimes infiltrates the dining room), it's a popular stop for people heading to the many movie houses in the area. ◆ Vietnamese ◆ Tu-Sa lunch and dinner; Su dinner. No credit cards accepted. 1574 California St (between Larkin and Polk Sts). 673.5637

5 Emerald Garden ★★$$ This restaurant was created in an alleyway, so the brick buildings on either side serve as its walls. The pink accents and leafy potted plants make everything seem intimate and comfortable. Some of the best items are the crepes, fried appetizers, and Saigon-style pork chops, which are marinated in soy sauce with sugar and black pepper, grilled over charcoal, and basted with rum. ◆ French/Vietnamese ◆ M-F lunch and dinner; Sa-Su dinner. Reservations recommended. 1550 California St (between Larkin and Polk Sts). 673.1155; fax 673.1253 &

6 Aromi ★★$$ Owner-chef Hoss Zare's stock-in-trade is lusty Italian food: veal shanks in a gutsy tomato sauce with white beans and wilted winter greens; risotto cakes stuffed with gorgonzola, shiitake mushrooms, and roasted garlic; sweetbreads laced with Marsala; and a bed of soft polenta soaked with an intense mushroom sauce. Other dishes worth ordering include penne with tomato and vodka, *pappardelle* (wide noodles) with veal, and linguine with grilled salmon, olives, capers, and fennel. For dessert, chocolate cake with a medley of fruit sauces drizzled

over the plate and *budino* (a warm chocolate soufflé cake) can't be beat. French doors separate an ornate, marble-floored bar from the attractive dining room, with its dark wood floor, bentwood chairs, and single flower on each table. More French doors lead to a heated patio overlooking the urban bustle of Polk Street. ◆ Italian ◆ Daily lunch and dinner. 1507 Polk St (between California and Sacramento Sts). 775.5977

6 Main Squeeze ★$ This juice bar/coffee shop has won many awards for its knockout design, which includes glazed cement floors and curving tabletops inset with constellations. Scattered throughout are bright green flats of wheat grass, which not only lend decoration but are squeezed into juice "shots" for health-conscious patrons. In case you haven't guessed, the emphasis here is on low- and nonfat preparations, fruit smoothies, and loads of salads. Near the counter, patrons can check out a chart of essential vitamins and minerals and the best foods for getting them. ◆ Cafe ◆ Daily. 1515 Polk St (between California and Sacramento Sts). 567.1515; fax 567.1515 &

6 Swan Oyster Depot ★★★$$ Since the early part of this century, this tiny storefront fish market has showcased some of the finest local products—salmon, sole, rockfish, sand dabs, lingcod, and oysters—as well as fish from other areas and a fine selection of smoked seafood. It's equally popular as a lunch destination for the steamy bowls of chowder and oysters on the half shell served at the old-fashioned marble counter. And if you like fish for breakfast, you can find it here. ◆ Seafood ◆ M-Sa breakfast, lunch, and early dinner. No credit cards accepted. 1517 Polk St (between California and Sacramento Sts). 673.1101

6 See's Candy These quaint candy stores, done in black and white, look as if they were plucked from a different era, and the sweet salesclerks from central casting. As you wait for your hand-packed order, the clerk will slip you a chocolate. For an unusual treat, try the chocolate-covered candied ginger. ◆ Daily. 1519 Polk St (between California and Sacramento Sts). 775.7049; fax 775.7049 & Also at: Numerous locations throughout the city

7 Ruth's Chris Steak House ★$$$ Popular with tourists, this New Orleans–based steak house chain has locations throughout the United States. The steaks, drowned in butter (unless you specify otherwise), are prime but pricey; vegetables, potatoes, and salads are ordered separately, pushing the tab even higher. Also, the service isn't what it should be at these prices. ♦ Steak house ♦ Daily dinner. 1700 California St (at Van Ness Ave). 673.0557; fax 673.5309 &

8 Hard Rock Cafe ★$ Even if you didn't notice the life-size black-and-white cow outside you couldn't miss this link in the popular chain because of the continuous line of people waiting to get in. This is where the younger set wants to hang out, snarf down burgers, and then take home a T-shirt bearing the famous logo. ♦ American ♦ Daily lunch and dinner. 1699 Van Ness Ave (at Sacramento St). 885.1699; fax 885.0701 &

9 Acquerello ★★★$$$ The service is consistently flawless at this chic, romantic Italian restaurant, and the *nuova cucina* (nouvelle cuisine) is imaginatively conceived and artfully presented. Chef/owner Suzette Gresham creates an ever-changing array of dishes that may include thin slices of raw beef stuffed with pickled vegetables in a lemon and truffle-oil sauce; quail stuffed with apple and thyme and presented on zucchini-and-potato pancakes; or tuna in a fennel-and-dill crust with saffron sauce and a refreshing confit of lemons. ♦ Italian ♦ Tu-Sa dinner. Reservations recommended. 1722 Sacramento St (between Polk St and Van Ness Ave). 567.5432; fax 567.6432 &

10 Bob's Donut and Pastry Shop Early morning traffic jams are common in front of this small, bare-bones bakery, as Mercedes, trucks, and taxis vie for a space so that drivers can rush in to get the city's best doughnuts. In a world filled with generic shops offering cookie-cutter products, these goods are actually made from scratch. The fried versions come out extra puffy and light with a thin, crackling glaze of sugar; the cake varieties crumble seductively with each bite; and the buttermilk bars have just a hint of tartness. The coffee is also freshly made and strong. ♦ Daily 24 hours. 1621 Polk St (between Sacramento and Clay Sts). 776.3141

10 Double Rainbow Ice Cream The almost magical rainbow reflected on the sidewalk in front of this parlor draws a wide cross section of people right in—some even sport the colors of the rainbow in their hair. "Double bow," as many refer to it, has been a favorite of ice-cream aficionados since the original shop opened on Castro Street in 1976. Ice cream is the star, but the frozen yogurts and baked goods are increasingly popular.

♦ M-Th, Su 11AM-11PM; F-Sa 11AM-midnight. 1653 Polk St (between Sacramento and Clay Sts). 775.3220 & Also at: Numerous locations throughout the city

HEART and SOUL

11 Julie Ring's Heart and Soul ★★$$ Julie Ring has launched such funky theme spots as the 1950s-style **Julie's Supper Club** and the lively Caribbean **Miss Pearl's Jam House.** Now she's exploring the sophisticated 1940s with a supper club that features piano music and jazz combos nightly. Dark green walls, red carpet, black accents, and a wrought-iron railing around the mezzanine give the room a moody, intimate atmosphere, and just about every table has a great view of the raised stage. The food is well executed and reasonably priced. Start with mussels served with aioli and pungent barbecue sauce, a classic whole-leaf Caesar salad, or a seafood sampler of shrimp and oysters with a variety of sauces. Main courses include a juicy steak with quartered portobello mushrooms and mashed potatoes; fettuccine with lemon, arugula, and a waft of chilies; and an earthy *posole,* pork stew with hominy, onions, and garlic. The homey desserts include fruit crisp and strawberry-rhubarb pie. ♦ Californian ♦ Cover. M, Su snacks; Tu-Sa dinner. 1695 Polk St (at Clay St). 673.7100; fax 673.6799 &

WING LEE RESTAURANT

12 Wing Lee Restaurant ★★$ What you lose in elegant decor you gain in good food at this family-owned Chinese cafe. Specialties include sizzling-rice soup; panfried noodles with chicken; and pork with fresh, nutty lotus root. For an impromptu dinner party, take home one of the bronzed roast ducks that hang upside down from hooks in the front window. ♦ Chinese ♦ M, W-Su lunch and dinner. 1810 Polk St (between Washington and Jackson Sts). 775.3210 &

13 The House of Prime Rib ★★$$ This eatery has been a San Francisco institution since the 1950s, and the staff is as cordial as you'll find anywhere (though the service can be a bit rushed when it's busy). This is the best place to get a slab of prime rib, carved tableside. The warren of richly appointed, clubby rooms, most with fireplaces, belies the reasonable prices. Included with each entrée are side dishes and salad (watch it being tossed in a spinning bowl filled with ice), but if that doesn't fill you up, seconds are even offered. ♦ American ♦ Daily dinner. 1906 Van Ness Ave (between Washington and Jackson Sts). 885.4605; fax 921.0854 &

14 Bell Tower ★★$ This comfortable bar/restaurant won the hearts of the Russian Hill crowd in short order. The older set comes in early; the younger crowd follows, either before, during, or after a night on the town. Chef Gary Ferry, who used to work in the kitchen at **Stars,** has refined the menu here, adding a grilled bluenose bass served with basil mashed potatoes and an olive-caper relish, and succulent roast chicken. The half-pound burger and french fries combo is good and very reasonably priced. ♦ Californian/ American ♦ Daily lunch and dinner until midnight. 1900 Polk St (at Jackson St). 567.9596 &

15 The Jug Shop People drive for miles to shop at this sprawling wine store, drawn by the enormous selection available, as well as the discounted prices. Here you'll find more than 2,000 wines, 400 beers, and just about every spirit imaginable. The clerks know their stuff and are fun, friendly, and helpful. They'll be happy to assist you in selecting and also shipping wines. A wine-tasting bar is open every Friday and Saturday. And wonder of wonders, there's even parking at the corner. ♦ Daily. 1567 Pacific Ave (between Larkin and Polk Sts). 885.2922; fax 885.6612 &

16 Rocco's Seafood Grill ★★$$ Restaurateur Sam Duvall, who also runs **Izzy's Steaks and Chops** in The Marina, has given this establishment (which used to be **Kiki's Paris 1920**) a complete overhaul. Although it still has the look of a 1920s Paris brasserie, it is now an American-style seafood place. The menu keeps things simple, offering straightforward dishes like sautéed sand dabs, cioppino, grilled petrale sole, Alaskan halibut, and king salmon caught in local waters. For carnivores, there's also roast chicken, New York sirloin steak, and prime rib.

♦ American/ Seafood ♦ Daily dinner. 2080 Van Ness Ave (between Jackson St and Pacific Ave). 567.7600; fax 673.8817 &

Harris'

17 Harris' Restaurant ★★★$$$ One of the best steak houses in San Francisco also sports the most sophisticated decor, with dark wood paneling, a bucolic mural, and deep, tufted booths. Start your meal with a martini and steak tartare or a Caesar salad and then try the New York cut, which has a caramelized exterior kissed with mesquite and a pink, juicy interior. The 100-plus wine list is appropriately weighted to full-bodied reds. For dessert the pecan pie is excellent. ♦ Steak house ♦ Daily dinner. Reservations recommended. 2100 Van Ness Ave (at Pacific Ave). 673.1888; fax 673.8817 &

18 Leonard's More than 200 types of cheese make this sunny, corner specialty store a prime draw. You'll also find many different grains and dried fruits as well as freshly ground peanut butter. The owner, Leonard Born, usually imparts great tidbits of information to his patrons about their purchases. ♦ Daily. 2001 Polk St (at Pacific Ave). 921.2001 &

19 Golden Turtle ★★★$ The city's prettiest Vietnamese restaurant is set in a converted house, where the husband-and-wife team of Kham Dinh Tran and Kim-Quy Tran has created an intimate, upscale dining room with intricately carved wood murals. Kim-Quy takes charge of the cooking duties, and she has a knack for balancing the sweet and spicy, crunchy and soft, and hot and cold elements that make this cuisine so intriguing. Try the cigar-shaped imperial rolls stuffed with ground pork, prawns, and crab; the platter of mint leaves, rice noodles, cilantro, marinated carrots, cucumbers, and spicy fish sauce that get rolled up together in lettuce leaves; or the rosy beef salad accompanied by black sesame seed–studded toasts. The kitchen is particularly adept with beef, whether it be minced and wrapped in edible leaves or skewered and grilled. The quail, flamed tableside in rum sauce, is also a must. And five-spice chicken and such fish as whole steamed sea bass with ginger and cilantro taste vibrant and fresh. In fact, nearly every dish is a winner. The only downside: The service is sometimes inefficient, though it is always gracious. ♦ Vietnamese ♦ Tu-Su lunch and dinner. 2211 Van Ness Ave (between Broadway and Vallejo St). 441.4419; fax 441.4419 ♿

20 Pasha ★$$$ This exotically decked-out oasis transforms an urban setting into a little piece of Morocco, with tented fabric draping from the ceiling, colorful rugs, low wood tables, and deep sofas. To cap it off, a belly dancer undulates by in a swirl of sequins and gauzy material. It seems a bit touristy when the dancer plucks people from their tables to join her, but the food is anything but hokey. The easiest, and most fulfilling, way to go is with the combination dinners (made for sharing), which consist of seven appetizers and four smaller-portioned main courses. Otherwise you might try quail with lime and sage, grilled chicken brochette, or smoky prawns served with basmati rice. ♦ Moroccan/ Middle Eastern ♦ Tu-Su dinner. Reservations recommended. 1516 Broadway (between Polk St and Van Ness Ave). 885.4477; fax 885.4477 ♿

20 Johnny Love's ★$$ John Meheny, with his good looks and 150-watt smile, became so popular as a bartender around town that he developed the nickname Johnny Love. Now he has his own place, and it's a singles' paradise. On weekends, when the live music cranks up at 10PM (it goes on until 2AM), lines wrap around the block. The menu has gone through a lot of changes over the years—from California cuisine to barbecue to pub grub—all with a limited amount of success. Your best bet is to stick to the simple items, like the burger. ♦ Eclectic/American ♦ Daily dinner. 1500 Broadway (at Polk St). 931.6053; fax 931.1712 ♿

¡WA-HA-KA!
OAXACA MEXICAN GRILL

20 WA-HA-KA! (Oaxaca Mexican Grill) ★$ This chic *taquería* has a Russian Hill pedigree but Mission District prices. Specializing in burritos with black beans and brown rice, the restaurant uses no lard and offers several lower-fat options, such as fish tacos and shrimp fajitas. The fresh salsa bar is a plus, and the sangria makes a cool refresher. ♦ Mexican ♦ Daily lunch and dinner. 2141 Polk St (between Broadway and Vallejo St). 775.1055 ♿ Also at: Numerous locations throughout the city

21 The Bagelry One of the oldest and most popular bagel emporiums in the city, it draws customers with its 14 varieties (more on weekends) and a big selection of flavored cream cheeses. ♦ Daily; W until noon. 2134 Polk St (between Broadway and Vallejo St). 441.3003; fax 441.8708 ♿

21 The Real Food Company The premier health food store in San Francisco has a deserved reputation for the best in organic produce at premium prices. There's always a great selection of whatever is in season, along with many hard-to-find and unusual items; excellent fresh fish, meat, and sausages; the city's best selection of dried beans; and all kinds of grains, flours, and specialty products, such as olive oils, natural body moisturizers, and vitamins. The one disadvantage to coming here is that there's no parking lot— just street parking, which can be hard to find in this very busy commercial area. ♦ Daily. 2140 Polk St (between Broadway and Vallejo St). 673.7420; fax 673.1787 ♿ Also at: Numerous locations throughout the city

21 The Real Food Company Deli ★$ Patrons have come to expect a wide selection here of bread from the best bakeries, well-prepared meat and vegetarian dishes, salads, and cheeses. The desserts, however, tend to be uneven. There's seating inside and outside for about 25 altogether. ♦ Deli/Takeout ♦ Daily. 2164 Polk St (between Broadway and Vallejo St). 775.2805; fax 673.1787 ♿ Also at: 1001 Stanyan St (at Carl St), Cole Valley. 564.1117; fax 564.4882 ♿

22 Royal Ground Coffee A branch of the chain started by Ramzi Faraj, this neighborhood stop is most popular on weekend mornings, when the locals gather for pastries and a brew. Like the other locations, this place has a simple, comfortable, and funky ambience. And it's hard to beat the selection of 40 to 50 kinds of beans, which are available either whole or ground to order. ♦ M-F 6:30AM-11PM; Sa-Su 8AM-11PM. 2216 Polk St (between Vallejo and Green Sts). 474.5957. Also at: Numerous locations throughout the city

22 Pure T ★★★$ This one-of-a-kind teahouse/ice-cream parlor observes the philosophy that's printed in bold letters on the wall: "Be Well and Enjoy Life to the Fullest." The stylish, Japanese-inspired interior, in earthy greens and browns, is a great place to do just that. Kick back with a pot of tea and rice wafers, or indulge in a dish of tea-flavored ice cream, which is the only variety served here. Although tea may seem like an unlikely flavor base for ice cream, it creates haunting, sophisticated blends. More than a dozen flavors are on hand, with new ones invented every day. The black currant is a good place to start; then sample the Earl Grey, German fruit, jasmine, and litchi. You can buy teas and pints of ice cream to take home, and unique brewing pots and cups, too. ♦ Teahouse/Ice-cream parlor ♦ Daily 11:30AM-10PM. 2238 Polk St (between Vallejo and Green Sts). 441.7878; fax 441.6878 ♿

23 Mario's Bohemian Cigar Store Cafe ★★$ A 60-seat branch of the original North Beach cafe, this one's decor boasts green wainscoting, yellow walls, and a mahogany bar. The menu is the same as at the North Beach location: grilled chicken, turkey, or meatballs, all served on warm focaccia bread; such main courses as cannelloni and polenta with sausages; and exceptional espresso drinks and fresh pastries. Like its sister, this branch stays open until midnight most evenings except Sunday (when it closes at 11PM). ♦ Italian ♦ Daily lunch and dinner. 2209 Polk St (between Vallejo and Green Sts). 776.8226; fax 776.3388 ♿ Also at: 566 Columbus Ave (at Union St), North Beach. 362.0536

23 Yabbies ★★★$$ Mark Lusardi, who used to run the kitchen at **Vertigo,** has now opened this new Asian-Mediterranean bistro (formerly **Salonika**). Seafood is the specialty here; indeed, the restaurant gets its name from a type of crayfish that is popular in Australia. Starters include oysters on the half shell, rich New England clam chowder, and chilled Dungeness crab salad; main courses range from light pasta dishes (like a combination of wild mushrooms and penne) to heavier entrées. Among the standouts are porcini mushroom–seared seabass served with velvety celery root and spinach; pine-crusted monkfish accompanied by artichokes; and ginger-lemongrass–grilled chicken with dry-fried long beans. The dining room has an inviting ambience, with whitewashed brick walls, warm woods, and tinted cement floors. There's also an oyster and wine bar. ♦ Seafood ♦ Daily dinner (oyster and wine bar: F-Sa to midnight). 2237 Polk St (between Vallejo and Green Sts). 474.4088; fax 474.4962 ♿

23 Wren & Culpeper's Vintages There may be better wine stores in the city, but few are as chic. The walls are covered with art, and the tasting bar is elegantly set with place mats and glasses. Customers can sample three selections, which change regularly, and wine classes and special tasting sessions are given

on occasion. Most of the bottles are from small American wineries. ♦ Tu-Su. 2253 Polk St (between Vallejo and Green Sts). 346.2713; fax 346.2718 ♿

24 Matterhorn Swiss Restaurant ★★$$$ Ignore the garishly lit entry; inside, most of the furnishings were crafted in Switzerland, from the chairs and tables up to the beamed ceiling. Hand-painted glass panes depicting Alpine scenes divide the room into dining alcoves. Chef-owner Andrew Thorpe creates rich fare rooted in classic techniques. Start with corn soup, full of sweet kernels and two light chicken quenelles. Among the main dishes are crisp sautéed halibut, which gets a flavor boost from a thin layer of smoked salmon. Pork tenderloin is wrapped in bacon and topped with an oniony breading. And the julienned veal, presented in a cream sauce with mushrooms, is worth the cholesterol surge. The crème brûlée looks like a mound of whipped cream, but tastes every bit as good as the more familiar version with the caramelized crust. ♦ Swiss ♦ Tu-Su dinner. 2323 Van Ness Ave (between Vallejo and Green Sts). 885.6116; fax 459.1967 ♿

25 Rex Cafe ★$$ Featuring an updated fern-bar look, this place attracts a good crowd after 10PM. Most patrons come for the lively bar scene, but the American-style fare can also be satisfying. ♦ American ♦ M-F dinner; Sa-Su brunch and dinner. 2323 Polk St (between Green and Union Sts). 441.2244; fax 441.2292 ♿

25 Aux Délices ★★$ The room is spare, with booths separated by open-slat partitions, and the Vietnamese food is fresh and light. Fans come for panfried catfish; lemongrass chicken; and crisp, gossamer spring rolls with pungent fish sauce. ♦ Vietnamese ♦ M-Sa lunch and dinner; Su dinner. 2327 Polk St (between Green and Union Sts). 928.4977 ♿

26 La Folie ★★★★$$$$ Without question, this is one of the top Californian/French restaurants in the city. French-born Roland Passot, his American wife, Jamie, and his brother George (the sommelier) have created a dreamy, casually elegant environment in which puffy white clouds dance across the sky-blue ceiling and rich, yellow print fabric hangs from the French windows and frames the doors. A copper hood creates a focal point above the open window to the kitchen, and a bar area and entryway constructed in light colored wood lend the restaurant a finished, polished look. Passot's presentations are breathtaking, and the menu (which changes seasonally) is better than ever. There might be roast quail leg stuffed with foie gras, backed by a lyonnaise salad topped with a poached quail egg; *rôti* (roast) of squab and quail; rack of lamb; or fricasseed lobster. Passot also offers an à la carte menu, a five-course Discovery Menu, and a four-course vegetarian menu. ♦ Californian/French ♦ M-Sa dinner. 2316 Polk St (between Green and Union Sts). 776.5577; fax 776.3431

26 Green World Mercantile Browsers will find a large selection of tea, pottery, cookware, and recycled glassware at this sunny, yellow-washed shop, which specializes in organic and ecologically correct products. A newsletter announces upcoming events and product demonstrations and offers inspiring reading. This place keeps late hours every night—a rarity among stores of this type. ♦ Daily 10AM-10PM. 2340 Polk St (between Green and Union Sts). 771.5717; fax 771.2809 ♿

27 Antica Trattoria ★★$$$ Ruggero Gadaldi, the owner/chef of this casual neighborhood eatery, first made a name for himself at the well-regarded **Etrusca** in Rincon Center. Now he's brought his brand of rustic Italian cooking to Russian Hill. The decor of the 60-seat dining room emphasizes lightness, with wood accents and off-white walls. The menu features excellent, reasonably priced regional specialties such as veal short ribs prepared osso buco–style and *bigoli* (a spelt-wheat spaghetti) with a wild-boar sauce Bolognese. Other lusty choices include duck-filled ravioli with sun-dried tomatoes, pinenuts, and basil; and *Maiale* (grilled pork tenderloin with polenta and gorgonzola); and *tonno brialo* (yellowfin tuna with red wine and capers). ♦ Italian ♦ Tu-Su dinner. 2400 Polk St (at Union St). 928.5797 ♿

28 City Discount In the garage of an old Victorian building, this rambling store offers home and restaurant supplies, including restaurant-quality bowls, whisks, ladles, and some food items. Oddly, a collection of furniture fills the back of the store. There's nothing exotic here, but it's fun and funky. ♦ Daily. 2436 Polk St (between Union and Filbert Sts). 771.4649

29 Zarzuela ★★★$ With its rough wood, stucco, and brick walls, this charming tapas place has a warm, welcoming look. Service is as friendly as you'll find anywhere; mention that you like a dish and the waiter may bring out the chef so you can tell him personally. Among the top hot tapas, lamb tenders are seared to a caramelized crustiness, all the better for the garlic-laced gravy that pools in the bottom of the plate. Scallops are golden outside and still silken inside and surround tender, wilted greens. The shrimp are spiced, cooked, cooled, and drizzled with a tomato-laced mayonnaise. Grilled vegetables, including eggplant and squash, get a boost from the smattering of olive oil and lemon. Big plates are also offered, including several rice dishes, but the tapas are so good we've never ventured beyond them. ♦ Spanish ♦ Daily lunch and dinner. 2000 Hyde St (at Union St). 346.0800

30 Hamada's Kebab-Key ★★$ You could easily miss this unobtrusive little Russian Hill eatery because it looks like just another neighborhood cafe—strictly bare-bones decor and no ambience to speak of. But take the trouble to venture in, and you'll find plenty of delicious Egyptian food. For lunch, try the red lentil soup and a falafel sandwich with fava beans. At dinner, only one entrée is offered—chicken kabobs with a quarter- or full-pound of white or dark meat—but there are no less than 15 side dishes, available à la carte. Among the best of these accompaniments are tangy tabbouleh, *baba ganooj* (grilled eggplant dip), hummus (chickpeas with tahini), cubed potato salad laced with onions and celery, butter-coated basmati rice, and couscous with herbs. The desserts vary in quality, but the coffee cake is a reliable choice. Prices are low, so you can eat a lot of food for very little money. ♦ Egyptian ♦ M-F breakfast, lunch, and dinner; Sa-Su brunch and dinner. 1207 Union St (between Hyde and Larkin Sts). 495.3222

30 Swensen's Ice Cream This is the original parlor, dating to the 1940s, that launched a huge ice-cream corporation. There may be better ice cream these days, but here you can watch the ice-cream maker at work in the front window. (The classic ice creams are made in-house, but the yogurt and fat-free creations are produced in Arizona.) Many people double park in front of the shop just to grab a cone. ♦ Daily till 10PM. 1999 Hyde St (at Union St). 775.6818 &

31 ZA Pizza ★$$ Top-quality ingredients go into these New York–style pizzas, while artsy inclinations are reflected in the picture-lined space and the inventively named pies: Vincent Van Dough (tomato and garlic), Pesto Picasso, and MOMA (mushrooms, onions, marinated artichokes). There's also a selection of fresh, crisp salads. Because the place has only 25 seats, more than half the pizzas made are for carryout; you can also buy slices. In addition, there's **LITTLE ZA,** for take-out pizza by the slice only (at 2162 Polk St, between Broadway and Vallejo St, 563.8515; fax 771.4675 &). ♦ Pizza ♦ ZA Pizza: M-Th dinner; F-Su lunch and dinner. LITTLE ZA: daily lunch and dinner. 1919 Hyde St (between Green and Union Sts). 771.3100; fax 771.4675

31 Frascati Restaurant ★★$$ A popular neighborhood gathering spot, this charming restaurant was purchased recently by Will Dodson and Ruth Schimmelpfennig. Although the new owners have changed the place from Italian to primarily American, they decided not to change the name, which may confuse people for a while. But the food has actually gotten better, particularly the meltingly tender honey-mustard pork chop with pineapple sauerkraut and sweet-potato chips; roast chicken; and walnut-encrusted sea bass. A bit of the old Italian influence remains on the menu, however, in the fusilli served with a grilled salmon fillet, olives, sun-dried tomatoes, and pesto. ♦ Contemporary ♦ Tu-Su dinner. 1901 Hyde St (at Green St). 928.1406; fax 928.1983

32 Café Chaise ★★$$ Owners Rae Dunn—a graphic designer—and Michael Berke transformed this space into a chic "attic" motif, with concrete floors, gold walls, and mismatched chairs. Eva Allard shows what a talented chef

can do with a six-burner stove: She roasts a free-range *poussin* (broiler chicken) to perfection and perches it upon a nest of garlic mashed potatoes and white-corn kernels tossed with nasturtium butter. Grilled tuna is served with a white bean and celery salad and moistened with a lemony anchovy vinaigrette, and the grilled trout is surrounded by a corn and squash hash. The vegetarian onion soup and the beet salad with the surprising addition of juicy watermelon are two great ways to begin the meal, and either the espresso or watermelon granita ensures a perfect ending. ♦ French ♦ Tu-Su dinner. 1556 Hyde St (between Jackson St and Pacific Ave). 775.5556 &

33 Nob Hill Noshery Cafe ★$ Located near the **Powell-Hyde** cable-car line, this deli-style cafe gets lots of tourist traffic. Bagels and coffee are the choice for breakfast, and the substantial sandwiches make a filling lunch. In between, there's a "nosh" menu of lighter tide-me-overs. ♦ Deli ♦ Daily breakfast, lunch, and dinner. 1400 Pacific Ave (at Hyde St). 928.6674

34 Ristorante Milano ★★$$ From the day it first opened in 1985, this Northern Italian restaurant has been building a loyal following. The contemporary decor is a mix of Asian and Italian accents, but the food and service are endearingly European. Top choices are the risottos, skewered chicken livers with grilled endive, and pasta *puttanesca* (a spicy, tomato-based Sicilian specialty). The tiramisù, a creamy classic dessert made with espresso, ladyfingers, and mascarpone cheese, is outstanding. ♦ Northern Italian ♦ Tu-Su dinner. 1448 Pacific Ave (between Hyde and Larkin Sts). 673.2961; fax 826.0448

35 Hyde Street Seafood House and Raw Bar ★$$ This charming, nautically inspired restaurant offers a cozy atmosphere and welcoming service. The best dish served here is the seafood in papillote. ♦ Seafood ♦ Daily dinner. 1509 Hyde St (between Jackson St and Pacific Ave). 928.9148; fax 921.9148

When word of the Gold Rush reached the East Coast and subsequently Europe in the 1850s, restaurateurs and French chefs swarmed to California to cash in on the boom. Although the 49ers had a reputation for being crude, many were educated, sophisticated men who frequented such elegant restaurants as Winn's Fountain Head, where diners enjoyed venison steaks, oysters, and partridge in a setting of Oriental rugs, rosewood chairs, and tables topped with Italian marble.

CHARLES
NOB HILL

36 Charles Nob Hill ★★★$$$ To staff this wonderful restaurant, owner Charles Condy has called on the same talented people who also run **Aqua,** his other outstanding San Francisco establishment. Executive chef Michael Mina has created a memorable dining experience. The tiny room, with bright white walls, gauzy window fabrics, recessed lighting, and slipcovered chairs, seats only 50 people, ensuring an intimate ambience. And almost all the dishes are a delight to behold (and taste), including starters such as pan-roasted Sonoma quail with quince puree; sautéed prawns with a cranberry bean ragout; and artichoke mascarpone agnolotti. Among the main dishes are a breast of squab with veal sweetbreads on a bed of lentils; veal tenderloin with creamed parsnips; and herb-roasted lamb chops with roasted eggplant ravioli. As at **Aqua,** the wine list here is long and carefully crafted to complement the food. ♦ Contemporary ♦ Tu-Sa dinner. Reservations recommended. 1250 Jones St (between Pleasant and Clay Sts). 771.5400; fax 771.3542 ♿

37 Nob Hill Cafe ★★$$ This charming cafe spreads over two storefronts: One room, with the stove wedged in at the front window, accommodates just a few tables; the other has forest green walls, fresh flowers on each table, and a terra-cotta floor. The printed menu emphasizes pasta—generous portions served in large bowls—with a few starters and pizzas to round out the offerings. Try the penne with tomato, cream, and vodka, or a stellar carbonara (cream with bacon). The pizza has a crisp, almost blackened crust and a cheese-and-tomato topping; additional ingredients are available at an extra charge. All main courses, such as fillet of sole or veal piccata, appear as blackboard specials. If it's available, don't miss the wonderful veal stew, which is flavored with fresh bell peppers and contains puffy gnocchi. Chocolate fans will swoon over the dense chocolate ganache, lightened with a generous dollop of whipped cream and served in a parfait glass. Many of the wines are reasonably priced, making this a great place for everyday meals as well as special occasions. ♦ Italian ♦ Daily lunch and dinner. 1152 Taylor St (between Sacramento and Clay Sts). 776.6500; fax 474.2000

38 The Big Four ★★$$$$ Few rooms capture that turn-of-the-century men's club ambience as well as this one, located in the **Huntington** hotel. An oasis of dark paneling, forest green leather, and sparkling beveled-glass windows, it offers a glimpse of what the privileged life must once have been like. It's a great place to have a drink to begin or cap off an evening. Game dishes are a specialty, and so is buffalo—an unusual offering these days and usually one of the main courses. A bar menu offers snacks as well. ♦ French/Californian ♦ M-F breakfast, lunch, and dinner; Sa-Su breakfast and dinner. Reservations recommended. 1075 California St (between Mason and Taylor Sts). 474.5400; fax 474.6227

39 The Fairmont Lobby ★★$$ The opulent lobby of the **Fairmont** hotel, with soaring columns, black walls, red-and-black-patterned carpet, and enough gilt to paint the Golden Gate Bridge, is a grand place to enjoy a cup of tea. Offered every afternoon, the fixed-price tea includes delicate sandwiches, pastries, cookies, and scones, which are served with a little pot of Devonshire cream. ♦ Teahouse ♦ M-Sa 3-6PM; Su 1-6PM. 950 Mason St (between California and Sacramento Sts). 772.5000; fax 837.0587 ♿

39 Tonga Restaurant and Hurricane Bar
$$$ Disneyland meets the South Pacific at this one-of-a-kind restaurant on the terrace level of the **Fairmont;** hourly lightning and thunderstorms are staged here, with water pouring down over a central pool. A waterfall behind the low-lit bar and artificial orchids and other plants evoke the tropics, as do the funky drinks (such as the Bora-Bora Horror, a mixture of rum, banana liqueur, Grand Marnier, and pineapple juice). The nightly hors d'oeuvres (including egg rolls, pot stickers, curried mussels, and barbecued pork loin) are a bargain, but the dinner menu is not well executed. The whole place is campy and can be fun with the right group of friends. ◆ Asian ◆ Daily dinner. 950 Mason St (between California and Sacramento Sts). 772.5278; fax 837.0587 ﬩

MASONS
R E S T A U R A N T

39 Masons Restaurant ★★$$$ One of the most striking rooms in the city, this restaurant on the arcade level of the **Fairmont** has an understated elegance, a beautiful wood ceiling, and deep chairs upholstered in pastel stripes and patterns. Flames from the copper-lined grill in the middle of the room romantically reflect in the leaded glass windows. Chef Katsuo Sugiura has just taken over the kitchen, putting an international spin on the menu. Starters include grilled prawns with a spicy edge, while entrées range from the outstanding five-spice loin of lamb with a garlic–red wine sauce to the too-elaborate pepper-honey-cured salmon over fennel-orange salad. A three-course fixed-price dinner, with choices from the regular menu, is offered before 7PM; it's the best deal here. For dessert, pastry chef Carlos Salazar produces a lovely coconut crème brûlée and a delicious roasted banana tart. ◆ American ◆ Daily dinner. 950 Mason St (between California and Sacramento Sts). 772.5233; fax 837.0587 ﬩

40 Fournou's Ovens ★★$$$ Although the chefs come and go, this restaurant, in the **Stouffer Stanford Court** hotel, remains a popular destination. Its classic European ambience complements a good wine list and some intriguing food combinations created by chef Mathew Dokoupil. Be sure to try the whole roasted portobello mushroom with polenta, or baked lobster strudel with artichoke and baby spinach, dressed with citrus crème fraîche. The oven specialty dishes are consistently good as well, including rack of veal perfumed with rosemary, roast lemon-pepper duck, and

tender rack of lamb with couscous. Pastas are also available in appetizer or entrée size. Vegetable side dishes are à la carte and served family style. One of the best bargains around is the Twilight Supper, served from 5:30PM to 6:30PM, featuring two or three courses. ◆ American ◆ Daily breakfast, lunch, and dinner. Reservations recommended. 905 California St (between Powell and Mason Sts). 989.3500; fax 391.0513 ﬩

41 The Dining Room ★★★$$$$ The restaurant in the **Ritz-Carlton San Francisco** is in transition, having just changed chefs. The new head of the kitchen is Sylvan Portay, who came here after establishing his culinary reputation at Le Cirque in New York. So far, Portay's creations have proved to be a mixed bag: The appetizer of risotto that incorporates a puree of butternut squash and is topped with crisp, rare squab couldn't be more perfect, but the combination of John Dory and sweetbreads relies too much on a sinfully rich, decidedly unfashionable butter sauce. However, the sage-and-pancetta-scented squab breast is succulent, and the accompanying foie gras enhances it splendidly. For dessert, try the soufflé. And the wine and cheese service by sommelier Emmanuel Kemiji and host Nick Peyton remains top-notch. The setting is formal and luxurious, ideal for romance and celebration. ◆ Californian/French ◆ Tu-Sa dinner. Reservations recommended. 600 Stockton St (at Pine St). 296.7465; fax 291.0147 ﬩

41 The Terrace ★★★$$$ This place, also at the **Ritz-Carlton San Francisco,** has an elegant French interior and also the prettiest outdoor dining facility in the city. Protected from the elements on three sides by the 86-year-old Neo-Classical hotel, the formal garden is lined with boxwood, roses, and azaleas and boasts a circular, tiered fountain. The menu juxtaposes Italian, French, and American dishes; lunch specials include classical French onion soup, smoked turkey breast sandwich, a pasta dish, and risotto. Main courses at dinner feature steak, grilled veal chop, sautéed Chilean sea bass, and roasted half chicken. A macrobiotic option for appetizer, main course, and dessert is offered as well. This spot is perfect for a leisurely lunch, accompanied by any of the 15 wines served by the glass. ◆ Italian ◆ Daily breakfast, lunch, and dinner. 600 Stockton St (at Pine St). 296.7465; fax 291.0147 ﬩

41 The Lobby Lounge This bar, on the fourth floor of the **Ritz-Carlton San Francisco,** offers live music, a formal English-style afternoon tea, and a unique sushi service in the evenings. ◆ Tea daily 2:30-4:30PM; sushi M-Sa until 8PM; bar M-Th, Su until midnight; F-Sa until 2AM. 600 Stockton St (at Pine Sts). 296.7465; fax 291.0147 ﬩

with fish, but the grilled salmon in red wine here will surprise you. Such classic desserts as crème brûlée and chocolate mousse are also excellent. ♦ French ♦ M-F lunch and dinner; Sa-Su dinner. 900 Pine St (at Mason St). 474.6070; fax 474.6187

42 Top of the Mark Dating from 1939, this renowned sky-high lounge, which boasts glorious views from its 19th-floor perch in the **Mark Hopkins Inter-Continental San Francisco,** set the standard for those that came later. After a recent remodeling that has enhanced the already-stunning views and removed some outdated disco-era touches, the place is more elegant and upscale than ever. Food is served during afternoon tea on weekdays (from 4-5PM), at the bar, and during the elaborate, expensive Sunday brunch. ♦ M-Th 4PM-1AM; F-Sa 4PM-2AM; Su brunch 10AM-2PM. 1 Nob Hill Cir (off Pine and Mason Sts). 392.3434; fax 421.3302 &

42 Nob Hill Restaurant ★★$$$$ Located in the **Mark Hopkins Inter-Continental San Francisco** and largely patronized by hotel guests, this restaurant serves food with a French accent. The menu changes often and might include consommé of pheasant with poached quail egg and chives, sea bass steamed with fennel and served with a parsnip-caviar mousse and grilled portobello mushrooms, or roast loin of veal with sun-dried–cherry sauce. One of the best deals is a prix-fixe, three-course dinner offered nightly. The interior has a clubby, Old World atmosphere in the tradition of grand-hotel dining. ♦ Californian/French ♦ Daily breakfast, lunch, and dinner. Reservations recommended. 1 Nob Hill Cir (off Pine and Mason Sts). 616.6944; fax 421.3302 &

43 Rue Lepic ★★$$$ This cheerful corner storefront, with an open kitchen carved out of one side of the room, has a lot of charm. Each table in the intimate, 35-seat dining room is set with a silver vase and a pink rose, and the traditional French food can be wonderful. The best deal is the five-course fixed-price menu. Few restaurants can pull off red wine sauces

44 Vanessi's ★$$$ During its glory days in North Beach, this Italian restaurant inspired the open kitchens seen at **Stars** and other places around the city. Unfortunately, after its migration to Nob Hill in 1986, both its food and its atmosphere have suffered. But the dining room, decked out in red upholstered chairs, is still pleasant, with a retro feel, and they still serve great hot zabaglione, a Marsala-laced egg dessert that's made to order and froths over the serving glass. Other specialties are veal chops and pasta. ♦ Italian ♦ M-F lunch and dinner; Sa-Su dinner. Reservations recommended. 1177 California St (between Taylor and Jones Sts). 771.2422; fax 771.7122 &

45 Buffalo Whole Food & Grain Company Started in 1975 by Rob Mitchell, this full-service store packs a lot into its little space. With an emphasis on organically grown foods, the shop has an adequate selection of produce and more than 200 items sold in bulk. The extensive variety of vitamins and supplements seems overwhelming, but the knowledgeable staff is happy to help. ♦ Daily. 1058 Hyde St (between Pine and California Sts). 474.3053 & Also at: 598 Castro St (at 19th St), Castro. 626.7038; fax 626.7511 &

Ever wonder why chefs wear those puffy hats (called toques)? In the days when kings were afraid of being poisoned by their enemies, the chef had to be a trusted member of the court. When he demonstrated his loyalty, he was awarded a "toque blanche," whose pleats represent the vertical bars of the monarch's golden crown.

Pacific Heights/Cow Hollow/
The Marina

Pacific Heights, Cow Hollow, and the Marina are three of the city's most affluent areas. The main business districts run north and south along **Fillmore Street** (in Pacific Heights) and east and west along **Union Street** (in Cow Hollow) and **Chestnut Street** (in the Marina). Pacific Heights, which sits on a hill above the other two neighborhoods, enjoys expansive views of the bay and is studded with mansions that cling to the hillsides and house some of the city's most prominent citizens. Union Street has evolved in recent years from a shopping mecca into a restaurant and bar destination for thirtysomethings. Chestnut Street also exploded with new restaurants and bars in the aftermath of the 1989 earthquake, which hit the Marina area hard; these places tend to

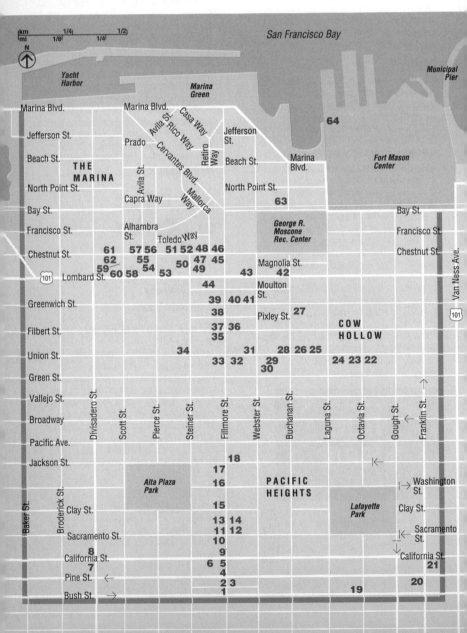

appeal to the postcollegiate singles who moved into the apartments vacated by the many longtime residents who left after the quake.

Only a decade ago, Fillmore Street was known mostly for its secondhand stores; these endure, but have been joined by chic flower shops, design galleries, and pretty cafes. Food lovers will find decadent pyramid cakes at **Le Chantilly,** Southern Italian takeout at **VIVANDE Porta Via,** and more than 200 bargain-priced Champagnes and sparkling wines at **D&M Liquors.** The dining-out options abound too. For example, **Oritalia** offers a creative blend of Asian and Italian fare, and the locals pack into **Via Veneto** and **Jackson Fillmore Trattoria** for Italian specialties, **Alta Plaza Bar and Restaurant** for contemporary California cuisine, **La Méditerranée** for Middle Eastern fare, **Leon's** for barbecue, the **Elite Cafe** for creole food, and **Osome** for Japanese dishes.

Union Street is one of the city's most popular shopping strips, where Victorian houses now serve as the setting for more than 300 boutiques, restaurants, and antiques stores. The area also boasts several fine eateries, with strong leanings to Italian, including **Pane e Vino, Bonta Ristorante,** and **Radicchio. Perry's,** a pioneer of the singles' scene when it opened almost 30 years ago, still draws crowds (including some of the original habitués). **Betelnut** is probably the most inventive restaurant to open on Union Street in some time; the concept—a stylish Asian beer house—was a hit from day one. And **Lhasa Moon** on Lombard Street is the West Coast's first Tibetan eatery.

Farther down Fillmore Street at **Greenwich Street** in Cow Hollow is the infamous "Bermuda Triangle," a cluster of restaurants and bars that is a weekend hub of singles' action. Here are the **Balboa Cafe,** the **City Tavern,** and the popular **Plumpjack Cafe.**

A few blocks farther down the hill, in the Marina, Chestnut Street is a popular hub, especially on Sunday mornings, when people congregate, sitting on the sidewalks and milling about the numerous coffeehouses (including **Peet's Coffee & Tea** and **Starbucks**) that have opened in the last decade. Many of the restaurants, too, appeal to the young, or at least the young at heart. **Cafe Marimba** serves up regional Mexican fare in a colorful, noisy setting; **Sweet Heat** and **Andalé Taqueria** are stylish, healthful *taquerías;* **Babaloo Restaurant** and **Allegria** make the most of the tapas trend; and **Paragon** mixes great cocktails and good food. Other places of interest in the area include **Ace Wasabi's Rock n' Roll Sushi** on **Steiner Street; Lucca Delicatessen,** an attractive Italian deli; and **Wild Oats Community Market,** a natural-foods supermarket that has quickly gained a loyal following.

ZINC details

1 Zinc Details Collections from more than 40 artists and craftspeople, among them 10 glassblowers, make this a great place to find a cutting-edge gift. Browse through the brightly colored frosted vases, delicate porcelain bowls, and wood furniture painted in a rainbow of colors. Fans of art glass probably won't be able to resist treating themselves to something, too. ♦ Daily. 1905 Fillmore St (between Bush and Wilmot Sts). 776.2100; fax 510/841.9700 ♿

1 Leon's Bar-B-Q ★$$ San Francisco may not be a barbecue kind of town, but it has supported Leon McHenry's rib joint for more than 30 years and prompted Leon's expansion to two other locations. All three sport the usual bare-bones backdrop that goes with this down-home fare. The thick red barbecue sauce veers toward the sweet end of the spectrum, but it goes particularly well with the hot links. Aficionados might be disappointed; at times the ribs can taste warmed over. ♦ Barbecue ♦ Daily lunch and dinner. 1911 Fillmore St (between Bush and Wilmot Sts). 922.2436 & Also at: Numerous locations throughout the city

2 Oritalia ★★★$$ Bruce Hill combines Italian and Asian cuisines in one of the few successful fusion restaurants in the city. Try the wonderful portobello mushrooms, sliced and stacked like Lincoln Logs and doused in a fresh plum sauce, or the mixed shrimp, salmon, and calamari served *moo shu* style with whole wheat Mandarin pancakes. On the Western side of the menu, salmon may be wrapped in pancetta and served with white beans and broccoli rabe, or a chicken breast will be accompanied by mashed celery root with artichokes and tarragon. The decor is also a marvelous cross-cultural blend, with Japanese accents, rich wood, and contemporary design combining to stunning effect. ♦ Asian/Italian ♦ Daily dinner. 1915 Fillmore St (between Wilmot and Pine Sts). 346.1333; fax 346.0610 &

Osome

2 Osome ★★$$ Many enthusiasts consider this one of the city's top neighborhood Japanese restaurants. The neutral colors and light wood give it a peaceful, casual feel, and the menu offers more than 40 kinds of sushi and sashimi. One of the most interesting is the *sakekawamaki*, which is grilled salmon skin with green onions. The *shabu shabu*, thin slices of beef, vegetables, and yam noodles cooked table-side in a broth, is a treat here. ♦ Japanese ♦ Daily dinner. 1923 Fillmore St (between Wilmot and Pine Sts). 346.2311

The "Big Four" moguls behind the Central Pacific Railroad—the Ralstons, Crockers, Stanfords, and Hopkins—entertained in lavish style. At one party held at the Palace Hotel in 1876, the banquet hall was decorated with oversize mirrors, flower and fruit arrangements—including a small grove of banana and orange trees—a profusion of candles, and 18 cages filled with songbirds. At each place setting, the menu was engraved upon a plate of solid silver from the Comstock lode.

2 Cedanna This shop specializes in modern home furnishings, mostly by local artists, that almost qualify as folk art. With inventory ranging from rough granite tables to rusted-metal objects, like candleholders and lamps, it is a good place to look for unusual accessories and gifts. ♦ Daily. 1925 Fillmore St (between Wilmot and Pine Sts). 474.7152; fax 726.3834 &

3 Mainline Gifts Among the wares at this trendy gift shop are fashionable place mats, candleholders, and other items for setting an interesting table. ♦ Daily. 1928 Fillmore St (at Wilmot St). 563.4438; fax 563.7528

3 Johnny Rockets ★$ The burgers are actually quite good at this 1950s-theme chain. This branch boasts large windows overlooking the street, plus a sunny patio n back; the shiny tile, polished chrome, and long counter give it all a well-scrubbed appeal. The burgers are served in old-fashioned paper wrappers, and the helpful waiters, decked out in traditional pointed caps, are so accommodating they even pour the ketchup for you. ♦ American/Hamburgers ♦ Daily lunch and dinner; F-Sa until 2AM. 1946 Fillmore St (at Pine St). 776.9878; fax 776.1189 & Also at: 81 Jefferson St (between Powell and Mason Sts), Fisherman's Wharf. 693.9120; fax 693.9404 &

4 Rory's Twisted Scoop As if the ice cream alone were not indulgence enough, the specialty here is add-ins, which include chunks of Reese's Peanut Butter Cups, M&Ms, and nuts. This is the shop's original location (there is also a Noe Valley store) and is where the ice cream for both units is produced. The shop also makes its own waffle cones and features several nonfat yogurts, including banana peanut butter and Ghirardelli chocolate. ♦ Daily 11AM-11PM; F-Sa until midnight. No credit cards accepted. 2015 Fillmore St (between Pine and California Sts). 346.3692. Also at: 4101 24th St (at Castro St), Noe Valley. 648.2837 &

5 The Straw, The Jar and The Bean "An environmental natural-food store" is how the owners bill this small, trendy shop, which features an excellent selection of high-quality products from specialty growers and manufacturers. An array of grains, seeds, and beans is sold in bulk; there's also a line of medicinal herbs, vitamins, and skin-care products. A flyer explains the effort that went into making the store environmentally friendly. For example, the galvanized sheet metal used in the construction was not hot-dipped (which would release toxic fumes), the stones for the counters were salvaged, and the woods used were from such fast-growing trees as birch. ♦ Daily. 2047 Fillmore St (between Pine and California Sts). 922.3811; fax 922.0407 ♿

5 Elite Cafe ★★$$ One of the few New Orleans–style restaurants in the city, it dishes up authentic Cajun and Creole fare. You'll find great-tasting raw oysters, seafood chowder, soft-shell crabs, baby back ribs, and pecan pie. The dark wood appointments, oyster bar in the window, and tall booths along the wall give the place a clubby ambience. Most of the time the service is professional and friendly, although occasionally, when they're jammed, it can be a bit curt. ♦ Creole/Cajun ♦ M-Sa dinner; Su brunch and dinner. 2049 Fillmore St (between Pine and California Sts). 346.8668; fax 346.9324 ♿

6 Grand Central Market Several independent purveyors sell under one roof at this grocery store, a combination that ensures personal service as well as the convenience of a one-stop supermarket. The produce isn't the best in town (that honor goes to **The Real Food Company** stores), but it's better than at many chain markets. The bakery is fairly standard, although it carries a good selection of breads from the best Bay Area producers. Excellent sandwiches and take-out food can be found at the deli area, and the meat market, one of the few remaining independents in the city, is a top draw with its wonderful beef, organic chicken, lamb, sausage, and fish. And the staff will capably roll a crown roast or butterfly a leg of lamb on request. ♦ Daily. 2435 California St (between Fillmore and Steiner Sts). 567.4902; fax 567.3215 ♿

7 Rasselas ★★$$ The city's best Ethiopian restaurant has the added attraction of nightly jazz performances. The comfortable dining room's high ceilings have been draped with swags of canvas to create an intimate, tentlike atmosphere, and the music spilling over from the bar area makes for a pleasant evening. The food mainly consists of stews, scooped up with a spongy bread called *injera,* which looks like a folded napkin. Main courses include fiery morsels of chicken topped with eggs, and tender cubes of beef in a thick, spicy sauce. Vegetarian entrées abound, one of the best being red and yellow lentils with greens, flavored with ginger and garlic. ♦ Ethiopian ♦ Two-drink minimum (if you come only for the music). Daily dinner. 2801 California St (at Divisadero St). 567.5010 ♿

8 Food Inc. ★★$ Terrific carry-out food and specialty products can be found at this charming storefront cafe with large windows. Homemade scones, pastries, and plum cakes are offered for breakfast, along with egg dishes and waffles. Lunchtime sandwiches include pear and brie, smoked salmon with cucumber, and Mediterranean chicken with olives and asparagus. There are homemade soups and salads, including Caesar, pasta, or warm goat cheese with mixed greens. Hot specials, available for eating in or out, might be stuffed peppers or eggplant parmigiana. ♦ Cafe/Takeout ♦ M-Sa 9AM-9PM; Su 9AM-3PM. 2800 California St (at Divisadero St). 928.3728; fax 928.0494 ♿

9 Le Chantilly Yellow walls and white-and-gold French provincial appointments lend elegance to this exclusive chocolate and pastry shop. Noteworthy delectables include impressive pyramid cakes made with Valhrona chocolate, and Ipanema cake layered with Cointreau and bitter chocolate mousse. More than a dozen kinds of truffles are sold, flavored with the likes of caramel and Cognac or white chocolate and mint. ♦ Daily. 2119 Fillmore St (between California and Sacramento Sts). 441.1500; fax 441.1380

9 VIVANDE Porta Via ★★★$$ Owner/chef Carlo Middione has gained national attention through his popular cookbooks and cooking show, and with good reason: He makes the best pasta in the city, as well as some marvelous desserts. His bustling trattoria specializes in Southern Italian fare; it also houses a deli that showcases prepared foods and high-quality specialty products to take out. (Customers can also sit at the counter and be served lunch.) Dining is a casual affair at tables that are arranged along a rough brick wall decorated with scores of ceramic pig heads. All the dishes are simply prepared and rich in flavor: Lamb chops are pounded flat and lightly sautéed; risotto is enhanced with lemon. For takeout, there's an impressive selection of Italian cheeses, such salads as white beans with caviar, and entrées that have saved many last-minute dinner parties. ♦ Italian/Takeout ♦ Daily lunch and dinner; deli, daily lunch; takeout 11:30AM-10PM. 2125 Fillmore St (between California and Sacramento Sts). 346.4430; fax 346.2877

10 Fillamento If it's new and different, you will find it first at this oh-so-chic furniture/accessory shop. Its three floors are filled with designer furniture, cutting-edge ceramics, and trend-setting glassware from some 2,000 vendors, of which more than 200 are local artisans. Owner Iris Fuller changes the merchandise so often that shoppers who want to keep up to date should drop by at least once a month. ♦ Daily. 2185 Fillmore St (between California and Sacramento Sts). 931.2224; fax 931.6304

11 R.H. This stylish shop's beautifully selected array of pottery and accessories for the home and garden includes herb topiary trees (English myrtle, lavender) and interesting table settings. ♦ Daily. 2506 Sacramento St (between Fillmore and Steiner Sts). 346.1460

11 Tea & Company This market/cafe offers an updated take on tea. There's brewed tea to sip (and seating for 25 sippers), bulk teas to buy, chocolates and jams to accompany your tea service, and—talk about being immersed in a subject!—even tea soaps. ♦ Daily 8AM-10:30PM; F-Sa until 11PM. 2207 Fillmore St (between Sacramento and Clay Sts). 929.TEAS; fax 929.8385 ♦

12 D&M Liquors The owners of this extraordinary wine shop claim to have the widest selection of Champagne outside France, and experience tells us they're probably right. They stock about 200 Champagnes, including 10 to 15 vintages of Dom Pérignon. What's more, the prices are better than at most other shops. And long before the single-malt scotch craze, this store carried about 150 selections. Other finds include vintage Calvados from as far back as 1955 and Armagnac dating to 1932. ♦ Daily. 2200 Fillmore St (at Sacramento St). 346.1325; fax 346.1812 ♦

12 La Méditerranée ★★$ Rock-bottom prices have helped this Middle Eastern eatery maintain a loyal following since it opened in 1979; the entrées even come with salad or a cup of soup. Start with the wonderful, lemony hummus, then try the ground lamb kebabs or the chicken drumsticks marinated and baked in pomegranate juice. The long, narrow restaurant can feel a little cramped, but the food is good, the service convivial. ♦ Mediterranean ♦ M-Sa lunch and dinner. 2210 Fillmore St (between Sacramento and Clay Sts). 921.2956 ♦ Also at: 288 Noe St (at Market St), Castro. 431.7210 ♦

13 Ten Ichi ★★$$ This venerable Japanese restaurant provides a simple, modern setting for its creative food, with blush-colored sponge-painted walls, polished wood accents, and an L-shaped sushi bar. The staff has fun naming the *maki* (rice and seafood wrapped in seaweed) rolls: There's Jurassic Park, with crab and vegetables; ELT (barbecued eel, lettuce, tomatoes, and avocado); and rainbow rolls, with five kinds of fish. Purists may sneer at some of the combinations, but if you're not overly serious about sushi, this place is fun. Try the golden, crisp tempura, the subtly sweet and never cloying teriyaki, or the sukiyaki, whose tasty broth contains chewy *udon* (white) noodles as well as the traditional glass noodles, chunks of button mushrooms, and still-crunchy scallions. Particularly friendly service enhances the meal. ♦ Japanese/Sushi ♦ M-F lunch and dinner; Sa-Su dinner. 2235 Fillmore St (between Sacramento and Clay Sts). 346.3477; fax 346.1816 ♦

14 Via Veneto ★★$$ With butter-colored walls painted with a harlequin pattern, plus a lively open kitchen, this Italian restaurant is chic and appealing. The 10 pastas on the menu—all good—are sauced sparingly, the way it's done in Italy. The fiery *penne puttanesca,* pungent with olives and anchovy, is our top choice. Also try the grilled chicken breast brushed with olive oil and served on a bed of spinach, or the classic veal with white wine, lemon butter, and capers. The tiramisù is an excellent way to end the meal. ♦ Italian ♦ M-Sa lunch and dinner; Su dinner. 2244

Fillmore St (between Sacramento and Clay Sts). 346.9211; fax 346.6948 &

15 Alta Plaza Bar and Restaurant ★★$$ Few restaurants rise from the ashes, but this one came back better than ever. After three years as the **Fillmore Grill** singles' bar, it was reborn under its original name; it now attracts a neighborhood crowd for early dining, followed by gay night owls. The bar is a popular gathering place until the wee hours. The decor has been spruced up with white-painted walls, and an open mezzanine overlooks the bar action. Chef Amey Shaw has created a solid, Italian-inspired menu. Best bets include an excellent Caesar salad; sautéed mushrooms; roast chicken with garlic mashed potatoes and broccoli rabe; and barbecued flank steak with a sweet-and-spicy sauce and fiery black beans. ◆ Californian ◆ M-Sa dinner; Su brunch and dinner; bar until 2AM. 2301 Fillmore St (at Clay St). 922.1444; fax 922.1767

16 Pauli's Cafe ★$$ With large windows overlooking Fillmore Street, this corner cafe is at its best for breakfast. The menu features omelettes with myriad fillings and buttermilk pancakes with real maple syrup. At dinner it's a come-as-you-are kind of place; for the same price you can find more stylish surroundings and better food elsewhere on Fillmore Street. ◆ Californian ◆ Daily breakfast, lunch, and dinner. 2500 Washington St (at Fillmore St). 921.5159

juicy NEWS

17 Juicy News A newsstand/juice bar, it carries many hard-to-find foreign food magazines, frozen yogurt, and freshly blended fruit concoctions. ◆ Daily. 2453 Fillmore St (between Washington and Jackson Sts). 441.3051 &

18 Jackson Fillmore Trattoria ★★★$$ Although this place is homey and unassuming, it serves top-notch Italian food and caters to the affluent Pacific Heights crowd. There's almost always a wait, especially for tables; many customers choose to sit at the diner-style counter overlooking the antipasto selections. Few appetizers can be better than the grilled portobello mushrooms: Roughly the size of a saucer, they are sliced, drizzled with olive oil, sprinkled with herbs and garlic, and arranged on a bed of peppery arugula. The gnocchi, occasionally on the menu, are as light as a feather and worth an hour's wait.

Sure bets among the entrées are such braised dishes as the woodsman-style chicken with sausage, mushrooms, and beans. End the meal with hot zabaglione, a frothy mixture of Marsala and eggs that practically spills over the wineglass in which it's served. ◆ Italian ◆ Daily dinner. Reservations accepted for three or more people. 2506 Fillmore St (between Jackson St and Pacific Ave). 346.5288

19 The Meetinghouse ★★★$$ Joanna Karlinsky and John Bryant Snell have created a charming eatery with Shaker-style decor, sunny yellow walls, and an American-centered menu. Appetizers include a crisp flatbread with caramelized onions, fingerling potatoes, sage, and sheep's milk ricotta; oyster stew with celery root and fennel; and potted rabbit with cranberry conserve. There are such delightful entrées as braised pork with juniper, and pan-roasted chicken with wild mushroom *jus*, savory bread pudding, and winter greens. But save room for the terrific desserts; it's hard to choose a favorite among the luscious Meyer lemon meringue pie, caramelized banana cream tart with dark rum sauce, and the chilled coconut-and-guava soup with pineapple sorbet. ◆ American ◆ W-Su dinner. 1701 Octavia St (at Bush St). 922.6733; fax 661.8565

20 Gourmet Carousel ★★$ In a neighborhood bereft of Chinese restaurants, this one is a nice surprise—and a bargain. A dinner for six featuring eight dishes even includes the 7-UP on the table. Be sure to try the pot stickers, crystal prawns (large shrimp stir-fried with vegetables), and pork with eggplant. Fearless eaters can opt for pork bellies in a clay pot, deep-fried intestines, crabmeat and fish-stomach soup, or pigskin with rice noodles. The pleasant room has a clean, simple look, with black metal chairs and white-clothed tables. ◆ Chinese ◆ Tu-Su dinner. 1559 Franklin St (between Bush and Pine Sts). 771.2044

21 Whole Foods Market With stores in Mill Valley, Berkeley, and throughout the Monterey Peninsula, this chain of natural-food markets has spread like wildfire through northern California, and now it's come to San Francisco. The market carries only the highest quality meats and produce—no artificial flavors, colors, preservatives, hormones, or other unnatural processes here. The first thing you see upon entering is a massive display of beautiful, fresh fruits and vegetables; there are also meats, bulk foods, a bakery, body care products, and the **Whole Foods Cafe,** where you can get noodle and grain dishes, sand-wiches, poultry cooked on a rotisserie, and fresh juices and coffee drinks. ◆ Daily. 1765 California St (between Van Ness Ave and Franklin St). 674.0500; fax 674.0505 &

Anchovies, Please

One of the most popular appetizers served at the **Betelnut** restaurant (2030 Union St between Buchanan and Webster Sts, 929.8855; fax 929.8894 &) in **Cow Hollow** is sun-dried anchovies with peanuts and chilies. Here's the recipe:

SUN-DRIED ANCHOVIES

1 cup sun-dried anchovies (found in Chinese or Vietnamese grocery stores under the name "ikan bilis," "ikan teri," or "kung yue")

1 cup roasted, skinless peanuts

1 cup green onion (white part, sliced)

1 tablespoon garlic, chopped

1 tablespoon hot red serrano chilies, chopped

Salt and white pepper to taste

Oil for deep-frying

Fry anchovies in medium hot, deep oil for one minute, until crisp. Pat dry on paper towels. Lightly oil a wok or sauté pan and add all the ingredients. Stir fry for 30 seconds until fragrant.

Serves four.

22 Sushi Chardonnay ★$$ It doesn't look like much—the well-worn interior is crowned by an industrial-style ceiling crisscrossed by pipes—but this Japanese restaurant has earned a reputation for its sushi buffet. It's an all-you-can-eat extravaganza, with 28 sushi and several tempura choices for a flat, per-person price. Just don't let your eyes get bigger than your stomach, because you'll be charged $1 for each piece left uneaten on your plate. ♦ Japanese ♦ M-F lunch and dinner; Sa-Su dinner. 1785 Union St (between Gough and Octavia Sts). 346.5070; fax 346.0581 &

23 Radicchio ★★$$ A generous spirit permeates this 50-seat Italian eatery that uses—you guessed it—radicchio in many dishes. The bitter purple lettuce makes a great wrapper for scallops and brings Caesar salad up to date. The kitchen is particularly proud of its black-and-white *tagliolini*, thin noodles made with squid ink and served with a saffron-infused sauce and a generous scattering of rock shrimp. Our favorite, however, is the penne with tomatoes, fresh artichokes, garlic, and herbs. For the meat course, try the flank steak served over mushrooms, or the New Zealand lamb chops. The tile floor in back and the mirrors that reflect the wine racks against one wall give the room an intimate feel. Owners Verniero Monti and Giacomo Ciabattini do wonders in the front of the house and with the food.♦ Italian ♦ Tu-Su dinner. 1809 Union St (between Octavia and Laguna Sts). 346.7373; fax 346.7374

24 Starbucks Coffee ★$ The Seattle-based chain, with more than 600 coffee bars across the country, entered the San Francisco market with a vengeance at this location back in 1992. Since then, its shops have been moving into just about every neighborhood and competing with the other major players. **Starbucks** blend, somewhat milder than most, is made from Central American coffee beans. Recently, this location of **Starbucks** has added a menu of sandwiches such as chicken on foccacia, turkey on seven-grain bread, and vegetarian. Gourmet they're not, but they provide a good accompaniment to the brew. ♦ Coffee/Sandwiches ♦ Daily lunch. 1899 Union St (at Laguna St). 921.4049 & Also at: Numerous locations throughout the city

25 Bepples Pies Thick-crusted pies beckon passersby from an open window overlooking the kitchen, which turns out all kinds of deep-dish pies—fruit, cream, and savory. The hearty savory pies, which are dense with chicken, herbs, carrots, peas, and other vegetables and crowned with a golden crust, make a great, quick meal at home; just heat them up and dig in. But be sure to ask for whatever is the freshest; at times, some of the pies can taste a tad old. Eat-in meals, including salad and soup, also are available at the Chestnut Street branch. ♦ Daily until midnight. No credit cards accepted. 1934 Union St (between Laguna and Buchanan Sts). 931.6225 & Also at: 2142 Chestnut St (between Steiner and Pierce Sts). 391.6226

25 Perry's ★★$$ Perry Butler escaped from Manhattan back in 1969, bringing with him the idea for this typical Upper East Side New York saloon. Originally popular as a singles' place, it has retained a fiercely loyal clientele over the years, but now the old regulars bring their kids. A smattering of singles can still be found at the traditional bar, which is reminiscent of the 1970s. Offerings include veal chops, steaks, calves' liver, *ahi* tuna, and such bar favorites as chicken fajitas, quesadillas, and excellent burgers and fries. ♦ American ♦ M-F breakfast, lunch, and dinner; Sa-Su brunch and dinner. 1944 Union St (between Laguna and Buchanan Sts). 922.9022. Also at: 185 Sutter St (between Montgomery and Kearny Sts), Union Square. 989.6895; fax 433.4409 ♿

26 WA-HA-KA! (Oaxaca Mexican Grill) ★$ This is the third branch of a *taquería* chain specializing in good, healthful Mexican fare, made without lard. Start with the fresh chips served with a delicious roasted tomato salsa. In the Northern Californian style, the burritos are stuffed to bursting with meat, beans, cheese, shredded lettuce, and rice. Also offered are quesadillas and tasty grilled meats. ♦ Mexican ♦ Daily lunch and dinner. 1980 Union St (between Laguna and Buchanan Sts). 775.4145 ♿ Also at: Numerous locations throughout the city

27 The Brazen Head Restaurant ★★$$ There's no sign to mark the entrance of this quaint place nestled in a residential area, and that is part of its mystique and charm. Inside, low, low lighting sets the stage for romance, with candles and flowers on each wooden table to enhance the mood. The classic food is all well prepared, including the onion soup and the garlicky Caesar salad. The melt-in-your-mouth tender filet mignon is accented with sautéed mushrooms and scalloped potatoes. Chicken breast is crusted with pepper and sautéed in a pungent brandy sauce. This place is popular with chefs and waiters. ♦ Continental ♦ Daily dinner until 1AM. No credit cards accepted. 3166 Buchanan St (at Greenwich St). 921.7600; fax 921.0164

28 Betelnut ★★★$$ George Chen has collaborated with Cecilia Chiang, the former owner of the **Mandarin,** and the Real Restaurant folks (they own **Fog City Diner**) to make this the restaurant of the moment. Thanks to the raves of local diners and reviewers, it's almost impossible to get in. The pan-Asian menu (chef Barney Brown is half Korean) includes delicious Singapore chili crab, spicy coconut chicken from Thailand, and a wonderful appetizer of sun-dried anchovies, peanuts, and chili from Taipei. All the food goes well with the Asian and American brews on tap and in bottles. The bar at the front has a somewhat mysterious air, with large, unusual looking ceiling fans, paintings of sensuous Asian beauties, and the sense that Peter Lorre or Sidney Greenstreet is about to be seated. ♦ Pan-Asian ♦ Daily lunch and dinner. Reservations recommended. 2030 Union St (between Buchanan and Webster Sts). 929.8855; fax 929.8894 ♿

28 Cafe de Paris L'Entrecôte
▲$$ The best features of this brasserie are the glassed-in patio built around a tree that overlooks Union Street, and the delicious hangar steak with crispy french fries and a wonderful sauce. The balance of the menu is just so-so, however. Still, the setting is bright and sunny during the day, glittering and romantic at night. ♦ French/Californian ♦ Daily lunch and dinner. 2032 Union St (between Buchanan and Webster Sts). 931.5006; fax 931.5383 ♿

29 Amici's East Coast Pizza ★$ The aroma of fresh-baked pizza filling this roomy place should be enough to convince you to stick with pizza and salad here. The pies have a medium-thick crust that's crisp enough to stand up to whatever toppings you concoct. Free delivery makes this one of the best take-out choices in town. ♦ Pizzeria ♦ Daily lunch and dinner; F-Sa until 1AM. 2033 Union St (between Buchanan and Webster Sts). 885.4500; fax 885.0152 ♿

29 Z-Gallerie Wonderful glasses and plates made by area artisans can be found at this poster-and-frame shop, which also carries trendy furniture and all kinds of decorative accessories. ♦ Daily. 2071 Union St (between Buchanan and Webster Sts). 346.9000 ♿

WRITER'S BOOKSTORE

30 Writer's Bookstore Here's where cookbook collectors from all over the Bay Area come to find great deals on current releases. Its selection and prices outclass the much-hyped chains. ♦ Daily. 2848 Webster St (between Green and Union Sts). 921.2620

Yoshida-ya

31 Yoshida-Ya ★★$$ One of only a handful of yakitori bars in the city, it is set in an expansive room with tasteful appointments. The extensive menu also offers tempura, sushi, and more, but the yakitori dishes—skewered and grilled combinations—are the best. Highlights include mushrooms stuffed with ground chicken; beef with pungent Japanese mustard; marinated shiitake mushrooms; and Japanese eggplant with ginger. ♦ Japanese ♦ Daily dinner. 2909 Webster St (between Union and Filbert Sts). 346.3431; fax 346.0907 &

31 Gordon Bennett A potpourri of accessories for the home and garden is featured at this delightful shop, including casual tabletop and kitchen wares, a small selection of first-rate packaged food, rusty garden sculptures, and seeds and bulbs. ♦ Daily. 2102 Union St (at Webster St). 929.1172; fax 929.7525 &

31 Terra Mia Ceramic Studios This shop is terrific for artistically inclined people who want to create personalized pottery. In stock here are hundreds of bowls, cups, teapots, plates, wine goblets, and other tableware, all unadorned. Once you have bought an item, you then can rent studio time so you can paint and decorate it. After that, the store fires your piece in their kiln for you to pick up a week later. If you need inspiration, there are books and stencils available, and the staff is very helpful. ♦ Daily. 2122 Union St (between Webster and Fillmore Sts). 351.2529; fax 921.6419. Also at: 4037 24th St (between Noe and Castro Sts), Noe Valley. 642.9911; fax 642.9922 &

31 Left at Albuquerque ★★$ The first San Francisco link in a popular California chain of Southwestern eateries, this place got its name from Bugs Bunny's frequent lament, "I knew I should've taken that left at Albuquerque." Owners Duke Rohlen and Maurice Werdegar have created a lively joint that has become an instant hit with the post-collegiate (but still young) crowd that hangs out on Union Street. The "calendar of salsas"—with a different one featured each day—and 101 varieties of tequila may have had something to do with that. The lineup of beverages also includes margaritas, sangria, and beers. Among the top menu choices are chicken or beef fajitas served with vegetables, salsa, guacamole, cheese, tortillas, and sour cream; brochette of grilled prawns and vegetables on corn mash with chipotle butter; burritos; and enchiladas. ♦ Southwestern ♦ Daily lunch and dinner (to 2AM). 2140 Union St (between Webster and Fillmore Sts). 775.7930 &

32 Union Street Coffee Roastery It may strike some as pretentious, but the bespectacled college-student types sitting on bags of coffee beans for hours while they pore over their Proust give this cafe a distinct personality. We think it makes a perfect retreat on a rainy or wintry day. The coffee is well balanced and strong; the pastries and light snacks are standard issue, but filling. Sit on the bench outside to sip your brew and people watch. The coffee served here is roasted at the **Chestnut Street Roastery,** which is also a cafe (2331 Chestnut St, between Scott and Divisadero Sts, 931.5282). ♦ Daily. 2191 Union St (at Fillmore St). 922.9559

33 Doidge's ★★$ Although it's a little frayed around the edges, this home-style cafe is a veritable breakfast institution; it draws throngs, especially on weekends. Choose from more than a dozen omelettes, including one filled with an unusual peach-walnut chutney, and 10 kinds of toast. The eggs Benedict are beautifully done, and the French toast and homemade scones also win raves. ♦ American ♦ Daily breakfast. Reservations recommended. 2217 Union St (between Fillmore and Steiner Sts). 921.2149

33 Bonta Ristorante ★★★$$ The flower boxes under the windows add a cheerful, European-style welcome to this always-crowded Italian restaurant. The tables are a bit close together, but that just contributes to the friendly, party atmosphere. An excellent starter is the smoked buffalo mozzarella, baked and crowned with sautéed mushrooms. Also try the ravioli stuffed with sea bass, ricotta, and spinach and covered with a creamy tomato sauce; the angel-hair pasta tossed with scallops and fresh tomatoes; or the marvelous beef fillet topped with bitter radicchio and soothed with a balsamic-vinegar sauce. For dessert, don't miss the warm pear crisp with hazelnut gelato. ♦ Italian ♦ Tu-Su dinner. Reservations recommended. 2223 Union St (between Fillmore and Steiner Sts). 929.0407

34 Pane e Vino ★★$$ The intimate dining room of this top-notch trattoria is dominated by a long, narrow table displaying a prosciutto ham, decorative vegetables, and parmesan cheese. The homey environment, the fresh aromas that greet you as you enter, the simply prepared but robust food, and the convivial spirit all evoke the best of Italy. This spot is so popular that even those with reservations may have to wait to be seated, but the food is worth it. All the pastas are superb, and if they're on the menu, try the braised rabbit (or any other long-simmered meat) or the whole roasted fish. ♦ Italian ♦ M-Sa lunch and dinner; Su dinner. Reservations recommended. 3011 Steiner St (between Union and Filbert Sts). 346.2111; fax 346.0741 ♿

35 **La Canasta** ★$ This is a good place to grab a quick bite, Mexican style, in a neighborhood that seems to host nothing but Italian eateries. The only seating is on a bench outside, but the food is so tasty that fans don't mind sitting there and trying to balance their *chalupas* (tortillas layered with beans, meat, cheese, and guacamole), burritos, and tamales—and inevitably splattering their clothes. (If you'd prefer eating at a set table, delivery is available for dinner.) The *chiles verdes* burrito with pork and the *tortas* (Mexican sandwiches made with crisp-crusted, nutty-tasting rolls) are outstanding. ♦ Mexican ♦ M-Sa lunch and dinner. No credit cards accepted. 2219 Filbert St (between Fillmore and Steiner Sts). 921.3003; fax 202.8582 ♿ Also at: 3006 Buchanan St (between Union and Filbert Sts). 474.2627; fax 202.8582

BREWCITY
PERSONAL BREWERY

36 **Brew City Personal Brewery** Here, at the city's first do-it-yourself brewery, customers choose a beer from about 40 recipes, then the trained staff guides them through the two-hour brewing process. The result is 13.5 gallons of beer, which must be cold fermented on-site for several weeks, when customers return to bottle it (bottles and personalized labels are included). The whole tab comes to a little more than $100, or less than $5 for the equivalent of a six pack. The smell of hops permeates the warehouse-size room, which is dominated by six copper tanks and a self-bottling line. No beer is served on premises, but customers can taste their own brew during the process. It makes a terrific personalized gift for your favorite "hop head." ♦ Tu-Su 3-8PM. Appointments recommended one week in advance. 2198 Filbert St (at Fillmore St). 929.2255; fax 929.2256 ♿

37 **PlumpJack Cafe** ★★$$ One of the city's most popular restaurants, this place has a celebrity pedigree: It was launched by Andrew and Billy Getty (sons of billionaire Gordon Getty) and Gavin Newsom (whose father, Bill, is a retired judge). The taupe–and–green-gray color scheme is appealing, as are all the subtle design details: A metal screen in front of the window enmeshes the traffic outside in a soft-focus artistic haze; a gold yin-yang–like fixture hovers over the center of the room, its oval shape repeated on the waiters' vests and on the buttons of the tufted banquettes. But the room can get noisy when it's packed, thanks to the many hard, uncushioned surfaces. Chef Maria Helm makes some terrific appetizers, including *bruschetta* topped with roasted beets, baby lettuces, goat cheese, and roasted garlic; gravlax with blini on the side; and a salad made from lettuce, gorgonzola, beets, and walnuts. The wine list offers some of the best bargains in the city: Its wines are priced at retail cost, without the premium usually paid in restaurants. But the entrées are sometimes overseasoned with salt and rosemary. ♦ Californian/Mediterranean ♦ M-F lunch and dinner; Sa dinner. Reservations recommended. 3127 Fillmore St (between Filbert and Pixley Sts). 346.9870; fax 346.9879 ♿

38 **Balboa Cafe** ★$$ Billy Getty and Gavin Newsom of **PlumpJack Cafe** (see above) recently bought this venerable bar and American eatery and gave it a beautiful face-lift. The society crowd and their kids are returning to rub shoulders, grab a bite, and down a few. The burger is terrific, but make sure you get it on a hamburger bun—trying to eat one served on a baguette will run up your cleaning bill. ♦ American ♦ Daily lunch and dinner. 3199 Fillmore St (at Greenwich St). 921.3944; fax 346.9879

39 **PlumpJack Wines** A companion to **PlumpJack Cafe**, this handsome wine store has become one of the city's best. The selection of boutique Californian wines is phenomenal, and all are elegantly displayed in surroundings worthy of the carriage trade—but at terrific prices. This is where you'll find wines you've never heard of, or small-vineyard wines that are distributed to the select few; because of the Getty-Newsom connection, all the wine makers want to showcase their wares here. ♦ Daily. 3201 Fillmore St (at Greenwich St). 346.9870; fax 346.9879 ♿

40 **City Tavern** ★$$ This eatery replaced the **Golden Gate Grill,** a singles' place known as much for its donnybrooks as its fare. The tone is more sedate now, and after a shaky opening, they've settled down a bit. Your best bet is to select a burger and a brew. Happy hour is a real bargain. ♦ American ♦ Daily

dinner. 3200 Fillmore St (at Greenwich St). 567.0918 &

40 Holey Bagel Here's a bagel to delight the most discriminating aficionado. The bagels are simmered in water, then baked to create a dense, chewy texture. The number of varieties now totals 18, with more than a dozen schmears. The shop also features such specialties as *rugalach* (filled crescent-shaped cookies), muffins, and croissants. And there's an espresso bar, a New York–style deli, and full-service catering. This bagelry has been in business since 1979 and has expanded to eight branches around the Bay Area. ♦ Daily. 3218 Fillmore St (between Greenwich and Moulton Sts). 922.1955; fax 626.2453 & Also at: Numerous locations throughout the city

41 Cassis Bistro ★★★$$ The neighborhood has embraced this sunny little bistro. It has cheerful blue-and-white striped banquettes, a copper-fronted bar that makes a pleasant place to wait for a table, and chef Erik Leroux's comforting bistro fare. There's an addictive individual onion tart, as well as warm sausage embedded in a slice of rosemary toast and paired with a veal sauce. Entrées include a toothsome spinach ravioli in a garlicky tomato sauce, several fish dishes, and a tender chicken breast. If it's offered, don't pass up the *tarte tatin;* it's one of the best in the city. The staff is very friendly and the whole experience is restorative. ♦ French ♦ Tu-Sa dinner. 2120 Greenwich St (between Webster and Fillmore Sts). 292.0770

41 North India Restaurant ★$$ Once considered the best Indian restaurant in the city, this place has lost some of its luster. The fixed-price meals are the best choice; they include many of the tastiest dishes (such as the chicken tandoori and chicken tikka), as well as all of the flavorful accompaniments (such as carrot chutney, basmati rice, and dals). Everything, including the breads, is made to order; glass windows offer glimpses of the chefs toiling in the pristine kitchen. The room, done in burgundy and pink, with rich, rose-colored wood, makes a comfortable (if a bit tired and outdated) backdrop for the food. One caveat: Service can be slow at some times and pushy at others. ♦ Indian ♦ M-F lunch and dinner; Sa-Su dinner. 3131 Webster St (between Greenwich and Moulton Sts). 931.1556; fax 931.1527 &

42 Byblos ★★$$ An array of *mezes,* the Middle Eastern version of tapas, makes the best meal at this pleasant Lebanese eatery. Labibi Maamari, mother of owner Anis Maamari, holds forth from the partly open kitchen. Choose from her more than 20 small appetizers, including *sambusik,* flaky braided pastries seasoned with ground chicken and pine nuts; *baba ganooj,* a spread of smoky

grilled eggplant infused with garlic; dill cakes, crisp fritters with loads of herbs; *crisor,* an outstanding version of hummus; and fantastic stuffed grape leaves plump with rice. The larger plates can be uneven, but lamb chops with pomegranate sauce and beef kabobs are winners. The house version of baklava is particularly good because it's not excessively sweet. ♦ Lebanese ♦ M-Sa lunch and dinner; Su dinner. 1910 Lombard St (between Buchanan and Webster Sts). 292.5672

43 Allegria ★★★$$ The tapas trend in San Francisco continues at this excellent dining spot. Cold dishes include authentic Spanish cured ham and imported pimientos, quail cooked in wine and sherry vinegar, and toast with anchovies, tomato, and manchego cheese; hot ones include meatballs, tripe Madrid style, and steamed mussels. But this restaurant also offers a dynamite paella, available in three versions (seafood, chicken and seafood, and vegetarian). And don't miss the thick crepes enveloped in a silky carame-lized milk sauce for dessert. A Spanish guitarist plays here at dinnertime. ♦ Spanish ♦ M-Tu dinner; W-Su lunch and dinner. 2018 Lombard St (between Webster and Fillmore Sts). 929.8888; fax 929.9215

43 Babaloo Restaurant ★$ The dishes at this tapas parlor have a decidedly Cuban influence. There's prawns with roasted paprika, salt, and garlic; turkey chorizo; and banana and pepper–stuffed shrimp in a *poblano* pepper sauce. The menu also offers several soups and salads, a burger served on Cuban bread, and grilled, marinated pork loin with chips and chayote slaw. You can wash it all down with any of the 16 microbrewed beers on tap or the tropical fruit–spiked sangria. However, this is not the place for a quiet meal: With the taped music, hard surfaces, and young exhuberant clientele, it can get pretty noisy here. ♦ Cuban/ Tapas ♦ Daily dinner. 2030 Lombard St (between Webster and Fillmore Sts). 346.5474 &

44 Mel's Drive-In ★$ A favorite with the preteen set, this idealized 1950s-style diner has a welcoming neon glow outside and an authentic look inside, with vinyl booths and tabletop jukeboxes. What to order? Hamburgers, cherry Cokes, banana splits, and, for a throw-back to the days before cholesterol became a household word, fried-egg sandwiches spread with mayo. ♦ American ♦ Daily breakfast, lunch, and dinner. No credit cards accepted.

2165 Lombard St (between Fillmore and Steiner Sts). 921.3039; fax 921.3521. Also at: Numerous locations throughout the city

45 Marina Central ★★$$$ Owners Doyle and Kathy Moon have been involved in some pretty high-profile area restaurants, including **Stars** and the **Balboa Cafe.** Now they've brought their extensive experience and talent to the former **Marina Joe's,** turning it into a glossy Italian trattoria with friendly service and a comfortable ambience. The pink exterior has changed to a creamy yellow with dark green trim, and the interior (painted yellow to match) features a curved metal railing around the mezzanine. Probably one of the best starters on the menu is the tender, garlic-baked squid topped with pungent garlic and anchovy bread crumbs in the Sicilian style. The Caesar salad is good, too, although the leaves are left whole (so the diner, not the kitchen, has to cut them up). Main courses include mustard-sauced roast chicken, grilled New York steak, a terrific marinated veal chop, and the ubiquitous burger. The accompaniments are excellent and often unusual, such as a wood-baked eggplant gratin, spinach with olive and lemon (which is a bit too tart at times), and roast cippolini (a type of onion) with grapes and rosemary. The prices are high, and the fact that side dishes are offered only à la carte raises the tab even more. ♦ Italian ♦ M-F lunch and dinner; Sa dinner; Su brunch and dinner. 2001 Chestnut St (at Fillmore St). 673.2222; fax 771.7907 ♿

45 Pasta Pomodoro ★★$ This quick-fix pasta house offers excellent pastas, salads, and sandwiches, all at rock-bottom prices. Tagliatelle is prepared with tomato, chicken, or alfredo sauce; a bowl of polenta is sprinkled with tomato-basil sauce or gorgonzola cheese. There's only counter seating, but called-in orders are ready in five minutes, which makes this neighborhood joint popular for takeout. ♦ Italian/Takeout ♦ Daily lunch and dinner. No credit cards accepted. 2027 Chestnut St (between Fillmore and Steiner Sts). 474.3400; fax 474.4511 ♿ Also at: Numerous locations throughout the city

45 Una Mas ★$ This chain of Mexican eateries is growing by leaps and bounds (there are already 19 in the Bay Area, with 12 more in the planning stages). Though the menu is rather unimaginative—burritos, tacos, enchiladas, tamales, nachos, and similarly standard fare—it's popular with people who like their Mexican food on the mild side. (If you prefer a bit more zing, there's a self-service bar with spicier condiments.) The cleanliness, low prices, pleasant outdoor seating, and bright, lively decor and atmosphere make this place an enjoyable, if uninspiring, stop. ♦ Mexican ♦ Daily lunch and dinner. No credit cards accepted. 2031 Chestnut St (between Fillmore and Steiner Sts). 756.TACO; fax 674.0700 ♿ Also at: Numerous locations throughout the city

46 Williams-Sonoma Another branch in the popular nationwide chain of housewares shops, it stocks all kinds of must-have kitchen gadgets and a wide variety of specialty foods. ♦ Daily. 2000 Chestnut St (at Fillmore St). 929.2520 ♿ Also at: Numerous locations throughout the city

46 Tây Việt ★★$ It's a tiny sliver of a restaurant, barely big enough for two rows of tables, but with its high ceiling hung with leaf-shaped white chandeliers, the white walls, and the changing artwork, this place has all the panache of an art gallery. The Vietnamese food offered here is as light and delicate as you could wish. Top choices include the imperial rolls, which are stuffed with mint and crabmeat, among other ingredients, and served with a refreshing dipping sauce; the quail, flamed table-side and served with salt and pepper and a wedge of lime; and beef fondue, featuring paper-thin slices of beef that quickly cook in a vinegar broth. Roast chicken, flavored with five-spice powder, and aromatic barbecued pork are other fine options. ♦ Vietnamese ♦ Daily lunch and dinner. 2034 Chestnut St (between Fillmore St and Mallorca Way). 567.8124 ♿

47 Noah's Bagels The green-and-white hexagonal floor tiles, dark green vinyl-covered stools, and tile work behind the bins of bagels and New York memorabilia give this place a snazzy look. The bagels here are more

breadlike than bagel-like, since they are steamed before baking rather than boiled, but they are tasty, particularly when spread with the wide selection of schmears. Espresso and good coffee are also available. ♦ Daily. No credit cards accepted. 2075 Chestnut St (between Fillmore and Steiner Sts). 775.2910; fax 775.1243 ♿ Also at: Numerous locations throughout the city

48 **Rosti** ★$ The first San Francisco branch of a popular Southern California chain of Italian restaurants, this place is part owned by bandleader Doc Severinsen. Tuscan-born Agostino Sciandri is the executive chef; his specialty is *pollo al mattone con patate,* a half-chicken seasoned with olive oil, rosemary, and garlic and then grilled under a brick. Other menu items include *bruschetta,* panini, pizzas, pastas, and risotto. The dining room is small (only 40-odd seats), and the decor is rustic; there is some outdoor seating which is pleasant in nice weather. ♦ Italian ♦ Daily lunch and dinner. 2060 Chestnut St (between Mallorca Way and Pierce St). 928.5930 ♿

49 **Parma Ristorante** ★★$$ The waiters at this fun, relaxed destination seem to have come from central casting; they banter with guests, peppering their speech with "Mamma Mia." The red banquette running the length of the brick wall makes diners feel they're sitting at a communal table, and the food is classic trattoria fare. There's minestrone thick with vegetables and several preparations of veal, including saltimbocca. One of the best pastas features sausage and tomato sauce spiked with vodka, which adds a complex, lingering spiciness. ♦ Italian ♦ M-Sa dinner. 3314 Steiner St (between Lombard and Chestnut Sts). 567.0500

SWEET HEAT

49 **Sweet Heat** ★★$ The slowly swinging palm fans over the service counter and the mismatched tables and chairs look as if they came straight from Old Mexico, but the food here has a modern, healthful bent. Spicy chicken wings are cooled with a nonfat cilantro-yogurt dipping sauce, and fire-roasted corn is slathered with either cilantro pesto or hot chipotle salsa. Tacos are stuffed with calamari or scallops, and burritos are plumped with fish or one of several other combinations, all at very reasonable prices. Even the Caesar salad gets a zippy twist with chili-flecked croutons, salsa, and Mexican cheese. ♦ Mexican ♦ Daily lunch and dinner until midnight. No credit cards accepted. 3324 Steiner St (between Lombard and Chestnut Sts). 474.9191; fax 292.6874 ♿

Bistro Aix marina

49 **Bistro Aix** ★★★$$ Formerly **Caffe Centro,** this little eatery gives the neighborhood just what it needed—great food at reasonable prices. The French-Californian dishes are all simple, tasty, and affordable. Start your meal off with mussels perfumed with white wine, shallots, or parsley; or grilled pear salad with endive, radicchio, arugula, gorgonzola cheese, and walnuts. Pasta dishes include *orecchiette* (meaning "little ears") with sautéed spinach and pancetta in a spicy tomato sauce, and spaghetti with rock shrimp, garlic, and fresh tomato. Other good choices are cracker-crust pizza, roast chicken, grilled *ahi* tuna, and a top sirloin burger on focaccia with aioli and fries. The prix-fixe menu—three courses for $9.95—is the bargain of the neighborhood; it's available from 6-8PM Sundays through Thursdays. Though the place has something of an industrial, warehouse-like look, there's a comfortable patio that's heated in cool weather. ♦ French/Californian ♦ Daily dinner. 3340 Steiner St (between Lombard and Chestnut Sts). 202.0100; fax 289.5775 ♿

49 **Barney's Gourmet Hamburgers** ★$ This branch of the well-known local chain has been spruced up with painted wood paneling and sailboat cutouts functioning as artwork. The menu is the same here as at the other locations: dozens of burgers, including some made of turkey or vegetables. Another draw is the outdoor patio in back. ♦ Hamburgers ♦ Daily lunch and dinner. No credit cards accepted. 3344 Steiner St (between Lombard and Chestnut Sts). 563.0307 ♿ Also at: 4138 24th St (between Castro and Diamond Sts), Noe Valley. 282.7770; fax 282.1920 ♿

50 **Izzy's Steak & Chops** ★★$$ One of the city's top steak houses, it boasts a lively, saloonlike ambience (which is only somewhat marred by the impersonal, sometimes rude service). The memorabilia-covered walls and the dark wainscoting—topped with a shelf that's lined with every steak sauce and condiment ever made—add considerable charm. The one thing to order here is steak. The assortment of accompaniments—potatoes, roasted carrots and onions, steamed broccoli, and especially the creamed spinach—are excellent, too. ♦ Steak/Seafood ♦ Daily dinner. Reservations recommended. 3349 Steiner St (between Lombard and Chestnut Sts). 563.0487; fax 563.4956 ♿

50 Ace Wasabi's Rock n' Roll Sushi ★★$$
The name of this funky, New-Wave Japanese restaurant tells you everything you need to know—if you're looking for the traditional sushi experience, this place isn't for you. Rather than serene music in the background, teakwood furnishings, and low lighting, you get bright yellow and red decor, uncushioned brick seating, piped-in reggae music, and Godzilla movies playing on a screen behind the bar. But the preparations of sushi are inventive and tasty. There's a menu of small appetizer plates (the Japanese version of tapas) that includes *hamachi* (yellow tail), *ahi* tuna potstickers served with a chili-soy vinegar dipping sauce, and a smoky-tasting grilled giant squid with a velvety roasted-pepper mayonnaise. Executive chef Kioshi Hayakawa turns out fine *nigiri* sushi, such as *ikura* (salmon roe), *maguro* (tuna) or *unagi* (grilled water eel). He has also designed 22 varieties of sushi rolls, including the Flying Kamikaze (spicy tuna and crunchy asparagus wrapped in sushi rice and then enclosed with albacore tuna). ◆ Sushi ◆ Daily dinner. 3339 Steiner St (between Lombard and Chestnut Sts). 567.4903 &

50 Jericho's Cafe & Deli ★★$ Set in a space that used to be a garage, this long, narrow little cafe is decorated with urns, plates, and vases from Palestine. The food is also from this region: enormous plates of such Middle Eastern dishes as hummus, dolmas, *baba ganooj,* tabbouleh, and *shwarma* (lamb pressed into a large cylinder and cooked on a skewer by indirect heat), all at ridiculously low prices. Try the shish kebab (which comes in meat or vegetarian varieties) and the souvlaki sandwiches. Beverage choices include Turkish coffee, mint tea, soda, and beer. ◆ Middle Eastern ◆ Daily lunch and dinner. 3321 Steiner St (between Lombard and Chestnut Sts). 474.7991 &

50 Szechuan Village Restaurant ★★$
This family-owned eatery in the trendy Marina district is as comfortable as an old shoe. Though the decor is nothing special—just bare-bones tables and chairs—the food definitely is. The menu focuses on Szechuan dishes, which makes it a rarity in San Francisco. Try the diced chicken with Szechuan sauce, which is redolent in minced garlic and hot chili peppers. It comes in a stir-fry with water chestnuts, green peppers, onions, and carrots. Another excellent dish is crispy shredded beef, in which beef is stir-fried with hot chilies and garlic and served over rice. The pot stickers, though not Szechuan, are very good, too. The staff is very friendly and helpful, offering advice if you need it. ◆ Chinese ◆ Daily lunch and dinner. 3317 Steiner St (between Lombard and Chestnut Sts). 567.9989

51 Peet's Coffee & Tea Started in Berkeley in 1966, this coffee bar and retail chain has grown to 20 shops (this was the first in San Francisco) and has amassed a following, thanks in part to the rich, earthy taste of the house blend produced by coffee roaster Alfred Peet. The high-ceilinged shop retains its old architectural moldings, and 30 kinds of beans from around the world are prominently displayed. If you buy a pound of coffee you get a free cup of the featured brew; or a free cup of tea for the purchase of a half pound of tea. Coffee and tea paraphernalia are also for sale. ◆ Daily. 2156 Chestnut St (between Mallorca Way and Pierce St). 931.8302 & Also at: Numerous locations throughout the area

Andalé
TAQUERÍA

51 Andalé Taquería ★★★$ Only in the Marina district would a taco place be as nattily put together as this architectural gem. A profusion of tables clutters an outdoor patio in front, all warmed by a corner fireplace. Inside, a copper pot filled with lacy palms, stippled walls, and wrought-iron fixtures gussy up what is really a fast-food restaurant. Diners order at a counter in front of the kitchen; the food is brought to the table. No lard, canned food, or preservatives are used. Traditional dinners feature *chiles rellenos,* tacos, and tamales, although the best menu choices here are the tacos and burritos filled with rotisserie-roasted chicken or mesquite-grilled beef. The *agua fresca* (freshly made fruit juices) and sangria are also excellent. ◆ Mexican ◆ M-F lunch and dinner; Sa-Su breakfast, lunch, and dinner. No credit cards accepted. 2150 Chestnut St (between Mallorca Way and Pierce St). 749.0506 &

52 Lucca Delicatessen The whole roast chicken with its bronzed skin flecked with black pepper, the marinated artichoke hearts, the pasta in meat sauce, and the roast turkey parts—all on view in the front window—speak volumes about the quality of this Italian deli. Inside, the tantalizing aromas of garlic and roasting meats make you want to buy one of everything—if you can ever reach the counter, which is always three-deep on weekends. In addition to the smoked tongue, sausage, and all manner of prepared take-away foods, the deli stocks pastas, wine, and other packaged goods. Very good selections of cheese and cold cuts are other draws. ◆ Daily. No credit cards accepted. 2120

Chestnut St (between Mallorca Way and Pierce St). 921.7873; fax 921.2402 &

52 Pottery Barn This California-based chain just opened its largest store here to carry most of the items previously available only through its catalog. Customers can now see for themselves those rustic pine tables and colorful stained-wood chairs, country cabinets to hold spices and mixing bowls, stainless steel flatware (including some with faux-bone handles), hand-painted pottery, bright kitchen towels, everyday bistro ware in white porcelain, and yellow pottery bowls that replicate Church Gresley's 1864 design. It all adds up to lots of style for not too much money. ♦ Daily. 2100 Chestnut St (between Mallorca Way and Pierce St). 441.1787; fax 441.5311 & Also at: 1 Embarcadero Center (Battery St, between Sacramento and Clay Sts), Financial District. 788.6810; fax 788.4819 &

53 Home Plate ★★$ Although this place changed hands a few years ago, the crowds that converge for breakfast every weekend don't seem to mind; it has become a neighborhood fixture. The interior has a pleasant minimalist look, with white walls and tables squeezed in a little too tightly. The homemade scones and coffee that arrive as you sit down make a nice start to the day. Then most people opt for one of the egg dishes—standard combinations, but done very well here. ♦ American ♦ Daily breakfast and lunch. 2274 Lombard St (between Steiner and Pierce Sts). 922.4663

54 The California Wine Merchant With its wooden shelves holding the bottles upright for easy browsing, this narrow shop is like a wine library. As the name implies, nearly all the wines are from California, and prices are better than at many of the high-volume shops. Personal service is the key here; the staff is happy to suggest appropriate wines for dinner, and the shop offers free local delivery; it also will ship anywhere in the US for a fee. A monthly newsletter highlights current releases and new arrivals. ♦ M-Sa. 3237 Pierce St (between Lombard and Chestnut Sts). 567.0646 &

55 The Chestnut Street Grill ★$ More than a hundred sandwiches named after well-known locals, and a penchant for making up whimsical quotations, have put this cafe on the culinary map. For example, the Andy Leitner sandwich "ruins roofs and razors," and consists of organic peanut butter, tomatoes, and bacon. The lengthy menu also lists more than a dozen burgers. The checkered tablecloths, bentwood chairs, brown ceiling, and white walls contribute to the place's cozy feel, but many people prefer the garden tables in back on sunny days. ♦ American ♦ Daily lunch and

dinner. 2231 Chestnut St (between Pierce and Scott Sts). 922.5558; fax 922.5274 &

55 World Wrapps ★$ The name refers to this place's flavored tortillas, which are stuffed with globally inspired designer combinations of meats and vegetables. There's mango salsa and grilled snapper in a spinach tortilla; Peking duck with *hoisin* sauce in a plain tortilla; barbecued chicken in a tomato tortilla; and teriyaki tofu in a whole wheat tortilla. Fruit smoothies are the featured drinks and the varieties include raspberry; banana date; pineapple ginger; and peanut butter banana. The food can be carried away or eaten in the bright blue-and-white room furnished with multicolored tables and chairs. ♦ International ♦ Daily lunch and dinner. No credit cards accepted. 2257 Chestnut St (between Pierce and Scott Sts). 563.9727 &

56 E'Angelo Restaurant ★★$ One of the city's most popular pasta houses, it has squeezed an open kitchen and a dining room into a narrow storefront. It's so crowded that parties fewer than six might as well be sharing tables. The fake wood paneling, linoleum, and blue-checkered tablecloths aren't much to look at, but no one seems to mind the downscale decor. Animated veteran waiters practically dance around the tables, and the simple pastas and salads are homey and satisfying. The carbonara combines thick noodles, mushrooms, and nubbins of crisp bacon enveloped in a delicious cream sauce. Eggplant parmigiana is liberally doused with homemade tomato sauce, mozzarella, and parmesan. Meat courses, such as leg of lamb, tend to taste warmed over, but such side dishes as garlicky sautéed spinach and crisply roasted potatoes are truly outstanding. Another winner is the thin-crusted pizza topped with anchovies, mushrooms, or salami. ♦ Italian ♦ Tu-Sa dinner. No credit cards accepted. 2234 Chestnut St (between Pierce and Avila Sts). 567.6164; fax 928.3727 &

57 The Grove ★★$ One of the best places to hang out in and get a feel for the neighborhood, this eatery is as comfortable as a well-worn leather chair. The rough plank flooring, dark wood wainscoting, heavy wood tables, and craftsmanlike lights and chairs add warm touches to the dining room's rustic interior. Display cases in back hold an array of sweets and pastries and such savory preparations as lasagna and burritos that can be heated up in the microwave. ♦ Cafe ♦ Daily breakfast, lunch, and dinner until 11PM; W-Sa until midnight. 2250 Chestnut St (between Avila and Scott Sts). 474.4843; fax 474.9734 ♿

58 Yukol's Place Thai Restaurant ★★★$ In this eatery that looks something like a Thai temple, owner/chef Yukol Nieltaweephong creates tasty, homestyle food with a flair that is entirely her own. In addition to the usual Thai standbys—well-prepared coconut-chicken soup, pad Thai, satay, and fish cakes—the menu features items that are much more unusual. Among the highlights are pastry cups, filled with chicken and vegetables, fried, and served in a mild curry sauce; chicken and corn patties accompanied by a cooling cucumber salad; and broiled Cornish hen, lovingly rubbed with curry and tumeric. If the mangoes and sticky rice dessert is on the menu, be sure to order it—it's a delightful way to finish off a meal. ♦ Thai ♦ M, Sa-Su dinner; Tu-F lunch and dinner. 2380 Lombard St (between Pierce and Scott Sts). 922.1599

58 Some Like It Hot! A Fiery Food Emporium The pungent aroma of chili pervades the air in this bright shop, which is lined with more than a hundred kinds of tantalizing hot sauces imported from around the world. Check out Habañero Hot Hot Hot! Pepper Sauce, and Ol' Gringo Gourmet Green Chile Sauce from Hatch Valley, New Mexico. They even publish a 12-page catalog, so you can keep up with what's hot without having to leave your home. ♦ Tu-Su. 3208 Scott St (between Lombard and Chestnut Sts). 441.7468, 800/806.4468; fax 510/482.1192 ♿

58 Saji Japanese Cuisine ★★★ $$ This modest little place may not look like much from the outside, but a wealth of expertly prepared sushi awaits within its walls. Sit at the bar and watch owner Hideki Makiyama do his magic with the sparkling fresh fish, or sit on cushions at one of the low-slung tables in the tatami room. Any of the *nigiri* sushi is wonderful, but once you've tried a few pieces

ask a chef to make you one of his specialties. In addition to sushi there's a full Japanese menu that features dishes such as chicken teriyaki, tempura, and crispy soft-shell crab. ♦ Japanese ♦ Daily dinner (F-Sa until midnight). 3232 Scott St (between Lombard and Chestnut Sts). 931.0563

BAR ✧ GRILL

59 Paragon ★★$$ The crowd of young diners at this handsome, bar-dominated restaurant gives it the feel of an ongoing college party—except that the food is every bit as good as the cocktails. The short, changing menu might include such choices as scallops topped with a mound of fried leeks, flank steak with garlic mashed potatoes and onion rings, and seared *ahi* tuna with a citrus aioli, ringed with potato chips and a salad of baby greens. ♦ American ♦ Daily dinner. 3251 Scott St (between Lombard and Chestnut Sts). 922.2456; fax 922.1740

59 Olive's Gourmet Pizza ★★$$ A slice of North Beach in the Marina, this eatery produces terrific pizzas with a delectable cornmeal–and–olive-oil crust. Toppings range from the traditional to the creative, but they never stray too far from the mainstream. The mushroom–and–roasted-eggplant pizza tastes so meaty that you'd hardly believe it's vegetarian; and the pizza with fennel-spiced sausage, roasted green peppers, tomato sauce, and mozzarella earns its status as a classic. A few well-prepared pastas and salads round out the menu. The lunch special (a slice of pizza, salad, and beverage) is a terrific deal at only $4.95. Try the dense almond cake for dessert. ♦ Italian ♦ Daily lunch and dinner. No credit cards accepted. 3249 Scott St (between Lombard and Chestnut Sts). 567.4488

60 Scott's Seafood ★$$ Popular with out-of-towners and local traditionalists, this seafood spot sails on safe waters with predictable preparations that disappoint only because they don't excite. The grilled fish is the best bet. This is also a good place to sample the classic San Francisco fish stew, cioppino. Other pluses are the comfortable, slightly nautical setting with dark wood and brass, and the crisp service. ♦ Seafood ♦ Daily lunch and dinner. 2400 Lombard St (at Scott St). 563.8988; fax 563.1897 ♿ Also at: 3 Embarcadero Center (Sacramento St, between Drumm and Davis Sts), Financial District. 981.0622; fax 296.9501 ♿

60 Samui Thai Cuisine ★★$ Named for an island off the coast of Thailand, this place evokes a tropical atmosphere with a long fish tank and a couple of artificial palm trees. It is one of the few restaurants in the city offering southern Thai fare. To best explore the flavors of that region, try the seafood specials and the hot-and-sour shrimp soup. Other good dishes include the green-papaya salad, which makes a refreshing, crunchy contrast to the soup. The coconut-flecked Thai crepe wraps around a filling of chicken and peanuts. Broiled eggplant gets a lift from both mint and basil. ♦ Thai ♦ Tu-Sa lunch and dinner; Su dinner. 2414 Lombard St (between Scott and Divisadero Sts). 563.4405; fax 563.3793

60 Lhasa Moon ★★$ Owner Losang Gyatso and his girlfriend, Tsering Wangmo, operate the first Tibetan restaurant to open west of the Rockies. Featured on the menu are a number of homestyle Tibetan dishes, some of which have Indian influences (such as a sauce made with onions, tomatoes, and ginger). Stews, soups, and hand-rolled pasta are also offered. Standouts include *momos*, a juicy dumpling similar to Chinese pot stickers that can be filled with a mixture of beef and herb-flavored vegetables, chicken, or a combination of vegetables; *churul*, blue cheese soup with minced beef; lamb curry; herbed fried chicken; and shredded beef with sliced potatoes and spinach. A few of the dishes are flavored with *emma,* a Tibetan wild peppercorn. The interior is painted white with hunter green wainscoting, and in keeping with their heritage, the owners display framed photographs of Tibet before it was occupied by China on the walls, and Tibetan music plays in the background. ♦ Tibetan ♦ Tu-F lunch and dinner; Sa-Su dinner. 2420 Lombard St (between Scott and Divisadero Sts). 674.9898

61 Bechelli's Coffee Shop ★★$ This is the real thing: an honest-to-goodness Deco-style diner with a horseshoe-shaped counter. The walls are lined with stills from films that opened in the theater next door back in the 1940s. It all conjures a nostalgia for the golden age of film, and for the food of that time. The hamburger and thick french fries are a delight, and the all-American, homemade apple pie, cherry pie, and chocolate cake are classic. ♦ American ♦ Daily breakfast and lunch. No credit cards accepted. 2346 Chestnut St (between Scott and Divisadero Sts). 346.1801

61 Wild Oats Community Market This branch of the Colorado-based natural foods store chain is a godsend to this neighborhood, which has no other really good markets. The specialty is organic items, including fruits, vegetables, juices, teas, hormone-free meat and poultry, vitamin supplements, and natural cosmetics. Some non-organic produce is available as well. ♦ Daily 7AM-10PM (F-Sa to 11PM). 2324 Chestnut St (between Scott and Divisadero Sts). 921.2992; fax 921.2244 &

62 Cafe Marimba ★$$ Louise Clement and Reed Hearon, who put together the wildly popular **LuLu,** here turn their talents to Mexican food. Highlights include mole dishes from Oaxaca and large family-style platters, each heaped with grilled chicken, pork ribs, rock shrimp, or mushrooms with tomato salsa. Among the unusual seafood dishes are tacos filled with octopus or red snapper. More traditional enchiladas and quesadillas also are offered, all served with homemade sauces. The decor is stunning: Two palm trees are stationed at the front entrance, and the boldly colored interior boasts a collection of Mexican folk art. The downside is the noise level and some sloppiness in the presentation— sometimes the entrées are not hot enough, temperature-wise. ♦ Mexican ♦ M dinner; Tu-F lunch and dinner; Sa-Su brunch and dinner. 2317 Chestnut St (between Scott and Divisadero Sts). 776.1506; fax 776.5104 &

62 Zinzino ★★$$ It took a while for this spot to catch on, but the wood-fired pizzas have proven to be truly addictive. The serpentine dining room is divided into several separate areas, with private nooks and crannies here and there. Crispy calamari, apple chicken salad, and *crostini misti* (with a choice of toppings that changes daily) are all good starters. The seared beef tenderloin, accompanied by Chianti mashed potatoes (they sound strange, but they're great) and sautéed red chard, is a winner. Other outstanding main courses include hearty lamb shank napped with a Marsala sauce; wild mushroom lasagna, rich with layers of provolone, walnuts, and ricotta cheese; and of course, those terrific pizzas. Dessert lovers will die for the Ghirardelli chocolate truffle cake and tiramisù gelato sundae. ♦ Italian ♦ Daily dinner. 2355 Chestnut St (between Scott and Divisadero Sts). 346.6623; fax 922.9391 &

THE BUCHANAN GRILL

63 Buchanan Grill ★★$$ "Classic" describes this busy bar/restaurant, where every inch of wall is covered with pictures of sports personalities. Many people eat in the green wainscoted area opposite the bar, but the back room, with six skylights, is quieter and more tranquil. Those who like their Buffalo chicken wings explosively hot will go for the ones here; they're doused in red-hot pepper sauce and accompanied by cooling celery sticks and blue cheese dipping sauce. Also try the crisp onion-potato pancake, topped with smoked salmon and capers and drizzled with sour cream. Main courses include such comfort food as pot roast and mashed potatoes in a rich mushroom gravy; there's also grilled salmon with avocado salsa, a stellar steak sandwich with sautéed onions and mushrooms, and a juicy, thick hamburger. And don't miss the thin-crusted hot apple tart, topped with a melting scoop of vanilla ice cream. ♦ American ♦ Daily lunch and dinner. 3653 Buchanan St (between Bay and North Point Sts). 346.8727; fax 346.8781 &

greens
RESTAURANT

64 Greens Restaurant ★★★$$ The Zen Buddhists who opened this place in 1979 brought vegetarian food into the mainstream; the bright flavors and creative combinations captivated even the most dedicated meat eaters. Lately, the menu (which changes daily) has been revised to eliminate many of the cheese-heavy dishes and to instill a more modern, vegetarian-oriented approach. Among the most popular favorites are *enchiladas verdes* with mushrooms, peppers, corn, red onions, two cheeses, and green sauce; curried vegetables; and light-as-air eggplant fritters, which come with a teriyaki-style dipping sauce and English cucumbers in an orange marinade. Another winner is the pizza with two kinds of mushrooms, onions, and two kinds of cheese. Among the best desserts are apricot-boysenberry cobbler, rich mocha *pots de crème* (custard), and chocolate-raspberry tart with whipped cream. Note: The five-course prix-fixe menu on Saturdays is a very good buy. The wine list, which covers nine pages, is exceptional as well. An added bonus is the spectacular location on a pier overlooking the scenic bay and the Golden Gate Bridge. The expansive dining room boasts a lofty, exposed-beam ceiling and striking flower arrangements. The bakery, just inside the door, features great breads and also sells take-out items. ♦ Vegetarian ♦ M dinner; Tu-Sa lunch and dinner, Su brunch. Reservations recommended. Fort Mason, Building A (at the foot of Buchanan St). 771.6222 &

Bests

Michael Cleary
Co-Host, "The Food & Travel Enthusiasts," a syndicated California radio show

The Big Four at the **Huntington**—late-night chili and a glass of red wine in the bar.

Scala's—Donna Scala keeps it simple and good.

Yank Sing—The wide variety of dim sum makes me feel like I'm a kid in a candy store.

Moose's—The ultimate East Coast hangout on the West Coast.

Aqua—Just plain elegant.

Gene Burns
Host, "Dining Around with Gene Burns" on KGO Radio 810

Yank Sing—Perhaps the best dim sum in the country. Pricey, but frankly worth more.

Byblos—Classic Middle Eastern food cooked, as if at home, and served with panache.

Tra Vigne—Chef Michael Chiarello has it and it shows. Well worth a drive to **St Helena.**

Billy Aquero
Nationally ranked professional billiards player and house pro at Chalkers Billiard Club

Bistro Rôti—Dress casually and order the spit-roasted chicken with garlic mashed potatoes.

Rubicon—Great spot for quail and vegetables. You never know who you might run into, since Robin Williams is an investor.

Zuni Cafe—Bring some friends and enjoy people watching on **Market Street.** The oysters and the wine list are the best.

Enrico's—The patio here is "the" place to people watch—great food and jazz to listen to at night.

Sugar built one of the city's most impressive homes, the Spreckels Mansion at 2080 Washington Street in Pacific Heights. Constructed in 1912 by sugar czar Claus Spreckels, the Beaux Arts structure is now owned by novelist Danielle Steel.

Japantown/Lower Haight

Japantown—"Nihonmachi" to its residents—is a surprising oasis, a pristine village located within the approximate boundaries of **Octavia** and **Fillmore Streets**, and **Geary Boulevard** and **California Street**. After World War II, when Japantown's residents returned from internment camps to find their former homes occupied, they scattered about the city and into the suburbs. Although the city's Japanese-Americans have fully integrated into the Bay Area, the heart of their community remains here.

The area's commercial and cultural focus is **Japan Center**, which covers a three-block stretch between Fillmore and **Laguna** Streets. It houses the North American headquarters of the **Ikenobo Ikebana Society**, the flower-arranging school, with its artful displays in the windows, as well as the **Kintetsu Mall** and **Kinokuniya Building**; they are connected by the arched **Webster Street Bridge of Shops**, fashioned after the Ponte Vecchio in Florence. Other attractions include the cobblestoned **Buchanan Mall**, with flowering plum and cherry trees, and **Peace Plaza**, with its towering pagoda, a gift from Japan. Relax with a shiatsu massage or enjoy a refreshing communal bath at the **Kabuki Hot Springs** (1750 Geary Blvd, at Fillmore St, 922.6002 ♿).

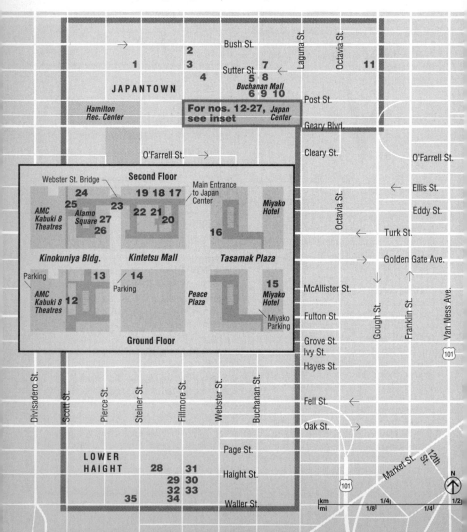

An 800-car parking lot makes the center easily accessible. And a block away is **Nichi Bei Kai** (1759 Sutter St, at Buchanan St, 921.1782; fax 931.1826), housing a cultural center and a small, peaceful room especially designed for the traditional Japanese tea ceremony (call for an appointment). The tearoom was actually brought from Japan and reassembled here.

To people unfamiliar with Japanese culture, Japantown may seem intimidating, but the staffs at restaurants and shops are generally friendly and welcoming. There are three major grocery stores, several bakeries and confection shops, and a great-for-browsing hardware store that stocks both Japanese and American wares. The Japanese aesthetic can be explored at the **Maruwa Foods** supermarket, with its displays of perfect, sushi-quality fish fillets; at sister shops **Asakichi** and **Asakichi II**, where bamboo shelves hold an impressive collection of metal and china teapots; and at **Ma-Shi-Ko Folkcraft**, with its antique oval sushi carriers.

Of the more than 40 traditional Japanese restaurants, **Mifune**, done in cheerful red with dark wood appointments, is a wonderful place to enjoy a generous bowl of *soba* (buckwheat) or *udon* (white) noodles. Sample tempura and a broad range of dishes in a rustic setting at **Sanppo**. One of the most popular eating attractions, though not necessarily the best, is **Isobune Sushi**, where sushi dishes travel around the counter on waterborne rafts. **YOYO Tsumami Bistro**, a stylish eatery at the **Miyako Hotel**, is a very good choice for a full dinner or drinks and *tsumami* (small plates of appetizers).

That this clean, orderly, almost serene area should butt up against the Lower Haight, which typifies urban grittiness, perfectly illustrates the diversity of San Francisco neighborhoods. In recent years, **Haight Street** has reinvented itself—evolving from the druggy peace-and-love era of the sixties through the outrageous punk rebellion to a new era of individuality in search of freedom. Here, body-pierced young people with brightly colored hair and leather clothing live in harmony with young marrieds with kids, gay couples, and seniors.

Ethnic restaurants, done on the cheap, cluster here. Catering to the young folk in the area, prices are low, service is casual (but can be absentminded), and many of the offerings are vegetarian. **India Oven** produces great tandoori and gutsy Indian food in soothing surroundings; **Thep Phanom** is one of the best Thai restaurants in the city and has the look of a well-heeled grandmother's parlor; and the **Squat & Gobble Cafe** serves hearty, fresh breakfasts and lunch to a mob of post-punk patrons. The Lower Haight may look rough, but it can be fun.

---

1 Neecha Thai ★★$ A neighborhood favorite, this place offers well-balanced Thai combinations that straddle the sweet-sour axis. No new ground is broken, but the coconut-chicken soup, chicken with basil, and Thai crepe are all winners. What with the brick and dark wood, the place is reminiscent of an English pub. ♦ Thai ♦ M-F lunch and dinner; Sa-Su dinner. 2100 Sutter St (at Steiner St). 922.9419 &

2 Patisserie Delanghe This is one of the top stops for classic French pastries. Owner Dominique Delanghe has a great feel for balance, which makes all her creations sparkle without being overly sweet. Napoleons are our favorites; order ahead and pick them up right before you want to serve them. The filling is cool and creamy, and the puff pastry crumbles at the touch of a fork. In fact, Delanghe's puff pastry is so excellent that many professional caterers buy sheets of the raw dough here. ♦ Tu-Su. 1890 Fillmore St (between Sutter and Bush St). 923.0711 &

Sushi is delicious with a dipping sauce of soy sauce and wasabi (green Japanese horseradish). The proper way to dip sushi is to pick it up gently, then rotate it so that just the fish touches the soy-wasabi mixture. Dipping the rice causes it to fall apart. Place the whole piece of sushi in your mouth, with the fish side touching your tongue first.

3 Trio Cafe ★$ Some years ago, under different ownership, this was the gathering place for a cross section of affluent business mavens, designers, and artists. All the hubbub has died down, but the cafe is still popular for a light breakfast and all-day fare, including poached eggs, scones, *pizzettas,* and simple open-face sandwiches. The sunny blue-and-white environment lends a cheery note to an early morning café au lait. ♦ Cafe ♦ Daily breakfast and lunch. 1830 Fillmore St (between Sutter and Bush Sts). 563.2248 &

3 Pizza Inferno ★$ True to this place's hellish name, the ceiling, walls, and floor are painted in a swirling pattern that seems to give off a red, vertiginous glow. Amid such surreal surroundings, the square pizzas, with a thin, crisp crust, fit right in. In addition to the classic toppings are some interesting variations, including one version with goat cheese, mozzarella, and walnuts, and another with spicy Thai chicken and cilantro or peanuts. The house salad with balsamic vinaigrette is a good way to start. ♦ Pizzeria ♦ Daily lunch and dinner. 1800 Fillmore St (at Sutter St). 775.1800 &

CAFE KATi

4 Cafe Kati ★★★$$ Kirk Webber is an artist, and this whimsical neighborhood restaurant is his studio. Few places in the city offer such interestingly designed presentations. In his version of Caesar salad, the romaine leaves are bunched together and stand straight up in the center of the plate. His desserts look like replicas of a Japanese garden. This all could come off as silly, but it's fun, and the flavors are always wonderful. The monthly-changing menu offers a host of intriguing combinations: steamed mussels and Thai salmon sausage with red curry; chicken breast stuffed with roquefort and walnuts and moistened with sage brown butter; crispy salmon fillet with Chinese five spices and a light oxtail broth; and filet mignon with house-dried tomatoes and a frothy herbed zabaglione. With all that fussing, dishes can emerge from the kitchen slowly. This is not the place to grab a bite; it's designed for an evening's entertainment, in cozy surroundings. ♦ Eclectic/Californian ♦ Tu-Su dinner. 1963 Sutter St (between Webster and Fillmore Sts). 775.7313; fax 379.9952 &

4 Yamada Seika Confectionery Since the early 1980s, the husband-and-wife team here has been turning out delicate rice crackers and sweet confections, many stuffed with bean paste. The sweets at this petite shop are displayed in the case in front and dried peas and other snacks and crackers occupy the side shelves. The husband is always toiling among the large sacks of flour and bakery equipment; the wife is so shy that she'll bolt to the back if asked too many questions. ♦ Tu-Su. 1955 Sutter St (between Webster and Fillmore Sts). 922.3848 &

5 Benkyodo Confectioners ★$ A popular gathering place for Japanese-Americans, this modest cafe features traditional bean-paste confections and light lunches. ♦ Japanese ♦ M-Sa breakfast and lunch. 1747 Buchanan Mall (at Sutter St). 922.1244 &

5 Sushi-A ★★★$$ The "A" of the name just might refer to the quality of the food here, because most of the numerous offerings are winners. The sushi and sashimi are exceptional, the tempura is light and feathery, and the clay-pot seafood dishes are not to be missed. The prawn, for example, combines at least a dozen shrimp, noodles, several types of mushrooms, scallions, cabbage, and tofu in a very light broth; the dipping sauce magically brings the food to life. If you can't make up your mind, try a combination dinner or the *kaiseki* dinner, which consists of many small seasonal dishes. The gray ceilings and recessed lighting create a restful backdrop for the exemplary fare. ♦ Sushi/ Japanese ♦ M, Th-Su lunch and dinner. 1737 Buchanan Mall (at Sutter St). 931.4685; fax 931.4120

6 Sanppo ★★$$ Celadon walls, dark wood screens, and the inset wood ceiling give this tiny spot a Japanese country feel. Although the food covers a broad range, it's all done surprisingly well. Offerings include yakitori (grilled skewered meat and vegetables), *nabemono* (clay-pot dishes), *udon* and *soba* noodles, *donburi* (rice), a particularly delicate and delicious tempura, and many other specialties, mostly seafood. Popular dishes include grilled seafood and *katsu*-marinated salmon, in which the fish is flavored with the lees of sake. Eggplant sandwiched between slices of marinated beef is a great choice for meat eaters. The meal comes with a pleasant miso soup and a salad with a light mustard dressing. ♦ Japanese ♦ Tu-Sa lunch and dinner; Su dinner. 1702 Post St (between Buchanan Mall and Webster St). 346.3486

7 Super Koyama This neat and clean full-service Japanese grocery store has a good selection of produce, packaged goods, and sweets. The fish is a standout. No other store in the city has such a wide selection of sushi-quality seafood. ♦ Daily. 1790 Sutter St (at Buchanan St). 921.6529 &

7 Now & Zen ★★$ This casual spot bills itself as a "gourmet vegetarian bistro and bakery." The menu is strictly vegan (that is, no eggs or dairy products are used in food preparation), and everything is made from scratch on the premises. A standout appetizer is the wild mushroom pâté with nuts served on grilled flatbread. Other good bets include the antipasto platter, with a variety of grilled vegetables, roasted garlic, tofu "feta cheese," flatbread, and kalamata olives dressed in a warm balsamic marinade; a stroganoff with mushrooms and seitan (a soy milk product); and "Zen kabobs," made with seitan, vegetables, and brown rice. ♦ Vegan ♦ Tu-F dinner; Sa-Su brunch and dinner. 1826 Buchanan St (between Sutter and Bush Sts). 922.9696; fax 922.1343 &

8 Sanko Cooking Supply For fun souvenirs, come here to buy those plastic sushi replicas seen in all the Japantown restaurant windows. The shop also carries teapots, sake sets, chopstick rests, rice cookers, rice bowls, serving plates, kitchen equipment, and just about everything else related to Japanese cooking and eating. ♦ Daily. 1758 Buchanan Mall (at Sutter St). 922.8331; fax 922.8365 &

9 Iroha ★★$$ Dark wood screens between the tables and rich red walls give this second-floor restaurant an upmarket look. Skip the heavy tempura and try the house specialty, *ramen* noodles, which come with toppings of chicken, beef, pork, seafood, or vegetables. Other winning dishes include yakitori and *gyoza* (Japanese pot stickers). ♦ Japanese ♦ Daily lunch and dinner. 1728 Buchanan Mall (between Post and Sutter Sts). 922.0321

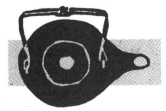

9 Soko Hardware Lovers of hardware stores and gadgets will be happy browsing this shop, where most of the wares are Japanese. This is the place for inexpensive tea and sake sets, rice bowls, vases, rice cookers, hibachis, cleavers, and utensils. Varieties of chopsticks and chopstick rests number more than a hundred and are very reasonably priced.

There's also a great selection of American products, including the indispensable Swing Away can opener. ♦ M-Sa. 1698 Post St (at Buchanan Mall). 931.5510; fax 931.4927

9 San Wang Restaurant ★★$$ This Northern Chinese eatery is one of the only places in the city that offers hand-pulled noodles. The chef pulls, stretches, kneads, and slaps a mass of dough on a table until long noodle strands miraculously form; the noodles are never cut with a knife. Other items on the menu are boiled dumplings, dry-braised shrimp, and pork salad. ♦ Chinese ♦ Daily lunch and dinner. 1682 Post St (between Laguna St and Buchanan Mall). 921.1453

9 Soko Interiors The window of this shop, a few doors down from **Soko Hardware** (see at left), displays primarily cement garden sculptures; inside, more upscale housewares are for sale, including tea sets. Either ask for admittance at **Soko Hardware** or call the store in advance for an appointment. ♦ M-Sa by appointment. 1672 Post St (between Laguna St and Buchanan Mall). 931.5510; fax 931.4927 &

10 Korea House ★★$$$ Join the crowds at this dark, woody restaurant for a late-night, do-it-yourself barbecue. In addition to such typical fare as thinly sliced beef and marinated chicken, there are a few exotic meats to toss on the table's grill, including beef tongue and tripe. ♦ Korean ♦ Daily lunch and dinner; F-Sa until 3AM. 1640 Post St (between Laguna St and Buchanan Mall). 563.1388; fax 563.3480

11 Cafe Majestic ★★$$$ Many people consider this restaurant in the **Hotel Majestic** one of the most romantic in the city. The Victorian ornamentation, flickering candles, gilded mirrors, and piano music put diners in the mood to woo. The seasonal menu has both Mediterranean and Asian accents: Roast breast of duck may be matched with fennel, caramelized pears, and cracked pepper gastrique; grilled lamb chops come with Japanese eggplant and crispy artichokes (which unfortunately aren't very crispy). The service is friendly but absentminded at times. ♦ Californian ♦ Daily breakfast and dinner; Su brunch. 1500 Sutter St (at Gough St). 776.6400; fax 673.7331 &

12 Asakichi More than 60 individual teapots and many styles of rice bowls are crowded into this tiny, pretty shop in **Japan Center**. Also on display are unique tea sets, pottery, and rectangular sushi plates. ♦ Daily. Kinokuniya Building, 1581 Webster St (between Geary Blvd and Post St). 921.2147; fax 921.2147 ♿ Also at: Webster St Bridge (above Webster St, near Post St). 921.3821; fax 921.3821 ♿

13 Isuzu Restaurant ★★$ The grandmotherly waitresses' friendly smiles light up this place. With round rice-paper lanterns, bamboo partitions, and red accents, it looks a bit like an upscale cafeteria, but the interesting menu boasts a wide selection, and the food is quite good. Spicy *udon* noodles are brought to the table in a lidded iron pot; nestling inside with the noodles are prawns, tofu, chunks of fish, carrots, cabbage, and scallions, all studded with chili flakes. The tempura has a light, feathery texture, and the standard array of sushi is better than average. Numerous clay-pot dishes also are offered. ♦ Sushi/Japanese ♦ M, W-Su lunch and dinner. Kinokuniya Building, 1581 Webster St (between Geary Blvd and Post St). 922.2290 ♿

14 Maruwa Foods Each shelf at this spotless modern grocery store is perfectly stacked, as if waiting to be filmed for a commercial. Most products are Japanese, and there's a full case of take-out fare, including breaded fish and noodle salads. The produce department stocks such ingredients for stir-fries as vacuum-packed slices of lotus root and cabbage, and the fish selections include sushi-quality octopus, tuna, and cuttlefish. Pork, beef, and chicken are thinly sliced for sukiyaki, and several kinds of marinated fish are ready to be taken home and placed on the grill. ♦ Daily. Kintetsu Mall, 1737 Post St (between Peace Plaza and Webster St). 563.1901; fax 563.0716 ♿

15 YOYO Tsumami Bistro ★★★$$ New chef Dominique Quelennec Crenn has dramatically improved this eatery in the **Miyako Hotel.** A native of Versailles, she has had a long and distinguished culinary career in San Francisco (other places she's worked include **Stars** and **Campton Place**), and she more than lives up to her reputation here. The menu is mostly French, but there are some Japanese influences, particularly in the list of *tsumami* (appetizers). For starters, don't miss the ginger-pickled salmon with wasabi crème fraîche; the *ahi* tuna tartare with miso and eggplant; or the roasted fennel with star anise and olives. Entrées include beef tenderloin grillade with fried artichokes and roasted potatoes; tempura salad; roasted cod with succotash; and braised lamb shank with *azuki*-bean ragout. The dining room is striking, yet comfortable and casual, with saturated colors and mobile-like light fixtures that seem to be in flight. ♦ French/Japanese ♦ Daily lunch and dinner. 1611 Post St (between Laguna St and Peace Plaza). 922.3200; fax 921.0417 ♿

16 Seoul Garden ★★$$ Deep in the heart of Japantown is one of the city's most beautiful Korean restaurants, which comprises two booth-lined rooms. On the grills set on the tables, diners get to cook their own marinated squid, beef, chicken, and seafood. Chef-prepared specialties include steamed fish and braised ribs. The *kimchi* (pickled cabbage) here is particularly good and packs a spicy punch. ♦ Korean ♦ Daily lunch and dinner. Tasamak Plaza (at Geary Blvd and Peace Plaza). 563.7664 ♿

17 Isobune Sushi ★$ At what is probably the most popular sushi bar in Japantown, diners pluck their selections from little boats that float around the counter while two sushi chefs continuously replenish the stock. At the end of the meal the waitress tabulates the bill according to the empty trays in front of each diner. Unfortunately, the sushi leaves a little to be desired, and the rice often is mushy. Best bets are the bright orange flying-fish roe that burst in the mouth and the bright-green fish roe flavored with wasabi. One tip: Keep an eye on what the chef places on the boat and nab it quickly to avoid any raw fish that's circled the counter too many times. ♦ Sushi ♦ Daily lunch and dinner. Kintetsu Mall, 1737 Post St (between Peace Plaza and Webster St). 563.1030; fax 921.3857 ♿

18 Koji Osakaya ★★$$ Yakitori, noodles, teriyaki, sushi—you name it, it's on the menu here. But it's best to bypass the sushi for the excellent *ramen* noodles in either miso or light soy broth, topped with deep-fried pork, vegetables, or barbecued meats. The crunchy tempura is served with an enticing, earthy dipping sauce with grated daikon. White walls and dark wood screens between the tables give this restaurant a clean, casual look, and the service is particularly pleasant. ♦ Japanese ♦ Daily lunch and dinner. Kintetsu Mall, 1737 Post St (between Peace Plaza and Webster St). 922.2728; fax 567.4211 ♦

19 **Benihana of Tokyo** ★$$$ Billed as the "Japanese Steakhouse," this chain is known for its chefs' fancy knife work as they cook to order on the hot iron grills inset on each table. All dinners include onion soup, salad, shrimp appetizer, vegetables, rice, and ice cream. ♦ Japanese/Steak house ♦ Daily lunch and dinner. Kintetsu Mall, 1737 Post St (between Peace Plaza and Webster St). 563.4844; fax 563.8022 ♦

20 **Murata's Café Hana** ★$ Perfect for a shopping break, this spot offers nothing but rich treats, including cream cakes and cookies, to have with coffee or tea. The free-form black tables spill out into the mall. ♦ Cafe ♦ Daily. Kintetsu Mall, 1737 Post St (between Peace Plaza and Webster St). 567.9133; fax 567.1710 ♦

21 **Mifune** ★★★$ People line up for quick bites at this inexpensive noodle emporium featuring 20 hot dishes, a dozen cold, and about as many *donburi* dishes. Each combination can be ordered with either *udon* or *soba*. The minimal interior with dark wood and red walls gives the bustling place a sleek look. ♦ Japanese ♦ Daily lunch and dinner. Kintetsu Mall, 1737 Post St (between Peace Plaza and Webster St). 922.0337 ♦

22 **Kushi Tsuru** ★★$$ This is a top stop for broiled salmon, mackerel, or eel, all crisply coated and slightly smoky. Other offerings include battered, skewered, then deep-fried meats and vegetables that are crisper and more substantial than tempura. The pork is a standout (the beef less so), and the whole asparagus spears are delicious. Tempura and sushi are respectable, but not outstanding. The *bento* box (a compartmentalized tray) contains tempura, tuna sashimi, cooked squash and daikon, broiled salmon, sushi rolls, and rice. Noodle cravers who can't get into **Mifune**, next door, can sample the fine *udon* here. ♦ Japanese ♦ M, W-Su lunch and dinner. Kintetsu Mall, 1737 Post St (between Peace Plaza and Webster St). 922.9902 ♦

23 **Asakichi II** Dozens of cast-iron teapots fill the bamboo shelves that zigzag across the center of this narrow shop, a sister to

Asakichi (see page 109). The teapots look more like museum pieces than functional kitchen equipment, but functional they are; they include detailed instructions on how to use and care for them. Also on display are wind chimes, sculptures, and other cast-iron and bronze pieces. ♦ Daily. Webster St Bridge (above Webster St, near Post St). 921.3821; fax 921.3821 ♦ Also at: Kinokuniya Building, 1581 Webster St (between Geary Blvd and Post St). 921.2147; fax 921.2147 ♦

24 **Sapporo-ya** ★$ With a noodle machine in the window and stacked boxes of noodles near the door, it's no surprise this country-style restaurant is most popular for its giant bowls of *ramen* noodles. An unusual offering is *okonomiyaki*, a rice-flour and egg pancake that is filled with either a shrimp or beef mixture, then sprinkled with dried bonito flakes and drizzled with Worcestershire sauce. ♦ Japanese ♦ Daily lunch and dinner. Kinokuniya Building, 1581 Webster St (between Geary Blvd and Post St). 563.7400 ♦

25 **Ma-Shi-Ko Folkcraft** Of particular interest here is the brushed Mashiko pottery, whose images are delicately painted on, often with enamel, a decorative technique that goes back seven centuries. The shop also sells interesting antique oval sushi carriers, cherry-wood teapots, cedar or kiri-wood vases, and classic Japanese pottery and serving pieces. ♦ M, W-Su. Kinokuniya Building, 1581 Webster St (between Geary Blvd and Post St). 346.0748 ♦

26 **Books Kinokuniya** This sprawling bookstore has the best inventory of Japanese books and magazines in the city. In addition to Japanese-language cookbooks, there are several shelves of all kinds of Asian cookbooks in English. The collection explores many traditional culinary arts, including sushi making, and also carries such newer-fangled titles as *New Salads: Quick Recipes from Japan*. Browsers will find vegetarian and macrobiotic guides, a selection of Japanese food magazines, as well as gardening books that show how to grow Japanese vegetables at home. ♦ Daily. Kinokuniya Building, 1581 Webster St (between Geary Blvd and Post St). 567.7625; fax 567.4109 ♦

Both the Chinese and the Japanese use chopsticks. In Chinese, they are called "quick little fellows," while the Japanese refer to them as "the bridge," because they are the bridge between the food and the mouth.

27 Maki ★★★$$ All of the dishes at this charming restaurant are created with a focus on the aesthetic and culinary harmony that typifies the best Japanese cuisine. The specialty is *wappa meshi*, a Northern Japanese dish consisting of rice steamed with fish, vegetables, or chicken in a cypress wood container. The *tsumami* (plates of small appetizers) are quite good as well, particularly the crisp okra, a pine-scented matsutake mushroom in a soy-based sauce, and taro root with red miso. Entrées include a tender teriyaki rib steak with artistically prepared vegetables. The menu does not list all of the appetizers and main courses, so ask your server what else may be available that day. ♦ Japanese ♦ Tu-Sa lunch and dinner. Kinokuniya Building, 1581 Webster St (between Geary Blvd and Post St). 921.5215 &

SPAGHETTI WESTERN

28 Spaghetti Western ★$ Plentiful portions and a grunge atmosphere are what this Haight hangout is all about. A dizzying black-and-white floor, bright colored walls, cow skulls, and yokes add up to a quirky decor. Eggs come in many guises: in an Irish breakfast with brown bread, bacon, and home fries; in a Cajun version with andouille sausage; and with chilies and cheese for a Mexican preparation. Other draws include fluffy homemade biscuits and moist pancakes served with maple syrup. The lunch menu includes hamburgers, vegetable burgers, and grilled chicken with chilies. Service is a little scattered but good-natured, which seems to suit the mood of the crowd. ♦ Californian ♦ Daily breakfast and lunch. 576 Haight St (between Fillmore and Steiner Sts). 864.8461

Some Japanese restaurants offer a special multicourse dinner that's arranged in advance with the chef, usually on a day's notice. Called a *kaiseki* dinner, it may include up to a dozen small dishes. Traditionally the meal begins with an hors d'oeuvre, followed by a clear soup, raw fish, special side dish, a broiled dish, a boiled dish, a salad, a fried dish, rice-miso soup, and a pickled vegetable. Green tea, fruit, and a sweet dish conclude the repast. The cost is usually about $50 per person.

What's the difference between sushi and sashimi? Sushi refers to combinations made from vinegared rice and raw fish (or other ingredients such as vegetables), and sashimi is the raw fish served by itself.

28 The Mad Dog in the Fog ★$ At this brew pub, locals like to kick back with a pint of bitters, throw a few darts, and scarf up some pub grub—there's a good version of shepherd's pie, a ploughman's lunch, and sausages and potatoes. The vinyl chairs may be a bit torn and shabby, but the barn-like space is comfortable and welcoming. ♦ English/Irish ♦ Daily lunch and dinner. 530 Haight St (between Fillmore and Steiner Sts). 626.7279 &

29 Ali Baba's Cave ★$ This Middle Eastern eatery has a peaceful and slightly exotic feel, thanks to the green fabric swags covering the ceiling and stucco walls, and the pounded copper surface behind the bar. From the kitchen come platters of falafel, hummus, cabbage rolls, and dolmas. Sandwiches and couscous are also available, as are many types of coffee, including strong Turkish cappuccino. ♦ Middle Eastern ♦ Daily lunch and dinner until midnight; F-Sa until 2AM. 531 Haight St (between Fillmore and Steiner Sts). 255.7820; fax 255.7820

29 Todos Santos ★$ A cheerful little joint, it features cheap but tasty Mexican food. The walls are a veritable shrine to the Virgin Mary, the tables covered in clear plastic over bright fabrics, and the rafters hung with angels. The waitress, with nose and lip pierced, is herself an angel of Haight Street. Specialties include burritos with *chorizo* (spicy sausage) and black beans, a mildly spiced enchilada, *huevos rancheros,* fajitas, nachos, and other typical fare. ♦ Mexican ♦ M-F lunch and dinner; Sa-Su breakfast, lunch, and dinner. No credit cards accepted. 521 Haight St (between Fillmore and Steiner Sts). 864.3721; fax 864.3721 &

29 Haight & Fillmore Whole Foods Although this full-service natural-foods store opened well after the Age of Aquarius, it's steeped in that era. With a peeling linoleum floor and faded walls, the crowded quarters can be overwhelming, but there's a good selection of produce, bulk items, and other staples. ♦ Daily. 503 Haight St (at Fillmore St). 552.6077

30 Kate's Kitchen ★★$ Breakfast buffs put this place at the top of their list, for good reason. Thick wedges of French toast are perfumed with orange zest and sprinkled with fresh berries and maple syrup. The hash, made with chunks of corned beef, potatoes, fried onions, carrots, and celery, is a great platform for two over-easy eggs. Sausage gravy is a perfect match for two biscuits laced with cheese and scallions, and buttermilk pancakes get a twist with cornmeal and a light lemon syrup. For lunch, there's a rich chicken soup to combat the sniffles, freshly made lemonade, and a meat loaf sandwich that, served either hot or cold, is worth a special trip. To end such a homey meal, try the freshly baked fruit pies, often still warm from the oven. The boxy dining room has a quasi-country look with blue-and-white-checkered tablecloths and cordial waitresses outfitted in 1950s-style housedresses. ◆ American ◆ Daily breakfast and lunch. No credit cards accepted. 471 Haight St (between Webster and Fillmore Sts). 626.3984

31 Ya Halla ★★★$ This little Middle Eastern place serves up huge plates of delicious hummus, *baba ganooj,* and tabbouleh salad, combined with main courses such as falafel, lamb or chicken shish kebab, or *shwarma* (a type of lamb loaf made by pressing raw meat into a cylindrical shape and cooked on a skewer). Unfortunately, the desserts are way too sweet; have a cup of mint tea instead. Beer and wine are also available. The dining room has a charming ambience, with yellow walls, curved moldings here and there, and photos of Palestinian scenes; often, Middle Eastern music plays softly in the background. ◆ Middle Eastern ◆ Daily lunch and dinner. 494 Haight St (at Fillmore St). 522.1509 ఉ

32 Squat & Gobble Cafe ★★$ You haven't experienced sensory overload until you've walk into this crowded, aptly named cafe. Those who don't sport a pierced nose, purple hair, grungy pants, and a ripped, baggy T-shirt may feel out of place. Take a number, order, jockey for a table (which you will probably find heaped with dirty dishes), then wait for your number to be called. Why come here? Because these people know something about good food, and the portions are large. Crepes have either sweet fillings or such savory combinations as feta, artichokes, olives, and tomatoes; the sandwiches are made with toasted multigrain bread and served with sautéed potatoes; and puffy omelettes practically push the sautéed potatoes off the oversize plates. ◆ American/ Creperie ◆ Daily breakfast, lunch, and dinner. No credit cards accepted. 237 Fillmore St (between Waller and Haight Sts). 487.0551 ఉ

33 Studio Cafe ★$ The chalkboard specials hold the most promise at this all-natural cafe and include vegetarian lasagna, polenta with turkey sausage, and *torta rustica* (marinated artichoke hearts, ricotta, and spinach in a corn bread crust). The housemade dishes are supplemented by first-rate pastries from **La Seine.** The decor has a homespun quality: The tables look like flea-market finds, and what appear to be recycled pieces of wood and tin are nailed to the wall and painted white. ◆ American ◆ Daily breakfast, lunch, and dinner until 6PM. No credit cards accepted. 248 Fillmore St (between Waller and Haight Sts). 863.8982

34 India Oven ★★$$ The aroma of curry and roasting meats is the first hint that the food here is fresh and exciting. The dining room, an airy Victorian storefront, has a contemporary feel, with white tablecloths, flowers, modern art on the walls, and an open kitchen with a tandoori oven. Although the service can be a little erratic and slow, patience is rewarded by the creative twists given even standard dishes. The lamb sausage is stuffed with pistachios, and the chicken *masala* in a tomato sauce has a cumin kick. ◆ Indian ◆ Daily dinner. 233 Fillmore St (between Waller and Haight Sts). 626.1628; fax 626.3945

34 Thep Phanom ★★★$ Hands down, this Lower Haight spot serves the best Thai food in the city. The homey surroundings—lots of wood and folk art—and the friendly service are serendipitous. Don't miss the fried quail or the chicken wings stuffed with glass noodles. The meat salads, particularly the chicken or beef, have an extraordinary sweet-sour balance. The Thai crepes also are good, as is the chicken with basil and the chicken and coconut-milk soup. ◆ Thai ◆ Daily dinner. 400 Waller St (at Fillmore St). 431.2526 ఉ

35 Bean There Bamboo chairs, a painted concrete floor, and artistically brushed walls give this coffeehouse an up-to-date look. Up to 16 coffees are for sale in bulk, as are 26 teas, including lemon hibiscus, apricot decaf, honey ginseng, and a mixture of mango, banana, and pineapple. Customers can choose a coffee blend, and the staff will grind and brew it to order. There also are soups, sandwiches, focaccia, and pastries. In one corner are free newspapers for perusing and a collection of mugs, teapots, and other coffee-and tea-related items for sale. It's a fun place to sit and sip outdoors. ◆ Daily. 201 Steiner St (at Waller St). 255.8855 ఉ

Civic Center/ Hayes Valley/ The Tenderloin

The Civic Center has long been the political and cultural heart of the city; it houses the impressively domed **City Hall**, as well as the high-tech new branch of the **San Francisco Public Library**, the **War Memorial Opera House**, and **Louise M. Davies Symphony Hall**. With curtain times and the daily schedules of city, state, and federal workers to consider, many of the area eateries are geared to fast lunches and quick bites for pre-performance noshers. But the district also boasts some fine restaurants that are destinations in their own right—places like **Stars**, Jeremiah Tower's famous (and frenetic) brasserie, and the **Zuni Cafe**, where a loyal crowd enjoys roast chicken and probably the best Caesar salad in the city.

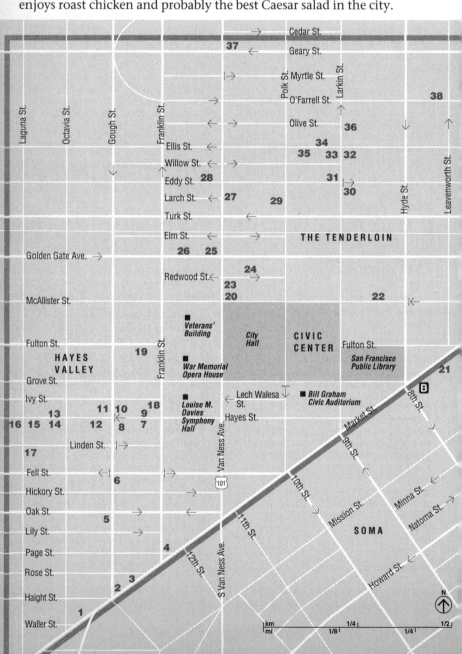

Vegetarians adore **Millennium,** the first restaurant in town to forgo not only meat but all dairy products and most added oil as well. Before or after the show, head to the plush, romantic **Act IV** for dinner or a nightcap. And the **California Culinary Academy,** also located here, trains professional chefs and runs two restaurants open to the public (of course, the food varies with the talents of the student chefs).

The two neighborhoods surrounding the area, Hayes Valley and the Tenderloin, are separated by **Van Ness Avenue,** the major north-south thoroughfare connecting San Francisco to **Marin.** Formerly a grand avenue, it has been transformed over the years into a mishmash of car dealerships, discount electronics stores, fast-food and mid-priced restaurants, and residential condominiums. **Hayes Street** received a much-needed boost when the interstate, which cut through the heart of the neighborhood, was damaged during the 1989 earthquake; it was later torn down. The street has been revitalized with new apartment buildings and a growing mix of restaurants, antiques shops, art galleries, and avant-garde clothing stores. Visitors as well as locals are drawn to the **Hayes Street Grill** for seafood, and the monastic-looking **Suppenküche** for modern German fare.

Perhaps the most interesting feature of the neighborhood's renaissance is the profusion of coffeehouses, cafes, and wine bars. **Place Pigalle** cafe provides sofas for cozy chats over wine, beer, coffee, and snacks, as well as live weekend entertainment and monthly art shows, and **Mad Magda's Russian Tea Room & Mystic Cafe** offers psychic readings in addition to tea, coffee, and light fare. **Momi Toby's Revolution Cafe** attracts 1960s-style political zealots and stages poetry readings on Monday nights. And the presence of **Hayes and Vine,** a stylish wine bar, is a sure sign that the neighborhood has been discovered by the mainstream. Still, the district's diversity is evident in such spots as **Moishe's Pippic,** a Chicago-style deli known for Vienna beef frankfurters and corned-beef sandwiches, and **Powell's Place,** which dishes up soul food along with first-rate fried chicken.

It's a big cultural leap across Van Ness Avenue to the Tenderloin, which suffers the highest crime rate in the city, although an influx of Vietnamese immigrants has helped soften the rough edges. Fortunately, some of the best cafes are located right on the Tenderloin's edge, along the relatively safe **Larkin Street.** Try the great fried quail at the Cambodian **Phnom Penh** or wonderful *bahn mi* (Vietnamese-French sandwiches) at **Saigon Sandwich.** During the day is the best time to explore the area east of Larkin, but even then it's a go-at-your-own-risk proposition.

1 Carta ★★$$ Under chef-owner Rob Zaborny (who spent 13 years at the **Hayes Street Grill**), this place offers what it calls "world cuisine": a menu of about a dozen small plates of appetizers and five entrées that focuses on a different country each month. Among the regions of the world Zaborny has explored in his cooking are India, Tuscany, and Greece. The setting is a storefront with an open kitchen in back; blue glassware on the tables adds a stylish note. ♦ World Cuisine ♦ Tu-Su dinner. Reservations recommended. 1772 Market St (between Gough and Waller Sts). Phone and fax 863.3516

2 Floogie's Swamp Cafe ★★$$ Jasper (Jazz) Boudreaux, who hails from Montegut, Louisiana, 75 miles south of New Orleans, has brought down-home Cajun food to San Francisco. The 1920s-style eatery has a classic Cajun look: ceiling fans, a corrugated tin roof covering a section of the bar, a saffron, green, and orange color scheme, and New Orleans memorabilia from Boudreaux's private collection. The space is tiny—just 48 seats, including the ones at the counter. The menu consists of such quintessential New Orleans fare as jambalaya, gumbo, barbecued shrimp, chicken-fried steak, and soft-shell crab, all prepared according to Boudreaux's family recipes. The "Swamp Cafe Sampler" combines small tastes of many of these dishes, with red beans and rice on the side. ♦ Cajun/Seafood ♦ Tu-F lunch and dinner; Sa brunch and dinner; Su dinner. 1686 Market St (between Franklin and Haight Sts). 864.3700

3 Zuni Cafe ★★★$$$ Most people who know and love food will put this restaurant at the top of their list of favorites. Since opening in the early 1980s with a menu of South-western fare (hence the name), the cafe has developed a Mediterranean flavor under the direction of chef-owner Judy Rodgers. Signature dishes include a grand selection of oysters, roast chicken with bread salad (bread and greens in a Champagne vinaigrette), juicy ground-to-order hamburgers on house-baked focaccia, and frosty espresso granita (coffee-flavored shaved ice). The Caesar salad is the best in the city. The unusual pie-shaped, two-story structure housing the restaurant has a bohemian feel, dovetailing with the eclectic crowd: artistic types, gays out on the town, and the city's most prominent citizens, all appearing to mix comfortably. ♦ American ♦ Tu-Su breakfast, lunch, and dinner. Reservations recommended for dinner. 1658 Market St (between Rose and Haight Sts). 552.2522; fax 552.9149 ♿

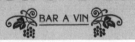

4 Bistro Clovis ★★$$ The style here comes straight from a Parisian wine bar, captured in the straight-back cane chairs, the impressive bar that commands one side of the room, the crocheted cafe curtains at the windows—and the menu. Classic country flavors come alive in the onion soup, shepherd's pie, smoked salmon, mushroom crepes, and light-as-air salmon mousse with marinated cucumbers. Be sure to do some wine sampling, too: Three two-ounce tastes of different wines are avail-able at a modest fee. ♦ French bistro ♦ M-Sa lunch and dinner. Reservations recommended. 1596 Market St (at Page St). 864.0231 ♿

5 Eliza's ★★★$$ Here's a stunning setting for fine Chinese fare. The restaurant preserved a Matisse-like mural and the art glass inherited from its French predecessor, and serves tea in Wedgwood demitasse cups and food on sophisticated Italian plates in a rainbow of colors. Start with the pot stickers and a refreshing celery salad, followed by a delicious sizzling-rice soup. Sunflower beef features thin slices of meat in a vibrant sauce surrounded by enoki mushrooms. Sesame chicken has a nutty flavor and is enhanced with julienned vegetables. Desserts are an afterthought, but what comes before is so good that only a sugarholic would object. ♦ Californian/Chinese ♦ M-F lunch and dinner; Sa dinner. Reservations recommended. 205 Oak St (between Gough and Octavia Sts). 621.4819 ♿

6 Thepin Thai Cuisine ★$ This pretty restaurant is popular with those who want a quick bite before the symphony (**Louise M. Davies Symphony Hall** is just four blocks away). The best bets are the chef's specialties and any of the salads that feature squid, duck, or chicken. But the food can be disappointing, missing the balance between sweet and acid and resulting in dishes that taste a bit sour. ♦ Thai ♦ M-F lunch and dinner; Sa-Su dinner. 298 Gough St (at Fell St). 863.9335

7 Nuts About You 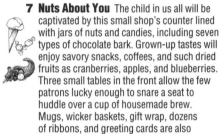 The child in us all will be captivated by this small shop's counter lined with jars of nuts and candies, including seven types of chocolate bark. Grown-up tastes will enjoy savory snacks, coffees, and such dried fruits as cranberries, apples, and blueberries. Three small tables in the front allow the few patrons lucky enough to snare a seat to huddle over a cup of housemade brew. Mugs, wicker baskets, gift wrap, dozens of ribbons, and greeting cards are also for sale in this charming, one-stop gift emporium. ♦ Daily. 327 Hayes St (between Franklin and Gough Sts). 864.6887

8 Hayes and Vine ★★$ This classy wine bar is a perfect stop before or after attending one of the nearby cultural events. It's a stylish, comfortable place to unwind. Thick cushions on the light wood chairs are upholstered in purple-and-gold-striped fabric, an attractive contrast to the earthy mustard-and-brick color scheme. The free-form white onyx bar glows (it's lit from below) and a black sculptural frame suspended above it holds gleaming stemware. Here, 350 bottles of wine are ready to be uncorked, and up to 35 wines can be ordered by the glass. Taste three similar wines—perhaps Pinot Blancs from California, Germany, and France—or compare the Rhônes of California and France. The food options are minimal, but all enhance the wine: There's caviar, pâté, cheese plates, smoked fish, and biscotti. ♦ Wine bar ♦ M-Th 5PM-midnight; F-Sa until 1AM. 377 Hayes St (between Franklin and Gough Sts). 626.5301; fax 626.5278 ♿

8 Caffè Delle Stelle ★★$$ The rustic pastas at this charming trattoria shine, whether with potatoes, sage, and truffle oil or blended with coarsely chopped tomatoes, garlic, arugula, and olive oil. Salads, especially the mixed greens with walnuts and blue cheese, are a good way to begin, and the mildly flavored, creamy tiramisù is a good way to end. ♦ Italian ♦ M-Sa lunch and dinner. Reservations recommended. 395 Hayes St (at Gough St). 252.1110; fax 863.5224 ♿

9 Hayes Street Grill ★★$$$ One of the city's most renowned seafood houses, it has built a reputation on serving the freshest fish with a choice of a half-dozen sauces. Salads all have unusual twists, such as grilled calamari with fennel, red onion, and arugula, or shrimp with grapefruit and lime. The 1930s-style light fixtures, bentwood chairs, white walls, and white tablecloths give the place a comfortable look. The service is erratic—anywhere from grill-room–surly (Heaven help you if you want to send anything back!) to diner-friendly. ♦ Seafood ♦ M-F lunch and dinner; Sa-Su dinner. Reservations recommended. 320 Hayes St (between Franklin and Gough Sts). 863.5545; fax 863.1873 ♿

10 City Picnic ★$ Passersby would never guess that this self-service restaurant has one of the most charming outdoor patios in the city. Tables cluster on cobblestone walkways, surrounded by flowers and grass under a canopy of Japanese maples. Stair-step benches on one side make a great spot for eating a sandwich (try the barbecued pork) and catching a few rays. There's also a good salad bar, Asian noodle salad, and Japanese *udon* soup. For the healthy set there are yogurt drinks mixed with fruit, bran, or whatever is trendy at the moment. ♦ American

♦ M-Sa 8AM-4PM. 384-A Hayes St (between Franklin and Gough Sts). 431.8814

11 Pendragon Bakery and Cafe ★$ On a busy corner, this popular spot turns out good muffins, scones, and salads. The shortbreads and cookies are particularly tasty, especially the Louisiana jumble, a huge cookie with chocolate chips, oatmeal, coconut, raisins, and an underlying flavor of brown sugar and butter. Savory hot dishes include vegetable roulade with a bronzed pastry and tamale pie. The few tables in front make it a good place for a quick bite. ♦ Cafe ♦ M-F 5AM-5PM; Sa-Su 6AM-5PM. 400 Hayes St (at Gough St). 552.7017

11 Stelline ★$ This cheerful eatery, with the kitchen half hidden behind stacks of beautifully arranged Italian products, is much more stylish than the low prices would indicate. Generous portions of pasta come with tossed salad and garlic bread. But if you want to splurge, try one of the large salads, the best being mixed greens surrounded by warm roasted potatoes, or one of the desserts, including a respectable tiramisù. This place is under the same ownership as **Caffè Delle Stelle** (see above). ♦ Southern Italian ♦ M-F lunch and dinner; Sa-Su dinner. No credit cards accepted. 429 Gough St (at Ivy St). 626.4292; fax 626.4282 ♿

12 Moishe's Pippic ★$ Midwesterners flock to this Chicago-style deli for the Vienna all-beef hot dogs, served heaped with Day-Glo green pickle relish and loads of mustard slathered on squishy poppyseed buns. Many Easterners swoon over the hot pastrami on chewy rye bread, but it's really pretty standard. And who else but a deli devotee could drool over the chopped liver sandwich with schmaltz? ♦ Deli ♦ M-F 8AM-4PM; Sa 9AM-4PM. No credit cards accepted. 425-A Hayes St (between Gough and Octavia Sts). 431.2440 ♿

The Return of the Smoke-Filled Room

Without a doubt, tobacco has been getting a lot of bad press lately. Tobacco company executives have had to go before Congressional hearings to testify about the safety of their product; presidential candidates give position statements on smoking (and often pay a political price for even appearing to support the tobacco industry); books like Christopher Buckley's *Thank You for Smoking* poke fun at the tobacco companies and their lobbyists; and the FDA is considering classifying nicotine as a drug. In response to this backlash, San Francisco and many other US cities have passed stringent laws prohibiting smoking in public places, including restaurants (for details on San Francisco's smoking policy, see page 7).

Strangely enough, at the same time as the tobacco industry has been under fire, cigar smoking has been on the rise. For example, an astounding $79 million was spent on cigars in the first half of 1996, according to statistics compiled by the Cigar Association of America. (That's an 83% increase over the first half of 1995.) There are cigar-oriented publications—including *Cigar Aficionado,* a monthly magazine largely credited with reigniting the cigar craze), books detailing cigar culture, and organized dinners where the participants can light up after eating without fear of censure.

The former image of the cigar smoker—a white-haired old man puffing away at a stogie—is now obsolete, in part because several high-profile celebrities have taken up the habit. Cigar-smoking public figures include President Bill Clinton, Bill Cosby, Rush Limbaugh, Arnold Schwarzenegger, and even actresses Whoopi Goldberg, Lauren Hutton, and Demi Moore. Basketball superstar Michael Jordan appeared on the cover of *Sports Illustrated* smoking a cigar after the **Bulls** won the 1994 world championship.

In short, cigar smoking has become cool, and baby boomers and Generation Xers—mostly well-heeled men and women in their 20s and 30s—are taking it up in droves. According to *Cigar Aficionado,* its readers boast an average annual salary of $150,000 and an average net worth of $1 million. The greater majority are professionals, and many run their own businesses.

The San Francisco restaurant industry, always quick to jump on any profitable bandwagon, decided it wanted to attract these high-rolling cigar lovers (and their bulging wallets) into their establishments, but it had those antismoking laws to contend with. The solution? Many of them have established cigar rooms on their premises. These rooms, which are usually luxurious and plush, are usually a good distance from the dining area and equipped with powerful exhaust fans to make sure that no one smells smoke who doesn't want to.

This way, the restaurants can have the best of both worlds: The dining rooms themselves remain smoke-free, but people who want to enjoy a cigar after a meal can retire to these retreats. High-quality cigars are always sold here, and there are often premium brandies, Cognacs, and other liqueurs available as well.

Cigars originate from such countries as Cuba, the Dominican Republic, Jamaica, Honduras, Mexico, and Nicaragua. And like the finest wines, cigars also come in a variety of strengths: mild (Casa Blanca or Macanudo), mild-to-medium (Te-Amo, Romeo y Julieta, or Don Diego), medium-to-full (Dunhill or Don Ramos), and full (Bolivar or Partagas).

The following are our choices for the best cigar rooms in town, where you can have a good meal *and* a good smoke.

The top cigar venue in the city is in the **Occidental Grill** (453 Pine St, between Montgomery St and Belden Pl, Union Square, 834.0484), which is always full of smokers. Six brands of cigars are sold here, including Dunhill and Partagas. Four times a year the restaurant hosts cigar dinners, featuring good food, fine wines and spirits, and the best cigars. They sell out quickly, so contact them far in advance if you want to attend. The cigar section, located in the bar, keeps the same hours as the restaurant, which is open Mondays through Fridays for lunch and dinner.

The Dining Room at the **Ritz-Carlton** (600 Stockton St, at Pine St, Nob Hill, 296.7465; fax 291.0147 ♿), one of the city's most elegant restaurants, has now added a classy cigar bar that fits in well with its formal surroundings. The bar is adjacent to the dining area, but powerful air cleaners have been installed so not a wisp of smoke escapes the glass walls. A dozen brands of cigar are sold here, including Don Asa, Partagas,

Macanudo, La Flora, Dominicana, Pleiades, La Gloria Cubana, and Hamiltons (a line by Upmann that is named for actor/cigar fancier George Hamilton). There's also an incredible selection of spirits: Rare Cognacs from 1968 and 1972, a 40-year-old Hennessey, and several well-aged Ports, just to name a few. And at last count, the bar served 110 single malt scotches, including one from 1972. The bar is open Monday through Saturday from 5:30PM to 11:30PM.

Fumé (101 Cyril Magnin St, at Ellis St, Union Square, 788.3863; fax 788.3864 &) is an upscale cigar bar run by local entrepreneur Tim Dale. Many *primo* cigar brands are offered here, such as Montecristo, Partagas, Hamiltons, Pheasant, Nat Sherman, and Dunhill. In addition, there's a lineup of more than a dozen single malt scotches, six bourbons, and six Cognacs. The bar is open Tuesday through Sunday from 4PM to 2AM.

At the venerable **North Beach Restaurant** (1512 Stockton St, between Green and Union Sts, 392.1587; fax 392.0230), a new cigar room has been created near the downstairs dining area. The bar sells Dunhill, Montecristo, Partagas, and Macanudo cigars, and humidor space can be rented. The cigar room is open at the same time as the restaurant, which serves lunch and dinner daily.

The cigar room at **Stars** (150 Redwood St, between Polk St and Van Ness Ave, Civic Center, 861.7827; fax 554.0351) is a glassed-off upstairs space with comfortable, plush leather easy chairs. Among the cigar brands available here are Dunhill, Partagas, Montecristo, and Hoyo de Monterey. The room is open from 11:30AM to 1:30AM daily, except when private parties are being held at J.T.'s Bistro, a small dining room right below it. Note: Although the restaurant itself is wheelchair accessible, the cigar room is not.

The decadently named **Bacchus Room** in the **Essex Supper Club** (847 Montgomery St, between Jackson St and Pacific Ave, Financial District, 397.5969; fax 397.3215 &) is very popular with a young, trendy crowd. Here, people leisurely sip top-flight brandies, play billiards, and, of course, smoke. Cigars featured for sale include Cohiba, Macanudo, Monte Cruz, Upmann, Hamiltons, Astral, and Don Thomas-Rothchild. The bar serves a lineup of 21 single-malt scotches and nine rare bourbons. The **Bacchus Room** is open Tuesday through Saturday from 5:30PM to 2AM.

At **Morton's of Chicago** (400 Post St, at Powell St, Union Square, 986.5830; fax 986.5829 &), patrons can smoke in the bar area to the left of the dining room. It's very popular because of the elegant, traditional surroundings and excellent service. Only Dunhill cigars are sold here. **Morton's** is open daily for dinner only.

13 Place Pigalle At this bar, art mixes with alcohol. In front, inviting sofas are arranged in cozy, conversational groupings; the back room is dedicated to monthly art exhibits and artsy metal tables. From the copper-topped bar come about 10 wines, 10 beers, and an array of coffee drinks. No food is served. Live performances of jazz are held several times a week. ♦ Daily. No credit cards accepted. 520 Hayes St (between Octavia and Laguna Sts). Phone and fax 552.2671

14 Powell's Place ★$ Soulful food draws locals to this bare-bones restaurant, owned by Emmit Powell, the well-known gospel singer. Great fried chicken, greens, and homemade pies top the list. You'll also find chicken-fried steak, pork chops, and braised short ribs. Just don't expect California-fresh vegetables; for example, the corn tastes as if it were picked by the Green Giant. ♦ Soul food ♦ Daily breakfast, lunch, and dinner. 511 Hayes St (between Octavia and Laguna Sts). 863.1404; fax 863.2368

15 Mad Magda's Russian Tea Room & Mystic Cafe ★$ "Great Food, Mystic Arts," reads the sign over this intimate cafe, summing up the focus here on baked goods, excellent coffee, and psychic readings (ask at the counter from early afternoon on). Tea is served in china pots and flowered cups from the 1940s. The cafe also offers soups, including borscht, a standard array of sandwiches and salads, and blintzes on weekends. A patio in back offers a hodgepodge of tables and chairs, set amid large splashes of greenery and vibrant clusters of pink and orange impatiens.

♦ Tearoom/Deli ♦ Daily lunch, afternoon tea, and dinner. 579 Hayes St (between Octavia and Laguna Sts). 864.7654

16 Suppenküche ★★$$ Popular with a hip crowd, the city's best German restaurant (whose name means "soup kitchen") serves the lighter kind of food now gaining increasing favor in Germany. Top dishes include venis on with red cabbage and cranberry sauce; bratwurst; chicken stew; and pork schnitzel with spaetzle. The cross in the corner of the dining room and the long, communal benches give the place a monastic look. ♦ German ♦ Daily dinner. Reservations recommended for parties over five. 601 Hayes St (at Laguna St). 252.9289

17 Momi Toby's Revolution Cafe The closest thing to the Age of Aquarius these days, this quirky coffeehouse offers poetry readings on Monday nights. Any day of the week, it's the place local hippies, beatniks, and other bohemians linger over strong cups of coffee. In the mornings, continental breakfast is available; and the lunch and dinner menu features enchilada pie, lasagna, soup, and one sandwich: tuna salad on a bagel. All of the food is brought in from outside and microwaved on the premises— not the most appetizing thought. ♦ Daily. 528 Laguna St (between Fell and Linden Sts). 626.1508

18 Vicolo Pizzeria ★$ If you like cornmeal-crust pizza, you'll like this place; if you don't, seek the pie of your dreams elsewhere. The pies have thick, crisp, cornmeal crusts and a choice of more than 30 combination toppings: Try the roast eggplant with blue cheese and garlic, or the fennel with mozzarella, fontina, red onions, and red bell peppers. A plus is that you can order by the slice to see if you like the combination. Green salads or marinated vegetable mixtures, such as black beans with jicama, are also available. Order at the counter, and the server will bring the food to the table. ♦ Pizzeria ♦ Daily lunch and dinner. 201 Ivy St (at Franklin St). 863.2382; fax 863.7202 &

19 Act IV ★★$$$ One of the most beautiful dining rooms in the city is located at the **Inn at the Opera** hotel. Decorated with wonderful oil paintings and flower arrangements, an ornate bar, dark wood appointments, an oversize fireplace, and deep, plush banquettes, it's the perfect spot for a drink and a bite either before or after a performance. The restaurant used to have a rather poor culinary reputation, but the owner has thoroughly overhauled the concept, and now the food lives up to the surroundings. The menu concentrates on steaks, chops, poultry, and fish, accompanied by inventive side dishes. Kick off the meal with the corn cakes with rock shrimp salsa enlivened with chipotle sour cream, or the tequila- and chili-cured gravlax with sour cream and flour tortillas. Winning main courses include grilled New York steak with roasted shallot butter; and beef tenderloin served with garlic mashed potatoes and a mushroom-onion demi-glace. The desserts, alas, are forgettable. ♦ American ♦ M-F breakfast, lunch, and dinner; Sa breakfast and dinner; Su brunch and dinner. 333 Fulton St (between Franklin and Gough Sts). 863.8400; fax 861.0821 &

20 Stars Cafe ★$$ Jeremiah Tower's less expensive version of **Stars** (see page 121) has an impersonal, corporate feel. The bar, which extends along one wall of the multilevel brasserie, has become a holding tank for expectant diners, since reservations are accepted only for large parties. Those waiting are poorly rewarded for their patience by a gougingly expensive by-the-glass wine list. Best food bets include hummus with fried *pappadams* (thin, crisp, lentil wafers), grilled rib-eye steak with mashed potatoes, and wood-oven–fired pizza. Among the out-standing, diverse desserts are a root-beer float, a mixed-berry napoleon, and a banana-cream pie with mounds of whipped cream. ♦ Californian ♦ Daily lunch and dinner. 500 Van Ness Ave (at McAllister St). 861.4344; fax 861.4322 &

CAFFE TRINITY

21 Caffe Trinity ★★$ At the end of City Hall Plaza, amid tacky T-shirt stores and pawnshops, this jewel has the rich appoint-ments found in espresso cafes in the best part of town—painted murals trimmed in gold leaf, Venetian glass chandeliers, a marble-and-mahogany bar, and matching bistro tables. The simple food is as lovely as the setting. Rich, strong coffee is served in oversized bowls. Breakfast features muffins, bagels, scones, and freshly squeezed juices.

Sandwiches, some of the best anywhere, include roast beef and turkey and are made with focaccia or a fresh-baked roll. Several pasta salads and freshly made soups are fine choices for a quick, light lunch. ♦ Cafe ♦ M-F breakfast and lunch. 1145 Market St (between Seventh and Eighth Sts). 864.3333 ₺

organic cuisine

MILLENNIUM

22 **Millennium** ★★$$ "Optimal health cuisine," which eschews meat, most oil, and dairy products, can present chefs with a stiff challenge. They've met it here. Start with the grilled portobello mushroom glazed with a sweet-and-spicy Moroccan sauce, or grilled rosemary polenta brightened with chopped red and yellow tomatoes. Main courses include a saffron and corn risotto, topped with a smoky stew featuring three beans and chunks of butternut squash; and chanterelle purse—phyllo dough filled with chanterelle and shiitake mushrooms, braised leek tofu "ricotta," and a barley-millet pilaf—served over a roasted shallot sauce and asparagus. If you're in San Francisco at Thanksgiving, try the restaurant's special feast, which boasts all of the trimmings—but none of the turkey. The centerpiece is a pumpkin that has been stuffed with seitan (a soy product), wild mushrooms, and root vegetables and then served over sage-perfumed polenta. Desserts are low-fat takeoffs on all-American favorites, including a nondairy butterscotch custard with an apple and cranberry compote. The cheerful setting, in the basement of a former carriage house for the 1920s-era **Abigail Hotel,** has a black-and-white tile floor, wall sconces, and sponge-painted walls. The wine list has a good selection of organic labels; organic beers are also offered. ♦ Vegetarian ♦ Tu-F lunch and dinner; Sa-Su dinner. 246 McAllister St (between Hyde and Larkin Sts). 487.9800; fax 487.9921

23 **Spuntino** $$ This high-tech Italian eatery has adopted the chaotic ordering process that's common all over Italy: semi–self-service. Diners order at the counter, pay, and head for a table to wait for the food. They have to fetch their own water and bus their own tables if they want the dishes cleared before they tackle dessert. The best way to go here is a salad (enough for two) and a simple pasta. Pizzas can be good but are sometimes underbaked and soggy, and the desserts look better than they taste. Given the food, ambience, and service, the place is a bit

overpriced. ♦ Italian ♦ Daily breakfast, lunch, and dinner; Sa-Su brunch. 524 Van Ness Ave (between McAllister and Redwood Sts). 861.7772; fax 861.7160 ₺

24 **Stars** ★★$$$$ After more than a decade, Jeremiah Tower's restaurant remains the archetypal American brasserie, and there's always a buzz at the tables, the bar, and the open kitchen overlooking the pizza oven. A new chef, Ralf Marhencke, recently took over the kitchen, and the menu now changes frequently. Among the best choices are the succulent rack of lamb; pasta with rabbit confit, capers, and tomato; grilled salmon; and sea bass paired with seafood ravioli and a Pernod-scented broth. (Skip the desserts, however, which are uniformly dreadful.) At peak times, the kitchen sometimes can't keep up with the crush of pretheater diners. Best to go at off-peak hours, or on a nonperformance weeknight. Upstairs is a separate room reserved for cigar smoking. ♦ Californian ♦ Daily lunch and dinner; limited bar menu daily 2PM-5:30PM and after 11:30PM. Reservations recommended for dinner. 555 Golden Gate Ave(between Polk St and Van Ness Ave). 861.7827; fax 554.0351 ₺

25 **Max's Opera Cafe** ★$ What it lacks in finesse, this eatery in the **Opera Plaza** apartment complex makes up for in quantity, like pastrami sandwiches as big as Arnold Schwarzenegger's biceps; one sandwich easily serves four. The blue-plate specials run from a chicken-wing dinner to barbecued brisket of beef, all served in such ample portions that leftovers are a given. Everything is large, but calorie counters can choose from such low-fat selections as salads with an oil-free mustard dressing, broiled chicken breast with tomato vinaigrette, and a turkey salisbury steak. The waitstaff also provides entertainment, breaking into song throughout the evening. ♦ Deli ♦ Daily lunch and dinner. 601 Van Ness Ave (at Golden Gate Ave). 771.7301; fax 771.2456

25 **Tempura House** ★★$$ This location, hidden away in the back of the **Opera Plaza** development, has been the kiss of death for restaurants: a steady succession of them has come and gone over the past several years. But this Japanese eatery has a good chance of surviving, thanks to the fact that it has a successful sister on Powell Street. The decor is understated and tranquil, with Japanese window treatments and plants, and the menu

boasts all the usual suspects: teriyaki; noodle dishes; chicken, pork, or fish *katsu* (cutlets); sashimi; and, of course, tempura. There's also a lively sushi bar where you can hobnob with other sushi lovers over sparkling fresh fish. Green tea ice cream and New York cheesecake are among the dessert offerings. ♦ Japanese ♦ Daily lunch and dinner. 601 Van Ness Ave (at Golden Gate Ave). 292.9997; fax 292.7767 ♿ Also at: 529 Powell St (between Sutter and Bush Sts), Union Square. 393.9911

26 **VIVANDE Ristorante** ★★$$$ Carlo Middione, who draws raves for his wonderful **VIVANDE Porta Via** in Pacific Heights, branched out by opening this impressive trattoria in the **Opera Plaza** complex. Known for his Southern Italian cooking, Middione has crafted a rustic menu where every pasta dish is a homemade winner—tagliatelle is tossed with oyster and shiitake mushrooms in a light olive-oil sauce. If rice is your fancy, try the risotto with sweet shrimp and fresh lemon. The buttery sea bass is served on a lightly charred wedge of cabbage that's drizzled with lemon oil and surrounded by roast potatoes. Finish the meal with the famous earthquake cake—a flourless chocolate cake with a cracked top. The Italian wine list is a bold move in a city where most restaurants offer California labels. The colorful frescoes, the bold orange-and-cream-striped lampshades on the ceiling fixtures and floor lamps, the orange-fronted brick oven, and the oversize wood chairs—which are branded with the distinctive "V" logo—are all examples of Middione's painstaking attention to detail. Before leaving, be sure to peek in the rest room to see the intricately painted, vaguely bawdy scenes—they're the talk of the town. ♦ Italian ♦ Daily lunch, tea, and dinner until midnight. 670 Golden Gate Ave (between Van Ness Ave and Franklin St). 673.9245; fax 673.2160 ♿

San Francisco
THAI BAR-B-Q

27 **Thai Bar-B-Q** ★★$ Good noodle dishes with a variety of meat and vegetable toppings—including squid, beef meatballs, and duck—are the staples here. Also available are such barbecued dishes as grilled prawns, trout, oysters, and veal, all served with carrot salad and sticky rice. To start, try the ever-popular flaky spring rolls or the chicken satay with peanut sauce. The cloth napkins and stylishly cool interior are unexpectedly elegant touches, considering the rock-bottom prices and in-a-hurry service. ♦ Thai ♦ M-F lunch and dinner; Sa dinner. No credit cards accepted. 730 Van Ness Ave (between Turk and Eddy Sts). 441.1640 ♿

28 **SF Scone Works** Mary Ann Woomer turns out some of the best scones in town in this small storefront. Baked throughout the day, they are dense but still crumbly, and come in such imaginative flavors as sun-dried cranberries and crystallized ginger with pecans. Those who want to eat scones fresh from the oven at home can buy them unbaked and frozen. ♦ M-F 6:30AM-4PM. 814 Eddy St (between Van Ness Ave and Franklin St). 922.0635

29 **California Culinary Academy** The West Coast's premier cooking school offers several training programs, including a 16-month professional chef's course. For the less committed culinarian, the continuing education department offers a series of one-shot or concentrated classes in catering and baking, as well as a kid's culinary college. In addition to preparing all the foods offered in the attractive ground-level retail shop, the students in the professional course run two dining rooms, but quality varies so widely that getting a good meal is as iffy as flipping a coin. ♦ 625 Polk St (between Turk and Eddy Sts). 771.3536; fax 775.5129 ♿

Within the California Culinary Academy:

Academy Grill $ Popular for lunch, this cafe is located in the culinary academy's basement. Among the offerings are burgers and deli items, as well as blue-plate specials: turkey florentine on Mondays, fried chicken on Wednesdays, and seafood gumbo on Fridays. ♦ American ♦ Call ahead; the hours vary with school sessions. 771.3536; fax 775.5129 ♿

Careme Room ★$$$ Set in a two-story atrium, this impressive room boasts soaring columns and walls of glass that let diners peek in on the culinary classrooms and kitchens. Early in the week, wait service is provided (including tableside preparations of Caesar salad and flaming desserts); Thursday and Friday offer buffets. Most dishes are continental classics; the menu continually changes. The high-priced wine list provides as much grief as pleasure: It's common to order vintages listed on the menu but be served something else because the selection wasn't available. ♦ French/Californian ♦ Call ahead; the hours vary with school sessions. Reservations recommended. 771.3536; fax 775.5129 ♿

30 **Saigon Sandwich** ★★$ The French influence found all over Vietnam adds a delightful twist to the fare at this typical Vietnamese cafe. The "Saigon sandwiches" here are made with French rolls slathered with mayonnaise and a pâté-like spread and heaped with a meat filling that might be pork or barbecued chicken. Then, for a wonderful crunch, cilantro and a few lightly pickled vegetables are added, including jalapeño,

daikon, carrots, and onions. Most sandwiches are very cheap and absolutely delicious and satisfying. ♦ Vietnamese ♦ Daily breakfast and lunch until 5PM. 560 Larkin St (between Turk and Eddy Sts). 474.5698

31 Bien Dong ★$ Incredibly cheap and surprisingly good Vietnamese food distinguishes this corner place from the look-alike storefronts up and down the block. Specialties include shrimp spring rolls, chicken with lemongrass over rice, and tofu with sautéed vegetables. ♦ Vietnamese ♦ Daily breakfast and lunch. 601 Larkin St (at Eddy St). 673.7604

31 Pacific Restaurant ★$ Open from morning to night, this Vietnamese eatery is known for its *pho* (beef and rice-noodle soup). The "soup" contains more noodles than broth, but those with big appetites can also opt for one of the inexpensive rice dishes. ♦ Vietnamese ♦ Daily breakfast, lunch, and dinner. 607 Larkin St (between Eddy and Willow Sts). 441.6722

32 Thai Noodle and Restaurant ★$ This bright new eatery offers well-prepared, if standard, Thai dishes, including chicken-lemongrass soup, pad thai, seafood dishes, curries, and barbecued meats. The decor is modern, with thin-slatted venetian blinds, sleek tables and chairs, and ethnic touches such as Thai artifacts. ♦ Thai ♦ Daily lunch and dinner. 670 Larkin St (between Eddy and Ellis Sts). 673.7220

33 Pagolac ★★$ Although this 50-seat place may look at first glance like a dreary Vietnamese coffee shop, it is spotless, which bodes well for the food. The best items to order here are the *com dai* (about 30 combinations of meat and vegetables served over rice), all very reasonably priced. Appetizers feature fragrant grilled pork balls served with rice noodles and pickled vegetables: Put together a bit of each ingredient on rice paper and wrap it all up. For dessert try the sweet red-bean paste layered with coconut milk and flavored gelatin and served in a parfait glass; it's challenging to eat it neatly, but the effort is definitely worth it. ♦ Vietnamese ♦ M-Tu, Th-Su lunch and dinner. 655 Larkin St (between Willow and Ellis Sts). 776.3234

34 New Chieu Fong Company Despite the somewhat run-down neighborhood, connoisseurs trek out to this market featuring Southeast Asian and Chinese products; it is one of the best in the city. Shoppers will find good produce, including young ginger, lemongrass, bitter melons, and lots of fresh noodles. There's also a fresh-fish display case, a wide variety of meats, which are butchered on-site, and dry goods. ♦ Daily. 724 Ellis St (between Larkin and Polk Sts). 776.7151 ♿

35 Racha Cafe ★★$ This Thai restaurant has won the affection of many local chefs, and it's gotten even better recently. You can always count on getting good meat salads, soups, whole fish, noodle dishes, and fried rice here. ♦ Thai ♦ Daily lunch and dinner. 771 Ellis St (between Larkin and Polk Sts). 885.0725 ♿

36 Thang Xuong Market With aisles barely wide enough to walk down with a hand-held basket, this tiny full-service market packs in lots of merchandise. Prices are lower here than at the **New Chieu Fong** market around the corner. ♦ Daily. No credit cards accepted. 724 Larkin St (between Ellis and O'Farrell Sts). 474.4004 ♿

37 Fina Estampa ★★$$ This successful tapas eatery based in the Mission has now opened a second location on Van Ness Avenue. The decor is rather glitzy, with an oversized chandelier dominating the high-ceilinged downstairs area, a grand staircase leading to the upper level (which is mainly used for private parties), and gilt-framed paintings of saints. The menu of appetizers features selections from Peru and Spain, including *anticuchos* (tender, cumin-scented pieces of skewered beef heart), *papa a huancaina* (potato chunks topped with a turmeric-colored feta-cheese sauce), and *patita de chancho a la criolla* (pickled pigs' feet served with pickled onions and bits of tomato). Main courses range from New York steak to *arroz con pollo* (chicken with rice). Seafood and vegetarian plates are offered as well. ♦ Peruvian/Spanish ♦ Tu-Su lunch and dinner. 1100 Van Ness Ave (at Geary St). 440.6343 ♿ Also at: 2374 Mission St (between 20th and 19th Sts), The Mission. 824.4437

38 German Cook ★★$ A warm ambience prevails at this tiny German restaurant. Diners can perch at the four seats at the counter in front of the open kitchen or sit in a wooden booth painted with delicate flowers. Everything has a lived-in look, but the waitress sparkles and has more than enough energy to cover the room by herself. Great, filling combinations include stuffed cabbage, sauerbraten with potato pancakes, and bratwurst with a fine consistency and a crisp, browned exterior. ♦ German ♦ M-Su dinner; W-F lunch. No credit cards accepted. 612 O'Farrell St (between Leavenworth and Hyde Sts). 776.9022

Around the boom time of the Gold Rush, fresh food was very expensive in San Francisco. A small loaf of bread cost 50¢, while onions were $1 per pound. Eggs, which were usually shipped from the East Coast, could cost as much as $10 a dozen.

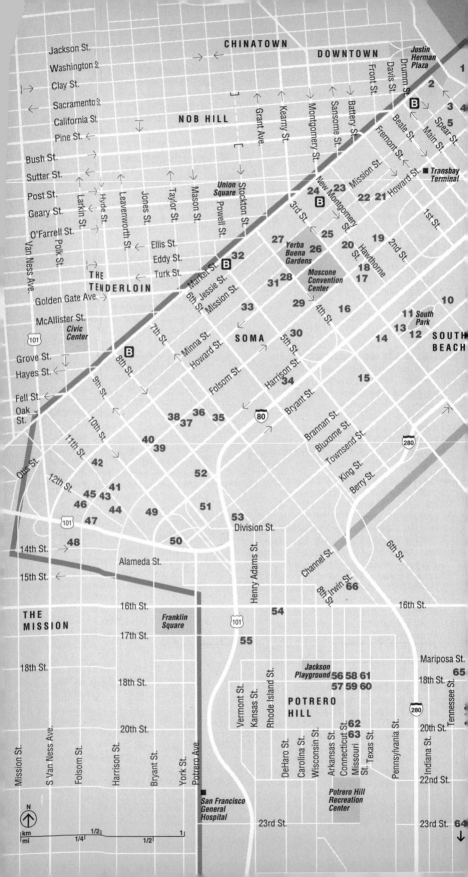

Ferries to Sausalito, Tiburon, Vallejo, Larkspur, Oakland, and Alameda

ng

to Oakland, Berkeley, and Alameda

80

Bay Bridge

Pier 30

Pier 40 **8**

South Beach Yacht Harbor

China Basin

0
Mission Rock St.

a Basin St.

San Francisco Bay

9
ua Vista
rk
entral
asin

SoMa (South of Market)/ South Beach/ Potrero Hill/ Bay View– Hunters Point

The South of Market area, popularly known as SoMa, has evolved into one of San Francisco's most eclectic and arty frontiers—and one of the city's most fun and casual districts for food. Bounded by **San Francisco Bay**, **Van Ness Avenue**, **I-80**, and **Market Street**, SoMa began as an industrial area. Several foundries established headquarters here in the 1850s, as did light industrial companies, wholesalers, and the **Southern Pacific Railroad.** When these industries moved out in the 1970s, blue-collar families and members of San Francisco's artistic community moved in, converting the cavernous warehouses into residential spaces. Still home to a community of families and artists today, SoMa has become a trendy neighborhood, ever-changing with the arrival of new restaurants, discos, and comedy clubs.

One cause of SoMa's rebirth was undoubtedly the 1981 arrival of the **Moscone Convention Center**, which was followed in 1989 by the **San Francisco Centre**, a vertical mall that is anchored by **Nordstrom.** The addition of such hotels as the **Marriott** and the **Sheraton Palace** also changed the face of the area, as did the 1994 debut of the dazzling **Yerba Buena Gardens** arts complex and cultural center and the 1995 unveiling of the **San Francisco Museum of Modern Art.**

The 1989 Loma Prieta earthquake actually provided another boon. Thanks to the temblor's devastation, the **Embarcadero Freeway** that had long blocked SoMa from the waterside

1·25

had to be dismantled. As a result, gorgeous views of the bay have been opened up, giving rise to the section of town known as South Beach, which is west of **The Embarcadero** and south of the **Bay Bridge**. The biggest residential building project in San Francisco in more than 30 years is currently being planned for South Beach; construction has been put on hold indefinitely, however, due to lack of funds. One of South Beach's best views of the Bay Bridge can be had from the patio of **Palomino Euro Bistro**, a glitzy branch of the Seattle-based chain at the **Hills Brothers Plaza** (once a coffee factory). The house-brewed beers and lively crowd at **Gordon Biersch Brewery Restaurant** make this pub worth a stop.

Potrero Hill, an up-and-coming residential area, is also enjoying a renaissance. Set on a hill above SoMa, it boasts some of the city's sunniest weather and awe-inspiring panoramas. The neighborhood's main shopping strip, a three-block stretch along **18th Street**, is so small-town picture-perfect that it could be a movie set. Yet the shops and restaurants here are charmingly diverse: There's **Aperto**, a fine Italian trattoria; **Eliza's**, for delicious Chinese food with a California twist; **San Francisco Bar-B-Que**, a Thai noodle house; **Asimakopoulos Cafe**, a top Greek spot; **The Daily Scoop**, an old-fashioned ice-cream parlor; and **Farley's**, an inviting coffeehouse.

Another bustling area is at SoMa's northern corner, around **Rincon Center** —a massive complex just south of Market Street and off The Embarcadero. Clustered within a few blocks of each other, such impressive places as **Boulevard** and **Harry Denton's** have made this the city's new Restaurant Row.

Changes may also be in store for one of the poorest neighborhoods in the city: Bay View–Hunters Point. This area runs along **Third Street** from **Army Street** to **Bayshore Boulevard** through what remains of San Francisco's light industrial, warehouse, and manufacturing districts. Most of the restaurants in this chiefly African-American neighborhood specialize in soul food, fried fish, and barbecue, with a few Chinese places here and there.

As with any burgeoning area, the attrition rate for restaurants has been high; but the quality of the eateries opening in SoMa has consistently improved. Among the wonderful spots with staying power are **LuLu**, known for great seafood and rotisserie meats and its impressively vast warehouse setting; **Fringale Restaurant**, a top French bistro; the pretty and lively **Bistro Rôti**; **Wu Kong Restaurant**, with its impressive menu of Shanghai specialties; the Parisian-style **South Park Cafe**; and **The Fly Trap**, which offers new twists on San Francisco classics. Other noteworthy spots are **Basil**, a sophisticated restaurant that melds California and Thai cuisines, **Kyo-ya**, one of the top Japanese eateries in the city; and **Hawthorne Lane**, a dining spot owned by Anne and David Gingrass, who—with Wolfgang Puck—put **Postrio** on the map.

Though the SoMa area still has rough edges, its fresh and appealing mix is drawing everyone from white-collar conventioneers to twentysomethings and stylish types of all ages, all eager to explore the culinary diversity here.

1 Ferry Plaza Farmers' Market Located on the beautiful waterfront in front of the **Ferry Building**, this certified market features fresh seasonal produce and such special events as a "Shop with the Chef" tour, during which a well-known cook chooses produce and offers shoppers advice on preparing it; some chefs include a cooking demonstration. There are also monthly tastings of one type of produce, such as greens, and activities for children, including cooking classes. The market has grown so popular that there's now a second branch near the **Hyatt Regency;** it's held on Tuesdays. ♦ Tu 11:30AM-3PM; Sa 8AM-1:30PM. Tuesday market: Market St (near the Hyatt Regency, 5 Embarcadero Center, between The Embarcadero and California St). No phone; Saturday market: Ferry Plaza (at The Embarcadero and Market St, near the Ferry Building). 981.3004 &

2 One Market Restaurant ★★★$$$
Celebrity chef Bradley Ogden made a name for himself at the illustrious **Campton Place;** then he moved to Marin County and opened the much-praised **Lark Creek Inn.** A couple of years ago, Ogden returned to San Francisco, opening this place in SoMa with Michael Dellar. Now he and Dellar have brought in a new partner, chef George Morrone, who has rejuvenated the entire menu and added more refined dishes. Appetizers like roasted foie gras with blackberry-balsamic essence and tuna carpaccio with lemon oil and celery juice are well worth their rather high price tags (none costs less than $10). Main courses include herb-poached baby chicken with white pepper dumplings on the side; New Zealand sea trout paired with a tomato coulis and a crisp calamari salad; and a truly decadent salmon steak resting atop foie gras mashed potatoes. Desserts are more homey, but feature the freshest seasonal fruits, home-made ice creams, and sorbets. Although the stylish interior design cost millions (the eggplant-colored walls are a particularly nice touch), the sea of tables, hard-surfaced floor, and high-tech open kitchen in back drive the noise level to deafening heights. ♦ Californian ♦ M-F lunch and dinner; Sa dinner. Reservations recommended. 1 Market St (at Steuart St). 777.5577; fax 777.3366 ♿

3 Boulevard ★★★$$$ Two of the city's top talents joined together for this venture—Nancy Oakes (formerly of **Pat O'Shea's Mad Hatter**), whom *Food & Wine* recently heralded as one of the country's top new chefs, and **Pat Kuleto,** who has designed some of the city's best restaurants (most notably **Postrio**). Here **Kuleto** has created a room with three distinct areas: the bar, defined by a domed brick ceiling and an intricate peacock-patterned tile floor; the informal central section, with an open kitchen and a counter; and the dramatically lit, more formal dining area. Oakes is known for her lusty combinations and innovative presentations. Her menu changes often, but when she features squab, be sure to try it. In one version, the bird comes accented with golden and red beets and red currants. The smoked sturgeon, served on a potato pancake and topped with a horseradish crème fraîche and golden caviar, is terrific, too, especially paired with a glass of Le Pigeoulet Blanc. Other items include a crisp roast duck with corn pancakes; tender grilled veal T-bone atop parmesan mashed potatoes; and, for vegetarians, wild mushroom risotto. For dessert, our pick is the orange walnut torte with honey ice cream and roasted peaches, which comes topped with a Sauterne-peach sauce. The wine list is a little pricey, but features some excellent, hard-to-find California vintages. ♦ French/Californian ♦ M-F lunch and dinner; Sa-Su dinner. Reservations recommended. 1 Mission St (at Steuart St). 543.6084; fax 543.8631 ♿

4 Longlife noodle & jook joint ★★$ For such an Asian-oriented city, San Francisco doesn't have a lot of big noodle houses. But now George Chen, co-owner of **Betelnut,** is seeking to fill the gap with this new pan-Asian eatery, whose name refers to the fact that in Chinese culture, noodles symbolize a long life. The kitchen produces a varied menu which includes Japanese *udon,* Vietnamese rice sticks, and Chinese egg noodles presented in soups, stir-fries, and salads. *Jook* (a savory Chinese rice gruel) is also prominently featured. Another fun dish to try is the yin-yang delight (wheat noodles served with five-spice beef and fresh spinach). The dining area is decorated with part-bamboo counters and jade green accents. ♦ Pan-Asian ♦ Daily lunch and dinner (F-Sa to midnight). 139 Steuart St (between Howard and Mission Sts). 281.3818; fax 281.9088 ♿

4 Bistro Rôti ★★★$$ Any seat in the house offers a good view of the action here: There's a lively bar scene up front; in the middle, a chef tends a rotisserie at an open brick fireplace; and, in the back of the room, counter seats overlook an open kitchen and tables have views of the Bay Bridge. The food has a French twist, as evidenced by such offerings as french fries with lemon aioli, or the grilled duck breast salad with peaches and a Port vinaigrette. The fireplace turns out grilled lamb sirloin, served with a silky polenta, and spit-roasted chicken, with garlic mashed potatoes. The griddled salmon with a thin mustard glaze and shiitake mushrooms, and the duck confit with lentils and garlic are also standouts. Dessert offerings include cherry-and-apricot brioche pudding, and an excellent crème brûlée topped with either light or dark chocolate. Although the food can be inconsistent, the service is efficient and the surroundings make up for the occasional lapses. ♦ Californian/French ♦ M-F lunch and dinner; Sa-Su dinner. Reservations recommended. 155 Steuart St (between Howard and Mission Sts). 495.6500; fax 495.3522 ♿

Harry Denton's

4 Harry Denton's ★$$ Operated by one of the city's most celebrated party guys, this posh watering hole is a favorite late-night haunt. The action at the bar (there's a cover charge for the live music after 9PM Thursday through Saturday) is better than the homey fare, although that can be pretty good, too. Pot roast with mashed potatoes and gravy is the signature dish. Other options include the blackened meat loaf (no, it wasn't burned, it's supposed to look that way); oak-fired pizzas; spaghetti marinara with rock shrimp and pesto; and country-style chicken with artichokes, escarole, and white beans. Parties of six or more can take advantage of an inexpensive five-course family-style dinner. ◆ American ◆ Daily breakfast, lunch, and dinner. Reservations recommended. 165 Steuart St (between Howard and Mission Sts). 882.1333; fax 979.0471 &

5 Rincon Center This multiuse complex contains several ethnic restaurants and many lunch places catering to office workers. What distinguishes the food court is that many of its eateries are branches of local restaurants, rather than generic chains. ◆ 101 Spear St (at Mission St)

Within Rincon Center:

CHALKERS
Billiard Club

Chalkers Billiard Club ★$ Shoot a game of pool and have a bite to eat at this elegant billiard parlor boasting more than 30 antique and custom pool tables. Appetizers veer toward the chip-and-dip genre: salsa with chips, tuna pâté, roasted-garlic almond spread, or country pâté with sourdough bread. Main courses include hearty salads, a pasta or two, and a large variety of sandwiches, including Mexican chicken, a salmon burger with jack cheese, and Italian sausage with marinara sauce. The most popular (and best) comestibles, however, are the 10 draft beers or the dozen wines available by the glass. ◆ American ◆ Daily lunch and dinner. 512.0450 &

Sorabol Noodles ★$ The area's top Korean restaurant is a scaled-down version of the original in Oakland, which has now closed. The menu features barbecue, noodles (try the seaweed noodles with beef, chicken, or pork), and a few side orders such as pot stickers and stir-fried vegetables. ◆ Korean ◆ M-F lunch until 4PM. 896.5959 &

Burger Gourmet ★$ All kinds of juicy hamburgers and fixings are available at one of the most popular lunch places around. ◆ American ◆ M-F breakfast and lunch. 777.9200 &

Tampico $ A safe bet for a quick Mexican fix. Burritos are filled with steak, pork, sausage, chicken, or cheese. Wash it all down with a fresh strawberry, pineapple, mango, banana, watermelon, or tangerine *agua fresca* soda. ◆ Mexican ◆ M-F lunch until 4PM. No credit cards accepted. 543.8616 &

Village Pizza ★$ Here's an outlet of the popular local pizza chain. Choose either a thick- or thin-crust pie, with all kinds of toppings, including clams and garlic.

◆ Pizzeria ◆ M-F lunch and dinner; Sa lunch until 4PM. 243.0666; fax 243.0917 & Also at: Numerous locations throughout the city

Thatcher's Dozens of flavors of sweet and savory popcorn, all available for sampling, are made here. Among the unique concoctions are low-fat caramel, honey vanilla and nuts, cookies and cream, pistachio crunch, sour cream and onion, jalapeño, barbecue, and white cheddar. ◆ M-F 10AM-6PM. 957.9601; mail-order sales 800/926.2676; fax 957.1217 & Also at: 180 Howard St (at Main St). 957.9601; fax 957.1217 &

Wu Kong Restaurant ★★$$ One of the city's prettiest Chinese restaurants, complete with glittering chandeliers and fine art, it's also the place to sample the cuisine of Shanghai province. Unfortunately, the food has gone a bit downhill of late. For an appetizer, try the drunken squab or drunken chicken (chilled and served in a wine sauce). Another must-have, whether as part of dinner or dim sum, is the Shanghai dumpling (a savory pork filling wrapped in gossamer-light noodle dough), which is best eaten in one bite. The vegetarian "goose," however, is rather bland, and the noodle dishes are prepared with too much oil. ◆ Chinese ◆ Daily lunch (including dim sum) and dinner. 957.9300; fax 957.0696 &

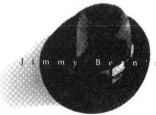

Jimmy Bean's ★★$ The menu at one of the most popular lunch spots in **Rincon Center** focuses on quesadillas, with fillings that range from duck with shiitake mushrooms and fennel, to grilled eggplant with potato and roasted tomato, scallops with parsley pesto, and vegetables with chipotle-and-cilantro pesto. The superb sandwiches include roast leg of lamb with red onions and eggplant, and pork loin with pears, arugula, red onions, and a red-pepper sauce. If none of these hits the spot, try one of the *soba* (buckwheat) noodle salads, chicken or seafood skewers, or *pizzettas*. ◆ Californian ◆ M-F breakfast and lunch. 495.2590; fax 495.2711 &

6 Palomino Euro Bistro ★$$ An offshoot of a Seattle-based chain, this eatery in **Hills Brothers Plaza** affords diners the best view of the Bay Bridge. The menu revolves around the wood-burning oven: Pizzas have cracker-thin crusts, and two of the best main courses are spit-roasted chicken and cedar-planked salmon with a hint of flavor picked up from the cedar. Even the apple tart gets a turn in the wood oven and comes out with a bronze glaze that is topped off with a drizzle of caramel sauce. ♦ Mediterranean ♦ M-F lunch and dinner; Sa dinner; Su brunch and dinner. 345 Spear St (between Harrison and Folsom Sts). 512.7400; fax 512.7358 ♿

6 Gordon Biersch Brewery Restaurant

★$$ The three types of beer (all brewed in-house), lovely view of the Bay Bridge, and lively after-work crowd are reasons enough to check out this pub, but the food served in the upstairs dining loft is also pretty good. The Korean-style short ribs and shrimp and chicken pot stickers are well-prepared appetizers. Try the signature garlic fries (with or without a cheeseburger on the side) or the wood-oven–scented pizza. Unfortunately the fried calamari is tough and doughy, and the grilled New York steak topped with Maytag blue cheese is inconsistent (tender one night, overcooked the next). Desserts are served in generous portions but aren't memorable. Service can be erratic at busy times, and bar noise sometimes intrudes on the dining area. ♦ Californian/Brew pub ♦ Daily lunch and dinner. 2 Harrison St (at Steuart St). 243.8246; fax 243.9214 ♿

7 Delancey Street Restaurant

$$ This self-described "ethnic American bistro" makes a social statement as well as a culinary one. It's run by residents of the Delancey Street Project, a residential community and training program for paroled criminals and former down-and-outers and drug addicts. The handsome copper bar, hand-crafted by the residents, and the wood and brass appointments create a modern bistro look. The outdoor patio provides a lovely view of the Bay Bridge and the waterfront area. On any given day, the menu might include matzoh-ball soup, Szechuan noodles with peanut sauce, Moroccan vegetable stew, or salmon mousse in phyllo. The American fare includes such staples as meat loaf, pot roast, barbecued baby back ribs, and chicken. ♦ Eclectic ♦ Tu-Su lunch and dinner. 600 The Embarcadero (at Brannan St). 512.5179 ♿

8 Red's Java House

★$ In contrast to all the new development going on around The Embarcadero since the freeway tumbled in the 1989 earthquake, this diner looks like an old crab shack. But for 36 years it has been a working-class gathering spot; and lately it's also being invaded by the white-collar crowd. The double cheeseburgers served here are legendary, and there's no need to delve much deeper. ♦ American ♦ M-Sa breakfast and lunch. Pier 40 (off The Embarcadero, between Berry and Townsend Sts). 495.7260 ♿

8 Pier 40 Roastery & Cafe

★$ Right on the wharf, this glass-enclosed cafe is a welcome addition to **Pier 40**. It serves good food for all three meals. Among the top breakfast items are corned beef hash with eggs and toast; a hazelnut French toast; and *gallo pinto,* a concoction of eggs, black beans, rice, and tortillas. Lunch dishes include cheeseburgers with potato salad; a roasted zucchini sandwich; and tuna nicoise. The dinner menu (served until 8PM) presents soups, salads, tapas, and such entrées as grilled eggplant and roasted peppers seasoned with balsamic vinegar and roasted garlic; and Chilean sea bass cakes served atop mashed potatoes and drizzled with chipotle chili sauce. In good weather, there's outdoor seating with a great view of the water, and there are live jazz performances Wednesday through Friday evenings. ♦ Contemporary ♦ Daily breakfast, lunch, and dinner (until 8PM). Pier 40 (off the Embarcadero, between Berry and Townsend Sts). 495.3815; fax 495.3818 ♿

9 Town's End Restaurant and Bakery

★★$$ The bakery here turns out chewy sourdough rye, poppy-seed wheat baguettes, parmesan bread sticks, and all kinds of delectable treats; in the restaurant, the basket of bread that graces the table is one of the best parts of the meal. The dining room is set off by curved partitions that combine with the bay views for a nautical ambience. The menu changes daily, but typical creations include a crisp triangle of polenta topped with shiitake, chanterelle, and portobello mushrooms; ravioli stuffed with caramelized onions; and fettuccine with rock shrimp in a light, but intensely flavored, tomato broth. If you're lucky, chocolate angel-food cake or lemon meringue pie will be among the desserts. ♦ American ♦ Tu-F breakfast, lunch, and dinner; Sa brunch and dinner; Su brunch. 2 Townsend St (at Delancey St). 512.0749; fax 512.0927 ♿

10 Infusion Bar & Restaurant

★★★$$ This South Beach eatery has made a name for itself very quickly, thanks to the delicious food and the wide variety of vodkas available here. Another draw is the live jazz music, which is performed nightly. Outstanding appetizers include the guava-filled empanada served with a wedge of Brie cheese, and roasted mussels steamed with a lemon-anise–infused vodka. For the main course, the menu offers salads, pastas (including a very satisfying linguine with grilled chicken and butternut squash), and a number of hearty meat entrées. Among the highlights are grilled New York steak, filet mignon, a thick-cut pork chop, a hamburger, and salmon fillet. The prices are fairly reasonable, but side orders come à la carte, which drives up the tab. The decor is modern, with stainless steel furnishings and accents, but a warm color scheme makes the atmosphere feel more welcoming. Service, however, can be frustratingly slow. ♦ Contemporary ♦ M-F lunch and dinner; Sa-Su dinner. 555 Second St (between Brannan and Bryant Sts). 543.2282; fax 543.3573

11 Caffe Centro ★★$ The perfect out-of-the-way retreat, an hour spent here is almost as relaxing as a weekend in the country. With bright paintings on the walls, a floor painted in warm tones of gold, green, and red, and an attractive wood bar, this mellow space is the ideal spot for savoring a light breakfast and a leisurely perusal of the morning paper. The menu changes slightly for lunch, but the mood is just as free-spirited. Try one of the generous salads or a focaccia sandwich with grilled vegetables or chicken. Good choices for dessert are the brownies and cookies, which taste freshly baked. ♦ Cafe ♦ M-F breakfast, lunch, and early dinner; Sa breakfast and lunch until 4:30PM. 102 South Park Ave (at Center Pl). 882.1500; fax 882.1502 ⴺ

S⊙UTH PARK CAFE

11 South Park Cafe ★★★$$ Here's a little bit of Paris overlooking the urban oasis of **South Park.** With the long, narrow room painted in ocher, the cozy bar, and the brief menu, the atmosphere is French cafe all the way. There's blood sausage, steamed mussels, roast pork tenderloin with potato puree, and duck breast with honey, ginger, and cinnamon. Desserts include a classic crème brûlée, profiteroles, and a bittersweet chocolate cake. ♦ French ♦ M-F breakfast, lunch, and dinner; Sa dinner. 108 South Park Ave (between Center Pl and Third St). 495.7275; fax 495.7255 ⴺ

12 Ristorante Ecco ★★$$ The simple but stylish dining room, which looks out onto

South Park, basks in warm earth tones. More dramatic is the impressive bar, which is set beneath a soaring ceiling along with some tables that accommodate dining room overflow. As at so many places, changes in the kitchen have caused the food to falter a bit. Still, an always reliable choice, *linguine al Ecco,* is one of the best dishes on the menu—an unlikely mix of linguine, pears, pecans, gorgonzola, and parmesan (ask to have it split into two portions for an appetizer). Another option for starters is the deep-fried squid with fennel and red onion. Main courses include *poussin* (broiler chicken) stuffed with olives, salmon served on white beans, or rabbit braised in red wine with mushrooms. ♦ Italian ♦ M-F lunch and dinner; Sa dinner. Reservations recommended. 101 South Park Ave (at Center Pl). 495.3291; fax 495.7225 ⴺ

12 Collections Gift Store It's quite a surprise to find this refined shop amid the urban sprawl here, and it's worth seeking out for the good selection of coffees and chocolates and stellar inventory of specialty foods. In addition, the shop sells great candles and candlesticks, water pitchers shaped like pelicans, handmade plates and platters emblazoned with fish, and even seed packets to grow a fragrant herb garden. ♦ M-Sa. 380 Brannan St (between Center Pl and Third St). 546.9298; fax 546.9397

13 Lumbini Garden statuary fills the windows of this shop, but the interior is stocked with all kinds of arty ceramic bowls and plates, some handmade by local artisans. Most items have a produce motif: earrings shaped like carrots, candles that replicate avocados, teapots that look like a head of cabbage, and the like. ♦ M-F noon-8PM. 156 South Park Ave (at Third St). 896.2666; fax 896.2995 ⴺ

14 The Wine House A warehouse-style shop with brick walls and wine stacked up in crates, it has one of the city's best inventories of French wines. Bordeaux, Burgundy, and Rhône selections are particularly strong; the store stocks multiple vintages of many of the best houses, including Château d'Yquem. Domestic and other non-French wines are also available. The knowledgeable staff can answer just about any question you can pose. ♦ M-Sa. 535 Bryant St (between Third and Fourth Sts). 495.8486; fax 495.4720 ⴺ

Fringale
RESTAURANT

15 Fringale Restaurant ★★★★$$ Chef Gerald Hirigoyen has created just about the best casual French restaurant you'll find outside of France. What's more, he's maintained his reasonable prices, despite his soaring popularity (a few years ago, *Food & Wine* named him one of the country's best new chefs). Some of the standout dishes on his Basque-influenced menu include Roquefort ravioli with pine nuts and basil; not-to-be-missed mussels flecked with parsley and crisp pieces of fried garlic; and a meltingly tender duck confit served with warm green lentil salad. Hirigoyen used to be a pastry chef, so look forward to finishing up with a rich crème brûlée, custardy fruit *clafouti* (a cross between a flan and a fruit-filled pancake), or a Basque chocolate cake. The restaurant's yellow facade and interior, curved bar, and large fresh flower arrangements are all the more charming in the semi-industrial location. Most of the staffers are French and are just as appealing as their surroundings. The place is so popular that there's often a wait, even with a reservation. ♦ French ♦ M-F lunch and dinner; Sa dinner. Reservations recommended. 570 Fourth St (between Brannan and Bryant Sts). 543.0573; fax 905.0317 ♿

BIZOU

15 Bizou ★★$$ Loretta Keller made her reputation at **Stars** before moving to South Beach to open her own place, an old-time bistro with hanging light fixtures and glazed mustard-colored walls. The bar dominates one side of the room, and the bar-side tables (by the windows overlooking Fourth Street) are perfect for those with romance in mind. Lately the quality of the food has dipped a bit, mainly because many of the dishes are too salty; however, the tempura-fried green beans, in a delicate batter with a bit of crunch and served with a fig dip, remain one of the best dishes of all time. The slow-simmered and gently baked dishes are just the thing on a foggy day. Sizzling Catalan shrimp and fresh grilled sardines are popular. Desserts are memorable, especially the summer berry pudding, with its dense, moist, cakey texture and plenty of fruit. ♦ French ♦ M-F lunch and dinner; Sa dinner. Reservations recommended. 598 Fourth St (at Brannan St). 543.2222; fax 543.2999 ♿

16 The CoffeeNet ★$ The idea behind this enterprise is to give the fanatical Internet user a comfortable place to surf the World Wide Web and hook up with other users while grabbing a bite to eat. So in addition to a menu of tasty deli-style sandwiches (like roast beef, Bay shrimp, or corned beef on a croissant or roll), coffee drinks, and desserts, patrons have access to six Pentium 100 workstations with color monitors and Web browser software. (And while other establishments of this type claim to be friendly and accommodating, **The CoffeeNet** puts its money where its mouth is: There's no charge to use the computers or set up an e-mail address with them.) ♦ Cafe ♦ M-Sa breakfast, lunch, and dinner (M-Tu to 6PM). 744 Harrison St (between Third and Fourth Sts). 495.7447; fax 495.7447; Web address www.coffee.net ♿

17 Pazzia ★$ The utilitarian interior and the kitchen exposed in back attract the young crowd that gathers at this popular spot at lunchtime and late in the evening. Pizzas have a cracker-thin crust, pastas are perfectly dressed with classic sauces, and the roast chicken with crisp roast potatoes is truly satisfying. ♦ Italian ♦ M-F lunch and dinner; Sa dinner. 337 Third St (between Harrison and Folsom Sts). 512.1693; fax 542.8455 ♿

17 Max's Diner and Bakery ★$ A sign on one side of the door reads "This is a good place for a diet." A sign on the other side says "This is a bad place for a diet." Both statements are true. Sandwiches are huge, big enough to feed two. There are also blue-plate diner specials, low-fat dishes, and lots of salads. Check out the "Salary Savers" section of the menu, where a turkey dinner with mashed potatoes and vegetables is a bargain. Cakes, pies, and crisps—in huge portions—are fine desserts. ♦ American ♦ Daily lunch and dinner, F-Sa until midnight. 311 Third St (between Harrison and Folsom Sts). 546.6297; fax 546.9231 ♿

18 Canton Restaurant ★★$ The dim sum at this pleasant, if plain, spot can rival the best in the city. And because the location is far from the bustle of Chinatown, there's less competition for the carts of wonderful dumplings that come rolling by. The parchment-wrapped chicken (actually wrapped in foil) is bronzed and gooey, and it practically melts in your mouth. The *ha gow* (shrimp with ginger and onions in a tapioca-flour dumpling) is simple and delicious. Even if it's not on the menu, order the bok choy in oyster sauce; the sautéed, but crunchy, bright green cabbage is perfectly topped by a light, salty sauce. ♦ Chinese/Dim sum ♦ Daily lunch and dinner. 655 Folsom St (at Hawthorne St). 495.3064 ♿

19 The Fly Trap ★★★$$ With walls washed in beige and punctuated by brass-framed architectural prints, this attractive room provides a modern stage for revitalized versions of San Francisco classics. For appetizers try the celery Victor (poached and served with hard-boiled egg, vinaigrette, and anchovies), sautéed chicken livers with polenta, or crab cakes. Main courses include Wiener schnitzel, sautéed sweetbreads with mushrooms, calves' liver with bacon and onions, and calves' brains in brown butter. The chef, Robert Morgenstein, has done a superb job maintaining the character of traditional dishes while cutting much of the fat, a feat few have accomplished with such style and success. The luscious tiramisù and cheese-cake, however, are still loaded with calories and fat. ♦ Californian ♦ M-F lunch and dinner; Sa dinner. 606 Folsom St (between Second and Hawthorne Sts). 243.0580; fax 243.9539 ♿

20 Hawthorne Lane ★★★$$$ One of the hottest restaurants in town, this place is run by David and Ann Gingrass, who made a name for themselves at Wolfgang Puck's **Postrio**. The Gingrasses have created a warehouse-size dining room that's as grand as their former digs. Metal sculptures of cherry blossoms serve as banisters and as polished insets in a light wood screen at the entrance. Crisscros-sing earthquake-bracing beams rise up to a huge skylight in the middle of the room. Another ceiling window above the open kitchen is filled with metal pipes from the exhaust fans that are as decorative as they are functional. The menu has equally unique offerings. Boldly flavored, the American food has a few Asian accents mixed in. Try grilled tenderloin of beef with spicy greens in fresh spring rolls; seared Maine scallops with mâche, Cabernet sauce, and horseradish crème fraîche; or slices of Sonoma lamb with artichoke risotto and tomato tarragon sauce. Another specialty is seared foie gras served with a rich chopped onion sauce and a vegetable-and-bread stuffed onion. Desserts also have an artistic bent: A light cheesecake, topped by a rich lemon curd, is on a poppy-seed cake and accompanied by swirls of blueberry sauce and whole blueberries; and a flaky almond tart with fresh peaches is served with delicate fresh peach ice cream topped with puff pastry and a chocolate butterfly. ♦ Californian ♦ M-F lunch and dinner; Sa-Su dinner. 22 Hawthorne St (between Folsom and Howard Sts). 777.9779; fax 777.9782 ♿

20 ThirstyBear Brewing Company and Spanish Cuisine ★$$ The explosive growth of microbreweries in San Francisco continues with this new brewpub-tapas parlor. It's the brainchild of immigration lawyer–turned-brewer Ron Silberstein. The dining area spans three floors and features exposed brick walls and ceramic tile accents. Under the stewardship of chef Daniel Olivella (formerly of **Zuni Cafe** and **Cafe Bastille**), the kitchen produces a menu of hot and cold tapas, such as deep-fried calamari; fish cheeks with garlic, lemon, and sherry; mixed seafood and vegetables; and a flavorful gazpacho. Soups, salads, and paella are also offered. And, of course, there's the house-brewed beer—pale and red ales, stouts, fruit beers, and wheat beers. ♦ Spanish/Brew pub ♦ Daily lunch and dinner (until 1AM). 661 Howard St (at Hawthorne St). 974.0905; fax 974.0955 ♿

21 Caribbean Zone ★$$ The airplane cabin suspended above the dining room is not just for decoration—it's a cocktail lounge that serves drinks with names like Sex in the Jungle, Goomba Boomba, and Belize Breeze. The dining room below offers a lush Kon Tiki setting, complete with an indoor waterfall. Not surprisingly, food isn't the major draw here, but it's pretty good. The tropics-inspired menu lists lots of munching options: conch fritters with a lime-mustard mayonnaise, grilled prawns with chipotle and orange juice, and panfried green plantains with salsa. Those who stick around for a main course can order vegetarian paella, jerk chicken, pecan-covered catfish, or curried goat. And don't miss the Key lime pie for dessert. ♦ Caribbean ♦ M-F lunch and dinner; Sa dinner. 55 Natoma St (between First and Second Sts). 541.9465; fax 974.6416

22 Eddie Rickenbacker's ★★$$ For a while this was a hot spot; now it's settled down into a popular after-work meeting place. The decor is an incongruous mix of Victoriana and sports bar, typified by the two enormous crystal chandeliers and three motorcycles hanging from the ceiling. The Caesar salad is good, as are the hamburgers and the crisp french fries. More substantial choices include grilled salmon, roast chicken, and other straightforward dishes. ♦ American ♦ M-F dinner; Sa lunch and dinner. 133 Second St (between Natoma and Minna Sts). 543.3498; fax 543.7526 ♿

MONDO CAFFE

23 Mondo Caffe ★★$ In marked contrast to the drab stretch of Mission Street on which it's located, this stylish cafe is visually arresting, with a patterned concrete floor, a polished wooden counter with a molded black cement top, sponge-painted walls, and copper-mesh-covered lights. The simple menu features focaccia sandwiches, frittatas, and a few appetizers (try the whole stuffed artichoke). Don't pass up the vegetable sandwich; it's layered with wilted greens, mushrooms, and paper-thin slices of zucchini, topped with cheese, flattened and grilled into a melting, yet crisp, masterpiece, and served with a pile of ultrafresh greens. Another good sandwich is made with thin slices of pork loin and topped with a generous dollop of tuna mayonnaise. ♦ Italian/Cafe ♦ M-F breakfast, lunch, and dinner (until 6:30PM). 602 Mission St (at Second St). 882.1682; fax 882.1683 ⑂

24 Garden Court ★★$$$$ There's no prettier room in San Francisco than this one in the lobby of the **Sheraton Palace** hotel. Beneath a spectacular glass roof, a sea of elegant tables, chairs, and willowy palms is arranged over a richly patterned carpet. The optimum time to visit is for afternoon tea; the aristocratic aura and attentive service bring a Victorian fantasy to life. But try it for other meals, too, as it's been much improved by more attentive service and chef Kerry Heffernan's updated menu. The chicken and beef salads are good choices. ♦ Contemporary ♦ Tu-Sa breakfast, lunch, afternoon tea, and dinner; Su brunch. Reservations recommended. 2 New Montgomery St (at Market St). 392.8600; fax 243.8062 ⑂

24 Kyo-ya ★★$$ One of the city's best Japanese restaurants lies within the **Sheraton Palace** hotel; the melt-in-the-mouth tuna sashimi here is unsurpassed. Full dinners begin with a vibrant miso and a small plate of pickled vegetables. Main courses include shrimp tempura—five prawns encased in a lacy batter—served with a rock-shrimp cake and fresh vegetables. The grilled sea bass is perfection, marinated and cooked to a mahogany hue, with a moist, snow-white interior. The ambience is serene, the decor, almost austere. Silk partitions separate the sushi bar from the dramatically lit dining room with black lacquered chairs and fresh flowers

on each highly glossed wood table. ♦ Japanese ♦ M, Sa dinner; Tu-F lunch and dinner. 2 New Montgomery St (at Market St). 546.5090; fax 243.8062 ⑂

24 Maxfield's $$ A cozy grill rounds out the dining options at the **Sheraton Palace** hotel. The specialty is spit-roasted meats, like leg of lamb and Cornish game hen. ♦ American ♦ Daily lunch and dinner. 2 New Montgomery St (at Market St). 392.8600; fax 243.8062 ⑂

CAFFÈ MUSEO

25 Caffè Museo ★★$ The **San Francisco Museum of Modern Art (SFMOMA)** has a cafe as chic as its environs. The eye-catching decor consists of wooden pegboards, a slatted ceiling, a striped granite floor, and leather directors' chairs. The cafeteria is run by Real Restaurants, which brought the Bay Area such eateries as **Rôti, Mustards Grill, Ristorante Tra Vigne,** and **Bix.** Sandwiches, including an excellent grilled vegetable version, are made with focaccia, and the salad choices range from barley with mushrooms and artichokes to saffron rice studded with bits of zucchini and whole rock shrimp. Skip the *pizzetta,* which tastes like an airy focaccia crust pulled from a grocery store freezer. ♦ Mediterranean ♦ Tu-Su breakfast, lunch, and dinner until 6PM, Th until 9PM. 151 Third St (between Howard and Minna Sts). 357.4500; fax 357.4506

26 Pasqua ★$ This chain's branch within the impressive **Yerba Buena Gardens** arts complex has a breezy open-air atmosphere. Surprisingly comfortable stainless-steel chairs and tables fill the glass-walled room and cluster under umbrellas on the outside terrace. At the cafeteria-style counter choose from fresh-baked muffins, scones, cookies, and desserts to go with coffee. Breakfast includes a choice of egg dishes, while lunchtime offerings consist of pizza, salads, and sandwiches made with baguettes and such fillings as smoked turkey with lemon, thyme, and caper sauce; roasted eggplant with ricotta; or roast beef with parmesan, sun-dried tomatoes, and a red pepper sauce. ♦ Cafe ♦ Daily breakfast and lunch until 5PM. 730 Howard St (between Third and Fourth Sts). 541.9962; fax 541.9964 ⑂ Also at: Numerous locations throughout the city

27 View Lounge The 39th floor of the **Marriott** hotel is an ideal place to enjoy an appetizer, a dessert, or a nightcap with the glittery skyline of San Francisco laid out before you. ♦ Daily. 55 Fourth St (between Mission and Market Sts). 896.1600; fax 777.2799 ♿

28 Chevys ★★$$ This enormous branch of the chain is supposed to look like a Mexican dive—bright colors, stacked boxes of beer—but the cardboard boxes that serve as partitions are empty; so it all comes across as less than authentic, thanks in part to its location in a glassy modern office building. The food can be very good, however. Tortillas are made in-house, and the chips and salsa are some of the best around. True to the "fresh Mex" trend, many of the dishes are low in fat and cholesterol. The fajitas are excellent, but avoid the *chiles rellenos* (stuffed chili peppers), which have a thick, greasy batter. ♦ Mexican ♦ Daily lunch and dinner. 150 Fourth St (between Howard and Minna Sts). 543.8060; fax 543.0410 ♿ Also at: Numerous locations throughout the city

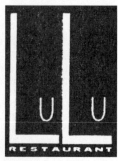

29 LuLu ★★★★$$ One of the best meals in San Francisco can be had here. Formerly three separate eateries, they are now connected throughout and serve the same menu (but each space has different hours). Fish and tender cuts of meat come slow-cooked from a rotisserie or a wood-burning oven. The food, presented on Italian pottery platters, is served family style. Best appetizer choices are the fried artichokes topped with thin shavings of parmesan cheese, and the roasted mussels with drawn butter. For entrées consider the roast chicken or the grilled rib eye for two, served over a bed of thinly sliced potatoes and artichokes. Don't miss the fire-roasted chestnuts with white truffle honey. Warm chocolate cake, with molten chocolate in the center, is the most popular dessert. The dramatic **Main Room** has a soaring ceiling with a skylight, seating on two levels, and an open kitchen; the **Bis** is a smaller, more intimate space; and the **Cafe** has the most casual ambience. ♦ French/Italian ♦ Main Room: M-F lunch and dinner; Sa-Su brunch and dinner. Bis: Daily dinner. Cafe: M-F breakfast, lunch, and dinner; Sa-Su dinner. Reservations recommended for the Main Room and the Bis. 816 Folsom St (between Fourth and Fifth Sts). 495.5775; fax 495.7810 ♿

Le Charm
FRENCH BISTRO

30 Le Charm ★★★$ Who would think that anyone would open a stylish French bistro in one of the ugliest strips south of Market Street? Well, the husband-and-wife team of Alain Delangle (former sous-chef at **Sherman House**) and Lina Yew (previously a pastry chef at **Fleur de Lys**) has done just that. They've created a charming place, with pretty lights, window boxes, awnings, soft yellow walls, an outdoor patio, and a copper-topped bar that separates the kitchen from the 45-seat dining room. Try the rich onion soup; sizzling-hot sautéed chicken livers; garlic roasted chicken with mashed potatoes and greens; or salmon topped with bread crumbs on a bed of spinach and mashed potatoes. Save room for the thinly glazed orange crème brûlée or the French apple tart. The lunch crowd is as diverse as the neighborhood: The reasonable prices attract filling-station attendants, artists, and postal workers, as well as the chi-chi crowd. ♦ French ♦ M lunch, Tu-F lunch and dinner; Sa dinner. 315 Fifth St (between Harrison and Folsom Sts). 546.6128 ♿

31 Cadillac Bar and Grill ★$ Pop in here around Happy Hour, when an array of free munchies can be had with the purchase of a margarita or a beer. Nibbling away on chimichangas or nachos, you'll be full before you know it. The warehouse-sized restaurant, behind the **Fifth and Mission Garage,** offers a few standouts, including multigrain chips and salsa; nachos smothered in guacamole, cheese, jalapeños, and sour cream; tamales; and enchiladas. ♦ Mexican ♦ Daily lunch and dinner. 325 Minna St (between Fourth and Fifth Sts). 543.8226; fax 543.8682 ♿

32 San Francisco Centre Across the street from the Powell Street cable-car turnaround, this vertical shopping mall of 90 stores is anchored by **Nordstrom,** and boasts multiple places to eat as well as to shop. The concourse level of the center is ringed with cafeteria-style restaurants. None of them will bring you back for more, but they're convenient for shoppers and people working nearby. ♦ 865 Market St (between Fourth and Fifth Sts). 495.5656; fax 512.6770 ♿

Within the San Francisco Centre:

Champagne Exchange $$ The wall-length display of Champagnes and sparkling wines underscores the focus of this burgundy-and-gray **Nordstrom** restaurant, whose food was designed to match the drink. The bill of fare highlights lighter meals, with lots of seafood, such as prawns, salmon, and caviar, and several entrée salads. The concept here of pairing food with wine started out wonderfully, but has become tired because of the slipshod preparation. ♦ Californian ♦ Daily lunch. N3 level. 978.5153; fax 978.5089 ♿

Williams-Sonoma A link in the chain of housewares shops, it stocks all kinds of must-have kitchen gadgets and specialty foods. ♦ Daily. Second floor. 546.0171 ♿ Also at: Numerous locations throughout the city

California Orchards This shop (formerly known as **Autumn Harvest**) has one of the best selections of edibles in the city, many from California. Along with the standard olive oils, flavored vinegars, and pastas are such unusual foodstuffs as court bouillons with thyme or dill and all kinds of flavored nuts, including honey-orange or anise almonds and chili-lemon pistachios. ♦ Daily. Concourse level. 543.0785; fax 543.1512 ♿

La Nouvelle Patisserie $ Old-fashioned marble-and-iron tables set the tone at this cafe, conveniently located by the center's Fifth Street entrance. The sandwiches, quiche, salads, and wide assortment of sweets are of varying quality. ♦ Cafe ♦ Daily lunch and snacks. Street level. 979.0553 ♿ Also at: 2184 Union St (between Webster and Fillmore Sts), Cow Hollow. 931.7655; fax 931.0544 ♿

33 **M & M Tavern** ★$ A block from the *Chronicle* and *Examiner,* this beloved greasy spoon is a real journalists' hangout. And the food's actually not greasy; every item is freshly prepared. Burgers are fat and juicy, and the hand-cut fries are the best (ask for them crispy). Any of the daily specials—like liver with onions, mashed potatoes, and mixed vegetables, or corned beef and cabbage—will fill you up for a pittance. The staff treats everyone like regulars, making this a cozy home away from home for locals and visitors alike. ♦ American ♦ M-Sa breakfast, lunch, and dinner. 198 Fifth St (at Howard St). 362.6386 ♿

34 **Wine Club** With its stacked rows of crates and bottles, this shop is far from posh, but the extraordinary wine selection makes it a connoisseur's delight, and the prices are hard to beat—it's unusual to be able to locate a hard-to-find wine *and* get a deal at the same time. In the back, there's a tasting bar and a small cache of serious wine paraphernalia for sale. Make a special trip. ♦ Daily. 953 Harrison St (between Fifth and Sixth Sts). 512.9086

35 **The Line-Up** ★$$ As popular for its drinks as its food, this is a good place to settle in at the bar with a margarita and crunch on a few chips. The Mexican fare here includes all the standards—we're talking tacos, *chiles rellenos,* and enchiladas. It's owned by the same people who run **La Posada** in Pacific Heights and **Leticia's** in the Castro. ♦ Mexican ♦ Daily lunch and dinner. 398 Seventh St (at Harrison St). 861.2887

36 **Julie's Supper Club** ★★$$ Every night is like a fraternity party at this 1950s-style joint. Push through the twentysomething crowd to the bar and sip a martini (the drink of choice here) while waiting for a table. After a few years of seesawing quality, the kitchen is on the upswing again. The menu showcases finger food like fried wontons, fried calamari, and chicken brochettes. For the main event, the grilled New York steak, leg of lamb, or pork chops will provide the fuel for partying the night away. ♦ American ♦ M-Sa dinner. Reservations recommended. 1123 Folsom St (at Langton St). 861.0707

36 **The Up & Down Club** $$ Part owner and supermodel Christy Turlington lends this place cachet. Upstairs is a bar and a disc jockey; downstairs is a restaurant with live jazz performances most nights. The short menu runs to such nibbles as polenta sticks with gorgonzola, deep-fried calamari, and duck quesadillas with red-pepper salsa. A few pastas and such main courses as seafood ragout and grilled rib eye round out the offerings. ♦ Californian ♦ Restaurant: M-Th, Sa dinner 8-10PM; F 7:30-10PM. Bar: M, W-Sa from 10PM to 2AM. 1151 Folsom St (between Langton and Eighth Sts). 626.2388; fax 626.4750

36 **San Francisco Patisserie Cafe** ★★$ The trompe l'oeil window and the crack painted on the cement wall in back give this industrial-chic cafe whimsical appeal. stylish decor is a bit cold, but the friendly service and well-crafted food warm up the place. A long bar holds the makings for a great cup of coffee and a sweet snack. From the kitchen come interesting breakfast and lunch dishes. Try the *koba* (a torpedo of ground lamb and herbs that's rolled in cracked wheat, fried to a crisp crust, and drizzled with a roasted-pepper-and-tomato sauce) or *croque madame,* a toasted ham sandwich dipped in melted cheese and topped with two eggs sunny side up. The delicious breads and sweets are baked in-house. ♦ Cafe/Takeout ♦ M-F breakfast and lunch until 5PM; Sa until 3PM. 1155 Folsom St (between Langton and Eighth Sts). 703.0557 ♿

Child's Play

It's a rite of passage experienced by many an adult restaurant goer: One day the bottles of wine, flowers, and candlelight disappear, replaced by plastic-topped tables and food wrapped in waxed paper. The microwave becomes a third hand at times. Suddenly a family includes a younger member and dining out becomes a different experience. But there's no need to worry—San Francisco has many child-friendly places that an adult can also enjoy:

1 **Alcatraz Bar and Grill** Children of all ages will be thrilled by the mock prison cell, the faux-prison decor, and such offerings as "killer shrimp." Pizza, burgers, and onion rings are featured; there's also a children's menu.

2 **Ghirardelli Chocolate Manufactory** Nobody can resist indulging in a luscious sundae, float, or a steaming cup of chocolate with whipped cream at this wonderful ice-cream parlor–cum–chocolate factory, where you can watch the chocolate being made.

3 **Mel's Drive-In** Preteens and nostalgia buffs love the 1950s-style vinyl booths and tabletop jukeboxes; and such diner eats as burgers and fries, meat loaf, fried-egg sandwiches—and, of course, cherry Cokes.

4 **Pizza Inferno** Square pizza is the specialty of this aptly named parlor, where devilishly colored, swirling-patterned murals cover the floor, walls, and ceiling. The pizzas are good, too.

5 **St. Francis Fountain** Not much has changed at this honest-to-goodness soda fountain since 1918: There are still grilled cheese sandwiches, blue-plate specials, scrumptious homemade ice cream in 20 flavors, and wonderful peanut brittle.

6 **Toy Boat Dessert Cafe** Children delight in riding the mechanical bucking horse in the center of the dining room and they can't resist the vast collection of toys lining the wall. Coffee drinks and old-fashioned berry pie will appeal to adults; the kids will go for the peanut-butter–and–chocolate-cookie sandwich.

7 **Isobune Sushi** Kids get a kick out of this sushi bar, where the raw fish and vegetable selections float by the diners on boats.

8 **Hard Rock Cafe** Teens are happy to line up and wait (sometimes for hours) to grab a hamburger and gawk at the rock memorabilia at this link in the worldwide chain.

9 **Planet Hollywood** Like the **Hard Rock Cafe,** it's a combination eatery and theme park, with plenty to look at. Kids will thrill to all the movie memorabilia on the walls, and the food isn't bad, either (if you stick to the simple stuff).

10 After romping through the games and play areas at **The Jungle,** grab a pizza or hot dog at **Mama Gorilla's Cafe.**

37 Basil ★★$$ This is one of the prettiest Thai restaurants in the city, with a sleek decor that includes a wall of glass bricks, a polished cement bar against a wall of midnight blue, yellow accents, wood floors, white tablecloths topped with butcher paper, and bistro-style chairs. The kitchen updates traditional fare: Huge prawns are splayed on a platter and seasoned with white pepper and garlic; spring rolls are cut on the diagonal to reveal a bright tangle of purple cabbage; beef short ribs get a lift from a mild, basil-laced curry with a confetti of lime leaves; and New Zealand mussels are steamed with Chardonnay. Save room for dessert: sweet coconut rice served with half a sliced mango. ♦ Thai ♦ M-F lunch and dinner; Sa dinner. 1175 Folsom St (between Langton and Eighth Sts). 552.8999; fax 552.8889 ♿

38 Ideal Deli/Border Cantina Cafe ★$ This "Mexicatessen" has a dual identity: During the day it's the **Ideal Deli,** and in the evening it becomes the **Border Cantina Cafe.** However, there's no real difference between the two, except that a few combination plates are added to the menu at night. No matter what you call it though, this is the place to try *tortas* (Mexican sandwiches) or to pick up a plump burrito stuffed with a choice of meat and beans—and don't forget the excellent salsa. Specials include chicken in red chili sauce, pork with green chilies, and beef Colorado with chilies. Sure, it looks like a dive, but a crowd of satisfied regulars keeps the kitchen busy, so they're clearly doing something right. ◆ Mexican/Takeout ◆ M-F breakfast, lunch, and dinner. 1198 Folsom St (at Eighth St). 626.6043 &

APPAM

39 Appam Indian Cuisine ★$ One of the prettier Indian restaurants, it's outfitted with a mahogany bar, murals of temple dancers and Indian landscapes, and a blue-tiled open kitchen; the small dining area overlooks a garden patio. Start with *samosas* (flaky pastries filled with curried potatoes and peas) and the stuffed breads. The kitchen specializes in *dum pukht* (clay-pot dishes) of meat and vegetable curries that are topped with dough and baked until golden and bubbling. Tandoori preparations, including squid and lamb, earn raves. ◆ Indian ◆ Daily dinner. 1259 Folsom St (between Eighth and Ninth Sts). 626.2798 &

40 Jessie's South of Market ★★$$ Haitian-born restaurateur Jessie Leonard-Corcia has opened this new eatery on the site of the **Acorn Restaurant,** which closed a few years ago. It's a tiny place, seating just 60 people in two narrow dining rooms and a back porch that overlooks a lovely garden. The stylish decor favors a terra-cotta, rust, and eggplant color scheme, and the ambience is cozy and intimate. Chef Glenn Thompson's menu features Caribbean fare at lunchtime and Creole food in the evening. A couple of standouts are the alligator sausage with wild mushroom and filet mignon Lafayette, a tender steak carved, fanned, and topped with a luscious crayfish and onion-custard sauce. The moist bread pudding studded with raisins and napped with a caramel-rum sauce makes a first-rate dessert. ◆ Creole/Caribbean ◆ Tu-Sa lunch and dinner; Su brunch and dinner. 1256 Folsom St (between Eighth and Ninth Sts). 437.2481

40 Stardust Restaurant and Lounge ★$ Taking the place of the short-lived **Icon Byte Bar & Grill,** this roadhouse looks so retro that it seems like Elvis could walk in any moment. It's decorated with gaudy flair: gold walls, pillars covered with shiny red vinyl, pyramid-shaped light fixtures, and thick leopard curtains. The menu is standard American fare, but it's done well. Try the thick Reuben sandwich, blackened catfish, grilled pork chop, or macaroni and cheese just like Mom used to make. For vegetarians, there's the portobello mushroom sandwich with spicy french fries. It's ideal for night owls, too, since it keeps its doors open until 4AM Thursday through Saturday and until 2AM the rest of the week. ◆ American ◆ Daily lunch and dinner. 299 Ninth St (at Folsom St). 861.2983

41 WA-HA-KA! (Oaxaca Mexican Grill) ★★$ A converted warehouse has become a popular refueling stop on the nightclub circuit in this part of town. The kitchen turns out excellent burritos and good, gooey quesadillas; the bar features scores of tequilas to sample straight or in margaritas. ◆ Mexican ◆ M-F lunch and dinner; Sa brunch and dinner; Su dinner. 1489 Folsom St (at 11th St). 861.1410; fax 861.1410 & Also at: Numerous locations throughout the city

42 Don Ramon's Mexican Restaurant ★$$ Friendly and casual, this venerable and popular SoMa eatery offers tasty Mexican specialties. Chef Dona Lupe's deluxe tostada is packed with beef or chicken, refried beans, lettuce, guacamole, and sour cream; other favorites include tender pieces of pork in a green tomatillo sauce garnished with tomato salsa; burritos; fajitas; Chili beef Colorado (which is made with beef and red chili sauce and seasoned with oregano); and steak ranchero (steak served in a sauce with onions, green chilies, and tomatoes). ◆ Mexican ◆ M-F lunch and dinner; Sa-Su dinner. 225 11th St (between Folsom and Howard Sts). 864.2700; fax 864.6497 &

43 Twenty Tank Brewery One of only four brew pubs in San Francisco, this gigantic watering hole features six house-brewed ales. Nachos and a few other beer-friendly noshes are on hand, and there's a shuffleboard table for entertainment. ◆ Daily 11:30AM-1:30AM. No credit cards accepted. 316 11th St (between Harrison and Folsom Sts). 255.9455; fax 255.MEAL &

44 Eleven Restaurant and Bar ★★$$ Now under new ownership (including Steve McPartland, the celebrated host of the local talk show "Mornings On Two"), this restaurant has made the transition from Italian to all-American. The casual, saloon-like ambience is reminiscent of **Perry's** (which isn't surprising, as several of the present owners worked there previously). The dramatic two-story dining room is a comfortable place to sit and listen to live music (performed Tuesday through Saturday nights) that ranges from rock to soul to jazz. The menu features well-prepared, standard dishes such as a center-cut pork chop with grain mustard sauce, fruit chutney, red potatoes, and green beans; a burger on a focaccia roll; filet mignon; fresh fish; pizzas; and pastas. Desserts include mango crème brûlée and a ricotta cheesecake that's as light as air. There's also a cigar room. ◆ American ◆ M-F lunch and dinner; Sa dinner. 374 11th St (between Harrison and Folsom Sts). 431.3337 &

45 Hamburger Mary's ★$ Pierce your nose, dye your hair (purple or cherry red would be appropriate), and add a tattoo, and you'll fit right in at this alternative universe. The decor looks like a collection of stuff from somebody's attic. The hamburgers are the main draw, although other sandwiches and soups can be very good. Still, the grazing is not nearly as satisfying as the gazing. ♦ American ♦ Daily lunch and dinner. 1582 Folsom St (between 12th and 11th Sts). 626.5767; fax 626.1985

46 Manora's Thai Cuisine ★★$$ There are two kinds of Thai restaurants: those that lean toward the sour side and those that veer to the sweet. This simple and unassuming spot is one of the city's best examples of the sweet type. Devoted customers swear by the curries, the pork infused with garlic and pepper, and the minced fish steamed in banana leaves. ♦ Thai ♦ M-F lunch and dinner; Sa-Su dinner. 1600 Folsom St (at 12th St). 861.6224. Also at: 3226 Mission St (between 29th and Valencia Sts), The Mission. 826.4639

47 Big Nate's Bar-B-Que ★$ Owned by basketball superstar Nate Thurman, this is your standard linoleum-and-Formica barbecue joint. The business consists mostly of takeout and catering, with a few seats for eating in-house. The ovens groan with bronzed chickens, crinkled sausage, charred hunks of brisket, and glazed slabs of ribs. Each of the sauces—mild, medium, and hot—carries an undercurrent of sweetness that combines perfectly with the smoky meats. ♦ Barbecue/Takeout ♦ Daily lunch and dinner. 1665 Folsom St (between 13th and 12th Sts). 861.4242; fax 861.1633 &

48 Homestead Ravioli Since 1917, this factory has been turning out stuffed pastas. At least a half-dozen kinds are offered in one- or two-pound boxes at near-wholesale prices. In addition to the traditional beef- or cheese-stuffed versions, there's ravioli filled with mushrooms, or sun-dried tomatoes and almonds, or a lean mix of seasoned veal, pork, and turkey. All are free of MSG and preservatives and can be frozen for several months. ♦ M-F 7AM-noon and 1PM-3:30PM. 120 14th St (between Folsom St and S Van Ness Ave). 864.2992 &

49 Costco Some of the best beef in the city is for sale at this members-only warehouse store (but the rather high membership fee makes it impractical for visitors to join). The meats are sold in bulk, which means you'd better have a big freezer (or a lot of friends) to stock up here. The steaks are of excellent quality, though, and the pork, lamb, and chicken are as good as or better than in most supermarkets. Check out the frozen-food aisles for designer items like Wolfgang Puck's pizza, Amy's lasagna and enchiladas, Nancy's bite-sized quiches, and more. There's also a wide assortment of olive oils, **Starbucks** coffee, and occasional bargains on wine. ♦ Daily. 450 10th St (between Bryant and Harrison Sts). 626.4288; fax 626.4599 &

GEORGE'S

50 George's Global Kitchen ★$ "Think globally, eat locally," says George, and you could hardly get more global than his cross-cultural cuisine, or more local than his quaint little diner tucked beneath the freeway. With a partly exposed kitchen and a dining counter, the atmosphere is homey and the eclectic fare ranges from seafood cannellini in red pepper pasta to a hearty pork chop with warm potato salad. The meatloaf and garlic mashed potatoes is a dish you can always count on. ♦ Californian ♦ M, Sa lunch; Tu-F lunch and dinner. 340 Division St (between 10th and Bryant Sts). 864.4224; fax 864.2332 &

51 Mama Gorilla's Cafe ★$ This child-oriented eatery is located at **The Jungle,** the West Coast's largest indoor play facility. With plenty of games and attractions (crawl-through tubes, ball ponds, cargo nets, and rides), the playhouse is tremendously popular for kids' parties. The cafe's menu is definitely on the informal side, stressing such finger foods as pizza, turkey dogs, turkey-corn dogs, chicken nuggets, nachos, and pretzels. Beverages run the gamut from soda and juice to coffee (to make sure the adults in the party keep on their toes). ♦ American ♦ Daily breakfast, lunch, and dinner (M-Th, Su to 8PM; F-Sa to 9PM). 555 Ninth St (between Brannan and Bryant Sts). 552.4386; fax 552.2937 &

51 Trader Joe's This branch of the popular Southern California discount specialty-foods chain offers nearly a thousand items under its own label, and many brand-name closeouts. Here's the place to pick up chili-lime tortilla chips and salsas, fruit juices, refrigerated sandwiches, salads, enchiladas, lasagnas, quiches, and frozen dinners. Also stocked are jams, vinegars, pickled vegetables, breads, and cookies. The wines offered are fine for everyday drinking; most are low-priced. ♦ Daily. 555 Ninth St (between Brannan and Bryant Sts). 863.1292 ♿

52 Stamp Francisco A mesmerizing array of rubber stamps, many with food themes, is sold here. With an ink pad and stamps of pears, berries, clusters of cherries, or ornate crossed forks and knives, anyone can create cool business cards, invitations, recipe cards, or stationery. It's easy to drop $50 quickly, so keep tabs on what you're tossing into the shopping basket. ♦ M-Sa. 466 Eighth St (between Bryant and Harrison Sts). 252.5975; fax 252.5978 ♿

53 Kiss ★★$$$ Hidden within a commercial-looking building is this romantic oasis: Fabric drapes from the ceiling, fresco-inspired murals cover the walls, and more gauzy drapery is loosely tied around each table. The creative food is a blend of East and West, and might include fillet of chicken with orange sauce, pork tenderloin with poached pears and red wine–and–cinnamon sauce, or venison in Port sauce. The only downside is that too many of the entrées are sweetly sauced. ♦ Californian/French ♦ M-Sa lunch and dinner. 680 Eighth St (between Townsend and Brannan Sts). 552.8757; fax 552.8758 ♿

54 Rustico ★$$ Famous for its excellent crisp-crusted pizza, this eat-in/take-out spot is small, but attractive. If none of the dozen or so fresh-tasting topping combinations appeals, create your own from a list of 25 ingredients. A few sandwiches, salads, soups, and pasta dishes round out the menu. ♦ Pizzeria/Takeout ♦ M-F 8AM-8PM; Sa 9AM-5PM; Su 10AM-4PM. 300 DeHaro St (at 16th St). 252.0180; fax 255.1533 ♿

55 Garden of Tranquility ★★$ This reasonably priced, country-style Chinese restaurant (on the former site of **Restaurant 2001**) is a welcome addition to Potrero Hill. An antique lamp hangs over every table; the bar, furnishings, and walls are made of rough-hewn, light-colored wood, and flowers, paintings, and a Chinese screen near the entrance add a touch of sophistication to the decor. Although the menu describes the food as Mandarin, it really shows influences from all over China, including Beijing, Canton, and Hunan. Try the bargain-priced combination appetizer plate for two—fried wontons, vegetarian eggrolls, two crab puffs, and pot stickers. Another option is the minced chicken in lettuce cups—a variation of the Northern Chinese minced squab dish. One noteworthy special is the sunflower chicken, which features chicken, mushrooms, julienned vegetables, and sunflower seeds, all stir-fried. ♦ Chinese ♦ M-F lunch and dinner; Sa-Su dinner. 2001 17th St (at Kansas St). 861.8610

56 Asimakopoulos Cafe ★★$$ One of the city's only Greek restaurants, it has garnered raves from residents and the local press for many years. One bite of the spinach in phyllo appetizer will make you a believer, too. The entrées are equally good, including skewered pork, chicken and lamb dishes, and moussaka. Save room for the flaky and delicious baklava; it's not overly sweet, so the flavors of the nuts and pastry shine through. On Tuesday or Sunday nights, bring a burning question along with an appetite; a fortune teller is on hand to read the coffee grounds in the bottom of your cup. ♦ Greek ♦ M-F lunch and dinner; Sa-Su dinner. 288 Connecticut St (at 18th St). 552.8789; fax 552.8798

57 Goat Hill Pizza ★$ The sourdough crust sets these pizzas above those of the competition. This popular Italian place also serves pasta, salads, and soups. Many regulars time their pizza feasts to coincide with the live music featured Thursday through Saturday nights. ♦ Pizzeria ♦ Daily lunch and dinner. 300 Connecticut St (at 18th St). 641.1440; fax 641.7262 ♿

57 Simply Breads Cafe Breads from around the world are the specialty of this small bakery located in a small organic produce market called **Dig It** (under separate ownership). Among the varieties are challah, croissants, Navajo bread, and potato bread (popular bread in Scotland). Other goods include focaccia, five flavors of coffee cake, 15 kinds of muffins, sweet breads, and twist rolls. All of the products are made from organic flours and grains. ♦ Daily 7AM-8PM. 301 Arkansas St (at 18th St). 821.2953; fax 626.5317

58 Aperto ★★★$$

There are few decorative frills here, but count on the lusty smells emanating from the open kitchen to provide enough atmosphere. The food is excellent, but it doesn't break any new creative ground. Crisp triangles of polenta topped with fresh chopped tomatoes and a dollop of melting gorgonzola make a good first course. To follow, the roast chicken—topped with wedges of salty, pungent, preserved lemons and surrounded by roasted potatoes and calamata olives—is a tasty choice. Best desserts are fresh fruit granita and warm chocolate soufflé cake. The high ceiling and windows on two sides add an airiness that helps disguise the fact that the tables are squeezed together. Since reservations are not accepted, hordes tend to line up, eyeing the occupied seats hungrily. ◆ Italian ◆ M-F lunch and dinner; Sa-Su brunch and dinner. 1434 18th St (at Connecticut St). 252.1625 &

59 Thanya and Salee ★★$ This top Thai eatery offers meticulous preparations of such standard dishes as duck salad, coconut-chicken soup, and pad thai, as well as more unusual fare. Sweet corn salad is infused with chilies, lime, thinly sliced red onion, roasted peppers, zucchini, and large cilantro leaves. Hot-and-sour prawn soup is scented with lemongrass and smoothed with coconut milk. Don't pass up the Southern Thai barbecue chicken with a mildly spicy red-curry dipping sauce or the garlic-marinated pork, which is crisply fried and served with a green chili sauce redolent of fresh lime. The mirror-backed bar under a replica Thai temple roof, the thick carpeting, and the tables freshly laid with white butcher paper and flowers contribute to the comfortable mood. ◆ Thai ◆ M-F lunch and dinner; Sa-Su dinner (from 2PM). 1469 18th St (at Connecticut St). 647.6469; fax 647.2910 &

59 Eliza's ★★★$ Ping and Jan Sung have crafted a Chinese restaurant that subtly reworks familiar preparations, giving them a modern California twist. Sunflower beef (thin slices of meat in a rich satay sauce spiked with scallions) is encircled by a burst of white enoki mushrooms. The sweet China prawns are matched with snow peas and toasted pine nuts in a velvety ginger sauce. Salmon is paired with asparagus tips in an equally refined black-bean sauce. The stylish decor features grand Matisse-like paintings, hand-crafted lights, and potted orchids on each table. Tea is served in white Wedgwood demitasse cups, and the food is presented on pastel Italian pottery. And all this creativity doesn't cost any more than a meal at the corner cafe. The only downside is dessert—nothing but fortune cookies and ice cream. ◆ Chinese ◆ Daily lunch and dinner. 1457 18th St (between Missouri and Connecticut Sts). 648.9999 &

59 Just For You Cafe ★$ This narrow little place is no more than a row of stools at a scarred wooden counter, with one table tucked into the front window. But on weekends customers line up for breakfast and for lunch specials that include shrimp creole, gumbo, and other New Orleans specialties. At dinner the menu takes on a Cajun edge with such dishes as red beans and rice and jambalaya. ◆ Creole/Cajun ◆ Daily breakfast and lunch (M-Th until 2:30PM; F-Su until 5PM). 1453 18th St (between Missouri and Connecticut Sts). 647.3033

59 The Daily Scoop ★$ With its tile floor, parlor chairs, and authentic soda fountain, this old-fashioned ice-cream parlor offers a glimpse of the past. The owner adds to the nostalgia with his growing collection of memorabilia that includes classic blenders and mixers. **Double Rainbow** ice cream is served in such flavors as banana-fudge-walnut. ◆ Ice-cream parlor ◆ Daily 7:30AM-10PM. 1401 18th St (at Missouri St). 824.3975 &

60 Hazel's Kitchen ★★$ Somehow, this closet-sized take-out place produces fabulous food. The aqua-and-white color scheme and the display of Bauer pottery add a bright note and reflect the homey character of the limited menu. A day's offerings usually include several sandwiches dressed with an herb-and-mustard mayonnaise, a refreshing soup (perhaps carrot-ginger), and salads. The Greek salad of pungent feta, cool mint, cucumbers, black olives, and tomatoes is outstanding. ◆ Deli ◆ Daily. 1331 18th St (between Texas and Missouri Sts). 647.7941 &

60 Mager's Wine Shop Just about the perfect neighborhood wine shop offers a small but well-selected array of California, French, and Italian wines. It also carries a small assortment of gourmet condiments and **Joseph Schmidt** chocolates. ◆ Daily. 1319 18th St (between Texas and Missouri Sts). 282.6650 &

60 Farley's A local institution, this coffeehouse has captured the spirit of the emerging Potrero Hill neighborhood, which has some of the most spectacular city and bay views in San Francisco. The wood floors and slatboard siding and ceiling lend a lived-in look that sets the tone of the place. People sit for hours, playing board games, nursing cups of the robust house blend of coffee, and perusing the large selection of magazines for sale. The pastries and light snack items are generally very good, and whole and ground beans are sold for home use. ◆ Daily. No credit cards accepted. 1315 18th St (between Texas and Missouri Sts). 648.1545

61 San Francisco Bar-B-Que ★$ With that name, this sounds like a traditional barbecue joint, but there are no slabs of ribs and brisket here. Actually, the menu lists all kinds of Thai-style noodles topped with chunks of barbecued meats. The portions are big and filling, and prices are rock-bottom. ◆ Thai ◆ Tu-F lunch and dinner; Sa-Su dinner. No credit cards accepted. 1328 18th St (between Texas and Missouri Sts). 431.8956

62 The Good Life Grocery Produce, cheese, packaged goods, bread from several of the city's best bakeries, and a limited meat selection (free-range chickens, sausages, and fresh fish) have made this a one-stop grocery store for the neighborhood. Although the quarters are small, it's one of the best natural-food stores in the city. ◆ Daily. 1524 20th St (between Missouri and Connecticut Sts). 282.9204 ம்

63 Klein's Deli ★$ Few delis are as personal as this one, where the female owners have named every sandwich after famous women: The Abzug celebrates Bella with tongue, muenster cheese, and dark rye bread; the Audrey Hepburn features salmon pâté on a sourdough roll; and the Minnie Mouse puts three kinds of cheese on a kaiser roll. It's become a popular hangout and working-lunch spot for an arty set of graphic designers, architects, and photographers. A small, reasonably priced selection of wine and a few choice packaged specialty foods fill a nook in the back of the store. ◆ Deli ◆ Daily breakfast, lunch, and dinner (M-Sa until 7PM; Su until

5:30PM). 501 Connecticut St (at 20th St). 821.9149; fax 821.0518

64 The Candy Jar Outlet Those with a serious sweet tooth and a penchant for bargains bypass the posh retail branch on Union Square and head for its outlet here, where truffles in more than a dozen flavors cost 30 to 50 percent less. Some goods are slightly flawed, some are overruns, but most are simply sold at wholesale prices. The sales counter, located in front of the candy factory, proffers such sweet treats as turtles, chocolate-covered Oreos, imported hard candies and jellies, and cooking chocolate, plus gift boxes, wrapping paper, and ribbon. ◆ M-Sa. 2065 Oakdale Ave (between Third and Industrial Sts). 550.8846; fax 550.8359 ம் Also at: 210 Grant Ave (between Post and Sutter Sts), Union Square. 391.5508 ம்

64 Heritage House Located in an industrial building on a sparsely traveled street in the warehouse district, this china, crystal, and flatware showroom glitters with up to 1,500 china patterns from the likes of Minton, Christian Dior, Fitz & Floyd, Lenox, Noritake, Rosenthal, Royal Doulton, Royal Worcester, Villeroy & Boch, and Wedgwood. In silverware, all the big names are covered, including such specialty producers as Georg Jensen, WMF Fraser, and Yamazaki. Crystal suppliers include Baccarat, Riedel, Waterford, and St. Louis. Many items are discounted by 20 to 40 percent. The store maintains a bridal registry; it will also replace broken pieces for half the retail price. ◆ M-F; Sa and evenings by appointment. 2190 Palou Ave (between Industrial St and Bayshore Blvd). 285.1331; fax 285.9840

64 Wendy's Cheesecake Bakery The friendly women who work here make some of the best cheesecakes, pecan pies, and sweet potato pies to be found in San Francisco. Established in the 1970s, the shop also does catering and offers light lunch fare, snacks, barbecued meats, and roast beef for takeout. But the baked goods are the reason people flock here; you should too. M-F 6AM-6PM; Sa 7AM-6PM. 4942 Third St (between Thornton and Oakdale Aves). 822.4959

Chicago may have deep-dish pizza but San Francisco has "It's It," an ice-cream sandwich made from oatmeal cookies dipped in chocolate. Created in 1928 at Playland-at-the-Beach (which was torn down in 1972 to make way for condominiums), It's It is now available commercially. There are four flavors in addition to the original vanilla (still the best): chocolate, mint, strawberry,

Lights, Camera, Dinner!

Thanks to San Francisco's spectacular scenery and proximity to Hollywood, scores of movies have been filmed here, among them the Alfred Hitchcock classic *Vertigo,* Clint Eastwood's five "Dirty Harry" films, and the James Bond flick *A View to a Kill.* The Nick Nolte–Eddie Murphy film *48 Hours* was also shot here, though its sequel, *Another 48 Hours,* was not (even though it too purportedly took place in San Francisco). Whoopi Goldberg spent two weeks filming *Sister Act* in Noe Valley, and Steve McQueen careened through Potrero Hill in *Bullitt.*

Since there are so many well-known restaurants in San Francisco, it was inevitable that some of them would make appearances on the silver screen. Here are just a few of them:

In *Jade* (1995), David Caruso and Linda Fiorentino were supposed to meet in the bar and trattoria area of **Ristorante Fior d'Italia,** but she stood him up.

The cavernous old **American Can Company** factory stood in for Cape Canaveral when *The Right Stuff* (1983) was shot here. The **Cow Palace,** a venue for exhibitions and conventions, was the setting the filmmakers used for a barbecue President Lyndon Johnson hosted for the astronauts.

In one scene of *The Graduate* (1967), Dustin Hoffman is seen sitting in **Berkeley's**

Mediterranee Caffè—still a popular student hangout.

Kim Novak and Jimmy Stewart supped at the elegant but now-closed **Ernie's** in *Vertigo* (1958). This classic citadel of French cuisine is now the Essex Supper Club.

The hilarious dining scene in *Mrs. Doubtfire* (1993), when Robin Williams, dressed as a female nanny, loses his false teeth, was filmed in the Bridges restaurant in San Ramon, about 30 miles east of San Francisco.

All the scenes set in **Meats of the World,** the butcher shop featured in *So I Married an Axe Murderer* (the 1993 farce starring Mike Myers of *Wayne's World)* were shot at the former **R. Iacoppi & Company** in **North Beach.** Last year, the owner sold the store to his goddaughter, Josette Prudente. With her husband, Daniel, she has turned it into the **Prudente Meat Market & Deli,** one of the best delis in the neighborhood.

64 Seafood Grotto ★★$ In this sparkling clean storefront operation, owner/chef Rich Alexander prepares some of the best down-home cooking you'll ever taste. The menu focuses on soul food, with fried fish (catfish, snapper, sole, whiting, and buffalo), salmon croquettes, chicken wings, and prawns or oysters. The main dishes are accompanied by either french fries or cole slaw. Everything is made on the premises, even the tartar sauce (which tends to be a little too sweet) and the refreshing lemonade. Enjoy your meal sitting at one of the stools in front of the L-shaped counter. In a display window, Alexander has collected a number of books by famous African-American and African authors, which he displays to "raise cultural awareness." ♦ Soul food ♦ M-Sa lunch and dinner. 5029 Third St (between Gilman and Palou Aves). 822.0774

64 James & James Ribs 'n' Thangs ★★★ $$ This rib joint, located on a stretch of small shops and bars in Bay View–Hunters Point, is a magnet for barbecue mavens from all over the city. The restaurant is classy (as barbecue joints go) and comfortable, with antique tables and chairs, a large open kitchen, and a barbecue pit. Paintings and posters of prominent African-American heroes from Malcolm X to Martin Luther King grace the walls. Upon entering, you'll be greeted by the luscious smell of barbecued meats and the blare of loud rock music. The most popular choice here (particularly with barbecue novices) is the "two-way," which offers a choice of two barbecued meats (such as beef, sausage links, chicken, or pork ribs), and a choice of two side dishes (creamy potato salad, cole slaw, collard greens, barbecued beans, cornbread muffins, or corn on the cob). White or wheat bread is also available so you can sop up the sauce (mild or hot) that's slathered over the meat. Other menu options include fried catfish, snapper, sole, and prawns. For dessert, try a slice of the moist and tasty sweet potato pie. ♦ Barbecue/Soul food ♦ Tu-Su lunch and dinner (F-Sa until 2AM). 5130 Third St (between Thornton and Oakdale Aves). 671.0269

65 Moshi Moshi ★★$ In a landscape dominated by warehouses, this bright corner restaurant serves skillfully prepared Japanese food. Start with the fine *gyoza* (Japanese dumplings), then move on to one of the classics—steak teriyaki, shrimp tempura, or chicken yakitori. The sushi is much better than at many places in Japantown, the service attentive, and the simple look of light wood tables and chairs and celadon walls attractive. Throw in the low prices, and this place warrants a special trip. ♦ Japanese ♦ M-F lunch and dinner; Sa-Su dinner. 2092 Third St (between 18th and Mariposa Sts). 861.8285; fax 861.8291 &

66 Economy Restaurant Fixtures The best

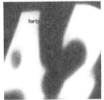

place in the city to shop for restaurant-grade pots, pans, and tableware is now even better. In early 1995 the store moved from its location on Howard Street to a new warehouse that's more than twice as big as the old shop. Professional stoves, industrial-strength cleaners, and cotton towels are among the thousands of other items on sale here. It's the spot to find an oversized stock pot or to pick up enough glassware to host a party (glasses come in boxes of 36). Prices are very low, and for an even better deal, check out the used equipment and tableware where the prices can be dirt cheap. ♦ M-Sa. 1200 7th St (at Irwin St). 626.5611; fax 252.9627 &

67 42 Degrees ★★★$$ It's unusual to find an exceptional late-night dining establishment in San Francisco (the joint doesn't start jumping until 9PM), another reason that this chic restaurant is so welcome. Located in a warehouse-size space, this place sports a high-tech look—there's a curving black metal staircase—mixed with a dash of nightclub style. Dine on purple banquettes upstairs while enjoying a view of the bay; eat downstairs in front of the exposed kitchen or near the 22-foot high windows that are opened in pleasant weather; or enjoy a lunchtime focaccia on the patio. Owner/chef Jim Moffat, who's also partner in **The Slow Club** in the Mission, offers a menu that changes daily and might include grilled quail and rich duck confit on a heap of truffled risotto with morels; and a whole *poussin* with hard cider sauce, baked apples, and rice studded with sour cherries. Also featured is a wide variety of small dishes that's perfect for the drinking crowd: Try the stuffed artichoke or grilled asparagus with cherries and a light vinaigrette. Sweets lovers will be quite content with the rich chocolate *pots de crème* or strawberries and blackberries over a warm pecan shortcake. ♦ Californian ♦ M-Tu lunch; W-Sa lunch, dinner, and late-night

meals. 235 16th St (east of Illinois St). 777.5559; fax 777.0278 &

68 The Ramp ★$$ Sunny weekends guarantee long waits at this bare-bones eatery, thanks to its large deck overlooking the bay. The menu includes average egg dishes, sandwiches, and burgers. In the summer there's live jazz, salsa, or rock Thursday through Sunday evenings, as well as outdoor barbecues on weekend afternoons through early evening. As cool weather sets in, the kitchen turns out hearty stews to ease the chill. It's a fun crowd—an eclectic mix of laborers, society matrons, singles, and gays. ♦ American ♦ M-F breakfast and lunch; Sa-Su brunch. 855 China Basin St (at Mariposa St). 621.2378

69 Mission Rock Resort ★$ With its terrace overlooking the slips and boats in dry dock on China Bay, this bar-restaurant attracts a fun-loving group of regulars. Sunday brunch, with the standard array of egg dishes, is a big draw, as are the barbecue and live music sessions on sunny weekend afternoons. The fare runs to burgers and deep-fried seafood—scallops, oysters, prawns, and fish-and-chips, served until 3PM. And the bar keeps hopping long after the kitchen closes. ♦ American ♦ M-Sa breakfast and lunch; Su brunch. 817 China Basin St (north of Mariposa St). 621.5538 &

70 Jelly's: A Dance Cafe ★$$ The outdoor terrace that opens onto the bay is a popular spot for lunch, when selections include a BLT with french fries, fish-and-chips, Caesar salad, and grilled chicken breast on a French roll. Daily lunch specials draw inspiration from far-flung destinations like the American Southwest, Italy, and France. ♦ International ♦ M-F lunch; Sa-Su brunch. 295 China Basin St (at Mission Rock St). 495.3099; fax 495.2884

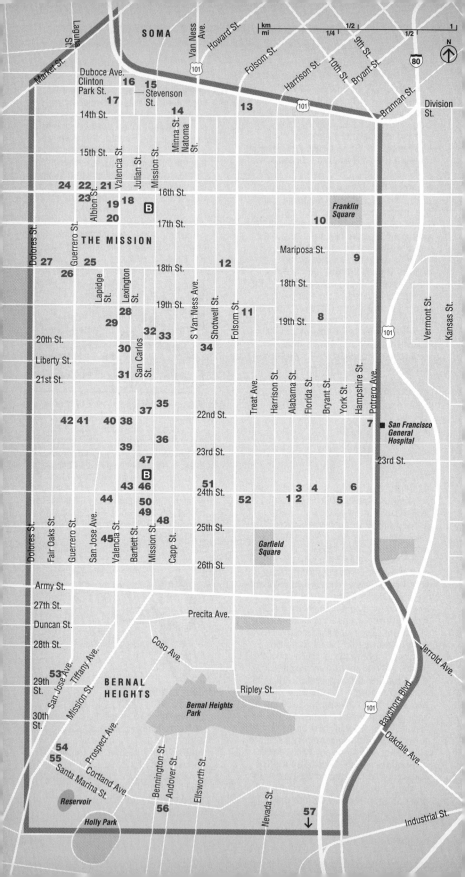

SOMA

Laguna St.

Market St.

Duboce Ave.
Clinton
Park St.   16
            15
Stevenson
17   St.

14th St.

15th St.

24 22 21
23
    19 18
    20

THE MISSION

27

26

25

Lapidge
St.

Lexington
St.

28

29

Dolores St.

Guerrero St.

Valencia St.

Julian St.

Mission St.

16th St.

B

17th St.

18th St.

19th St.

S Van Ness Ave.

Shotwell St.

Folsom St.

12

32 33

30

31

San Carlos
St.

34

20th St.

Liberty St.

21st St.

37 35

42 41 40 38

39

36

47

B

43 46

44

50 49

45

48

Dolores St.

Fair Oaks St.

Guerrero St.

San Jose Ave.

Valencia St.

Bartlett St.

Mission St.

Capp St.

22nd St.

23rd St.

24th St.

25th St.

26th St.

Army St.

27th St.

Duncan St.

28th St.

53
29th
St.

30th
St.

San Jose Ave.

Tiffany Ave.

Mission St.

**BERNAL
HEIGHTS**

54

55

Santa Marina St.

Reservoir

Holly Park

Prospect Ave.

Cortland Ave.

Bennington St.

Andover St.

Ellsworth St.

56

Coso Ave.

Precita Ave.

Ripley St.

**Bernal Heights
Park**

Nevada St.

57
↓

Van Ness Ave.

Howard St.

101

Folsom St.

Harrison St.

10th St.

9th St.

Bryant St.

Brannan St.

km
mi   1/4   1/2   1

N

80

Division
St.

Minna St.
Natoma St.

13

Mariposa St.

Franklin
Square

10

9

18th St.

11

19th St.

8

Treat Ave.

Harrison St.

Alabama St.

Florida St.

Bryant St.

York St.

Hampshire St.

Potrero Ave.

101

Vermont St.

Kansas St.

7 ■ San Francisco
General
Hospital

23rd St.

3 4
1 2   6
52   5

Garfield
Square

51

Jerrold Ave.

101

Bayshore Blvd.

Oakdale Ave.

Industrial St.

The Mission

North Beach was a magnet for the Beat generation of the 1950s; the Haight captured the hearts of the flower children of the 1960s; the Castro was the mecca for the gay movement of the 1970s; and the Mission is becoming home to what writer Herb Gold and others have dubbed the "New Bohemia"—the favorite hangout of young, white, underemployed coffeehouse philosophers, former punk rockers, and political activists, among others.

Sandwiched between Potrero Hill to the east, the Castro to the west, and downtown to the north, the Mission is more diverse culturally and culinarily than any other neighborhood in San Francisco. This flat, expansive area, one of the warmest and sunniest in the city, has a long history as an ethnic enclave, beginning with the arrival of Irish and German immigrants in the 19th century and continuing with Italians, Mexicans, and most recently Central Americans and Asians.

This diversity has given birth to a veritable United Nations of restaurants, including Brazilian, Peruvian, Salvadoran, Spanish, Italian, French, Chinese, Cambodian, Laotian, Korean, Thai, and Indian places. Most are true mom-and-pop operations, but the low rents are beginning to attract such destination establishments as **Bruno's**, as well as many of the city's most innovative kitchens: **The Flying Saucer**'s eccentric chef creates a menu of wild, cross-cultural dishes, and **The Rooster** serves peasant fare from southern Europe and Asia.

One indicator of the area's growing sophistication was the transformation of **Picaro**. For more than a decade, it was a popular gathering place for the New Bohemians, who would linger for hours discussing art, films, and life. But **Picaro** turned into one of the city's hottest tapas bars a few years ago, and more recently it's been joined by the nearby **Paella la Movida**. Sylvie Le Mer's creperie, **Ti Couz**, continues to attract the urban set as well as the bridge-and-tunnel crowd.

The Mission is a laid-back kind of neighborhood, designed for hanging out, which is what draws the current generation of dreamers. There's a cafe for just about every persuasion: **Radio Valencia Cafe** has quickly become the place to showcase new jazz acts; **The Slow Club** attracts a trendy young crowd; and **Cafe Istanbul** offers the flavors and atmosphere of the Middle East. And 1960s idealism lives on at **Rainbow Grocery**, one of the few true communal efforts still prospering. In utilitarian surroundings, it has accumulated the city's best collection of natural foods, fresh herbs, and food items in bulk.

Despite the diversity, the real heart of the Mission is Central American. Much of the neighborhood's Central American character can be found on **Mission Street** and along **24th Street**, the bustling area that contains the bulk of the city's Latino restaurants, markets, and bakeries. The Mission, like many other parts of the city, suffers from some street crime, gang activity, and drug problems. It's safe to visit during the day, when the streets are filled with ordinary folks going about their lives. At night, however, visitors should exercise common-sense precautions: Always try to know where you're going (or at least look like you do), and pay attention to where you are and what is happening around you. Don't flash cash or expensive jewelry and keep an eye on your wallet or purse. And if in doubt, take a taxi to and from your destination. Just remember that the road to culinary nirvana isn't always smooth, but it is always worth the trip.

1 Dominguez Mexican Bakery People have been known to drive for miles for the *churros* here. The long twists of doughnutlike dough, fried crisp and rolled in sugar, can be addictive, so fans buy them in dozens to freeze (with minimal loss in quality). The display windows contain electric pink, blue, and green cookies and gingerbread that look garish but taste wonderful. The bakery is also known for its breads; they're all winners. ♦ Daily. No credit cards accepted. 2951 24th St (at Alabama St). 821.1717

"La Victoria"

2 La Victoria Mexican Bakery Since it opened in the mid-1960s, this bakery has been turning out delicious, plump, and moist macaroons called *cocadas* and Mexican wedding cookies dusted with powdered sugar. Unlike those at some other bakeries, the sweet breads here have the traditional dry, sandy texture. ♦ Daily. No credit cards accepted. 2937 24th St (between Florida and Alabama Sts). 550.9292

3 Casa Lucas This Latino market carries many products from the Caribbean and Central America that can't be found elsewhere: canned breadfruit for Jamaican dishes; burnished palm oil for Brazilian cuisine; cans of small Colombian potatoes; and a whole shelf of fruit products, including guava. The produce section boasts such hard-to-find fruits as green coconuts, bitter oranges, and huge Mexican mangoes. ♦ Daily. No credit cards accepted. 2934 24th St (between Florida and Alabama Sts). 826.4334 &

4 La Palma A rapid-fire slapping sound means tortillas are being made by hand at this "Mexicatessen." Women lined up at a counter pat the dough into tortillas and then places them on the griddle, where they release a seductive aroma of corn. The steam table along

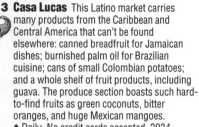

the back wall offers all kinds of take-out specialties, including wonderful tamales swathed in corn husks, *papusas* (stuffed tortillas), and *chiles verdes* (pork, chilies, and onions in a green sauce). The shelves hold several kinds of red and green salsas, which make perfect accompaniments to the best tortilla chips in the Bay Area. There's also an exceptionally large selection of canned, ground, dried, and bottled chilies. ♦ Daily. No credit cards accepted. 2884 24th St (at Florida St). 647.1500; fax 647.1710 &

5 Roosevelt Tamale Parlor ★★$ Very good Tex-Mex food has been packing fans into this eatery since 1922. With its bright blue ceiling, glowing Pepsi clock, and baseball pennants, it's a deceptively simple joint. Tamales are a specialty, and so are the combination platters, which include great enchiladas, *chiles rellenos* (stuffed chili peppers), and tacos. The green-chili burrito, with chunks of stewed pork and pungent strips of chilies, is marvelous. ♦ Mexican ♦ Tu-Su lunch and dinner. No credit cards accepted. 2817 24th St (between York and Bryant Sts). 550.9213

5 St. Francis Fountain ★★$ Still looking much as it did when it opened in 1918, this is a childhood fantasy come true. It is flanked by a soda fountain on one side and a display case of candy on the other; the peanut brittle alone is worth a visit. Sit at the counter or at one of the tables in back and indulge in a soda or a cone of luscious homemade ice cream in one of 20 flavors. More substantial fare includes wonderful comfort food of days gone by, like grilled cheese sandwiches and blue-plate specials. ♦ American/Ice-cream parlor ♦ Daily lunch and dinner. No credit cards accepted. 2801 24th St (at York St). 826.4200

6 Casa Sanchez Mornings are the time to visit this family shop: That's when the staff is busy working amid steaming vats of corn and cranking up dough machines that turn out fresh tortillas in all sizes. Connoisseurs head for the regular corn tortillas, recognized as the city's best. The shop also sells staples and such take-out fare as sausages, stuffed *poblano* chilies, and excellent salsas, particularly *salsa verde* (green sauce) made with tomatillos. ♦ Daily. No credit cards accepted. 2778 24th St (between Hampshire and York Sts). 282.2400; fax 550.4463 &

7 La Paz Restaurant and Pupuseria ★★$
This clean, well-lit hole-in-the-wall across the street from **San Francisco General Hospital** is quite a find. Not only does it serve well-prepared authentic Salvadoran fare, the prices are incredibly low—an entire meal can cost as little as $6. The delicious *pupusas* (tortillas stuffed with cheese alone or meat and cheese) are served with a sharply flavored cole slaw, and the pork or chicken tamales are so light they practically float over your plate. Other dishes include tongue in salsa, chicken in red sauce, and beef cooked with tomatoes, peppers, and eggs. It's a bit out of the way, but the journey is well worth it. ♦ Salvadoran ♦ Daily breakfast, lunch, and dinner. 1028 Potrero Ave (between 23rd and 22nd Sts). 550.8313

8 Universal Cafe ★★★$$
Despite the hard-to-find location in an unlikely industrial-residential neighborhood, this place attracts a wide range of young (or young-at-heart) diners with its excellent food. (Its conversion from a coffee-roasting company into a sunny, high-style, urban

hangout has also attracted the attention of design magazines.) At lunch the sandwiches on focaccia are unsurpassed: Try the grilled beef tenderloin with gorgonzola, roast chicken with aioli, or Italian meat loaf with provolone. At dinner the candlelit room takes on a magical glow. Great appetizers include the grilled flatbread topped with sautéed arugula, prosciutto, and asiago cheese; warm greens with pancetta and leeks; or baked gnocchi with oyster mushrooms and scallions. Only about three main courses are offered on any given evening; they might include roast chicken with tomato *coulis*, semolina, and braised greens, or roast salmon with avocado-leek salad and crispy potatoes. For dessert, try the seasonal fruit crisps.
♦ Cafe ♦ Tu-F breakfast, lunch, and dinner; Sa-Su brunch, lunch, and dinner. 2814 19th St (between Bryant and Florida Sts). 821.4608; fax 285.6760 ♿

9 The Slow Club ★★$$ Never mind the name—a fast-paced crowd fills this trendy cafe with its quasi-industrial feel and slick, California-inspired menu. From the closet-size kitchen behind a colorful plywood bar comes a United Nations of flavors. The menu changes daily, but appetizers might be an array of tapas, a designer salad, or soft polenta enriched with parmesan and brightened with fava beans. Entrées might include monkfish presented on risotto or braised short ribs with roasted apples. Seductive endings: a rich *pots de crème*

(custard) or polenta pound cake topped with fruit compote. ♦ Californian ♦ M lunch; Tu-F lunch and dinner; Sa dinner. 2501 Mariposa St (at Hampshire St). 241.9390 ♿

10 Moxie ★$ On the former site of **Eichelberger's** is a new place that calls itself an "Eastern European bistro." So what does that mean? Basically, it amounts to New York deli–style food, such as latkes (potato pancakes), matzoh ball soup, turkey Reuben, and house-cured salmon gravlax. The decor is plain—brick walls, uninteresting tables and chairs, and little ambience to speak of. The food comes in large quantities and is very filling, so come hungry. ♦ Bistro ♦ Tu-F lunch and dinner; Sa dinner (F-Sa to midnight). 2742 17th St (between Bryant and Florida Sts). 863.4177

11 Dylan's Set in a building that dates from 1902, this funky nightspot is the only Welsh bar in the city (and possibly on the entire West Coast). Owner Titch Jones, a Welshman, and his French-Canadian wife, Danielle, have decorated the place with lots of Wales-related memorabilia. Photos of illustrious Welsh boxers, writers, and poets (including the bar's namesake, Dylan Thomas) hang on the walls, as does a colorful flag from Conwy Castle. There's also a mural painted on one wall that depicts famous Welsh actors Sir Anthony Hopkins and Sir Richard Burton. The bar serves nine brews on tap and 12 single malt scotches, as well as a limited menu of pub grub. Poetry readings are held on Tuesday evenings, and various kinds of live music are performed Wednesday through Saturday evenings. ♦ Daily 4PM-2AM. 2301 Folsom St (at 19th St). 641.1416

12 Chava's Mexican Restaurant ★★$
Brightly painted in primary colors, this eatery is particularly popular on weekends, when it serves goat and *menudo,* the hearty tripe stew that Mexicans consider the only cure for a hangover; many other places cook up this rich, hominy-studded stew, but few do it better. The kitchen is also known for its egg dishes, especially the *huevos rancheros.* Other top draws are the homemade corn tortillas and the *chiles verdes.* ♦ Mexican ♦ Daily lunch and dinner. No credit cards accepted. 3248 18th St (at Shotwell St). 552.9387

Menudo, a rib-sticking stew made with tripe and hominy, is supposed to be a good hangover cure, according to Mexican folklore. It's available at several San Francisco restaurants, but the best one is Chava's Mexican Restaurant (3248 18th St, at Shotwell St) in the Mission.

13 Rainbow Grocery This natural-foods co-op, owned by a very ecologically aware collective, stocks a staggering array of vitamins and a truly amazing range of foodstuffs, including produce, cheese, and top-quality organic fruits and vegetables. The store recently moved from its original Mission Street location to new, larger digs—it even has a parking lot now! The aisles are filled with bins of various flours, grains, and fruits, including dried persimmons, mangoes, and papayas. More than 30 teas, 80 spices, and 200 roots and herbs (including Irish moss and Jamaican dogwood) are also sold in bulk. One thing is certain—you won't find environmentally "incorrect" products on the shelves. Under the same roof (and ownership) is a general store that carries everything from housewares to natural-fiber clothing to gemstones. ◆ Daily. 1745 Folsom St (between 14th and 13th Sts). 863.0620, general store 863.9200; fax 863.8955 ౼

14 San Francisco Herb Company Spices in *serious* bulk—that is, one-, five-, or 20-pound portions—are all that this wholesale-retail shop sells. The savings are huge, too, so many people divide their purchases with friends. All the standard seasonings are available, as are spices used for ethnic cooking, such as annatto, lemongrass, and chicory root. The store also carries seeds for sprouting, including mung bean, radish, alfalfa, and clover. ◆ M-F 10AM-4PM; Sa 10AM-2PM. 250 14th St (between S Van Ness Ave and Mission St). 861.3018; fax 864.4440 ౼

15 Woodward's Garden ★$$ Practically abutting the multilevel freeway, this place in a brick building on a dingy corner is a true find. Inside, the kitchen dominates an L-shaped room big enough for just nine tables. The menu, which changes weekly, showcases everything good about California cuisine. Whether it's a massive pork chop accompanied by a hillock of mashed potatoes and a vibrant tomato-and-mushroom ragout, or roasted salmon topped with aioli and

arranged over a bed of white beans and spinach, it's fresh and delicious. Lemon *pots de crème* and moist ginger cake with fruit compote and rum-scented whipped cream show up from time to time, along with other satisfying sweets. ◆ American ◆ W-Su dinner. No credit cards accepted. 1700 Mission St (at Duboce Ave). 621.7122 ౼

16 Greek American Food Imports This small shop is packed with all the products needed to put an authentic Greek meal on the table, including wine. Several kinds of phyllo are available, both fresh and frozen; the selection of cheeses includes *kasseri* (similar to cheddar) and feta from the United States, Greece, and France. A display case in front holds baklava and other pastries. ◆ Tu-Su 10AM-1PM. No credit cards accepted. 223 Valencia St (between Clinton Park St and Duboce Ave). 864.0978 ౼

PAULINE'S

17 Pauline's Pizza ★★$ A prime stop for pizza with crisp, cornmeal-dusted crusts, this spot has even been spiffed up recently. The cloth-covered tables and enthusiastic service make clear that this is no ordinary pizza parlor, but the bars across the windows hint that it's not in the best neighborhood. Pizza toppings run from the traditional to combinations that would make even Wolfgang Puck shake his head in wonder: Consider smoked ham, braised leeks, fontina cheese, and bell-pepper puree, for instance. The best-known dish is pesto pizza, in which the vibrant topping is spooned over a prebaked crust. The salad is generous enough for sharing. ◆ Pizzeria ◆ Tu-Sa dinner. 260 Valencia St (between 14th and Clinton Park Sts). 552.2050 ౼

18 Pancho Villa Taqueria ★$ Similar fresh fare is offered here as at its sister *taquería* **El Toro** (see page 149), but in spacious, bare-bones surroundings. There's a larger selection of fruit drinks, as well as such dishes as tequila-marinated prawns, served with rice and beans. ◆ Mexican ◆ Daily lunch and dinner. No credit cards accepted. 3071 16th St (between Mission and Valencia Sts). 864.8840; fax 864.3484 ౼

Sauerkraut, meaning "sour cabbage" in German, was originally a Chinese vegetable dish made by fermenting the vegetable in rice wine.

18 Taquería La Cumbre ★$ In its 1970s heyday, this was the best *taquería* in town. But over the years, it grew into a large chain, and the style and food have become more impersonal. But the food is still pretty good: The made-to-order burritos weigh in at well over a pound each, the *carne asada* (beef) is a winner, and the burritos made with tongue or pork stomach have legions of fans. However, many of the authentic Mexican specialties have been eliminated. ♦ Mexican ♦ Daily lunch and dinner. No credit cards accepted. 515 Valencia St (between 17th and 16th Sts). 863.8205; fax 863.2322 ♿

18 Cafe Istanbul $ A peaceful oasis, this blue-tented room with cushions on the floor is the place to relax with tea made with anise, sage, apple, or licorice, or to linger over a Turkish coffee. Light snacks include falafel, hummus, and other standard Middle Eastern fare. The service is relaxed, too—almost to the point of nonexistence. ♦ Middle Eastern ♦ Daily lunch and dinner. No credit cards accepted. 525 Valencia St (between 17th and 16th Sts). 863.8854

19 Bombay Bazar Pungent incense pervades this well-stocked Indian grocery store, which sells most items in bulk. The selection of beans and grains is far wider than at any health-food store. Gunnysacks of basmati rice are stacked high, and *dal* (lentils) seem to come in every color of the rainbow. On one shelf alone are more than 20 kinds of flour. Drums of raw peanuts and garbanzo beans and huge bins of *masala,* cumin, and other spices are offered at rock-bottom prices. ♦ Tu-Su. 548 Valencia St (between 17th and 16th Sts). 621.1717 ♿

20 The Slanted Door ★★$ Decorated in soothing shades of blue and featuring paintings by local artist Judy North, this restaurant offers a wide variety of well-prepared Asian dishes. The menu changes weekly, but typical items include stir-fried beans, five-spice chicken, and curried tofu. The desserts, however, are undistinguished; finish your meal with a pot of jasmine pearl tea instead. ♦ Asian ♦ Tu-Su lunch and dinner. 584 Valencia St (between 17th and 16th Sts). 861.8032; fax 861.8329 ♿

20 Amira ★$$ Ceilings draped with purple fabric, low tables topped with brass trays, and artfully painted walls lend an exotic air to this "pan-Arabic" restaurant. It's like a visit to a foreign land, even without the belly dancers, who entertain on weekends. The walnut dip, a specialty of the chef, is the best way to begin. Follow with one of the couscous dishes, succulent kabobs, or another of the Middle Eastern standards. (Be prepared to linger over your meal, though: To say that the service is slow is an understatement.) ♦ Middle Eastern ♦ Tu-Su dinner. 590 Valencia St (between 17th and 16th Sts). 621.6213

20 El Toro Taqueria ★★$$ The owners are so meticulous that they regularly scrape off the flyers that are plastered on the lampposts in front of their corner restaurant. The fresh-tasting food, even better than at **Pancho Villa Taqueria** (see page 148), reflects that same persnicketiness. Offerings include the standard soft tacos, a burrito generously filled with plump shrimp, and a tamale made with a *masa* (corn) dough that's so light it's almost a soufflé. ♦ Mexican ♦ Daily. No credit cards accepted. 598 Valencia St (at 17th St). 431.3351

21 La Hacienda Rows of colorful piñatas hang above a marble floor and below an ornate gilded ceiling—clues that this popular grocery once was a bank. It has one of the best selections of chilies in the Mission, a small produce aisle, meats, cheeses, and canned goods. There are also at least a hundred different kinds of religious candles—even one to light to win the lottery. ♦ Daily. 3100 16th St (at Valencia St). 431.8445; fax 431.8455 ♿

21 Ti Couz ★★★$ Sylvie Le Mer's Breton creperie is a winner—so popular, in fact, that it expanded next door a couple of years ago. The interior design comes straight from a French village, but the real focus is at the counter, where the cooks make crepes in assembly-line fashion. There are dozens of fillings: Savory ones include sausage, mushrooms, and ratatouille, while the sweet options might be apples, caramel, or chocolate. The beverage of choice is hard cider—a novelty in San Francisco—which is perfect with the light fare.

At the adjacent bar, the cozy seating is conducive to conversation. Young, old, rich, poor, conservative, liberal—everyone comes here. ◆ Creperie ◆ Daily lunch and dinner. 3108 16th St (between Valencia and Albion Sts). 252.7373; fax 252.7712 &

PicaRO

21 **Picaro** ★★$ Bright, bold colors and flavors dominate this warehouse-size tapas bar. The bar is painted in tribute to Miró, and the art on the walls evokes Picasso and Dalí. The tables are arranged helter-skelter, and the service can be painfully slow, but the kitchen successfully turns out a laundry list of tapas, which are as big as the entrées at most restaurants. Grilled mussels are redolent of garlic, the grilled quail needs nothing more than a gentle squeeze of lemon, and chicken croquettes ooze béchamel sauce. The beet-and-mushroom salad is an excellent antidote for all the garlic. For dessert, try the chocolate mousse, rice pudding, or creamy custard. ◆ Spanish/Tapas ◆ Daily lunch and dinner. No credit cards accepted. 3120 16th St (between Valencia and Albion Sts). 431.4089; fax 431.4089 &

22 **Maya Taqueria** ★$ Although it looks as big as a dance hall, this busy *taquería*'s dimensions can't dwarf the enormous portions of its food. It's all hearty (and priced at rock-bottom), but the specialty is the Azteca taco, a flour tortilla stuffed with beans, rice, a choice of meat, cheese, and salsa. It's heated quickly, ladled with spicy enchilada sauce, and crowned with creamy guacamole sauce and tangy sour cream sauce that help quell the chili-induced fire. ◆ Mexican ◆ Daily lunch and dinner. No credit cards accepted. 3198 16th St (at Guerrero St). 621.8025

23 **Katz Bagels** ★$ The chewy, slightly doughy bagels here come in 18 varieties, from traditional versions to dill cheddar and jalapeño. Smear them with a choice of spreads that includes honey date and dill cucumber, and eat in or carry them out. Loyal Mission residents keep this place hopping; they, and their diverse lifestyles, are celebrated by color portraits of them covering the walls. ◆ Cafe ◆ Daily. No credit cards accepted. 3147 16th St (between Albion and Guerrero Sts). 552.9122; fax 642.1255

23 **Malai Lao Restaurant** ★$ One of the few Laotian restaurants in the city, this small storefront eatery has tasty food. The *larb gai* (chicken with rice flour) here is similar to the Thai version, but better. Grilled quail is served with a dipping sauce of salt, pepper, and lemon—an accompaniment familiar to those who frequent Vietnamese and Thai restaurants. Another interesting dish is the fish steamed in banana leaves. ◆ Laotian/Thai ◆ M-F lunch and dinner; Sa-Su dinner. 3189 16th St (between Albion and Guerrero Sts). 626.8528

24 **Jack's Elixir Bar** A tavern has stood on this spot since 1932. In 1988, the place was purchased by Bill Carlson, who has turned six other locations throughout the city into multi-tap venues, all incorporating **Jack's** in the name (e.g., **Jack's Bar** in Fisherman's Wharf). There are no fewer than 50 beers on tap here (try the Pyramid apricot—it's fabulous). The wood bar, with a silver footrest and chrome stools, is the focal point of this dark room; there also are tables below the windows. No food is served. ◆ Daily 2PM-2AM. 3200 16th St (at Guerrero St). 552.1633

24 **Paella la Movida** ★★$$ Named for the movement that came into being in Spain after the death of Franco in 1975, this restaurant does indeed serve a very good paella, as well as some of the best tapas around (but at a rather high price). The dining room is decorated in a rainbow of colors, including bright yellow walls, a green wood floor, and red tables; paintings depicting Spanish landscapes and street scenes hang on the walls. ◆ Spanish ◆ Tu-F dinner; Sa-Su brunch and dinner. 3228 16th St (between Guerrero and Dolores Sts). 552.3889 &

25 **Anna's Danish Cookies** With Danish butter cookies this crisp and rich, it's no wonder this family business has been going strong since the 1930s; it ships up to 300 boxes of cookies across the country every day. (The cookies also are available in dietetic and chocolate-dipped versions.) The storefront windows and the shelves behind the service counter are filled with marvelous ceramic cookie jars in the shapes of pineapples, strawberries, whimsical animals, and Victorian houses. ◆ M-Sa. 3560 18th St (between Valencia and Guerrero Sts). 863.3882 &

26 **Carl's Pastry** This bakery produces superb American-style pastries in surroundings that evoke memories of its 1950s debut. The bear claws, with a crispy exterior and a flaky interior, are a sharp contrast to the doughy versions found at most places today. Carl's special, an almond, cinnamon, and buttercream ring, generally sells out first thing in the morning. If you want a treat for your pooch, pick up a bag of Bone Appetit, a bakery-made version of dog biscuits. ◆ Tu-Su. 600 Guerrero St (at 18th St). 552.1141

26 **Canto do Brazil** ★$ Bright green walls, yellow cafe curtains, and colored oilcloth tablecloths transform this small storefront into a fun setting for Brazilian food. The deep-fried croquettes made with chicken or beef are

outstanding; the *feijoada* (the bean-based national dish of Brazil), which is made on weekends, is one of the best in the city. ♦ Brazilian ♦ Tu-Su dinner. 3621 18th St (between Guerrero and Dolores Sts). 626.8727

27 Jivano's Cutlery Service Make an appointment to explore the fine selection of new and used knives here. Even when the place is closed and the curtains are drawn, you can drop your dull knives through the door slot with your name and phone number; they'll be sharpened to about the best edge in town. ♦ By appointment only. 3674 18th St (between Guerrero and Dolores Sts). 552.7997

28 Burger Joint ★$ The neon decor of this diner, with vivid aqua tabletops and vinyl booths in lime green and red, draws crowds—and so do the hamburgers made with chic Niman-Schell beef and the chicken-breast sandwiches made from free-range chicken. The limited menu also includes hot dogs, a vegetarian burger, and milk shakes. ♦ American/Hamburgers ♦ Daily lunch and dinner. No credit cards accepted. 807 Valencia St (between 20th and 19th Sts). 824.3494 &

28 Arabian Nights ★★$$ This new Arabian eatery has a refined atmosphere and an elegant appearance, with comfortable seating, attractive urns, and knicknacks and other decorative items from the Middle East. Among the tasty appetizers are hummus, *baba ganooj*, falafel, tabbouleh salad, and *foul moudames* (flavored fava beans). Main dishes include "The Sultan's Pleasure," rack of lamb with fresh herbs, accompanied by vegetables and couscous; "The Bedouin's Feast," roast chicken with couscous and vegetables; and "The Plate of 40 Thieves," which features sample tastes of all the salads on the menu, prepared vegetarian style. The best choice for dessert is baklava, washed down with mint tea or rich Turkish coffee. Two belly dancing shows are performed every night (with live music on Wednesdays and Thursdays). ♦ Middle Eastern ♦ Tu-Sa dinner (F-Sa until midnight). 811 Valencia St (between 20th and 19th Sts). 821.9747

29 Timo's Tapas Bar ★★$ Tapas lovers flock to this popular bar; it's aglow in bright colors, from the aqua-and-blue–trimmed exterior to the tables of electric yellow and black Formica. Among the outstanding tapas are grilled mushrooms punched up with garlic and parsley; new potatoes drizzled with aioli; and a masterful, chunky salt-cod and potato cake, crisp outside and creamy within. Other showstoppers include a ramekin of shrimp, glistening with butter and olive oil and studded with crisp slices of garlic, and duck confit ringed by baby turnips. Dish after dish is fresh and vibrant. Unfortunately, the service is amateurish. ♦ Spanish ♦ Daily dinner. 842 Valencia St (between 20th and 19th Sts). 647.0558

30 La Rondalla ★$$ It's always Christmas at this Mexican restaurant, which is bedecked with blazing tree lights 365 days a year and has developed something of a cult following (it's also a late night hangout for bar-hoppers). Stuffed birds and other kitsch fill the dining rooms and compete with the strolling mariachis for attention. The open kitchen turns out delicious guacamole and *carne asada,* and several creations made with goat meat. ♦ Mexican ♦ Tu-Su lunch and dinner until 3AM. No credit cards accepted. 901 Valencia St (at 20th St). 647.7474

31 VAL 21 ★★$$ The corrugated-tin walls are softened by a curved, emerald green bar, red-cushioned chairs, and cobalt blue vases of fresh tulips, all contributing to a finished, dramatic look. It's a fitting setting for the California-inspired menu, which changes every six weeks but always includes several impressive vegetarian dishes (for example, the twice-baked miniature pumpkins, one stuffed with mushrooms and the other with ratatouille). A roasted baby chicken may be glazed with cranberries and served with corn-bread dressing and wilted chard; *ahi* tuna may be paired with coconut-scented couscous, baked baby bananas, and pineapple salsa. Desserts include a hearty, spiced bread pudding with cranberries and a dense, steamed chocolate pudding. ♦ Californian ♦ M-F dinner; Sa-Su brunch and dinner. 995 Valencia St (between 21st and 20th Sts). 821.6622 &

31 Valencia Whole Foods As far as selection goes, this natural-foods store doesn't compare to **The Real Food Company** or **Rainbow Grocery,** but it earns high marks for its presentation. The bulk merchandise is stored in wood- and glass-fronted bins, the vitamins are perfectly aligned behind the counter, and the shelves display all kinds of high-quality convenience products, like organic dry soup mixes. ♦ Daily. 999 Valencia St (at 21st St). 285.0231; fax 285.5267 &

32 Fina Estampa ★★$ It's nothing fancy, but the food keeps this place packed with regulars (in fact, it's so popular that it recently expanded to a second location in the Tenderloin). Among the tapas from Spain and Peru are marinated beef hearts, and potato slices drizzled with a feta-based sauce and topped with hard-cooked egg and black olives. There's also excellent paella, and fried chicken nuggets tossed with marinated onions and tomatoes. The shrimp in garlic, served both as a tapa and a main course, is a stunner. The decor features faux-wood paneling, a matted red carpet, and tables topped with glass. ◆ Spanish ◆ Tu-Su lunch and dinner. 2374 Mission St (between 20th and 19th Sts). 824.4437. 1100 Van Ness Ave (at Geary St), The Tenderloin. 440.6343 ᕈ

33 Bruno's ★★★$$ From the moment it opened in the 1940s, **Bruno's** was a popular favorite among labor leaders, city politicians, and just plain folks. It seemed that everybody loved to come here and feast on classic Italian dishes like veal parmigiana and *spaghetti Bolognese*. In the 1990s, it wore out its welcome a bit, closing for four years. But now **Bruno's** is back, reopened by restaurant veterans (and Mission residents) John Varnedoe and Wayne Neithold. Together, they've created a retro setting that celebrates and yet refines the old, friendly ambience of the place. The partners rescued the restaurant's 14 handsome red leather booths from a salvage yard, shined up its original stained-glass light fixtures, and moved the kitchen to the back of the main dining room. Chef James Ormsby's best appetizers include Prince Edward Island mussels in an orange-saffron-mint broth and petite tuna steak au poivre. Featured entrées are roasted chicken breast and leg served with garlic mashed potatoes and portobello mushroom sauce; and braised Dutch Valley veal breast with turnip gratin and chanterelle mushroom jus. Desserts are also special, particularly the chocolate mousse and any warm fruit crisp. There's also a lounge with music every night. ◆ Mediterranean ◆ Restaurant Tu-Su dinner; lounge daily until 1AM. 2389 Mission St (at 20th St). 550.7455; fax 642.9059 ᕈ

34 Mi Rancho Market An all-purpose source of imported and local Latino food supplies, the market is equipped with a butcher shop, a bakery, and a wine section that stocks bottles from Chile and Argentina. Unlike many of the smaller stores in the Mission, this one—bigger, and with a more complete selection of merchandise—has a supermarket atmo-sphere. ◆ Daily. No credit cards accepted. 3365 20th St (between Shotwell St and S Van Ness Ave). 647.0580; fax 647.0582 ᕈ

35 Casa Felix Produce and packaged goods are stacked high at this popular store specializing in Latino products. It offers great deals on produce, baked goods, dried chilies, spices, and canned foods. ◆ Daily. No credit cards accepted. 2567 Mission St (between 22nd and 21st Sts). 824.4491. Also at: 2840 Mission St (between 25th and 24th Sts). 824.4474 ᕈ

36 Lucky Pork Store This shop stocks a wide variety of hard-to-find organ meats—pig's head for headcheese, pig's feet for pickling, pork intestines for sausage casings, for example. Suckling pigs can be ordered, and goat meat is available most days. The constant traffic ensures freshness. ◆ Daily. 2659 Mission St (between 23rd and 22nd Sts). 285.3611 ᕈ

37 Mission Market Fish & Poultry To find this vendor, walk through the marketplace clutter of the enclosed Mission mall. At the rear, under a red awning, you'll find free-range chickens, fresh turkey parts, fat stewing hens, and the like. Everything is freshly cut on-site. The seafood includes an array of clams, oysters, shrimp, and other shellfish, and many kinds of fish, including tilapia from Taiwan, "Gasper Goo" from Louisiana, and carp. ◆ M-Sa. 2590 Mission St (at 22nd St). 282.3331 ᕈ

37 Mission Meat Market Just across the aisle from the seafood and poultry market, this meat market is the place to find Harris Ranch beef and all kinds of lamb and pork, including pork hearts. The honeycomb tripe is especially good. ◆ M-Sa. No credit cards accepted. 2590 Mission St (at 22nd St). 282.1030 ᕈ

38 Esperpento ★★$ The Spanish name loosely translates as "weird," but the restaurant and the customers just look arty. With bright pink walls stippled with yellow splotches, hand-painted tabletops, and Dalíesque paintings, the compact room feels like an artists' retreat. Nearly 40 tapas are offered for big-time noshing. Chicken croquettes come out crisp, golden, and moist inside with béchamel sauce. Squid is infused with its own ink; most people will probably prefer the more familiar fried calamari. Try the shrimp, which come from the kitchen sizzling in olive oil studded with garlic and red chili flakes. The paella is an excellent rendition of this classic dish of rice, seafood, chicken, and pork, served in the traditional cast-iron skillet. ◆ Spanish/Tapas ◆ Daily lunch and dinner.

3295 22nd St (at Valencia St). 282.8867; fax 282.8867 ♿

38 The Rooster ★★$$ Peasant cooking from Southern Europe and Asia draws diners to this stylishly rustic new spot. The floor has the texture of sandpaper, the walls look scraped of a century of paint, and the chandeliers are made of rusted iron and shards of glass. Starters might be polenta with mushrooms, mussels in a spicy Asian-inspired broth, or roasted beets with crumbled creamy goat cheese. Entrées include such clay-pot dishes as lamb *tajine* (a Moroccan stew with olives and couscous) and beef stew in a red wine sauce perfumed with orange, as well as paella. Roast chicken and mashed potatoes get a twist with a compote of prunes and apricots. Dessert is not a strong point, except for the poached pear: One half is poached in red wine, the other in white wine, then the fruit is reassembled and presented upright on the plate with the red-wine poaching liquid. ♦ Mediterranean/Asian ♦ Daily dinner. 1101 Valencia St (at 22nd St). 824.1222; fax 824.1222

39 Radio Valencia Cafe ★$ Young people love this energetic cafe/bar, where they huddle around the tables—actually painted cable spools. All the standard coffee drinks are offered, as well as five beers on tap and Wyder's Pear Cider. The food is prepared to order, and the main attractions are sandwiches, focaccia, and pizzas. There's live blues and rock on Friday nights, bluegrass on Saturday, and jazz on Sunday; the jazz has a modest music charge, but there's no cover. ♦ Cafe ♦ M-F dinner until midnight; Sa-Su lunch and dinner. 1199 Valencia St (at 23rd St). 826.1199 ♿

40 Lucca Ravioli Co., Inc. Loyal customers take a number and stand in line, and their patience is rewarded by great homemade ravioli, fresh pasta, Italian cheese, sausage, superb cold cuts, sauces, frozen pesto, and excellent Italian wines—all at reasonable prices. No wonder this place has been in business so long (it opened in the 1920s). ♦ M-Sa. 1100 Valencia St (at 22nd St). 647.5581; fax 647.1948 ♿

40 Saigon Saigon ★★$ A bright urban oasis in a drab section of the Mission, this place sets a cheerful tone with the flower arrangements at the door. Begin with soft-shell crabs with a spicy dipping sauce, papaya-beef salad with nuances of fresh mint, or a gingery duck salad. Move on to black-peppered catfish or lamb kebabs with peanut sauce. If you insist on dessert, the crème caramel is simple, soothing, and satisfying. ♦ Vietnamese ♦ M-F lunch; Sa-Su dinner. 1132 Valencia St (between 23rd and 22nd Sts). 206.9635

41 Mangiafuoco ★★$$ This 50-seat dining spot serves incredible risotto, featherweight gnocchi, and great pasta, including the eponymous *mangiafuoco:* fettuccine coated with tomato sauce, topped with seafood, and then baked in parchment paper. Other excellent choices are the salads and the carpaccio drizzled with mustard. Since the restaurant's name means "fire eater," it's ironic that grilled dishes are its weak point; they aren't bad, they just pale by comparison to the other preparations. The cozy interior has hand-painted tabletops, ocher walls, halogen lighting, an open kitchen, and picture windows overlooking a row of Victorian houses. ♦ Italian ♦ Daily dinner. No credit cards accepted. 1001 Guerrero St (at 22nd St). 206.9881 ♿

FLYING SAUCER

42 The Flying Saucer ★★★$$$ The far-out food and decor have made this quirky restaurant a winner from the day it opened. There are black wooden booths, pressed-tin panels, and folk art on the walls, and a store mannequin lying across the ledge above the window. The menu, crafted by chef-owner Albert Trodjman, changes every six weeks and reflects what he calls "world-beat cuisine," meaning unusual cross-cultural combinations and dramatic presentations. Duck confit may share a plate with cabbage-peanut salad and ginger-infused Asian noodles. Rack of lamb might be coated with pecans and served with wild rice and a tart mint-fig compote; salmon might be blackened and served with spicy shrimp bread pudding. ♦ Californian ♦ T-Su dinner. Reservations recommended. 1000 Guerrero St (at 22nd St). 641.9955 ♿

A Tasteful Reading List

Unfortunately, you can't wrap up the flavors of San Francisco and take them home with you as a souvenir. And even if you take a doggie bag home from a restaurant, it'll only last a day or so. However, many of the city's culinary secrets have been captured in books by famous local chefs and food writers. These recipes have been a major influence on both professional and recreational chefs across the country. The following are among the best:

Beth's Basic Bread Book by Beth Hensperger (1996, Chronicle Books). This cookbook focuses on bread making, both by hand and using machines. It also includes good tips that make the process less daunting for beginners.

Bistro: The Best of Casual French Cooking by Gerald Hirigoyen (1995, Sunset Books). If you've ever wanted to try your hand at cooking homestyle French comfort food, this is the book for you. Among more than 50 recipes, Hirigoyen tells readers how to make one of his most popular dishes: roast chicken stuffed with bread and garlic.

Chez Panisse Vegetables by Alice Waters (1996, HarperCollins Publishers). The renowned chef who is credited with inventing California cuisine salutes the vegetable with more than 250 recipes that make good use of the garden's bounty. This is the latest of several **Chez Panisse** cookbooks; others include *Fanny at Chez Panisse* (1992, HarperCollins Publishers), which focuses on recipes that children can prepare with minimal assistance (Fanny is Waters's daughter); *The Chez Panisse Menu Cookbook* (1982, Random House); and *Chez Panisse: Pasta, Pizza, and Calzone* (1984, Random House).

The Cuisine of Hubert Keller by Hubert Keller (1996, Ten Speed Press). Every knowledgeable food lover in San Francisco knows the name and reputation of Hubert Keller, the owner/chef of the great **Fleur de Lys** restaurant. In this book, Keller gives detailed instructions on how to make some of his most famous dishes, including roasted chicken breasts on leeks with truffle sauce and wild mushrooms and caramelized vegetables in a potato shell.

From the Earth to the Table: John Ash's Wine Country Cuisine by John Ash (1996, Dutton). John Ash, food consultant to the Fetzer Vineyards in Mendocino and a former restaurateur, has put together a collection of more than 300 recipes for healthy, flavorful dishes using fresh California produce; also included is a section on tasting and evaluating wines.

James McNair Cooks Southeast Asian (1996, Chronicle Books). Best-selling author McNair has produced yet another excellent cookbook, this one on Southeast Asian fare.

Mostly Mediterranean by Paula Wolfert (1996, Penguin Books). Here is a collection of straightforward, easy-to-follow recipes for Mediterranean dishes.

La Parilla: The Mexican Grill by Reed Hearon (1996, Chronicle Books). This book, written by the popular owner of **Rose Pistola** and **Cafe Marimba**, covers everything you could ever want to know about doing a Mexican-style barbecue. Topics include dry rubs, marinades, grill temperatures, and working with wraps like banana leaves.

Roy's Feasts from Hawaii by Roy Yamaguchi (1996, Ten Speed Press). Yamaguchi is the founder of a chain of fusion restaurants with outposts in Hawaii and in Northern California and Asia. His innovative approach to fusion cuisine, influenced by his Japanese heritage and the native seafood and produce of Hawaii, is demonstrated in this collection of recipes.

The San Francisco Chronicle Cookbook by Michael Bauer and Fran Irwin (1997, Chronicle Books). Bauer, the food columnist for the *San Francisco Chronicle,* and Irwin have compiled a collection of the best recipes from the last ten years of the newspaper's award-winning food section.

Stars Desserts by Emily Luchetti (1993, HarperPerennial). The former pastry chef at **Stars** has compiled a volume of 150 of her favorite dessert recipes.

The Vegetarian Table: America by Deborah Madison (1996, Chronicle Books). Madison, the founder/chef of **Greens** restaurant, goes well beyond tofu burgers in this beautifully illustrated book of vegetarian recipes.

La Vera Cucina: Traditional Recipes from the Homes and Farms of Italy by Carlo Middione (1996, Simon and Schuster). Middione, a local restaurateur (**VIVANDE Ristorante** and **VIVANDE Porta Via**) and popular TV personality (who can be seen on the Discovery Channel), has compiled a collection of Tuscan recipes for main dishes, appetizers, and desserts.

43 Taqueria Goyaz ★$ The Mission hardly needs another *taquería*, but this spot has a twist: In addition to the standard Mexican selections (the pork burritos are excellent), it offers a range of Brazilian fare. Skewers of marinated beef are served on a bed of greens, and the Brazilian-style grilled chicken is tender and succulent. The plain environment doesn't encourage lingering, but prices are low even by Mission standards. ◆ Mexican/Brazilian ◆ Daily lunch and dinner. 3392 24th St (at Valencia St). 821.4600; fax 695.9295 &

44 Muddy's Coffee House With all its clutter and its faux-grungy crowd, this coffeehouse fits right into the neighborhood. Most people come here for a dose of caffeine and to hang out. There's also the standard array of pastries and other cafe fare. ◆ Daily. 1304 Valencia St (between 25th and 24th Sts). 647.7994. Also at: Numerous locations throughout the city

45 Suriya Thai Restaurant ★★$$ Chef-owner Suriya Srithongt adds pizzazz to her dishes with such fanciful garnishes as radishes carved into elephants, elevating this spot a step above most of the competition. The decor features Asian antiques, bamboo-backed chairs, and large urns of bamboo. The food veers toward the sweet side, making it popular with Western palates. Best dishes include chicken salad, garlic-pepper pork with red peppers and scallions, and chicken wrapped in banana leaves with cashews and raisins. The shrimp with ginger makes a dazzlingly hot contrast to the sweeter items. ◆ Thai ◆ Tu-F lunch and dinner; Sa-Su dinner. No credit cards accepted. 1432 Valencia St (between 26th and 25th Sts). 824.6655

46 Latin Freeze *Paletas* (fruit purees frozen on a stick) are produced at this tiny shop in dozens of seasonal flavors, including papaya, mango, melon, pineapple, coconut, and strawberry; all taste as if they were made from fresh-picked fruit. For a refreshing change, try the intriguingly sour tamarind. ◆ Daily. No credit cards accepted. 3338 24th St (between Mission and Bartlett Sts). 282.5033 &

47 23rd and Mission Produce The produce overflows onto the street at this clean shop, which has some of the best-priced fruits and vegetables in the city. Don't be discouraged by the long lines at the checkouts; the system is so efficient, you'll be through in a flash. ◆ Daily. No credit cards accepted. 2700 Mission St (at 23rd St). 285.7955 &

48 Dianda's Italian and American Pastries Just before the holidays, aficionados of Italian baked goods line up around the block to pick up their special orders. After one taste, you'll understand why. The amaretto cookies are soft and delicious; the fillings for zuppa inglese and zabaglione tortes are whipped by hand in copper bowls. *Paneforte,* a dense Italian fruitcake popular at Christmas, is moist and somewhat lighter here; it's available year-round. ◆ Daily. No credit cards accepted. 2883 Mission St (between 25th and 24th Sts). 647.5469 &

48 La Taqueria ★★$ The terra-cotta–colored floor and Mexican-tile walls here are always scrupulously clean, as is the open kitchen that turns out juicy grilled steak, tender *carnitas* (pork), and moist chicken, all wrapped in delicate flour tortillas. The salsa, even in winter, is fresh and vibrant, and the quesadillas are also good. *Agua fresca* sodas, which come in at least a half-dozen flavors, taste like the fruit's very essence (the cantaloupe and tangerine are incredible). The friendly service and rock-bottom prices are icing on the cake. ◆ Mexican ◆ Daily lunch and dinner. No credit cards accepted. 2889 Mission St (at 25th St). 285.7117 &

49 La Traviata ★★$$ An elegant outpost in a drab part of the Mission, the narrow room boasts an arched wooden ceiling, window frames holding mirrors instead of glass, and bronze carpeting that matches the upholstery on the booths and chairs; the tables are adorned by fresh pink roses and candles under frosted pink shades. Pictures of opera stars and scenes from famous operas bedeck the walls, and opera music plays continuously—a fitting backdrop for the dramatic fare. The gnocchi are wonderful—light, slightly chewy puffs of potato dough in a creamy tomato sauce with a hint of sweet spices. The tortellini is served in a white cream sauce perfumed with nutmeg. And don't miss the stews: The lamb stew is rich with the flavor that comes from slow simmering, yet the meat remains juicy. Other selections on the classic menu include veal with artichokes and chicken rolled around prosciutto and served with a mushroom sauce. Desserts mostly come from **Dianda's Italian and American Pastries** (see left), but the creamy tiramisù is made in-house. Avoid the cannoli: It's prepared in advance and tastes like it. ◆ Italian ◆ Tu-Su dinner. 2854 Mission St (between 25th and 24th Sts). 282.0500 &

50 Taqueria San Jose ★★★$ This is one of the best taco and burrito joints in the city. The grilled beef burrito is always worth sampling, and aficionados of more unusual Mexican fare can also find tripe, brains, chicken, pork stomach, and other delicacies on the menu. Prices are good and portions are big. ♦ Mexican ♦ Daily lunch and dinner. No credit cards accepted. 2830 Mission St (between 25th and 24th Sts). 282.0203

51 El Pollo Supremo ★★$ The bright yellow-and-orange exterior has dulled over time and the colorful interior looks the worse for wear, but this modest place produces some of the best chicken in the city, either to eat in or to take out. The limited menu also offers such side dishes as yucca (a starchy root) in garlic sauce, but chicken is the main event. ♦ Rotisserie/Mexican ♦ Daily lunch and dinner. No credit cards accepted. 3150 24th St (at Shotwell St). 550.1193; fax 550.2433

52 El Nuevo Frutilandia ★$ The dishes of Cuba and Puerto Rico are showcased in this small storefront restaurant with vivid coral walls and a cozy dining counter. Plantains, rice, and yucca show up in many of the mildly seasoned dishes—for example, in a Brazilian tamale, which is steamed in a plantain leaf. Lunch includes Cuban sandwiches, while dinner features substantial plates like chicken breasts in a bright green salsa. The nightly specials generally include a homey braised dish, always a good choice. ♦ Cuban/Puerto Rican ♦ Daily lunch and dinner. 3077 24th St (between Treat Ave and Folsom St). 648.2958 &

A famous chronicler of the Gold Rush era was Samuel Upham. His first business venture in San Francisco, in 1849, was making pickles. He wrote in his journal, "Pickles are scarce and sell at fabulous prices. The beach . . . for miles is lined with discarded pickle-jars and bottles, and I have gathered up, cleaned and stored them, having several hundred ready for use. I boarded a vessel just arrived from Boston and persuaded the captain to sell me a barrel of salted cucumbers and half a barrel of cider vinegar." According to his reports, Upham cleared $300 on the sale of his pickles in just one week—a small fortune in those days.

The legendary Poodle Dog Cafe in San Francisco was the site of a rather embarassing incident in 1885. It seems that a female patron's bustle caught on fire, and she was saved by a quick-thinking gentleman who poured Champagne on her smoldering backside.

53 Mitchell's Ice Cream Even though it's a bit off the beaten track, this parlor is a local legend. The ice creams are as rich as gelato, and many come in exotic tropical flavors, including avocado, litchi, *ube* (a root similar to a yam), *langka* (a tart melon), and *buko* (baby coconut). The Mexican chocolate ice cream has an enticing whisper of cinnamon, and the rich caramel is studded with toasted pecans. Three display cases hold half gallons for takeout, and an attendant sequestered behind glass, much like a bank teller, sells coffee and cones to those who want to lick and run. ♦ Daily. No credit cards accepted. 688 San Jose Ave (between 29th and Guerrero Sts). 648.2300 &

54 Angkor Borei ★★$ San Francisco was the first city in the United States to have a Cambodian restaurant. Although that one has closed, it paved the way for the others, of which this modest place is among the best. Juicy grilled beef balls, encasing water chestnuts and presented with pickled vegetables, are a wonderful introduction to this aromatic cuisine. Delicate Cambodian spring rolls, which crack like a thin layer of ice, are stuffed with vegetables, noodles, and pork. Green curries are laced with the fresh tastes of basil and lemongrass. The simple room in the outer Mission isn't up to the caliber of the food, but it's pleasant enough. ♦ Cambodian ♦ M-Sa lunch and dinner; Su dinner. 3471 Mission St (between Cortland Ave and Eugenia Aves). 550.8417

55 Inca ★★$ This small blue-and-white Peruvian cafe specializes in seafood; the deep-fried seafood platter—prawns, red snapper, mussels, clams, and calamari—is a standout. Also excellent is the appetizer of marinated and grilled beef heart with fried potatoes. Just be warned that service in this mom-and-pop operation can be slow. ♦ Peruvian ♦ M, W-Su lunch and dinner. No credit cards accepted. 3515 Mission St (between Santa Marina St and Cortland Ave). 821.5852; fax 206.0783 &

56 The Liberty Cafe ★★★$$ Finally, the Bernal Heights neighborhood has its first three-star hangout, thanks to this charming cafe. The menu features about four appetizers and as many main courses, but each is perfectly executed. Spears of asparagus are drizzled with a jalapeño-shallot vinaigrette, sprinkled with crisp bread crumbs, and topped with two halved quail eggs, and the Caesar salad is among the best in the city. Chicken potpie has a burnished puff-pastry crust and a lightly thickened filling of roasted pearl onions, carrots, and big chunks of potatoes and chicken. A whole trout is coated in a cornmeal crust, pan-seared, and served with lemony spinach, sautéed baby artichokes, and browned potatoes. For dessert the banana cream pie is unbeatable: a buttery, crisp crust, rich, creamy custard studded with slices of fruit, and billowy whipped cream. The decor of this 38-seat cafe is simple but attractive, with sky blue wainscoting and golden walls stenciled with ivy. White-clothed tables are topped with butcher paper and set with ceramic candleholders from Guatemala. All in all, it's an excellent destination. ♦ American ♦ Tu-F lunch and dinner; Sa brunch and dinner; Su brunch. 410 Cortland Ave (at Bennington St). 695.8777 &

56 The Good Life Grocery One of the city's most complete natural-food stores, it offers an impressive display of organic produce, plus a full-service deli featuring prepared salads and sandwiches. In addition, it carries beer and wine. ♦ Daily. 448 Cortland Ave (between Andover and Bennington Sts). 648.3221 &

57 Alemany Farmers' Market This market has been around since the 1940s and features all kinds of California-grown fruits and vegetables, as well as hard-to-find Asian products, dried fruits, nuts, eggs, herbs, honeys and jams, and crabs and oysters from Half Moon Bay. Street musicians often set up around the market. ♦ Sa 6AM-5PM. 100 Alemany Blvd (between Hwy 101 and Nevada St, near the intersection of I-280). 647.9423 &

Norry Beth Carrel
Bay Area Restaurant Designer

My favorite restaurants, from a design perspective:

Garden Court, Sheraton Palace Hotel—The gorgeous glass atrium dining room, with thousands of panes of leaded glass, was lovingly restored in 1991. While neither the food nor the service measures up to the beauty of the room, it is well worth a visit for brunch or tea.

Fleur de Lys—Designed by the late Michael Taylor, this elegant dining room is draped in a hand-painted floral "tent." The setting is simple, yet romantic, and the food is superb.

South Park Cafe—The atmosphere transports one to a bistro in Paris . . . the menu is authentic Gallic fare . . .

Caroline Bates
Restaurant Reviewer/Contributing Editor, *Gourmet* magazine

Two new restaurants that excite me are **EOS**, where Arnold Wong cooks artistic fusion dishes, and Ruggero Gadaldi's **Antica Trattoria,** which looks and tastes like his native Lombardy. In **Berkeley**, I like the inventive but grounded cooking of Wendy Bruckner at **Rivoli**. In **Napa Valley,** it's **Catahoula** in **Calistoga** for Jan Birnbaum's soulful and sophisticated New Orleans food. And for espresso and a good cry, it's **Caffè Trieste** in **North Beach.** On Saturday afternoon, I get tears in my eyes when someone sings "Torna a Sorrento," where I've never been, never mind returned to.

Bella Farrow
Socialite/Fund-Raiser

Nob Hill Cafe—Charming storefront and relaxed atmosphere, personal attention.

Downtown, I like **Postrio** and **Scala's**—both have exciting atmospheres and delicious food.

Joan Goldman
Owner, Reservations Tonight!, a concierge service

I really enjoy family-run restaurants where the chef's personality really comes through, like **Zax**, which is a perfect example—great food and a bit of whimsy. The **Universal Cafe** is a lunch favorite and **Palio d'Asti**'s moon shaped ravioli floating in a truffle flavored broth is one of my all-time favorites.

Across the Bay, I like **Citron**, **Ajanta**, and **Lalime's**. In **Marin**, on a warm night it's worth a drive to the **Lark Creek Inn,** where you can enjoy dessert, Cognac, and cigars under the stars among the redwoods.

Castro/Noe Valley

A stroll past **Chloe's Cafe** on a Sunday morning can tell even casual observers everything they need to know about the Castro and Noe Valley, two neighborhoods settled on the eastern slopes of **Twin Peaks**. While waiting outside for a table, two men lean against the building, holding hands; a young father bounces a baby on his knee while the mother watches; two women pushing a stroller down the sidewalk zigzag around the crowd. And no one seems to notice anything unusual about this scene; that's just the way this neighborhood is. In the Castro and Noe Valley, Boys Town meets Baby Town. That's a big change from just a decade or so ago. When young

heterosexuals moved into the area, and the **Walgreen's** at **18th** and **Castro Streets** began to carry Pampers, it was front-page news in the mainstream press.

The center of San Francisco's gay culture from about the 1970s on, the Castro has never been known for great food, but it does have a keen sense of culinary humor. **RoCocoa's Faerie Queene Chocolates,** for example, with fairies flying from the ceiling and faux-pearl–encrusted candy cases, is a campy (and pricey) place to buy Belgian chocolates. And although the phrase "hot 'n' hunky" may have certain connotations to some people, it also happens to be the name of a popular diner in this neighborhood specializing in hamburgers. Still, there's a lot to recommend here: delicious cross-cultural meals at **Ma Tante Sumi,** sparkling fresh oysters at **Anchor Oyster Bar,** and creative American fare at **Ryan's Restaurant,** whose downstairs deli features some of the best takeout in the city.

Good wine shops and cheese shops can be found along Castro and **Market Streets,** and a few blocks up, the excellent specialty grocer **Harvest Ranch Market** displays nature's bounty in baskets. Just about everywhere you look there's a coffeehouse, and none is as popular as **Cafe Flore.** Known by the gay locals as "Cafe Hairdo" because of the funky hairstyles worn by many of its customers, this spot is a prime place to relax and get a snapshot view of the neighborhood.

Coffeehouses fuel Noe Valley, too, a quaint neighborhood of Victorian storefronts and homes. The main shopping strip, **24th Street,** is the home of the original **Spinelli Coffee Company,** a well-known specialty roaster. Also on the street, **The Real Food Company** offers wonderful organic produce, **Caruso Wine and Liquor Store** can set you up with a great wine from a small California producer, and the **Noe Valley Bakery & Bread Co.** is one of the top spots for baked goods.

The restaurants didn't used to appeal to anyone from beyond the neighborhood, but that's beginning to change. In the last few years **Bacco Ristorante Italiano** and **Firefly** have brought three-star dining status to this three-star neighborhood. And then there are **Miss Millie's,** a fantastic place to enjoy Sunday brunch; and **2223 Restaurant** (formerly **John Cunin's No-Name Restaurant**). Even without a name, it became a huge hit; now that it's got one, who knows how much higher it can go?

---

1 It's Tops Coffee Shop ★★$ Amid all the glitzy faux diners popping up, it's a treat to find an authentic one like this place, which dates to 1935. Even the table-side jukeboxes play nothing more recent than early Beatles tunes. The knotty pine covering the walls and peaked ceiling are original; the eight bright orange booths and the counter with 12 stools were installed in the 1950s. The classic breakfasts include waffles, pancakes, and omelettes. The hamburgers are terrific—loosely formed, crisp on the outside, and sandwiched between grilled, cornmeal-dusted buns. Dinners include excellent grilled chicken breast, lamb chops, or liver and onions. The pies are average-tasting, but the homemade brownies and the milk shakes are exceptional. It's a great stop for night owls, as it's open late several nights a week. ♦ American ♦ M-Tu, Su breakfast and lunch; W-Sa breakfast, lunch, and dinner until 3AM. 1801 Market St (at McCoppin St). 431.6395; fax 431.6395

1 Dame—a restaurant ★★$ Though it's just a hole-in-the-wall kind of place—no atmosphere to speak of—this eatery is a hot hangout for locals in the know. The menu offers a modest selection of well-prepared American dishes. Starters include Caesar salad, gorgonzola french fries, and mussels steamed in a roasted red pepper broth. Entrées, which change frequently, include fettuccine with grilled chicken, spinach, onions, and pesto; and moist and tasty smoked pork loin served with rosemary polenta and oven-roasted vegetables. Friendly and fun, this is a great place to mingle with neighborhood residents. ♦ American ♦ Tu-F lunch and dinner; Sa dinner; Su brunch. 1815 Market St (between McCoppin and Guerrero Sts). 255.8818

2 The Orbit Room ★$ This trendy hangout cranks up early in the morning and continues into the wee hours. Daytime bites include sandwiches of roast beef or turkey, and salads topped with tuna, lemon chicken, or stilton cheese. There are strong espresso drinks, pastries, and desserts. At night the focus is on the bar, which stocks a full line of spirits and nine beers on tap (plus 12 bottled brews). The decor is impressive: the Deco building, the intricate period ceiling, cement vases on the tables, and large ornate windows overlooking the street. ♦ Cafe/Bar ♦ Daily breakfast, lunch, and dinner (M-Th until midnight; F-Su until 2AM). 1900 Market St (at Laguna St). 252.9525 ₺

3 Mecca ★$$ The centerpiece of this stylish supper club is a circular bar that seats 28; surrounding it are five distinct dining rooms, each with a different ambience. The atmospheres range from French bistro to 1930s supper club, but the menu throughout (by chef Lynn Sheehan) is Mediterranean. The food can be pretty uneven; your best bet is a pizza or appetizer enjoyed at the bar, where you can get a good view of the happening scene. ♦ Mediterranean ♦ M-Sa dinner. 2029 Market St (between Dolores and 14th Sts). 621.7000 ₺

4 Amazing Grace Vegetarian Restaurant ★$ The amazing thing about this clean but earthy-looking restaurant, with its slatted-wood ceiling and chairs, is that it's been in the same location since 1969, serving cafeteria-style vegetarian food at rock-bottom prices. Don't be surprised to find that the pungent smell of curry pervades the place. You'll find a southern Indian version with carrots and cashews and another with mushrooms. The salad bar offers more than 30 items. ♦ Vegetarian ♦ M-Sa lunch and dinner. No credit cards accepted. 216 Church St (between 15th and Market Sts). 626.6411 ₺

5 Just Desserts

This is the original retail location (there are now a dozen) that the Hoffmans, a husband-and-wife team, founded in the 1970s as an outlet to sell their immensely popular cheesecakes. Their made-it-big story may be unique: The company, which has also acquired the popular **Tassajara Bread Bakery,** maintains strict quality control and still uses butter and hand-cracked eggs. Such care really shows in its popular cheesecakes and super-moist chocolate cake. Just about any of the baked goods—pastries, cookies, and pies—are winners. ♦ Daily. ♦ 248 Church St (between 15th and Market Sts). 626.5774; fax 626.7212 ₺ Also at: Numerous locations throughout the city

6 Nippon Sushi ★★$ Since there's no signage at this 1980s-era eatery, locals have taken to calling it "No-Name Sushi." Although it's just a sliver of a place—with a well-worn sushi bar, bare tables, and only 26 seats, including at the counter—its good, inexpensive sushi attracts a cultlike following; fans begin to line up before 6PM. Upon being seated, customers are served a pot of toasted-barley tea, which goes well with the tasty *maki* (rice and seaweed with fish or vegetables rolled in the center). There's no telephone—only a pay phone that is never answered—and no liquor license, but that hasn't dampened its popularity one whit. ♦ Japanese ♦ M-Sa lunch and dinner. No credit cards accepted. 314 Church St (between 16th and 15th Sts). No phone

7 Thai House Bar and Café ★$ Opened only a few years ago, this outpost of **Thai House Restaurant** (see page 161) features an outdoor patio and a full bar. The warm meat salads and the soups are good, although main courses can be oily. Try the chicken satay, panfried shrimp, or chicken and coconut-milk soup. ♦ Thai ♦ Daily lunch and dinner. 2200 Market St (at Sanchez St). 864.5006 ₺ Also at: 151 Noe St (at Henry St). 863.0374

8 2223 Restaurant ★★★$$ John Cunin is nothing if not a smart entrepreneur who keeps ahead of (and sometimes starts) the latest trends. The opening of his **Cypress Club** in 1989 helped spark the renaissance of the supper club in San Francisco. Now, he's got a stylish and moderately priced dining establishment here in the Castro, a neighborhood that has always been short on contemporary cuisine. The sunny walls and fanciful light fixtures (with sculptured metal, opaque shades, and bulbs in various interesting shapes) set a friendly and almost magical tone, preparing you for the wonderful food to come. Star appetizers include warm duck confit salad with seasonal fruits, spiced pecans and pomegranate vinaigrette; wild mushroom soup with puff pastry; and grilled sea scallops with shaved fennel and citrus salad. Leading entrées are herb brioche–crusted pork loin served with yams and sage-buttered escarole; fillet of salmon poached in Champagne accompanied by potato puree; and a whole roasted guinea hen. The chocolate cake with Champagne-citrus granita is a heavenly way to round out the meal. The full bar serves a wide variety of cocktails, and the vintages on the wine list have been carefully chosen to complement the foods. ◆ Contemporary American ◆ M-Sa lunch and dinner; Su brunch and dinner. 2223 Market St (between Sanchez and Noe Sts). 431.0692 ♿

9 Thai House Restaurant ★$ Smaller than the branch on Market Street (see page 160), this place has a more intimate feel and a more loyal neighborhood clientele. The menu is virtually the same, although the food tends to be a little better balanced. Best bets include the shrimp rolls, the yellow (with turmeric) chicken curry, and the sirloin with spinach in peanut sauce. ◆ Thai ◆ Daily dinner. 151 Noe St (at Henry St). 863.0374. Also at: 2200 Market St (at Sanchez St). 864.5006 ♿

10 Cafe Flore ★★$ Probably the most popular coffeehouse with the gay community, this place looks like an overgrown lean-to and is easy to miss because of the planters obscuring the windows. The patio is the place to be on fine days, and the cozy, crowded interior is warming in the chilly winter. Quarters are so close, in fact, that at Christmas the tree is suspended upside down from the ceiling. Nobody is ever hassled; frustrated poets spend hours writing in their diaries, while other customers nurse their brew, trying to catch the eye of potential dates. People don't come for the food, but the eggs are fine and the organic greens taste as fresh as any you'll find. ◆ Californian ◆ M-Th, Su 7:30AM-11PM; F-Sa 7:30AM-midnight. 2298 Market St (at 16th St). 621.8579

11 Metro Bar and Restaurant ★$ Customers flock to this restaurant, up a flight of stairs, for the pot stickers, General Tso's chicken in hot sweet-and-sour sauce, and the squid *kung pao* (in a spicy sauce with peanuts). The bar, opposite, serves as a way station and is also a popular gay watering hole featuring drink specials on most nights. Its narrow outdoor patio wrapping around two sides is a prime place to hang out, listen to ear-blasting disco music, and watch the street action on Market. ◆ Chinese ◆ Daily dinner; bar M-F 2:30PM-2AM; Sa-Su 1PM-2AM. 3600 16th St (at Noe St). 703.9750; fax 241.9493

11 La Méditerranée ★★$ This Middle Eastern–inspired restaurant offers good food in intimate surroundings at excellent prices. The lemony hummus with fresh herbs is a good starter. Among the popular main courses are the "Levant" sandwiches, pinwheels of cream cheese and other ingredients, which change daily; ground lamb kebab served with rice; and chicken drumsticks marinated in pomegranate sauce and baked. Main courses come with salad or a cup of soup. ◆ Middle Eastern ◆ Tu-Su lunch and dinner. 288 Noe St (between 16th and 15th Sts). 431.7210 ♿ Also at: 2210 Fillmore St (between Sacramento and Clay Sts), Pacific Heights. 921.2956 ♿

12 Harvest Ranch Market One of the top specialty groceries, this place is always lively. People fill up the benches outside, eating takeout from the elaborate salad bar. Produce, most of it organic and looking hand-selected, is displayed in baskets, and breads from all the best bakeries fill the front window. The bins of bulk items, good olive oils, condiments, and hard-to-find products make this a popular destination. ◆ Daily 9AM-11PM. 2285 Market St (between Sanchez and 16th Sts). 626.0805; fax 626.0809

13 Port Cafe ★$ After a slight name change (it used to be the **Port Deli**) and a complete change of menu, this place has quickly won the affection of neighborhood residents for its good, inexpensive Cuban food. The surroundings—harsh lighting, Day-Glo orange walls, minimal furniture—aren't much to look at, but the owners may be contemplating a renovation in the near future. However, the menu has plenty to excite the taste buds. Among the best choices are *ropa vieja* (Spanish for "old clothes"), skirt steak, onions, and tomatoes which have been shredded to look like rags and served over rice and black beans; leg of pork; *arroz con pollo* (chicken and rice); and steak marinated in citrus juice, pounded thin, and grilled. A few American dishes are available too, like meatloaf, shepherd's pie, burgers, sandwiches, roast turkey, and fried chicken. ◆ Cuban/American ◆ M-Th, Su lunch (to 4PM); F-Sa lunch and dinner. 3499 16th St (at Sanchez St). 552.7645

General Mariano Guadalupe Vallejo may have been a California pioneer, but his daughter was renowned in her own right as a cook. Here's her recipe for Spanish eggs: Add two cups of peeled, seeded, and chopped tomatoes to a large skillet. Thicken with bits of crustless bread. Add two or three jalapeño peppers (for hotter flavor, mince the peppers beforehand) and a finely sliced onion. Add a little butter, salt, and pepper. Simmer gently 20 minutes to meld the flavors, then break three whole eggs on top. Baste with the sauce until the eggs are set.

14 Pozole ★★$ It looks like a Mexican folk art museum, but it's a burrito parlor specializing in low-fat, low-salt Mexican food, and the quesadillas and burritos have interesting fillings. The *burrito Californiano* combines cactus, *pasilla* (dried chili pepper), tomatoes, and roasted garlic; the *Mexicano* has chicken and roasted peppers with tomatillo and lime. Order at the counter and the food is brought to you. ◆ Mexican ◆ M-Th dinner; F-Sa lunch and dinner until midnight; Su lunch and dinner until 11PM. 2337 Market St (between Noe and 17th Sts). 626.2666; fax 252.8083 ♿

15 RoCocoa's Faerie Queene Chocolates Owner Jeoffrey Douglas says he's serious about chocolate, but not to the extent that he found in the exclusive shops in Europe, where chocolates are treated like precious jewels. He's put a drag-queen twist on his shop by draping the ceiling and walls with pink and white satin, gilding just about everything that could be painted, and adding dried nosegays and dozens of flying fairies (they're for sale, too). He's even glued pearls around the edges of the two cases that hold the pricey Belgian, French, and American chocolates. Douglas makes his own fudge—peanut butter and chocolate leading the pack. Among the specialty items: a chocolate phallus for the bawdy; delicate, pink-chocolate long-stem roses for the romantic. You can fax your orders. ◆ Daily noon-10PM. 415 Castro St (between 18th and Market Sts). 252.5814; fax 255.2016

15 Castro Cheesery This may be called a cheese shop, but when you walk in and smell the wake-up aroma of fresh-ground beans you know that coffee is the real attraction. Stacked in the corner, ceiling high, are plastic sacks of beans, and the area behind the counter displays more than 40 varieties, plus 20 flavored blends. Most of the coffees are surprisingly cheap; among the premium types are Kona, Yemen Mocha, and Jamaican Blue Mountain—considered by many to be the finest in the world. There is cheese, of course, a dozen cheddars and nine blues, but when it comes to aroma, coffee wins by a nose. ◆ Daily. 427 Castro St (between 18th and Market Sts). 552.6676; fax 552.0663 ♿

16 Rossi's Delicatessen Although small, this Italian-style deli makes great use of its space. Besides sandwiches and salads, you'll find a good sampling of wines, a growing collection of coffee beans, and a surprising selection of coffee filters. ◆ M-Sa 8AM-10PM; Su 10AM-

8PM. No credit cards accepted. 426 Castro St (between 18th and Market Sts). 863.4533 ♿

17 Slider's Diner ★$ Hamburgers are the tour de force of this restaurant featuring a 25-item self-service condiment bar. The burgers are thick and juicy, with thick fries to match—you order and pick up from the counter. It's a quick in and out, although some people linger to enjoy the music videos, concerts, and games that play on the television suspended from the ceiling in the clean, tiled dining room. ◆ Hamburgers ◆ Daily lunch and dinner (M-Th, Su until midnight; F-Sa until 3AM). 449 Castro St (between 18th and Market Sts). 431.3288; fax 431.3288 ♿

17 Cliff's Variety Established in 1936, this one-stop hardware store carries a large assortment of kitchenware, small appliances, and dishes. It's one of the most complete variety stores in the city. ◆ M-Sa 9:30AM-8PM. 479 Castro St (between 18th and Market Sts). 431.5365; fax 431.0803 ♿

18 Cafe Lupann's ★$$ Although the atmosphere suggests fine dining, the food and service can be uneven. Retro appetizers go from fried brie wedge (1970s) to pâté and escargot (1960s French). Main courses are more interesting: American pot roast, pork tenderloin grilled and served with Bourbon sauce and dried cherries, and boneless chicken breast topped with a spicy cucumber-and-mint yogurt sauce. ◆ Californian ◆ Daily dinner. 4072 18th St (between Hartford and Castro Sts). 552.6655

19 The Sausage Factory ★$ Since the 1960s, this local Italian restaurant has been dishing up pizzas, pastas, and salads in ample portions at reasonable prices. The dark wood paneling and narrow design of the winding dining rooms make for a cozy dinner but a rather dimly lit lunch. ◆ Italian ◆ Daily lunch and dinner. No credit cards accepted. 517 Castro St (between 19th and 18th Sts). 626.1250 ♿

19 Bad Man Jose's ★★$ A terrific place for a quick snack, this self-serve parlor features interesting burritos made of whole-wheat tortillas, black beans, brown rice, and grilled chicken or steak. Ingredients taste fresh and prices are low. The pleasant, modern surroundings are a plus, too, with a granite bar (ideal for the single diner) and, along the opposite wall, tables with straight-back wooden chairs. ♦ Mexican ♦ Daily lunch and dinner. No credit cards accepted. 4077 18th St (between Hartford and Castro Sts). 861.1706; fax 861.2426

20 Rosie's Cantina ★$ This pleasant corner restaurant features a menu of burritos, tacos, enchiladas, and other simple Mexican fare. After ordering at the counter, you can sit at one of the tables or have your food wrapped to go. ♦ Mexican ♦ Daily lunch and dinner. No credit cards accepted. 4001 18th St (at Noe St). 864.5643 ⑤

20 Hot 'N' Hunky ★$ Yet another chrome-and-tile burger joint, this one capitalizes on the gay clientele in both its name and its interior appointments, such as pictures of Marilyn Monroe. Fans contend that this eatery has the best burger in the city; we'd argue otherwise, but they are thick and the fries are crisp. ♦ Hamburgers ♦ M-Th, Su lunch and dinner until midnight; F-Sa lunch and dinner until 1AM. No credit cards accepted. 4039 18th St (between Noe and Hartford Sts). 621.6365

21 Taqueria Zapata ★$ This spare, cafeteria-style taco joint offers a large selection of fillings. Be patient, though; the many choices tend to slow and confuse both customers and employees. ♦ Mexican ♦ Daily lunch and dinner until midnight. No credit cards accepted. 4150 18th St (at Collingwood St). 861.4470 ⑤

MA TANTE

22 Ma Tante Sumi ★★$$ Featuring a creative menu that blends Japanese and French dishes, this small, intimate space, with tables on several levels, has a cozy aura and cross-cultural accents. The wasabi-cured salmon with pickled ginger is always a popular starter and so is the warm goat cheese served with *shiso* (a peppery Japanese herb), Asian pears, and walnut vinaigrette. Some of the more unusual dishes include grilled tuna with *wasabi-tobiko* (Japanese horseradish with flying-fish roe); pan-roasted duck with *hoisin* vinaigrette; and roast chicken with lemon and garlic sauce and a sesame *udon* (white noodle) salad. Sometimes the food soars, and only the amateurish service keeps this restaurant from playing in the big

leagues. ♦ Californian/Japanese ♦ Daily dinner. 4243 18th St (between Collingwood and Diamond Sts). 626.7864; fax 626.7886

23 Ryan's Charcuterie This is one of the city's top carryout places, and chef and co-owner Lenore Nolan-Ryan stocks two cases with freshly made products. Chicken may be Jamaican barbecued, crusted with mustard, simply grilled, or roasted whole with herbs and lemon. You can always find roasted garlic bulbs (great spread over bread), artichokes stuffed with aioli and croutons, a wonderful chicken potpie, and an excellent version of *pasta primavera*. The dessert crumble, made with fresh fruit in season, is a particular favorite. ♦ Daily. 4230 18th St (between Collingwood and Diamond Sts). 621.6131

23 Ryan's Restaurant ★★$$ Few establishments have such a charming, speakeasy atmosphere as this one, located above the carryout shop and accessed by a narrow, curving staircase that spills into a warren of rooms. The solid antique tables and chairs and white walls hung with modern art give the place distinction.While the decor is classic, the food is imaginative. A game hen may be stuffed with gruyère cheese and served with a warm potato-and-wild-mushroom salad. Pork loin is coated with garlic and comes with soft polenta and a fresh-tasting marinara sauce. Sometimes the creativity can go a little too far, such as soft pork taco with chipotle, aioli, and coriander salad. But such desserts as the fruit crumble are winners. ♦ Californian ♦ W-F dinner; Sa brunch and dinner; Su brunch. 4230 18th St (between Collingwood and Diamond Sts). 621.6131

24 The Patio Cafe $$ People love to knock the food here, but this is probably the most popular place in the Castro, thanks to the tree-shaded patio in back that fosters a pleasant atmosphere in good weather. It's particularly busy during the day for brunch, when 15 omelettes and a half-dozen kinds of pancakes are featured. There's something for everyone on the laundry-list menu, which leans toward sandwiches, burgers, and such generic American food as meat loaf, spaghetti, grilled chicken breast, and fried calamari. ♦ American ♦ Daily breakfast, lunch, and dinner. 531 Castro St (between 19th and 18th Sts). 621.4640 ⑤

The food in this city is fantastic. Better than London.
John Lennon and Yoko Ono

The first San Francisco restaurant owned by an African-American was Live and Let Live, opened by Joseph Watkins in 1860.

Exotic Ingredients: A Glossary

Chefs in San Francisco pride themselves on their cutting-edge cooking techniques and innovative recipes using unusual ingredients. This creativity is what makes the city such an exciting culinary destination. But it also means that as you explore all the dining possibilities here, you will probably come across terms that you've never heard of before. The following glossary defines the exotic foods you are most likely to find on San Francisco menus:

achiote a bright orange seed used in Hispanic cooking to color and flavor dishes.

amaranth a highly nutritious green that is usually cooked; the seed of this plant is also used in bread.

arugula a spicy salad green that can be served raw or cooked.

balsamic vinegar an Italian vinegar that is aged in wooden casks for as long as 25 years; it is used in sauces and salad dressings.

caul fat lacy fat that comes from near an animal's kidneys; it is used to wrap sausage patties or pâtés.

cranberry beans cream-colored beans with red streaks and a delicious, nutlike flavor; they are also known as *shell beans* or *shellouts.*

fava beans similar in appearance to lima beans (only fatter), these beans have a slightly bitter flavor.

fennel a popular vegetable that looks like celery

but has a mild licorice flavor; it is either braised or served raw.

flageolets tiny, tender French kidney beans with a delicate flavor; they are often served with lamb.

free-range refers to poultry that has been raised in a larger-than-usual space and has been fed a diet free of antibiotics, hormones, by-products, and other artificial ingredients.

haricots verts skinny French green beans.

harisa a hot chili paste used in Moroccan cooking, though now it is used in other ethnic cooking as well.

jicama a mild tasting root vegetable resembling a turnip, with light brown skin and a juicy white interior; it is great either raw or cooked and is usually served in salads or stir-fries.

lemongrass a pungent Southeast Asian herb with a strong, citrus-like taste; it is used in salads, stir-fries, and soups.

mesclun a mix of wild salad greens.

quinoa a Peruvian grain which, when cooked, is similar to couscous.

rocket See *arugula.*

sorrel a green with a slightly lemony taste; popular in French cuisine, it is used primarily in soups.

24 Anchor Oyster Bar ★★$$ Fresh seafood served in tiled, vaguely nautical surroundings is the draw of this small oyster bar with seating divided about equally between the counter and the stainless steel tables. The oysters are good, but what keeps customers coming back are the well-prepared clam

chowder and the classic crab or shrimp Louis salad, made with a dressing that is similar to Thousand Island. ◆ Seafood ◆ M-Sa lunch and dinner; Su dinner. 579 Castro St (between 19th and 18th Sts). 431.3990

25 Pachá ★$ The setting of this tapas bar— the only one in the area—is whimsical and modern with bright colors and unusual chairs with squiggly legs. Some of the best dishes are the chunks of roasted potatoes drizzled with garlicky aioli; Chinese-style chicken with a bronzed exterior cut into irregular chunks; eggplant doused in an oregano-flecked tomato sauce and covered with cheese and green olives; plump shrimp accented with a spicy tomato sauce; and fried calamari enhanced by a lemony dipping sauce. Service can be erratic, though, and the quality of the food varies. ♦ Spanish ♦ Daily lunch and dinner. No credit cards accepted. 544 Castro St (between 19th and 18th Sts). 431.7622 ዉ

25 Suzanne's Muffins This bakery has earned a reputation for big, fist-size muffins—more than 80 kinds. The top seller is the cakelike blueberry, followed by the likes of buttermilk spice and bran. Savory selections include "chile cheese corn" and "broccoli cheddar quiche." Those with a sweet tooth will find such dessert varieties as chocolate Grand Marnier and rum raisin. And many fans go for the "Very Very Lowfat Muffins," such as pumpkin, apple, banana walnut, and cranberry orange. ♦ Daily from 7AM. 564 Castro St (between 19th and 18th Sts). 864.4266 ዉ

26 Buffalo Whole Food & Grain Company Smaller than the Nob Hill branch, this health-food store is packed with select organic produce, plentiful breads, packaged convenience foods, and lots of vitamins and supplements. ♦ Daily. 598 Castro St (at 19th St). 626.7038; fax 626.7511 ዉ Also at: 1058 Hyde St (between Pine and California Sts), Nob Hill. 474.3053 ዉ

27 Castro Village Wine Co. Specializing in small California wine producers, the shop employs a knowledgeable staff to help the committed wine lover find just the right bottle. In the corner is a tasting bar featuring a different selection of varietals each week, and customers get a 10 percent discount on the purchase of a featured bottle. Rare wines might include a 1980 Stony Hill Chardonnay or a 1989 Groth Cabernet Sauvignon. There's also a small selection of premium spirits. Prices are competitive, often lower than other full-service shops in the area. ♦ Daily. 4121 19th St (between Castro and Collingwood Sts). 864.4411; fax 864.4411 ዉ

28 Firefly ★★★$$ You might miss this small chef-owned place, tucked into a row of houses, if it weren't for the bumblebee-yellow door and the glowing firefly above the entrance. A comfortable eclectic spirit

pervades the restaurant, started on a shoestring by Brad Levy and Veva Edels on. Despite the improvised decor—such as the mismatched tables and chairs from a garage sale—the look comes together. Levy characterizes his food as home cooking from around the world. That translates to pot stickers (Chinese dumplings) plump with shrimp and scallops, potato latkes with apple sauce, and chopped chicken livers. Main courses may be grilled tuna with *soba* (buckwheat) noodles, sesame orange–glazed yams, and wasabi aioli; hearty beef brisket; spicy gumbo; barbecued chicken with mashed potatoes; or cabbage stuffed with turkey in a sweet-and-sour sauce. Desserts are based on such down-home favorites as a dense chocolate chip cake layered with peanut butter. ♦ Californian ♦ Daily dinner. 4288 24th St (between Diamond and Douglass Sts). 821.7652; fax 821.5812

29 Bacco Ristorante Italiano ★★★$$ Persimmon and pumpkin hues lend a modern, stylish Italian feel to this establishment. It covers several storefront spaces, and the three-tiered dining room faces a wall of windows overlooking the quiet side street. Although the menu seems pedestrian at first glance, the preparations are anything but. Try the gnocchi, tender and light, or the simply sauced pastas, cooked exactly as they should be with just a little bite. The main courses are as good as the rest of the meal, especially the lamb chops and any veal dish. For dessert the warm chocolate cake, with a slightly runny center, is a real winner. To top it all off, the consummate Italian waiters are efficient yet friendly, with a good sense of humor. ♦ Italian ♦ Daily dinner. Reservations recommended. 737 Diamond St (between 24th and Elizabeth Sts). 282.4969; fax 282.1315 ዉ

In the late 19th century two exotic restaurants (now, unfortunately, defunct) opened in San Francisco. One was the Cobweb Palace, located down at Meig's Wharf at the foot of Powell Street. Owner Abe Warner served seafood in three dining rooms whose ceilings were festooned with cobwebs. Odder still was the Cabaret de la Mort, where guests were seated at empty coffins instead of tables and the dining room was illuminated by candles stuck in skulls.

What today appears on menus as an "oyster loaf"—half a loaf of bread, hollowed out, toasted, then filled with fried oysters and condiments—was invented at Gobey's Restaurant in the late 1880s. Considered a sure-fire cure for hangovers, in those days the dish was called "The Squarer."

30 Barney's Gourmet Hamburgers ★$
Barney's developed such a following in the East Bay that the owners decided to try their luck in Noe Valley. The specialty here is the big, fat beef patty (one-third of a pound) with all kinds of toppings that span the globe for flavor inspiration. You can also find tofu burgers, chicken, and salads, if you're not a beef eater. Located in a Victorian house, the restaurant has given over the front yard to tables shaded by green canvas umbrellas, making it a prime alfresco dining spot. ♦ American ♦ Daily lunch and dinner. 4138 24th St (between Castro and Diamond Sts). 282.7770; fax 282.1920 & Also at: 3344 Steiner St (between Lombard and Chestnut Sts), The Marina. 563.0307 &

31 Tom Peasant Pies An offshoot of a pie shop in Paris, this tiny bakery chain sells both sweet and savory pies, baked twice a day to ensure freshness. They're a real bargain, taste great at room temperature, and are ideal for picnics. The savories are reminiscent of piroshki. Generally four or five vegetable offerings are waiting to be snapped up, the most popular made of potato and onion laced with rosemary. Close behind are the seafood pies—shrimp, calamari, or clam. The fruit pies, made with a brown-sugar crust, are plumped with whatever is in season. Although most people prefer takeout, there's a counter with 10 seats and a bench outside. ♦ Daily. No credit cards accepted. 4108 24th St (between Castro and Diamond Sts). 642.1316 & Also at: Numerous locations throughout the city

32 Miss Millie's ★★★$ Great word of mouth on this retro-looking diner has drawn customers from all over the city. Breakfast is a big deal here, featuring fat, sticky cinnamon rolls, citrus-flavored scones, and French toast topped with bananas, whipped butter, and real maple syrup. And don't miss the lemon ricotta pancakes with blueberry syrup—yum! More healthy alternatives are also available, such as the side dish of roasted root vegetables and the entrée of scrambled curried tofu. Lunch is also popular; try the great grilled cheese sandwich made with two kinds of cheddar (New York sharp, made with cow's milk, and goat cheese). Now the restaurant has expanded its menu, serving a short dinner menu of vegetarian dishes as well. The specifics change from day to day, but every item is well prepared. The pizza is good (try

the chard and caramelized red onion), as is the appetizer of potato-and-leek pancakes with horseradish crème fraîche and chives. Millie's rib-sticking macaroni and cheese comes gussied up with roasted mushrooms, fontina, gruyère, and thyme, and risotto incorporates bitter greens, roasted butternut squash, and brussels sprouts. There's a long wait at times, especially for Sunday brunch, but this place is worth it. ♦ American ♦ Tu-Sa breakfast, lunch, and dinner; Su breakfast. 4123 24th St (between Castro and Diamond Sts). 285.5598; fax 585.5030

32 Little Italy Ristorante ★★$$ If the food-labeling act extended to restaurants, the sign in front of this tiny eatery would read: "Garlic-shy diners should go elsewhere." The pungent aroma of the stinking rose is everywhere, and it shows up on just about every dish: At least a quarter-cup is strewn over the marvelous veal chop, and it's the main ingredient in the spaghetti with prawns and anchovies. Garlic even shows up on the stuffed artichoke, the asparagus side dishes, and the half chicken broiled with garlic vinegar and olive oil. To clean your palate, finish with the zabaglione, one of the top preparations in the city. ♦ Southern Italian ♦ Daily dinner. 4109 24th St (between Castro and Diamond Sts). 821.1515

32 Rory's Twisted Scoop The idea here is to choose an ice-cream flavor and combine it with such add-ins as chunks of Reese's Peanut Butter Cups, M&Ms, and nuts. The scoopmaster plops the ice cream on a marble slab and cuts in customers' selections with paddles. The shop makes its own waffle cones and also features such nonfat yogurts as banana peanut butter and Ghirardelli chocolate. The original store on Fillmore Street is where they actually make the ice cream. ♦ M-Th, Su until 11PM; F-Sa until midnight. No credit cards accepted. 4101 24th St (at Castro St). 648.2837 & Also at: 2015 Fillmore St (between Pine and California Sts), Pacific Heights. 346.3692

33 Hamano Sushi ★★$
The light wood used in the hand-tooled sushi bar and raised dining area in back give this narrow restaurant an understated feel of serenity. Full meals are offered, but the specialty is *makimono* (sushi rice roll), which includes tuna with green onions, salmon with avocado, or eel with cucumber. The equally impressive vegetarian rolls are filled with pickled burdock, radish sprouts, or fermented soybeans. Be sure to try the *mirugai* (giant geoduck clams) for their nutty flavor. ♦ Japanese ♦ Daily dinner. 1332 Castro St (between Jersey and 24th Sts). 826.0825

34 Out of Hand

American contemporary crafts are featured here, and shoppers should drop in regularly to keep abreast of the ever-changing merchandise. You might come upon a special exhibition/ sale, such as the *Ultimate Ice Cream Dish Show,* a collection of glass and ceramic dishes commissioned from top artists across the United States, including Lisa Scroggin's *Original Sin,* an ice-cream goblet encircled with a snake. ♦ M-Sa 10:30AM-6:30PM; Su noon-6PM. 1303 Castro St (at 24th St). 826.3885; fax 510.526.1743 ♦

34 Noe Valley Bakery & Bread Co.

Owners Michael Gassen and Mary Gaylord-Gassen met at **Il Fornaio,** one of the city's premier Italian bakeries, and they have brought their combined skills and experience to this place. Their gorgeous breads, displayed in baskets, come in many unusual flavors: One chewy loaf is studded with figs, another with dried apricots and a whisper of ginger, another with cherries and chocolate. Cinnamon twists have a crackling glaze and a seductively buttery, spicy essence. The brioche is finely textured and barely sweet, and the bread sticks are crisp and flavorful. Focaccia is offered plain, with scallions, or with fresh rosemary. The scones are some of the best around; try the intense lemon almond or blueberry pecan versions. Other irresistible treats include oatmeal-raisin or chocolate chip cookies, lemon pound cake, fruit tarts, pear frangipani, and carrot cake. ♦ Daily. 4073 24th St (between Noe and Castro Sts). 550.1405; fax 550.1485 ♦

35 Caruso Wine and Liquor Store

Steve Kerr has assembled a fine collection from small-production wineries, with special emphasis on California, French Rhône, and central Italian wines. He also stocks 40 kinds of single-malt scotches, a half-dozen premium tequilas, up to a dozen small-batch American whiskeys, and dozens of Cognacs and Armagnacs. Prices are good, considering the hand-picked nature of his collection. If you don't see what you want, just ask; Kerr stashes some of the rarer wines in back. ♦ Daily. 4011 24th Street (between Noe and Castro Sts). 282.3841; fax 282.6109 ♦

36 Panos' $$

Popular with neighborhood residents, this restaurant leans toward chic with its white walls, granite-topped wine bar, and black marble floor, although the Greek food is pretty standard and can be salty. Good bets are the grilled lamb, the avgolemono soup with its bright lemon kick, and the *spanikopita* (spinach pie). ♦ Californian/Greek ♦ M-F lunch and dinner; Sa-Su brunch and dinner. 4000 24th St (at Noe St). 824.8000 ♦

37 Herb's Fine Foods ★$

Since 1943 this has been the place to go for a longshoreman-style breakfast of eggs and bacon or corned beef hash. The sea of vinyl chairs, red-plaid Formica tabletops, and the horseshoe counter foster a comfortable, "Happy Days"–like atmosphere. ♦ Diner ♦ M-F 6:30AM-3:30PM; Sa-Su 7AM-4PM. 3991 24th St (between Sanchez and Noe Sts). 826.8937

37 Bakers of Paris

Croissants and baguettes, crispy outside and soft and slightly airy inside, are the specialties of one of the city's best-known bakeries. On any given day you'll find more than a dozen kinds of bread, such as Alsatian rye or multigrain walnut. There's limited seating for those who want to sip a coffee while indulging in one of the delectable offerings. ♦ Daily. No credit cards accepted. 3989 24th St (between Sanchez and Noe Sts). 863.8725 ♦

37 The Chef Specialty Foods

Hardly big enough to turn around in, this shop packs a lot into its small space. In addition to made-to-order sandwiches and salads, you'll find dried shiitake and morel mushrooms, crystallized ginger and candied violets, and all kinds of pâtés. Other specialty products include such jarred condiments as hot mango chutneys and a choice selection of coffee beans. ♦ Daily. 3977 24th St (between Sanchez and Noe Sts). 550.7982

37 Chocolate Covered

This shop has a great assortment of chocolates and chocolate-covered goodies from 15 manufacturers and five countries. Among the tempting treats are candied fruits, creams, nuts, and espresso nuggets. Everything comes professionally wrapped, and if you buy enough items, the staff will place them in a beautiful tin. ♦ Hours are erratic; call ahead. 3961 1/2 24th St (between Sanchez and Noe Sts). 641.8123 ♦

38 Spinelli Coffee Company

Opened in 1984, this is the original location of the popular chain that's known for its strong coffee with a slightly bitter edge. The house blend is a medium-body mixture of Central American beans. There are also 15 coffees for takeout. ♦ Daily 6:30AM-10PM. 3966 24th St (between Sanchez and Noe Sts). 550.7416; fax

550.0301 & Also at: Numerous locations throughout the city

39 The Real Food Company The produce here is top-of-the-line organic, as it is at the other branches, but this shop is smaller. There's no meat or fish and the cheese selection is not as extensive. Service here is marginally better than at the other branches. ♦ Daily. 3939 24th St (between Sanchez and Noe Sts). 282.9500; fax 282.9190 & Also at: Numerous locations throughout the city

39 Panetti's Gifts On sale here is a charming selection of decorative accessories and some food-related products, such as place mats and napkins; jewelry in the shape of chilies, fruits, and other food motifs; copper cookie cutters; picnic baskets; mushroom-shaped garlic crushers; and blue-and-white tin plates. ♦ Daily. 3927 24th St (between Sanchez and Noe Sts). 648.2414

39 Savor ★★$ Noe Valley is nicknamed "the baby belt of San Francisco," and this family-oriented spot suits the area to a T. The decor (sparkling white walls, an exhibition kitchen, and a paved patio for outdoor dining) and casual ambience is very kid-friendly, and the menu specializes in crepes. There are lots of varieties, many of them international, including the Barcelona (with Fontina cheese, glazed onions, spinach, and mushrooms), the Cypress (with feta cheese and kalamata olives), and the Kyoto (with smoked tofu, shiitake mushrooms, ginger, and green onions). Other items include egg dishes, crab cakes topped with spicy hollandaise sauce, French toast, frittatas, and ordinary pancakes. And don't get us started on the dessert crepes. . . ♦ Creperie ♦ M-Sa breakfast, lunch, and dinner; Su breakfast and lunch. 3913 24th St (between Sanchez and Noe Sts). 282.0344; fax 282.3881 &

40 Twenty-Fourth Street Cheese One of the best cheese shops in the city for both variety and price, this 1970s-era establishment has a quaint European atmosphere. The front window is decorated with wheels of gruyère and a barrel-size round of parmesan reggiano. Customers can choose among 250 kinds of cheese and about 30 types of crackers and bread sticks (including the much-admired Cuneo), as well as **Acme** bread, **Molinari** sausage, a small selection of wines, and a dozen varieties of olives. The shop also rents raclette ovens and sells fondue sets. ♦ Daily. 3893 24th St (between Vicksburg and Sanchez Sts). 821.6658; fax 648.3361

41 Martha and Brothers Coffee Co. The coffee aroma lures people in; the earthy house blend of Sumatra and Guatemalan keeps them coming back. Fifty kinds of coffee are offered, with scones, muffins, and biscotti available to complement the heady brews. ♦ Daily. No

credit cards accepted. 3868 24th St (between Vicksburg and Sanchez Sts). 641.4433; fax 641.0193. Also at: Numerous locations throughout the city

42 Chloe's Cafe ★$ Marked with a blue awning, this small storefront is a neighborhood gathering place, especially for breakfast on the weekend. You sign up outside and wait your turn. Different configurations of couples touch and chat comfortably while babies in strollers create a traffic jam in the middle of the sidewalk; it's just another Noe Valley Sunday. Pancakes are the specialty here and might be banana nut or Swedish-style with oatmeal. Scrambled eggs are enhanced with such additions as bacon and tomato and served with ho-hum wedges of sautéed potatoes. Pasta, pork chops, grilled chicken, quesadillas, and soup and salad combos draw the locals at dinnertime. ♦ American ♦ M-F breakfast and dinner; Sa-Su breakfast. No credit cards accepted. 1399 Church St (at 26th St). 648.4116

43 Lady Sybil's Closet This shop, specializing in tea accessories, is as tiny as the name implies. The windows are filled with antique teapots, cups and saucers, hand-crocheted potholders, and embroidered dish towels; the interior is draped with all types of lace, crocheted doilies, and tablecloths. Most items are vintage and handmade. ♦ Th-Su 1-6PM. No credit cards accepted. 1484 Church St (between 27th and Army Sts). 282.2088; fax 285.7452

What's For Dessert?

44 What's for Dessert? ★$ Owner Mervyn Mark has acquired a faithful clientele for breakfast and lunch and is also the creator of the unique "Gâteau San Francisco," featuring an intricate chocolate design of the San Francisco skyline. The cookies, whether flavored with ginger or chocolate, are first-rate. ♦ Cafe ♦ Tu-Su breakfast and lunch. No credit cards accepted. 1497 Church St (at 27th St). 550.7465 &

45 Eric's ★★$ On most nights, this place has the atmosphere of a nightclub rather than a Chinese restaurant; purple and green neon lights up the outside and illuminates the milling throng waiting for tables. The interior features plain white walls and plank floors, and only the tasteful, hand-carved wood screen hints at the ethnic origin of the food. Some dishes miss the mark because of too much oil and cloying sweetness, but the hits can be sensational: Try the spicy eggplant with shrimp and loads of chilies or the walnut prawns (sugar-glazed walnuts with fried shrimp and creamy mayonnaise sauce served in a fried-potato nest). Among the more unusual dishes are the spicy smoked pork with leeks and the Shanghai chicken nuggets laced with crunchy seaweed. ♦ Chinese ♦ Daily lunch and dinner. 1500 Church St (at 27th St). 282.0919 ♿

46 Speckmann's ★★$$ The food is traditional at this out-of-the-way *bierstube* that looks as if it was created for a movie set: dark paneling, austere wood chairs, and tables draped in red-and-white–checkered cloths, which are placed so close together that you brush up against the waiter's lederhosen as he serves. Cheerful music completes the stereotype. The sauer-braten is more sweet than sour, and so is the cabbage, but the crunchy potato pancakes are a welcome accompaniment. Wiener schnitzel, another specialty, is fried to a crisp and served with roasted potatoes and peas and carrots. Wash it down with an excellent German beer. All dinners come with soup: meaty lentil, thick potato leek, or goulash dense enough to be a pasta sauce. Desserts are mostly rich pastries. The deli in the front of the restaurant is the place to buy German sausages, cold cuts, cheeses, and specialty items. ♦ German ♦ Daily lunch and dinner. 1550 Church St (at Duncan St). 282.6850

47 Lehr's German Specialties This shop, chockablock with teacups, mugs, and beer steins, is one of the few businesses catering to the German community in the Bay Area. It sells everything German from bath salts to decorative accessories to salad dressings, cookies, and candies. ♦ M-Sa 10AM-6PM; Su noon-6PM. 1581 Church St (between 28th and Duncan Sts). 282.6803; fax 282.0565 ♿

48 Drewes Meats With a history dating back to 1889, this landmark meat market has been selling free-range chickens since the mid-1970s. The shop retains an old-fashioned look with blue and white hexagonal tiles and service counters that stretch along two walls. Benches line the opposite walls, so weary customers can sit while waiting their turn. The shop also prepares a meat loaf "ready for the

oven" and stuffed pork chops. ♦ Daily 10AM-5PM. No credit cards accepted. 1706 Church St (between Day and 29th Sts). 821.0555 ♿

49 Star Bakery Irish soda bread is the main reason to come to this 1950s-style bakery that's been in business since the 1890s. Whether you prefer your soda bread plain, with raisins, or with raisins and caraway, it makes great breakfast toast. Other items sold here can be chancy. ♦ M-Sa 6:30AM-6PM; Su 7:30AM-4PM. No credit cards accepted. 1701 Church St (at 29th St). 648.0785 ♿

50 Mikey Tom's Market In this small, chic grocery housed in a Deco-style building with bright yellow walls, a checkout stand doubles as an espresso bar. The limited but carefully chosen produce offers several upscale varieties of potatoes and mushrooms. Choice specialty products line the shelves, and in the refrigerated display case are such fresh carryout items as mustardy chicken potpies. ♦ Daily. 1747 Church St (at Day St). 826.5757; fax 695.7932 ♿

51 Valentine's Cafe ★★★$ Vegetarian food, superbly prepared and thoughtfully priced, is created at this delightfully cozy, out-of-the-way spot decorated with many gold-rimmed mirrors, a yellow and white color scheme, and a large picture window looking onto the street. Owners Kunal Mukkherjee and Daniel Morrison have put together a veggie menu with true international flair. The *samosas* come filled with curried potato and accompanied by herbal-mint chutney; vegetarian spring rolls, totally free of grease, are stuffed with glass noodles, sun-dried tomatoes, and wild mushrooms; and crisp-fried tofu with roasted root vegetables is eminently satisfying. The desserts are good, but not remarkable. ♦ Vegetarian ♦ Tu dinner; W-F lunch and dinner; Sa-Su brunch and dinner. 1793 Church St (between 30th and Day Sts). 285.2257 ♿

52 Church Produce This corner shop provides a little bit of everything edible and offers an interesting selection of natural foods, breads, and produce. ♦ Daily. No credit cards accepted. 1798 Church St (at 30th St). 282.1153 ♿

Bests

Ronald Mar

Food & Wine Columnist for the Asian editions of *Esquire* and *Penthouse* magazines

Alain Rondelli—Alain can be almost world class—my favorite since the closure of **Amelio's**.

Pane e Vino—My favorite trattoria for Italian contemporary food—always delightful.

Masa's or **Fleur de Lys**—Don't miss either of these two places—probably the best.

The Haight/Cole Valley/
West Portal/Glen Park

The Haight is virtually synonymous with the psychedelic 1960s, and the philosophy and the aesthetic of the flower children who arrived here in droves back then still lives on. The bright blue, yellow, red, and green storefronts that line the streets are filled with used bookstores, occult shops, and ice-cream parlors; vintage-clothing shops display tie-dyed shirts and patent-leather go-go boots; and wafts of marijuana sometimes perfume the air. The last of the longhaired hippies pass time on the street corners, along with the homeless, new-wave hipsters, and ex-punk rockers, who are pierced and earringed to the nines.

Food is cheap and basic in the Haight, a neighborhood mainly populated by young college students and recent graduates. To appeal to these environmentally conscious (and relatively poor) residents, many of the

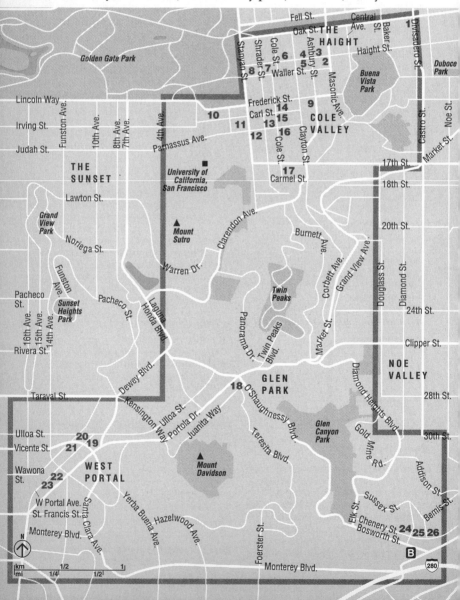

restaurants here offer a good selection of vegetarian dishes on their menus. Almost every kind of food is represented in this culinarily diverse area: **Taquería El Balazo** offers Mexican fare (burritos, enchiladas, and the like); **Massawa Restaurant** serves African specialties; **Cha Cha Cha** features Latin and Caribbean food in a colorful setting filled with folk art; and **Zare** is the place for Middle Eastern fare. And just off **Haight Street**, on **Divisadero Street**, is **Cookin'**, a tiny cookware shop stacked to the ceiling with used (and some vintage) baking and cooking accessories, appliances, glasses, dishes, and other assorted kitchenware.

While the Haight may be a tourist destination, the neighborhoods to its south tend to focus on the activities of everyday residential life. Just below the Haight lies Cole Valley, an up-and-coming district filled with charming shops and former hippie haunts gone mainstream. Among its many claims to fame, the original **Tassajara Bread Bakery** was started here by Zen Buddhists, and Cole Valley also boasts one of the city's finest natural-foods stores, **The Real Food Company**, along with a great cheese shop, **Say Cheese.** Its true culinary beacon, however, is **Ashbury Market,** which proffers the gamut of gourmet products and has earned a citywide reputation for its selection of fine wines. **EOS Restaurant & Wine Bar** is breaking new culinary ground with its Asian-fusion cuisine and stylish wine bar.

Twin Peaks, situated south of Cole Valley and in the geographic center of the city, is the site of San Francisco's second- and third-tallest hills, which offer spectacular panoramas of the Bay Area. (You can enjoy the views by car by following **Twin Peaks Boulevard,** which winds around the whole district, or on foot by mounting one of the steep stairways that rise from the streets to the slopes' magnificent terraces.) The Twin Peaks neighborhood also is home to a not-to-be-missed supermarket, **Tower Market,** which boasts an enviable selection of specialty foods and high-quality meat, fish, and produce. The market also sells a good selection of wines.

Middle-class West Portal, located to the southwest of Twin Peaks, is the main shopping district for **Sir Francis Woods** and **Forest Hill,** two of the city's more affluent neighborhoods. Its name derives from its location at the western entrance of the streetcar tunnel that was cut through the hills of Twin Peaks early in the century. Nestled at the base of three hills—including **Mount Davidson,** which, at 925 feet, is the city's highest spot—West Portal has the feel of a European village, with curvy streets, streetcars, and a romantic, foggy shroud. It's a charming place to spend an afternoon. For a taste of Eastern Europe, stop in at **Old Krakow,** the city's only Polish restaurant. The most popular neighborhood hangout is **Cafe for All Seasons,** which serves straight-forward American cuisine with an emphasis on the freshest ingredients—perfectly prepared and presented.

Glen Park, located on the southeastern slope of Twin Peaks, is a mostly residential area. It still has no restaurants that would attract people from outside the neighborhood, but it's beginning to develop a shopping district. Tucked away in this neighborhood lies **Glen Canyon,** where, according to old-timers, Russian Smugglers once hid their contraband.

Today, it's a favorite spot to enjoy a picnic. Among the other spots of interest to locals and visitors are the **Cheese Boutique,** a bakery branch of the Twin Peaks district's **Creighton's Cheese & Fine Foods** (go for the marvelous sticky buns), and **Sweet Sue's** (don't miss the lemon pound cake).

1 Cookin' Specializing in used merchandise, this is the best-stocked cookware shop in the city; it's the place food stylists call when they're looking for one-of-a-kind props. Although the owners had to clear up some of the clutter to provide access to people with disabilities, the merchandise is still arranged in piles on the floor and in stacks on baker's racks. It's an awesome sight. There are vintage dishes, glasses, and appliances from the 1940s and 1950s, but most of the store's merchandise is modern. One area is devoted to cast-iron skillets, another to an enviable selection of French pastry equipment—including intricate molds, cutting utensils, and pans. And you won't find a better selection of copper pots or Le Creuset cookware anywhere. ◆ Tu-Su. 339 Divisadero St (between Page and Oak Sts). 861.1854; fax 861.1971 ₷

2 People's Cafe ★★$ This spot was quickly embraced by the neighborhood, with its simple, light fare that attracts lines of fans at peak hours. The generous sandwiches are made with French rolls, and the salads are served in huge glass bowls. The stylish room has a tile floor, traditional bentwood chairs, and clever tables with coffee beans pressed under the glass tops. And it's immaculate—something of a rarity in this part of town. ◆ Cafe ◆ Daily breakfast, lunch, and dinner. 1419 Haight St (between Masonic Ave and Ashbury St). 553.8842 ₷

2 Manhattan Bagel The home of jalapeño bagels, this bakery also has pumpkin, blueberry, onion, honey-corn, and about a dozen other kinds of bagels, plus an equal number of cream cheeses, including sun-dried tomato, herb and garlic, and vegetable. It also serves **Caffè Trieste** coffee (from a well-known North Beach roaster) and a few select pastries. ◆ Daily. No credit cards accepted. 1206 Masonic St (between Waller and Haight Sts). 626.9111; fax 626.2730. Also at: Numerous locations throughout the city

3 Ben & Jerry's Locals have made it clear that chain stores are unwelcome in the Haight, but this ice-cream franchise is a different story. More than merely making Cherry Garcia a household name, the corporation has made its presence felt in the political arena as well—serving the community's heart as well as its stomach. The ice cream comes in almost every flavor imaginable—including chocolate fudge brownie, chocolate chip cookie dough, peanut butter cup, and vanilla caramel fudge swirl— and patrons can linger at the tables over sundaes and baked goods. ◆ Daily. No credit cards accepted. 1480 Haight St (between Masonic Ave and Ashbury St). 249.4685; fax 249.4682 ₷ Also at: Numerous locations throughout the city

4 Massawa Restaurant ★$ The setting is uninspired—a bright blue, barnlike space broken up with rattan screens—but the aromatic East African fare is enticing. Everything is served with *injera,* a spongelike bread used to scoop up the stews that are this cuisine's staple. Choices include a thick chicken stew with red peppers, lamb and vegetables simmered with spices, and a tuna stew with spinach. About half the offerings are vegetarian. For those who want to avoid culinary adventures, there's spaghetti with meat sauce. ◆ East African ◆ Tu-Su lunch and dinner. 1538 Haight St (between Ashbury and Clayton Sts). 621.4129 ₷

4 Martin Macks Bar and Restaurant ★$ A traditional Irish bar in the heart of the Haight? Well, it *is* a diverse neighborhood. Sports fans fill the front bar area with a haze of smoke, but through the saloon doors in back is a kitchen/dining counter and tables. The bric-a-brac along the walls and the copper pots hanging from the latticework behind the counter give the place a Victorian feel, despite the movie-size screen that keeps fans abreast of the game. Weekend brunch may offer eggs Benedict with salmon or sautéed trout with a tarragon-and-mushroom sauce, served with eggs and home fries. The kitchen is also known for its fish-and-chips, hamburgers, shepherd's pie, and other substantial pub grub. ◆ Irish ◆ M-F lunch and dinner; Sa-Su brunch and dinner. 1568 Haight St (between Ashbury and Clayton Sts). 864.0124 ₷

5 Pork Store Cafe ★$ One of the most popular spots in the Haight, this place is known for its hearty breakfasts. No one seems to mind crowding in at the counter or the cramped tables for huge plates of eggs with all the traditional trimmings. The name, incidentally, comes from the meat market that once occupied the space. ◆ American ◆ Daily breakfast and lunch. 1541 Haight St (between Ashbury and Clayton Sts). 864.6981

Take in the beautiful San Francisco scenery with a picnic along the 3.5-mile long Golden Gate Promenade. Don't forget a loaf of sourdough bread, a bottle of Napa Valley wine, and some cheese and drink up those spellbinding views of the bay, the boats, and, of course, the bridge.

6 Coffee, Tea & Spice In business since the 1970s, this coffee store does its own roasting; its distinctive house blend has slightly burned nuances. The coffee comes from Costa Rica, Ethiopia, Sumatra, Tanzania, and other countries that produce high-quality beans. The shop also sells various herbs and spices in bulk. A room upstairs—with a charming fireplace and tables for drinking brewed cups of coffee—also displays unusual mugs, coffeepots, and teapots for sale. ♦ Daily. 1630 Haight St (between Clayton and Cole Sts). 861.3953; fax 861.0535 ♿

6 Zare ★$$ One of the few places to serve creative food in the Haight, it also has a more refined ambience than most. Sun-dried tomatoes are the principal flavoring for a smoked-chicken linguine, and a rich lamb ragout is thick with beans, tomatoes, and other vegetables. The baked brie appetizer is a dish of the 1970s, but for the frozen-in-time Haight, even that's progress. ♦ Middle Eastern ♦ M-F lunch and dinner; Sa-Su brunch and dinner. 1640 Haight St (between Clayton and Cole Sts). 861.8868

6 Taquería El Balazo ★★$ This *taquería* only dates back to 1993, but it looks as if it's been around forever. There's a marble floor, a copper-topped counter, and a garish red, yellow, and orange paint job; the menu is printed on old-fashioned calendars decorated with Mexican scenes and images of buxom women with off-the-shoulder blouses. The top seller is the vegetarian burrito, given a meaty flavor by grilled vegetables, black beans, and saffron rice; it's served with tortilla chips and lime-cabbage salad. Full plates include fish tacos, enchiladas, vegetarian tamales, chicken mole, and *tortas* (Mexican sandwiches)—all very reasonably priced. ♦ Mexican ♦ Daily lunch and dinner. No credit cards accepted.

1654 Haight St (between Clayton and Cole Sts). 864.8608 ♿

7 Zona Rosa ★$

Compared with most others up and down the street, this upscale corner *taquería* is a civilized place for a quick bite. A loyal clientele munches on the good burritos, with meats grilled to order, at the counters in front of the windows and down the center of the room. Fajitas, fried tacos, and nachos round out the limited menu. ♦ Mexican ♦ Daily lunch and dinner. No credit cards accepted. 1797 Haight St (at Shrader St). 668.7717

8 Cha Cha Cha ★★★$ Bright, bold, Latin-inspired flavors make this the area's best and most popular restaurant. The wild interior, ablaze with color, is filled with altars and other Hispanic folk art. Weekend brunch consists of such dishes as polenta with grilled red bell peppers and eggs, or a guacamole omelette. Lunch and dinner selections might be roast leg of pork marinated with Cuban spices and served with rice and black beans, or marinated chicken with pimientos, capers, and olives. Among the dozen tapas offered are mussels in a saffron broth and barbecued-pork quesadillas. Service tends to be a little lax, but the food is excellent, and the people watching is delicious. It's a perfect place to absorb the Haight's atmosphere while eschewing the nitty-gritty. ♦ Latin ♦ Daily lunch and dinner. No credit cards accepted. 1805 Haight St (at Shrader St). 386.5758 ♿

9 Ashbury Market No other mom-and-pop grocery in the city can compare with this market. The exterior is reminiscent of France, with the name printed in gold on a burgundy background, white canvas umbrellas at the entrance, fresh raspberries and other produce on one side, and flowers on the other. Though the window displays Jolly Time Popcorn and Kool-Aid—after all, it's an all-purpose neighborhood market—the shop also proffers wonderful specialty merchandise. There are more than two dozen kinds of olive oil, hazelnut oil, truffle oil, and grape-seed oil with chilies; teas from the chic Republic of

Teas; dozens of mustards; and boutique-bakery breads. A passageway leads to a wine shop and deli. The wine department is legendary, with the best in French, Italian, and California wines—and at competitive prices, too. The deli is filled with house-baked scones, salads, and smoked fish and meat delicacies such as lemon-pepper cod, duck breast, and trout. ♦ Daily. 205 Frederick St (at Ashbury St). 566.3134; fax 566.0266 ㅎ

10 The Ganges ★★$ Sari-clad waitresses serve customers who lounge on cushions at low tables at this vegetarian Indian spot. Top starters include a cilantro-and-potato puree, dipped in batter and fried until golden, or *pappadams,* crisp lentil-flour wafers with a touch of hot spice. Among the main courses, the curries get star billing: Try the *mater paneer,* fried cheese and peas in a rich tomato gravy with garam masala, a spice mixture with chilies. Another often-ordered dish is *kofta,* meatless "meatballs" made with black-eyed peas. ♦ Indian ♦ Tu-Sa dinner. 775 Frederick St (between Willard St and Arguello Blvd). 661.7290; fax 661.4059

11 The Real Food Company The ground floor of this excellent natural-foods store is chock-full of organic produce and bins holding beans, flours, granola, rice, and other bulk goods. Upstairs is a storehouse of packaged goods and vitamins, and a small anteroom has a collection of natural-food cookbooks, coffees, teas, pastas, and spices sold in bulk. ♦ Daily. 1023 Stanyan St (between Parnassus Ave and Carl St). 564.2800; fax 564.4882 ㅎ Also at: Numerous locations throughout the city

11 The Real Food Company Deli Next door to the **The Real Food Company** (see above) is a fine selection of baked goods and a changing array of main courses and salads, all prepared in-house. The temptations may include *samosas* (fried pastries filled with vegetables or meat), curried vegetables, and Szechuan cabbage. The small wine collection in back is nothing to speak of, though, especially given the impressive wine shops down the street. ♦ Daily. 1001 Stanyan St (at Carl St). 564.1117; fax 564.4882 ㅎ Also at: 2164 Polk St (between Broadway and Vallejo St), Russian Hill. 775.2805; fax 673.1787 ㅎ

Lucius Beebe, a columnist for the *San Francisco Chronicle* at the turn of the century, once said, "Everything in San Francisco smells deliciously of money or sauce Mornay." And what goes into a Mornay sauce? Just add some good cheese, usually swiss or parmesan, to a béchamel or simple white sauce. Serve with eggs, fish, vegetables, or chicken.

12 Sun Country Foods Nowhere else in the city can you pick up a bunch of flowers at midnight. With a splashy fire-engine red exterior and 20 feet of sidewalk lined with bouquets stacked four deep on risers, this corner grocery attracts attention. The utilitarian interior houses such goods as beans, flours, and grains in bulk, along with sandwiches and a small but nicely selected array of produce. ♦ Daily 6AM-midnight. 1100 Stanyan St (at Parnassus Ave). 566.2511; fax 566.1336 ㅎ

13 EOS Restaurant & Wine Bar ★★★$$ Arnold and Richard Wong, sons of the founder of the well-regarded **Ashbury Market** (see page 173), have opened Cole Valley's first truly upscale restaurant, a real change of pace from the casual, ethnic eateries that characterize this area. Lively and fun, this place is bustling and very noisy much of the time. The room has a modern, sleek look, with high ceilings, light-colored wood accents, and black granite tables. Arnold Wong's menu features fresh, California-grown ingredients and Asian influences. Dishes include shiitake mushroom dumplings and sake-lemongrass-steamed clams as appetizers, and five-pepper calamari, pan-roasted salmon, and free-range chicken with green onions as main courses. Don't miss the wine bar (whose entrance is around the corner), with 400 vintages from countries around the world. ♦ Asian/Fusion ♦ Daily dinner. Restaurant: 901 Cole St (at Carl St). Wine bar: Entrance at 101 Carl St (at Cole St). 566.3063; fax 566.2663 ㅎ

13 Zazie ★★$$ It's just a bit bigger than a shoe box, but this charming French bistro has plenty of dash. The green-and-yellow–painted concrete floor, brick wall, and gold accents make a fine setting for the impressive food, which is served by a cheerful staff. At breakfast, the Belgian waffles with caramelized pecans and the omelette specials win raves; lunch selections include a large variety of sandwiches. The dinner menu offers such hearty dishes as a bone-warming daube (a marinated beef stew), free-range chicken roasted with garlic and herbs, and trout prepared in a different way each day. The homey desserts include fruit crumble, served warm with crème fraîche in a handmade ceramic bowl, and a charlotte with chocolate mousse, ladyfingers, and raspberry sauce. ♦ French ♦ Daily breakfast, lunch, and dinner. No credit cards accepted. 941 Cole St (between Parnassus Ave and Carl St). 564.5332

13 GRANDEHO KAMEKYO Sushi Bar ★★★ $$ What sets this place apart from the ordinary sushi bar is the unusual, elegant interior and the superior quality of the food. The dining room has gold walls and a lavender ceiling, and the bar is fashioned of light-colored wood. Chef Yoshihiko Fujita, formerly of the acclaimed **Kyo-ya** restaurant at the **Sheraton Palace** hotel, offers a creative menu: In addition to the usual varieties of sushi, there are some that are vegetarian (such as avocado combined with pickled and fresh vegetables), and some that feature cooked fish rather than raw (including smoked salmon and fried soft-shell crab). The main courses are extremely well done, including the delicate fried shrimp tempura and panko-encrusted chicken or pork cutlet. Desserts include green tea ice cream and fruit drizzled with a soy-based sauce. ♦ Japanese ♦ M-F lunch and dinner; Sa-Su dinner. 943 Cole St (between Parnassus Ave and Carl St). 759.8428

14 Taqueria la Coqueta ★$ When **The Crepery Cafe** folded at this sunny location, it was replaced by yet another San Francisco *taquería*. But it's a good one, with huge portions of well-prepared Mexican dishes such as burritos, tacos, nachos, and various types of sandwiches. The prices are very reasonable, too. The dining room is small, cozy, and bright, with yellow tables and pictures of Mexican scenes on the walls; there's also outdoor seating, so you can soak up the sun while enjoying your meal. ♦ Mexican ♦ Daily lunch and dinner. 86 Carl St (between Clayton and Cole Sts). 566.1274 ♿

14 Say Cheese One of the best cheese shops in the city, it carries up to 400 types; look for those by Laura Chenel, the top specialty producer of goat cheese. The store also stocks caviar, salsas, crackers, breads, pâtés, sandwich meats, nine kinds of olives, goat-milk yogurt, marmalades, and vinegars, all carefully selected. It's a one-stop shop for gifts and elegant munchies for entertaining. ♦ Daily. 856 Cole St (between Carl and Frederick Sts). 665.5020; fax 566.9776

15 Val de Cole Wines and Spirits A sea of boxes gives this shop the look of a well-organized grocery store. Spirits are lined up behind the counter, and a hundred or more kinds of beer can be found in a nook at the rear and in a refrigerator case. The wines, arranged down the center of the room, feature many hard-to-find labels and vintages. The wine display in the window includes many inexpensive options, and a rack of hand-picked bargain wines is displayed prominently by the cashier. ♦ M-Th; F-Sa until midnight.

906 Cole St (between Parnassus Ave and Carl St). 566.1808; fax 566.3564 ♿

16 Tassajara Bread Bakery ★$ Renowned for its fabulous rustic breads, this Zen bakery-cafe was created by the group that made **Greens** one of the country's best-known vegetarian restaurants. Although it is now owned by the local **Just Desserts** chain, it still carries products found nowhere else, such as a ginger-plum tart and a berry-cheese tart. A dozen kinds of bread are always on hand, as well as such **Just Desserts** staples as triple lemon cake, big, chewy cookies, cheesecakes, and seasonal pastries. The cafe tables are usually packed with people relaxing over a cup of coffee and a breakfast pastry, a salad, vegetarian chili, or a vegetarian sandwich (no meat is served). ♦ Vegetarian/Cafe ♦ Daily breakfast, lunch, and dinner. 1000 Cole St (at Parnassus Ave). 664.8947; fax 664.3747 ♿

17 Adel's Wine Cellar Up the steps inside **17th & Cole Market,** this shop is chock-a-block with bottles—more than a thousand labels from California, France, and Italy. Prices are a bit higher here than at other wine shops in the city, but the selection of older vintages is better. There may be multiple vintages of Ridge Howell Mountain Zinfandel, or Pine Ridge or Steltzner Cabernet Sauvignon. ♦ M-Sa until 10:30PM; Su until 10PM. 1400 Cole St (at 17th St). 731.6319 ♿

18 Tower Market One of the city's best supermarkets, this independently owned full-service store was opened in 1942 by Mark Pommon. His 77-year-old son, Daniel, now runs it. To compete with the grocery chains, the market emphasizes upscale products. It carries a fine supply of organic produce, an array of breads from boutique bakeries, cheeses as varied as at any specialty shop, and at least a dozen olive oils. The deli is a godsend for anyone short on time (or desire) to cook and offers a variety of prepared foods. The meat market is leased to John Vigglizzio, who has built a reputation on his high-quality cuts. Many of the staffers have been here for years

and they know loyal customers by name.
♦ Daily. 635 Portola Dr (between O'Shaughnessy Blvd and Fowler Ave). 664.1600, meats 664.1609, deli 661.7333; fax 664.7406 ♿

18 Creighton's Cheese & Fine Foods ★$ This deli-cafe supplies the Twin Peaks area with more than 140 kinds of cheeses, a modest selection of wine, a variety of coffee drinks, and prepared fare to take out or eat at one of the tables. Salads range from sesame noodle and celery root with crème fraîche, mustard, and mayonnaise, to tarragon chicken with walnuts and sour-cream dressing; the standard array of sandwiches includes turkey and roast beef. The deli also sells pastries and other treats produced at **Creighton's American Bakery,** its sister shop (598 Chenery St, at Castro St, 239.5525); the most popular are the lemon curd tart, its buttery crust flecked with cornmeal; and the terrific sticky buns. ♦ Cafe/Takeout ♦ Daily breakfast and lunch. 673 Portola Dr (between O'Shaughnessy Blvd and Fowler Ave). 753.0750; fax 753.0938.

19 Spiazzo ★★$$ Stippled walls and an open kitchen make this the neighborhood's trendiest-looking spot; adding friendly service to the formula makes it a favorite gathering place. The pizzas, which are assembled before your eyes and baked in a brightly tiled wood-burning oven, boast a thin, slightly smoky crust. Simple toppings include sausage and prosciutto; and mushrooms, fresh tomatoes, and seasonal vegetables. Such pastas as penne with onions, tomatoes, red chili peppers, and pecorino cheese or linguine with smoked salmon, garlic, parmesan, tomato, and béchamel sauce are worth a try. The few grilled dishes—chicken and pork loin among them—are not the kitchen's strength. ♦ Italian ♦ Tu-Su dinner. 33 W Portal Ave (between Vicente and Ulloa Sts). 664.9511

20 El Toreador ★★$ A local favorite here since the 1960s, this eatery reigned unabashedly in the kitschy fun of colorful stuffed parrots, fake flowers, piñatas, and sombreros long before such folk art touches became staples of Mexican restaurant decor. The food breaks no new ground, but it's freshly prepared, tasty, and filling. Try the taco and chicken tamale plate; fajitas; or *gorditas*, plump with Mexican sausage, *salsa verde*,

sour cream, and guacamole. All plates are served with soup, refried beans, Spanish rice, salad, and fresh corn tortillas. For dessert, be sure to have the silky flan, which comes topped with caramel sauce and whipped cream. ♦ Mexican ♦ Tu-Su lunch and dinner. 50 W Portal Ave (between Vicente and Ulloa Sts). 566.8104

20 French Village Cafe ★$ The decor is nothing special—standard coffee-shop—but the food is good enough to merit a visit if you're in the neighborhood. There are nice grilled sandwiches, such as eggplant on a baguette with pesto or tapenade, tomatoes, and Bermuda onions. The menu offers cold sandwiches as well, such as tuna salad, roast beef, and a bagel with lox, cream cheese, or perhaps a shmear of pesto; salad plates, quiches, and *tortas* are also available. (Take a pass on the soup, though—it tastes canned.) On Saturday afternoons, various local singers and musicians entertain diners with French *chansons*. ♦ Coffee shop ♦ M-Sa breakfast and lunch (M-F until 5PM; Sa until 4PM). 60 W Portal Ave (between Vicente and Ulloa Sts). 681.6726

21 Shaw's Confections At one time, branches of this chain of candy shops, founded in 1931, were scattered all over the Bay Area. Now only two remain—this one and another at the manufacturing plant in Millbrae, where the company makes private-label chocolates. The selection here includes cream-filled chocolates, nuts, all kinds of gooey jelly candies, hard candies, and jelly beans. There are mugs and other gift items, and a fountain in back that serves ultra-rich Mendocino ice cream. ♦ Daily. No credit cards accepted. 122 W Portal Ave (between 14th Ave and Vicente St). 681.2702 ♿

21 Cafe for All Seasons ★★★$$ Donna Katzl, who studied with James Beard, carries on her teacher's romance with solid American fare at the eatery she owns with her husband, Frank. The light wood interior and the long kitchen that stretches along one wall provide an informal appeal in keeping with the straightforward food. There are wonderful salads and one of the best hamburgers in the city. The delicious main courses include grilled rainbow trout with herb butter and french fries; sautéed chicken breast with mushrooms, lemon, and a light cream sauce, served with orzo pasta; and pork, which is distinguished by a creamy mustard sauce. The pasta dishes are simply great; all of them are made with *capellini*, a long, flat, thin noodle, which may be served simply with garlic, fresh tomato, olive oil, and grated asiago cheese, or dressed up with a light cream sauce and an array of fresh vegetables. For dessert, the apple cake with warm caramel sauce is the favorite; a close second is the sweet molded French cream with fresh berries and raspberry sauce. ◆ American ◆ M-F lunch and dinner; Sa-Su brunch and dinner. 150 W Portal Ave (between 14th Ave and Vicente St). 665.0900 &

22 Fuji Japanese Restaurant ★★$$

Adorned with bamboo umbrellas, *tansu* wooden chests, kimonos, and plants everywhere, this spot defies the minimalist decor of most other Japanese eateries. From his perch at the sushi counter, chef Makoto Kobayashi greets just about everyone who enters. The sashimi, particularly the tuna, has an exceptional buttery quality, and the *maki* (rolls of tidbits wrapped in rice and seaweed) are unusual; the one called Gilroy (after the garlic capital of California) combines marinated salmon with avocado and a hefty dose of fresh garlic. All the standard dishes— tempura, teriyaki, and sukiyaki—are well prepared, too. The pork *katsu* is superb, with a crisp coating and a pleasant, slightly smoky dipping sauce. To sample almost all the specialties, try the Fuji special, a combination platter for two or more people. ◆ Japanese ◆ M-Sa lunch and dinner; Su dinner. 301 W Portal Ave (at 14th Ave). 564.6360; fax 564.2247 &

23 Old Krakow ★★$$ As far as we know, this is San Francisco's only Polish restaurant. The antique wood tables and chairs (no two are alike), the original artwork by Polish artists, and the red swags at the windows and over the kitchen area re-create some of the atmosphere of a Krakow cafe. The food is homey: rich beef stew in a thick, tomato-infused broth; huge cabbage rolls stuffed with seasoned ground beef and rice; crisp crepes filled with finely chopped mushrooms; and tender pieces of boneless duck rolled around apples and prunes, served with red cabbage and potatoes. For dessert, the crumbly cheesecake is a perfect rendition of the European original. A dense and satisfying poppy-seed cake (made from a breadlike dough) is prepared every Friday. ◆ Polish ◆ M dinner; Tu-Su lunch and dinner. 385 W Portal Ave (between 15th and 14th Aves). 564.4848 &

24 Sweet Sue's Although this bakery sells primarily to wholesale clients and is off the beaten path (as are most spots in the Glen Park area), it's worth seeking out. Try the lemon pound cake, which has an intense flavor and moist texture; the *rugelach* and seasonal pies are also winners. ◆ M-F. No credit cards accepted. 732 Chenery St (between Diamond St and Lippard Ave). 587.7837 &

25 Cheese Boutique Glen Park's first gourmet specialty store has quickly become a neighborhood favorite. Cheese lovers can choose among 170 varieties, all at lower-than-supermarket prices, and are welcome to taste before they buy. The packaged goods cover all the bases and most cuisines; there are several brands of *arborio* rice and polenta, for example. With a nod to the health-conscious, the shop also stocks juices and assorted dried fruits and vegetables. One of the most popular items is a locally made vegetarian ravioli. ◆ M-Sa. No credit cards accepted. 666 Chenery St (between Castro and Diamond Sts). 333.3390; fax 333.5450 & Also at: 1298 12th Ave (at Irving St), The Sunset. 566.3155; fax 333.5450

26 Creighton's American Bakery The tiny branch of Creighton's Cheese & Fine Foods (see page 176) is devoted to the production and sale of delicious baked goods. People flock here for sticky buns and scones, as well as for lemon bars, orange-pecan bars, and the not-to-be missed fresh-fruit tarts, which are very reasonably priced. ◆ Daily 598 Chenery St (at Castro St). 239.5525; fax 753.0538 & Also at: 673 Portola Dr (between O'Shaughnessy Blvd and Fowler Ave). 753.0750; fax 753.0938

Bests

Bill Wallace

Culinary Director, Draegers Markets, and Host of "Chef's Edition," a PBS radio show

Ton Kiang # 2—I eat here the most . . . great Hakka cuisine—salt-baked chicken and vegetable dishes.

Fringale—I go there whenever I can get in.

Carta—Every month their menu focuses on a different part of the world.

Masa's and **Fleur de Lys**—Two of the top places— I'll go anytime I can afford it.

Helmand Restaurant—The best bargain in San Francisco, unusual Afghani food and excellent service.

The Sunset

The Sunset is one of the city's least explored areas, metaphorically—and literally—shrouded in fog. This residential neighborhood—the last one to be developed in San Francisco—is bordered by **Golden Gate Park** to the north, **Twin Peaks** to the east, and the ocean to the west. More popular with tourists than locals, it's best known for being the home of the **San Francisco Zoo** and for its proximity to **Golden Gate Park.**

Yet for those who love food, the Sunset is a rewarding destination. Through the years, the neighborhood has attracted people from Thailand, Japan, Greece, Mexico, the Middle East, and other foreign lands (including, most recently, Russia and Northern Ireland), and the shops and restaurants reflect these diverse ethnic heritages. One of the city's best grocery stores—**Andronico's Market**—is here; its staggering array of goods includes at least 10 varieties of dates, 18 types of olives, and 25 kinds of apples under one sleek, modern roof.

The Sunset also boasts two unique ice-cream purveyors: **Marco Polo**, offering Italian gelato in Asian-influenced flavors such as guava; and **Polly Ann Ice Cream**, which dishes up ice cream flavored with durian, a tasty exotic fruit that has such a pungent odor that it is actually banned from airplanes and some hotel rooms in its native Thailand. The area is also home to **Shaharazad Bakery**, one of the few bakeries that still makes phyllo dough by hand.

The main shopping areas are along **Irving**, **Judah**, **Noriega**, and **Taraval Streets**, which are lined with great produce markets, Chinese and Middle Eastern delis, and all kinds of shops for the home cook. (Notice that the streets here—known as the "alphabet streets"—are named in alphabetical order from north to south, beginning with **Lincoln** and proceeding to **Wawona**.) Thanks to their proximity to the **University of California San Francisco Medical Center**, a teaching hospital, many spots cater to a student's budget and taste. One such place is **Cafe Mirabelle**, a popular hangout. The outer edge of Sunset is a favorite destination for San Francisco residents from other neighborhoods, who shop at a number of Asian, Middle

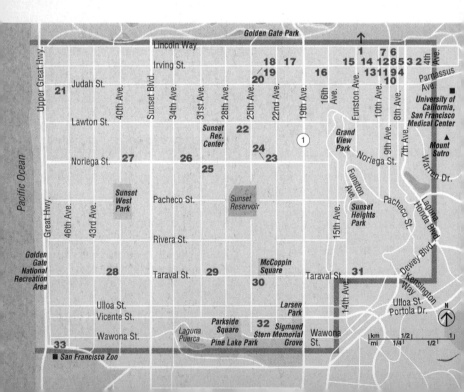

Eastern, and European-American markets, including the venerable **22nd & Irving Market**, one of the best places for fresh produce.

The Sunset's restaurants tend to be small and neighborhood-oriented, but that doesn't mean the kitchens are unambitious. There is **Marnee Thai,** a top Thai spot; a good Greek place, **Stoyanof's;** and two excellent Middle Eastern eateries, the stylish **YaYa Cuisine** and **Just Like Home** deli/cafe. And **Raw Living Foods,** the most unusual kid on the block, features a menu consisting solely of uncooked food—and its daring cuisine has quickly won an enthusiastic local following.

Because of its proximity to the ocean, the Sunset can be gray, cold, and foggy sometimes. But on a sunny day, hopping from ethnic market to ethnic market and stopping for lunch at one of the great cafes in the area can make a visit here a heart- and stomach-warming adventure.

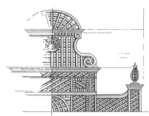

Cafe de Young
IN THE DE YOUNG MUSEUM

1 Cafe de Young ★★$ Located in the **M. H. de Young Memorial Museum** in **Golden Gate Park,** this boasts one of the city's most charming garden settings: Handsome metal tables with umbrellas are arranged around a small pool, all surrounded by lush rhododendrons and other flowers. Before settling in, diners make their choices—all prepared to order—at a short counter. The menu, which changes daily, showcases seasonal produce in such dishes as Greek-style salad with spirals of pasta, chunks of juicy chicken, chickpeas, roasted peppers, and feta, or tuna salad on soft sourdough bread with crisp coleslaw in a celery-seed dressing. For a light meal, adults can order from a children's menu of half sandwiches with soups. On the first Wednesday of each month, when the museum is open late and admission is free, dinner is served until 8PM. ♦ American ♦ W-Su lunch 10AM-4PM. North side of the Music Concourse (off J.F. Kennedy Dr), Ground level. 752.0116; fax 752.3313 &

1 Teahouse in Japanese Tea Garden ★$ Since it opened in the late 19th century, the five-acre tea garden has been a highlight of **Golden Gate Park.** It's a serene spot for reflective strolling along groomed paths winding past flowers, shrines, and pools. Complete a visit by relaxing at the teahouse over a steaming pot of tea and a plate of simple cookies, served by the traditionally costumed staff. ♦ Teahouse ♦ Daily. Next to the Asian Art Museum, north side of the Music Concourse (off J.F. Kennedy Dr). 752.1171

2 Hana Restaurant ★★$ One of the oldest Japanese restaurants in the area, it maintains a loyal following and a cheerful spirit, thanks to the longtime staff and the lively setting. Oversize round lanterns hang from the plum-colored ceiling above dark wood beams; the walls are a rich blue, accented with blue print fabric and black tile floors. In a little room next door, chefs at the sushi bar fashion sushi with firm, chewy rice and the freshest-tasting fish. Try the eponymous Hana roll, containing yellowtail, avocado, and rice flecked with flying-fish roe. The sukiyaki is a model of all the dish should be, with paper-thin beef, tofu, cabbage, carrots, onions, and a richly sweet sauce. The kitchen also does a great job with tempura, which has an almost buttery flavor. ♦ Japanese ♦ M-F lunch and dinner; Sa dinner. 408 Irving St (between Fifth and Sixth Aves). 665.3952 &

3 Mae-Thip ★$ Walk through an intricate Thai shrine to a cozy dining room with gray walls, blue-and-white dishes, and tapers flickering on each table. One of the best choices here is the soup, a clear broth with shrimp, mushrooms, the seductive, sour citrus taste of lemongrass, and a touch of spice from chilies. The rest of the menu tends to be humdrum; daily specials sometimes show creative twists, such as a bite-sized dumpling filled with curried sweet potatoes and served with a salad of tiny cucumbers in a sweet-and-sour sauce. ♦ Thai ♦ M-Sa lunch and dinner; Su dinner. 524 Irving St (between Sixth and Seventh Aves). 759.9644 &

San Francisco has a long coffee tradition. During the Gold Rush, such entrepreneurs as James Folger sold specially roasted beans to miners and other fortune seekers. At the turn of the century, the Hills Brothers invented vacuum packing, which brought good coffee to a broader audience. Today, hundreds of coffee bars dot the city's culinary landscape.

4 Tart to Tart ★★★$ Few places in the city make pastries better than this one. The setup is basic—shoulder-high display cases of baked goods separate the kitchen from the cafe, which is a hodgepodge of wooden tables—but the aromas of freshly brewed coffee and pastries are irresistible. Fruit tarts are a specialty, with an almost runny pastry cream and a buttery, flaky crust; don't miss the Key lime tart, which has an intense, puckery richness. Other delights include thick peanut butter cookies with concentrated flavor and a great, sandy texture; big, crumbly, and nutty chocolate chip cookies; and three-layer chocolate-mocha cake, with a light butter-cream filling and whipped-cream frosting. For special occasions, there are two-layer sheet cakes in such flavors as apricot-mango, lemon-blueberry, or raspberry-coconut. Customers eating in-house can also choose among such sandwiches as curry chicken and roast turkey, a selection of salads, and a few hot dishes, including three-bean chili and vegetable pasties. ♦ Cafe ♦ Daily breakfast, lunch, and dinner (until 2AM). 641 Irving St (between Seventh and Eighth Aves). 753.0643; fax 753.3274 ♿

5 Crepevine ★★$ Just about every neighborhood in the city seems to be getting its own creperie nowadays, but the budding competition will have to work hard to beat the crepes at this cafe. We're not talking teatime fare; these crispy crepes, served with home fries, make a complete meal. The Florentine version has a good, savory mix of cheddar, onions, spinach, and cottage cheese; the lasagna crepe is made with mozzarella, cottage cheese, eggplant, tomatoes, onions, and marinara sauce. Dessert crepes may be filled with apples and cheese; bananas and

brown sugar; or strawberries and chocolate. A trio of soufflé-light omelettes, sandwiches, salads, and bagels with a variety of toppings round out the menu. The simple cafe is accented with tile floors, pine, and large, industrial-looking, copper chandeliers. ♦ Cafe/Creperie ♦ Daily breakfast, lunch, and dinner. No credit cards accepted. 624 Irving St (between Seventh and Eighth Aves). 681.5858 ♿

6 YaYa Cuisine ★★★$$ Many restaurants serve Middle Eastern fare, but we can name only one that mixes the food of Mesopotamia with a hefty dose of Californian creativity. Yahya Salih, who grew up near the ruins of Nineveh in northern Iraq, has created a beautiful retreat. An impressive mural stretches along one wall, expansive arches separate the dining areas, and decorative halogen lighting casts a glow over the stippled walls. Salih also has inventively updated the traditional foods of his mother's kitchen, which are aromatically flavored with cardamom, sumac, dried limes, pomegranate syrup, cinnamon, and mint. Baby chicken is stuffed with rice, raisins, and cashews and served with an apricot sauce. Lamb stew is studded with eggplant and lifted by a sweet-sour pomegranate sauce. Other lamb dishes are perked up with onions, lime, and cinnamon, all blended to exotic dimensions. It's an amazing culinary reach, and at times the attempt doesn't quite make it, but the food is never boring. ♦ Middle Eastern ♦ Tu-F lunch and dinner; Sa-Su dinner. 1220 Ninth Ave (between Irving St and Lincoln Way). 566.6966 ♿

6 Raw Living Foods ★$ In a city like San Francisco, which boasts just about every kind of restaurant, it's tough to come up with a new concept. But the folks here have done it: This New Age–style eatery serves nothing but raw food. (This is in keeping with a health-food philosophy that cooked food interferes with the body's natural balance.) So the only heated item you'll find here is the water for the herbal teas; the rest of the menu consists of things like fruit smoothies, organic salads, sandwiches, and pizzas that are topped with cured vegetables or dried fruit and then "baked" in the sun for six hours. The owners also claim to have the first organic, vegan sushi bar in the city (and we certainly don't know of any other). You can enjoy your meal sitting on Japanese-style cushions at low tables or in more conventional seating. New Age music plays in the background, creating a very peaceful atmosphere. ♦ Vegan ♦ Daily lunch and dinner. 1224 Ninth Ave (between Irving St and Lincoln Way). 665.6519

6 Stoyanof's Cafe and Restaurant ★★★ $$ One of only a handful of Greek restaurants in San Francisco, this place has earned a devoted following with its excellent cuisine. At lunch it has the air of a neighborhood cafeteria, but at night the room takes on a romantic glow, and the wooden tables are set with fresh flowers. The traditional starters are all great: avgolemono soup with chicken, rice, and loads of lemon; dolmas; hummus; and tabbouleh. Also try *taramasalata,* red mullet caviar whipped with olive oil and served with fresh lemon and pita, or the smoked eggplant blended with bell peppers, tomatoes, and olive oil. The *spanakopita* (spinach pie) and *tiropetes* (cheese pie), both made with phyllo, are superb. Main courses include grilled chicken in a creamy hazelnut sauce; grilled salmon; Greek fisherman's stew; and beef, lamb, or swordfish kabobs. The kitchen consistently produces some of the best leg of lamb in the city. Although Angel Stoyanof largely has taken over day-to-day operations, his father, Georgi Stoyanof, still makes the pastries and his own phyllo dough. His quince tart is utterly delicious. ♦ Greek ♦ Tu-Su lunch and dinner. No credit cards accepted at lunch. 1240 Ninth Ave (between Irving St and Lincoln Way). 664.3664; fax 665.9914 &

6 The Coffee Merchant Few shops offer a more complete selection of teas and coffees. More than a hundred kinds of teas, both bagged and loose, and about 90 kinds of coffee are stacked so high behind a counter here that customers need assistance reaching them. Hundreds of mugs also line the wall, along with coffeepots and specialty food items. ♦ Daily. 1248 Ninth Ave (between Irving St and Lincoln Way). 665.1915; fax 665.1915

7 Avenue 9 ★★$$ Lovingly created by Jeff Rosen, who used to run the kitchens of the Savannah Grill in Marin and the Big Horn Grill in San Ramon, this small space has the casual look and ambience of a diner. But the bistro-style food is much better than the decor might lead you to expect. Leading menu choices include barbecued quail with buttered hominy and pepper marmalade; seared salmon and potato napoleon; grilled flatiron steak; and

large, juicy burgers. ♦ American bistro ♦ Daily lunch and dinner. 1243 Ninth Ave (between Irving St and Lincoln Way). 664.6999; fax 664.7099 &

8 Noah's Bagels This bakery's products are steamed, not boiled in the traditional fashion. The resulting texture has attracted a large following (though detractors say the bagels here are nothing more than bread with a hole in it). The franchise, which is now part of the Boston Market chain, has enjoyed tremendous success—there are outlets all over the city, with more planned. The bagels, which come in more than a dozen flavors, are fatter than the competition's, and there are plenty of go-withs available, including flavored cream-cheese spreads and sliced smoked fish. ♦ Daily. No credit cards accepted. 742 Irving St (between Eighth and Ninth Aves). 566.2761; fax 566.9258 & Also at: Numerous locations throughout the city

9 PJ's Oysterbed ★★$$ Lovers of Louisiana-style seafood have loyally patronized this nonstop Mardi Gras since the late 1970s. Reservations are accepted, but people don't seem to mind arriving unannounced, putting their names on the list, and waiting for an hour or more; they simply head across the street for a drink at **Yancy's.** Once guests are seated, though, the open kitchen turns out mounds of food just as quickly as the zydeco music bounces. Start with heaps of crayfish, or try the shrimp bisque with a dollop of jalapeño puree. And there's no better jambalaya in the city than the version here, made with rice, tomatoes, chicken, and spicy andouille sausage. **PJ's** also houses a thriving fish market and, next to the sales area, a counter where people can enjoy bowls of steaming clam chowder. ♦ Seafood ♦ Daily lunch and dinner. 737 Irving St (between Eighth and Ninth Aves). 566.7775; fax 566.8088 &

9 Cafe Mirabelle ★★$ This earthy eatery (formerly the **Owl & Monkey Cafe**), with the rough-hewn look of pine tables and plank flooring, is usually packed with college students. A recent change in ownership has brought a few changes to the menu as well: The previously pedestrian sandwiches are now more creative and sophisticated. Options include smoked turkey and avocado on toasted levain bread; roasted eggplant; and Black Forest ham and Swiss cheese. The Greek, Caesar, and house salads are enlivened with yogurt or blue cheese dressings; other selections include pastries, a quiche of the day, and **Noah's** bagels. Live acoustic music is performed Thursday through Saturday nights. ♦ Cafe ♦ Tu-Su breakfast, lunch, and dinner (Su until 7PM). 1336 Ninth Ave (between Judah and Irving Sts). 665.4840; fax 665.0335

10 Tamnan Thai ★★$ The story to wheedle out of the owners is what brought Mick Jagger to this small Thai place after a concert in October 1994. (A photo of the rock star posing with them graces the front window.) The answer could be the food. The sweetness of the silken *tom kha gai* (chicken and coconut-milk soup) is perfectly tempered by sour flavoring from lime juice. The traditional ground chicken with basil is above average, too, thanks to the profusion of herbs that provide a licorice aftertaste. Specials always include at least one curry, including one of the best we've had in any Thai restaurant: shrimp with fresh asparagus, doused in a green curry that's fragrant with basil. With a canopied service area in one corner, candles on the tables, and friendly service, enjoying a meal here is like eating in the home of a relative. ♦ Thai ♦ Tu-Su lunch and dinner. 1360 Ninth Ave (between Judah and Irving Sts). 564.5771 &

11 Organic Grounds While San Francisco has many, many coffeehouses, this one is unique in that it uses only beans organically grown in Guatemala. Whether it's the way the beans are grown or just that these folks know how to make a cup of coffee, the brew is complex, full, and rich, with a touch of bitterness. The narrow shop has a stylish look, with light wood tables, banquettes lining cheery yellow walls, and a pretty wood floor. Health drinks also are served, including shots of wheat grass, smoothies (the orange, banana, and cinnamon smoothie has a bright and lively flavor and tastes as rich as a milk shake), and all kinds of vegetable juices. Even the bagels and granola are organic. ♦ Daily. No credit cards accepted. 1307 Ninth Ave (between Judah and Irving Sts). 661.1255 &

11 Chika ★★$ The sushi chef at work in the shoe-box–size kitchen at this Japanese spot offers a good show. The dining room is spare and attractive, with a high-gloss, blond wood

sushi bar and rice-paper screens softening the windows. Diners munch on complimentary plates of steamed beans as they peruse the menu, which offers the standard array of sushi (barbecued eel, tuna, and shrimp) and limited hot options, including tempura and teriyaki. The blackboard lists such specials as bonito, as well as paper-thin slices of lemon and salmon hand-rolled in rice. ♦ Japanese ♦ M-Tu, Th-Su dinner. 841 Irving St (between Ninth and 10th Aves). 681.5539 &

12 HOUSE ★★$$ Entrepreneur Larry Tse and wife Angela have followed up their immensely successful North Beach restaurant with this location in the Sunset. It is much bigger than the original, with soaring ceilings and three times the seating capacity; cone-shaped light fixtures and comfortable banquette seating help break up the large space, but all the hard surfaces tend to make the noise level high. The menu features light preparations of classic Mediterranean dishes; appetizers include five-spice fried calamari, Tse's signature taro spring rolls, deep-fried salmon rolls served with Chinese hot mustard, steamed mussels, and cream of carrot soup with ginger. For the main course, try the perfect softshell crab, enhanced with a spicy vinegar sauce and fresh baby lettuce salad; Peking duck with pickled ginger; or New Zealand lamb. Wine buyer Mark Ellenbogen's list is well chosen, and the prices are reasonable. The desserts still need work, though. ♦ Asian/Californian ♦ Tu-Su lunch and dinner. 1269 Ninth Ave (between Irving St and Lincoln Way) 682.3898; fax 682.3892 & Also at: 1230 Grant Ave (at Columbus Ave), North Beach. 986.8612 &

12 Just Desserts The draw at this sweet shop—which serves only desserts—is the long counter and soda fountain. It's the place for milk shakes, all kinds of sundaes in traditional fluted glass dishes, or sinful baked goods. Chocoholics will love the rich fudge cake. The bakery also has a way with lemon. Try the lemon tart; the triple lemon cake with layers of lemon sponge, lemon custard filling, and a lemon butter-cream filling; or the densely textured lemon-buttermilk pound cake. ♦ Daily. 836 Irving St (between Ninth and 10th Aves). 681.1277; fax 681.0308. Also at: Numerous locations throughout the city

13 New Eritrea Restaurant ★★$ From the front window this East African place appears to be a bar. But just beyond the quaffing space is a small, dark dining room with a pass-through window to the kitchen. Combination dinners appear on enameled platters the size of a small tabletop, laid with *injera* (spongy Ethiopian bread) and ringed with shredded romaine. The vegetarian combo includes okra with tomatoes and aromatic spices, a spicy vegetable curry, and zucchini and spinach. The meat combo has beef simmered in a red pepper sauce, chicken in clarified butter with a spicy red pepper sauce, lamb curry, and spinach. The braised dishes are fork tender and the flavors are excellent, although the sauces do begin to taste alike. ◆ East African ◆ Tu-Su lunch and dinner. 907 Irving St (between 10th and 11th Aves). 681.1288 &

14 Cheese Boutique A sister shop to the one in Glen Park, this neighborhood favorite boasts more than a hundred kinds of cheese and imported foods. Although the selection at **Andronico's Market** (see below) is more visually impressive, regulars here are loyal to the friendly staff and caring service. ◆ M-Sa. 1298 12th Ave (at Irving St). 566.3155; fax 333.5450. Also at: 666 Chenery St (between Castro and Diamond Sts), Glen Park. 333.3390; fax 333.5450 &

15 Andronico's Market This pricey supermarket has one of the best selections of upscale products in the city, beginning with 25 varieties of apples and 10 types of dates. Consider seven kinds of mushrooms, every fresh herb imaginable, and four varieties of pearl onions. On any given day, the store is likely to surprise customers with something they've never seen before, such as cocktail avocados—creamy, delicious baby avocados without pits. Chic chrome shelves are filled with oils and other essentials, and the terrific selection of bulk items includes 15 kinds of granola. The fresh meat cases display venison, and the fish tanks are swimming with carp, trout, catfish, lobsters, and crabs. Browse the deli for seven pâtés, cold cuts, and myriad take-out treats, the "Hofbrau" department for ribs and pastrami, and the "Hot Wok" for lemon chicken, *egg foo yong,* and barbecued pork. The bread department stocks loaves from most of the boutique bakeries in the area, and the bins are filled with three kinds of bread sticks and four flavors of croutons. We could go on and on, but we're still dizzy with delight. ◆ Daily. 1200 Irving St (at Funston Ave). 661.3220; fax 661.5294 &

16 Sagami-Ya Restaurant ★★$ Ignore the decor at this mom-and-pop Japanese cafe—it's a find. So what if the place looks a bit worn, and the chairs are covered in orange vinyl? It's all immaculate. Ask about the not-to-be-missed sukiyaki, and the cook will wax eloquent about the balance of sake, onions, and broth that flavor the paper-thin slices of beef. The *yosenabe,* an aromatic pot of broth brimming with seafood, is another specialty. Also try the *gyoza,* tasty pot stickers filled with plump shrimp and a hint of dill. Sushi selections are more limited than most, but they're absolutely fresh. ◆ Japanese ◆ Tu-Sa lunch and dinner; Su dinner. 1525 Irving St (between 16th and 17th Aves). 661.2434

17 Just Like Home ★★$ The food at this Middle Eastern cafe/deli is just as homey as the name implies. Up front is the deli, a wall of packaged products, and bins of rice and grains. Beyond an arched doorway lies the dining room, which has booth seating and few other amenities. The vegetarian combination includes the classics: tangy tabbouleh, creamy hummus, delicately flavored dolmas, refreshing cucumbers in yogurt with mint and garlic, and boldly seasoned falafel. Rustic meat dishes include chicken Musakhan (baked with grilled onions and spooned over pita bread) and lamb *shwarma* (thinly sliced rotisseried lamb served over hummus or rice). Wash it all down with the great homemade lemonade. ◆ Middle Eastern/Deli ◆ Daily lunch and dinner. 1924 Irving St (between 20th and 21st Aves). 681.3337 &

18 Irving Seafood Market Since its expansion into a second storefront, this market now carries more than seafood, but the fish here is particularly fresh. As many as 15 types of whole fish are available, as well as mussels, conch, oysters, and tanks of crabs, lobster, catfish, and rock cod. Packaged products, including a shelf of Thai wonton wrappers, cram the other half of the store. ◆ Daily. No credit cards accepted. 2130 Irving St (between 22nd and 23rd Aves). 681.5000 &

18 Irving Little Cafe & Sandwiches ★$ *Banh mi,* traditional Vietnamese sandwiches, are served at this tiny spot (just big enough for four tables and a counter). For a pittance, feast on half a French roll slathered with a mayonnaise and chili sauce, spiked with five-spice powder, peppers, shredded carrots, and cilantro, and filled with pâté, chicken, barbecued pork, sardines, or meatballs. It's a taste treat. The cafe also serves rice and noodle dishes. ◆ Vietnamese ◆ Daily breakfast, lunch, and dinner until 6:30PM. No credit cards accepted. 2146 Irving St (between 22nd and 23rd Aves). 681.2326

San Francisco claims about 3,200 eating and drinking establishments, or one restaurant for every 230 residents.

A (Dining) Room with a View

There's no question that San Francisco has plenty of gorgeous assets, both natural and man-made: the **Golden Gate Bridge,** the **Bay Bridge, Treasure Island, Alcatraz,** the towering skyscrapers of the skyline, and, above all, the **San Francisco Bay** itself.

These picture-postcard views can be enjoyed from any one of myriad eateries. The trouble with most view-oriented dining rooms, though, is that the food often becomes a secondary consideration, and given the hefty prices usually charged at treetop restaurants, the visitor comes away short-changed—culinarily, that is.

But not to worry. There are a few places in this city that offer good to excellent food to go with their scenic floor show. The **Cityscape Restaurant** (333 O'Farrell St, between Mason and Taylor Sts, 771.1400; fax 673.5163 ♿), located on the 46th floor of the **San Francisco Hilton and Towers** in **Union Square,** offers a 360-degree picture of the entire city, as well as some pretty good food. Stick to the basics: prime rib, surf and turf, Maine lobster, or New York steak. The **Carnelian Room** (555 California St at Kearny St, 433.7500; fax 291.0815 ♿), another **Downtown** dining room, perches atop the 52nd floor of the **Bank of America** world headquarters. Particularly romantic at night, it boasts brass chandeliers,

dark wood paneling, and the spectacle of the lit-up Golden Gate and Bay Bridges. Again, your best bet is to order simple dishes; the three-course, prix-fixe menu, offering straightforward choices, is a good value.

The fact that a restaurant doesn't have to be elevated to afford a good view is evidenced by two places in the **Fisherman's Wharf/The Embarcadero** area. **The Waterfront Restaurant** (Pier 7, at The Embarcadero and Broadway, 391.2696; fax 391.7125 ♿) capitalizes on a grand view of the Bay Bridge and Treasure Island. Crowds flock here at lunch and brunch for the fresh seafood, which is prepared with Asian flavors and influences. And **Timo's Norte** (900 North Point St, at Larkin St, across from Aquatic Park, 440.1200; fax 440.3192 ♿), on the second floor of the **Mustard Building** in **Ghirardelli Square,** boasts lovely views of the bay and Fisherman's Wharf. Owner/ chef Carlos Corredor has created a menu of terrific tapas ranging from tender veal kidneys in a sherry sauce to Catalan-style spinach with pine nuts and raisins; main courses are good, too, including the house specialty: *ajiaco*, a hearty chicken-potato soup.

19 22nd & Irving Market Since the late 1960s, this neighborhood market has attracted customers from all over the city. Fresh olives are just waiting to be brined and cured; the quince is picture-perfect; Italian chestnuts are ready for roasting; and the herbs are some of the freshest around. There are also bags of basmati and jasmine rice, nuts, dried fruits, and beans. The dairy department carries feta and Mexican cheeses, and many of the makings for Latin and Asian fare are on hand—though **May Wah** (see page 185) is a better bet for stocking up on the most esoteric Asian ingredients. A couple of tables are available for eating takeout food from the other shops and cafes in the area.
♦ Daily. No credit cards accepted. 2101 Irving St (at 22nd Ave). 681.5212; fax 681.3285 ♿

19 Sunrise Deli and Cafe ★$ The falafel made here is sold to many of the corner markets around the city. These tasty croquettes are made from highly spiced, ground chickpeas that are deep-fried and either tucked into pita bread or served with a yogurt or tahini sauce. The front window showcases a spit of layered lamb slices, all

brown, succulent, and ready to be carved. The deli also proffers salads, including tabbouleh.
♦ Middle Eastern ♦ Daily lunch and dinner. No credit cards accepted. 2115 Irving St (between 22nd and 23rd Aves). 664.8210

Yum Yum Fish

19 Yum Yum Fish Shoppers in the know seek out this store for the freshest fish fillets in town. At the rear is a sushi counter, where more than a dozen first-rate sushi and sashimi items are prepared to order. You can get a sushi snack to go, too. The party trays are hugely popular. ♦ Tu-Su. No credit cards accepted. 2181 Irving St (between 22nd and 23rd Aves). 566.6433 ♿

19 New Hai Ky ★$ Cheap, good food attracts crowds to this popular spot. The window is full of mahogany-hued Peking ducks and other roasted meats that taste as good as they look; flavorful noodle soups are also a draw. It's enough to make you overlook the Formica tables and bare floors that contrast oddly with the sea of bright, crystal chandeliers above them. ♦ Chinese ♦ Daily breakfast, lunch, and dinner. No credit cards accepted. 2191 Irving St (at 23rd Ave). 731.9948

20 May Wah Trading Company A full-service Asian market, this store is more compact than its branches in Chinatown and Richmond. The narrow aisles and merchandise are stacked high. Those who can overcome their claustrophobia will find a grand selection of packaged products, produce, well-trimmed meat, up to a dozen kinds of fish, and everything else needed to put an Asian meal on the table. The younger staffers are helpful, but the older ones can be brusque. ♦ Daily. 2201 Irving St (at 23rd Ave). 665.4756 ♿ Also at: Numerous locations throughout the city

20 Marnee Thai ★★$ The peaked room lined in bamboo and the walls covered in woven palm-frond mats give this Thai restaurant a tropical feel. Although it's one of the most popular in the city, the food has lost a bit of its edge recently. The signature dish is a fresh, thin corn-and-ginger cake deep-fried to a honey brown. Other top choices are raw spinach leaves filled with shrimp and ginger, and spicy green papaya salad with wedges of tomatoes and whole green beans. Among the main courses, the spicy chicken with cashews is studded with chunks of white onions, scallions, and red peppers. The chicken with chili sauce and fresh basil is another popular standby. For dessert, few can resist the fried bananas with a scoop of rich ice cream laced with coconut. ♦ Thai ♦ M, W-Su lunch and dinner. 2225 Irving St (between 23rd and 24th Aves). 665.9500

21 Thanh Long ★★$$ People travel from all over the city to feast on roast crab at this Vietnamese restaurant that was opened by Helene and Danny An in 1969—and for good reason. It's served either with sweet-and-sour sauce or "drunken" (in a vibrant wine broth with scallions). Diners, outfitted for battle with plastic bibs and nutcrackers, are amply rewarded with delighted palates, full stomachs, and hot towels to clean their fingers. Those who don't crave crab can opt for Saigon beef, the meat rolled around cooked onions and topped with more sweet, gooey onions, or lemongrass chicken with its edge of garlic. A good way to start is the multivitamin roll, a crisp-skinned imperial roll

stuffed with pork and vegetables; also don't miss the garlic noodles. The dining room is always crowded, and it's not hard to understand why. ♦ Vietnamese/Seafood ♦ Tu-Su dinner. 4101 Judah St (at 46th Ave). 665.1146

JOUBERT'S

21 Joubert's ★★$$ This new vegetarian restaurant reflects the flavors of South Africa, which is where the owners are from. The country's inhabitants are of French, English, Cape Dutch, Malay, and Indian extraction, and all of those cuisines are represented on the menu—with Indian food dominating. One appetizer is olive tapenade (a puree of black olives, garlic, and herbs) spread on bread; main courses include kidney-bean meat loaf with mushroom gravy and a portobello mushroom baked in aioli and served with rice, seasonal greens, and a relish. Daily specials are also available, such as Durban red lentil dal, curried stew, and cassoulet with butter beans. The wine list offers several excellent South African vintages. The tiny dining room is soothingly decorated with bright paintings, a homey fireplace, fresh flowers, and sparkling white tablecloths. One element that needs work is the service—though friendly, the staff is a bit absentminded. ♦ South African/Vegetarian ♦ W-Su dinner. 4115 Judah St (between 46th and 47th Aves). 753.5448; fax 753.5497 ♿

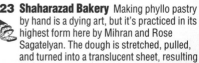

22 Sweet Endings Cookies This all-purpose bakery has a retail outlet in front and a production facility in back, which supplies biscotti and other baked goods to many cafes in the city. Its biscotti (the dry Italian biscuit) are denser and not as crisp as most, but the flavors are just as good, particularly the chocolate. The ovens also turn out a variety of Middle Eastern cookies. ♦ Tu-Sa. No credit cards accepted. 1935 Lawton St (between 25th and 26th Aves). 665.4748 ♿

23 Shaharazad Bakery Making phyllo pastry by hand is a dying art, but it's practiced in its highest form here by Mihran and Rose Sagatelyan. The dough is stretched, pulled, and turned into a translucent sheet, resulting in a phyllo that is flakier and moister than any other. The cheery aqua-and-white bakery makes the most of the artful phyllo in such not-to-be missed treats as the *spanakopita,* baklava, apple turnover, or pistachio birds' nests, freshly made and dripping with honey. ♦ M-Sa. No credit cards accepted. 1586 Noriega St (at 23rd Ave). 661.1155 ♿

24 House of Coffee One of the first shops to introduce the city to the full range of fresh roasted coffees, this has been a popular neighborhood stop since the mid-1960s. In addition to the coffees, roasted in the rear, it proffers coffeepots, espresso machines, and such specialty products as jars of baby eggplants, sour cherries, and Australian dried apricots. ♦ M-Sa. 1618 Noriega St (between 23rd and 24th Aves). 681.9363; fax 566.0768 ♿

25 Cheung Hing ★★$ The space is cramped, the decor utilitarian, but the wonderful aromas emanating from this little Chinese eatery have fans lining up even on Sunday nights, when other places wind down. Three frenzied workers behind the counter serve up roast pig, soy-sauce chicken, and barbecued pork and duck. And it seems almost everyone orders the lo mein noodles (try the ones topped with barbecued pork). All delicious, and for ridiculously low prices. ♦ Chinese/Barbecue ♦ Daily breakfast, lunch, and dinner. 2339 Noriega St (between 30th and 31st Aves). 665.3271

26 Hong Kong Seafood Restaurant ★★$ One of the best of the growing number of Hong Kong–style restaurants serving dim sum in the Sunset, it boasts Sunday-morning queues. People even line up at the take-out area, which has its own entrance and is separated from the dining room by a folding screen. The dim sum is terrific, each preparation given a slight twist: The pork in the *siu mai* dumpling is chopped into fairly large pieces along with equally large pieces of shrimp. Each *ha gow* (a shrimp dumpling made with a thin tapioca-flour casing) holds three shrimp smeared with a ginger-and-garlic paste. And the steamed dumplings' pork-and-cilantro filling is finely chopped, creating a creamy contrast to the al dente wrapping. The red swagged drapes at the storefront windows have faded to pink, but the room is a cut above most in the area, with tapestry-like upholstery and crystal chandeliers. ♦ Chinese/Dim sum ♦ Daily lunch and dinner; dim sum Sa-Su 9:30AM-2:30PM. 2588 Noriega St (at 33rd Ave). 665.8338 ♿

27 Polly Ann Ice Cream Unique in its decor and its ice cream, this parlor dishes up 400 flavors (50 on any given day), including passion fruit, litchi, guava, jackfruit, and taro. For less exotic tastes, owner Charles Wu offers Bumpy Road (his answer to Rocky Road) and coffee rum fudge. If it's too hard to decide what to order, spin the flavor wheel and hope you like what it lands on. The walls of the tiny shop are papered with slogans like "If there's anything a depressed person hates, it's a cheerful person." But it's hard not to feel cheerful at a place that offers a free ice-cream cone to any pup accompanied by a human customer. ♦ Daily. No credit cards accepted. 3142 Noriega St (between 38th and 39th Aves). 664.2472 ♿

28 Win's ★$ Roast ducks and spareribs hang in the window of this Chinese spot, and just inside the door cooks pull noodles and wontons from steaming pots. At eight pages, the menu is too long for the kitchen to manage consistently, but the duck is always a must-have. Start with pot stickers and barbecued baby pork ribs, served on a bed of lightly sauced white beans. The *congees,* rich rice soups that constitute a meal, are also very good—especially the combination with shrimp, scallops, squid, chicken, and pork. For a really inexpensive, filling meal, choose one of the rice plates topped with all kinds of stir-fries or curries. ♦ Chinese ♦ Tu-Sa lunch and dinner. 3040 Taraval St (between 40th and 41st Aves). 759.1818

29 Rick's Restaurant & Bar ★★★$$ Richard and Victoria Oku's stylish place has a somewhat remote setting near the ocean, where it was sorely needed. The dining room resembles that of an exclusive cruise ship, with Philippine mahogany paneling, an ornate bar, gleaming brass trim, starched white tablecloths, bentwood chairs, and a forest green carpet. In keeping with the theme, brass porthole-framed mirrors are hung on the paneling. Oku, the former chef at the **Washington Square Bar and Grill** and a native of Hawaii, includes a few island-inspired dishes—such as *poki* (a tuna seviche) and *goliah* (a fish stew). But most of the fare is what he calls "San Francisco comfort food." That translates to lamb shanks with polenta, pork tenderloin over herbed bread stuffing, and New York steak with green-peppercorn sauce. Among the seafood selections are mahimahi with avocado-papaya salsa and red snapper in lime vinaigrette. Vegetarian dishes include ravioli with sun-dried tomatoes and almonds, and a mixed vegetable platter. ♦ American ♦ Daily dinner. Reservations recommended. 1940 Taraval St (between 29th and 30th Aves). 731.8900 ♿

30 Marco Polo This parlor, an East-West hybrid, is aptly named for the explorer who supposedly brought ice cream to Europe from the Orient. Two signs stretch across the building: one in English printed on the colors of the Italian flag, the other with Chinese characters. The ice cream is Italian-style gelato, which is dense in texture and rich in taste; it comes in both Asian flavors (red bean, litchi, and guava) and such Italian classics as double chocolate and *arcobaleno* (rainbow), with its stripes of vanilla, chocolate, and pistachio. ♦ Daily. No credit cards accepted. 1447 Taraval St (between 24th and 25th Aves). 731.2833 ♿

31 Mr. Liquor The top wine shop in the Sunset, and one of the best in the city, it will meet or beat any competitor's prices. It's the only San Francisco outlet for Kermit Lynch wines (a well-known importer in Berkeley) and carries about two-thirds of the entire line. It also stocks a good selection of current-release wines, particularly from California. Many older Bordeaux and Californian wines are stored off-premises in a 10,000-square-foot warehouse; a newsletter lists what's available. The store also carries up to 130 beers and 60 single-malt scotches. The tasting bar by the front window offers self-service wine tastings at a minimal charge, and wine-tasting seminars are held regularly. To double-check your choices, consult the binders full of wine ratings by the *Wine Advocate, Grapevine, Connoisseur's,* and the *Wine Journal.* ♦ Daily. 250 Taraval St (between 12th and Funston Aves). 731.6222; fax 731.0155 ♿

32 Just Won Ton ★★$ That's what to order at this little restaurant: just won tons. They may well be the best you ever ate. The skin is almost translucent, and the delicate fillings burst with flavor. The best bet is a bowl of broth brimming with the stuffed noodles and another ingredient, maybe fish balls or barbecued chicken or pork. Other noodles include *chow mei fun* (thick rice noodles) and chow mein. The white-painted room is nothing fancy and has fewer than a dozen tables covered with bright oilcloth. ♦ Chinese ♦ Tu-Su lunch and dinner. No credit cards accepted. 1241 Vicente St (between 23rd and 24th Aves). 681.2999

33 Leon's Bar-B-Q ★$ After spending a day at the **San Francisco Zoo,** head across the street to this diner. Specialties are greasy ribs with a sweet barbecue sauce, jambalaya, and homemade sweet-potato pie. All the barbecue comes with corn bread, baked beans, potato salad, coleslaw, and fries or spaghetti. For something a little different, try the barbecued smoked turkey sandwich. There are also branches on Fillmore Street and at Fisherman's Wharf. ♦ Barbecue ♦ Daily lunch and dinner. 2800 Sloat Blvd (at 46th Ave, across from the zoo entrance). 681.3071. Also at: Numerous locations throughout the city

Bests

Stuart Whitman
Actor

Postrio—For its ambience and superb food.

John's Grill—Any of the veal dishes.

Calzone's—For their unique Italian food.

The Stinking Rose—For the garlic dishes and the baked garlic—a treat I now do at home.

Gary Goldberg
Executive Director, Culinary Arts at The New School, NYC

French Laundry—Thomas Keller is an artist on par with the best chefs in the world. His food is superb, and you will dream about some dishes forever. We also love the understated minimalist dining rooms and cosseting service.

Tra Vigne—Once you get over hypertension-provoking crowdedness . . . there still is surprisingly wonderful food and great wine by the glass. I recommend the eggplant and tomato bruschetta, whole fish from the brick oven, and even the tiramisù.

Pinot Blanc—Order the grilled chicken with the house *frites* (french fries)—it costs $12.95. It's the best I've ever had!

Daryl Sattui
Owner/Winemaker, V Sattui Winery, St. Helena

Yuet Lee—Looks like a dump, but great Hong Kong–style food. Salt and pepper prawns, oyster clay pot . . . fresh crab and eel in a clay pot.

Moose's—My favorite in **North Beach,** but not Italian.

Scala's—Great Italian food.

Bistro Ralph, Healdsburg—Really good . . . eclectic style.

The Richmond/ Presidio Heights

A largely residential district, the Richmond is family-oriented to be sure. But those families are a diverse lot, with roots that cover the globe. The traditions of Asia, the Middle East, and Eastern and Western Europe mingle in this excitingly varied community, making for a bracing cultural and culinary stew.

Russians were the first group to settle the area, when some 10,000 immigrants arrived here after the 1917 Revolution. Many second- and third-generation Russians gradually moved away from the city beginning in the 1970s, but they were replaced by a large number of Russian-Jewish émigrés who came

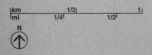

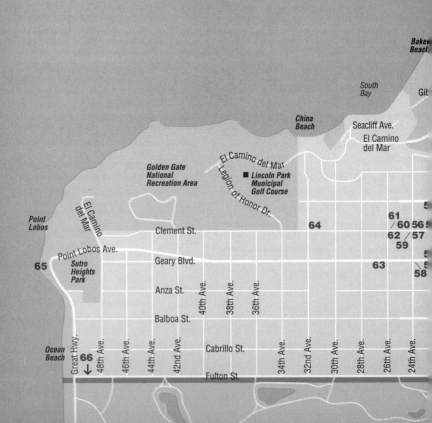

Pacific Ocean

Baker Beach

South Bay

Gib

China Beach

Seacliff Ave.

El Camino del Mar

El Camino del Mar

Golden Gate National Recreation Area

El Camino del Mar

Legion of Honor Dr.

■ Lincoln Park Municipal Golf Course

Point Lobos

61

/ 60 56

64

62 / 57

59

Clement St.

Point Lobos Ave.

Sutro Heights Park

65

Geary Blvd.

63

58

Anza St.

40th Ave.

38th Ave.

36th Ave.

Balboa St.

Ocean Beach

Great Hwy.

66

↓

48th Ave.

46th Ave.

44th Ave.

42nd Ave.

Cabrillo St.

34th Ave.

32nd Ave.

30th Ave.

28th Ave.

26th Ave.

24th Ave.

Fulton St.

km   1/2   1
mi   1/4   1/2

N

here in the 1980s to escape repression in the former Soviet Union. In subsequent years, non-Jewish Russians came here as well. More than 25,000 strong today, this community clusters around the impressive, onion-domed **Holy Virgin Cathedral**, a Russian Orthodox church on **Geary Boulevard** at **26th Avenue**. At least a half-dozen bakeries and several stores and delis have opened in the last few years to cater to this growing group of residents.

Many people of Japanese descent moved to the central areas of the Richmond after World War II, and today more Japanese-Americans live in this district than in any other part of the city. The Chinese have likewise put down deep roots here—so much so that the Richmond is often called New Chinatown. In the mid-1970s, the main shopping district of **Clement Street**, from **Fourth** to

Tenth Avenues, had one small dim sum restaurant and no Asian groceries. Today there are numerous shops and restaurants catering to the burgeoning Asian community. But stores in the "original" Chinatown generally carry products that appeal primarily to the Chinese cook, while Richmond merchants branch out to cater to a more diverse market.

At **El Chico Produce Market**, for example, Asian and Hispanic products share shelf space with bread and pastries from **Cinderella Restaurant and Bakery**, one of the city's oldest Russian bakeries. And at **Cinderella**'s restaurant, diners may favor an order of traditional stuffed cabbage with the soy sauce that always sits on the tables.

The ethnic diversity in the Richmond has also given rise to a number of diverse Asian venues, such as the delightful, family-run **Jasmine House**, with some of the best Vietnamese food in the city; **Mandalay**, San Francisco's first Burmese eatery; and several three-star Hong Kong–style dim sum parlors, including **Hong Kong Flower Lounge Restaurant** and **Ton Kiang**. These places happily coexist with such neighborhood institutions as **Haig's Delicacies**, where people have stocked up on Middle Eastern goods for almost half a century, and **Shenson's**, renowned for its Jewish delicatessen fare.

Western Europe is well represented here, too. Such French classics as coq au vin or sweetbreads in Madeira cream sauce are served at the romantic **Le Cyrano**; modern Mediterranean fare stars at **Socca Restaurant**, and the area even boasts a prominent French restaurant, **Alain Rondelli**. Some of the best cracker-crisp–crusted pizza in the city is offered at **Mescolanza**, along with great pasta and veal dishes. And you can get your Irish up debating the fine points of a soccer match at **Pat O'Shea's Mad Hatter**—and enjoy a lunch of roast salmon or leg of lamb washed down with a brew. A fine spot to appreciate the community's family spirit is the **Toy Boat Dessert Cafe**, where youngsters climb up on a mechanical horse, ogle the tin toys for sale, and slurp ice-cream cones. Their older siblings may prefer a burger and malted at **Mel's Drive-In.**

The Richmond spills into one of the city's most affluent areas: Presidio Heights, home to some of its most distinguished citizens, including US senator Dianne Feinstein. North of Geary Boulevard are the expensive homes of **Seacliff**, with many wealthy and famous residents (such as actor-comedian Robin Williams). And **Laurel Village** offers some of the best shopping in the city. **Wine Impression** has a vast selection of vintages from all over the world; the **Cal-Mart** supermarket proffers an impressive selection of goods, including breads from more than a half-dozen bakeries; **Bryan's** market sells top-quality meat, fish, and poultry (including the Prime grade of beef, which non-restaurateurs find difficult to obtain). **Forrest Jones**, on **Sacramento Street**, was the first store in the country to carry Calphalon pots and pans among its wide range of fine housewares. On the same street are several antiques stores that also provide ample opportunities to fantasize and window shop. Here, too, the clubby **Garibaldis** serves up a fine hamburger and Caesar salad; a more elegant dining option is **The Heights**, a four-star French-California eatery. Presidio Heights, Seacliff, and Laurel Village are decidedly upscale enclaves, but they harmonize nicely with the staunchly middle-class Richmond district. Together they provide another example of the unified diversity that is San Francisco.

Baker St. Bistro

1 Baker Street Bistro ★★$$ Classic French food is the draw of this cozy storefront dining room with only 24 seats and tables brightened by pots of herbs. Throughout the evening, the chef emerges from the kitchen to make sure everything is going smoothly. Selections include snails sautéed in garlic and cream, and a rich ragout of lamb with carrots and other vegetables. Fish specials are offered nightly, and might include yellowtail tuna in a brown butter sauce, served with vegetables and a crusty wedge of baked polenta. The four-course prix-fixe dinner is a great deal. On Friday and Saturday nights, the seating area spills over into a small space next door. At other times, the extra room is a casual cafe serving breakfast and lunch. The menu includes pastries, baguette sandwiches, salads, and egg dishes, among them a great quiche. ♦ French ♦ Tu-Su breakfast, lunch, and dinner. 2953 Baker St (at Lombard St). 931.1475 ♿

2 Liverpool Lil's ★$$ When the Presidio was an army base, military personnel as well as civilians hung out at this cozy English pub. Still popular, it's one of the few places in the city where you can indulge in a steak-and-kidney pie. Other traditional English fare includes fish-and-chips, beef ribs with barbecue sauce, and Manchester Wellington—ground chuck swaddled in ham and puff pastry and finished with béarnaise sauce. With the kitchen open until 1AM most nights (until midnight on Sundays), this is a great place for a late snack of sausage-stuffed mushrooms, French onion soup, or baked brie. ♦ English ♦ M-F lunch and dinner; Sa-Su brunch and dinner. 2942 Lyon St (between Greenwich and Lombard Sts). 921.6664; fax 921.1019

3 Sue Fisher King This is the place for beautiful, expensive linens, wonderful plates, and glass- and tableware. One area is devoted to hotel silver, many in classic Deco designs; there's also a

collection of unusual napkin rings. Watch for announcements of sales—the buys can be great. ♦ M-Sa 10AM-6PM; Su noon-5PM. 3067 Sacramento St (between Broderick and Baker Sts). 922.7276; fax 922.9241 ♿

3 Virginia Breier Whimsical, unique artwork is this shop's claim to fame. Some of the found-object sculptures incorporate silverware; shoppers with more traditional tastes will find incredible one-of-a-kind plates, cups, and saucers. ♦ M-Sa. 3091 Sacramento St (at Baker St). 929.7173; fax 929.7173 ♿

American Pie

4 American Pie This general store displays candles in an unimaginable range of colors. A counter at the back features hard candy, coffee beans, and candy cordials. ♦ Daily Nov-Dec; M-Sa Jan-Oct. 3101 Sacramento St (at Baker St). 929.8025 ♿

5 The Heights ★★★★$$$ Chef Charles Solomon made a name for himself in New York before moving west and opening this charming restaurant in a converted house. One dining room faces the street; the other two overlook a garden. The decor is simple and pleasant; the chairs are slipcovered either in an attractive green linen, or patterned with black-and-white artichokes. Solomon is truly a genius at creating vibrant, light combinations for his à la carte and fixed-price menus, which change weekly. One perennial is lobster in a balsamic-Port reduction, sometimes paired with hedgehog mushrooms or parsnips. Carpaccio of Diver sea scallops are sliced transparently thin and topped with caviar. Other great appetizers are Washington State belon oysters with fennel and salmon roe in a curry sauce; and cream of organic pumpkin soup. It seems Solomon can do no wrong, even with dessert, which might be apple napoleon with green apple sorbet or steamed persimmon pudding with crème anglaise and vanilla ice cream. ♦ French/Californian ♦ Tu-Su dinner. Reservations recommended. 3235 Sacramento St (between Lyon St and Presidio Ave). 474.8890; fax 474.1713

6 Ella's ★★★$ Line up here on weekends for one of the best brunches in San Francisco. It's a comfortable place with an open kitchen, a dining counter that's always bedecked with fresh flowers, and simply set, closely placed tables. The sticky buns alone are worth a visit. Other noteworthy items include chicken hash, buttermilk pancakes, and the fresh punch of ginger and orange juice. All the baking is done in-house. The lunch menu ranges from grilled fish of the day and chicken potpie to a warm spinach salad with bacon, mushrooms, and a sherry vinaigrette. ♦ American ♦ M-F breakfast, lunch, and dinner; Sa-Su brunch. 500 Presidio Ave (at California St). 441.5669

7 Forrest Jones A pioneer in the housewares industry, this 1970s-era shop was the first retail outlet for Calphalon pots and pans. The aisles are crammed with Chinese pots, lamps, kitchen towels, dishes, kitchen equipment, and a variety of other high-quality but reasonably priced goods. ♦ Daily. 3274 Sacramento St (between Lyon St and Presidio Ave). 567.2483; fax 567.7604

8 Garibaldis ★★$$$ This charming neighborhood restaurant has an understated beige-and-white decor and windows that open onto Presidio Avenue. Great appetizers include grilled radicchio; fat crab cakes; and green beans sautéed with pancetta, garlic, hot chili oil, and oyster sauce. Burgers, skirt steak, and a Mediterranean lamb tenderloin marinated in Zinfandel are always good choices, and grilled salmon makes frequent appearances in different guises. Pastas comprise a large part of the menu, but they can be oversauced and overcomplicated with too many ingredients. ♦ Californian ♦ M-F lunch and dinner; Sa dinner; Su brunch and dinner. 347 Presidio Ave (between Sacramento and Clay Sts). 563.8841; fax 563.1227 ⚹

9 Ken Groom's Dogs and cats deserve gourmet treats, too, so don't overlook this chic pet shop, which carries Bowser Brittle, Haute Canine Gourmet dog cookies, and huge, bone-shaped biscuits with oatmeal and raisins. There's also a selection of crystal Waterford-inspired dishes for the truly pampered pooch. ♦ M-Sa. 3429 Sacramento St (between Walnut and Laurel Sts). 673.7708 ⚹

10 Tortola ★★$ Healthful and tasty Southwestern and Mexican fare is the specialty of this casual place, which has spun off four quick-service shops in Northern California. It offers burritos, tostadas, and tacos with various fillings, but is known for its "cup tamale," a fresh *masa* (pasta) shell filled with chicken, moistened with a smoky chili sauce, and topped with black beans and salsa. Sausages from the Yucatán are mildly spiced

with chilies and garlic and served with grilled polenta and black beans. Also try the stewlike Santa Fe pork, which wins the most accolades. ♦ Southwestern/Mexican ♦ Tu-Sa lunch and dinner; Su dinner. 3640 Sacramento St (between Locust and Spruce Sts). 929.8181; fax 929.8181 ⚹

11 Rosmarino ★★$$ Tucked away behind two buildings, this restaurant boasts a pretty, ivy-trimmed patio. Inside, the focal point is a whimsical metal sculpture of the Golden Gate Bridge and the city that stretches along one wall. Unfortunately, frequent changes in the kitchen make the food unpredictable, although ricotta gnocchi are always on hand, accompanied by various seasonal toppings. Other Italian-inspired dishes include whole sea bass rubbed with thyme and olive oil and sprinkled with orange zest and *niçoise* olives. Dessert might be a fresh-fruit crumble or buckwheat crepes bulging with fruit and served with a scoop of homemade ice cream. ♦ Mediterranean ♦ Tu-Sa lunch and dinner; Su brunch. 3665 Sacramento St (between Locust and Spruce Sts). 931.7710; fax 931.5013

11 Magic Flute ★$$ The best features of the dining experience here are the cozy French ambience and the outdoor patio. The service adds a warm note, too; it's professional and efficient without being pretentious. On recent visits the food was mediocre, but one dish always worth ordering is the polenta lasagna, which changes nightly; sandwiched between layers of polenta may be fillings of duck, ricotta, greens, tomatoes, and a mix of herbs, all topped with cheese. The Caesar salad is a good way to begin, but the desserts consistently disappoint. ♦ Italian/American ♦ M-F lunch and dinner; Sa dinner. 3673 Sacramento St (between Locust and Spruce Sts). 922.1225; fax 922.1225

12 Wine Impression The majority of the stock at this high-end wine store isn't on display; it's in a 10,000-bottle warehouse. There John Brennan, the fine-wine specialist and one of the owners, stores every vintage of BV Private Reserve dating back to 1936; other California wines date to 1890. The French collection begins with the 1870 vintage. These rare wines can be in the customer's hand within 24 hours. The store prides itself on having extraordinary wines from around the world at exceptional values. Within the shop is a display of incredible wines by varietal at very reasonable prices, as well as up to 50 single-malt scotches and as many Cognacs—and the selection nearly triples during holidays. ◆ Daily. 3461 California St (between Laurel and Spruce Sts). 221.WINE; fax 221.5505 ﹠

12 Eppler's/Fantasia Once a magical name in San Francisco pastry making, **Fantasia** was bought several years ago by **Eppler's**, a high-volume, American-style bakery. However, the store continues to produce some of **Fantasia**'s most popular cakes, including espresso torte, "Ecstasy" (a flourless chocolate cake made with ganache), Black Forest cake, Grand Marnier Sacher torte, and "Better-than-sex," containing a layer each of dense chocolate, truffle cream, and chocolate ganache, all topped with a layer of fudge. Most of the other baked goods, including the Danish pastries and cookies, are **Eppler's** recipes. ◆ Daily. 3465 California St (between Laurel and Spruce Sts). 752.0825; fax 752.1251 ﹠

12 Bryan's Since 1963, when it opened in **Cal-Mart** (see below), this meat market has catered to the carriage trade. The butchers are knowledgeable about Midwestern beef, milk-fed veal, foie gras, and such game as pheasant, squab, guinea hen, and free-range geese. This is also the only place in the city that stocks Prime grade beef, and sushi-grade *ahi*, Dover sole from France, and Russian caviar can be found in the fish department. And homemade stocks and demi-glace (rich brown sauce) are popular with home cooks trying to prepare a gourmet meal in a hurry. ◆ M-Sa. 3473 California St (between Laurel and Spruce Sts). 752.3430; fax 752.0714 ﹠

13 Judith Ets-Hokin's Home Chef This comprehensive one-stop shop for the budding or experienced cook has been in business since 1972. In addition to a vast range of cookware, it offers classes in its fully equipped kitchen; enrolled students receive a 10 percent discount on their purchases. And on the first Monday of each month, customers can trade in old knives, pots, pans, and bakeware for discounts up to 20 percent on new Home Chef knives, All-Clad, Calphalon, and Zani cookware, and Kaiser LaForme bakeware. ◆ Daily. 3525 California St (between Laurel and Spruce Sts). 668.3191; fax 668.0902 ﹠ (classes not ﹠)

14 Cal-Mart A cruise down the aisles reveals that this is no run-of-the-mill supermarket. It's where the elite meet (or at least their maids do). The store has a fine selection of staples, and the produce section carries such items as lemon cucumbers and fava beans. The meat market offers a good selection of veal, including shanks for osso buco. Fresh bread comes in regularly from the best

bakeries in San Francisco. There are also about two dozen olive oils, as well as walnut, hazelnut, almond, and avocado oils, every kind of vinegar, and endless rows of specialty jams, jellies, and packaged products. ◆ Daily. 3585 California St (at Spruce St). 751.3516; fax 751.2744 ﹠

15 Ton Kiang ★★$ The long menu specializes in the food of China's Hakka region, but is rounded out with Cantonese and Northern Chinese selections; the waiters will helpfully lead you through it all. Best bets are the clay-pot dishes: braised pork in a rich sauce lightened with tofu and vegetables, or delicious squares of pork-stuffed tofu stewed with carrots, celery, and pieces of pork. Other excellent choices include salt-baked chicken, served in a vinegar sauce with chilies and garlic, and wonderful fish balls, lightly seasoned and finely textured. A low brick building houses the two large dining rooms, which are brightly lit and separated from the kitchen by fish tanks. Tablecloths soften the look at dinner. A more elaborate sister restaurant, with the same name, serves dim sum (see page 202). ◆ Chinese ◆ Daily lunch and dinner. 3148 Geary Blvd (at Spruce St). 752.4440. Also at: 5821 Geary Blvd (between 22nd and 23rd Aves). 386.8530 ﹠

Straits Café

16 Straits Café ★★$$ Hairstylist-turned-cook Chris Yao has crafted a unique menu of foods from Singapore. For example, he stuffs trout with lemongrass and other herbs, wraps it in a banana leaf, then grills the package. The herbs and smoke permeate the fish, making for a complex combination of flavors. Whole okra is cooked in a slightly spicy chili sauce with dried shrimp—an earthy, unusual taste. And don't miss the deliciously prepared curry dishes, especially the chicken version. The dining room evokes a village courtyard; there's a mural of houses with shutters and ornate roof ornaments and, draped across it, a real clothesline with baby clothes. ◆ Singaporean/Chinese ◆ Daily lunch and dinner. 3303 Geary Blvd (at Parker Ave). 668.1783; fax 668.3901

Top o' the Morning:
Breakfast and Brunch in San Francisco

Although breakfast and brunch are not the exclusive province of San Francisco restaurants, the city's extraordinary cultural diversity and high culinary standards mean that the breakfast experience here can be anything you want it to be. You can partake of eggs Benedict and Champagne in an elegant hotel dining room; indulge in a hearty, down-home meal of flapjacks and maple syrup at a family-style cafe; select from a bountiful cart of dim sum at a Chinese restaurant; or have a typical Irish breakfast with eggs, rashers of bacon, cereal, and even blood sausage. If you're a morning person, the places listed below are among our favorite wake-up calls.

French Room With its massive crystal chandelier and classy Louis XV decor, this dining room in the **Clift Hotel** offers a truly international menu. For breakfast and Sunday brunch, there's Belgian waffles, *huevos rancheros* (fried eggs served over a corn tortilla with spicy tomato sauce), smoked-salmon eggs Benedict, and frittatas (prepared with egg whites for the low-cholesterol set). ♦ Daily breakfast 6:30AM-11AM; Su brunch 10AM-2PM. 495 Geary St (at Taylor St), Union Square. 775.4700; fax 441.4621 ♿

Gold Mountain Restaurant Grand and elegant, this **Chinatown** restaurant offers some of San Francisco's best dim sum. The dumplings come in many varieties—stuffed with shrimp, pork, fish, and scallops and chives, for example—but all of them are delicious. The *siu mai* (traditional steamed dumplings) come with whole shrimp on top, an unusual touch. One of the most delicious preparations is a ground shrimp mixture, dotted with carrots and a whole cilantro leaf, dipped in a tempura-like batter and deep-fried. ♦ M-F 10:30AM-3PM; Sa-Su 8AM-3PM. 644 Broadway (between Grant Ave and Stockton St). 296.7733; fax 296.7782 ♿

Mama's Girl If you're a fan of omelettes, join the crowds who line up early to get into this venerable cafe in **North Beach**. There are more than 15 variations of omelettes on the menu (including a low-cholesterol egg-white rendition with mushrooms and green onions), in addition to other egg dishes and grilled items. ♦ Tu-Su 8AM-3PM. No credit cards accepted. 1701 Stockton St (at Filbert St). 362.6421

Miss Millie's If you eat breakfast out only once during your San Francisco visit, have it at this retro diner in the **Noe Valley**. They make a big fuss over their morning fare, and it shows: You'll find it hard to choose among fat, sticky cinnamon rolls; citrus-flavored scones; roasted vegetables; French toast topped with bananas, whipped butter, and real maple syrup; and lemon ricotta pancakes with blueberry syrup. You may have to wait, especially if you come for Sunday brunch, but it's worth it. ♦ M-F 7:30AM-11:30AM; Sa-Su 9AM-2PM. 4123 24th St (between Castro and Diamond Sts). 285.5598; fax 585.5030

O'Reilly's
Bar & Restaurant

Owned by Dubliner Miles O'Reilly, this pub brings the taste of Ireland to the Italian neighborhood of North Beach. Everyone who works here seems to have come from the old country, including the chef, who has designed a quintessential Irish brunch menu. Dishes include French toast made with Irish soda bread; farm eggs prepared any way you like and accompanied by bacon, sausages, or ham steak; and black or white pudding. ♦ Su 10AM-4PM. 622 Green St (between Columbus Ave and Powell St). 989.6222

Postrio Set in the heart of **Downtown,** Wolfgang Puck's Northern California outpost is well known as a great lunch and dinner spot—especially if you're into people watching—but it's largely overlooked at breakfast time. Too bad, because the master chefs here cook just as well in the morning as they do the rest of the day. Don't miss the oyster and pancetta omelette; the apple pancakes with a caramelized apple syrup; or the three-cheese omelette. And the glamorous dining room with its huge, dramatic staircase makes an impressive setting for the wonderful food. ♦ M-F 7AM-10AM; Sa-Su 9AM-2PM. 545 Post St (between Mason and Taylor Sts), Union Square. 776.7825; fax 776.6702 ♿

Rendezvous du Monde If you find yourself downtown on a weekday morning, this family-run cafe is a good choice for breakfast. During the week, the fare is simple, with various kinds of toast (including whole-wheat raisin), homemade pastry and muffins, bagels and cream cheese, and a fruit plate. (The special, featuring a large orange juice, pastry, and coffee, costs less than $5—a real bargain.) And on Saturday, there's a more extensive brunch menu with herb-scrambled eggs, Italian mushroom and egg scramble, an Applewood-smoked bacon omelette, granola, and a variety of coffees, including espresso drinks. ♦ M-F 8:30AM-11AM; Sa 11AM-3:30PM. 431 Bush St (between Claude La and Grant Ave), Union Square. 392.3332

Sears Fine Foods The setting is decidedly informal, the environment bare-bones, but this downtown spot gets awfully crowded nevertheless. Perhaps it's the menu of straightforward breakfast classics, prepared from scratch with skill and dedication; or maybe it's the down-to-earth, matronly waitresses who give every customer a warm welcome. At any rate, this place is definitely worth a stop. The most popular dish—and with good reason—is the Swedish pancakes. Breakfast is served all day. ♦ W-Su. 439 Powell St (between Post and Sutter Sts), Union Square. 986.1160

17 Mel's Drive-In ★$ A branch of the chain of glitzy diners, it appeals to kids and those who once used "neat" to mean "cool." The fare includes respectable hamburgers and fries, sandwiches, meat loaf, pork chops, chicken-fried steaks, salads, and all the breakfast standards. Small jukeboxes sit on almost every table and dot the bowling alley–length counter. ◆ American ◆ Daily breakfast, lunch, and dinner. No credit cards accepted. 3355 Geary Blvd (between Parker and Beaumont Aves). 387.2244; fax 387.1259 ₺ Also at: Numerous locations throughout the city

18 Pat O'Shea's Mad Hatter ★★$$ Don't be intimidated by the sign out front that says, "We cheat tourists and drunks." This popular, convivial Irish pub serves some of the best lunches in the city in a room chock-full of television sets and sports paraphernalia. Renowned chef Nancy Oakes of the glitzy **Boulevard** got her start here. Tony Ngo, then her sous-chef, now works the kitchen, turning out roast salmon on a bed of garlicky mashed potatoes with a touch of herbal beurre blanc; fish-and-chips served with cole slaw; homey chicken potpie; and pot roast with mashed potatoes. For lighter appetites, the menu offers several salads, including Caesar salad with grilled chicken breast and autumn salad with grilled chicken, greens, apples, and bacon. And the crème brûlée in this drinkers' paradise is much better than average. ◆ American ◆ M-F lunch and dinner; Sa-Su brunch and dinner. 3848 Geary Blvd (between Second and Third Aves). 752.3148; fax 751.2285 ₺

18 Bella Trattoria ★★$$ In the former site of **L'Avenue** is this new trattoria with light-colored walls, disc-shaped halogen lights, and a friendly ambience. Co-owner Alessandro Iacobelli can always be found in the dining room, greeting people with an ingratiating charm that makes regulars and new customers alike feel right at home. You can't go wrong ordering one of the seafood specials; other good choices are gratinée polenta with mushrooms and gorgonzola; carpaccio accented with lemon, capers, parmesan cheese, and extra virgin olive oil; and boneless breast of duck stuffed with mushrooms and pancetta and napped with a sauce flavored with orange. The star of the dessert list is the tiramisù, a creamy confection with just the right amount of chocolate and alcohol. In good weather, there's outdoor seating. ◆ Italian ◆ Daily dinner. 3854 Geary Blvd (at Third Ave). 221.0305

19 Le Soleil ★★$ This Vietnamese spot extends a warm family welcome amid pleasant surroundings. Tables are dressed with gray cloths and napkins, the walls with muted pink-and-aqua–striped wallpaper. The terrific appetizers include the chicken salad—a mound of steamed meat with a tangle of cabbage, carrots, and browned garlic—and the flavorful marinated-beef salad. Another top starter is the do-it-yourself imperial rolls: You roll up rice noodles, cilantro, mint, and fish sauce in lettuce leaves, then bite into their excitingly varied tastes and textures. For main courses, try the aromatic five-spice chicken; spicy lemongrass chicken accented with citrus; or crunchy fried egg noodles topped with shrimp, chicken, mushrooms, sugar snap peas, carrots, and other vegetables. With more than 60 dishes on the menu, however, the kitchen is bound to have a weakness: It's seafood. ◆ Vietnamese ◆ Daily lunch and dinner. 133 Clement St (between Second and Third Aves). 668.4848; fax 751.2616

ALAIN RONDELLI
SAN FRANCISCO

20 Alain Rondelli ★★★$$$ Chef Alain Rondelli arrived in San Francisco from France with impressive credentials. He had worked for six years in Marc Meneau's three-star restaurant, cooked at Palais de L'Elysée (the French White House), and been executive chef at Le Mas de Chastelas in Saint-Tropez. However, San Francisco so captivated him that he gave up his quest for Michelin stars and took a job at **Ernie's.** Three years later he opened this intimate 48-seat establishment. The simple decor, with pearlescent white walls and upholstered banquettes, provides a serene stage for Rondelli's creations. His changing menu features a half-dozen appetizers and as many main courses. One starter is mussels in orange soup with a hint of saffron; while the pears and roquefort with Champagne vinegar and black pepper make a stunning starter, as does foie gras molded around a black Mission fig and served with warm brioche. Thai snapper is pan roasted with eggplant; while a crispy fried salmon is accompanied by black chanterelles and wild rice pilaf. Six-, nine-, and 12-course tasting menus are available by prior arrangement. Desserts are often preceded by a pink, billowy cone of cotton candy—Rondelli's attempt at whimsy. Fantastic finales include apple upside-down cake with caramel ice cream and crème anglaise, and a selection of flavorful sorbets, ice cream, and madelines. One occasional glitch, however, is that sometimes food is not hot enough when served. ◆ French ◆ T-Su dinner. Reservations recommended. 126 Clement St (between Second and Third Aves). 387.0408

21 Murasaki ★★★$ Chef/owner Toshi Sasaki works with quiet intensity at this comfortable restaurant favored by local sushi chefs. He produces some of the freshest sushi in the city, including mellow *hamachi* (yellowtail) with its silken texture, more strongly flavored *saba* (pickled mackerel), and sake-cured velvety salmon. What also makes the sushi so wonderful is the perfect rice that has enough stickiness to hold the grains together, yet is not starchy or mushy. Other menu items include tempura and deep-fried, soft-shell crabs in season. The simple decor features white, battened walls, a well-worn carpet, and chairs adorned with cartoon characters. There are even pictures of Sasaki's children on the walls behind where he produces his wonders, and on slower nights you'll find his family here enjoying the fruits of his labors. Unfortunately, the staff tends to shower its attention on regulars only; occasional or first-time visitors often get a cool reception. ♦ Japanese ♦ Daily dinner. 211 Clement St (between Third and Fourth Aves). 668.7317

22 Fountain Court ★★$ The Shanghai-inspired fare here is a delight. A good way to start is with the Shanghai steamed buns, which are filled with ginger-laced pork and herbs and set on thin slices of cucumber in a bamboo steamer. Braised beef, served in half-moon slices, is redolent of five-spice powder, and lion's head is a well-executed classic: Five browned balls of ground pork are arranged over crunchy bok choy and a pool of intensely flavored meat sauce. Another standout is plump prawns combined with rice wine, garlic, ginger, and minced pork. The friendly host will guide overwhelmed diners through the long menu. The only drawback: the glaring lightbulbs; choose seats on the more subdued lower level, where large windows overlook the street. ♦ Chinese ♦ Daily lunch and dinner. Reservations recommended. 354 Clement St (at Fifth Ave). 668.1100; fax 668.1123

22 Happy Supermarket If the name doesn't make you smile, surely the ceiling-high selection of Asian products will. The aisles are packed with all kinds of ingredients—Chinese, Thai, and Filipino. The produce is pristine, including mustard greens with their yellow flowers intact, big water chestnuts, and delicate pea shoots. Fresh meat and fish are featured, and frozen foods include sausages, dim sum, and grated coconut. Also available are durian (whole or cleaned), green soy beans, an array of canned and powdered curries, and hundreds of sauces. ♦ Daily. No credit cards accepted. 400 Clement St (at Sixth Ave). 221.3195; fax 221.8137 ♿

23 New Golden Turtle ★$$ Once, this and its sister restaurant (the **Golden Turtle** in Pacific Heights) were *the* outposts for the city's best Vietnamese food. But the owners sold this

location about a year ago, and although the menu has remained the same, the food no longer rates as highly as that found in the Pacific Heights branch. The best dishes are crisp imperial rolls and five-spice chicken. The interior is an exotic oasis of plants and bamboo appointments, including a bamboo ship on the wall. ♦ Vietnamese ♦ M dinner; Tu-Su lunch and dinner. 308 Fifth Ave (between Geary Blvd and Clement St). 221.5285

24 Toy Boat Dessert Cafe ★★$ The squeals of delighted children fill this classic ice-cream and dessert parlor. Kids love climbing onto the mechanical prancing horse in the center of the room, and they can't resist the vast collection of playthings, ranging from nostalgic tin toys to rubber figures of such popular characters as the Lion King, the Hunchback of Notre Dame, and the Muppets. In addition to ice cream, there are coffee drinks and some killer desserts with adult appeal. Try the peanut-butter-and-chocolate-cookie sandwich; the good old-fashioned blackberry pie with a flaky crust; the Black Satin cake; or the mildly tart Key lime pie. ♦ Cafe/Ice-cream parlor ♦ Daily. 401 Clement St (at Fifth Ave). 751.7505

24 Taiwan Restaurant ★★★$ Don't miss the pork-filled boiled dumplings, roasted chicken, or lion's head (big pork balls in a clay pot with cabbage) among the Shanghai dishes available here. Another winner is wok-fried Shanghai noodles—fat, doughy noodles topped with strips of pork and other vegetables. The small dining room, cast in shades of pink, is packed with tables and always busy, so the waiters move at a frantic pace. Expect a wait unless you go early or late. The Chinatown branch is generally less busy. ♦ Chinese ♦ Daily lunch and dinner; F-Sa until midnight. 445 Clement St (at Sixth Ave). 387.1789 ♿ Also at: 289 Columbus Ave (at Broadway), Chinatown. 989.6789

25 Café Riggio ★$$ The main challenge here is getting in; no reservations are accepted for parties smaller than six, so patrons squeeze into a small bar area to wait. Once seated in the dining room—which is decorated with photos of Italy and light fixtures made of inverted terra-cotta flowerpots—they're served at a rapid clip. The food's good, but it may not be worth the wait. Spinach salad topped with marinated squid is a nice starter. Follow with pasta or one of the half-dozen veal dishes, including scaloppini topped with a mound of mushrooms infused with basil, garlic, and sun-dried tomatoes. ♦ Italian ♦ Daily dinner. 4112 Geary Blvd (between Fifth and Sixth Aves). 221.2114; fax 387.9119 &

25 Brothers Restaurant ★★$$ One of the best Korean places featuring tabletop barbecues, this dining spot offers a long list of grilling possibilities, including beef hearts. The *kimchi*, a spicy pickled cabbage that ests a Korean kitchen's mettle, is excellent here. If you're not up for do-it-yourself cooking, several hot and cold noodle dishes are available. ♦ Korean ♦ Daily lunch and dinner. 4128 Geary Blvd (between Fifth and Sixth Aves). 387.7991

25 Le Cyrano ★★$ A charming French restaurant with tieback curtains separating the dining areas, gleaming chandeliers, and an atmosphere that encourages conversation, it's a throwback to another era. But the food isn't tired, just a tad indulgent: Many sauces are lavished with butter and cream, bringing harmony to the dish and a smile to the face. With a nod to today's restraint, the menu also offers a number of low-fat choices. Most of the entrées are very reasonably priced, and for a slight additional charge, rich onion soup, house salad, and a choice of desserts are included. Best bets include rack of lamb marinated with juniper berries and served with hunter's sauce (wine, shallots, and herbs); red snapper poached in wine with mushroom cream sauce; frogs' legs with garlic and tomatoes; and sweetbreads with Madeira cream sauce. For dessert, go for the classic profiteroles or the ambrosial Grand Marnier soufflé—you won't be sorry. ♦ French ♦ Tu-Su dinner. 4134 Geary Blvd (between Fifth and Sixth Aves). 387.1090; fax 387.1090

26 Angkor Wat ★★$$ Established in the early 1980s, this is thought to be the first Cambodian restaurant in the US. And it still remains one of the best today. Start with the minted carrots with peanuts, pork, and shrimp in a lemon dressing; the vegetable soup, which gets added texture from toasted rice; or the Cambodian-style crepe, filled with chicken, shrimp, bean sprouts, and other vegetables. Main courses include a duck curry with undercurrents of tropical fruit, and a fiery lamb curry in a rich, red sauce. The grilled chicken, marinated overnight, also is outstanding. The dining room has an exotic, cavelike feel, enhanced by the handsome folk art collection and the Cambodian dancer who performs on a stage in the rear. ♦ Cambodian ♦ M-Sa lunch and dinner; Su dinner. 4217 Geary Blvd (between Sixth and Seventh Aves). 221.7887; fax 221.4408 &

27 Cinderella Restaurant and Bakery ★$ This place has been touted as one of San Francisco's top Russian restaurants and bakeries since the mid-1960s. Top items include *pelmeny,* Russian ravioli stuffed with seasoned beef and served in a pleasant chicken broth; lamb with kasha; and stuffed peppers and cabbage. The soft-crusted homemade breads are excellent examples of the Russian baking style. There's often a wait, but never for too long. ♦ Russian ♦ Tu-Su lunch and dinner. 436 Balboa St (between Fifth and Sixth Aves). 751.9690 &

KATIA'S

28 Katia's ★★$$ Although it calls itself a Russian tearoom, it's actually a full-fledged restaurant, serving home-style food lightened with a Californian touch. Start with smoked salmon or piquant marinated mushrooms to wake up the palate. Then there's *pozharski* (a patty of herbed, minced chicken), sautéed and served with roasted potatoes; beef stroganoff rich with mushrooms; golden, flaky piroshki; and cabbage stuffed with beef and rice, baked in an intense tomato sauce. And don't miss the homemade dill pickles. Desserts—perhaps cheesecake or berry pudding—are uneven in quality. The service tends to be friendly but inefficient. Cheerful African violets are set on each white-clothed table, and mirrors expand the tiny room. The floor-to-ceiling windows in front are opened in warm weather. ♦ Russian ♦ Tu-Su lunch and dinner. 600 Fifth Ave (at Balboa St). 668.9292 &

29 Jakarta ★★$$ Charming and popular, this Indonesian restaurant is painted white, a dramatic backdrop for its folk-art collection of hand puppets, masks, and figurines. Tables set with batik place mats under glass, upholstered chairs, and a burgundy carpet make a pretty setting for the often fiery food. Crisp shrimp cakes studded with corn, bean sprouts, and chilies are an excellent way to begin. Main courses are divided into vegetarian dishes, grills, and fried and braised options, and the kitchen handles each technique with aplomb. Chicken is soaked in a spicy marinade to produce a tongue-tingling treat; rock cod, wrapped in banana leaves and grilled, boasts a moist, silken texture; and oxtails, infused with a chili-laced coconut-milk sauce, come out fork tender. ◆ Indonesian ◆ Tu-F lunch and dinner; Sa-Su dinner. 615 Balboa St (between Seventh and Eighth Aves). 387.5225; fax 387.0233

30 Mandalay ★★$ Opened in 1984, San Francisco's first Burmese restaurant is still one of the best. The storefront surroundings don't add much to the dining experience, but the pleasant service and exotic food certainly do. In general, the Burmese specialties are much better than the Mandarin (Chinese) selections. Start with the tea salad—piles of green tea leaves, toasted lentils, ground shrimp, fried garlic, green pepper, and sesame seeds, all tossed tableside in a sprightly vinaigrette. A similar rendition substitutes shredded fresh ginger for the tea and is just as enticing. Other attractions: Burmese-style fish chowder, thick with coconut milk and noodles; Mandalay squid, served steamed on a bed of spinach; fried onions in a hot-and-sour sauce; and crisp, stir-fried green beans. ◆ Burmese/Mandarin ◆ Daily lunch and dinner. 4348 California St (between Fifth and Sixth Aves). 386.3895; fax 386.3895 &

GREEN APPLE BOOKS

31 Green Apple Books Lavish displays of glossy books aren't this bookstore's forte, but it has one of the best selections of new and used cookbooks in the city (and it keeps late hours to accommodate the insomniac bookworms among us). There's even a full shelf of classics, which might include *Thoughts for Buffets,* published in 1958; *The Home Dietitian's Cook Book,* published in 1938; or *Cooking For Two,* first published in 1909. ◆ Daily (M-F until 11PM; F-Sa until midnight). 506 Clement St (between Sixth and Seventh Aves). 387.2272; fax 387.2377 &

32 Richmond New May Wah Market A branch of the Chinatown **May Wah Market,** this supermarket likewise offers all the essential products for Vietnamese, Chinese, Korean, and Thai cooking. Fish and poultry are arranged on tubs in front of the display case and in crates in the narrow aisles (making it hard for two people to squeeze by), and *kimchi* is dished up from open containers in the refrigerator case. The produce aisles hold roots and tubers (including lotus, sweet potatoes, and onions), plus huge bins of Thai purple basil, lemongrass, and other specialty herbs. ◆ Daily. 547 Clement St (between Sixth

and Seventh Aves). 668.2583; fax 666.3933 & Also at: Numerous locations throughout the city

32 6th Avenue Cheese Shop Blue and white checkered curtains freshen this tiny shop, which has a small selection of cheese, all kinds of take-out salads and sandwiches, breads, and other gourmet products. A few small tables in the front are available for eating in-house. ◆ Daily. 311 Sixth Ave (between Geary Blvd and Clement St). 387.1436

HAIG'S
Middle Eastern Specialty Foods

33 Haig's Delicacies Established in 1956, this shop is the place to go for Middle Eastern take-out treats—sheep's milk feta from three countries, piquant dolmas, hummus, excellent tahini, falafel and *kufta* (a spiced hamburger) sandwiches, coffees and teas, and a half-dozen phyllo desserts. Customers can also eat at one of the tables in the front. In addition, the shop also stocks such unusual products as pomegranate syrup (great for marinating ducks or pork, or for sprinkling on desserts) and packaged soups from Turkey. And the array of spices available here will dazzle the senses of any gourmet cook. ◆ M-Sa. 642 Clement St (between Seventh and Eighth Aves). 752.6283 &

The Village Market

34 The Village Market This popular neighborhood market stands out from other similar food shops because of its organic merchandise. Its shelves are stocked with a variety of organic fresh and frozen fruits and vegetables, coffees, specialty mustards, canned truffles, and some organic wines. ◆ Daily. No credit cards accepted. 4555 California St (at Eighth Ave). 221.0445 &

35 San Francisco Chicken/New On Sang Market Here's a Chinese spin on fast food, and it's also a study in cultural amalgamation. The decor is Western, with ceramic tiles, neon logos, and illuminated menu boards. And a rotisserie turns out stupendous herb-crusted chicken, served with corn on the cob, Caesar salad, and baked beans. But other sections display bins of raw chicken parts, trays of Chinese stir-fried dishes, and ribs and ducks hanging on hooks. The focal point, however, is a whole suckling pig; the chef hacks off pieces to your specifications, and the pork has a marvelous crisp skin, robust taste, and succulent texture. Takeout is the mainstay here, although there are a half-dozen stools and a low counter for eating in-house. This place is under the same ownership as

Chinatown's **New On Sang Poultry Company.** ◆ Tu-Su 4-9PM. 617 Clement St (between Seventh and Eighth Aves). 752.4100; fax 750.8242 ᕐ Also at: 1114 Grant Ave (between Pacific Ave and Broadway), Chinatown. 982.9228 ᕐ

36 **Cafe Maisonette** ★★★$$ Chef Ronald Tseng turns out impressive French fare in his shoe-box–size restaurant (there are just nine tables), decorated with sky-blue walls, lace curtains, and a latticework ceiling. The soups are excellent, and the duck confit salad with tiny greens is a classic. Tseng prepares a perfect rack of lamb with a Port-and-shallot demi-glace, drizzled with a creamy dressing of chopped mint and served with garlic-thyme potato pancakes, a specialty. Pork medaillons get a zing from green peppercorns and mustard, and chicken is rolled around a spinach stuffing before being roasted to bronze perfection. Generally, a choice of two desserts is offered, perhaps truffle cake with Grand Marnier or a fresh fruit torte. And Tseng often presents each departing diner with a small box containing a triangle of rich chocolate cake. ◆ French ◆ Tu-Su dinner. Reservations recommended. 315 Eighth Ave (between Geary Blvd and Clement St). 387.7992

37 **Clement Street Bar and Grill** ★$$ In traditional San Francisco fashion, this grill has a masculine ambience, with dark wood paneling and white tablecloths. In addition to the simple grilled meats, poultry, and seafood, it's one of the few places in the neighborhood that serve such creative pastas as rigatoni with fresh tuna, roasted peppers, and tomatoes, and asparagus ravioli with spinach, garlic, and parmesan. ◆ American ◆ Tu-F lunch and dinner; Sa-Su brunch. 708 Clement St (between Eighth and Ninth Aves). 386.2200

38 **Seafood Center** On any given day, the dozen enormous fish tanks here are packed with live fish, shellfish, turtles, and frogs. There also are periwinkles, Manila and cherrystone clams, and green-lipped mussels, all at much-lower-than-supermarket prices. Iced and refrigerated cases hold octopus, Hawaiian *hasa hasa,* and other whole and filleted fish. ◆ Daily. No credit cards accepted. 831 Clement St (between Ninth and 10th Aves). 752.3496; fax 752.3518 ᕐ

39 **No. 1 Dumpling House** ★★$ Most of the menu at this plain, tiny storefront operation is run-of-the-mill, but the *chiao-tzu* (boiled dumplings) are truly wonderful. The owner is originally from Northern China, where these dumplings are a specialty. The irregularly shaped treats are filled with enticing ingredients, such as minced shrimp, flat pungent chives and garlic, and minced pork with cabbage. They come with a good dipping sauce—perhaps

chicken stock with soy sauce and green onions or hot chili paste. A couple of orders of dumplings and a plate of sautéed spinach or Chinese broccoli make a great meal—and the prices are unbelievably low. ◆ Chinese ◆ Daily lunch and dinner. 832 Clement St (between Ninth and 10th Aves). 221.2699

39 **Singapore Malaysian** ★$ Malaysian food is quite distinct from other Asian cuisines, but it's not well represented in the United States. That's why this tiny restaurant is such a treat. It's known for its salad of fruits and vegetables, which is tossed in a dressing spiced with fermented shrimp, chilies, and sesame seeds. Green beans are sautéed until crisp with a fiery mixture of chilies, herbs, and spices, an interesting variation on a standard Chinese dish. Rice noodles are another specialty ◆ Malaysian ◆ M, W-Su lunch and dinner. 836 Clement St (between Ninth and 10th Aves). 750.9518

CORIYA

39 **Coriya** ★★$ This Korean cook-it-yourself place has been packed from its opening day a few years ago. Mirrored walls, white tile floors, and black accents give it a bright, modern appeal. Each table is equipped with a burner, a hot pot of steaming water, a foil-covered tray for sautéing, and a strong vent to disperse the cooking smoke. Diners line up at the all-you-can-eat buffet to choose their ingredients from the heaps of raw sea-food, meat, poultry, eggs, vegetables, and condiments. It's amazingly inexpensive, and it's fun creating your own dishes. If you don't like the results, you know who's to blame. ◆ Korean ◆ M-Tu, Th-Su lunch and dinner; W dinner. 852 Clement St (at 10th Ave). 387.7888 ᕐ

40 **Royal Thai** ★$ Although many say this is the city's best Thai restaurant, it's not nearly as good as the original outpost in San Rafael. The kitchen washes many of the dishes in sweetness and tones down the spicing. But all the standards are here, including chicken and coconut-milk soup; chicken with basil; and Thai crepe, an airy pancake filled with shrimp, pork, peanuts, and tofu. Regulars also like the pad thai and the green papaya salad with green beans, carrots, and peanuts. The room is divided into a bar and dining areas; tables by the windows are best. ◆ Thai ◆ M-F lunch and dinner; Sa-Su dinner. 951 Clement St (at 11th Ave). 386.1795 ᕐ

41 **Boudin Bakery** One of the best-known bakery chains in the Bay Area, it started at this modest location with a retail shop in front and the plant in back. The sourdough bread is a

classic; also not to be missed is the *pain au chocolat,* a buttery croissant that is loaded with chocolate. Just skip the weak, bitter coffee. ♦ M-Sa. No credit cards accepted. 399 10th Ave (at Geary Blvd). 221.1210; fax 221.3854 ♿ Also at: Numerous locations throughout the city

Heavenly Hot Restaurant

麻辣潮烤自助火鍋城

42 Heavenly Hot ★$$ Specializing in *shabu shabu* (the cook-it-yourself hot pots), this tiny, popular Korean place was originally owned by the same people who run **Coriya**. Its booths are separated by light wood screens that look like a cross between Korean and Craftsman. The buffet line is stocked with raw fish, meat, and vegetables; diners make their selections, take them back to the table, and cook them all up in a copper pot. Some tables are also equipped with an aluminum-foil tray for sautéing. ♦ Korean ♦ Daily lunch and dinner. 4627 Geary Blvd (between 10th and 11th Aves). 750.1818 ♿

43 Chiang Mai Thai ★★$$ Silk plants and flowers splash color all over this Thai cafe, where each table is set with a bright bouquet of silk posies. Other adornments include a rose-colored ceiling, intricate wood detailing, and paned windows in back that reveal a fountain and lush greenery. The food is fresh-tasting, too. The kitchen produces standard Thai dishes and isn't afraid to use spices liberally: Green-curry chicken, smoothed with coconut milk, is fiery enough to clear the sinuses. The sautéed ground pork is served in a bowl, accompanied by cooling cucumber slices. Beef salad, another standard menu item, has a wonderful balance of flavors and leans toward savory seasoning rather than sweet. Plus, the service is unusually accommodating. ♦ Thai ♦ M-F lunch; daily dinner. 5020 Geary Blvd (between 14th and 15th Aves). 387.1299

43 House of Bagels Popular since the early 1960s, this shop resembles a bakery warehouse, piled high with bags of bagels. In addition to the dozen or so kinds of bagels, it sells good bread, including egg twists, whole wheat, and corn. ♦ Daily. No credit cards accepted. 5030 Geary Blvd (between 14th and 15th Aves). 752.6000; fax 752.6003 ♿

44 Kabuto Sushi ★★★$$ By most accounts, this is the top place for sushi in the entire city; it's certainly the most entertaining and friendly sushi bar around. Owner Sachio Kojima and his young assistant are in constant motion, and the best views are from the long, curved counter (there is also table seating). Kojima always offers diners a complimentary tidbit, perhaps a bowl of cooked tuna pieces. Barbecued eel is served piping hot, and conch, cooked in its shell in a sake broth, is brought flaming to the table. Everything is fresh as can be. Among the exceptional offerings are white tuna and the flying-fish roe served with a raw quail egg nestled in the middle. A full Japanese menu is also available, but sushi is the main attraction. Upon leaving, you'll get a bow and a warm goodbye from the staff. ♦ Sushi/Japanese ♦ Tu-Su dinner. 5116 Geary Blvd (between 15th and 16th Aves). 752.5652; fax 386.0149

44 Shenson's The oldest Jewish deli in San Francisco, it's been around since 1933. The corned-beef sandwiches and egg creams are winners, and the dill pickles and pickled green tomatoes are the best in town. The deli also offers homemade soups and entrées for takeout, as well as frozen kreplach (chewy dumplings) for you to use in your own chicken soup. ♦ Daily. 5120 Geary Blvd (between 15th and 16th Aves). 751.4699; fax 751.4794 ♿

Hong Kong Flower Lounge Restaurant

45 Hong Kong Flower Lounge Restaurant ★★★$$ Among the best and prettiest of the Hong Kong–style restaurants, this branch of the decade-old place on the Peninsula is always bustling. Glazed green tiles and red swagged valences add a dash of style to the warren of rooms. Fish tanks in back display the daily seafood selection, but don't expect much help from the harried staff. Top menu choices are Peking duck; crab bathed in wine sauce; minced squab in lettuce cups; wok-charred calamari topped with fried peppers; roast chicken; dry-braised green beans; and roast baby pig with pickled vegetables (a frequent special). ♦ Chinese ♦ Daily lunch and dinner. 5322 Geary Blvd (between 17th and 18th Aves). 668.8998; fax 668.0318 ♿

46 Joe's ★★$ A classic ice-cream parlor, this utilitarian place makes its own ice cream. The chocolate–peanut butter and the mocha–chocolate chip versions win raves, as do just about all of the 40 flavors. The root beer swirl, something like a frozen float, is worth the visit alone. There's also a grill here, so if you prefer savory to sweet, opt for a good hot dog, grilled cheese sandwich, or hamburger. ♦ Ice-cream parlor/American ♦ M-Th, Su until 10PM; F-Sa until 11PM. No credit cards accepted. 5351 Geary Blvd (at 18th Ave). 751.1950 ♿

47 Tip Toe Inn Many Russian families make an Easter tradition of a trip to this 1950s-era shop to purchase *kulich* (a tall, cylindrical Russian fruitcake). While they're here, they might also pick up bread and select from a case of frozen main courses and classic Russian favorites, many of which are produced on site. ◆ M-Sa. No credit cards accepted. 5423 Geary Blvd (between 18th and 19th Aves). 221.6422

47 Odessa One of the Russian delicatessens to spring up in recent years, this bright, clean shop offers a broad array of individually wrapped Russian candies; the selection fills most of one wall. Other products include Russian mineral water, farmer cheese, very rich Russian-style yogurt, at least a dozen kinds of smoked fish, and *pelmeny*. Most of the staff speaks little or no English, so you may have to point to what you want. ◆ Daily. No credit cards accepted. 5427 Geary Blvd (between 18th and 19th Aves). 666.DELI; fax 666.3370 ♿

48 Moscow and Tbilisi Bakery On Sunday afternoons, when most bake shops are quiet, customers line up at this Russian bakery. It turns out at least eight kinds of breads, cream puffs, and other confections, as well as sweet yeast rolls and piroshki. The display case at the entrance holds such savory deli items as pickled tomatoes and sour cabbage. ◆ Daily. No credit cards accepted. 5540 Geary Blvd (between 19th and 20th Aves). 668.6959 ♿

49 Laghi ★★★$$$ The spirit of a true Italian trattoria is captured at this corner storefront. (Just overlook the decor: The blue-heart ceiling borders would be more at home in a Midwestern country kitchen.) The short menu—only a few appetizers, four pastas, five main courses, and two desserts—changes nightly, and every item's a winner. All pasta is made in-house. The polenta, topped with a variety of mushrooms, is smooth and creamy. Equally good entrées might be a combination of roast duck and venison topped with sliced portobello mushrooms, or wonderful oxtails braised in red wine. And the service couldn't be more convivial; chef/owner Gino Laghi makes the rounds to see if diners are enjoying their meal, and he basks in their praise. ◆ Northern Italian ◆ Tu-Su dinner. 1801 Clement St (at 19th Ave). 386.6266

50 Vegi Food ★$ No dairy, meat, onions, or garlic are served at this Chinese vegetarian eatery, but the food still has a rib-sticking quality. Dumplings are plumped with cabbage, braised eggplant acquires a meaty flavor from its rich sauce, and brown rice mixed with mushrooms is moistened with an explosively spicy curry sauce. One of the best dishes on the menu is fried walnuts coated with a delicate sweet-and-sour sauce studded with carrot coins, pineapple, and bits of tomato and bell pepper. The spicy fare cries out for beer, but soft drinks will have to do; there's no liquor license. The servers are friendly, but the spartan decor (brown paneling, Formica tables, bare floors) doesn't encourage lingering. ◆ Chinese/Vegetarian ◆ Tu-Su lunch and dinner. No credit cards accepted. 1820 Clement St (between 19th and 20th Aves). 387.8111

51 Israel Kosher Meats The only kosher meat market in San Francisco, it has a homey feel—just a bit frayed around the edges, with boxes stacked helter-skelter. Long a gathering place for the area's Russian-Jewish population, it also draws shoppers from all over the city. A complete line of fresh beef, chicken, and lamb is cut to order. A freezer case holds fish and all kinds of kosher convenience foods, including frozen dinners. The deli department features a number of sandwich meats, freshly prepared pierogi and kugel, as well as desserts like strudel. Also available are packaged products and kosher wines. ◆ M-F, Su. 5621 Geary Blvd (between 20th and 21st Aves). 752.3064 ♿

51 Vishal India Restaurant ★$ Chef Surinder Kuman worked at **Gaylord India Restaurant** before opening this place, where vegetarian dishes are among the best choices. Garlic nan, onion *kulcha* (onion-filled nan), *baigan bharta* (eggplant with potatoes and peas), and *saag paneer* (spinach with cheese) are all winners. From the tandoori oven come chicken wings and boneless chicken breast marinated in mint and cilantro; both are excellent. The restaurant stretches over three rooms; the blue walls are bedecked with sequined hangings depicting the Taj Mahal. ◆ Indian ◆ Daily lunch and dinner. 5625 Geary Blvd (between 20th and 21st Aves). 751.2975; fax 751.2979

In the Gay Nineties, the Cliff House was not just a place with a great view. It also had a racy reputation for its wild parties, featuring drunkenness and general disorderly conduct. Perhaps not surprisingly, it caught fire three times, which local clergymen claimed was the work of God.

An immigrant Chinese cook in San Francisco invented the dish that is called a Denver sandwich west of the Mississippi and a Western sandwich in the eastern US. Recipe: In a little oil, sauté some chopped ham with finely chopped onion and green bell pepper. Add one beaten egg and cook until set, turning once. Serve between two pieces of toast with a little ketchup.

The Sporting Life

Baseball great Joe DiMaggio was descended from a long line of Sicilian fishermen; his father, Giuseppe Paolo DiMaggio, fished in **San Francisco Bay** for his living. So it seemed the natural thing for DiMaggio to open a seafood restaurant in his hometown. **DiMaggio's** operated at 245 Jefferson Street on **Fisherman's Wharf** from 1937 until it was sold in 1984; it eventually became **Bobby Rubino's Place for Ribs,** which still is in business today.

Probably the most famous San Francisco eatery owned by a sports figure is **Lefty O'Doul's** (333 Geary St, between Powell and Mason Sts, 982.8900), located near **Union Square.** O'Doul gained prominence as a pitcher for the **Boston Red Sox** in the 1920s. His restaurant has been open since 1958, offering hofbrau-style food in a room filled with sports memorabilia.

Dante Benedetti became a local hero as the coach of the **University of San Francisco** baseball team, which he led from 1968 to 1989. His family established the **New Pisa Restaurant** (550 Green St, between Grant Ave and Stockton St, North Beach, 989.2289) in 1918; today it's owned by Tom Ginella. **The Trophy Room** is filled with Dante's prized trophies, and old-timers and sports buffs stop by frequently to talk sports with the famed ex-coach, who shows up here at lunch most days.

Of course San Francisco also has many sports bars that, while not owned by former athletes, are nonetheless magnets for lovers of football, baseball, soccer, and other sports. Even a stylish restaurant like **Moose's** in **North Beach** has two jumbo TV screens. Here's a list of some of the top sports spots in town:

Barley & Hops (55 Cyril Magnin St, between Eddy and Ellis Sts, Union Square, 392.8000), on the second floor of the **Parc 55 Hotel,** offers a casual menu of burgers and sandwiches in a smoke-free environment.

The Bus Stop (1901 Union St, at Laguna St, Cow Hollow, 567.6905) does not serve food, but it's a good place to hang out, grab a beer, and take in the sports action.

Greens Sports Bar (2239 Polk St, between Vallejo and Green Sts, Russian Hill, 775.4287) displays lots of sports memorabilia on the walls, and of course, there are plenty of TV sets; no food is served.

Pat O'Shea's Mad Hatter (3848 Geary Blvd, between Second and Third Aves, The Richmond, 752.3148) is a friendly Irish pub that serves a menu of terrific American snacks and entrées.

Perry's (1944 Union St, between Laguna and Buchanan Sts, Cow Hollow, 922.9022) offers tasty meat and fish dishes in a typically New York saloon setting.

52 Ton Kiang ★★★$$ A dressier and more ambitious version of its sister restaurant of the same name (see page 193), this Hakka-inspired, Hong Kong–style eatery is adorned with light wood booths, rose-colored walls, Chinese lanterns, patterned carpets, and white tablecloths. The dim sum, particularly the Shanghai dumplings, are excellent, and the kitchen adeptly prepares vegetables, be they bok choy, spinach, or *ong choy* (Chinese watercress). An entire menu of specialties is offered at night, but the one-page "special menu" highlights the best bets, perhaps tender pea shoots (in spring), thin slices of geoduck sautéed with chives and bean sprouts, or fresh frogs' legs served with ginger and asparagus. The delicious salt-baked chicken is always available. ◆ Chinese ◆ Daily lunch and dinner.
5821 Geary Blvd (between 22nd and 23rd Aves). 386.8530 ♿ Also at: 3148 Geary Blvd (at Spruce St). 752.4440

52 Thom's Natural Foods In business since 1964 (and at this location for about a decade), this market carries a fine selection of produce, including such hard-to-find items as Spanish black radishes and burdock root, as well as cheese and fresh chickens. Sunflower meal, soya flour, and protein powder are in the refrigerator section. A staffer is generally on hand to provide nutritional information and help customers choose from the wide selection of vitamins and herb extracts. There is also an excellent collection of natural-foods books. ◆ Daily. 5843 Geary Blvd (between 22nd and 23rd Aves). 387.6367; fax 387.9215

Socca

53 Socca Restaurant ★★★$$ This charming restaurant is named after the chickpea cake sold on the streets in southern France. The green-and-yellow–striped walls, lapis-colored bar, and tile floor have a modern, warm feel, making the dining room a fine showcase for John Caputo, former chef at the tony Jordan Winery in Sonoma and sous-chef at **Campton Place.** Caputo's food is much more complex than one might expect at a neighborhood spot, and it's only gotten better with time. The changing menu might list rich goose confit, topped with a stack of beer-battered, fried green beans, all moistened with an earthy truffle vinaigrette. Grilled pork chops, accompanied by crispy potato pancakes and creamy leeks, are the best in town. Lamb shank, browned and glazed, is served in a shallow pool of white beans with carrot spears, parsnips, and celery. And the trio of crème brûlées—lime, maple, and pumpkin—is a great way to end a meal. ◆ Mediterranean ◆ Tu-Su dinner. 5800 Geary Blvd (at 22nd Ave). 379.6720; fax 379.9666

53 La Vie Vietnamese Cuisine ★★$ The roast crab is not quite as good at this modern, plain establishment as at the **Jasmine House,** but it is still very satisfying. Other good bets are *banh xeo* (a delicate crepe made from rice flour) filled with tender bean sprouts, chicken, and shrimp; *banh hoi chao tom* (minced shrimp wrapped around a piece of sugar cane and served with rice noodles and a shrimp and bean dipping sauce); five-spice chicken; coconut prawns cooked in a clay pot; and (in season) pan-fried softshell crab. ◆ Vietnamese ◆ Daily lunch and dinner. 5830 Geary Blvd (between 22nd and 23rd Aves). 668.8080 ⌖

54 Yet Wah ★$$ Several **Yet Wah**s are scattered around the Bay Area, but only the name is the same—they are all under different ownership and offer very different dining experiences. This outpost offers larger quarters and a more civilized ambience than the popular Chinatown branch. Specialties on the menu here include glazed walnut prawns, scallops with ginger and garlic, chicken chow mein, and lemon chicken. ◆ Chinese ◆ Daily lunch and dinner. 2140 Clement St (between 22nd and 23rd Aves). 387.8040; fax 387.8333

55 La Belle Saison ★★$$ East meets West at chef Tadayuki Tani's welcoming corner restaurant. The exceptional onion soup is classic Paul Bocuse, topped with flaky puff pastry; the seafood salad falls in the Japanese camp, coming bathed in a dressing of plum paste, rice vinegar, miso, and olive oil (after all, a little Italian flair never hurt anyone). Presentation plays a major role here: Duck breast is splayed on a plate drizzled with blackberry sauce; salmon is brightened with tarragon and truffles. For dessert, the poached pear is a work of fine art, a perfect pear half filled with ice cream, perched on a pool of berry sauce. The dining room's not fancy, but makes a comfortable setting for the innovative and surprisingly moderately priced fare. ◆ Eclectic ◆ Tu-Su dinner. 200 23rd Ave (at California St). 751.7066; fax 751.7074

56 El Chico Produce Market The produce spilling onto the sidewalk and the milling crowds give this shop a farmers' market ambience. The quality of the produce offered here can be a bit tired sometimes, but prices are good, and there are always a few surprises, such as fresh horseradish and arrowroot. In addition to basic products and breads and pastries from **Cinderella Bakery** (see page 197), the shop also sells ingredients for Russian, Mexican, and Chinese cooking. ◆ Daily. No credit cards accepted. 2214 Clement St (between 23rd and 24th Aves). 752.7372 ⌖

57 Mescolanza ★★★$$ Squeezed into a block of Chinese restaurants, this homespun eatery is easy to miss, but it's definitely worth seeking out for the delicious Italian food. The pizza's cracker-crisp crust doesn't need any fancy toppings, and the gnocchi rivals that prepared by the most experienced Italian grandmother. Pastas are excellent, but the kitchen tends to ladle on too much sauce; if you prefer a bit more restraint, tell the waiters. Standouts among the meat courses are roast chicken and the veal with lemon and capers. The understated decor includes gray-blue walls adorned with plates and copper pots, blue-and-white checkered tablecloths, and a china cabinet near the entrance. ◆ Italian ◆ Daily dinner. 2221 Clement St (between 23rd and 24th Aves). 668.2221; fax 668.1905 ⌖

NARAI RESTAURANT

57 Narai ★★$ Glass bricks separating the kitchen from the dining room and metallic wallpaper are attractive enough, but the food here is much more stylish than the decor. The kitchen turns out both Thai and Chiu Chow Chinese dishes. Among the Thai offerings are chicken and coconut-milk soup and *larb ped,* chicken infused with lime and chilies. One of the Chinese delights is pompano, lightly breaded with rice flour, deep-fried, and sprinkled with garlic. The crisp fish comes with a choice of sauces, of which the best is the zingy lemon; it's accented with diced chilies, bell peppers, and carrots. Another standout is duck simmered in a sweet soy-based sauce and served with a puckery vinegar sauce. To round out the meal, try the Chinese broccoli, cooked to a tender crunch and laced with a confetti of fried garlic and strands of smoked fish. Attention, adventurous dessert eaters: This is one of the few places to sample durian, a spiky fruit with a pungent smell; it's served with taro pudding. ♦ Chinese/Thai ♦ Tu-Su lunch and dinner. 2229 Clement St (between 23rd and 24th Aves). 751.6363 &

58 Khan Toke Thai House ★★★$$ Far and away the prettiest Thai restaurant in the city, it resembles a serene Thai temple. Diners leave their shoes at the entrance and are seated at low, intricately carved tables positioned over pits that accommodate their legs. The rich wood paneling and ceiling work exhibit the best Thai craftsmanship, and the patio filled with blooming orchids lends a tropical feel to the place. Coconut-chicken soup is a velvety broth with succulent pieces of chicken and mushrooms; the prawn salad tastes intensely of lime and lemongrass, with just a touch of heat, creating a wonderfully balanced blend; and the duck salad has an earthy flavor and texture, thanks to the powdered rice that is sprinkled on top. An unusual main course is clear, chewy noodles tossed with Napa cabbage, celery, pork, shrimp, and squid in a faintly sweet sauce of pickled garlic. For dessert, have the fried bananas topped with a scoop of ice cream, which is decorated with cashews and currants. With its good wine list and food prices only slightly higher than at the city's more modest Thai places, this makes a fine setting for special occasions. ♦ Thai ♦ Daily dinner. 5937 Geary Blvd (between 23rd and 24th Aves). 668.6654; fax 386.1352

59 Jasmine House ★★★$ San Franciscans can get very passionate about good crab restaurants—and this Vietnamese place ranks high on nearly everybody's list. Among chef Nhan Nguyen's best creations is an authentic Vietnamese roast crab; the huge crustacean is quartered, then cooked in a butter and black pepper sauce. The result is heavenly. Another tasty item featured on the menu is barbecued catfish—its crackling skin caramelized from the heat of the grill—served with thin rice crepes and a dipping sauce of ginger, lemon grass, sugar, and fish. If you're unfamiliar with Vietnamese food, the staff is happy to assist you. ♦ Vietnamese ♦ Daily lunch and dinner. 2301 Clement St (at 24th Ave). 668.3382 &

60 Hong Kong Villa ★★★$$ Those in the know here start with prawns, scooped from a three-tiered fish tank, quickly steamed to sweet succulence, and served with a scallion-flecked soy dipping sauce. They're so good that diners don't mind having to do the messy chore of removing the heads, peels, and tails. Black cod, also netted from the tanks, is served salt-baked or steamed in sweet rice wine. Seafood is the prime attraction here, but don't ignore the crispy fried chicken, the clay-pot dishes, and the vegetable stir-fries (especially when pea shoots are in season). To end the meal, try the sweet soup of the day, which might be taro with swirls of egg whites and flecks of fresh water chestnuts. The lighting from two crystal chandeliers is harsh, but the room is softened by white tablecloths and walls painted in mint green and blue with pink trim. ♦ Chinese ♦ Daily lunch and dinner. 2332 Clement St (at 25th Ave). 752.8833 &

60 25th & Clement Produce Market Top-quality produce is the hallmark at this market; the selection isn't vast, but it's well chosen and maintained. There are also breads from some of the best bakeries, plus other specialty and everyday products. ♦ Daily. 2354 Clement St (at 25th Ave). 387.8222; fax 387.2437 &

61 Courtyard Bar and Grill ★$$ Bamboo furniture, leafy palms, skylights, and steel beams crisscrossing the ceiling imbue this expansive restaurant with the feel of a woodland retreat. Chef Tim Whalen has created a straightforward menu featuring lots of salads, pastas, and such dishes as chicken stuffed with ham, petrale sole stuffed with crab in a lobster cream sauce, and grilled filet mignon with béarnaise sauce. Sports fans happily gather around the bar's oversize video monitor to watch their favorite teams in action. ♦ Californian ♦ Daily lunch and dinner. 2436 Clement St (between 25th and 26th Aves). 387.7616; fax 387.6227 &

61 Greco-Romana ★★$$ Greek and Italian specialties are offered in a courtyardlike setting, with shuttered windows and flowerpot-filled balconies. Pizzas, tossed in the air and shaped before your eyes, are as good as the show. The thin crust is substantial enough to stand up to the dozen toppings, which include Canadian bacon with pineapple, and pesto with pine nuts and sun-dried tomatoes. Pasta with meat sauce and pasta shells with tuna are just as tasty. On the Greek side, just about any lamb dish is a winner; try the moussaka with ground lamb and eggplant, or the flaky *spanakopita* (spinach pie). ♦ Mediterranean ♦ Tu-Su lunch and dinner. 2448 Clement St (between 25th and 26th Aves). 387.0626; fax 751.1964 ♿

62 Blue Point ★★$$ This restaurant has a sleek, sophisticated look, with walls the color of pale buttercups, rich mahogany chairs and tables, and a serene atmosphere. Chef Tony Batchon offers a refined menu of classic seafood dishes like plump oysters on the half shell; house-smoked salmon served with *lebanni* (a Middle Eastern yogurt cheese); pasta with sautéed clams, prosciutto, sweet peas, and cream sauce; grilled salmon with Chardonnay sauce; and crab cioppino. And there's a succulent rib-eye steak splashed with olive oil for confirmed carnivores. ♦ Seafood ♦ Tu-Su dinner. 2415 Clement St (between 25th and 26th Aves). 379.9726

62 India Clay Oven ★★★$ This narrow dining room was a phenomenal success almost immediately. Luscious, marinated meats cooked in a 1,000° tandoori oven are the main attraction, but the rest of the menu is pretty good, too. Try the *bhaigan bharta* (a tandoori-roasted eggplant dish with a smoky flavor). The rather spartan decor is enlivened by some knicknacks and artifacts from India, and the service is friendly and helpful. ♦ Indian ♦ Daily lunch and dinner. 2435 Clement St (between 25th and 26th Aves). 751.0505

63 Mayflower Seafood Restaurant ★★★★$$ The four-page menu is filled with many Chinese favorites, but the specialty here is seafood. For a good sampling, try the seafood dinner (for four people), which includes steamed crab in wine sauce, sautéed conch, and scallops with tender greens. Other recommended dishes are minced squab; shrimp accompanied by fried milk (cubes of milk curd that are crisp outside and barely set inside); sweet shrimp and deep-fried milk

dumplings, with a silky interior; and roast chicken. Tapioca makes a warm, comforting finale. At lunch, there's excellent dim sum. Crystal chandeliers dominate the large room, making it brighter than day, whatever the hour. ♦ Chinese/Seafood ♦ Daily lunch and dinner. 6225 Geary Blvd (at 27th Ave). 387.8338; fax 387.1760

64 Shanghai King ★$ Don't be put off by the gaudy gold exterior or by the baskets of artificial plants hanging from the ceiling inside: This place makes some of the best dumplings in the city. Shanghai steamed dumplings as well as the boiled version with hot-and-spicy sauce will satisfy the most persnickety palates. Twenty soups are also featured, as well as nine chow mein dishes and a dozen noodle preparations, all at ridiculously low prices. ♦ Chinese ♦ Daily lunch and dinner. 3038 Clement St (between 31st and 32nd Aves). 751.8866; fax 751.6368

65 Upstairs at the Cliff House ★$$ Omelettes are served here from early morning to mid-afternoon. Among the 20 different combinations are Joe's Special, with ground beef, spinach, and onions, and a seafood version with shrimp, scallops, and mushrooms. The lunch menu also includes hot Reuben sandwiches, burgers, and cold sandwiches filled with tuna-pecan salad and shrimp salad. ♦ American ♦ Daily breakfast, lunch, and dinner. 1090 Point Lobos Ave (at Great Hwy), Second floor. 386.3330; fax 387.7837

66 Beach Chalet Restaurant & Brewery ★★★$$ For many years, **The Chalet** was a restaurant and meeting hall, but it closed in the 1980s, and the historic building was boarded up and abandoned. It continued to stand empty until 1994, when Lara and Greg Truppelli decided to buy it from the city and re-open it as a restaurant/brewpub. The dining room occupies the entire second floor of the building, right above the new **Golden Gate Visitors' Center,** and it houses a 15-barrel brewery. Five English-style ales are produced here, and there's a menu of such casual staples as spicy chicken wings, lamb braised in stout, a smoked trout platter, a double-cut pork chop, and rotisserie chicken. ♦ American ♦ Daily breakfast, lunch, and dinner. 1000 Great Hwy (between Lincoln Way and Fulton St). 386.8459; fax 753.5607 ♿

Beyond the Bridges

All the culinary wealth of the Bay Area isn't confined to San Francisco. In fact, **Chez Panisse**—the restaurant generally considered to be the birthplace of California cuisine—is in **Berkeley**, in the **East Bay.** Today the East Bay area is still on the gastronomic cutting edge, boasting dining spots with proven staying power, like **Bay Wolf** in **Oakland**, as well as newer ones that are destined to become lasting favorites, such as **Rivoli** in Berkeley. The East Bay is also more multicultural than San Francisco, hosting some of the best ethnic restaurants in the area, including **Ajanta Restaurant** in Berkeley and **Le Cheval Restaurant** and **Battambang** in Oakland. Just minutes from San Francisco across the **Bay Bridge**, Berkeley and Oakland are appropriate places to begin an exploration of restaurants beyond the city limits. Also nearby—just north of the **Golden Gate Bridge**—are the rolling hills and quaint towns of **Marin County**, a place synonymous with hot tubs and New Age thinking, perhaps because the terrain is so magical. Many of Marin's restaurants have wonderful outdoor decks, all the better to enjoy a climate that is more reliably sunny than the city.

Currently, the hottest area for new culinary ventures is the grapevine-covered **Napa Valley**, less than 100 miles northeast of San Francisco. The **Culinary Institute of America,** which has a campus geared to educating food industry professionals on the site of the former **Greystone** winery, has also established the **Wine Spectator Greystone Restaurant,** staffed by its graduates and students. In addition, a number of famous chefs have moved to the county, including Joachim Splichal, whose **Pinot Blanc** dining room has raised the level of culinary excellence in the Napa Valley; Jeremiah Tower, who opened **Stars Oakville Cafe,** an outpost of **Stars** and **Stars Cafe** in **Downtown** San Francisco; Jan Birnbaum, who left **Campton Place** to open the **Catahoula Restaurant and Saloon** in **Calistoga** as a showcase for his take on modern Creole cooking; and Thomas Keller, who made his reputation at Checkers Restaurant in Los Angeles and Rakel in New York before taking over the ever-popular **French Laundry** in **Yountville.**

Sprawling **Sonoma County,** birthplace of the California wine industry, is home to much of the state's general farmland. Perhaps the two best known areas are **Sonoma Valley** (which runs roughly from the town of **Sonoma** to **Santa Rosa**), and **Russian River Valley,** whose hub is the little town of **Healdsburg.** Only about an hour from San Francisco, the region abounds with charming restaurants, from the tiny **Babette's** in the town of Sonoma, to the cutting-edge **Bistro Ralph** in Healdsburg, to **Willowside Cafe** in Santa Rosa, which showcases the incredible bounty of locally grown meat and produce.

These areas are generally relaxed and informal, and most of the restaurants here follow suit, so you don't need to dress up. Reservations, however, are suggested for the more popular places.

The East Bay

In addition to the legendary **Chez Panisse** in **Berkeley,** the East Bay is also home to many other excellent and popular restaurants. This area is accessible via **Bay Area Rapid Transit (BART),** by ferry, and by car over the **Bay Bridge.** Our coverage begins in **Oakland,** moves to Berkeley, then north to **Marin.**

1 Soizic Bistro ★★★$$ San-Ju Dong and her husband Hi-Suk Dong (formerly of the now-closed **Cafe Pastoral** in Berkeley) have given fusion cooking an innovative spin at this new eatery. San-Ju sometimes adds Asian flavors to her beautifully arranged creations. At lunch, choose from a selection of light salads, such as spinach with goat cheese; roast chicken salad with a soy vinaigrette and hazelnuts; and soul-warming duck confit salad paired with red cabbage and a poached pear. Dinner entrées include such tasty concoctions as ravioli stuffed with white corn, summer squash, parmesan, and ricotta; grilled salmon marinated in a soy-sake sauce and placed atop Chinese eggplant and noodles; and rib-eye steak accented with a tangy mustard sauce and with a hearty potato gratin. Desserts include a luscious chocolate torte and a spicy ginger custard. ♦ Contemporary ♦ Tu lunch; W-F lunch and dinner; Sa-Su dinner. 300 Broadway (at Third St), Oakland. 510/251.8100 ♿

1 Battambang ★★★$ This modest little restaurant, located on the ground floor of a high-rise condominium complex in downtown Oakland, is not just the best Cambodian restaurant in the Bay Area; it's one of the area's best restaurants of any kind. Here, you can explore the wonders of Cambodian food, which is similar to Thai and Vietnamese cuisine (but less spicy). The best way to sample a cross-section of Cambodian dishes is to order the inexpensive "Special Combo," which consists of a generous portion of shredded chicken breast in a julienne cabbage salad served in a lime vinaigrette with fresh mint; red lemongrass soup with pineapple, chilies, and chicken chunks in a coconut milk broth; a plate with grilled chicken, pork, and beef, plus a skewer threaded with prawns and vegetables; and a mound of rice, dipping sauce for the meats, and fried soft rice noodles with vegetables on the side. All of the above items are also available as separate entrées. The staff is friendly and very helpful. ♦ Cambodian ♦ Daily lunch and dinner. 850 Broadway (at Ninth St), Oakland. 510.839.8815 ♿

Napa's grapevines were pulled out during Prohibition, and the area became known as the nation's prune capital.

1 Le Cheval Restaurant ★★★$ In the 1970s, when US immigration laws were relaxed, large numbers of Vietnamese people settled in Oakland. Many of the newcomers established successful businesses here, revitalizing the area. Among them was the Tran family, whose two branches of **Le Cheval Restaurant** have popularized Vietnamese cuisine in Oakland. The creative menu gives an Asian flavor to such familiar staples as poultry, beef, pork, seafood, and tofu. One top choice is *cha gio*, a crispy egg roll wrapper made from rice flour and filled with noodles, shredded vegetables, and pork. The proper way to eat this dish is to wrap pieces of the roll in lettuce and dip them in a rice-vinegar sauce. Or try an entrée of lemongrass beef (lean steak panfried with lemongrass, onions, and a touch of curry), or either *pho* or beef noodle soup (which is large enough to make a tasty meal in itself). The prices are incredibly low, especially considering the large size of the portions. ◆ Vietnamese ◆ M-Sa lunch and dinner; Su dinner. 1007 Clay St (between 10th and 11th Sts), Oakland. 510/763.8495; fax 510/763.0555 &

2 Bay Wolf ★★★$$$ A few years after Alice Waters launched the culinary revolution in Berkeley with **Chez Panisse,** Michael Wild followed suit in Oakland. This charming restaurant, perfectly situated in a converted house, has dark wainscoting lightened by cream walls and bright artwork. The dining rooms on either side of the bar are a perfect setting for the food. Duck is one of Wild's specialties and has a permanent place on the menu, which changes weekly: It can be grilled with bacon, chanterelles, and peas; or served over pasta with okra, corn, bell peppers, and andouille sausage. Duck liver also plays a major role—it may appear warm, in a salad of dandelion greens and hazelnuts; or as an ethereal flan. Other excellent dishes include artichoke fritters with an herbed rice timbale, grilled salmon with sorrel sauce, and a pan-seared pork chop with sherry vinegar. Desserts of the day might be a lemon almond tart or chocolate pecan cake. The wine list boasts a few unusual labels (especially European). ◆ Californian ◆ M-F lunch and dinner; Sa-Su dinner. 3853 Piedmont Ave (between MacArthur Blvd and 40th St), Oakland. 510/655.6004; fax 510/652.0429 &

2 Oliveto ★★★$$ Paul Bertolli, who was the chef for a decade at **Chez Panisse,** is now a partner at this ever-popular restaurant. The Tuscan-inspired menu, with Bertolli giving an inspired twist to traditional dishes, is alive with rustic, straightforward flavors; nothing can beat the salad with radicchio, walnuts, and homemade duck "proscuitto" (duck that has been seasoned, salt-cured, and air-dried). There's roast stuffed pork with flageolet beans; a rotisseried rabbit whose flavor melds with the white baby onion that accompanies it; and pan-seared quail with turnips braised in balsamic vinegar. The dessert offerings vary with the season: luscious strawberries and cream atop an old-fashioned biscuit, or caramelized mango upside-down cake, served with an extraordinary lime sorbet. There's a traditional dining room upstairs; downstairs is a more casual cafe with an open kitchen, rustic terra-cotta–colored walls, open-beamed ceiling, and windows that overlook one of the most jam-packed food shopping areas in the East Bay. (Be sure to stop by the **Market Hall** a few doors down where there are all kinds of wonderful fresh and prepared products for sale.) ◆ Californian ◆ M-F lunch and dinner; Sa-Su dinner. 5655 College Ave (at Hwy 24), Oakland. 510/547.5356; fax 510/547.4624 &

3 Chez Panisse ★★★★$$$ This restaurant has been turning out a set rustic French/Italian–style menu for the last 25 years, and the packed house at each of the nightly four seatings is the best evidence of its lasting success. Founder Alice Waters's philosophy is to find the best ingredients and to present them as simply as possible, and the results are outstanding. On Monday a three-course meal is offered; four courses are served Tuesday through Thursday; and a five-course dinner is offered on Friday and Saturday nights. A typical midweek, four-course meal might begin with grilled leeks and fennel served with olive toasts, followed by a green-garlic custard with Dungeness crab, and grilled pork loin accompanied by preserved lemons and a mélange of sautéed cabbage, potatoes, and leeks. An apple tart with pink-apple sherbet is a perfect ending to the meal. The California Craftsman–style interior mirrors the food, which is sophisticated and rustic at the same time. The open kitchen flows right into the dining room where copper light fixtures and wall sconces add a warming glow. The table settings are as straightforward as the food—no candles or flowers, just good wine glasses to showcase the fine wines from the carefully selected list. Hearty eaters, however, may be disappointed by the small portions.
◆ Californian ◆ M-Sa dinner. Reservations required. 1517 Shattuck Ave (between Cedar and Vine Sts), Berkeley. 510/548.5525; fax 510/548.0140

Upstairs at Chez Panisse:

3 Cafe at Chez Panisse ★★★★$$ Meals are served à la carte at this casual offspring of **Chez Panisse**. The brick oven, positioned behind a long service counter, turns out some of the best pizzas in Northern California. The toppings aren't elaborate, but everything tastes like it just came from the garden. Pastas and salads enticingly showcase seasonal vegetables, and simple meat dishes, grilled or baked, are succulent. Don't pass up dessert; the cookies, fruit tarts, cobblers, and ice creams are all marvelous. ♦ Californian ♦ M-Sa lunch and dinner 510/548.5049; fax 510/548.0140

4 O Chamé ★★★$$ Chef David Vardy creates Japanese-style food with a California twist at this attractive and peaceful restaurant on Fourth Street, Berkeley's culinary center. Using local produce in addition to traditional Japanese foodstuffs, Vardy's menu consists of appetizers and salads and a selection of meals in a bowl, featuring *udon* (buckwheat) or *soba* (white) noodles, augmented with about four daily specials. Winning appetizers include young greens blanched and served with a sesame dressing, and delicately vinegared cucumbers enlivened with *wakame* seaweed. One particularly memorable dish features two pristine salmon fillets, wet-roasted in a wood oven to create an almost poached texture, tucked under tender carrots that have been roasted and glazed with sweet sake, and accompanied by chunks of grilled portobello mushrooms—all surrounded by a tomato-lemon broth. The focal point of the dining room is an Oriental carpet, centered under a long table that holds a vase with an arrangement of grasses and blooms as well as platters of wonderful cookies and a few other baked goods. The Japanese country ambience is further enhanced by the straight-back rough wooden chairs and a round window inset with bamboo. There's also a tea kiosk outdoors where cookies, tea, and bento boxes are available at lunchtime—either to take away or enjoy at the heavy wooden table under a leafy green tree. ♦ Japanese ♦ M-Sa lunch and dinner. 1830 Fourth St (between Hearst Ave and Virginia St), Berkeley. 510/841.8783 ♿

4 Bette's Oceanview Diner ★★$ The black-and-white floor and curved white walls create the ambience of a 1930s Deco diner. Customers can sit at the long counter overlooking the open kitchen or at one of the burgundy booths that line the wall. Breakfast covers all the ethnic bases: *huevos rancheros*, lox scramble, or a Philadelphia breakfast (poached eggs with scrapple). And don't miss the best buttermilk pancakes west of the Mississippi (probably east of it too). The sandwich selection is equally broad, ranging from a panfried fish fillet, to a chicken sandwich, to kosher New York franks. The diner is famous for its desserts, so leave room for the pie of the day, bread pudding, or fresh fruit crisp. ♦ American ♦ Daily breakfast and lunch; F-Su until 4PM. 1807 Fourth St (between Hearst Ave and Virginia St), Berkeley. 510/644.3230; fax 510/644.3209 ♿

4 Bette's-to-Go Just as the name says, here you can get all of Bette's goodies, from fresh baked goods—rich double-chocolate pecan or moist peanut-butter cookies, almond cakes, apple pie—to Chinese chicken salad, sandwiches, and pizza by the slice. Home chefs can pick up the famous buttermilk pancake mix, lemon-currant scone mix, and other essentials. ♦ Daily. 1804 Fourth St (between Hearst Ave and Virginia St), Berkeley. 510/548.9494; fax 510/644.3209 ♿

4 Crate & Barrel Outlet Store Here's the place to find terrific bargains on everything for the home, including good kitchen towels for as little as 50 cents each. There are loads of serving pieces, glasses, plates, stainless steel flatware, chefs' knives, mugs, candlesticks, and just about everything else. Area bargain hunters stop in at least once a month to see what's new. ♦ Daily. 1785 Fourth St (between Hearst Ave and Virginia St), Berkeley. 510/528.5500; fax 510/528.3466 ♿

5 Lalime's ★★★$$ This neighborhood restaurant forges a close bond with the community through special theme dinners, charity benefits, and a monthly newsletter that keeps its regulars abreast of what's going on in the kitchen. The à la carte menu changes daily, and there's also a fixed-price menu that varies in price and offerings every day. It might be a Spanish-influenced evening that begins with an assortment of tapas, followed by paella, and a refreshing blood-orange granita for dessert; or a French meal, with a *tajine* of mussels perfumed with coriander, followed by grilled Cornish hens with stuffed mushrooms and roast garlic mashed potatoes, and warm pear strudel. Although it's always crowded in the two-level dining room, the light colors give the space a restful, celebratory feeling. ♦ Mediterranean ♦ Daily dinner. 1329 Gilman St (near Neilson St), Berkeley. 510/527.9838; fax 510/527.1350 ♿

Eighty percent of all avocados in the US are grown in California.

6 Ajanta Restaurant ★★★$ With this comfortable, refined Indian restaurant in one of North Berkeley's busiest shopping districts, owner Lachu Moorjani has achieved something very special. His menu (which changes monthly) goes beyond standard tandoori dishes, nan bread, and rice to offer interesting entrées from all over India, including Tamil Indian curry, flavored with poppy seeds and fennel; *lobhia aur khumbi,* a dish featuring fresh black-eyed peas with mushrooms, onions, tomatoes, garlic, and other spices; and chicken in coconut-onion-tomato sauce. The dining room is decorated in bright yellow fabrics accented with burnt sienna woodwork and carpeting; there is a number of striking murals depicting the Ajanta caves, a popular archaeological area in central India. ♦ Indian ♦ Daily lunch and dinner. 1888 Solano Ave (between The Alameda and Fresno Ave), Berkeley. 510/526.4373; fax 510/526.3885

6 Rivoli ★★★$$ This restaurant was an instant sensation, thanks to the reputations of chef/owner Wendy Brucker (**Stars, Square One, Ernie's**) and her husband and host, Roscoe Skipper (**Square One, Maza, Bijou**). Start with portobello mushroom fritters with lemon aioli, parmesan, peppery leaves of arugula, and caper vinaigrette. One of the best salads combines endive, pear *frisée* (curly endive), and arugula with spiced hazelnuts, pickled onions, and a hazelnut-balsamic vinaigrette. Main courses include braised lamb shank, accompanied by pomegranate-and-bulgur wheat pilaf, accented with a mint-garlic yogurt sauce and cumin oil. The day's vegetarian plate might be potato-cauliflower curry, basmati rice, and steamed or grilled seasonal vegetables. Desserts are equally delectable, from blood-orange granita to chocolate *pots de crème* (custard) with hazelnut cookies. This is a great place to learn the wonders of the sweet Meyer lemon, which stars in a flaky tart with pistachio, cranberry, and apricot sauces. ♦ Californian ♦ Daily dinner. 1539 Solano Ave (at Peralta Ave), Albany. 510/526.2542; fax 510/525.8412

When writer Robert Louis Stevenson visited the wine country of California, he remarked, "One corner of land after another is [planted] with one kind of grape after another. . . the smack of Californian earth shall linger on the palate of your grandson."

Marin County

This charming county has some of the prettiest villages and most dramatic vistas in the Bay Area. In **Sausalito** and **Tiburon,** visitors can spend the day strolling through quaint seaside villages, poking in shops and art galleries, and enjoying the sun that across the bay may be obscured by fog. The well-known **Lark Creek Inn,** in airy, Victorian surroundings in **Larkspur,** draws crowds for Bradley Ogden's American food with a twist. And travelers bogged down in traffic near the **Golden Gate Bridge** will be glad to stop for a bite at the Buckeye **Roadhouse** or **Frantoio Ristorante,** an eatery that boasts its own working olive oil press. Marin is reachable from San Francisco by bus, ferry, and the Golden Gate Bridge, and from the **East Bay** via the **Richmond–San Rafael Bridge.** We start our tour in Tiburon and work north to **San Rafael**.

7 Guaymas ★★$$ On a sunny afternoon take a ferry from The Embarcadero to Tiburon, where the boat debarks at the door of this pretty Mexican restaurant. Take a seat on the deck and enjoy an enchanting view of the San Francisco skyline while indulging in nachos and margaritas. You can dine outside if it's warm, or head inside to try some of the creative dishes that pepper the menu. Start with grilled shrimp, marinated in lime juice and cilantro, or tiny tamales filled with chicken and coated with a pumpkin-seed sauce. If there's a nip in the air (remember, you're on the water), try the tortilla soup with chunks of chicken and avocado floating in a rich smoky broth. Such main course offerings as slow-roasted pork sirloin or mesquite-grilled lamb loin with salsa can't be beat. ♦ Mexican ♦ Daily lunch and dinner. 5 Main St (near Tiburon Blvd), Tiburon. 415/435.6300; fax 415/435.6802 ♿

7 Tutto Mare Ristorante & Taverna ★★★$$ In the last few years, the town of Tiburon has become a popular dining center, and this place is just one of the reasons. Under the same ownership as **Guaymas** (see above), it's a bi-level replica of an Italian boathouse, only this one offers spectacular views of the San Francisco skyline. Another striking feature of the decor is the three-dimensional ceramic murals. Be sure to try the portobello mushroom–filled ravioli with slivered asparagus and truffle oil. Other great choices are fried calamari with aioli; seafood salad with shrimp, octopus, and vegetables; freshly shucked oysters; and steamed shellfish. For landlubbers, there are pizzas, charcoal-grilled meat and poultry, and homemade pastas. The deck is a perfect place to sit and enjoy a sunny afternoon or relax and watch the sun set in the evening. ♦ Italian/Seafood ♦ M-Sa lunch and dinner; Su brunch and dinner. 9 Main St (near Tiburon Blvd), Tiburon. 415/435.4747; fax 415/435.4766 ♿

BUCKEYE
R O A D H O U S E

8 Buckeye Roadhouse ★★$$ Owned by
Real Restaurants, the same people who
brought **Bistro Rôti, Bix, Fog City Diner,
Ristorante Tra Vigne,** and **Mustards Grill** to
fruition, this popular roadhouse just on the
other side of the Golden Gate Bridge has a
lodgelike ambience. The high-pitched ceiling
adds drama, but the massive rock fireplace
holds center stage. The food style is a
mélange of classic American, French, and
Italian cuisine, with a few Asian touches
added to spice up the menu. An appetizer of
pan-roasted artichoke with creamy tarragon
dip is an ideal way to celebrate California's
favorite vegetable. Onion rings with home-
made ketchup, and warm spinach salad with
smoked bacon are other excellent ways to
launch a meal. Heartier appetites will enjoy
barbecued baby back ribs accompanied by
cole slaw and garlic mashed potatoes are
delicious; as are the smoked half chicken and
grilled pork chops. Don't miss the butter-
scotch crème brûlée or baked lemon pudding
for dessert. ♦ American ♦ M-Sa lunch and
dinner; Su brunch and dinner. 15 Shoreline
Hwy (near Hwy 101), Mill Valley.
415/331.2600; fax 331.6067 ♿

9 Piazza D'Angelo ★★★$$ One of the
most popular spots in Marin, the patio or
light-filled interior of this active restaurant is
an ideal place to end a walk around Mill Valley
(check out **Smith and Hawkins** for chic
gardening finds, **Mill Valley Market** for
gourmet foods, and several cookstores
and accessory shops). For a light meal,
two excellent choices are a simple *pizza
margherita* with mozzarella, basil, and tomato
sauce, and a heartier *pizza rustica* with
calamata olives, sun-dried tomatoes, feta
cheese, and arugula. The menu changes
daily, but there's always a pasta dish—maybe
penne with fresh tomatoes, artichokes, and
wild mushrooms—and such entrées as red
snapper alla Calabrese - a spicy sauce to wake
up the taste buds. Anything from the rotisserie
is recommended: rabbit, duck with balsamic
vinegar, or chicken. The chef is from Sardinia,
so dishes from that area are worth a try,
especially the *bottarga* (dried tuna roe) with
spaghetti and garlic and the carpaccio with
celery and touches of olive oil. ♦ Italian
♦ Daily lunch and dinner. 22 Miller Ave
(between Sunny Side and Throckmorton
Aves), Mill Valley. 415/388.2000; fax
388.1234 ♿

9 The Frog and the Peach ★★$$ The
British comedy team of Dudley Moore and
Peter Cook had a classic sketch about a
restaurant called "The Frog and the Peach,"
whose menu consisted only of those two
foods in hideous combinations. Now an eatery
of the same name has opened in Mill Valley,
but this one is anything but a joke. It's the
creation of local restaurant mogul Nancy
Mootz (who also co-owns **Vertigo** in San
Francisco). Try the Mediterranean dishes,
such as potato and roasted shallot soup with
smoked salmon; hearts of romaine salad with
creamy anchovy dressing; and roast chicken
with wild mushrooms and sweet onion bread
pudding. The leg of lamb with pearl couscous,
carrots, and thyme is exquisite. For dessert,
try the popular Valrhona chocolate tart with
orange mousse. The dining room is decorated
in a lovely pastiche of pale peach, green,
white, and eggplant. ♦ Contemporary
♦ M-F lunch and dinner; Sa-Su dinner. 106
Throckmorton Ave (at Miller Ave), Mill Valley.
415/381.3343; fax 415/381.8649 ♿

10 Frantoio Ristorante ★★★$$ The unique
centerpiece of the dining room—a massive,
working olive oil press—is second only to the
distinctive Italian dishes served here.
Milanese-born Duilio Valenti has recently taken
over the kitchen, bringing new inspiration and
more authenticity to the cooking. The appetizer
of oak-roasted portobello mushroom with
fennel, olives, and roasted bell pepper with
marjoram-infused olive oil is an excellent
starter. In addition, carpaccio is available in
two versions, one with beef and the other with
tuna. The list of main courses includes thin-
crust pizzas, pastas, and meat, poultry, and
fish dishes. Top choices are fillet of veal with
Yukon potatoes in a rosemary sauce and
succulent Sonoma duck with honey glazed
figs, eggplant caponata, and a tangy balsamic
vinegar sauce. While you enjoy your food, you
can watch the floor show—olives being
crushed by the two 3,600-pound granite

wheels of the olive oil press. The well-chosen wine list offers mainly Italian vintages. ♦ Italian ♦ Daily lunch and dinner. 152 Shoreline Hwy (between Hwy 101 and Panoramic Hwy), Mill Valley. 415/289.5777; fax 415/289.5775 ♿

11 Lark Creek Inn ★★★$$$ A large and airy Victorian house surrounded by redwoods showcases the style of New American cuisine invented by founding chef Bradley Ogden. Ogden, who earned his stripes at the American Restaurant in Kansas City and at **Campton Place** in San Francisco, has become known for his twists on familiar comfort food. And a new chef de cuisine, Todd Davies, has rejuvenated the menu (which changes frequently). Dishes might include a yummy sweet pea soup with tarragon; an appetizer of oven-baked onion flatbread with pancetta, Swiss chard, and mozzarella; grilled cider-marinated double-cut pork chops atop braised cabbage and cheddar scalloped potatoes; oven-roasted chicken accompanied by buttered spinach and mashed red potatoes (which are, unfortunately, gummy); and braised lamb shank dressed up with horseradish mashed potatoes and roasted root vegetables. Desserts are definitely worth a splurge, particularly the warm country apple crisp with vanilla ice cream or butterscotch pudding with shortbread cookies. When the weather permits, people can sit on the deck overlooking the proverbial babbling brook. ♦ Californian ♦ M-F lunch and dinner; Sa dinner; Su brunch and dinner. 234 Magnolia Ave (at William Ave), Larkspur. 415/924.7766; fax 924.7117 ♿

11 Left Bank ★★★$$ A little bit of Paris has been captured in this brasserie, which is partly owned by Roland Passot of **La Folie** in San Francisco. For this venture in charming downtown Larkspur, Passot has scaled back his grand style and offers stick-to-your-ribs fare. Stop at the ornate bar and order one of the fruit- or vegetable-infused vodkas (fennel, kumquat, or pear, to name a few), which are impressively displayed in huge glass jars. The menu changes seasonally; in spring two can share the generous warm new-potato salad with mussels and roasted artichoke; on a late summer's night nothing can beat the cooling salad of mixed organic greens and yellow wax beans with roasted peppers and vine-ripened tomatoes. You'll swear you're in France when you order salad *lyonnaise,* composed of *frisée* tossed with lardoons of bacon and topped with a poached egg. Steamed salmon glistens in an herbed broth with a medley of vegetables; duck confit is enriched with braised lentils; and roast chicken is a perfect foil to roasted vegetables. For dessert try the fruit shakes or classic chocolate mousse. ♦ French ♦ M-Sa lunch and dinner; Su brunch and dinner. 507 Magnolia Ave (at Ward St), Larkspur. 415/927.3331; fax 927.3034 ♿

11 Chai of Larkspur ★★$$ Just a stone's throw from **Left Bank** is this gem of a tea salon. Decorated by Candra Scott (who also designed **VIVANDE** in Pacific Heights), the room features tomato-red walls, oversize green wicker chairs, and persimmon accents. Owner Betty Shelton prepares a wide variety of sandwiches, pastries, and cookies to go with the tea service. There's also a shop selling more than 70 imported teas, accessories, and tea-themed gifts. ♦ Tea salon ♦ Tu-Su tea (Tu-Th, Su until 7PM, F-Sa until 10:30PM). 25 Ward St (at Magnolia Ave), Larkspur. 415/945.7161; fax 415/945.7164 ♿

12 Bay Area Certified Farmers' Market Started in 1983 as a Thursday market, it is now held on Sunday as well, year-round at the **Marin Civic Center.** On both days it draws thousands of people who relish the cornucopia of locally grown, mostly organic fruits, vegetables, and herbs, free-range poultry and lamb, ranch eggs, local honey, homemade jams, freshly squeezed juices, fresh fish and shellfish, multigrain breads, pastries, and specialty pastas, sauces, and vinegars. ♦ Th, Su 8AM-1PM. Marin Civic Center, 3501 Civic Center Dr (Thursday in the parking lot of the Veterans Auditorium, at the Avenue of the Flags; Sunday in the main parking lot, parallel to Hwy 101), San Rafael. 415/456.FARM; fax 415/453.7502 ♿

12 Kasbah Moroccan Restaurant ★★★$$ This opulent dining room brings the atmosphere of Marrakesh to sunny California. Diners sit at low brass tables and eat their food with their hands, and most nights there's a floor show of sensual belly dancing. Among the best dishes on the lengthy menu are lamb with prunes; chicken with honey and almonds; rabbit tajine (a stewlike concoction cooked in a clay pot); and chicken brochettes served with couscous and topped with crisp vegetables. The fixed-price meal (consisting of your choice of as many appetizers as you like, savory lentil soup, a main course, and cookies and spearmint tea for dessert) is a bargain. ♦ Moroccan ♦ M-F lunch and dinner; Sa-Su dinner. 200 Merrydale Rd (at Willow Ave), San Rafael. 415/472.6666; fax 415/472.6666 ♿

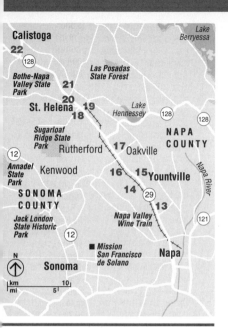

Calistoga
22
(128)
Bothe-Napa
Valley State   21
Park   20
    St. Helena 19
              18
Sugarloaf
Ridge State
Park   Rutherford   17 Oakville
(12)
Annadel
State   Kenwood   16 15 Yountville
Park   14
SONOMA   (29)
COUNTY   13
Jack London   Napa Valley
State Historic   Wine Train
Park   (12)
                ■ Mission
N   San Francisco   Napa
                de Solano
    Sonoma
km   10
mi   5

Lake
Berryessa

Las Posadas
State Forest

Lake
Hennessey   (128)   (128)

NAPA
COUNTY

Napa River

(121)

Napa Valley

Once a series of quiet little farm towns, today the
Napa Valley wine-growing region gets almost as
many tourists in a year as Disneyland. It boasts
hundreds of wineries, shops, art galleries, and some
of the hottest restaurants in Northern California, all
within a 1.5-hour drive of San Francisco. Some of
the best dining spots in the valley are located along
the **St. Helena Highway** (also called **Highway 29**)
spine, starting from the city of **Napa** and extending
north to **Calistoga.** The following are our favorites.

13 Bistro Don Giovanni ★★$$ Surrounded
by vineyards, this Italian restaurant is owned by
Donna and Giovanni Scala, who also have an
interest in **Scala's Bistro** in San Francisco. The
place has a rustic look, with country fabrics,
antique copper pots, Italian ceramics, a
Mediterranean garden, and an outdoor
fireplace. The food takes on the warm gutsy
notes of Italian cooking. Start with *fritto misto*,
fried crispy rock shrimp, purple onions, and
green beans, served with spicy aioli on the side.
The *pappardelle* (wide ribbon noodles) are a
perfect bed for the stew of rabbit with baby
artichokes. *Capellini* (thin spaghetti-like
noodles) tossed with tomato, basil, and garlic
make a simple, soul-satisfying dish. The lunch
menu features several focaccia sandwiches—
the grilled vegetable version is outstanding.
Roast chicken is another winner, as is braised
lamb shank with Tuscan white-bean stew. The
wine list is dominated by California selections
and includes Italian wines, Armagnacs, and
grappas. ♦ Italian ♦ Daily lunch and dinner.
Reservations recommended. 4110 St. Helena
Hwy (north of Salvador Ave), Napa.
707/224.3300; fax 707/224.3395 ♿

14 Domaine Chandon ★★★★$$$$ On the
grounds of this eponymous winery is one of
the most impressive restaurants in Northern
California, thanks to the cuisine of Philippe
Jeanty who has been in charge of the kitchen
since it opened in 1977, and the magnificent
setting overlooking a pond and vineyards.
During the day it's a magical experience to
enjoy Jeanty's French/Californian creations
on the patio with the gentle breeze tickling
your face. At night the arch-roofed dining
room glows with candlelit romance. The
menu changes often but the chef might pair
seared tuna crusted in black pepper with
buttery mashed potatoes and a mustard sauce;
tender slices of lamb tongue accented with
warm potatoes, *frisée*, and capers; or quail
presented over a rich risotto with caramelized
mushrooms. Dessert may be a seductive
warm chocolate cake with a truffle-like center,
or crème brûlée sandwiched between perfect
layers of puff pastry. As you would expect,
the restaurant has one of the best wine lists
in the valley for both selection and price.
♦ French/Californian ♦ M-Tu lunch, W-Su
lunch and dinner May-Oct; W-Su lunch and
dinner Jan-Apr, Nov-Dec. Reservations
recommended; jackets required at dinner.
1 California Dr (off St. Helena Hwy), Yountville.
707/944.2892; fax 707/944.1123 ♿

THE FRENCH LAUNDRY

15 French Laundry ★★★★$$$$ Thomas
Keller has taken over this old stone laundry
and has turned it into a fine-dining destination
in the tradition of France. The dining room has
an almost austere simplicity, in contrast to the
luxurious style of the table settings with
oversized napkins and sparkling crystal. Keller
has also added a touch of whimsy: a starched
chef's coat hangs to "dry" over the fireplace,
wooden laundry pins hold the napkins in place,
and laundry tags are used to itemize the check.
There are four- or five-course prix-fixe menus,
with as many as five choices for each course
and one all-vegetarian option. A fish choice
could be a snowy fillet of sea bass moistened
by a bright, fresh carrot broth—which gets its
intense flavor from dehydrating the vegetables
before juicing them—presented on a bed of
couscous. Meat courses are particularly good,
especially when Keller takes humble cuts and
transforms them into heavenly creations. He
roasts the breast of veal for hours, cools it,
doubles it over, and cuts it into perfect rounds.
It is then brushed with mustard and bread
crumbs and seared, forming a crackling crust
that creates an alluring contrast to the velvety
meat. The wine list is one of the best in the

wine country; it concentrates on Napa Valley and boasts a mix of classics and selections from small wineries. Also, 25 half-bottles are offered, allowing parties of two to match the wine with the food. And for dessert, you've surely never had "coffee and doughnuts" like this—a freshly made doughnut and a cup of cappuccino mousse topped with a froth of whipped cream. ◆ Californian ◆ Tu-Su dinner; call ahead about lunch hours, as they vary with the season. Reservations required. 6640 Washington St (at Creek St), Yountville. 707/944.2380; fax 707/944.1974 &

16 **Mustards Grill** ★★★$$ A popular restaurant from the day it opened over a decade ago, this low-slung, ranch-style building is still one of the best destinations for casual dining. The menu features such all-American standards as hamburgers and great onion rings, but with a twist; for example, the ketchup is homemade, as is everything else. Smoked salmon is given distinction with corn cakes spiced with mild *pasilla* chilies and topped by fresh dill cream cheese; wild mushrooms are baked in a flaky tart; and crab cakes are served with a three-pepper salad. Liver with caramelized onions and bacon is always on the menu, as is a delicious slab of barbecued baby back ribs served with corn bread and slaw. Occasionally braised lamb shanks with polenta, grilled rabbit with wild mushrooms, or a grilled pork chop with mashed potatoes appear as specials. There is an enticing selection of the more unusual wines produced in the Napa Valley, with more than a dozen good wines available by the glass. Prices tend to be a little high. Try the caramel apple cake with cinnamon ice cream, or the Jack Daniel's chocolate cake with an intense chocolate sauce. ◆ Californian ◆ Daily lunch and dinner. Reservations recommended. 7399 St. Helena Hwy (between California Dr and Dwyer Rd), Yountville. 707/944.2424; fax 707/944.0824 &

Without the influence of Italian immigrant growers, who brought the necessary seeds with them, there wouldn't be acres and acres of artichokes growing around Half Moon Bay, 20 miles south of San Francisco. Other commercial crops linked to the influx of Italians are bell peppers, eggplant, broccoli, and fava beans. Some of the first farms were established in the Outer Mission in the late 19th century by Italian immigrants.

Mt. St. Helena, the mountain that looms above the Napa Valley, was an active volcano millions of years ago. Its ash and lava flows formed much of the rich substrata that make the surrounding acreage so suited to wine growing.

17 **Stars Oakville Cafe** ★$$$ Jeremiah Tower has re-created a little bit of San Francisco's **Stars Cafe** in the Napa Valley. The menu changes daily, crafted to the season, and may include house-smoked salmon with pickled red onions, oysters on the half shell, or a baby romaine salad. Salmon is grilled and served with vegetable-studded orzo; and grilled lamb sirloin is accompanied by baked white beans with spinach. Many meat dishes, including delectable chicken and duck, are prepared in the wood-burning oven. The 75 wines—Californian, French, and Italian— are a good mix of classics and more unusual bottles, but prices can be high, with few bargains to be found. The interior doesn't have the flash of its big-city brother, but the single room is given dimension by a cathedral ceiling at the entrance and a small bar area tucked next to the kitchen, which is separated from the dining area by glass so you can watch the action. In summer, a seating area is created on a tented outdoor patio and, beyond that, a white lattice fence encloses a garden filled with olive trees and lavender, centered with an aviary filled with doves. ◆ Cafe ◆ M, Th-Su lunch and dinner. Reservations recommended. 7848 St. Helena Hwy (near Oakville Cross Rd), Oakville. 707/944.8905; fax 707/944.0469 &

18 **Pinot Blanc** ★★★$$ The latest celebrity chef to grace the Napa Valley is Joachim Splichal, the mastermind behind several Los Angeles restaurants, including Patina, Pinot Bistro, and Pinot Hollywood. With such impressive credentials, this was a highly anticipated restaurant opening. After some growing pains and a change in the chef de cuisine (who is now Sean Knight), this place seems to have gotten on the right track. The boxy-looking building is enhanced with a lovely pergola and grounds landscaped with olive trees, flowers, and an herb garden. The menu features French country bistro classics prepared with a California twist, including rotisserie beef and chicken; herring salad served with a potato pancake and mustard greens; caramelized onion tart with marinated salmon and cream; calf's liver with roasted fingerling potatoes; spinach casserole and sweet and sour shallot *jus;* and crispy duck leg confit with a warm salad of *frisée*, apples, and walnuts. ◆ French/Californian◆ Daily lunch and dinner. 641 Main St (between Grayson and Vidovich Aves), St. Helena. 707/963.6191; fax 707/963.6192 &

19 **Ristorante Tra Vigne** ★★$$ No restaurant in the valley captures the feel of the wine country better than this impressive stone building in St. Helena which has grape vines on the front lawn. The restaurant is always crowded; you can sit outside on the impressive patio underneath fig trees, or

inside, which sports a magnificent casual trattoria feel with an open kitchen hung with hams, strings of garlic, and garlands of herbs. Most products, including the prosciutto, sausage, and even the olive oil is produced in-house by chef Michael Chiarello. Because of the volume of business the food can some-times be uneven. The regularly changing menu includes a list of thin-crusted pizzas, great pasta with interesting sauces—such as a mushroom ragout or braised rabbit—and many grilled dishes, like excellent lamb. The wine list includes Italian and Californian vintages (try one of the Californian wines using the Italian varietals), but prices are a bit high. ♦ Italian ♦ Daily lunch and dinner. Reservations recommended. 1050 Charter Oak Ave (at Main St), St. Helena. 707/963.4444; fax 707/963.1233 ♿

Next to Ristorante Tra Vigne:

Cantinetta Tra Vigne ★★★$ This upscale deli and wineshop offers such simple fare as panini (Italian sandwiches on focaccia bread) and interesting salads that can be eaten outside on the patio or taken away for a glorious picnic. Wines, house-produced conserves, vinegars and oils, mustards, and some fresh produce items are also offered. ♦ Italian/Takeout ♦ Daily lunch and early dinner (until 6PM). 1050 Charter Oak Ave (at Main St), St. Helena. 707/942.8888 ♿

TERRA

Terra ★★★★$$$$ Chef/owner Hiro Sone and his wife, Lissa Doumani, met at Spago in Los Angeles: He was on the line with Wolfgang Puck and she worked in the pastry kitchen. Their partnership has produced a magnificent cross-cultural restaurant where Italian and Asian flavors play against each other in a setting reminiscent of a Tuscan village. Located one block off the main street in St. Helena, the stone building has exposed rock walls, a terra-cotta floor, and bright modern art that work together to create a simultaneously rustic and refined setting. The menu changes often, but the combin-ations are always creative—try the ragout of sweetbreads with prosciutto and mushrooms in a broth perfumed with white truffle oil. Follow with rack of lamb flanked by ratatouille, hummus, and a refreshing *raita* (yogurt and chopped cucumber). Spicy tripe with

spaghetti is another winning dish, though it may not appeal to everyone. There's an extensive collection of Napa Valley wines, which are clearly labeled by varietal. Less common varietals are characterized as "the other side of red" on the wine list; French selections are called "intruders." The desserts are also unusual: Consider sampling the gently warmed strawberries in a Cabernet sauce spiked with black pepper, and cooled by a slowly melting scoop of vanilla ice cream. ♦ Asian/Mediterranean ♦ M, W-Su dinner. Reservations recommended. 1345 Railroad Ave (between Hunt Ave and Adams St), St. Helena. 707/963.8931; fax 707/963.8933 ♿

20 Wine Spectator Greystone Restaurant ★★$$ When the **Culinary Institute of America** (based in Hyde Park, New York) wanted to create a Northern California campus in the early 1990s, they chose to take over the beautiful building that once housed the **Christian Brothers Winery–Greystone Cellars.** The campus now features a restaurant staffed by **CIA** graduates and students; its name acknowledges a generous donation from the *Wine Spectator* magazine. One good starter is pureed Mediterranean dips: garlicky yogurt dill, a bland chick pea hummus, and *muhammara,* a combination of red pepper and walnuts. Pizza prepared with cooked sweet onions, *niçoise* olives, and bits of anchovies on a crispy flat bread is another outstanding choice. Although tasty, the duck cooked on the rotisserie and flavored with honey and lavender was a little too fatty. The rich, dense Valrhona chocolate cake sitting on a sauce of espresso Sambuca and vanilla bean cream makes a fine finish. The dining room's rough stone walls (from the former winery) are brightened by the generous use of tile, wrought iron, and blond wood furnishings. The tasting and antipasto bar is a good place to watch the cooks on display in the open kitchen and to sample up to 16 wines by the glass (the wine list offers helpful hints for beginners). But the staff can be a bit absentminded. ♦ Californian ♦ M, W-Su lunch and dinner. 255 Main St (north of Madrona St), St. Helena. 707/967.1010; fax 707/963.1113 ♿

Legend has it that nature, not man, produced California's first raisin crop. A devastating heat wave hit the San Joaquin Valley in 1873, right before the grapes could be harvested. Most of the crop withered on the vine before it could be picked, and all seemed lost. But then one enterprising grower went to San Francisco and persuaded a local grocer to try to market the shriveled grapes (which he termed "raisins"). And the rest, as they say, is history.

Late-Night Dining by the Bay

Unlike New York, "the city that never sleeps," San Francisco does slow down at night. But for the sizable segment of people who stay out quite late—theatergoers, restaurant workers, nightclub hoppers, and the like—and want to grab a bite to eat in the wee hours, the City by the Bay has an impressive number of options, with a surprising variety of cuisines—everything from a nosh to a soup-to-nuts supper. These are our favorite places, many of which keep their doors open until 3 or 4AM (and one that never closes at all):

The Brazen Head Restaurant Popular with chefs, waiters, and other restaurant staff who come here after their evening shift, this quaint, elegant **Cow Hollow** place presents a full menu of well-prepared continental fare until 1AM. The onion soup, garlicky Caesar salad, and meltingly tender filet mignon with sautéed mushrooms and scalloped potatoes are all excellent. The restaurant is easy to miss because there's no sign, but it's worth seeking out if you want a late-night bite. ◆ Daily dinner until 1AM. No credit cards accepted. 3166 Buchanan St (at Greenwich St). 921.7600; fax 921.0164

42 Degrees At this restaurant/nightclub in **Potrero Hill,** the action doesn't even begin to heat up until after 9PM. With a high-tech, glossy veneer and striking design (a curving black metal staircase, purple banquettes), it offers a menu of Californian fare that changes nightly. Among owner/chef Jim Moffat's most popular dishes are grilled quail and rich duck confit on a heap of truffled risotto with morels; and a whole *poussin* with hard-cider sauce, baked apples, and rice studded with sour cherries. Full dinner can be ordered until 11:30PM. ◆ W-Sa. 235 16th St (east of Illinois St). 777.5559; fax 777.0278 ◇

Johnny Rockets Okay, it's a chain, but this juke joint straight out of "Happy Days" serves a pretty good hamburger. The waiters, wearing traditional pointed caps, are so helpful they even pour the ketchup for you (and some of the late-night, pre-hangover partyers who frequent this place on Fridays and Saturdays need the assistance). ◆ F-Sa until 2AM. 1946 Fillmore St (at Pine St), Pacific Heights. 776.9878; fax 776.1189 ◇ Also at: 81 Jefferson St (between Powell and Mason Sts), Fisherman's Wharf. 693.9120; fax 693.9404 ◇

La Rondalla Judging from the blazing tree lights that decorate this Mexican restaurant in the **Mission**, you'd think it was Christmas. But that's the way the dining room always looks. It's developed something of a cult following around here, perhaps because of its kitschy charm (stuffed birds, strolling mariachis) or perhaps because the kitchen produces such great food: delicious guacamole, *carne asada,* and several dishes featuring goat meat. ◆ Tu-Su until 3AM. No credit cards accepted. 901 Valencia St (at 20th St). 647.7474

Silver Restaurant The glittering silver marquee in front raises expectations of glamour, so it's a bit of a shock when you enter the rather utilitarian dining room. But no doubt you'll recover in time to enjoy the good, inexpensive food. The best time to visit this busy **Chinatown** spot is during crab season (November through April), when a whole crab can be had for about $9. And the *congees* and thin noodles with wontons topped with barbecued pork or duck make a fine end to a long night of partying. The place usually fills to the rafters around 2AM, when the bar crowd stops by for "breakfast." ◆ Daily 24 hours. 737 Washington St (between Portsmouth Sq and Grant Ave). 433.8888 ◇

Stardust Restaurant and Lounge This roadhouse looks so retro that it seems like Elvis might walk in any moment. It's a bit gaudy, but the food is good. Try the thick Reuben sandwich, blackened catfish, grilled pork chop, portobello mushroom sandwich with spicy french fries, or macaroni and cheese just like Mom used to make. It's ideal for night owls, too, since it keeps its doors open until 4AM Thursday through Saturday and until 2AM the rest of the week. ◆ M-W, Su until 2AM; Th-Sa until 4AM. 299 Ninth St (at Folsom St), SoMa. 861.2983

Yuet Lee Seafood One of San Francisco's most popular late-night eateries, this restaurant in Chinatown always seems to produce the freshest seafood dishes. Every bar-hopper in town makes a pilgrimage here when hunger strikes, as do cops, restaurant workers, and other night owls. Menu items include whole crab, shrimp with scrambled eggs, and salt-and-pepper squid, quickly stirred in a dry wok. Other good choices are steamed rock cod and, for landlubbers, roast duck. The bright lighting and bare-bones decor may be a little jarring, but the food helps ease the blow. ◆ M, W-Su until 3AM. No credit cards accepted. 1300 Stockton St (at Broadway). 982.6020

21 Brava Terrace ★★★$$ The redwood deck overlooking the creek is the place to be in the summer at this dining spot; in the winter, it's in front of the massive rock fireplace that holds center stage in the peaked roof dining room. Owner/chef Fred Halpert offers a hearty Mediterranean menu, and many of his herbs and lettuces are fresh picked from the restaurant's adjacent garden. Long-cooked dishes are a standout, particularly the cassoulet, and another great main course is pan-seared Alaskan halibut with slivers of vegetables in a soy-butter sauce. The menu includes several excellent sandwiches for lunch, and the risotto of the day is always superb. Halpert hosts interesting food and wine tastings as special events; for example, California Zinfandel paired with barbecue is a match made in heaven. Because the restaurant is located just north of St. Helena, it's often a bit less crowded than the places in the lower valley. ♦ Mediterranean ♦ Daily lunch and dinner May-Oct; M-Tu, Th-Su lunch and dinner Nov-Apr. Reservations recommended. 3010 St. Helena Hwy N (at Lodi La), St. Helena. 707/963.9300; fax 707/963.9581 ♿

22 Wappo Bar Bistro ★★$$ This restaurant takes its name from a Native American tribe that used to occupy the area. Its decor is California Craftsman and the fare consists of continually changing offerings that span the globe: Mexican spicy meatball soup, Indian fish fritters, Spanish seafood vermicelli, and Asian grilled chicken with sesame-ginger sauce. American-influenced dishes include a homey rabbit pie and roast chicken with chive-mashed potatoes. The 40-bottle wine list is an eccentric mix containing unusual varietals that have clearly been selected to go with the spicy food. Desserts are formidable: The warm steamed chocolate cake with a brownielike texture and a strawberry-rhubarb pie could win a prize at any state fair. The brick patio in back, with a grape arbor overhead and a wall of climbing vines with pink and yellow roses, makes this one of the loveliest outdoor stops in the upper Napa Valley. ♦ International/Californian ♦ M, W-Su lunch and dinner. Reservations recommended. 1226B Washington St (off Lincoln Ave), Calistoga. 707/942.4712; fax 707/942.4741 ♿

22 Catahoula Restaurant and Saloon ★★★★$$$ For this venture within the **Mount View Hotel**, Jan Birnbaum returned to his native Louisiana roots (where he worked for Paul Prudhomme) to create a host of spicy foods. Menu offerings range from spicy rooster gumbo to pizza with andouille sausage to hominy cakes with vegetables and smoked-onion vinaigrette. Locally raised lamb is encrusted with sassafras and served with potato-salsify pie; whole roast fish is stuffed with fennel and onion; braised short ribs are paired with mashed potatoes and pungent mustard greens; and, in an unusual combination, wild boar sausage is served with pecorino ravioli. There's an excellent wine list, and Birnbaum also offers food and wine tastings where he matches a dish with three different wines. Dessert could be buttermilk pie, a rich apple grunt (where the fruit is stewed and topped with biscuit dough), or almond upside-down cake with caramelized mangoes. The restaurant's interior has an urban, sophisticated look: salvaged wood tables edged with wrought iron, rusted animal sculptures, and portraits of dogs (the Catahoula is the state dog of Louisiana). A granite bar separates the open kitchen from the brick oven and the rest of the dining room. There's additional seating in the bar and around the pool in back. ♦ Contemporary Creole ♦ M, W-Su lunch and dinner; closed in January. Reservations recommended. 1457 Lincoln Ave (between Washington and Fairway Sts), Calistoga. 707/942.2275; fax 707/942.5338 ♿

Sonoma County Farm Trails, founded in 1972, produces a map of small farms, wineries, and other food-related businesses that sell to the public. Free maps are available by writing PO Box 6032, Santa Rosa, CA, 95406, or they can be picked up at member businesses throughout the county. Napa, Sonoma, Alameda, and other counties produce their own farm trail maps.

Sonoma County is home to four cheese manufacturers: Vella Cheese Company (known for its dry Monterey jack), the Sonoma Cheese Factory, Laurel Chenel Cheese (which put goat cheese on the map in this country), and Joe Matos Cheese Factory (which produces St. George, a semihard cheese otherwise made only in the Azores). Thirty-four wineries in the Sonoma Valley produce 25 types of wine—more than 5 million cases yearly.

Sonoma County

Unlike the **Napa Valley,** where wine grapes are about the only crop, Sonoma County is an agricultural region that happens to grow grapes. The terrain is varied, with orchards scattered among the grapevines, and cows and lambs grazing just about everywhere you look. The setting is so bucolic it's easy to forget that you are only an hour or two from San Francisco. **Sonoma** has quickly become a hotbed of restaurant activity. Here's a rundown of the best, starting from the town of Sonoma and heading north to **Healdsburg.**

23 Piatti ★★$$ The perfect meal here begins with grilled vegetables, including whole roasted garlic cloves that can be spread like butter. From there it's on to spinach-and-ricotta ravioli topped with lemon-infused cream sauce, or grilled meat from the rotisserie, such as a pork chop served with creamy mashed potatoes and a heady mushroom sauce. Those who are in the mood for a lighter midday snack can opt for tasty thin-crusted pizza. An open kitchen, terra-cotta floor, light walls painted with big fruits and vegetables, and massive chairs give this trattoria an Italian country look. The feeling is further enhanced by a wisteria-draped outdoor patio complete with a massive fig tree. For dessert, hope that a fruit ice is on the menu; if not, the tiramisù is rich, creamy, and refreshing. ◆ Italian ◆ Daily lunch and dinner.

Reservations recommended. 405 First St W (between W Napa and W Spain Sts), Sonoma. 707/996.2351; fax 707/996.3148 ᐸ Also at: Numerous locations throughout the area

23 Babette's ★★★★$$ Owned by chef Daniel Patterson and his wife Elizabeth Ramsey, this French restaurant probably serves the finest food in Sonoma County. In all of his preparations, Patterson uses mostly local ingredients, including the freshest organic produce. His menu changes frequently, but no matter what the choices are, you can't go wrong. Among the best recent dishes is a truffle-infused puree of yellow corn soup with a silky, shrimp-filled ravioli. The main dining room, aptly named the "Feast Room," has an elegant but friendly atmosphere, and Ramsey is a graceful, welcoming hostess. There's also a more casual (and even cheaper) bistro in the front of the house, offering a lighter menu; try the burger or the French-style steak with shoestring potatoes. You can opt to finish your meal with a luscious dessert or with French cheeses and wine. ◆ French ◆ Feast Room: Tu-Sa dinner. Bistro: Tu-Sa lunch and dinner. 464 First St W (near E Napa St), Sonoma. 707/939.8921; fax 707/939.9360 ᐸ

24 Kenwood Restaurant and Bar ★★★ $$$ One of the most popular restaurants in this part of the valley is frequented by local wine folks, including comedian/gentleman farmer Tommy Smothers, who owns a winery in the area. The gently peaked roof lined in natural pine and large windows overlooking lush greenery combine with comfortable bentwood and bamboo chairs and bright art to create an airy feel. The food can be uneven, although the Caesar salad is a consistent winner, as is poached salmon served with a lemon cream sauce kissed with mustard. Sweetbreads are always on the menu in different guises, sometimes sprinkled with capers and accompanied by marinated mushrooms and an arugula salad. Fat crab cakes get a lift from an intense red bell pepper sauce, and duck is prepared with orange sauce and accompanied by wild rice or locally grown berries. Tapioca pudding with brandied cherries finishes the meal in a comforting fashion. ◆ Californian ◆ Tu-Su lunch and dinner. 9900 Sonoma Hwy (at Warm Springs Rd), Kenwood. 707/833.6326; fax 707/833.2238 ⑤

24 Cafe Citti ★★$ It looks like a modest roadside eatery, but once you see the open kitchen, the deli case filled with great salads, and the glistening bronzed chickens on the rotisserie, you'll know you've found a winner. The chicken, redolent of rosemary, tastes as good as it looks. The place is frequented mostly by locals who swear by such fresh, simply sauced pastas as rigatoni with garlic, black-pepper pancetta, and olive oil. This is a good place to pick up wine and fixings for a picnic. If you decide to eat in, order, take a seat, and the food will be delivered to your table. The outside deck is close to the highway, but plantings block the traffic so you see only rustling trees and hillsides. ◆ Italian ◆ Daily lunch and dinner. No reservations accepted. 9049 Sonoma Hwy (at Shaw Rd), Kenwood. 707/833.2690 ⑤

CAFE Lolo

25 Cafe Lolo ★★★$$ Located in downtown Santa Rosa, this restaurant has a simple clean look, a convivial backdrop for the food of Michael Quigley, who was a sous chef at Meadowood in Napa Valley before venturing out on his own. The menu changes seasonally and might include rock shrimp with shaved raw artichokes and asiago cheese, topped with lemon dressing; or roasted beets with caramelized shallots, toasted walnuts, and *frisée,* bathed in sherry vinaigrette. Main courses could be a pork chop in Merlot sauce paired with Swiss chard, or roast duck with mushrooms and a rhubarb chutney. The sophisticated food and moderate prices have quickly made this place a local favorite. ◆ Californian ◆ M-F lunch and dinner; Sa dinner. Reservations recommended. 620 Fifth St (between D St and Mendocino Ave), Santa Rosa. 707/576.7822

26 Willowside Cafe ★★★$$ This modest, low-slung barn-red roadhouse attracts little attention from the highway, but within it owners Michael and Carole Hale and chef

Richard Allen have created one of the best restaurants in California wine country. The light paneled ceiling, whirling fans, dark wood floors, and copper-top tables add a dash of style, as do cheerfully painted wainscoting and bright oil paintings created by employees. The weekly changing menu might start with mussels coated with a mustardy broth thickened with crème fraîche. Leg of lamb, roasted to a perfect pink, is served on a bed of artichokes and barely crunchy onions with cheese and tarragon. The wine list is as refreshing as the menu and concentrates on unusual and hard-to-find selections. The desserts—intense lemon tart, angel food cake layered with lemon mousse, or chocolate silk pie with a nut crust—are all delicious. ◆ Californian ◆ W-Su dinner. Reservations recommended. 3535 Guerneville Rd (at Willowside Rd), Santa Rosa. 707/523.4814

27 Bistro Ralph ★★★$$ Ralph Tingle's cutting-edge cuisine makes use of fresh local ingredients and takes its inspiration from the Southwest, Italy, and Asia. Never pass up the Szechuan pepper calamari, which is fried crispy and served with a lemon-ginger dipping sauce. Sonoma lamb stars in *niçoise* stew at dinner and as a lamb burger with goat cheese and delightful shoestring potatoes at lunch. Grilled *ahi* tuna is served with an olive sauce and horseradish-flavored mashed potatoes. The staff is friendly and well-informed, and there's a reasonably priced wine list. ◆ Californian ◆ M-F lunch and dinner; Sa-Su dinner. Reservations recommended. 109 Plaza St (on Healdsburg Plaza), Healdsburg. 707/433.1380 ⑤

California's greatest culinary contribution to this country has been the fact that its climate allows for the cultivation of a wide variety of fruits and vegetables year-round. Today, the state supplies more than 50 percent of the nation's produce and 70 percent of its wine.

The grape industry of California was started by Spanish missionaries, who planted grapevines around their missions so they could produce sacramental wine.

Santa Cruz/Monterey/ Carmel-by-the-Sea/Environs

Located approximately two hours south of San Francisco, the Santa Cruz–Monterey–Carmel area encompasses spectacular stretches of the California coastline, bucolic farmland, vineyards, and several towns and small cities that offer plenty of recreational and culinary possibilities. Beginning in the north at Santa Cruz, the coastline curves around **Monterey Bay** and ends its sweep in the towns of Monterey, **Pacific Grove**, and Carmel.

A drive along **Cabrillo Highway 1** passes through a diverse countryside: contorted cypress and pine forests, fog-shrouded mountains, fertile valleys,

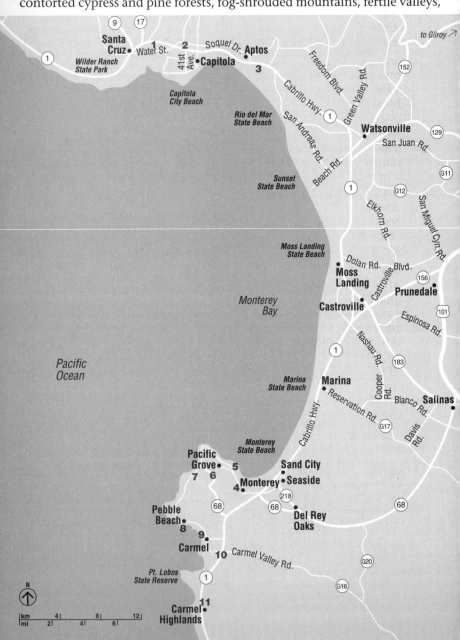

and miles of sandy beaches. Not surprisingly, agriculture is a very important industry in this region, particularly around **Salinas, Gilroy** and **Castroville.** The area is particularly well known for its many vineyards; **Monterey County** ranks as the third-largest wine-producing region in the United States, eclipsed only by Napa and Sonoma Counties. Wine grapes, artichokes, and garlic jockey for prominence in the local economy—and make their way onto the menus of area restaurants.

Santa Cruz is the site of a campus of the **University of California,** so its population is dominated by college students most of the year. Its eight colleges form an impressive campus nestled among the redwoods. The town's other major attraction is its boardwalk (the only one in Northern California), with the famous **Giant Dipper** roller coaster (considered by most wooden-roller-coaster aficionados to be the best in the world) , video arcades, and a lovely beach. The fishing trade flourishes here, and the day's catch is likely to appear on the tables of local restaurants like **Bittersweet Bistro** and **Cafe Cruz.**

Immortalized in John Steinbeck's novel *Cannery Row,* the city of Monterey also has roots in the fishing industry; dining options here range from the elegant **Ferrante's,** which features classic Italian food, to the somewhat kitschy **Bubba Gump Shrimp Co.,** a theme restaurant rife with references to the Oscar-winning film *Forrest Gump.* Other outstanding choices include **Stokes Adobe,** serving contemporary food in a charming 19th-century setting; and **Montrio,** which boasts a menu of excellent continental fare. Some of California's best and most famous vintners are located within an hour's drive of Monterey, including **Paul Masson Vineyards** and **Chalone;** the area lends itself to self-guided winery tours. Near Monterey are the residential town of Pacific Grove and the exclusive **Pebble Beach 17-Mile Drive,** a gated resort community with a number of excellent restaurants, including CLUB XIX, whose menu has been revamped by local star chef Hubert Keller; **Roy's at Pebble Beach;** and the **Bay Club.**

Just south of Monterey is Carmel-by-the-Sea, which was established around 1900 as an artists' colony. The town has a charming (if touristy) air, with Victorian houses and rustic stone structures co-existing with more modern commercial and residential developments. In addition, there is a staggering number of restaurants (especially for such a small place); the more note-worthy ones include **Robert Kincaid's Bistro on the Boulevard,** a traditional French bistro, and **Mondo's,** an eatery that combines Italian and French influences. If you're really looking to splurge, visit **Pacific's Edge at the Highlands Inn** in nearby **Carmel Highlands,** one of the best contemporary restaurants in the entire area (and the host of the **Masters of Food & Wine** festival, a world-famous culinary event held in February). The experience carries a high price tag, but it's more than worth it.

Not only do all of these dining spots benefit from the bounty of sparkling fresh seafood and vegetables so abundant in this region, but many of them also boast stunning views of the Pacific. For food lovers, there could be no better destination.

Santa Cruz

Being the site of a campus of the **University of California,** Santa Cruz has a predominantly young (and budget-conscious) population. As a result, vegetarianism and health and organic foods have become popular trends here. The town has a farmers' market; **Staff of Life/Cafe del Sol,** a large natural-foods grocery and restaurant; and a reasonably priced Tuscan eatery called **Cafe Cruz.** There are also some good mid-priced dining spots in the nearby town of Aptos, including the contemporary **Italian Bittersweet Bistro.** In the mountains looming above the seashore here, there are about 30 small wineries (most notably the excellent **Ridge Vineyards)**, and you're bound to see their names on more than a few wine lists in this area.

STAFF OF LIFE
CAFE DEL SOL

1 Staff of Life/Cafe Del Sol ★★$ **Staff of Life** is a large, modern, natural-foods grocery. It offers a wide selection of herbs, teas, bulk foods, fresh produce, and candles, as well as books on subjects ranging from astrology to wheat grass.The store itself has a small deli that offers vegetarian dishes and sweets for takeout, and in a separate building next door is **Cafe del Sol,** a dining room with a more extensive menu. Like most casual cafes in Santa Cruz, this high-ceilinged space is creatively decorated with colorful artworks and always offers a pile of the local alternative newspapers for patrons to browse through. The clientele includes families with kids in tow, ex-hippies, college students, and workers from the nearby stores. This place has the only organic salad bar in town. The entrées, all vegetarian, come in large or small sizes (and even the large portion can be had for less than $5, which makes for a pretty unbeatable deal). Good choices include any of the Mexican dishes, marinated tofu cutlet, and mushroom-nut casserole with cashew gravy and cabbage. A separate counter sells a selection of homemade muffins, cookies, and filled knishes, as well as some adventurous—though less successful—tofu-based confections. Note: The cafe stops serving its hot entrées an hour before closing. ♦ Vegetarian ♦ Daily lunch and dinner (M-Sa to 9PM; Su to 8PM). 1305 Water St (between Morrissey Blvd and Poplar Ave), Santa Cruz. 408/423.8041 ♿

CAFÉ CRUZ
ROSTICCERIA & BAR

2 Cafe Cruz ★★$$ Don't drive too fast along this busy shopping strip in Santa Cruz, or you'll miss this Tuscan restaurant. Just inside the door is the signature rotisserie, where two versions of roast chicken are cooked (one honey-cured and Alder-smoked, the other perfumed with garlic and herbs). The interior is divided into two areas: a space near the partially open kitchen, where you can watch the chefs at work, and a main dining room decorated with colorful murals. Among the best appetizers are a Castroville artichoke with balsamic mayonnaise; homemade bread with pesto spread, organic tomatoes, and melted gorgonzola; and crab cakes served with a lemon *beurre blanc.* There are seven salads, including a Tuscan version featuring pieces of that delectable garlic-and-herb roasted chicken. The list of main courses includes a dozen pastas and several meat dishes, such as New York steak stuffed with roasted garlic, gorgonzola cheese, and rosemary. In good weather there is seating at an outdoor patio. ♦ Italian ♦ M-Sa lunch and dinner; Su dinner. 2621 41st Ave (across from Kmart), Santa Cruz. 408/476.3801; fax 408/476.7887 ♿

Bittersweet
BISTRO

3 Bittersweet Bistro ★★★$$ **Culinary Institute of America** graduate Thomas Vinolus and his wife, Elizabeth, run this local favorite that serves good contemporary Italian fare. It's in the town of Aptos, which is 15 minutes outside Santa Cruz. The building itself has rough-textured stone and stucco walls; and the dining room is decorated in sedate, neutral colors, with a mahogany bar and bistro-style seating. As a starter, try the antipasto sampler: a roasted head of garlic, sliced meats and cheeses, olives, and marinated vegetables. There's a good Caesar salad with parmesan cheese and garlic croutons (they also offer a low-fat "mock" version for the benefit of the diet-conscious). The entrées are all delicious, especially black-pepper linguine tossed with olives, tomatoes, garlic, herbs, and pine nuts; garlic chicken; Black Angus rib-eye steak; mushroom moussaka; and veal medaillons with a wild mushroom sauce. An expert pastry chef, Vinolus uses only the finest ingredients in his desserts, including the luscious Valrhona chocolate and ricotta cheesecake served with mango and raspberry coulis. ♦ Contemporary Italian ♦ Tu-Su dinner. 787 Rio del Mar Blvd (at Hwy 1), Aptos. 408/662.9799; fax 408/662.9779 ♿

Thirty-four wineries in the Sonoma Valley produce 25 types of wine—more than 5 million cases yearly.

Hangtown Fry, a mixture of eggs, bacon, and oysters, is said to have been invented for a successful miner wishing to show off his wealth. He walked into a restaurant in Hangtown (the heart of the Gold Rush country, north of San Francisco) and ordered the three most expensive items on the menu: oysters, bacon, and eggs. Source: West Coast Cookbook, by Helen Brown (Alfred A. Knopf, 1991).

From Hangout to Haute Cuisine: The Rise of the Neighborhood Restaurant

It used to be that when you thought "upscale San Francisco restaurant," you immediately thought of **Downtown.** After all, **Union Square** and the **Financial District** are where business and tourist activity is concentrated, so it follows that they would be the dining center of the city as well. But while there is certainly no shortage of three- and four-star places in that part of town, in the last few years a number of equally good eateries have sprung up in the outlying, less-traveled neighborhoods, such as the **Mission**, **Pacific Heights,** the **Marina,** the **Castro,** the **Haight,** and **SoMa.** What's more, many of these are owned and operated by top chefs, including James Ormsby, Arnold Wong, and Rob Zaborny.

The obvious draw for these restaurateurs is the lower rents. Another reason is that in a food-savvy city like San Francisco, it's impossible to over-saturate the market with high-quality restaurants—in any location. In addition, city residents have a tendency to "cocoon"—i.e., they favor patronizing nearby places rather than travel beyond their neighborhood. This means a restaurant aimed at a particular clientele (such as gays, young trendies, or families) has a better chance of succeeding if it's located right in the neighborhood where they live.

Visitors to San Francisco, however, often keep to the well-worn tourist track. Diana Nelson, chief concierge at the **Grand Hyatt Hotel** in Union Square, says that the only guests who ask her about neighborhood spots are the truly committed foodies: "Unfortunately, most visitors don't stray too far from their hotel." More's the pity, for it would be a shame to let ignorance, ennui, or habit distract you from exploring all the culinary delights San Francisco has to offer.

Each of the following eateries offers a dining experience that's well worth a trip across town. The Mission, for example, boasts **Bruno's** (2389 Mission St, at 20th St, 550.7455; fax 642.9059 &), serving creative interpretations of Mediterranean dishes such as Prince Edward Island mussels in an orange-saffron-mint broth, petite tuna steak au poivre, and braised veal breast with turnip gratin and chanterelle mushroom *jus;* and **The Slanted Door** (584 Valencia St, between 17th and 16th Sts, 861.8032; fax 861.8329 &), presenting ever-changing Vietnamese/Californian dishes in a tranquil setting. **Carta** (1772 Market St, between Gough and Waller Sts, 863.3516), in the

Hayes Valley, offers a menu that focuses on a different cuisine each month, served in a casual storefront setting; the **Cole Valley's EOS Restaurant & Wine Bar** (901 Cole St, at Carl St, 566.3063; fax 566.2663 &) features Asian/fusion cuisine such as pan-roasted salmon, free-range chicken with green onions, and five-pepper calamari; and the cheerful **Cassis Bistro** (2120 Greenwich St, between Webster and Fillmore Sts, 292.0770) brings simple French cooking to the **Cow Hollow** neighborhood.

For contemporary American cooking, try **Infusion** (555 Second St, between Brannan and Bryant Sts, 543.2282), a new SoMa eatery boasting a lengthy menu of meat, seafood, and pasta dishes, as well as a number of flavored vodkas; **The Meetinghouse** (1701 Octavia St, at Bush St, 922.6733; fax 661.8565), on the edge of Pacific Heights, offering Shaker-style decor and a menu of such hearty dishes as braised pork, roast chicken, and oyster stew; and **2223 Restaurant** (2223 Market St, between Sanchez and Noe Sts, 431.0692 &), a stylish eatery in the Castro serving such contemporary American dishes as fillet of salmon poached in Champagne accompanied by potato puree; grilled sea scallops with shaved fennel and citrus salad; and a whole roasted guinea hen. Other good Castro eateries include **Bacco Ristorante Italiano** (737 Diamond St, between 24th and Elizabeth Sts, 282.4969; fax 282.1315 &), serving exquisitely prepared Italian dishes; and **Firefly** (4288 24th St, between Diamond and Douglass Sts, 821.7652; fax 821.5812), a tiny place with an extensive, internationally inspired menu.

Monterey

The original capital of California, Monterey is the major city on the peninsula, with many remnants of California's early Spanish-Mexican heritage. Although the area near the old canneries and waterfront (in which John Steinbeck set part of his novel *Cannery Row*) have been commercialized by a proliferation of T-shirt and souvenir shops, this town offers a number of outstanding dining options.

4 Montrio ★★★$$$ Brian Whitmer, the longtime chef at the excellent **Pacific's Edge at the Highlands Inn,** struck out on his own a few years ago, opening this eatery set in a former firehouse in downtown Monterey. The menu of contemporary classics is creative and well executed: For a starter, try the terrine of goat cheese, eggplant, and roasted peppers or the delicate herb ravioli stuffed with goat cheese and artichokes. Then move on to one of the terrific entrées, such as rotisserie chicken with garlic whipped potatoes, mushrooms, rosemary, and a green vegetable; locally caught salmon with mushrooms, tomatoes, and a basil-pea sauce; or polenta topped with oven-roasted portobello mushrooms and a vegetable ragout. All of the desserts are good, but we're particularly fond of the bread pudding, which comes flavored with chocolate and topped with a warm banana compote and vanilla ice cream. But while the food is unusual and wonderful, the decor is a bit jarring. It's basically a mishmash of design elements that look like they've been plucked from every successful Northern Calfornia restaurant in the past ten years: dashes of Art Nouveau, etched glass dividers, Southwestern coverings on the banquettes, brick walls, and, most oddly, clouds of white insulation on the ceiling. These last were installed to help alleviate the dining room's high noise level, but they don't really work and just look weird. Still, the food is worth enduring the discordant surroundings. ◆ Contemporary ◆ M-Sa lunch and dinner; Su brunch and dinner. 414 Calle Principal (between Pearl and Franklin Sts), Monterey. 408/648.8880; fax 408/648.8241 ♿

4 Stokes Adobe ★★★★$$$ This is a joint venture by chef Brandon Miller (who used to work at San Francisco's **Campton Place** and **LuLu** restaurants) and entrepreneurs Kirk and Dorothea Probosco. Set in an early-19th-century adobe building in the historic district of Old Monterey, the dining room features a beautiful rustic bar and furnishings, pale pink walls, and views of a splendid garden. This exquisite space has seen quite a few restaurants come and go through the years, but finally it has a tenant worthy of its opulence. The menu of contemporary classics includes a selection of creative, tasty tapas (mussels with *salsa verde,* fava bean crostini, Basque veal meatballs flavored with allspice, and the like) and such entrées as white corn bisque with a dab of chili crème fraîche; oven-roasted spinach gratin with mussels; lamb shank; chicken cooked under a brick; and hanger steak with truffled parsnip puree. The desserts are succulent as well, especially the lemon polenta pound cake and parfait with strawberries. This is the perfect place to celebrate a special event or enjoy a romantic evening. ◆ Contemporary ◆ Daily lunch and dinner. 500 Hartnell St (at Calle Principale), Monterey. 408/373.1110; fax 408/373.1202 ♿

ferrante's

4 Ferrante's ★★$$ With views of **Cannery Row, Fisherman's Wharf,** and miles of coastline, this elegant dining room at the **Monterey Marriott Hotel** is a spectacular place to enjoy a drink and hors d'oeuvres, dinner, or Sunday brunch. This used to be just a boring hotel restaurant, but executive chef Silvano Merlo, who comes from Northern Italy, has livened up the entire menu, from the antipasti to the *dolci* (desserts). Appetizers include braised mussels, grilled portobello mushrooms, and fried rice balls stuffed with mozzarella and garnished with a light tomato sauce. The lineup of entrées features a number of pastas, such as spaghetti with toasted garlic and crushed hot pepper; angel hair pasta with a simple accompaniment of toasted pine nuts, garlic, and basil; and the pasta sampler (which varies). Rack of lamb, saltimbocca, roasted half chicken, and steak stuffed with mozzarella and toasted pine nuts wrapped in pancetta are other good selections. For dessert, try the sinfully delicious tiramisù. At the Sunday Champagne Brunch, a buffet of American-style breakfast selections, as well as prime rib and turkey, is offered to the strains of live jazz. ◆ Italian ◆ M-Sa dinner; Su brunch and dinner. 350 Calle Principal (at Del Monte Ave), Monterey. 408/647.4020; fax 408/372.2968 ♿

5 Bubba Gump Shrimp Co. ★$$ If this name rings a bell, it's because it's the company Tom Hanks founded in the movie *Forrest Gump.* In general, theme restaurants concentrate too much on the theme and not enough on the food, and this one is no different. Our advice would be to stick to the simpler seafood items and avoid everything else. Try the peel-and-eat shrimp, which has been steamed in beer and comes with two spicy dips, or the grilled mahimahi with french fries and cole slaw. Of course, the decor is a bit overdone (with fishing nets and a shrimp boat jutting from the wall), and the dishes have cute names like "Forrest's Shrimp Net Catch." But if you're looking for a kitschy experience, this place isn't bad. ♦ Seafood ♦ Daily lunch and dinner. 720 Cannery Row (between Drake and David Aves), Monterey. 408/373.1884 ♿

Pacific Grove

A tiny residential town, Pacific Grove has several restaurants worth visiting, including **Vito's**, a Sicilian place, and the casual **Taste Cafe & Bistro.**

6 Taste Cafe & Bistro ★★★$$ Ask any local foodie for a list of favorite restaurants, and this place will probably appear prominently on it. Set in a modest shopping center, it's rather informal and unprepossessing, but the homestyle food sets it apart. All of the dishes are made from scratch on the premises, from the house-cured salmon carpaccio to the grilled rabbit with gnocchi in a green peppercorn sauce. Herb-scented roast chicken is another delight. And the prices are very reasonable. ♦ Mediterranean/Californian ♦ Tu-Su dinner. 1199 Forest Ave (near Sunset Dr), Pacific Grove. 408/655.0324

6 Vito's ★★★$$ In an unlikely setting—a strip shopping mall—this outstanding Sicilian restaurant offers first-rate fare in a modern dining room decorated with soft peach colors, track lighting, and a wall-sized mural of Sicily. The potato gnocchi in creamy gorgonzola sauce are to die for (they also can come with pesto or tomato sauce, but the gorgonzola's the best), and there are 16 different varieties of pasta. Meat and fish dishes are available as well. ♦ Italian ♦ M-F lunch and dinner; Sa-Su dinner. 1180 Forest Ave (near Sunset Dr), Pacific Grove. 408/375.3070 ♿

Garlic wasn't cultivated in the United States until World War II, when the government asked a few farmers in the Northern California town of Gilroy to grow the crop so that the dehydrated garlic could be used in food supplies for the troops.

The fad for putting edible flowers in salads and sprinkling them over entrées was said to have originated in California. But which kinds of flowers are best for this purpose? Many San Francisco chefs use chives, calendulas, daylillies, marigolds, mint, nasturtiums, pansies, roses, and sage.

The Pebble Beach 17-Mile Drive

This exclusive residential resort between **Pacific Grove** and **Carmel** boasts a number of renowned golf courses (including **Pebble Beach** and **Spyglass Hill)** and several hotels with excellent restaurants. There are three gated entrances, one at Pacific Grove and two in Carmel-by-the-Sea; although there's a charge to enter, the fee will be applied to your bill if you're visiting one of the restaurants here.

7 Bay Club ★★$$$$ At this modern dining room at the **Inn at Spanish Bay,** chef Drew Previti produces outstanding antipasti dishes, which can be ordered in combination to make a meal—and we suggest you do just that, since the entrées are altogether unsatisfying and overpriced. Top choices include beef carpaccio with white truffle oil, shaved parmesan, and arugula; puree of asparagus soup enriched with lobster; an oxtail agnolotti pasta dish; and penne with truffles and lobster sauce. ♦ Italian ♦ Daily dinner. 2700 17 Mile Dr (near the Pacific Grove gate), Pebble Beach. 408/647.7433; fax 408/644.7955 ♿

7 Roy's at Pebble Beach ★★$$$ Chef Roy Yamaguchi is a major player in the restaurant business, with establishments in Hawaii, on the mainland US, and in Asia. This enterprise at the **Inn at Spanish Bay** is a trendy spot that appeals to the baby-boom crowd—both locals and visitors—that Pebble Beach seems to be attracting these days. Most likely, they're drawn by the lively atmosphere, attractive, Asian-influenced decor, and over-the-top menu of fusion Euro-Asian dishes. For lunch, there's dim sum, salads, and wood-fired pizzas; in the evenings, fish and meat entrées are served. In general, the food is good, but in some cases the presentation is too elaborate and overdone (some dishes arrive napped with as many as five sauces). Good choices include lemongrass-crusted fish satay, pot stickers filled with seafood, charbroiled garlic-mustard short ribs with mashed potatoes, and tender filet mignon with a silky wild-mushroom sauce. Breakfast is offered as well, with egg dishes, corned beef hash, and other traditional items. ♦ Euro-Asian ♦ Daily breakfast, lunch and dinner. 2700 17 Mile Dr (near the Pacific Grove gate), Pebble Beach. 408/647.7423; fax 408/644.7957 &

8 **CLUB XIX** ★★★$$$$ Hubert Keller, the mastermind behind San Francisco's four-star **Fleur de Lys,** has completely updated and improved the cuisine at the formerly stodgy CLUB XIX. Working with chef Lisa Magadini, he has created a menu of lighter French cuisine. The look of the place has been updated as well, which is a welcome change: Paintings of modern art hang on the walls, there are gold accents here and there, and an outdoor patio with a working fireplace is a pleasant place to sit and watch the action on the adjacent golf course. At lunch, you can have a club sandwich, a refined version of crab bisque with artichoke pieces wrapped in a phyllo pouch, or black quinoa salad with toasted pine nuts, basil, and cream of sweet peas. The dinner lineup includes herb-crusted rack of lamb, black-pepper–crusted filet mignon, and boneless squab served in a wine sauce with an array of vegetables and capers. ♦ Contemporary French ♦ Daily lunch and dinner. 17-Mile Dr (at Cypress Dr, 2 miles northwest of the Carmel gate), Pebble Beach. 408.625.8519; fax 408/625.8598

A San Francisco original, steam beer is named for the way it used to be brewed. The process used lager yeast at ale temperatures; the resulting brew was so effervescent that, when a keg was tapped, the beer erupted like steam escaping a pipe. These days, steam beer is still produced (Anchor Steam Beer is one of the leading brands), but more modern methods are used.

During the wild Barbary Coast era in San Francisco, bartender Michael "Mickey" Finn was notorious for spiking customers' drinks with knockout drops, which occasionally ended in their deaths. His name became synonymous with that practice, and also led to the phrase "to slip someone a Mickey."

Carmel-by-the-Sea

This quaint, lovely village has more than its share of art galleries, upscale shops selling clothing, housewares, and antiques, and fine eateries. Easy to explore on foot, Carmel is so small it doesn't even need to use numbers in its street addresses. Among the places worth stopping at are **Mondo's,** a lively trattoria, and **Robert Kincaid's Bistro on the Boulevard.** And just outside of Carmel, in **Carmel Highlands,** is **Pacific's Edge at the Highlands Inn,** one of the best restaurants in the entire area.

9 **Il Fornaio** ★★$$ Like the other members of this popular Northern California chain, this Italian eatery in the **Pine Inn** is casual, comfortable, and pretty in a generic sort of way. Wood-fired pizzas, rotisserie-cooked meats, and fresh regional pastas are well represented on the menu. One of the most popular dishes is artichoke halves stuffed with garlic, bread crumbs, a touch of anchovy, and crushed red pepper flakes. The breads and pastries, which are made fresh daily in the on-site bakery, are wonderful, too. ♦ Italian ♦ Daily breakfast, lunch, and dinner. Ocean Ave (between Lincoln and Monte Verde Sts), Carmel-by-the-Sea. 408/622.5100; fax 408/622.9095 & Also at: Numerous locations throughout the area

9 **Mondo's** ★★$$ What happens when a young Frenchman falls in love with an Italian chef in the heart of Northern California? Well, in the case of Philippe Tardivet and Michelle Mondo, they decided to start this lively trattoria influenced by the tastes of both Italy and France. The food, prepared by Mondo, includes a variety of bruschetta, homemade pizzas, and a tempting array of pastas (when in doubt, go for the scrumptious linguine with clams). And to accompany the food, Tardivet has put together a wine list dominated by excellent French vintages. The dining room itself has a rustic decor; when it fills up (as it almost always does), the noise level goes through the roof. But this is a great place to have a good—if not peaceful—time. ♦ Italian ♦ Daily lunch and dinner. Dolores St (between Seventh and Ocean Aves), Carmel-by-the-Sea. 408/624.8977

9 **Piatti** ★★$$ Another link in the popular Northern California chain, this restaurant offers Italian fare that is well prepared, if not particularly innovative. The atmosphere is casual, and the dining room has light-colored walls, wood accents, and bright Italian pottery; the rooftop patio is a welcoming place to dine in warm weather. Spit-roasted chicken with garlic mashed potatoes, fritto misto, carpaccio, and "white pizza" with goat cheese, sliced tomatoes, and a touch of pesto are among the better menu items. ♦ Italian ♦ Daily lunch and dinner. Sixth Ave and Junipero St, Carmel-by-the-Sea. 408/625.1766; fax 408/625.1883 &

10 Robert Kincaid's Bistro on the Boulevard ★★★$$$ The name is a bit misleading: This eatery isn't actually on the boulevard—rather, it's hidden away in a shopping center a mile south of central Carmel. But when you step through the door, you'll think you've been magically transported to a streetside bistro in Paris. Decorated with rough woods, touches of lace here and there, Belle Epoque antiques, and fresh flowers, the room has a rustic though elegant look. And owner/chef Robert Kincaid does classical French cuisine (enlivened with a few Californian influences) better than anyone else in the area. The delights begin with the onion tart, kissed with *fromage blanc* and cream; sausage in puff pastry accented with Madeira and white wine sauces; and escargot swimming in garlic-butter sauce. French onion soup gratinée, Caesar salad with prosciutto, lobster ravioli, osso buco Milanese, and tequila-marinated steak are other outstanding dishes. ♦ Bistro ♦ M-F lunch and dinner; Sa dinner. 217 Crossroads Blvd (at Hwy 1 and Rio Rd), Carmel-by-the-Sea. 408/624.9626

11 Pacific's Edge at the Highlands Inn ★★★★$$$$ Executive chef Cal Stamenov spent many years working with Philippe Jeanty at the excellent restaurant of the famous Domaine Chandon winery in Yountville. All that training and influence has paid off, as Stamenov's heavenly cooking is displayed to the fullest advantage in this restaurant perched high above the Pacific. Located in Carmel Highlands, a few miles outside Carmel, the elegant dining room boasts a panoramic view of the ocean. Stamenov's creations (which change seasonally) constantly test the limits of culinary invention—with great success. For example, one night's dinner menu might feature potato soup with smoked salmon garnished with horseradish crème fraîche; portobello mushroom soup with goat cheese and truffle oil; and roast squab breast on sweet white corn, foie gras, and Madeira sauce. Other possible choices might be Maine lobster salad with mango, avocado, and passion fruit–curry vinaigrette; roasted beet salad with asparagus, *frisée*, and feta; lamb steak with a porcini mushroom stew; or, for those with more traditional tastes, grilled New York steak with a red onion–green peppercorn sauce. The wine list is extensive and quite impressive. The prices are high—this is one of the region's most expensive restaurants—but the "sunset dinner" is a relatively good value. ♦ Contemporary ♦ Daily lunch and dinner. On Hwy 1 (4 miles south of Carmel), Carmel Highlands. 408/624.3801; fax 408/626.1574 &

Bests

Harvey Steiman
Editor at Large, *Wine Spectator* magazine

Masa's—For elegance and top-level cuisine.

Cafe at Chez Panisse, Berkeley—Bistro of the gods.

Pastis—Great atmosphere, inspired casual cuisine.

Kabuto Sushi—No atmosphere, but the best sushi in town.

Hayes Street Grill—Perfect for fish and salads.

Manora's Thai Cuisine—Family-run ethnic restaurant.

El Toro—Biggest, best grilled beef burritos in town. . . good agua fresca also.

Jeremiah Tower
Owner/Chef, Stars Restaurant

42 Degrees—I love the industrial style interior and the chalkboard specials are always great. I often order four or five of those and nosh on them with a bottle of wine—young, energetic crowd.

Zuni Cafe—One of the few San Francisco restaurants that caters to the greatest cross section of customers—everything from businessmen to bohemians and tourists. Great food!

Yank Sing—I try to dine here once a week—delicious dim sum and courteous service.

Aqua—I go here when I'm in the mood for delicious seafood, like Le Bernardin in New York City. Great service!

The Slanted Door—I love Asian food . . . outstanding spring rolls and vegetable crepes; reminds me of Cafe Indochine in Paris.

Fringale—Whenever I want delicious, perfect comfort food, I head to this **SoMa** bistro. I love the waiters' French accents.

Index

Index

Index

Index

Restaurants by Star Ratings

Only restaurants with star ratings are listed below. All restaurants are listed alphabetically in the main (preceding) index. Always call in advance to ensure a restaurant has not closed, changed its hours, or booked its tables for a private party. The restaurant price ratings are based on the average cost of an entrée for one person, excluding tax and tip.

★★★★ An Extraordinary Experience
★★★ Excellent
★★ Very Good
★ Good

$$$$ Big Bucks ($25 and up)
$$$ Expensive ($15-$25)
$$ Reasonable ($10-$15)
$ The Price Is Right (less than $10)

★★★★

Aqua $$$$ 30
Babette's $$ 218
Cafe at Chez Panisse $$ 209
Catahoula Restaurant and Saloon $$$ 217
Chez Panisse $$$ 208
Domaine Chandon $$$$ 213
Fleur de Lys $$$$ 13
French Laundry $$$$ 213
Fringale Restaurant $$ 130
The Heights $$$ 191
La Folie $$$$ 82
LuLu $$ 134
Masa's $$$$ 19

Index

Index

Restaurants by Description

The following index lists restaurants by the type of food served. All restaurants are listed alphabetically in the main index (above) and restaurants with stars are listed in the ratings index (also above).

Afghanl

African

See East African, Egyptian, Ethiopian, Moroccan, and South African.

American

Index

Argentine

Asian

Barbecue

Index

Index

Index

SAN FRANCISCO PUBLIC TRANSPORTATION

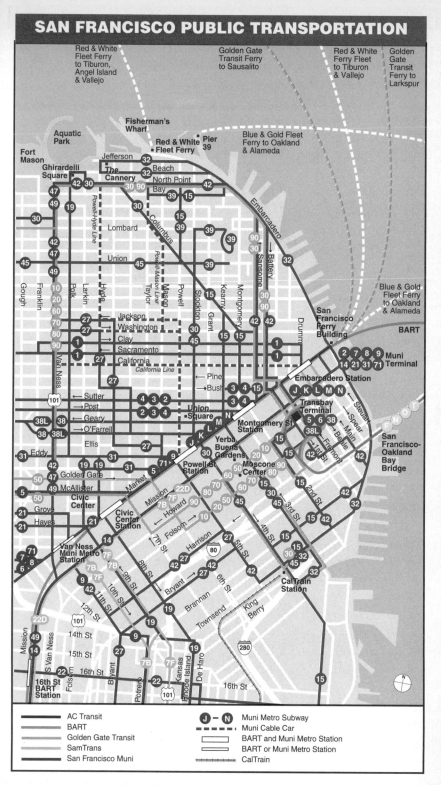

Base map courtesy of the Metropolitan Transportation Commisson.

Credits

Writer and Researcher
GraceAnn Walden

Writer and Researchers (Previous Edition)
Michael Bauer
Dan Bowe

ACCESS®PRESS

Editorial Director
Lois Spritzer

Managing Editor
Laura L. Brengelman

Senior Editors
Mary Callahan
Beth Schlau

Associate Editors
Patricia Canole
Gene Gold
Susan McClung

Map Coordinator
Jonathan Goodnough

Editorial Assistant
Susan Cutter Snyder

Senior Art Director
C. Linda Dingler

Design Supervisor
Joy O'Meara

Designers
Alexandra Lindquist
Elizabeth Paige Streit

Map Designer
Patricia Keelin

*Associate Director
of Production*
Dianne Pinkowitz

*Director, Electronic
Publishing*
John R. Day

Special Thanks
**Ann Roberti, Librarian,
Alice S. Statler
Culinary Library,
San Francisco City
College
Tracy F. Shaffer**

The publisher and authors assume
no legal responsibility for the
completeness or accuracy of the
contents of this book nor any legal
responsibility for the appreciation or
depreciation in the value of any
premises, commercial or otherwise,
by reason of inclusion in or exclusion
from this book. All contents are based
on information available at the time of
publication. Some of the maps are
diagrammatic and may be selective
of street inclusion.

ACCESS®PRESS does not solicit
individuals, organizations, or
businesses for inclusion in our books,
nor do we accept payment for inclusion.
We welcome, however, information
from our readers, including comments,
criticisms, and suggestions for new
listings. Send all correspondence to:
ACCESS®PRESS, 10 East 53rd
Street, 18th Floor, New York, NY 10022

PRINTED IN THE UNITED STATES

ACCESS® Guides

Order by phone, toll-free: 1-800-331-3761

Name _____ Phone _____

Address _____

City _____ State _____ Zip _____

Please send me the following ACCESS® Guides:

☐ **ATLANTA** ACCESS® $18.50
0-06-277156-6

☐ **BARCELONA** ACCESS® $17.00
0-06-277000-4

☐ **BOSTON** ACCESS® $18.50
0-06-277197-3

☐ **BUDGET EUROPE** ACCESS® $18.50
0-06-277171-X

☐ **CAPE COD, MARTHA'S VINEYARD,
& NANTUCKET** ACCESS® $18.50
0-06-277159-0

☐ **CARIBBEAN** ACCESS® $20.00
0-06-277165-5

☐ **CHICAGO** ACCESS® $18.50
0-06-277196-5

☐ **FLORENCE/VENICE/MILAN** ACCESS® $18.50
0-06-277170-1

☐ **HAWAII** ACCESS® $18.50
0-06-277142-6

☐ **LAS VEGAS** ACCESS® $18.50
0-06-277177-9

☐ **LONDON** ACCESS® $18.50
0-06-277161-2

☐ **LOS ANGELES** ACCESS® $18.50
0-06-277167-1

☐ **MEXICO** ACCESS® $18.50
0-06-277166-3

☐ **MIAMI & SOUTH FLORIDA** ACCESS® $18.50
0-06-277178-7

☐ **MONTREAL & QUEBEC CITY** ACCESS®
$18.50 0-06-277160-4

☐ **NEW ORLEANS** ACCESS® $18.50
0-06-277176-0

☐ **NEW YORK CITY** ACCESS® $18.50
0-06-277162-0

☐ **NEW YORK RESTAURANTS** ACCESS®
$13.00 0-06-277218-X

☐ **ORLANDO & CENTRAL FLORIDA** ACCESS®
$18.50
0-06-277175-2

☐ **PARIS** ACCESS® $18.50
0-06-277163-9

☐ **PHILADELPHIA** ACCESS® $18.50
0-06-277155-8

☐ **ROME** ACCESS® $18.50
0-06-277195-7

☐ **SAN DIEGO** ACCESS® $18.50
0-06-277185-X

☐ **SAN FRANCISCO** ACCESS® $18.50
0-06-277169-8

☐ **SAN FRANCISCO RESTAURANTS** ACCESS®
$13.00
0-06-277219-8

☐ **SANTA FE/TAOS/ALBUQUERQUE** ACCESS®
$18.50
0-06-277194-9

☐ **SEATTLE** ACCESS® $18.50
0-06-277198-1

☐ **SKI COUNTRY** ACCESS®
Eastern United States $18.50
0-06-277189-2

☐ **SKI COUNTRY** ACCESS®
Western United States $18.50
0-06-277174-4

☐ **WASHINGTON DC** ACCESS® $18.50
0-06-277158-2

☐ **WINE COUNTRY** ACCESS® France $18.50
0-06-277193-0

☐ **WINE COUNTRY** ACCESS®
Northern California $18.50
0-06-277164-7

Prices subject to change without notice.

Total for **ACCESS®** Guides:	$
Please add applicable sales tax:	
Add $4.00 for first book S&H, $1.00 per additional book:	
Total payment:	$

☐ Check or Money Order enclosed. Offer valid in the United States only.
Please make payable to HarperCollins*Publishers*.

☐ Charge my credit card   ☐ American Express   ☐ Visa   ☐ MasterCard

Card no. _____ Exp. date _____

Signature _____

Send orders to: HarperCollins*Publishers*
P.O. Box 588
Dunmore, PA 18512-0588